INFORMATION TECHNOLOGY AUDITING and ASSURANCE

THIRD EDITION

JAMES A. HALL
Lehigh University

SOUTH-WESTERN
CENGAGE Learning

Australia • Brazil • Japan • Korea • Mexico • Singapore • Spain • United Kingdom • United States

SOUTH-WESTERN
CENGAGE Learning

Information Technology Auditing and Assurance, Third Edition

James A. Hall

Editor-in-Chief: Rob Dewey

Acquisition Editor: Matt Filimonov

Developmental Editor: Margaret Kubale

Editorial Assistant: Ann Mazzaro

Senior Marketing Manager: Natalie King

Content Project Management: PreMediaGlobal

Senior Art Director: Stacy Jenkins Shirley

Manufacturing Coordinator: Doug Wilke

Production House/Compositor: PreMediaGlobal

Permissions Acquisition Manager/Photo: Deanna Ettinger

Permissions Acquisition Manager/Text: Mardell Glinski Schultz

Cover Designer: cmiller design

Cover Image: © Getty Images

For product information and technology assistance, contact us at **Cengage Learning Customer & Sales Support, 1-800-354-9706.**

For permission to use material from this text or product, submit all requests online at **www.cengage.com/permissions**
Further permissions questions can be e-mailed to
permissionrequest@cengage.com

Library of Congress Control Number: 2010928362

ISBN-13: 978-1-4390-7911-9

ISBN-10: 1-4390-7911-0

South-Western Cengage Learning
5191 Natorp Boulevard
Mason, OH 45040
USA

Cengage Learning is a leading provider of customized learning solutions with office locations around the globe, including Singapore, the United Kingdom, Australia, Mexico, Brazil, and Japan. Locate your local office at: **www.cengage.com/global**

Cengage Learning products are represented in Canada by Nelson Education, Ltd.

To learn more about south-western **cengage.com/south-western**

Purchase any of our products at your local college store or at our preferred online store **www.cengagebrain.com**

Printed in the United States of America
3 4 5 6 7 14 13

INFORMATION TECHNOLOGY
AUDITING and ASSURANCE

DEDICATION

To my wife, Eileen, for her unwavering support, encouragement, and patience.

Brief Contents

Contents

Preface

The third edition of this text contains key improvements and changes that continue to provide instructors and students with the best information technology auditing text available. This edition has been reorganized and expanded to address the internal control and audit issues mandated by Sarbanes-Oxley legislation. The third edition includes a full range of new and revised homework assignments, up-to-date content changes, a new chapter on transaction processing, and new appendix material in several chapters to provide the reader with background and perspective. All of these changes add up to more student and instructor enhancements than in previous editions. We have made these changes to keep students and instructors as current as possible on issues such as business processes, general controls, application controls, fraud issues, and relevant aspects of Sarbanes-Oxley legislation in a changing IT auditing environment.

DISTINGUISHING FEATURES

- A **risk-based approach.** This text presents a risk-based approach for identifying significant IT threats and describes the audit tests and procedures for evaluating internal controls in the following general control areas:
  1. IT Governance, including IT organizational structure, disaster recovery planning, and IT outsourcing;
  2. System security, including security issues pertaining to operating systems, networks, and database systems.
  3. Systems development and program change procedures.

  It also provides extensive treatment of accounting application risks, application controls for mitigating risk, tests of controls and substantive testing techniques.
- **CAATTs.** Business organizations use Computer Aided Audit Tools and Techniques (CAATTs) for testing internal controls to provide evidence of compliance with Sarbanes-Oxley legislation (SOX). These technologies and techniques are discussed and illustrated in an easy-to-understand manner.
- **ACL software.** ACL is the leading data extraction CAATT software. An instructional version is included with each NEW copy of the book. The text integrates ACL into relevant discussions and end-of-chapter problems. Data files to support ACL cases and tutorials are also included on the book's Website.
- Structured Presentation of Chapter Content. For clarity and comparability, most chapters are structured along similar lines. They begin with a discussion of the operational features and technologies employed in the area. They then lay out the nature of the risks and explain the controls needed to mitigate such risks. Finally, the chapters define specific audit objectives and present suggested audit procedures to achieve those objectives.

NEW AND REVISED FEATURES

- **Completely updated.** The third edition has been rigorously updated to include SAS 109, SAS 99, and the COSO internal control model.
- **REVISED ERP systems chapter.** Chapter 11 now provides extensive coverage of enterprise resource planning (ERP) systems. This revised chapter examines a number of audit issues related to the implementation, control, and audit of ERP.
- **EXPANDED transaction processing coverage.** Several chapters of this book deal with various issues involving AIS applications including automated procedures, internal controls, audits test, and fraud schemes. As background, a new chapter 6 provides an overview of transaction processing systems (TPS) and Financial Reporting Systems (FRS) and presents preliminary topics that are common to all TPS and FRS applications. In addition, supporting appendixes have been added to chapter 9 (revenue cycle) and chapter 10 (expenditure cycle).
- **Revised ACL tutorials.** These 'how to' tutorials on the product Website have been revised to be compliant with ACL 9.0. They make it easy for students to quickly understand ACL's extensive capabilities and master its use.
- **Revised ACL fraud and auditing case.** Due to popular demand for increased integration of ACL software into the text, we have revised the Bradmark ACL case that spans chapters 9, 10, and 12. This case will enable students to apply many concepts presented in the book using ACL software.
- **NEW chapter-ending projects.** Selected chapters conclude with projects and cases on disaster recovery, fraud, internal controls, emerging technologies, ERP, and XBRL. These new cases and projects enable students to apply current concepts covered in the text.

ORGANIZATION AND CONTENT

Chapter 1   Auditing and Internal Control

This chapter provides an overview of IT auditing. It describes the various types of audits that organizations commission. The chapter distinguishes between the auditor's traditional attestation responsibility and the emerging field of advisory services. It goes on to explain the structure of an IT audit: the relationship between management assertions, audit objectives, tests of controls, and substantive tests are explained. The chapter also outlines the key points of the COSO control framework, which defines internal controls in both manual and IT environments. The final section of the chapter examines audit issues and implications related to Sarbanes-Oxley legislation and provides a conceptual framework that links general controls, application controls, and financial data integrity. This framework is a model for the remainder of the text.

Chapter 2   Auditing IT Governance Controls

This chapter presents the risks, controls, and tests of controls related to IT governance. It opens by defining IT governance and identifying elements of IT governance that have internal control and financial reporting implications. The topics covered include structuring of the IT function, computer center threats and controls, and disaster recovery planning. The chapter also examines the risks and benefits of IT outsourcing. It concludes with a discussion of audit issues in an outsourcing environment and the role of the SAS 70 report.

Chapter 3 Security Part I: Auditing Operating Systems and Networks

This chapter focuses on Sarbanes-Oxley compliance regarding the security and control of operating systems, communication networks, Electronic Data Interchange, and PC based accounting systems. The chapter examines the risks, controls, audit objectives, and audit procedures that may be performed to either satisfy compliance or attest responsibilities.

Chapter 4 Security Part II: Auditing Database Systems

The focus of this chapter is on Sarbanes-Oxley compliance regarding the security and control of organization databases. The chapter opens with a description of flat-file data management, which is used in many older (legacy) systems that are still in operation today. The chapter then presents a conceptual overview of the database model and illustrates how problems associated with the flat-file model are resolved under this approach. The chapter outlines the key functions and defining features of three common database models: the hierarchical, the network, and the relational models. Both centralized and distributed database systems are discussed. The chapter concludes by presenting the risks, audit objectives, and audit procedures relevant to flat files, centralized databases, and distributed database systems.

Chapter 5 Systems Development and Program Change Activities

This chapter concludes our treatment of general control issues as they relate to management and auditor responsibilities under SOX Section 404. It begins by describing the roles of the participants involved in developing an organization's information system, including systems professionals, users, and stakeholders. Then it outlines the key activities that constitute the systems development life cycle (SDLC). These include systems planning, systems analysis, conceptual design, system selection, detailed design, system implementation, and program change procedures (systems maintenance). This multistage procedure is used to guide systems development in many organizations. Finally, it discusses SDLC risks, controls, and audit issues.

NEW: Chapter 6 Transaction Processing and Financial Reporting Systems Overview

This chapter provides an overview of transaction processing systems (TPS) and Financial Reporting Systems (FRS) and presents topics that are common to all TPS and FRS applications. Subsequent chapters draw heavily from this material as we examine the individual systems in detail. The chapter is organized into seven major sections. The first is an overview of transaction processing. This section defines the broad objectives of the three primary transaction cycles and specifies the roles of their individual subsystems. The second section describes the relationships among accounting records in forming an audit trail in both manual and computer-based systems. The third section examines documentation techniques used to represent both manual and computer-based systems. The fourth section reviews the fundamental features of batch and real-time technologies and their implication for transaction processing. The fifth section examines data coding schemes and their role in transaction processing. The sixth section of the chapter illustrates the central role of the general ledger as a hub that connects TPS applications and provides input to the FRS. Finally, the seventh section outlines imminent changes to the traditional financial reporting process as a result of XBRL (extendable business reporting language) initiatives by the SEC.

Chapter 7   Computer-Assisted Audit Tools and Techniques

Chapter 7 presents the use of Computer Assisted Audit Tools and Techniques (CAATTs) for performing tests of application controls. The chapter begins with an extensive description of application controls organized into three classes: input controls, process controls, and output controls. It examines both the *black box* (audit around) and *white box* (audit through) approaches to testing application controls. The latter approach requires a detailed understanding of the application's logic. The chapter discusses five CAATT approaches used for testing application logic. These are the *test data method, base case system evaluation, tracing, integrated test facility,* and *parallel simulation.*

Chapter 8   Data Structures and CAATTs for Data Extraction

Chapter 8 examines the uses of CAATTs for data extractions and analysis. Auditors make extensive use of these tools in gathering accounting data for testing application controls and in performing substantive tests. In an IT environment, the records needed to perform such tests are stored in computer files and databases. Understanding how data are organized and accessed is central to using data extraction tools. For this reason, a thorough review of common flat-file and database structures is provided. Considerable attention is devoted to relational databases, since this is the most common data structure used by modern business organizations. The coverage includes relational concepts, terminology, table-linking techniques, database normalization, and database design procedures.

Data extraction software fall into two general categories: *embedded audit modules* (EAM) and *general audit software* (GAS). The chapter describes the features, advantages, and disadvantages of both. The chapter closes with a review of the key features of ACL, the leading GAS product on the market.

Chapters 9 and 10   Auditing the Revenue Cycle and Auditing the Expenditure Cycle

Auditing procedures associated with the revenue and expenditure cycles are examined in Chapters 9 and 10, respectively. Each chapter begins with a review of alternative technologies employed in legacy systems and modern computer systems. This review is followed by the audit objectives, controls, and tests of controls that an auditor would normally perform to gather the evidence needed to limit the scope, timing, and extent of substantive tests. Finally, the substantive tests related to audit objectives are explained and illustrated using ACL software. End-of-chapter material contains several ACL assignments including a comprehensive assignment, which spans chapters 9, 10, and 12. An appendix to each chapter provides the reader with a detailed description of the activities and procedures that constitute the respective cycle and with the key accounting records and documents employed in transaction processing.

Chapter 11   Enterprise Resource Planning Systems

This chapter presents a number of issues related to the **implementation and audit of enterprise resource planning (ERP) systems**. It is comprised of five major sections.

- The first section outlines the key features of a **generic ERP system** by comparing the function and data storage techniques of a traditional flat-file or database system to that of an ERP.
- The second section describes various ERP configurations related to **servers, databases, and bolt-on software**.

- Data warehousing is the topic of the third section. A **data warehouse** is a relational or multidimensional database that supports online analytical processing (OLAP). A number of issues are discussed, including data modeling, data extraction from operational databases, data cleansing, data transformation, and loading data into the warehouse.
- The fourth section examines **risks associated with ERP implementation**. These include "big bang" issues, opposition to change within the organization, choosing the wrong ERP model, choosing the wrong consultant, cost overrun issues, and disruptions to operations.
- The fifth section reviews **control and auditing issues related to ERPs**. The discussion follows the COSO control framework and addresses the significant risks associated with role granting activities.

Chapter 12   Business Ethics, Fraud, and Fraud Detection

Perhaps no aspect of the independent auditor's role has caused more public and professional concern than the external auditor's responsibility for detecting fraud during an audit. Recent major financial frauds have heightened public awareness of fraud and the terrible damage it can cause. This chapter examines the closely related subjects of ethics and fraud and their implications for auditing. It begins with a survey of ethical issues that highlight the organization's conflicting responsibilities to its employees, shareholders, customers, and the general public. Management, employees, and auditors need to recognize the implications of new information technologies for such traditional issues as working conditions, the right to privacy, and the potential for fraud. The section concludes with a review of the code of ethics requirements that SOX mandates.

The chapter then considers basic fraud issues beginning with a definition of fraud. The chapter examines the nature and meaning of fraud, differentiates between employee fraud and management fraud, explains fraud-motivating forces, and reviews common fraud techniques. The chapter outlines the key features of SAS 99, "Consideration of Fraud in a Financial Statement Audit," and presents the results of a fraud research project conducted by the Association of Certified Fraud Examiners (ACFE). Finally, the chapter presents a number of specific fraud schemes and fraud detection techniques that are used in practice. The discussion follows the fraud classification format derived by the ACFE, which defines three broad categories of fraud schemes: fraudulent statements, corruption, and asset misappropriation. The chapter presents several ACL tests that auditors can perform to help them detect fraud. The end-of-chapter material contains a number of ACL fraud exercises as well as an integrated fraud case. The fraud assignments and their associated data may be downloaded from this book's Website.

SUPPLEMENTS

The third edition contains enhanced learning and teaching aids: a new and improved version of ACL, new PowerPoint slides, and increased integration of ACL in our online resources.

       ACL™ Desktop Edition (full educational version) CD, is bundled with each NEW copy of the text. ACL is the preferred software tool of audit and financial professionals for data extraction, data analysis, fraud detection, and continuous monitoring. Robust yet easy-to-use, **ACL™** Desktop Edition, Version 9.0 software expands the depth and breadth of your analysis, increases your personal productivity, and gives you confidence in your findings.

With **ACL** you can:

- Perform analysis more quickly and efficiently.
- Produce easy-to-understand reports—easily design, preview, and modify your results on-screen with drag-and-drop formatting.
- Identify trends, pinpoint exceptions, and highlight potential areas of concern.
- Locate errors and potential fraud by comparing and analyzing files according to end-user criteria.
- Identify control issues and ensure compliance with standards.

NEW Microsoft® PowerPoint slides provide invaluable lecture and study aids, charts, lists, definitions, and summaries directly correlated with the text.

The **Solutions Manual** contains answers to all of the end-of-chapter problem material in the text.

The **Product Website** contains revised ACL tutorials, a revised ACL case, and data files along with instructor solutions. These exercises and cases are tied to chapters in the text.

ACKNOWLEDGMENTS

We wish to thank the following reviewers for their useful and perceptive comments:

Faye Borthick
(Georgia State University)

John Coulter
(Western New England College)

Lori Fuller
(Widener University)

Jongsoo Han
(Rutgers University)

Sharon Huxley
(Teikyo Post University)

Louis Jacoby
(Saginaw Valley State University)

Orlando Katter
(Winthrop University)

Jim Kurtenbach
(Iowa State University)

Nick McGaughey
(San Jose State University)

Rebecca Rosner
(Long Island University—
CW Post Campus)

Hema Rao
(SUNY-Oswego)

Chuck Stanley
(Baylor University)

Tommie Singleton
(University of Alabama at Birmingham)

Brad Tuttle
(University of South Carolina)

Douglas Ziegenfuss
(Old Dominion)

Thanks also go to Sabrina Terrizzi (LeHigh University) for writing the solutions manual.

We wish to thank ACL Services, Ltd. for its cooperation in the development of the third edition, for its permission to reprint screens from the software in the text, and for granting use of an educational version of the software to accompany our text.

Finally, we are grateful to the publishing team at Cengage South-Western for all their work: Matt Filimonov, acquisitions editor; Maggie Kubale, developmental editor; Natalie King, marketing manager; Chris Valentine, media editor; and Doug Wilke, senior buyer.

ABOUT THE AUTHOR

James A. Hall is the Peter E. Bennett Chair in Business and Economics at Lehigh University, Bethlehem, PA. After his discharge from the U.S. Army, he entered the University of Tulsa in 1970 and received a BSBA in 1974 and an MBA in 1976. He earned his Ph.D. from Oklahoma State University in 1979. Hall has worked in industry in the fields of systems analysis and computer auditing and has served as consultant in these areas to numerous organizations. Professor Hall has published articles in the Journal of Accounting, Auditing & Finance, Journal of Management Information Systems (JMIS), Communications of the ACM, Management Accounting, Journal of Computer Information Systems, The Journal of Accounting Education, The Review of Accounting Information Systems, and other professional journals. He is the author of Accounting Information Systems, 7th Edition, published by South-Western Publishing. His research interests include computer controls, database design, and IT outsourcing.

INFORMATION TECHNOLOGY
AUDITING and ASSURANCE

1

Auditing and Internal Control

LEARNING OBJECTIVES

After studying this chapter, you should:

- Know the difference between attest services and advisory services and be able to explain the relationship between the two.
- Understand the structure of an audit and have a firm grasp of the conceptual elements of the audit process.
- Understand internal control categories presented in the COSO framework.
- Be familiar with the key features of Section 302 and 404 of the Sarbanes-Oxley Act.
- Understand the relationship between general controls, application controls, and financial data integrity.

Recent developments in **information technology (IT)** have had a tremendous impact on the field of **auditing**. IT has inspired the reengineering of traditional business processes to promote more efficient operations and to improve communications within the entity and between the entity and its customers and suppliers. These advances, however, have introduced new risks that require unique internal controls. They have engendered the need for new techniques for evaluating controls and for assuring the security and accuracy of corporate data and the information systems that produce it.

This chapter provides an overview of IT auditing. We begin by describing the various types of audits that organizations commission and distinguish between the auditor's traditional attestation responsibility and the emerging field of advisory services. We go on to explain the structure of an IT audit: the relationship between management assertions, audit objectives, tests of controls, and substantive tests are explained. The chapter also outlines the key points of the COSO control framework, which defines internal controls in both manual and IT environments. The final section of the chapter examines audit issues and implications related to Sarbanes-Oxley legislation and provides a conceptual framework that links general controls, application controls, and financial data integrity. This framework is a model for the remainder of the text.

OVERVIEW OF AUDITING

Business organizations undergo different types of audits for different purposes. The most common of these are external (financial) audits, internal audits, and fraud audits. Each of these is briefly outlined in the following sections.

External (Financial) Audits

An external audit is an independent attestation performed by an expert—the auditor—who expresses an opinion regarding the presentation of financial statements. This task, known as the **attest service**, is performed by Certified Public Accountants (CPA) who work for public accounting firms that are independent of the client organization being audited. The audit objective is always associated with assuring the fair presentation of financial statements. These audits are, therefore, often referred to as *financial audits*. The Securities and Exchange Commission (SEC) requires all publicly traded companies be subject to a financial audit annually. CPAs conducting such audits represent the interests of outsiders: stockholders, creditors, government agencies, and the general public.

The CPA's role is similar in concept to a judge who collects and evaluates evidence and renders an opinion. A key concept in this process is **independence**. The judge must remain independent in his or her deliberations. The judge cannot be an advocate of either party in the trial, but must apply the law impartially based on the evidence presented. Likewise, the independent auditor collects and evaluates evidence and renders an opinion based on the evidence. Throughout the audit process, the auditor must maintain independence from the client organization. Public confidence in the reliability of the company's internally produced financial statements rests directly on an evaluation of them by an independent auditor.

The external auditor must follow strict rules in conducting financial audits. These authoritative rules have been defined by the SEC, the Financial Accounting Standards Board (FASB), the AICPA, and by federal law (**Sarbanes-Oxley [SOX] Act of 2002**). With the passage of SOX, Congress established the Public Company Accounting Oversight Board (PCAOB), which has to a great extent replaced the function served by the FASB, and some of the functions of the AICPA (e.g., setting standards and issuing reprimands and penalties for CPAs who are convicted of certain crimes or guilty of certain infractions). Regardless, under federal law, the SEC has final authority for financial auditing.

Attest Service versus Advisory Services

An important distinction needs to be made regarding the external auditor's traditional attestation service and the rapidly growing field of advisory services, which many public accounting firms offer. The attest service is defined as:

> ... an engagement in which a practitioner is engaged to issue, or does issue, a written communication that expresses a conclusion about the reliability of a written assertion that is the responsibility of another party. (SSAE No. 1, AT Sec. 100.01)

The following requirements apply to attestation services:

- Attestation services require written assertions and a practitioner's written report.
- Attestation services require the formal establishment of measurement criteria or their description in the presentation.

- The levels of service in attestation engagements are limited to examination, review, and application of agreed-upon procedures.

Advisory services are professional services offered by public accounting firms to improve their client organizations' operational efficiency and effectiveness. The domain of advisory services is intentionally unbounded so that it does not inhibit the growth of future services that are currently unforeseen. As examples, advisory services include actuarial advice, business advice, fraud investigation services, information system design and implementation, and internal control assessments for compliance with SOX.

Prior to the passage of SOX, accounting firms could provide advisory services concurrently to audit (attest function) clients. SOX legislation, however, greatly restricts the types of nonaudit services that auditors may render audit clients. It is now unlawful for a registered public accounting firm that is currently providing attest services for a client to provide the following services:

- bookkeeping or other services related to the accounting records or financial statements of the audit client
- financial information systems design and implementation
- appraisal or valuation services, fairness opinions, or contribution-in-kind reports
- actuarial services
- internal audit outsourcing services
- management functions or human resources
- broker or dealer, investment adviser, or investment banking services
- legal services and expert services unrelated to the audit
- any other service that the board determines, by regulation, is impermissible

The advisory services units of public accounting firms responsible for providing IT control-related client support have different names in different firms, but they all engage in tasks known collectively as IT risk management. These groups often play a dual role within their respective firms; they provide nonaudit clients with IT advisory services and also work with their firm's financial audit staff to perform IT-related tests of controls as part of the attestation function.

The material outlined in this chapter relates to tasks that risk management professionals normally conduct during an IT audit. In the pages that follow, we examine what constitutes an audit and how audits are structured. Keep in mind, however, that in many cases the *purpose* of the task, rather than the task itself, defines the service being rendered. For example, a risk management professional may perform a test of IT controls as an advisory service for a nonaudit client who is preparing for a financial audit by a different public accounting firm. The same professional may perform the very same test for an audit client as part of the attest function. Therefore, the issues and procedures described in this text apply to a broader context that includes advisory services and attestation, as well as the internal audit function.

Internal Audits

The Institute of Internal Auditors (IIA) defines **internal auditing** as an independent appraisal function established within an organization to examine and evaluate its activities as a service to the organization.[1] Internal auditors perform a wide range of activities on behalf of the organization, including conducting financial audits, examining an operation's

---

1   AAA Committee on Basic Auditing Concepts, "A Statement of Basic Auditing Concepts," *Accounting Review*, supplement to vol. 47, 1972.

compliance with organizational policies, reviewing the organization's compliance with legal obligations, evaluating operational efficiency, and detecting and pursuing fraud within the firm.

An internal audit is typically conducted by auditors who work for the organization, but this task may be outsourced to other organizations. Internal auditors are often certified as a Certified Internal Auditor (CIA) or a Certified Information Systems Auditor (CISA). While internal auditors self-impose independence to perform their duties effectively, they represent the interests of the organization. These auditors generally answer to executive management of the organization or the audit committee of the board of directors, if one exists. The standards, guidance, and certification of internal audits are governed mostly by the Institute of Internal Auditors (IIA) and, to a lesser degree, by the Information Systems Audit and Control Association (ISACA).

External versus Internal Auditors

The characteristic that conceptually distinguishes external auditors from internal auditors is their respective constituencies: while external auditors represent outsiders, internal auditors represent the interests of the organization. Nevertheless, in this capacity, internal auditors often cooperate with and assist external auditors in performing aspects of financial audits. This cooperation is done to achieve audit efficiency and reduce audit fees. For example, a team of internal auditors can perform tests of computer controls under the supervision of a single external auditor.

The independence and competence of the internal audit staff determine the extent to which external auditors may cooperate with and rely on work performed by internal auditors. Some internal audit departments report directly to the controller. Under this arrangement, the internal auditor's independence is compromised, and the external auditor is prohibited by professional standards from relying on evidence provided by the internal auditors. In contrast, external auditors can rely in part on evidence gathered by internal audit departments that are organizationally independent and report to the board of directors' audit committee (discussed below). A truly independent internal audit staff adds value to the audit process. For example, internal auditors can gather audit evidence throughout a fiscal period, which external auditors may then use at the year's end to conduct more efficient, less disruptive, and less costly audits of the organization's financial statements.

Fraud Audits

In recent years, fraud audits have, unfortunately, increased in popularity as a corporate governance tool. They have been thrust into prominence by a corporate environment in which both employee theft of assets and major financial frauds by management (e.g., Enron, WorldCom, etc.) have become rampant. The objective of a fraud audit is to investigate anomalies and gather evidence of fraud that may lead to criminal conviction. Sometimes fraud audits are initiated by corporate management who suspect employee fraud. Alternatively, boards of directors may hire fraud auditors to look into their own executives if theft of assets or financial fraud is suspected. Organizations victimized by fraud usually contract with specialized fraud units of public accounting firms or with companies that specialize in forensic accounting. Typically, fraud auditors have earned the Certified Fraud Examiner (CFE) certification, which is governed by the Association of Certified Fraud Examiners (ACFE).

THE ROLE OF THE AUDIT COMMITTEE

The board of directors of publicly traded companies form a subcommittee known as the audit committee, which has special responsibilities regarding audits. This committee usually consists of three people who should be outsiders (not associated with the families of executive management nor former officers, etc.). With the advent of the Sarbanes-Oxley Act, at least one member of the audit committee must be a "financial expert." The audit committee serves as an independent "check and balance" for the internal audit function and liaison with external auditors. One of the most significant changes imposed by SOX has been to the relationship between management and the external auditors. Prior to SOX, external auditors were hired and fired by management. Many believe, with some justification, that this relationship erodes auditor independence when disputes over audit practices arise. SOX mandates that external auditors now report to the audit committee who hire and fire auditors and resolve disputes.

To be effective, the audit committee must be willing to challenge the internal auditors (or the entity performing that function) as well as management, when necessary. Part of its role is to look for ways to identify risk. For instance, it might serve as a sounding board for employees who observe suspicious behavior or spot fraudulent activities. In general, it becomes an independent guardian of the entity's assets by whatever means is appropriate. Corporate frauds often have some bearing on audit committee failures. These include lack of independence of audit committee members, inactive audit committees, total absence of an audit committee, and lack of experienced members on the audit committee.

FINANCIAL AUDIT COMPONENTS

The product of the attestation function is a formal written report that expresses an opinion about the reliability of the assertions contained in the financial statements. The auditor's report expresses an opinion as to whether the financial statements are in conformity with *generally accepted accounting principles (GAAP)*; external users of financial statements are presumed to rely on the auditor's opinion about the reliability of financial statements in making decisions. To do so, users must be able to place their trust in the auditor's competence, professionalism, integrity, and independence. Auditors are guided in their professional responsibility by the ten *generally accepted auditing standards (GAAS)* presented in Table 1.1.

Auditing Standards

Auditing standards are divided into three classes: general qualification standards, field work standards, and reporting standards. GAAS establishes a framework for prescribing auditor performance, but it is not sufficiently detailed to provide meaningful guidance in specific circumstances. To provide specific guidance, the American Institute of Certified Public Accountants (AICPA) issues *Statements on Auditing Standards (SASs)* as authoritative interpretations of GAAS. SASs are often referred to as *auditing standards*, or *GAAS*, although they are not the ten generally accepted auditing standards.

The first SAS (SAS 1) was issued by the AICPA in 1972. Since then, many SASs have been issued to provide auditors with guidance on a spectrum of topics, including methods of investigating new clients, procedures for collecting information from

TABLE 1.1	Generally Accepted Auditing Standards	
General Standards	**Standards of Field Work**	**Reporting Standards**
1. The auditor must have adequate technical training and proficiency.	1. Audit work must be adequately planned.	1. The auditor must state in the report whether financial statements were prepared in accordance with generally accepted accounting principles.
2. The auditor must have independence of mental attitude.	2. The auditor must gain a sufficient understanding of the internal control structure.	2. The report must identify those circumstances in which generally accepted accounting principles were not applied.
3. The auditor must exercise due professional care in the performance of the audit and the preparation of the report.	3. The auditor must obtain sufficient, competent evidence.	3. The report must identify any items that do not have adequate informative disclosures.
		4. The report shall contain an expression of the auditor's opinion on the financial statements as a whole.

attorneys regarding contingent liability claims against clients, and techniques for obtaining background information on the client's industry.

Statements on Auditing Standards are regarded as authoritative pronouncements because every member of the profession must follow their recommendations or be able to show why a SAS does not apply in a given situation. The burden of justifying departures from the SASs falls upon the individual auditor.

A Systematic Process

Conducting an audit is a systematic and logical process that applies to all forms of information systems. While important in all audit settings, a systematic approach is particularly important in the IT environment. The lack of physical procedures that can be visually verified and evaluated injects a high degree of complexity into the IT audit (e.g., the audit trail may be purely electronic, in a digital form, and thus invisible to those attempting to verify it). Therefore, a logical framework for conducting an audit in the IT environment is critical to help the auditor identify all-important processes and data files.

Management Assertions and Audit Objectives

The organization's financial statements reflect a set of **management assertions** about the financial health of the entity. The task of the auditor is to determine whether the financial statements are fairly presented. To accomplish this goal, the auditor establishes **audit objectives**, designs procedures, and gathers evidence that corroborate or refute management's assertions. These assertions fall into five general categories:

1. The **existence or occurrence** assertion affirms that all assets and equities contained in the balance sheet exist and that all transactions in the income statement actually occurred.
2. The **completeness** assertion declares that no material assets, equities, or transactions have been omitted from the financial statements.

3. The **rights and obligations** assertion maintains that assets appearing on the balance sheet are owned by the entity and that the liabilities reported are obligations.
4. The **valuation or allocation** assertion states that assets and equities are valued in accordance with GAAP and that allocated amounts such as depreciation expense are calculated on a systematic and rational basis.
5. The **presentation and disclosure** assertion alleges that financial statement items are correctly classified (e.g., long-term liabilities will not mature within one year) and that footnote disclosures are adequate to avoid misleading the users of financial statements.

Generally, auditors develop their audit objectives and design **audit procedures** based on the preceding assertions. The example in Table 1.2 outlines these procedures.

Audit objectives may be classified into two general categories. Those in Table 1.2 relate to transactions and account balances that directly impact financial reporting. The second category pertains to the information system itself. This category includes the audit objectives for assessing controls over manual operations and computer technologies used in transaction processing. In the chapters that follow, we consider both categories of audit objectives and the associated audit procedures.

Obtaining Evidence

Auditors seek evidential matter that corroborates management assertions. In the IT environment, this process involves gathering evidence relating to the reliability of computer controls as well as the contents of databases that have been processed by computer programs. Evidence is collected by performing tests of controls, which establish whether internal controls are functioning properly, and substantive tests, which determine whether accounting databases fairly reflect the organization's transactions and account balances.

Ascertaining Materiality

The auditor must determine whether weaknesses in internal controls and misstatements found in transactions and account balances are material. In all audit environments,

---

TABLE 1.2 **Audit Objectives and Audit Procedures Based on Management Assertions**

Management Assertion	Audit Objective	Audit Procedure
Existence of Occurrence	Inventories listed on the balance sheet exist.	Observe the counting of physical inventory.
Completeness	Accounts payable include all obligations to vendors for the period.	Compare receiving reports, supplier invoices, purchase orders, and journal entries for the period and the beginning of the next period.
Rights and Obligations	Plant and equipment listed in the balance sheet are owned by the entity.	Review purchase agreements, insurance policies, and related documents.
Valuation or Allocation	Accounts receivable are stated at net realizable value.	Review entity's aging of accounts and evaluate the adequacy of the allowance for uncorrectable accounts.
Presentation and Disclosure	Contingencies not reported in financial accounts are properly disclosed in footnotes.	Obtain information from entity lawyers about the status of litigation and estimates of potential loss.

assessing materiality is an auditor judgment. In an IT environment, however, this decision is complicated further by technology and a sophisticated internal control structure.

Communicating Results

Auditors must communicate the results of their tests to interested users. An independent auditor renders a report to the audit committee of the board of directors or stockholders of a company. The audit report contains, among other things, an **audit opinion**. This opinion is distributed along with the financial report to interested parties both internal and external to the organization. IT auditors often communicate their findings to internal and external auditors, who can then integrate these findings with the non-IT aspects of the audit.

AUDIT RISK

Audit risk is the probability that the auditor will render an unqualified (clean) opinion on financial statements that are, in fact, materially misstated. Material misstatements may be caused by errors or irregularities or both. Errors are unintentional mistakes. Irregularities are intentional misrepresentations associated with the commission of a fraud such as the misappropriation of physical assets or the deception of financial statement users.

Audit Risk Components

The auditor's objective is to achieve a level of audit risk that is acceptable to the auditor. Acceptable audit risk (AR) is estimated based on the *ex ante* value of the components of the audit risk model. These are inherent risk, control risk, and detection risk.

Inherent Risk

Inherent risk is associated with the unique characteristics of the business or industry of the client.[2] Firms in declining industries have greater inherent risk than firms in stable or thriving industries. Likewise, industries that have a heavy volume of cash transactions have a higher level of inherent risk than those that do not. Furthermore, placing a value on inventory when the inventory value is difficult to assess due to its nature is associated with higher inherent risk than in situations where inventory values are more objective. For example, the valuation of diamonds is inherently more risky than assessing the value of automobile tires. Auditors cannot reduce the level of inherent risk. Even in a system protected by excellent controls, financial data and, consequently, financial statements, can be materially misstated.

   Control risk is the likelihood that the control structure is flawed because controls are either absent or inadequate to prevent or detect errors in the accounts.[3] To illustrate

---

2   Institute of Internal Auditors, *Standards of Professional Practice of Internal Auditing* (Orlando, FL.: Institute of Internal Auditors, 1978).

3   Auditing Standards Board, *AICPA Professional Standards* (New York: AICPA, 1994), AU Sec. 312.20.

control risk, consider the following partial customer sales record, which is processed by the sales order system.

Quantity	Unit Price	Total
10 Units	$20	$2,000

Assuming the Quantity and Unit Price fields in the record are correctly presented, the extended amount (Total) value of $2,000 is in error. An accounting information system (AIS) with adequate controls should prevent or detect such an error. If, however, controls are lacking and the value of Total in each record is not validated before processing, then the risk of undetected errors entering the data files increases.

Auditors assess the level of control risk by performing tests of internal controls. In the preceding example, the auditor could create test transactions, including some with incorrect Total values, which are processed by the application in a test run. The results of the test will indicate that price extension errors are not detected and are being incorrectly posted to the accounts receivable file.

Detection Risk

Detection risk is the risk that auditors are willing to take that errors not detected or prevented by the control structure will also not be detected by the auditor. Auditors set an acceptable level of detection risk (planned detection risk) that influences the level of substantive tests that they perform. For example, more substantive testing would be required when the planned detection risk is 10 percent than when it is 20 percent.

Audit Risk Model

Financial auditors use the audit risk components in a model to determine the scope, nature, and timing of substantive tests. The audit risk model is

$$AR = IR \times CR \times DR$$

Assume that acceptable audit risk is assessed at a value of 5 percent, consistent with the 95 percent confidence interval associated with statistics. By illustration, assume IR is assessed at 40 percent, and CR is assessed at 60 percent. What would be the level of planned detection risk (DR) needed to achieve the acceptable audit risk (AR) of 5 percent?

$$5\% = 40\% \times 60\% \times DR$$
$$DR = .05/.24$$
$$DR = .20$$

Let's now reduce the control risk (CR) value to 40 percent and recalculate DR.

$$5\% = 40\% \times 40\% \times DR$$
$$DR = .31$$

Notice that to achieve an acceptable level of audit risk in the first example. the auditor must set planned detection risk lower (20 percent) than in the second example (31 percent). This is because the internal control structure in the first example is more risky (60 percent) than it is in the second case (40 percent). To achieve the planned detection of 20 percent in the first example, the auditor will need to perform more substantive tests than in the second example, where the risk is lower. This relationship is explained below.

The Relationship Between Tests of Controls and Substantive Tests

Tests of controls and substantive tests are auditing techniques used for reducing audit risk to an acceptable level. The stronger the internal control structure, as determined through tests of controls, the lower the control risk and the less substantive testing the auditor must do. This relationship is true because the likelihood of errors in the accounting records is reduced when controls are strong. In other words, when controls are in place and effective, the auditor may limit substantive testing. In contrast, the weaker the internal control structure, the greater the control risk and the more substantive testing the auditor must perform to reduce total audit risk. Evidence of weak controls forces the auditor to extend substantive testing to search for misstatements.

In summary, the more reliable the internal controls, the lower the CR probability. That leads to a lower DR, which will lead to fewer substantive tests being required. Because substantive tests are labor intensive and time-consuming, they drive up audit costs and exacerbate the disruptive effects of an audit. Thus, management's best interests are served by having a strong internal control structure.

THE IT AUDIT

The public expression of the auditor's opinion is the culmination of a systematic financial audit process that involves three conceptual phases: audit planning, tests of controls, and substantive testing. Figure 1.1 illustrates the steps involved in these phases. An IT audit focuses on the computer-based aspects of an organization's information system; and modern systems employ significant levels of technology. For example, transaction processing is automated and performed in large part by computer programs. Similarly source documents, journals, and ledgers that traditionally were paper-based are now digitized and stored in relational databases. As we will see later, the controls over these processes and databases become central issues in the financial audit process.

The Structure of an IT Audit

Audit Planning
The first step in the IT audit is **audit planning**. Before the auditor can determine the nature and extent of the tests to perform, he or she must gain a thorough understanding

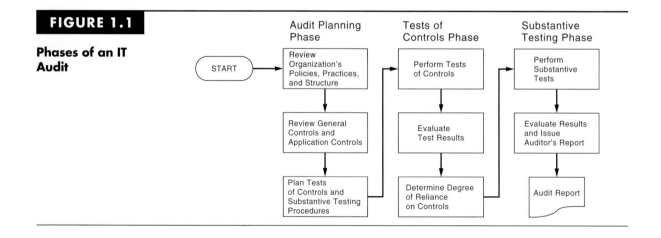

FIGURE 1.1

Phases of an IT Audit

of the client's business. A major part of this phase of the audit is the analysis of audit risk. The auditor's objective is to obtain sufficient information about the firm to plan the other phases of the audit. The risk analysis incorporates an overview of the organization's internal controls. During the review of controls, the auditor attempts to understand the organization's policies, practices, and structure. In this phase of the audit, the auditor also identifies the financially significant applications and attempts to understand the controls over the primary transactions that are processed by these applications.

The techniques for gathering evidence at this phase include conducting questionnaires, interviewing management, reviewing systems documentation, and observing activities. During this process, the IT auditor must identify the principal exposures and the controls that attempt to reduce these exposures. Having done so, the auditor proceeds to the next phase, where he or she tests the controls for compliance with pre-established standards.

Tests of Controls

The objective of the **tests of controls** phase is to determine whether adequate internal controls are in place and functioning properly. To accomplish this, the auditor performs various tests of controls. The evidence-gathering techniques used in this phase may include both manual techniques and specialized computer audit techniques. We shall examine several such methods later in this text.

At the conclusion of the tests-of-controls phase, the auditor must assess the quality of the internal controls by assigning a level for control risk. As previously explained, the degree of reliance that the auditor can ascribe to internal controls will affect the nature and extent of substantive testing that needs to be performed.

Substantive Testing

The third phase of the audit process focuses on financial data. This phase involves a detailed investigation of specific account balances and transactions through what are called **substantive tests**. For example, a customer confirmation is a substantive test sometimes used to verify account balances. The auditor selects a sample of accounts receivable balances and traces these back to their source—the customers—to determine if the amount stated is in fact owed by a bona fide customer. By so doing, the auditor can verify the accuracy of each account in the sample. Based on such sample findings, the auditor is able to draw conclusions about the fair value of the entire accounts receivable asset.

Some substantive tests are physical, labor-intensive activities, such as counting cash, counting inventories in the warehouse, and verifying the existence of stock certificates in a safe. In an IT environment, the data needed to perform substantive tests (such as account balances and names and addresses of individual customers) are contained in data files that often must be extracted using **Computer-Assisted Audit Tools and Techniques (CAATTs)** software. In a later chapter of this text, we will examine the role of CAATTs in performing traditional substantive tests and other data analysis and reporting tasks.

INTERNAL CONTROL

Organization management is required by law to establish and maintain an adequate system of internal control. Consider the following Securities and Exchange Commission statement on this matter:

> The establishment and maintenance of a system of internal control is an important management obligation. A fundamental aspect of management's stewardship responsibility

is to provide shareholders with reasonable assurance that the business is adequately controlled. Additionally, management has a responsibility to furnish shareholders and potential investors with reliable financial information on a timely basis.[4]

Brief History of Internal Control Legislation

Since much of the internal control system relates directly to transaction processing, accountants are key participants in ensuring control adequacy. This section begins with a brief history of internal controls, and then provides a conceptual overview of internal control. Lastly, it presents the COSO control framework.

SEC Acts of 1933 and 1934

Following the stock market crash of 1929, and a worldwide financial fraud by Ivar Kruegar, the U.S. legislature passed two acts to restore confidence in the capital market. The first was the Securities Act of 1933, which had two main objectives: (1) require that investors receive financial and other significant information concerning securities being offered for public sale; and (2) prohibit deceit, misrepresentations, and other fraud in the sale of securities. The second act, the Securities Exchange Act, 1934, created the Securities and Exchange Commission (SEC) and empowered it with broad authority over all aspects of the securities industry, which included authority regarding auditing standards. The SEC acts also required publicly traded companies to be audited by an independent auditor (i.e., CPA). But is also required all companies that report to the SEC to maintain a system of internal control that is evaluated as part of the annual external audit. That portion of the Act has been enforced on rare occasions. That leniency changed with the passage of Sarbanes-Oxley Act in July 2002, discussed later.

Copyright Law–1976

This law, which has had multiple revisions, added software and other intellectual properties into the existing copyright protection laws. It is of concern to IT auditors because management is held personally liable for violations (e.g., software piracy) if "raided" by the software police (a U.S. marshal accompanied by software vendors' association representatives), and sufficient evidence of impropriety is found.

Foreign Corrupt Practices Act (FCPA) of 1977

Corporate management has not always lived up to its internal control responsibility. With the discovery that U.S. business executives were using their organizations' funds to bribe foreign officials, internal control issues, formerly of little interest to stockholders, quickly became a matter of public concern. From this issue came the passage of the **Foreign Corrupt Practices Act of 1977 (FCPA)**. Among its provisions, the FCPA requires companies registered with the SEC to do the following:

1. Keep records that fairly and reasonably reflect the transactions of the firm and its financial position.
2. Maintain a system of internal control that provides reasonable assurance that the organization's objectives are met.

The FCPA has had a significant impact on organization management. With the knowledge that violation of the FCPA could lead to heavy fines and imprisonment, managers have developed a deeper concern for control adequacy.

---

4   Ibid.

Committee of Sponsoring Organizations–1992

Following the series of S&L scandals of the 1980s, a committee was formed to address these frauds. Originally, the committee took the name of its chair, Treadway, but eventually the project became known as **COSO (Committee of Sponsoring Organizations)**. The sponsoring organizations included Financial Executives International (FEI), the Institute of Management Accountants (IMA), the American Accounting Association (AAA), AICPA, and the IIA. The Committee spent several years promulgating a response. Because it was determined early on that the best deterrent to fraud was strong internal controls, the committee decided to focus on an effective model for internal controls from a management perspective. The result was the COSO Model. The AICPA adopted the model into auditing standards and published SAS No. 78—*Consideration of Internal Control in a Financial Statement Audit.*

Sarbanes-Oxley Act of 2002

As a result of several large financial frauds (e.g., Enron, Worldcom, Adelphia, etc.) and the resulting losses suffered by stockholders, pressure was brought by the U.S. Congress to protect the public from such events. This led to the passage of the Sarbanes-Oxley Act (SOX) on July 30, 2002. In general, the law supports efforts to increase public confidence in capital markets by seeking to improve corporate governance, internal controls, and audit quality.

In particular, SOX requires management of public companies to implement an adequate system of internal controls over their financial reporting process. This includes controls over transaction processing systems that feed data to the financial reporting systems. Management's responsibilities for this are codified in Sections 302 and 404 of SOX.

Section 302 requires that corporate management (including the CEO) certify their organization's internal controls on a quarterly and annual basis. Section 302 also carries significant auditor implications. Specifically, external auditors must perform the following procedures quarterly to identify any material modifications in controls that may impact financial reporting:

- Interview management regarding any significant changes in the design or operation of internal control that occurred subsequent to the preceding annual audit or prior review of interim financial information.
- Evaluate the implications of misstatements identified by the auditor as part of the interim review that relate to effective internal controls.
- Determine whether changes in internal controls are likely to materially affect internal control over financial reporting.

In addition, Section 404 requires the management of public companies to assess the effectiveness of their organization's internal controls. This entails providing an annual report addressing the following points:

1. Understand the flow of transactions, including IT aspects, in sufficient detail to identify points at which a misstatement could arise.
2. Using a risk-based approach, assess both the design and operating effectiveness of selected internal controls related to material accounts.[5]
3. Assess the potential for fraud in the system and evaluate the controls designed to prevent or detect fraud.
4. Evaluate and conclude on the adequacy of controls over the financial statement reporting process.

---

5   Securities and Exchange Commission, Securities Release 34-13185 (19 January 1977).

5. Evaluate entity-wide (general) controls that correspond to the components of the COSO framework.

Regarding the control framework, the SEC has made specific reference to COSO as a recommended model. Furthermore, the PCAOB Auditing Standard No. 5 endorses the use of COSO as the framework for control assessment. Although other suitable frameworks have been published, any framework used should encompass all of COSO's general themes.[6] The key elements of the COSO framework are presented in a later section.

INTERNAL CONTROL OBJECTIVES, PRINCIPLES, AND MODELS

An organization's **internal control system** comprises policies, practices, and procedures to achieve four broad objectives:

1. To safeguard assets of the firm.
2. To ensure the accuracy and reliability of accounting records and information.
3. To promote efficiency in the firm's operations.
4. To measure compliance with management's prescribed policies and procedures.[7]

Modifying Principles

Inherent in these control objectives are four modifying principles that guide designers and auditors of internal control systems.[8]

Management Responsibility
This concept holds that the establishment and maintenance of a system of internal control is a management responsibility. Although the FCPA supports this principle, SOX legislation makes it law!

Methods of Data Processing
The internal control system should achieve the four broad objectives regardless of the **data processing** method used (whether manual or computer based). However, the specific techniques used to achieve these objectives will vary with different types of technology.

Limitations
Every system of internal control has **limitations** on its effectiveness. These include (1) the possibility of error—no system is perfect, (2) circumvention—personnel may circumvent the system through collusion or other means, (3) management override—management is in a position to override control procedures by personally distorting transactions or by directing a subordinate to do so, and (4) changing conditions—conditions may change over time so that existing effective controls may become ineffectual.

---

6   A popular competing control framework is Control Objectives for Information and related Technology (COBIT®) published by the IT Governance Institute (ITGI). This framework maps into COSO's general themes.

7   American Institute of Certified Public Accountants, *AICPA Professional Standards*, vol. 1 (New York: AICPA, 1987) AU Sec. 320.30–35.

8   American Institute of Certified Public Accountants, Committee on Auditing Procedure, Internal Control—Elements of a Coordinated System and Its Importance to Management and the Independent Public Accountant, *Statement on Auditing Standards No. 1*, Sec. 320 (New York: AICPA, 1973).

Reasonable Assurance

The internal control system should provide **reasonable assurance** that the four broad objectives of internal control are met. This reasonableness means that the cost of achieving improved control should not outweigh its benefits.

To illustrate the limitations and reasonable-assurance principles, Figure 1.2 portrays the internal control system as a shield that protects the firm's assets from numerous undesirable events that bombard the organization. These include attempts at unauthorized access to the firm's assets (including information); fraud perpetrated by persons both in and outside the firm; errors due to employee incompetence, faulty computer programs, and corrupted input data; and mischievous acts, such as unauthorized access by computer hackers and threats from computer viruses that destroy programs and databases.

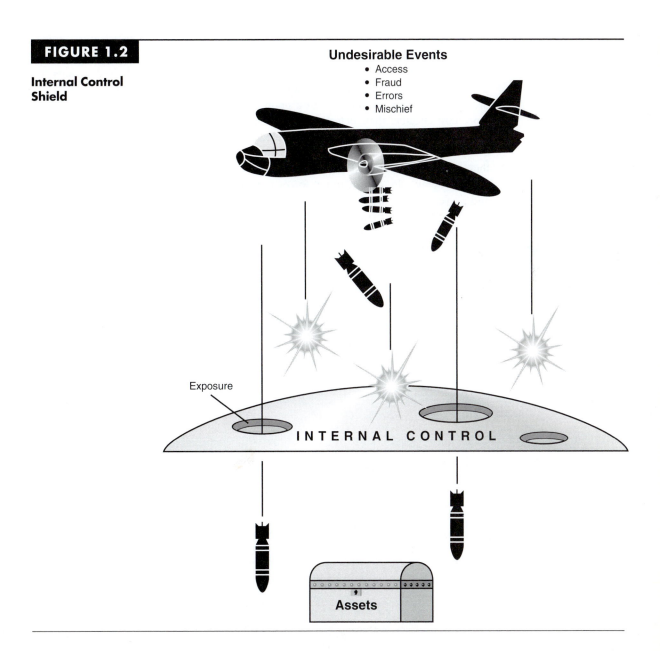

FIGURE 1.2

Internal Control Shield

Undesirable Events
- Access
- Fraud
- Errors
- Mischief

Exposure

INTERNAL CONTROL

Assets

Absence of or weakness in controls are illustrated in Figure 1.2 as holes in the control shield. Some weaknesses are immaterial and tolerable. Under the principle of reasonable assurance, these control weaknesses may not be worth fixing. Material weaknesses in controls, however, increase the firm's risk to financial loss or injury from the undesirable events. The cost of correcting these weaknesses is offset by the benefits derived.

The PDC Model

Figure 1.3 illustrates that the internal control shield represented in Figure 1.2 actually consists of three levels of control: preventive controls, detective controls, and corrective controls. This is called the **PDC control model**.

Preventive Controls

Prevention is the first line of defense in the control structure. **Preventive controls** are passive techniques designed to reduce the frequency of occurrence of undesirable events. Preventive controls force compliance with prescribed or desired actions and thus screen out aberrant events. When designing internal control systems, an ounce of prevention is most certainly worth a pound of cure. Preventing errors and fraud is far more cost-effective than detecting and correcting problems after they occur. The vast majority of undesirable events can be blocked at this first level. For example, a well-designed data entry screen is an example of a preventive control. The logical layout of the screen into zones that permit only specific types of data, such as customer name, address, items sold, and quantity, forces the data entry clerk to enter the required data and prevents necessary data from being omitted.

FIGURE 1.3

Preventive, Detective, and Corrective Controls

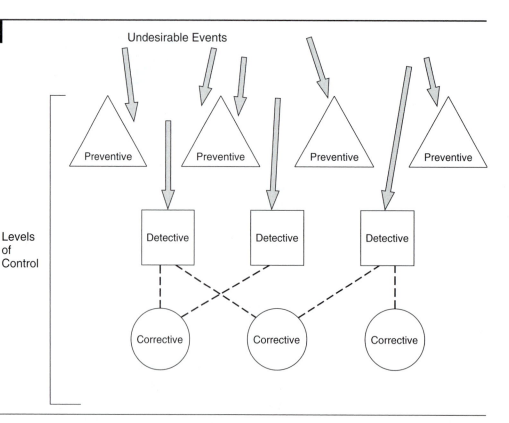

Detective Controls

Detection of problems is the second line of defense. **Detective controls** are devices, techniques, and procedures designed to identify and expose undesirable events that elude preventive controls. Detective controls reveal specific types of errors by comparing actual occurrences to preestablished standards. When the detective control identifies a departure from standard, it sounds an alarm to attract attention to the problem. For example, assume that because of a data entry error, a customer sales order record contains the following data:

Quantity	Unit Price	Total
10	$10	$1,000

Before processing this transaction and posting to the accounts, a detective control should recalculate the total value using the price and quantity. Thus, this error above would be detected.

Corrective Controls

Corrective actions must be taken to reverse the effects of detected errors. There is an important distinction between detective controls and corrective controls. Detective controls identify undesirable events and draw attention to the problem; **corrective controls** actually fix the problem. For any detected error, there may be more than one feasible corrective action, but the best course of action may not always be obvious. For example, in viewing the preceding error, your first inclination may have been to change the total value from $1,000 to $100 to correct the problem. This presumes that the quantity and price values in the record are correct; they may not be. At this point, we cannot determine the real cause of the problem; we know only that one exists.

Linking a corrective action to a detected error, as an automatic response, may result in an incorrect action that causes a worse problem than the original error. For this reason, error correction should be viewed as a separate control step that should be taken cautiously.

The PDC control model is conceptually pleasing but offers little practical guidance for designing or auditing specific controls. The current authoritative document for specifying internal control objectives and techniques is the **Statement on Auditing Standards No. 109**, which is based on the COSO framework. SAS 109 describes the complex relationship between the firm's internal controls, the auditor's assessment of risk, and the planning of audit procedures. SAS 109 provides guidance to auditors in their application of the COSO framework when assessing the risk of material misstatement. We now discuss the key elements of this framework.

Coso Internal Control Framework

The COSO framework consists of five components: the control environment, risk assessment, information and communication, monitoring, and control activities.

The Control Environment

The **control environment** is the foundation for the other four control components. The control environment sets the tone for the organization and influences the control awareness of its management and employees. Important elements of the control environment are:

- The integrity and ethical values of management.
- The structure of the organization.

- The participation of the organization's board of directors and the audit committee, if one exists.
- Management's philosophy and operating style.
- The procedures for delegating responsibility and authority.
- Management's methods for assessing performance.
- External influences, such as examinations by regulatory agencies.
- The organization's policies and practices for managing its human resources.

SAS 109 requires that auditors obtain sufficient knowledge to assess the attitude and awareness of the organization's management, board of directors, and owners regarding internal control. The following paragraphs provide examples of techniques that may be used to obtain an understanding of the control environment.

1. Auditors should assess the integrity of the organization's management and may use investigative agencies to report on the backgrounds of key managers. Some of the "Big Four" public accounting firms employ former FBI agents whose primary responsibility is to perform background checks on existing and prospective clients. If cause for serious reservations comes to light about the integrity of the client, the auditor should withdraw from the audit. The reputation and integrity of the company's managers are critical factors in determining the auditability of the organization. Auditors cannot function properly in an environment in which client management is deemed unethical and corrupt.

2. Auditors should be aware of conditions that would predispose the management of an organization to commit fraud. Some of the obvious conditions may be lack of sufficient working capital, adverse industry conditions, bad credit ratings, and the existence of extremely restrictive conditions in bank or indenture agreements. If auditors encounter any such conditions, their examination should give due consideration to the possibility of fraudulent financial reporting. Appropriate measures should be taken, and every attempt should be made to uncover any fraud.

3. Auditors should understand a client's business and industry and should be aware of conditions peculiar to the industry that may affect the audit. Auditors should read industry-related literature and familiarize themselves with the risks that are inherent in the business.

4. The board of directors should adopt, as a minimum, the provisions of SOX. In addition, the following guidelines represent established best practices.
   - *Separate CEO and chairman.* The roles of CEO and board chairman should be separate. Executive sessions give directors the opportunity to discuss issues without management present, and an independent chairman is important in facilitating such discussions.
   - *Set ethical standards.* The board of directors should establish a code of ethical standards from which management and staff will take direction. At a minimum, a code of ethics should address such issues as outside employment conflicts, acceptance of gifts that could be construed as bribery, falsification of financial and/or performance data, conflicts of interest, political contributions, confidentiality of company and customer data, honesty in dealing with internal and external auditors, and membership on external boards of directors.
   - *Establish an independent audit committee.* The audit committee is responsible for selecting and engaging an independent auditor, ensuring that an annual audit is conducted, reviewing the audit report, and ensuring that deficiencies are addressed. Large organizations with complex accounting practices may need to create audit subcommittees that specialize in specific activities.

- *Compensation committees.* The compensation committee should not be a rubber stamp for management. Excessive use of short-term stock options to compensate directors and executives may result in decisions that influence stock prices at the expense of the firm's long-term health. Compensation schemes should be carefully evaluated to ensure that they create the desired incentives.
- *Nominating committees.* The board nominations committee should have a plan to maintain a fully staffed board of directors with capable people as it moves forward for the next several years. The committee must recognize the need for independent directors and have criteria for determining independence. For example, under its newly implemented governance standards, General Electric (GE) considers directors independent if the sales to, and purchases from, GE total less than 1 percent of the revenue of the companies for which they serve as executives. Similar standards apply to charitable contributions from GE to any organization on which a GE director serves as officer or director. In addition, the company has set a goal that two-thirds of the board will be independent nonemployees.[9]
- *Access to outside professionals.* All committees of the board should have access to attorneys and consultants other than the corporation's normal counsel and consultants. Under the provisions of SOX, the audit committee of an SEC reporting company is entitled to such representation independently.

Risk Assessment

Organizations must perform a **risk assessment** to identify, analyze, and manage risks relevant to financial reporting. Risks can arise or change from circumstances such as:

- Changes in the operating environment that impose new or changed competitive pressures on the firm.
- New personnel who have a different or inadequate understanding of internal control.
- New or reengineered information systems that affect transaction processing.
- Significant and rapid growth that strains existing internal controls.
- The implementation of new technology into the production process or information system that impacts transaction processing.
- The introduction of new product lines or activities with which the organization has little experience.
- Organizational restructuring resulting in the reduction and/or reallocation of personnel such that business operations and transaction processing are affected.
- Entering into foreign markets that may impact operations (that is, the risks associated with foreign currency transactions).
- Adoption of a new accounting principle that impacts the preparation of financial statements.

SAS 109 requires that auditors obtain sufficient knowledge of the organization's risk assessment procedures to understand how management identifies, prioritizes, and manages the risks related to financial reporting.

Information and Communication

The accounting information system consists of the records and methods used to initiate, identify, analyze, classify, and record the organization's transactions and to account for

---

9   Rachel E. Silverman, "GE Makes Changes in Board Policy," The Wall Street Journal (New York: November 8, 2002).

the related assets and liabilities. The quality of information that the accounting information system generates impacts management's ability to take actions and make decisions in connection with the organization's operations and to prepare reliable financial statements. An effective accounting information system will:

- Identify and record all valid financial transactions.
- Provide timely information about transactions in sufficient detail to permit proper classification and financial reporting.
- Accurately measure the financial value of transactions so their effects can be recorded in financial statements.
- Accurately record transactions in the time period in which they occurred.

SAS 109 requires that auditors obtain sufficient knowledge of the organization's information system to understand:

- The classes of transactions that are material to the financial statements and how those transactions are initiated.
- The accounting records and accounts that are used in the processing of material transactions.
- The transaction processing steps involved from the initiation of a transaction to its inclusion in the financial statements.
- The financial reporting process used to prepare financial statements, disclosures, and accounting estimates.

Monitoring

Management must determine that internal controls are functioning as intended. **Monitoring** is the process by which the quality of internal control design and operation can be assessed. This may be accomplished by separate procedures or by ongoing activities.

An organization's internal auditors may monitor the entity's activities in separate procedures. They gather evidence of control adequacy by testing controls and then communicate control strengths and weaknesses to management. As part of this process, internal auditors make specific recommendations for improvements to controls.

Ongoing monitoring may be achieved by integrating special computer modules into the information system that capture key data and/or permit tests of controls to be conducted as part of routine operations. Embedded modules thus allow management and auditors to maintain constant surveillance over the functioning of internal controls. In Chapter 7, we examine a number of embedded module techniques and related audit tools.

Another technique for achieving ongoing monitoring is the judicious use of management reports. Timely reports allow managers in functional areas such as sales, purchasing, production, and cash disbursements to oversee and control their operations. By summarizing activities, highlighting trends, and identifying exceptions from normal performance, well-designed management reports provide evidence of internal control function or malfunction.

Control Activities

Control activities are the policies and procedures used to ensure that appropriate actions are taken to deal with the organization's identified risks. Control activities can be grouped into two distinct categories: *physical controls* and *information technology (IT) controls*. Figure 1.4 illustrates control activities in their respective categories.

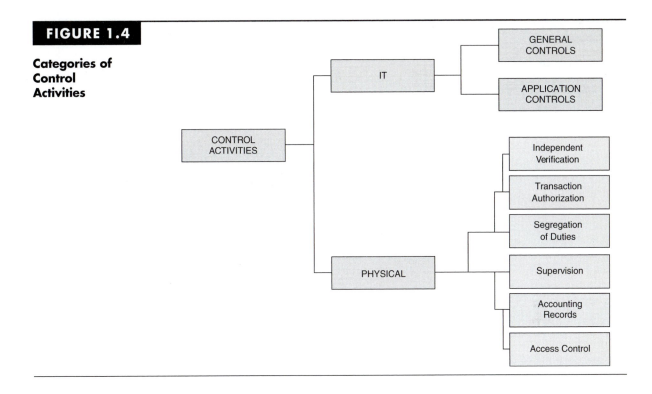

FIGURE 1.4

Categories of Control Activities

Physical Controls

This class of controls relates primarily to the human activities employed in accounting systems. These activities may be purely manual, such as the physical custody of assets, or they may involve the *physical* use of computers to record transactions or update accounts. Physical controls do not relate to the computer logic that actually performs accounting tasks. Rather, they relate to the human activities that trigger and utilize the results of those tasks. In other words, physical controls focus on people, but are not restricted to an environment in which clerks update paper accounts with pen and ink. Virtually all systems, regardless of their sophistication, employ human activities that need to be controlled.

Our discussion will address the issues pertaining to six categories of physical control activities: transaction authorization, segregation of duties, supervision, accounting records, access control, and independent verification.

Transaction Authorization. The purpose of **transaction authorization** is to ensure that all material transactions processed by the information system are valid and in accordance with management's objectives. Authorizations may be general or specific. General authority is granted to operations personnel to perform day-to-day activities. An example of general authorization is the procedure to authorize the purchase of inventories from a designated vendor only when inventory levels fall to their predetermined reorder points. This is called a programmed procedure (not necessarily in the computer sense of the word) in which the decision rules are specified in advance, and no additional approvals are required. On the other hand, specific authorizations deal with case-by-case decisions associated with nonroutine transactions. An example of this is the decision to extend a particular customer's credit limit beyond the normal amount. Specific authority is usually a management responsibility.

FIGURE 1.5				
			TRANSACTION	

**Segregation of
Duties
Objectives**

Control Objective 1	Authorization	Processing		
Control Objective 2	Authorization	Custody	Recording	
Control Objective 3	Journals	Subsidiary Ledgers	General Ledger	

Segregation of Duties. One of the most important control activities is the segregation of employee duties to minimize incompatible functions. **Segregation of duties** can take many forms, depending on the specific duties to be controlled. However, the following three objectives provide general guidelines applicable to most organizations. These objectives are illustrated in Figure 1.5.

Objective 1. The segregation of duties should be such that the authorization for a transaction is separate from the processing of the transaction. For example, the purchasing department should not initiate purchases until the inventory control department gives authorization. This separation of tasks is a control to prevent individuals from purchasing unnecessary inventory.

Objective 2. Responsibility for asset custody should be separate from the record-keeping responsibility. For example, the department that has physical custody of finished goods inventory (the warehouse) should not keep the official inventory records. Accounting for finished goods inventory is performed by inventory control, an accounting function. When a single individual or department has responsibility for both asset custody and record keeping, the potential for fraud exists. Assets can be stolen or lost and the accounting records falsified to hide the event.

Objective 3. The organization should be structured so that a successful fraud requires collusion between two or more individuals with incompatible responsibilities. For example, no individual should have sufficient access to accounting records to perpetrate a fraud. Thus, journals, subsidiary ledgers, and the general ledger are maintained separately. For most people, the thought of approaching another employee with the proposal to collude in a fraud presents an insurmountable psychological barrier. The fear of rejection and subsequent disciplinary action discourages solicitations of this sort. However, when employees with incompatible responsibilities work together daily in close quarters, the resulting familiarity tends to erode this barrier. For this reason, the segregation of incompatible tasks should be physical as well as organizational. Indeed, concern about personal familiarity on the job is the justification for establishing rules prohibiting nepotism.

Supervision. Implementing adequate segregation of duties requires that a firm employ a sufficiently large number of employees. Achieving adequate segregation of duties often presents difficulties for small organizations. Obviously, it is impossible to separate five incompatible tasks among three employees. Therefore, in small organizations or in functional areas that lack sufficient personnel, management must compensate for the absence of segregation controls with close **supervision**. For this reason, supervision is often called a compensating control.

An underlying assumption of supervision control is that the firm employs competent and trustworthy personnel. Obviously, no company could function for long on the alternative assumption that its employees are incompetent and dishonest. The competent and trustworthy employee assumption promotes supervisory efficiency. Firms can thus establish a managerial span of control whereby a single manager supervises several employees. In manual systems, maintaining a span of control tends to be straightforward because both manager and employees are at the same physical location.

Accounting Records.   The **accounting records** of an organization consist of source documents, journals, and ledgers. These records capture the economic essence of transactions and provide an audit trail of economic events. The audit trail enables the auditor to trace any transaction through all phases of its processing from the initiation of the event to the financial statements. Organizations must maintain audit trails for two reasons. First, this information is needed for conducting day-to-day operations. The audit trail helps employees respond to customer inquiries by showing the current status of transactions in process. Second, the audit trail plays an essential role in the financial audit of the firm. It enables external (and internal) auditors to verify selected transactions by tracing them from the financial statements to the ledger accounts, to the journals, to the source documents, and back to their original source. For reasons of both practical expedience and legal obligation, business organizations must maintain sufficient accounting records to preserve their audit trails.

Access Control.   The purpose of **access controls** is to ensure that only authorized personnel have access to the firm's assets. Unauthorized access exposes assets to misappropriation, damage, and theft. Therefore, access controls play an important role in safeguarding assets. Access to assets can be direct or indirect. Physical security devices, such as locks, safes, fences, and electronic and infrared alarm systems, control against direct access. Indirect access to assets is achieved by gaining access to the records and documents that control the use, ownership, and disposition of the asset. For example, an individual with access to all the relevant accounting records can destroy the audit trail that describes a particular sales transaction. Thus, by removing the records of the transaction, including the accounts receivable balance, the sale may never be billed and the firm will never receive payment for the items sold. The access controls needed to protect accounting records will depend on the technological characteristics of the accounting system. Indirect access control is accomplished by controlling the use of documents and records and by segregating the duties of those who must access and process these records.

Independent Verification.   **Verification procedures** are independent checks of the accounting system to identify errors and misrepresentations. Verification differs from supervision because it takes place after the fact, by an individual who is not directly involved with the transaction or task being verified. Supervision takes place while the activity is being performed, by a supervisor with direct responsibility for the task. Through independent verification procedures, management can assess (1) the performance of individuals, (2) the integrity of the transaction processing system, and (3) the correctness of data contained in accounting records. Examples of independent verifications include:

- Reconciling batch totals at points during transaction processing.
- Comparing physical assets with accounting records.

- Reconciling subsidiary accounts with control accounts.
- Reviewing management reports (both computer and manually generated) that summarize business activity.

The timing of verification depends on the technology employed in the accounting system and the task under review. Verifications may occur several times an hour or several times a day. In some cases, verification may occur daily, weekly, monthly, or annually.

IT Controls

Information technology drives the financial reporting processes of modern organizations. Automated systems initiate, authorize, record, and report the effects of financial transactions. As such, they are inextricable elements of the financial reporting processes that SOX considers and must be controlled. COSO identifies two broad groupings of IT controls: *application controls* and *general controls*. The objectives of **application controls** are to ensure the validity, completeness, and accuracy of financial transactions. These controls are designed to be application-specific. Examples include:

- A cash disbursements batch balancing routine that verifies that the total payments to vendors reconciles with the total postings to the accounts payable subsidiary ledger.
- An account receivable check digit procedure that validates customer account numbers on sales transactions.
- A payroll system limit check that identifies and flags employee time card records with reported hours worked in excess of the predetermined normal limit.

These examples illustrate how application controls have a direct impact on the integrity of data that make their way through various transaction processing systems and into the financial reporting process.

The second broad group of controls defined by the COSO framework is **general controls**. They are so named because they are not application-specific but, rather, apply to all systems. General controls have other names in other frameworks, including **general computer controls** and **information technology controls.** Whatever name is used, they include controls over IT governance, IT infrastructure, security and access to operating systems and databases, application acquisition and development, and program change procedures.

Although general controls do not control specific transactions, they have an effect on transaction integrity. For example, consider an organization with poor database security controls. In such a situation, even data processed by systems with adequate built-in application controls may be at risk. An individual who is able to circumvent database security (either directly or via a malicious program) may then change, steal, or corrupt stored transaction data. Thus, general controls are needed to support the functioning of application controls, and both are needed to ensure accurate financial reporting.

Audit Implications of SOX

Prior to the passage of SOX, external auditors were not required to test internal controls as part of their attest function. They were required to be familiar with the client organization's internal controls, but had the option of not relying on them and thus not performing tests of controls. Therefore the audit could, and often did, consist primarily of substantive tests.

SOX legislation dramatically expands the role of external auditors by mandating that they attest to the quality of their client organizations' internal controls. This constitutes the issuance of a separate audit opinion on the internal controls in addition to the opinion on the fairness of the financial statements. The standard for this new audit opinion is high. Indeed, the auditor is precluded from issuing an unqualified opinion if only one material weakness in internal control is detected. Interestingly, auditors are permitted to simultaneously render a qualified opinion on internal controls and an unqualified opinion on the financial statements. In other words, it is technically possible for auditors to find internal controls over financial reporting to be weak, but conclude through substantive tests that the weaknesses did not cause the financial statements to be materially misrepresented.

As part of the new attestation responsibility, PCAOB Standard No. 5 specifically requires auditors to understand transaction flows, including the controls pertaining to how transactions are initiated, authorized, recorded, and reported. This involves first selecting the financial accounts that have material implications for financial reporting. Then, auditors need to identify the application controls related to those accounts. As previously noted the reliability of application controls rests on the effectiveness of the general controls that support them. Figure 1.6 illustrates this IT control relationship. The sum of these controls, both application and general, constitutes the relevant IT controls over financial reporting that auditors need to review.

This book deals systematically with this substantial body of control and audit material. Chapters 2, 3, 4, and 5 address respectively the general control areas of IT governance, operating system and network security, database security, and systems development and program change procedures. Applications, and the design and audit of application controls are the subjects of Chapters 6, 7, 8, 9, 10, and 11.

Finally, SOX places responsibility on auditors to detect fraudulent activity and emphasizes the importance of controls designed to prevent or detect fraud that could lead to material misstatement of the financial statements. Management is responsible for implementing such controls, and auditors are expressly required to test them. Because computers lie at the heart of the modern organizations' accounting and financial reporting systems, the topic of **computer fraud** falls within the management and audit responsibilities imposed by SOX. Fraud drivers, fraud schemes and fraud detection techniques are covered in Chapter 12.

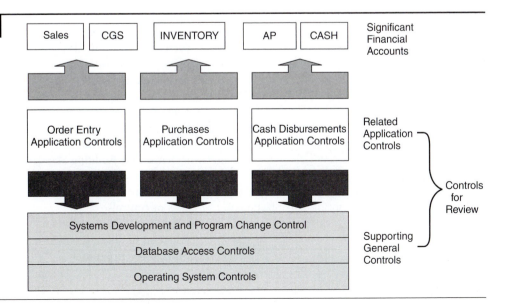

FIGURE 1.6

Information Technology Control Relationship

With this backdrop in place, the scene is set for viewing control techniques and tests of controls that might be required under SOX. PCAOB Auditing Standard No. 5 emphasizes that management and auditors use a risk-based approach rather than a one-size-fits-all approach in the design and assessment of controls. In other words, the size and complexity of the organization needs to be considered in determining the nature and extent of controls that are necessary. The reader should recognize, therefore, that the controls and audit procedures presented in the chapters that follow describe the needs of a generic organization and may not apply in specific situations.

SUMMARY

This chapter provided an overview of IT auditing and a backdrop for the remainder of the book. We began by describing the various types of audits and distinguishing between the auditor's traditional attestation responsibility and the emerging field of advisory services. The structure of an IT audit, management assertions, audit objectives, tests of controls, and substantive tests were explained. The chapter also outlined the key points of the COSO control framework, which defines internal controls in both manual and IT environments. The final section of the chapter examined audit issues and implications related to Sarbanes-Oxley legislation and provided a conceptual framework that links general controls, application controls, and financial data integrity. The remainder of the text is based upon this framework.

KEY TERMS

access controls
accounting record
Advisory services
application controls
attest service
audit objective
audit opinion
audit planning
audit procedure
audit risk
auditing
completeness
Computer-Assisted Audit Tools and Techniques
    (CAATTs)
control activities
control environment
computer fraud
control risk
corrective controls
COSO (Committee of Sponsoring Organizations)
detection risk
detective controls
existence or occurrence
Foreign Corrupt Practices Act of 1977 (FCPA)

general controls
independence
information technology (IT)
inherent risk
internal auditing
internal control system
management assertion
monitoring
PDC control model
presentation and disclosure
preventive controls
reasonable assurance
rights and obligations
risk assessment
Sarbanes-Oxley Act 2002
segregation of duties
Statement on Auditing Standards No. 109 (SAS 109)
substantive test
supervision
tests of controls
transaction authorization
valuation or allocation
verification procedure

REVIEW QUESTIONS

1. What is the purpose of an IT audit?
2. Discuss the concept of independence within the context of a financial audit. How is independence different for internal auditors?
3. What are the conceptual phases of an audit? How do they differ between general auditing and IT auditing?
4. Distinguish between internal and external auditors.
5. What are the four primary elements described in the definition of auditing?
6. Explain the concept of materiality.
7. How does the Sarbanes-Oxley Act of 2002 affect management's responsibility for internal controls?
8. What are the four broad objectives of internal control?
9. What are the four modifying assumptions that guide designers and auditors of internal control systems?
10. Give an example of a preventive control.
11. Give an example of a detective control.
12. Give an example of a corrective control.
13. What are the five internal control components described in the COSO framework?
14. What are the six broad classes of control activities defined by COSO?
15. Give an example of independent verification.
16. Differentiate between general and application controls. Give two examples of each.
17. Distinguish between tests of controls and substantive testing.
18. Define audit risk.
19. Distinguish between errors and irregularities. Which do you think concern auditors the most?
20. Distinguish between inherent risk and control risk. How do internal controls affect inherent risk and control risk, if at all? What is the role of detection risk?
21. What is the relationship between tests of controls and substantive tests?
22. SOX contains many sections. Which sections does this chapter focus on?
23. What control framework does the PCAOB recommend?
24. COSO identifies two broad groupings of information system controls. What are they?
25. What are the objectives of application controls?
26. Give three examples of application controls.
27. Define general controls.
28. What is the meaning of the term *attest services*?
29. List four general control areas.

DISCUSSION QUESTIONS

1. Discuss the differences between the attest function and advisory services.
2. A CPA firm has many clients. For some of its clients, it relies very heavily on the work of the internal auditors, while for others it does not. The amount of reliance affects the fees charged. How can the CPA firm justify the apparent inconsistency of fees charged in a competitive marketplace?
3. Accounting firms are very concerned that their employees have excellent communication skills, both oral and written. Explain why this requirement is so important by giving examples of where these skills would be necessary in each of the three phases of an audit.
4. Explain the audit objectives of existence or occurrence, completeness, rights and obligations, valuation or allocation, and presentation and disclosure.
5. How has the Foreign Corrupt Practices Act of 1977 had a significant impact on organization management?
6. Discuss the concept of exposure and explain why firms may tolerate some exposure.
7. If detective controls signal errors, why should they not automatically make a correction to the identified error? Why are separate corrective controls necessary?
8. Most accounting firms allow married employees to work for the firm. However, they do not allow an employee to remain working for them if he or she marries an employee of one of their auditing clients. Why do you think this policy exists?

9. Discuss whether a firm with fewer employees than there are incompatible tasks should rely more heavily on general authority than specific authority.
10. An organization's internal audit department is usually considered to be an effective control mechanism for evaluating the organization's internal control structure. The Birch Company's internal auditing function reports directly to the controller. Comment on the effectiveness of this organizational structure.
11. According to COSO, the proper segregation of functions is an effective internal control procedure. Comment on the exposure (if any) caused by combining the tasks of paycheck preparation and distribution to employees.
12. Discuss the key features of Section 302 of SOX.
13. Discuss the key features of Section 404 of SOX.
14. Section 404 requires management to make a statement identifying the control framework used to conduct its assessment of internal controls. Discuss the options in selecting a control framework.
15. Explain how general controls impact transaction integrity and the financial reporting process.
16. Prior to SOX, external auditors were required to be familiar with the client organization's internal controls, but not test them. Explain.
17. Does a qualified opinion on management's assessment of internal controls over the financial reporting system necessitate a qualified opinion on the financial statements? Explain.
18. The PCAOB Standard No. 5 specifically requires auditors to understand transaction flows in designing their tests of controls. What steps does this entail?
19. What fraud detection responsibilities (if any) does SOX impose on auditors?

PROBLEMS

1. Audit Committee
CMA 6898 3-3

Micro Dynamics, a developer of database software packages, is a publicly held company whose stock is traded over the counter. The company recently received an enforcement release proceeding through an SEC administrative law judge that cited the company for inadequate internal controls. In response, Micro Dynamics has agreed to establish an internal audit function and strengthen its audit committee.

A manager of the internal audit department has been hired as a result of the SEC enforcement action to establish an internal audit function. In addition, the composition of the audit committee has been changed to include all outside directors. Micro Dynamics has held its initial planning meeting to discuss the roles of the various participants in the internal control and financial reporting process. Participants at the meeting included the company president, the chief financial officer, a member of the audit committee, a partner from Micro Dynamics' external audit firm, and the newly appointed manager of the internal audit department. Comments by the various meeting participants are presented below.

President: "We want to ensure that Micro Dynamics complies with the SEC's enforcement release and that we don't find ourselves in this position again. The internal audit department should help to strengthen our internal control system by correcting the problems. I would like your thoughts on the proper reporting relationship for the manager of the internal audit department."

CFO: "I think the manager of the internal audit department should report to me since much of the department's work is related to financial issues. The audit committee should have oversight responsibilities."

Audit committee member: "I believe we should think through our roles more carefully. The Treadway Commission has recommended that the audit committee play a more important role in the financial reporting process; the duties of today's audit committee have expanded beyond mere rubber-stamp approval. We need to have greater assurance that controls are in place and being followed."

External audit firm partner: "We need a close working relationship among all of our roles. The internal audit department can play a significant role in monitoring the control systems on a continuing basis and should have strong ties to your external audit firm."

Internal audit department manager: "The internal audit department should be more involved in operational auditing, but it also should play a significant monitoring role in the financial reporting area."

Required:

a. Describe the role of each of the following in the establishment, maintenance, and evaluation of Micro Dynamics' system of internal control.
   i. Management
   ii. Audit committee
   iii. External auditor
   iv. Internal audit department
b. Describe the responsibilities that Micro Dynamics' audit committee has in the financial reporting process.

2. Role of Internal Auditor
CMA 1290 4-Y8

Leigh Industries has an internal audit department consisting of a director and four staff auditors. The director of internal audit, Diane Bauer, reports to the corporate controller, who receives copies of all internal audit reports. In addition, copies of all internal audit reports are sent to the audit committee of the board of directors and the individual responsible for the area of activity being audited.

In the past, the company's external auditors have relied on the work of the internal audit department to a substantial degree. However, in recent months, Bauer has become concerned that the objectivity of the internal audit function is being affected by the nonaudit work being performed by the department. This possible loss of objectivity could result in more extensive testing and analysis by the external auditors. The percentage of nonaudit work performed by the internal auditors has steadily increased to about 25 percent of the total hours worked. A sample of five recent nonaudit activities follows.

- One of the internal auditors assisted in the preparation of policy statements on internal control. These statements included such things as policies regarding sensitive payments and the safeguarding of assets.
- Reconciling the bank statements of the corporation each month is a regular assignment of one of the internal auditors. The corporate controller believes this strengthens the internal control function because the internal auditor is not involved in either the receipt or the disbursement of cash.
- The internal auditors are asked to review the annual budget each year for relevance and reasonableness before the budget is approved. At the end of each month, the corporate controller's staff analyzes the variances from budget and prepares explanations of these variances. These variances and explanations are then reviewed by the internal audit staff.

- One of the internal auditors has been involved in the design, installation, and initial operation of a new computerized inventory system. The auditor was primarily concerned with the design and implementation of internal accounting controls and conducted the evaluation of these controls during the test runs.
- The internal auditors are sometimes asked to make the accounting entries for complex transactions as the employees in the accounting department are not adequately trained to handle such transactions. The corporate controller believes this gives an added measure of assurance to the accurate recording of these transactions.

Required:

a. Define objectivity as it relates to the internal audit function.
b. For each of the five nonaudit activities presented, explain whether the objectivity of Leigh Industries' internal audit department has been materially impaired. Consider each situation independently.
c. The director of internal audit reports directly to the corporate controller. Does this reporting relationship affect the objectivity of the internal audit department? Explain your answer.
d. Would your evaluation of the five situations in Question b change if the director of internal audit reported to the audit committee of the board of directors? Explain your answer.

3. Segregation of Function
CMA 1288 3-22

An effective system of internal control includes the segregation of incompatible duties. Some of the examples presented represent incompatible duties. Comment on the specific risks (if any) that are caused by the combination of tasks.

a. The treasurer has the authority to sign checks but gives the signature block to the assistant treasurer to run the check-signing machine.
b. The warehouse clerk, who has custodial responsibility over inventory in the warehouse, may authorize disposal of damaged goods.
c. The sales manager, who works on commission based on gross sales, approves credit and has the authority to write off uncollectible accounts.
d. The shop foreman submits time cards and distributes paychecks to employees.
e. The accounting clerk posts to individual account receivable subsidiary accounts and performs the reconciliation of the subsidiary ledger and the general ledger control account.

4.   Segregation of Duties

CMA 1288 3-23

Explain why each of the following combinations of tasks should, or should not, be separated to achieve adequate internal control.

a. Approval of bad debt write-offs and the reconciliation of accounts payable subsidiary ledger and the general ledger control account.
b. Distribution of payroll checks to employees and approval of sales returns for credit.
c. Posting of amounts from both the cash receipts and the cash disbursements journals to the general ledger.
d. Distribution of payroll checks to employees and recording cash receipts in the journal.
e. Recording cash receipts in the journal and preparing the bank reconciliation.

5.   Internal Control

CMA Adapted 1289 3-4

Oakdale, Inc., is a subsidiary of Solomon Publishing and specializes in the publication and distribution of reference books. Oakdale's sales for the past year exceeded $18 million, and the company employed an average of 65 employees. Solomon periodically sends a member of its internal audit department to audit the operations of each of its subsidiaries, and Katherine Ford, Oakdale's treasurer, is currently working with Ralph Johnson of Solomon's internal audit staff. Johnson has just completed a review of Oakdale's investment cycle and prepared the following report.

General

Throughout the year, Oakdale has made both short-term and long-term investments in securities; all securities are registered in the company's name. According to Oakdale's bylaws, long-term investment activity must be approved by its board of directors, while short-term investment activity may be approved by either the president or the treasurer.

Transactions

Oakdale has a computer link with its broker; thus, all buy and sale orders are transmitted electronically. Only individuals with authorized passwords may initiate certain types of transactions. All purchases and sales of short-term securities in the year were made by the treasurer. In addition, two purchases and one sale of long-term securities were executed by the treasurer. The long-term security purchases were approved by the board. The president, having online authorization access to all transactions, was able to approve a sale of a long-term security. The president is given access to authorize all transactions engaged in by the firm. Because the treasurer is listed with the broker as the company's contact, all revenue from these investments is received by this individual, who then forwards the checks to accounting for processing.

Documentation

Purchase and sales authorizations, along with brokers' advice, are maintained in an electronic file with authorized access by the treasurer. Brokers' advice is received verbally on the phone, and this advice is noted on a broker advice form. This form is filed by the treasurer. The certificates for all long-term investments are kept in a safe deposit box at the local bank; only the president of Oakdale has access to this box. An inventory of this box was made, and all certificates were accounted for. Certificates for short-term investments are kept in a locked metal box in the accounting office. Other documents, such as long-term contracts and legal agreements, are also kept in this box. There are three keys to the box, held by the president, treasurer, and the accounting manager. The accounting manager's key is available to all accounting personnel, should they require documents kept in this box. Certificates of investments may take up to four weeks to receive after the purchase of the investment. An electronic inventory list is kept perpetually. The data are keyed in by accounting personnel who receive a buy/sale transaction sheet from the treasurer. The president, treasurer, and accounting manager all have passwords to access and update this inventory list. The accounting manager's password is known by two of the accounting supervisors in case the inventory list needs to be updated when the accounting manager is not available. Documentation for two of the current short-term investments could not be located in this box; the accounting manager explained that some of the investments are for such short periods of time that formal documentation is not always provided by the broker.

Accounting Records

Deposits of checks for interest and dividends earned on investments are recorded by the accounting department, but these checks could not be traced to the cash receipts journal maintained by the individual who normally opens, stamps, and logs incoming checks. These amounts are journalized monthly to an account for investment revenue. Electronic payments for investment purchases are authorized by the treasurer. If the amount is in excess of $15,000, an authorization code given by the treasurer or president is necessary.

Each month, the accounting manager and the treasurer prepare the journal entries required to adjust the short-term investment account. There was insufficient backup documentation attached to the journal entries reviewed to trace all transactions; however, the balance in the account at the end of last month closely approximates the amount shown on the statement received from the broker. The amount in the long-term investment account is correct, and the transactions can be clearly traced through the documentation attached to the journal entries. No attempts are made to adjust either account to the lower of aggregate cost or market.

Required:

To achieve Solomon Publishing's objective of sound internal control, the company believes the following four controls are basic for an effective system of accounting control.

- Authorization of transactions
- Complete and accurate record keeping
- Physical control
- Internal verification

a. Describe the purpose of each of the four controls listed above.

b. Identify an area in Oakdale's investment procedures that violates each of the four controls listed above.

c. For each of the violations identified, describe how Oakdale can correct it.

6. Internal Control

CMA 1290 4-2

Arlington Industries manufactures and sells component engine parts for large industrial equipment. The company employs over 1,000 workers for three shifts, and most employees work overtime when necessary. Arlington has had major growth in its production and has purchased a mainframe computer to handle order processing, inventory management, production planning, distribution operations, and accounting applications. Michael Cromley, president of Arlington, suspects that there may be internal control weaknesses due to the quick implementation of the computer system. Cromley recently hired Kathleen Luddy as the internal control accountant.

Cromley asked Luddy to review the payroll processing system first. Luddy has reviewed the payroll process, interviewed the individuals involved, and compiled the flowchart shown on the next page. The following additional information concerns payroll processing:

- The personnel department determines the wage rate of all employees at Arlington. Personnel starts the process by sending an authorization form for adding an employee to the payroll to Marjorie Adams, the payroll coordinator. After Adams inputs this information into the system, the computer automatically determines the overtime and shift differential rates for the individual, updating the payroll master files.

- Arlington uses an external service to provide monthly payroll tax updates. The company receives a magnetic tape every month, which the data processing department installs to update the payroll master file for tax calculations.

- Employees at Arlington use a time clock to record the hours worked. Every Monday morning, Adams collects the previous week's time cards and begins the computerized processing of payroll information to produce paychecks the following Friday. Adams reviews the time cards to ensure that the hours worked are correctly totaled; the system will determine whether overtime has been worked or a shift differential is required.

- All the other processes displayed on the flowchart are performed by Adams. The system automatically assigns a sequential number to each payroll check produced. The checks are stored in a box next to the computer printer to provide immediate access. After the checks are printed, Adams uses an automatic check-signing machine to sign the checks with an authorized signature plate that Adams keeps locked in a safe.

- After the check processing is completed, Adams distributes the checks to the employees, leaving the checks for the second- and third-shift employees with the appropriate shift supervisor. Adams then notifies the data processing department that she is finished with her weekly processing, and data processing makes a backup of the payroll master file to magnetic tape for storage on the tape shelves in the computer room.

Required:

By referring to the information in Problem 6 and the *flowchart*, identify and describe:

a. Five different areas in Arlington's payroll processing system where the system controls are inadequate.

b. Two different areas in Arlington's payroll processing system where the system controls are satisfactory.

7. Evaluation of Controls

Gaurav Mirchandaniis is the warehouse manager for a large office supply wholesaler. Mirchandaniis receives two copies of the customer sales order from the sales department. He elects the goods from the shelves and sends them and one copy of the sales order to the shipping department. He then files the second copy in a temporary file. At the end of the day, Mirchandaniis retrieves the sales orders from the temporary file and

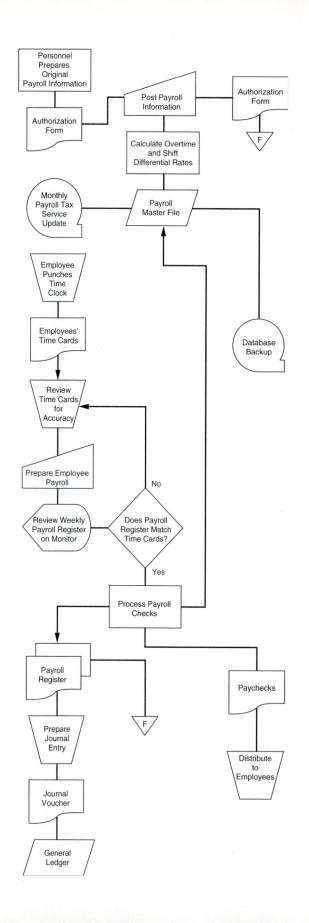

updates the inventory subsidiary ledger from a terminal in his office. At that time, he identifies items that have fallen to low levels, selects a supplier, and prepares three copies of a purchase order. One copy is sent to the supplier, one is sent to the accounts payable clerk, and one is filed in the warehouse. When the goods arrive from the supplier, Mirchandaniis reviews the attached packing slip, counts and inspects the goods, places them on the shelves, and updates the inventory ledger to reflect the receipt. He then prepares a receiving report and sends it to the accounts payable department.

Required:

 a. Prepare a systems flowchart of the procedures previously described.
 b. Identify any control problems in the system.
 c. What sorts of fraud are possible in this system?

8. Evaluation of Controls

Matt Demko is the loading dock supervisor for a dry cement packaging company. His work crew is composed of unskilled workers who load large transport trucks with bags of cement, gravel, and sand. The work is hard, and the employee turnover rate is high. Employees record their attendance on separate time cards. Demko authorizes payroll payments each week by signing the time cards and submitting them to the payroll department. Payroll then prepares the paychecks and gives them to Demko, who distributes them to his work crew.

Required:

 a. Prepare a systems flowchart of the procedures described here.
 b. Identify any control problems in the system.
 c. What sorts of fraud are possible in this system?

PROJECTS

1. Visit a Web site for one of the audit professional organizations. Find the answers to the following questions:

 a. What relevant certification(s) is(are) supported by the organization? What is the cost to take the certification exam?
 b. What requirements does the organization have for continuing education requirements?
 c. How does the organization support IT auditors? Be specific.
 d. What publications are provided by the organization? How does the publication relate to IT audits?
 e. What services are provided by the organization to its members?
 f. Where is the closest chapter?
 g. Does a student membership program exist for the organization? If so, what is the cost for student members?
  TIPS: AICPA, ISACA, IIA, and ACFE

2. Financial frauds perpetrated by companies such as Enron, WorldCom, and Adelphia led to the passage of the Sarbanes-Oxley Act of 2002. Using the Internet, find answers to the following questions about changes being made regarding audit committees in SOX:

 a. Describe a requirement for audit committees in SOX.
 b. Describe a requirement for internal controls in SOX.
 c. How do these changes affect IT auditors?
 d. How do these changes affect internal auditors?
 e. How do these changes affect financial auditors?

CHAPTER 2

Auditing IT Governance Controls

LEARNING OBJECTIVES

After studying this chapter, you should:

- Understand the risks of incompatible functions and how to structure the IT function.
- Be familiar with the controls and precautions required to ensure the security of an organization's computer facilities.
- Understand the key elements of a disaster recovery plan.
- Be familiar with the benefits, risks, and audit issues related to IT outsourcing.

This chapter presents risks, controls, and tests of controls related to IT governance. It opens by defining IT governance and the elements of IT governance that have internal control and financial reporting implications. First, it presents the exposures that can arise from inappropriate structuring of the IT function. Next, the chapter reviews computer center threats and controls, which include protecting it from damage and destruction from natural disasters, fire, temperature, and humidity. The chapter then presents the key elements of a disaster recovery plan, including providing second-site backup, identifying critical applications, performing backup and off-site storage procedures, creating a disaster recovery team, and testing the plan. The final section of the chapter presents issues concerning the growing trend toward IT outsourcing. The logic behind management decisions to outsource is explored. The chapter also reveals the expected benefits and the risks associated with outsourcing. The chapter concludes with a discussion of audit issues in an outsourcing environment and the role of the SAS 70 report.

INFORMATION TECHNOLOGY GOVERNANCE

Information technology (IT) governance is a relatively new subset of corporate governance that focuses on the management and assessment of strategic IT resources. Key objectives of IT governance are to reduce risk and ensure that investments in IT resources add value to the corporation. Prior to the Sarbanes-Oxley (SOX) Act, the common practice regarding IT investments was to defer all decisions to corporate IT professionals. Modern IT governance, however, follows the philosophy that all corporate stakeholders, including boards of directors, top management, and departmental users (i.e., accounting and finance) be active participants in key IT decisions. Such broad-based involvement reduces risk and increases the likelihood that IT decisions will be in compliance with user needs, corporate policies, strategic initiatives, and internal control requirements under SOX.

IT Governance Controls

Although all IT governance issues are important to the organization, not all of them are matters of internal control under SOX that may potentially impact the financial reporting process. In this chapter, we consider three IT governance issues that are addressed by SOX and the COSO internal control framework. These are:

1. Organizational structure of the IT function
2. Computer center operations
3. Disaster recovery planning

The discussion on each of these governance issues begins with an explanation of the nature of risk and a description of the controls needed to mitigate the risk. Then, the audit objectives are presented, which establishes what needs to be verified regarding the function of the control(s) in place. Finally, example tests of controls are offered that describe how auditors might gather evidence to satisfy the audit objectives. These tests may be performed by external auditors as part of their attest service or by internal auditors (or advisory services professionals) who are providing evidence of management's compliance with SOX. In this regard, we make no distinction between the two types of services.

STRUCTURE OF THE INFORMATION TECHNOLOGY FUNCTION

The organization of the IT function has implications for the nature and effectiveness of internal controls, which, in turn, has implications for the audit. In this section, some important control issues related to IT structure are examined. These are illustrated through two extreme organizational models—the centralized approach and the distributed approach. The risks, controls, and audit issues related to each model are then discussed. The reader should recognize, however, that most organizational structures embody elements of both models.

Centralized Data Processing

Under the **centralized data processing** model, all data processing is performed by one or more large computers housed at a central site that serves users throughout the organization. Figure 2.1 illustrates this approach, in which IT services activities are consolidated and managed as a shared organization resource. End users compete for these resources on the basis of need. The IT services function is usually treated as a cost center whose operating costs are charged back to the end users. Figure 2.2 illustrates a centralized IT services structure and shows its primary service areas: database administration,

FIGURE 2.1

Centralized Data Processing Approach

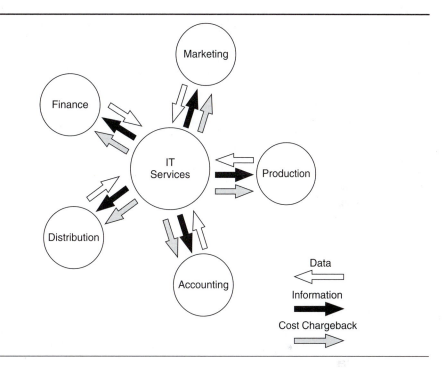

FIGURE 2.2

Organizational Chart of a Centralized Information Technology Function

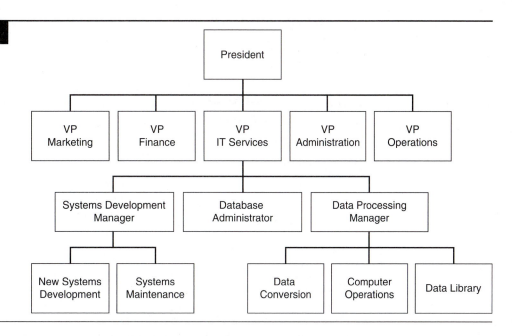

data processing, and systems development and maintenance. A description of the key functions of each of these areas follows.

Database Administration

Centrally organized companies maintain their data resources in a central location that is shared by all end users. In this shared data arrangement, an independent group headed by the database administrator (DBA) is responsible for the security and integrity of the database.

Data Processing

The data processing group manages the computer resources used to perform the day-to-day processing of transactions. It consists of the following organizational functions: **data conversion**, **computer operations**, and the **data library**.

Data Conversion.   The data conversion function transcribes transaction data from hard-copy source documents into computer input. For example, data conversion could-involve keystroking sales orders into a sale order application in modern systems, or transcribing data into magnetic media (tape or disk) suitable for computer processing in legacy type systems.

Computer Operations.   The electronic files produced in data conversion are later processed by the central computer, which is managed by the computer operations groups. Accounting applications are usually executed according to a strict schedule that is controlled by the central computer's operating system.

Data Library.   The data library is a room adjacent to the computer center that provides safe storage for the off-line data files. Those files could be backups or current data files. For instance, the data library could be used to store backup data on DVDs, CD-ROMs, tapes, or other storage devices. It could also be used to store current operational data files on magnetic tapes and removable disk packs. In addition, the data library is used to store original copies of commercial software and their licenses for safekeeping. A data librarian, who is responsible for the receipt, storage, retrieval, and custody of data files, controls access to the library. The librarian issues data files to computer operators in accordance with program requests and takes custody of files when processing or backup procedures are completed. The trend in recent years toward real-time processing and the increased use of direct-access files has reduced or even eliminated the role of the data librarian in many organizations.

Systems Development and Maintenance

The information systems needs of users are met by two related functions: system development and systems maintenance. The former group is responsible for analyzing user needs and for designing new systems to satisfy those needs. The participants in system development activities include systems professionals, end users, and stakeholders.

> *Systems professionals* include systems analysts, database designers, and programmers who design and build the system. Systems professionals gather facts about the user's problem, analyze the facts, and formulate a solution. The product of their efforts is a new information system.
>
> *End users* are those for whom the system is built. They are the managers who receive reports from the system and the operations personnel who work directly with the system as part of their daily responsibilities.

Stakeholders are individuals inside or outside the firm who have an interest in the system, but are not end users. They include accountants, internal auditors, external auditors, and others who oversee systems development.

Once a new system has been designed and implemented, the systems maintenance group assumes responsibility for keeping it current with user needs. The term *maintenance* refers to making changes to program logic to accommodate shifts in user needs over time. During the course of the system's life (often several years), as much as 80 or 90 percent of its total cost may be incurred through maintenance activities.

Segregation of Incompatible IT Functions

The previous chapter stressed the importance of segregating incompatible duties within manual activities. Specifically, operational tasks should be segregated to:

1. Separate transaction authorization from transaction processing.
2. Separate record keeping from asset custody.
3. Divide transaction-processing tasks among individuals such that short of collusion between two or more individuals fraud would not be possible.

The IT environment tends to consolidate activities. A single application may authorize, process, and record all aspects of a transaction. Thus, the focus of segregation control shifts from the operational level (transaction processing tasks that computers now perform) to higher-level organizational relationships within the computer services function. Using the organizational chart in Figure 2.2 as a reference, the interrelationships among systems development, systems maintenance, database administration, and computer operations activities are examined next.

Separating Systems Development from Computer Operations

The segregation of systems development (both new systems development and maintenance) and operations activities is of the greatest importance. The relationship between these groups should be extremely formal, and their responsibilities should not be commingled. Systems development and maintenance professionals should create (and maintain) systems for users, and should have no involvement in entering data, or running applications (i.e., computer operations). Operations staff should run these systems and have no involvement in their design. These functions are inherently incompatible, and consolidating them invites errors and fraud. With detailed knowledge of the application's logic and control parameters and access to the computer's operating system and utilities, an individual could make unauthorized changes to the application during its execution. Such changes may be temporary ("on the fly") and will disappear without a trace when the application terminates.

Separating Database Administration from Other Functions

Another important organizational control is the segregation of the database administrator (DBA) from other computer center functions. The DBA function is responsible for a number of critical tasks pertaining to database security, including creating the database schema and user views, assigning database access authority to users, monitoring database usage, and planning for future expansion.[1] Delegating these responsibilities to others who perform incompatible tasks threatens database integrity. Thus, we see from Figure 2.2

---

1   The role of the DBA is examined in more detail in Chapter 4.

FIGURE 2.3

Alternative Organization of Systems Development

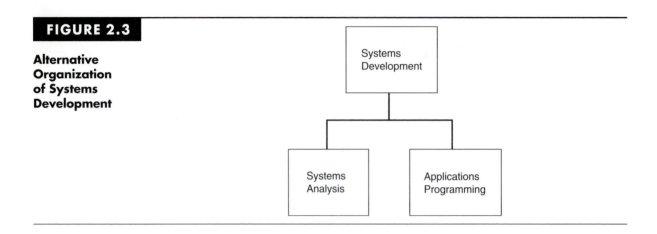

how the DBA function is organizationally independent of operations, systems development, and maintenance.

Separating New Systems Development from Maintenance

Some companies organize their in-house systems development function into two groups: systems analysis and programming (see Figure 2.3). The systems analysis group works with the users to produce detailed designs of the new systems. The programming group codes the programs according to these design specifications. Under this approach, the programmer who codes the original programs also maintains the system during the maintenance phase of the systems development life cycle (discussed in Chapter 5). Although a common arrangement, this approach is associated with two types of control problems: **inadequate documentation** and the potential for **program fraud**.

Inadequate Documentation. Poor-quality systems documentation is a chronic IT problem and a significant challenge for many organizations seeking SOX compliance. There are at least two explanations for this phenomenon. First, documenting systems is not as interesting as designing, testing, and implementing them. Systems professionals much prefer to move on to an exciting new project rather than document one just completed.

The second possible reason for poor documentation is job security. When a system is poorly documented, it is difficult to interpret, test, and debug. Therefore, the programmer who understands the system (the one who coded it) maintains bargaining power and becomes relatively indispensable. When the programmer leaves the firm, however, a new programmer inherits maintenance responsibility for the undocumented system. Depending on its complexity, the transition period may be long and costly.

Program Fraud. When the original programmer of a system is also assigned maintenance responsibility, the potential for fraud is increased. Program fraud involves making unauthorized changes to program modules for the purpose of committing an illegal act. The original programmer may have successfully concealed fraudulent code among the thousands of lines of legitimate code and the hundreds of modules that constitute a system. For the fraud to work successfully, however, the programmer must be able to control the situation through exclusive and unrestricted access to the application's programs. The programmer needs to protect the fraudulent code from accidental detection by another programmer performing maintenance or by auditors testing application controls. Therefore, having sole responsibility for maintenance is an important element in the duplicitous programmer's scheme. Through this maintenance authority, the programmer may freely access the system, disabling fraudulent code during audits and then restoring the code when the coast is clear. Frauds of this sort may continue for years without detection.

A Superior Structure for Systems Development

Figure 2.2 presents a superior organizational structure in which the systems development function is separated into two different groups: *new systems development* and *systems maintenance*. The new systems development group is responsible for designing, programming, and implementing new systems projects. Upon successful implementation, responsibility for the system's ongoing maintenance falls to the systems maintenance group. This restructuring has implications that directly address the two control problems just described.

First, documentation standards are improved because the maintenance group requires documentation to perform its maintenance duties. Without complete and adequate documentation, the formal transfer of system responsibility from new systems development to systems maintenance simply cannot occur.

Second, denying the original programmer future access to the program deters program fraud. That the fraudulent code, once concealed within the system, is out of the programmer's control and may later be discovered increases the risk associated with program fraud. The success of this control depends on the existence of other controls that limit, prevent, and detect unauthorized access to programs (such as source program library controls). Although organizational separations alone cannot guarantee that computer frauds will not occur, they are critical to creating the necessary control environment.

The Distributed Model

For many years, economies of scale favored large, powerful computers and centralized processing. Today, however, small, powerful, and inexpensive systems have changed this picture dramatically. An alternative to the centralized model is the concept of **distributed data processing (DDP)**. The topic of DDP is quite broad, touching upon such related topics as end-user computing, commercial software, networking, and office automation. Simply stated, DDP involves reorganizing the central IT function into small IT units that are placed under the control of end users. The IT units may be distributed according to business function, geographic location, or both. All or any of the IT functions represented in Figure 2.2 may be distributed. The degree to which they are distributed will vary depending upon the philosophy and objectives of the organization's management. Figure 2.4 presents two alternative DDP approaches.

Alternative A is actually a variant of the centralized model; the difference is that terminals (or microcomputers) are distributed to end users for handling input and output. This eliminates the need for the centralized data conversion groups, since the user now performs this tasks. Under this model, however, systems development, computer operations, and database administration remain centralized.

Alternative B is a significant departure from the centralized model. This alternative distributes all computer services to the end users, where they operate as standalone units. The result is the elimination of the central IT function from the organizational structure. Notice the interconnections between the distributed units in Figure 2.4. These connections represent a *networking* arrangement that permits communication and data transfers between the units. Figure 2.5 shows a possible organizational structure reflecting the distribution of all traditional data processing tasks to end-user areas.

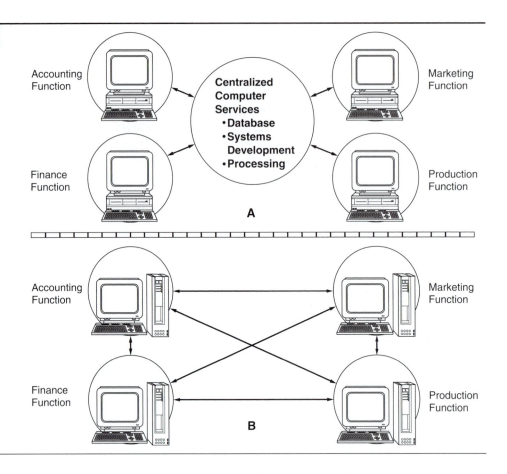

FIGURE 2.4

Two Distributed Data Processing Approaches

Risks Associated with DDP

This section discusses the organizational risks that need to be considered when implementing DDP. The discussion focuses on important issues that carry control implications that auditors should recognize. Potential problems include the inefficient use of resources, the destruction of audit trails, inadequate segregation of duties, increased potential for programming errors and systems failures, and the lack of standards.

Inefficient Use of Resources. DDP can expose and organization to three types of risks associated with inefficient use of organizational resources. These are outlined below.

First, is the risk of mismanagement of organization-wide IT resources by end users. Some argue that when organization-wide IT resources exceed a threshold amount, for example 5 percent of the total operations budget, effective IT governance requires central management and monitoring of such resources. For many organizations, IT services including computer operations, programming, data conversion, and database management meet or exceed this threshold.

Second, DDP can increase the risk of operational inefficiencies because of redundant tasks being performed within the end-user committee. Autonomous systems development initiatives distributed throughout the firm can result in each user area reinventing

FIGURE 2.5

Organization Chart for a Distributed Data Processing Environment

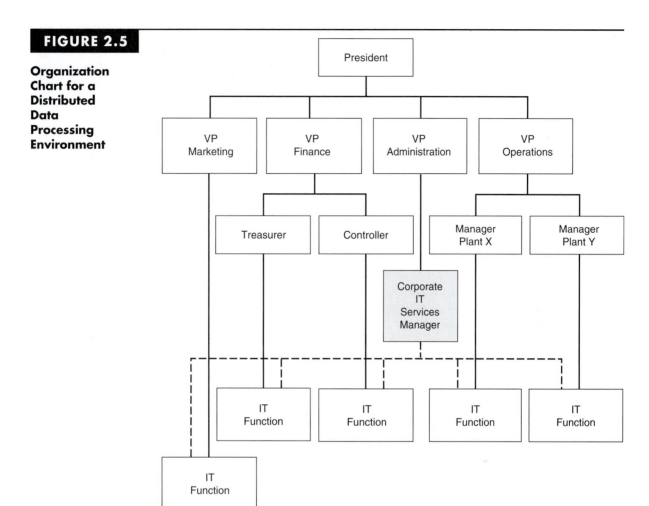

the wheel rather than benefiting from the work of others. For example, application programs created by one user, which could be used with little or no change by others, will be redesigned from scratch rather than shared. Likewise, data common to many users may be recreated for each, resulting in a high level of data redundancy. This situation has implications for data accuracy and consistency.

Third, the DDP environment poses a risk of incompatible hardware and software among end-user functions. Distributing the responsibility for IT purchases to end users may result in uncoordinated and poorly conceived decisions. For example, decision makers in different organizational units working independently may settle on dissimilar and incompatible operating systems, technology platforms, spreadsheets, word processors, and database packages. Hardware and software incompatibilities can degrade and disrupt connectivity between units, causing the loss of transactions and possible destruction of audit trails.

Destruction of Audit Trails. An audit trail provides the linkage between a company's financial activities (transactions) and the financial statements that report on those activities. Auditors use the audit trail to trace selected financial transactions from the source documents that captured the events, through the journals, subsidiary ledgers, and general ledger accounts that recorded the events, and ultimately to the financial statement themselves. The audit trail is critical to the auditor's attest service.

In DDP systems, the audit trail consists of a set of digital transaction files and master files (Chapter 6 deals with transaction processing techniques) that reside in part or entirely on end-user computers. Should an end user inadvertently delete one of the files, the audit trail could be destroyed and unrecoverable. Similarly, if an end user inadvertently inserts transaction errors into an audit trail file, it could become corrupted.

Inadequate Segregation of Duties.   Achieving an adequate segregation of duties may not be possible in some distributed environments. The distribution of the IT services to users may result in the creation of small independent units that do not permit the desired separation of incompatible functions. For example, within a single unit the same person may write application programs, perform program maintenance, enter transaction data into the computer, and operate the computer equipment. Such a situation would be a fundamental violation of internal control.

Hiring Qualified Professionals.   End-user managers may lack the IT knowledge to evaluate the technical credentials and relevant experience of candidates applying for IT professional positions. Also, if the organizational unit into which a new employee is entering is small, the opportunity for personal growth, continuing education, and promotion may be limited. For these reasons, managers may experience difficulty attracting highly qualified personnel. The risk of programming errors and system failures increases directly with the level of employee incompetence.

Lack of Standards.   Because of the distribution of responsibility in the DDP environment, standards for developing and documenting systems, choosing programming languages, acquiring hardware and software, and evaluating performance may be unevenly applied or even nonexistent. Opponents of DDP argue that the risks associated with the design and operation of a DDP system are made tolerable only if such standards are consistently applied.

Advantages of DDP

This section considers potential advantages of DDP, including cost reductions, improved cost control, improved user satisfaction, and backup.

Cost Reductions.   For many years, achieving economies of scale was the principal justification for the centralized data processing approach. The economics of data processing favored large, expensive, powerful computers. The wide variety of needs that centralized systems were expected to satisfy also called for computers that were highly generalized and employed complex operating systems. The overhead associated with running such a system, however, can diminish the advantages of its raw processing power. Thus, for many users, large centralized systems represented expensive overkill that they should escape.

Powerful and inexpensive microcomputers and minicomputers that can perform specialized functions have changed the economics of data processing dramatically. In addition, the unit cost of data storage, which was once the justification for consolidating data in a central location, is no longer a prime consideration. Moreover, the move to DDP has reduced costs in two other areas: (1) data can be edited and entered by the end user, thus eliminating the centralized task of data preparation; and (2) application complexity can be reduced, which in turn reduces systems development and maintenance costs.

Improved Cost Control Responsibility.   End-user managers carry the responsibility for the financial success of their operations. This responsibility requires that they be properly empowered with the authority to make decisions about resources that influence their overall success. When managers are precluded from making the decisions necessary to achieve their goals, their performance can be negatively influenced. A less aggressive and less effective management may evolve.

Proponents of DDP contend that the benefits of improved management attitudes more than outweigh any additional costs incurred from distributing these resources. They argue that if IT capability is indeed critical to the success of a business operation, then management must be given control over these resources. This argument counters the earlier discussion favoring the centralization of organization-wide resources.

Improved User Satisfaction. Perhaps the most often cited benefit of DDP is improved user satisfaction. DDP proponents claim that distributing system to end users improves three areas of need that too often go unsatisfied in the centralized model: (1) as previously stated, users desire to control the resources that influence their profitability; (2) users want systems professionals (analysts, programmers, and computer operators) to be responsive to their specific situation; and (3) users want to become more actively involved in developing and implementing their own systems.

Backup Flexibility. The final argument in favor of DDP is the ability to back up computing facilities to protect against potential disasters such as fires, floods, sabotage, and earthquakes. The only way to back up a central computer site against such disasters is to provide a second computer facility. Later in the chapter we examine disaster recovery planning for such contingencies. The distributed model offers organizational flexibility for providing backup. Each geographically separate IT unit can be designed with excess capacity. If a disaster destroys a single site, the other sites can use their excess capacity to process the transactions of the destroyed site. Naturally, this setup requires close coordination between the end-user managers to ensure that they do not implement incompatible hardware and software.

Controlling the DDP Environment

DDP carries a certain leading-edge prestige value that, during an analysis of its pros and cons, may overwhelm important considerations of economic benefit and operational feasibility. Some organizations have made the move to DDP without considering fully whether the distributed organizational structure will better achieve their business objectives. Many DDP initiatives have proven to be ineffective, and even counterproductive, because decision makers saw in these systems virtues that were more symbolic than real. Before taking an irreversible step, decision makers must assess the true merits of DDP for their organization. Nevertheless, careful planning and implementation of controls can mitigate some of the DDP risks previously discussed. This section reviews several improvements to the strict DDP model.

Implement a Corporate IT Function

The completely centralized model and the distributed model represent extreme positions on a continuum of structural alternatives. The needs of most firms fall somewhere between these end points. Often, the control problems previously described can be addressed by implementing a *corporate IT function* such as that illustrated in Figure 2.5.

This function is greatly reduced in size and status from that of the centralized model shown in Figure 2.2. The corporate IT group provides systems development and database management for entity-wide systems in addition to technical advice and expertise to the distributed IT community. This advisory role is represented by the dotted lines in Figure 2.5. Some of the services provided are described next.

Central Testing of Commercial Software and Hardware.   A centralized corporate IT group is better equipped than are end users to evaluate the merits of competing commercial software and hardware products under consideration. A central, technically astute group such as this can evaluate systems features, controls, and compatibility with industry and organizational standards. Test results can then be distributed to user areas as standards for guiding acquisition decisions. This allows the organization to effectively centralize the acquisition, testing, and implementation of software and hardware and avoid many problems discussed earlier.

User Services.   A valuable feature of the corporate group is its user services function. This activity provides technical help to users during the installation of new software and in troubleshooting hardware and software problems. The creation of an electronic bulletin board for users is an excellent way to distribute information about common problems and allows the sharing of user-developed programs with others in the organization. In addition, a chat room could be established to provide threaded discussions, frequently asked questions (FAQs), and intranet support. The corporate IT function could also provide a help desk, where users can call and get a quick response to questions and problems. In many organizations user services staff teach technical courses for end users as well as for computer services personnel. This raises the level of user awareness and promotes the continued education of technical personnel.

Standard-Setting Body.   The relatively poor control environment imposed by the DDP model can be improved by establishing some central guidance. The corporate group can contribute to this goal by establishing and distributing to user areas appropriate standards for systems development, programming, and documentation.

Personnel Review.   The corporate group is often better equipped than users to evaluate the technical credentials of prospective systems professionals. Although the systems professional will actually be part of the end-user group, the involvement of the corporate group in employment decisions can render a valuable service to the organization.

Audit Objective

The auditor's objective is to verify that the structure of the IT function is such that individuals in incompatible areas are segregated in accordance with the level of potential risk and in a manner that promotes a working environment. This is an environment in which formal, rather than casual, relationships need to exist between incompatible tasks.

Audit Procedures

The following audit procedures would apply to an organization with a centralized IT function:

- Review relevant documentation, including the current organizational chart, mission statement, and job descriptions for key functions, to determine if individuals or groups are performing incompatible functions.
- Review systems documentation and maintenance records for a sample of applications. Verify that maintenance programmers assigned to specific projects are not also the original design programmers.
- Verify that computer operators do not have access to the operational details of a system's internal logic. Systems documentation, such as systems flowcharts, logic flowcharts, and program code listings, should not be part of the operation's documentation set.

- Through observation, determine that segregation policy is being followed in practice. Review operations room access logs to determine whether programmers enter the facility for reasons other than system failures.

The following audit procedures would apply to an organization with a distributed IT function:

- Review the current organizational chart, mission statement, and job descriptions for key functions to determine if individuals or groups are performing incompatible duties.
- Verify that corporate policies and standards for systems design, documentation, and hardware and software acquisition are published and provided to distributed IT units.
- Verify that compensating controls, such as supervision and management monitoring, are employed when segregation of incompatible duties is economically infeasible.
- Review systems documentation to verify that applications, procedures, and databases are designed and functioning in accordance with corporate standards.

THE COMPUTER CENTER

Accountants routinely examine the physical environment of the computer center as part of their annual audit. The objective of this section is to present computer center risks and the controls that help to mitigate risk and create a secure environment. The following are areas of potential exposure that can impact the quality of information, accounting records, transaction processing, and the effectiveness of other more conventional internal controls.

Physical Location

The physical location of the computer center directly affects the risk of destruction to a natural or man-made disaster. To the extent possible, the computer center should be away from human-made and natural hazards, such as processing plants, gas and water mains, airports, high-crime areas, flood plains, and geological faults. The center should be away from normal traffic, such as the top floor of a building or in a separate, self-contained building. Locating a computer in the basement building increases its risk to floods.

Construction

Ideally, a computer center should be located in a single-story building of solid construction with controlled access (discussed next). Utility (power and telephone) lines should be underground. The building windows should not open and an air filtration system should be in place that is capable of extracting pollens, dust, and dust mites.

Access

Access to the computer center should be limited to the operators and other employees who work there. Physical controls, such as locked doors, should be employed to limit access to the center. Access should be controlled by a keypad or swipe card, though fire exits with alarms are necessary. To achieve a higher level of security, access should be monitored by closed-circuit cameras and video recording systems. Computer centers should also use sign-in logs for programmers and analysts who need access to correct program errors. The computer center should maintain accurate records of all such traffic.

Air Conditioning

Computers function best in an air-conditioned environment, and providing adequate air conditioning is often a requirement of the vendor's warranty. Computers operate best in a temperature range of 70 to 75 degrees Fahrenheit and a relative humidity of 50 percent. Logic errors can occur in computer hardware when temperatures depart significantly from this optimal range. Also, the risk of circuit damage from static electricity is increased when humidity drops. In contrast, high humidity can cause molds to grow and paper products (such as source documents) to swell and jam equipment.

Fire Suppression

Fire is the most serious threat to a firm's computer equipment. Many companies that suffer computer center fires go out of business because of the loss of critical records, such as accounts receivable. The implementation of an effective fire suppression system requires consultation with specialists. However, some of the major features of such a system include the following:

1. Automatic and manual alarms should be placed in strategic locations around the installation. These alarms should be connected to permanently staffed fire-fighting stations.
2. There must be an automatic fire extinguishing system that dispenses the appropriate type of suppressant for the location.[2] For example, spraying water and certain chemicals on a computer can do as much damage as the fire.
3. Manual fire extinguishers should be placed at strategic locations.
4. The building should be of sound construction to withstand water damage caused by fire suppression equipment.
5. Fire exits should be clearly marked and illuminated during a fire.

Fault Tolerance

Fault tolerance is the ability of the system to continue operation when part of the system fails because of hardware failure, application program error, or operator error. Implementing fault tolerance control ensures that no single point of potential system failure exists. Total failure can occur only if multiple components fail. Two examples of fault tolerance technologies are discussed next.

1. **Redundant arrays of independent disks (RAID).** Raid involves using parallel disks that contain redundant elements of data and applications. If one disk fails, the lost data are automatically reconstructed from the redundant components stored on the other disks.

---

2 Some fire-fighting gases, such as halon, have been outlawed by the federal government. Make sure any gas used does not violate federal law.

2. **Uninterruptible power supplies.** Commercially provided electrical power presents several problems that can disrupt the computer center operations, including total power failures, brownouts, power fluctuations, and frequency variations. The equipment used to control these problems includes voltage regulators, surge protectors, generators, and backup batteries. In the event of a power outage, these devices provide backup power for a reasonable period to allow commercial power service restoration. In the event of an extended power outage, the backup power will allow the computer system to shut down in a controlled manner and prevent data loss and corruption that would otherwise result from an uncontrolled system crash.

Audit Objectives

The auditor's objective is to evaluate the controls governing computer center security. Specifically, the auditor must verify that:

- Physical security controls are adequate to reasonably protect the organization from physical exposures
- Insurance coverage on equipment is adequate to compensate the organization for the destruction of, or damage to, its computer center

Audit Procedures

The following are tests of physical security controls.

Tests of Physical Construction. The auditor should obtain architectural plans to determine that the computer center is solidly built of fireproof material. There should be adequate drainage under the raised floor to allow water to flow away in the event of water damage from a fire in an upper floor or from some other source. In addition, the auditor should assess the physical location of the computer center. The facility should be located in an area that minimizes its exposure to fire, civil unrest, and other hazards.

Tests of the Fire Detection System. The auditor should establish that fire detection and suppression equipment, both manual and automatic, are in place and tested regularly. The fire-detection system should detect smoke, heat, and combustible fumes. The evidence may be obtained by reviewing official fire marshal records of tests, which are stored at the computer center.

Tests of Access Control. The auditor must establish that routine access to the computer center is restricted to authorized employees. Details about visitor access (by programmers and others), such as arrival and departure times, purpose, and frequency of access, can be obtained by reviewing the access log. To establish the veracity of this document, the auditor may covertly observe the process by which access is permitted, or review videotapes from cameras at the access point, if they are being used.

Tests of Raid. Most systems that employ RAID provide a graphical mapping of their redundant disk storage. From this mapping, the auditor should determine if the level of RAID in place is adequate for the organization, given the level of business risk associated with disk failure. If the organization is not employing RAID, the potential for a single point of system failure exists. The auditor should review with the system administrator alternative procedures for recovering from a disk failure.

Tests of the Uninterruptible Power Supply.   The computer center should perform periodic tests of the backup power supply to ensure that it has sufficient capacity to run the computer and air conditioning. These are extremely important tests, and their results should be formally recorded. As a firm's computer systems develop, and its dependency increases, backup power needs are likely to grow proportionally. Indeed, without such tests, an organization may be unaware that it has outgrown its backup capacity until it is too late.

Tests for Insurance Coverage.   The auditor should annually review the organization's insurance coverage on its computer hardware, software, and physical facility. The auditor should verify that all new acquisitions are listed on the policy and that obsolete equipment and software have been deleted. The insurance policy should reflect management's needs in terms of extent of coverage. For example, the firm may wish to be partially self-insured and require minimum coverage. On the other hand, the firm may seek complete replacement-cost coverage.

DISASTER RECOVERY PLANNING

Disasters such as earthquakes, floods, sabotage, and even power failures can be catastrophic to an organization's computer center and information systems. Figure 2.6 depicts three categories of disaster that can rob an organization of its IT resources:

FIGURE 2.6

Types of Disasters

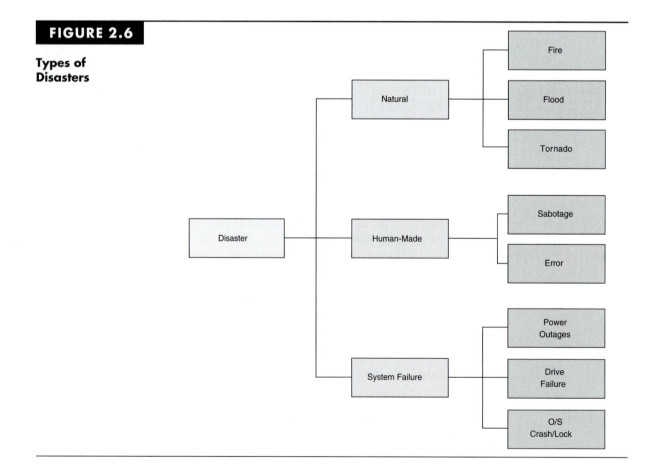

natural disasters, human-made disasters, and system failure. Natural disaster such as hurricanes, wide-spread flooding, and earthquakes are the most potentially devastating of the three from a societal perspective because they can simultaneously impact many organizations within the affected geographic area. Human-made disasters, such as sabotage or errors, can be just as destructive to an individual organization, but tend to be limited in their scope of impact. System failures such as power outages or a hard-drive failure are generally less severe, but are the most likely to occur.

All of these disasters can deprive an organization of its data processing facilities, halt those business functions that are performed or aided by computers, and impair the organization's ability to deliver its products or services. In other words, the company loses its ability to do business. The more dependent an organization is on technology, the more susceptible it is to these types of risks. For businesses such as Amazon.com or eBay, the loss of even a few hours of computer processing capability can be catastrophic.

Disasters of the sort outlined above usually cannot be prevented or evaded. Once stricken, the victim firm's survival will be determined by how well and how quickly it reacts. Therefore, with careful contingency planning, the full impact of a disaster can be absorbed and the organization can recover. To survive such an event, companies develop recovery procedures and formalize them into a **disaster recovery plan (DRP)**. This is a comprehensive statement of all actions to be taken before, during, and after any type of disaster. Although the details of each plan are unique to the needs of the organization, all workable plans possess four common features:

1. Identify critical applications
2. Create a disaster recovery team
3. Provide site backup
4. Specify backup and off-site storage procedures

The remainder of this section is devoted to a discussion of the essential elements of an effective DRP.

Identify Critical Applications

The first essential element of a DRP is to identify the firm's critical applications and associated data files. Recovery efforts must concentrate on restoring those applications that are critical to the short-term survival of the organization. Obviously, over the long term, all applications must be restored to predisaster business activity levels. The DRP, however, is a short-term document that should not attempt to restore the organization's data processing facility to full capacity immediately following the disaster. To do so would divert resources away from critical areas and delay recovery. The plan should therefore focus on short-term survival, which is at risk in any disaster scenario.

For most organizations, short-term survival requires the restoration of those functions that generate cash flows sufficient to satisfy short-term obligations. For example, assume that the following functions affect the cash flow position of a particular firm:

- Customer sales and service
- Fulfillment of legal obligations
- Accounts receivable maintenance and collection
- Production and distribution decisions
- Purchasing functions
- Cash disbursements (trade accounts and payroll)

The computer applications that support these business functions directly are critical. Hence, these applications should be identified and prioritized in the restoration plan.

Application priorities may change over time, and these decisions must be reassessed regularly. Systems are constantly revised and expanded to reflect changes in user requirements. Similarly, the DRP must be updated to reflect new developments and identify critical applications. Up-to-date priorities are important, because they affect other aspects of the strategic plan. For example, changes in application priorities may cause changes in the nature and extent of second-site backup requirements and specific backup procedures, which are discussed later.

The task of identifying critical items and prioritizing applications requires the active participation of user departments, accountants, and auditors. Too often, this task is incorrectly viewed as a technical computer issue and therefore delegated to IT professionals. Although the technical assistance of IT professionals will be required, this task is a business decision and should be made by those best equipped to understand the business problem.

Creating a Disaster Recovery Team

Recovering from a disaster depends on timely corrective action. Delays in performing essential tasks prolongs the recovery period and diminishes the prospects for a successful recovery. To avoid serious omissions or duplication of effort during implementation of the contingency plan, task responsibility must be clearly defined and communicated to the personnel involved.

Figure 2.7 presents an organizational chart depicting the composition of a disaster recovery team. The team members should be experts in their areas and have assigned tasks. Following a disaster, team members will delegate subtasks to their subordinates. It should be noted that traditional control concerns do not apply in this setting. The environment created by the disaster may make it necessary to violate control principles such as segregation of duties, access controls, and supervision.

Providing Second-Site Backup

A necessary ingredient in a DRP is that it provides for duplicate data processing facilities following a disaster. Among the options available the most common are **mutual aid pact**; **empty shell** or *cold site*; **recovery operations center** or *hot site*; and internally provided backup. Each of these is discussed in the following sections.

Mutual Aid Pact. A mutual aid pact is an agreement between two or more organizations (with compatible computer facilities) to aid each other with their data processing needs in the event of a disaster. In such an event, the host company must disrupt its processing schedule to process the critical transactions of the disaster-stricken company. In effect, the host company itself must go into an emergency operation mode and cut back on the processing of its lower-priority applications to accommodate the sudden increase in demand for its IT resources.

The popularity of these reciprocal agreements is driven by economics; they are relatively cost-free to implement. In fact, mutual aid pacts work better in theory than in practice. In the event of a disaster, the stricken company has no guarantee that the partner company will live up to its promise of assistance. To rely on such an arrangement for substantive relief during a disaster requires a level of faith and untested trust that is uncharacteristic of sophisticated management and its auditors.

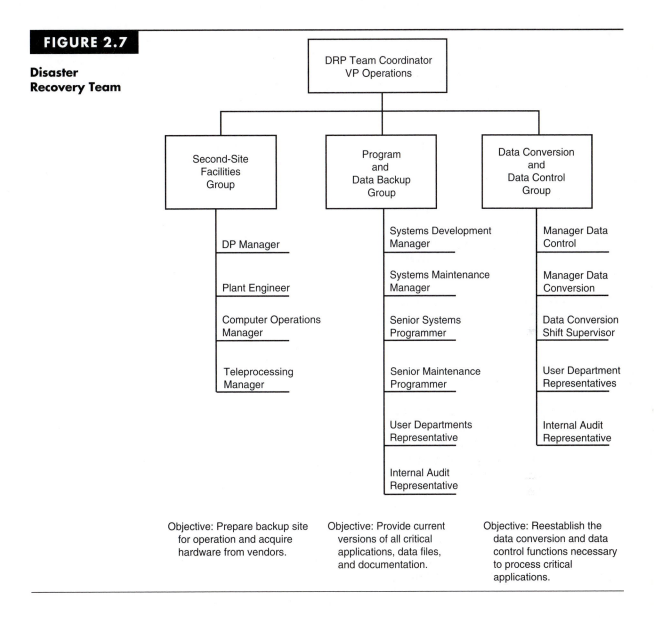

FIGURE 2.7

Disaster Recovery Team

DRP Team Coordinator
VP Operations

Second-Site Facilities Group

DP Manager

Plant Engineer

Computer Operations Manager

Teleprocessing Manager

Objective: Prepare backup site for operation and acquire hardware from vendors.

Program and Data Backup Group

Systems Development Manager

Systems Maintenance Manager

Senior Systems Programmer

Senior Maintenance Programmer

User Departments Representative

Internal Audit Representative

Objective: Provide current versions of all critical applications, data files, and documentation.

Data Conversion and Data Control Group

Manager Data Control

Manager Data Conversion

Data Conversion Shift Supervisor

User Department Representatives

Internal Audit Representative

Objective: Reestablish the data conversion and data control functions necessary to process critical applications.

Empty Shell. The empty shell or cold site plan is an arrangement wherein the company buys or leases a building that will serve as a data center. In the event of a disaster, the shell is available and ready to receive whatever hardware the temporary user needs to run essential systems. This approach, however, has a fundamental weakness. Recovery depends on the timely availability of the necessary computer hardware to restore the data processing function. Management must obtain assurances through contracts with hardware vendors that, in the event of a disaster, the vendor will give the company's needs priority. An unanticipated hardware supply problem at this critical juncture could be a fatal blow.

Recovery Operations Center. A recovery operations center (ROC) or hot site is a fully equipped backup data center that many companies share. In addition to hardware and backup facilities, ROC service providers offer a range of technical services to their clients, who pay an annual fee for access rights. In the event of a major disaster, a subscriber can occupy the premises and, within a few hours, resume processing critical applications.

September 11, 2001, was a true test of the reliability and effectiveness of the ROC approach. Comdisco, a major ROC provider, had 47 clients who declared 93 separate disasters on the day of the attack. All 47 companies relocated and worked out of Comdisco's recovery centers. At one point, 3,000 client employees were working out of the centers. Thousands of computers were configured for clients' needs within the first 24 hours, and systems recovery teams were on-site wherever police permitted access. By September 25, nearly half of the clients were able to return to their facilities with a fully functional system.

Although the Comdisco story illustrates a ROC success, it also points to a potential problem with this approach. A widespread natural disaster, such as a flood or an earthquake, may destroy the data processing capabilities of several ROC members located in the same geographic area. All the victim companies will find themselves vying for access to the same limited facilities. Because some ROC service providers oversell their capacity by a ratio of 20:1, the situation is analogous to a sinking ship that has an inadequate number of lifeboats.

The period of confusion following a disaster is not an ideal time to negotiate property rights. Therefore, before entering into a ROC arrangement, management should consider the potential problems of overcrowding and geographic clustering of the current membership.

Internally Provided Backup.   Larger organizations with multiple data processing centers often prefer the self-reliance that creating internal excess capacity provides. This permits firms to develop standardized hardware and software configurations, which ensure functional compatibility among their data processing centers and minimize cutover problems in the event of a disaster.

Pershing, a division of Donaldson, Lufkin & Jenrette Securities Corporation, processes more than 36 million transactions per day, about 2,000 per second. Pershing management recognized that a ROC vendor could not provide the recovery time they wanted and needed. The company, therefore, built its own remote **mirrored data center**. The facility is equipped with high-capacity storage devices capable of storing more than 20 terabytes of data and two IBM mainframes running high-speed copy software. All transactions that the main system processes are transmitted in real time along fiber-optic cables to the remote backup facility. At any point in time, the mirrored data center reflects current economic events of the firm. The mirrored system has reduced Pershing's data recovery time from 24 hours to 1 hour.

Backup and Off-Site Storage Procedures

All data files, applications, documentation, and supplies needed to perform critical functions should be automatically backed up and stored at a secure off-site location. Data processing personnel should routinely perform backup and storage procedures to obtain and secure these critical resources.

Operating System Backup.   If the company uses a cold site or other method of site backup that does not include a compatible operating system (O/S), procedures for obtaining a current version of the operating system need to be clearly specified. The data librarian, if one exists, would be a key person to involve in performing this task in addition to the applications and data backups procedures discussed next.

Application Backup. Based on results obtained in the critical applications step discussed previously, the DRP should include procedures to create copies of current versions of critical applications. In the case of commercial software, this involves purchasing backup copies of the latest software upgrades used by the organization. For in-house developed applications, backup procedures should be an integral step in the systems development and program change process, which is discussed in detail in Chapter 5.

Backup Data Files. The state-of-the-art in database backup is the remote mirrored site, which provides complete data currency. Not all organizations are willing or able to invest in such backup resources. As a minimum, however, databases should be copied daily to high-capacity, high-speed media, such as tape or CDs/DVDs and secured off-site. In the event of a disruption, reconstruction of the database is achieved by updating the most current backed-up version with subsequent transaction data. Likewise, master files and transaction files should be protected.

Backup Documentation. The system documentation for critical applications should be backed up and stored off-site along with the applications. System documentation can constitute a significant amount of material and the backup process is complicated further by frequent application changes (see Chapter 5). Documentation backup may, however, be simplified and made more efficient through the use of Computer Aided Software Engineering (CASE) documentation tools. The DRP should also include a provision backing up end-user manuals because the individuals processing transactions under disaster conditions may not be usual staff who are familiar with the system.

Backup Supplies and Source Documents. The organization should create backup inventories of supplies and source documents used in processing critical transactions. Examples of critical supplies are check stocks, invoices, purchase orders, and any other special-purpose forms that cannot be obtained immediately. The DRP should specify the types and quantities needed of these special items. Because these are such routine elements of the daily operations, they are often overlooked by disaster contingency planners. At this point, it is worth noting that a copy of the current DRP document should also be stored off-site at a secure location.

Testing the DRP. The most neglected aspect of contingency planning is testing the DRP. Nevertheless, DRP tests are important and should be performed periodically. Tests measure the preparedness of personnel and identify omissions or bottlenecks in the plan.

A test is most useful when the simulation of a disruption is a surprise. When the mock disaster is announced, the status of all processing affected by it should be documented. This approach provides a benchmark for subsequent performance assessments. The plan should be carried through as far as is economically feasible. Ideally, that would include the use of backup facilities and supplies.

The progress of the plan should be noted at key points throughout the test period. At the conclusion of the test, the results can then be analyzed and a DRP performance report prepared. The degree of performance achieved provides input for decisions to modify the DRP or schedule additional tests. The organization's management should seek measures of performance in each of the following areas: (1) the effectiveness of DRP team personnel and their knowledge levels; (2) the degree of conversion success (i.e., the number of lost records); (3) an estimate of financial loss due to lost records or facilities; and (4) the effectiveness of program, data, and documentation backup and recovery procedures.

Audit Objective

The auditor should verify that management's disaster recovery plan is adequate and feasible for dealing with a catastrophe that could deprive the organization of its computing resources.

Audit Procedures

In verifying that management's DRP is a realistic solution for dealing with a catastrophe, the following tests may be performed.

Site Backup. The auditor should evaluate the adequacy of the backup site arrangement. System incompatibility and human nature both greatly reduce the effectiveness of the mutual aid pact. Auditors should be skeptical of such arrangements for two reasons. First, the sophistication of the computer system may make it difficult to find a potential partner with a compatible configuration. Second, most firms do not have the necessary excess capacity to support a disaster-stricken partner while also processing their own work. When it comes to the crunch, the management of the firm untouched by disaster will likely have little appetite for the sacrifices that must be made to honor the agreement.

More viable but expensive options are the empty shell and recovery operation center. These too must be examined carefully. If the client organization is using the empty shell method, then the auditor needs to verify the existence of valid contracts with hardware vendors that guarantee delivery of needed computer hardware with minimum delay after the disaster. If the client is a member of a ROC, the auditor should be concerned about the number of ROC members and their geographic dispersion. A widespread disaster may create a demand that cannot be satisfied by the ROC facility.

Critical Application List. The auditor should review the list of critical applications to ensure that it is complete. Missing applications can result in failure to recover. The same is true, however, for restoring unnecessary applications. To include applications on the critical list that are not needed to achieve short-term survival can misdirect resources and distract attention from the primary objective during the recovery period.

Software Backup. The auditor should verify that copies of critical applications and operating systems are stored off-site. The auditor should also verify that the applications stored off-site are current by comparing their version numbers with those of the actual applications in use. Application version numbers is explained in detail in Chapter 5.

Data Backup. The auditor should verify that critical data files are backed up in accordance with the DRP. Specific data backup procedures for both flat files and relational databases are discussed in detail in Chapter 4.

Backup Supplies, Documents, and Documentation. The system documentation, supplies, and source documents needed to process critical transactions should be backed up and stored off-site. The auditor should verify that the types and quantities of items specified in the DRP such as check stock, invoices, purchase orders, and any special-purpose forms exist in a secure location.

Disaster Recovery Team. The DRP should clearly list the names, addresses, and emergency telephone numbers of the disaster recovery team members. The auditor should verify that members of the team are current employees and are aware of their assigned responsibilities. On one occasion, while reviewing a firm's DRP, the author discovered that a team leader listed in the plan had been deceased for nine months.

OUTSOURCING THE IT FUNCTION

The costs, risks, and responsibilities associated with maintaining an effective corporate IT function are significant. Many executives have therefore opted to outsource their IT functions to third-party vendors who take over responsibility for the management of IT assets and staff and for delivery of IT services, such as data entry, data center operations, applications development, applications maintenance, and network management. Often-cited benefits of **IT outsourcing** include improved core business performance, improved IT performance (because of the vendor's expertise), and reduced IT costs. By moving IT facilities offshore to low labor-cost areas and/or through economies of scale (by combining the work of several clients), the vendor can perform the outsourced function more cheaply than the client firm could have otherwise. The resulting cost savings are then passed to the client organization. Furthermore, many IT outsourcing arrangements involve the sale of the client firm's IT assets—both human and machine—to the vendor, which the client firm then leases back. This transaction results in a significant one-time cash infusion to the firm.

The logic underlying IT outsourcing follows from **core competency** theory, which argues that an organization should focus exclusively on its core business competencies, while allowing outsourcing vendors to efficiently manage the non–core areas such as the IT functions. This premise, however, ignores an important distinction between commodity and specific IT assets.

Commodity IT assets are not unique to a particular organization and are thus easily acquired in the marketplace. These include such things as network management, systems operations, server maintenance, and help-desk functions. **Specific IT assets**, in contrast, are unique to the organization and support its strategic objectives. Because of their idiosyncratic nature, specific assets have little value outside their current use. Such assets may be tangible (computer equipment), intellectual (computer programs), or human. Examples of specific assets include systems development, application maintenance, data warehousing, and highly skilled employees trained to use organization-specific software.

Transaction Cost Economics (TCE) theory is in conflict with the core competency school by suggesting that firms should retain certain specific non–core IT assets in-house. Because of their esoteric nature, specific assets cannot be easily replaced once they are given up in an outsourcing arrangement. Therefore, if the organization should decide to cancel its outsourcing contract with the vendor, it may not be able to return to its preoutsource state. On the other hand, TCE theory supports the outsourcing of commodity assets, which are easily replaced or obtained from alternative vendors.

Naturally, a CEO's perception of what constitutes a commodity IT assets plays an important role in IT outsourcing decisions. Often this comes down to a matter of definition and interpretation. For example, most CEOs would define their IT function as a non–core commodity, unless they are in the business of developing and selling IT applications. Consequently, a belief that *all* IT can, and should, be managed by large service organizations tends to prevail. Such misperception reflects, in part, both lack of executive education and dissemination of faulty information regarding the virtues and limitations of IT outsourcing.[3]

---

3   This knowledge disconnect is not unique to IT outsourcing; it has been observed by Ramiller and Swanson in their research on how executives respond to what is termed organizing visions for IT [101].

Risks Inherent to IT Outsourcing

Large-scale IT outsourcing events are risky endeavors, partly because of the sheer size of these financial deals, but also because of their nature. The level of risk is related to the degree of asset specificity of the outsourced function. The following sections outline some well-documented issues.

Failure to Perform

Once a client firm has outsourced specific IT assets, its performance becomes linked to the vendor's performance. The negative implications of such dependency are illustrated in the financial problems that have plagued the huge outsourcing vendor Electronic Data Systems Corp. (EDS). In a cost-cutting effort, EDS terminated seven thousand employees, which impacted its ability to serve other clients. Following an 11-year low in share prices, EDS stockholders filed a class-action lawsuit against the company. Clearly, vendors experiencing such serious financial and legal problems threaten the viability of their clients also.

Vendor Exploitation

Large-scale IT outsourcing involves transferring to a vendor "specific assets," such as the design, development, and maintenance of unique business applications that are critical to an organization's survival. Specific assets, while valuable to the client, are of little value to the vendor beyond the immediate contract with the client. Indeed, they may well be valueless should the client organization go out of business. Because the vendor assumes risk by acquiring the assets and can achieve no economies of scale by employing them elsewhere, the client organization will pay a premium to transfer such functions to a third party. Further, once the client firm has divested itself of such specific assets it becomes dependent on the vendor. The vendor may exploit this dependency by raising service rates to an exorbitant level. As the client's IT needs develop over time beyond the original contract terms, it runs the risk that new or incremental services will be negotiated at a premium. This dependency may threaten the client's long-term flexibility, agility, and competitiveness and result in even greater vendor dependency.

Outsourcing Costs Exceed Benefits

IT outsourcing has been criticized on the grounds that unexpected costs arise and the full extent of expected benefits are not realized. One survey revealed that 47 percent of 66 firms surveyed reported that the costs of IT outsourcing exceeded outsourcing benefits. One reason for this is that outsourcing clients often fail to anticipate the costs of vendor selection, contracting, and the transitioning of IT operations to the vendors.

Reduced Security

Information outsourced to offshore IT vendors raises unique and serious questions regarding internal control and the protection of sensitive personal data. When corporate financial systems are developed and hosted overseas, and program code is developed through interfaces with the host company's network, U.S. corporations are at risk of losing control of their information. To a large degree U.S. firms are reliant on the outsourcing vendor's security measures, data-access policies, and the privacy laws of the host country. For example, a woman in Pakistan obtained patient-sensitive medical data from the University of California Medical Center in San Francisco. She gained access to the data from a medical transcription vendor for whom she worked. The woman threatened to publish the records on the Internet if she did not get a raise in pay. Terrorism in

Asia and the Middle East raises additional security concerns for companies outsourcing technology offshore. For example, on March 5, 2005, police in Delhi, India, arrested a cell of suspected terrorists who were planning to attack outsourcing firms in Bangalore, India.

Loss of Strategic Advantage

IT outsourcing may affect incongruence between a firm's IT strategic planning and its business planning functions. Organizations that use IT strategically must align business strategy and IT strategy or run the risk of decreased business performance. To promote such alignment, firms need IT managers and chief information officers (CIOs) who have a strong working knowledge of the organization's business. A survey of 213 IT managers in the financial services industry confirmed that a firm's IT leadership needs to be closely aligned with the firm's competitive strategy. Indeed, some argue that the business competence of CIOs is more important than their IT competence in facilitating strategic congruence.

To accomplish such alignment necessitates a close working relationship between corporate management and IT management in the concurrent development of business and IT strategies. This, however, is difficult to accomplish when IT planning is geographically redeployed offshore or even domestically. Further, because the financial justification for IT outsourcing depends upon the vendor achieving economies of scale, the vendor is naturally driven to toward seeking common solutions that may be used by many clients rather than creating unique solutions for each of them. This fundamental underpinning of IT outsourcing is inconsistent with the client's pursuit of strategic advantage in the marketplace.

Audit Implications of IT Outsourcing

Management may outsource its organization's IT functions, but it cannot outsource its management responsibilities under SOX for ensuring adequate IT internal controls. The PCAOB specifically states in its Auditing Standard No. 2, "The use of a service organization does not reduce management's responsibility to maintain effective internal control over financial reporting. Rather, user management should evaluate controls at the service organization, as well as related controls at the user company, when making its assessment about internal control over financial reporting." Therefore, if an audit client firm outsource its IT function to a vendor that processes its transactions, hosts key data, or performs other significant services, the auditor will need to conduct an evaluation of the vendor organization's controls, or alternatively obtain a SAS No. 70 auditor's report from the vendor organization.

Statement on Auditing Standard No. 70 (SAS 70) is the definitive standard by which client organizations' auditors can gain knowledge that controls at the third-party vendor are adequate to prevent or detect material errors that could impact the client's financial statements. The SAS 70 report, which is prepared by the vendor's auditor, attests to the adequacy of the vendor's internal controls. This is the means by which an outsourcing vendor can obtain a single audit report that may be used by its clients' auditors and thus preclude the need for each client firm auditor to conduct its own audit of the vendor organization's internal controls.

Figure 2.8 illustrates how a SAS 70 report works in relation to the vendor, the client firms, and their respective auditors. The outsourcing vendor serves clients 1, 2, 3, and 4 with various IT services. The internal controls over the outsourced services reside at the vendor location. They are audited by the vendor's auditor, who expresses an opinion and

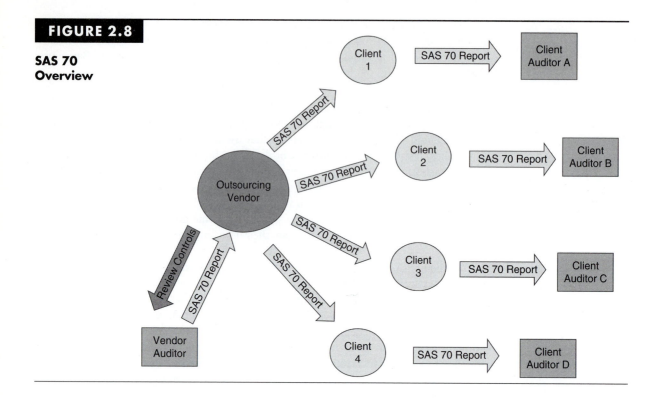

FIGURE 2.8

**SAS 70
Overview**

issues a SAS 70 report on the control adequacy. Each of the client firms is audited by different auditors A, B, C, and D, respectively, who as part of their respective audits, rely on the vendor's SAS 70 report and are thus not compelled to individually test the vendor's controls. Given that a vendor may have hundreds or even thousands of clients, individual testing under SOX would be highly disruptive to the vendor's operations, costly to the client, and impractical.

Service provider auditors issue two types of SAS 70 reports. An SAS 70 Type I report is the less rigorous of the two and comments only on the suitability of the controls' design. An SAS 70 Type II report goes further and assesses whether the controls are operating effectively based on tests conducted by the vendor organization's auditor. The vast majority of SAS 70 reports issued are Type II. Because Section 404 requires the explicit testing of controls, SAS 70 Type I reports are of little value in a post-SOX world.

SUMMARY

This chapter presented risks and controls related to IT governance. It began with a brief definition of IT governance and identified its implications for internal control and financial reporting. Next it presented exposures that can arise from inappropriate structuring of the IT function within the organization. The chapter turned to a review of computer center threats and controls, which include protecting it from damage and destruction from natural disasters, fire, temperature, and humidity. The chapter then presented the key elements of a disaster recovery plan. Several factors need to be considered in such a plan, including providing second-site backup, identifying critical applications, performing backup and off-site storage procedures, creating a disaster recovery team, and testing the DRP. The final section of the chapter examined issues surrounding the growing trend toward IT outsourcing. In particular, it reviewed the logic underlying outsourcing and its expected benefits. IT outsourcing is also associated with significant risks, which were addressed. The chapter concluded with a discussion of audit issues in an outsourcing environment.

KEY TERMS

centralized data processing
computer operations
core competency
Commodity IT assets
data conversion
data library
disaster recovery plan (DRP)
distributed data processing (DDP)
empty shell
fault tolerance

inadequate documentation
Information technology (IT) governance
IT outsourcing
mirrored data center
mutual aid pact
recovery operations center (ROC)
redundant arrays of independent disks (RAID)
Specific IT assets
Transaction Cost Economics (TCE)

REVIEW QUESTIONS

1. What is IT governance?
2. What are the objectives of IT governance?
3. What is distributed data processing?
4. What are the advantages and disadvantages of distributed data processing?
5. What types of tasks become redundant in a distributed data processing system?
6. Explain why certain duties that are deemed incompatible in a manual system may be combined in a CBIS computer-based information system environment. Give an example.
7. What are the three primary CBIS functions that must be separated?
8. What exposures do data consolidation in a CBIS environment pose?
9. What problems may occur as a result of combining applications programming and maintenance tasks into one position?
10. Why is poor-quality systems documentation a prevalent problem?
11. What is RAID?
12. What is the role of a data librarian?
13. What is the role of a corporate computer services department? How does this differ from other configurations?
14. What are the five risks associated with of distributed data processing?
15. List the control features that directly contribute to the security of the computer center environment.
16. What is data conversion?
17. What may be contained in the data library?
18. What is an ROC?
19. What is a cold site?
20. What is fault tolerance?
21. What are the often-cited benefits of IT outsourcing?
22. Define commodity IT asset.
23. Define specific asset.
24. List five risks associated with IT outsourcing.

DISCUSSION QUESTIONS

1. How is pre-SOX IT governance different from post-SOX IT governance?
2. Although IT governance is a broad area, only three aspects of IT governance are discussed in the chapter. Name them and explain why these topics were chosen.
3. What types of incompatible activities are prone to becoming consolidated in a distributed

data processing system? How can this be prevented?

4. Why would an operational manager be willing to take on more work in the form of supervising an IT function?

5. How can data be centralized in a distributed data processing system?

6. Should standards be centralized in a distributed data processing environment? Explain.

7. How can human behavior be considered one of the biggest potential threats to operating system integrity?

8. A bank in California has thirteen branches spread throughout northern California, each with its own minicomputer where its data are stored. Another bank has ten branches spread throughout California, with the data being stored on a mainframe in San Francisco. Which system do you think is more vulnerable to unauthorized access? Excessive losses from disaster?

9. End-user computing has become extremely popular in distributed data processing organizations. The end users like it because they feel they can more readily design and implement their own applications. Does this type of environment always foster more efficient development of applications? Explain your answer.

10. Compare and contrast the following disaster recovery options: mutual aid pact, empty shell, recovery operations center, and internally provided backup. Rank them from most risky to least risky, as well as from most costly to least costly.

11. Who should determine and prioritize the critical applications? How is this done? How frequently is it done?

12. Why is it easier for programmers to perpetrate a fraud than operators?

13. Why should an organization centralize the acquisition, testing, and implementation of software and hardware within the corporate IT function?

14. Organizations sometimes locate their computer centers in the basement of their buildings to avoid normal traffic flows. Comment on this practice.

15. The 2003 blackout that affected the U.S. Northeast caused numerous computer failures. What can an organization do to protect itself from such uncontrollable power failures?

16. Discuss a potential problem with ROCs.

17. Discuss two potential problems associated with a cold site.

18. Discuss three techniques used to achieve fault tolerance.

19. Explain the outsourcing risk of failure to perform.

20. Explain vendor exploitation.

21. Explain why reduced security is an outsourcing risk.

22. Explain how IT outsourcing can lead to loss of strategic advantage.

23. Explain the role of a SAS 70 report in reviewing internal controls.

MULTIPLE-CHOICE QUESTIONS

1. Segregation of duties in the computer-based information system includes
   a. separating the programmer from the computer operator.
   b. preventing management override.
   c. separating the inventory process from the billing process.
   d. performing independent verifications by the computer operator.

2. A disadvantage of distributed data processing is
   a. the increased time between job request and job completion.
   b. the potential for hardware and software incompatibility among users.
   c. the disruption caused when the mainframe goes down.
   d. that users are not likely to be involved.
   e. that data processing professionals may not be properly involved.

3. Which of the following is NOT a control implication of distributed data processing?
   a. redundancy
   b. user satisfaction
   c. incompatibility
   d. lack of standards

4. Which of the following disaster recovery techniques may be least optimal in the case of a disaster?
   a. empty shell
   b. mutual aid pact
   c. internally provided backup
   d. they are all equally beneficial

5. Which of the following is a feature of fault tolerance control?
   a. interruptible power supplies
   b. RAID
   c. DDP
   d. MDP

6. Which of the following disaster recovery techniques is has the least risk associated with it?
   a. empty shell
   b. ROC
   c. internally provided backup
   d. they are all equally risky

7. Which of the following is NOT a potential threat to computer hardware and peripherals?
   a. low humidity
   b. high humidity
   c. carbon dioxide fire extinguishers
   d. water sprinkler fire extinguishers

8. Which of the following would strengthen organizational control over a large-scale data processing center?
   a. requiring the user departments to specify the general control standards necessary for processing transactions
   b. requiring that requests and instructions for data processing services be submitted directly to the computer operator in the data center
   c. having the database administrator report to the manager of computer operations.
   d. assigning maintenance responsibility to the original system designer who best knows its logic

9. The following are examples of commodity assets except
   a. network management
   b. systems operations
   c. systems development
   d. server maintenance

10. Which of the following is true?
   a. Core competency theory argues that an organization should outsource specific core assets.
   b. Core competency theory argues that an organization should focus exclusively on its core business competencies.
   c. Core competency theory argues that an organization should not outsource specific commodity assets.
   d. Core competency theory argues that an organization should retain certain specific non-core assets in-house.

PROBLEMS

1. Internal Control

In reviewing the processes, procedures, and internal controls of one of your audit clients, Steeplechase Enterprises, you notice the following practices in place. Steeplechase has recently installed a new computer system that affects the accounts receivable, billing, and shipping records. A specifically identified computer operator has been permanently assigned to each of the functions of accounts receivable, billing, and shipping. Each of these computer operators is assigned the responsibility of running the program for transaction processing, making program changes, and reconciling the computer log. In order to prevent any one operator from having exclusive access to the tapes and documentation, these three computer operators randomly rotate the custody and control tasks every two weeks over the magnetic tapes and the system documentation. Access controls to the computer room consist of magnetic cards and a digital code for each operator. Access to the computer room is not allowed to either the systems analyst or the computer operations supervisor.

The documentation for the EDP system consists of the following: record layouts, program listings, logs, and error listings.

Once goods are shipped from one of Steeplechase's three warehouses, warehouse personnel forward shipping notices to the accounting department. The billing clerk receives the shipping notice and accounts for the manual sequence of the shipping notices. Any missing notices are investigated. The billing clerk also manually enters the price of the item, and prepares daily totals (supported by adding machine tapes) of the units shipped and the amount of sales. The shipping notices and adding machine tapes are sent to the computer department for data entry.

The computer output generated consists of a two-copy invoice and remittance advice and a daily sales register. The invoices and remittance advice are forwarded to the billing clerk, who mails one copy of the invoice and remittance advice to the customer and files the other copy in an open invoice file, which serves as an accounts receivable document. The daily sales register contains the total of units shipped and sales amounts. The computer operator compares the computer-generated totals to the adding machine tapes.

Required:

Identify the control weaknesses present and make a specific recommendation for correcting each of them.

2. Internal Control

Gustave, CPA, during its preliminary review of the financial statements of Comet, Inc., found a lack of proper segregation of duties between the programming and operating functions. Comet owns its own computing facilities. Gustave, CPA, diligently intensified the internal control study and assessment tasks relating to the computer facilities. Gustave concluded in its final report that sufficient compensating general controls provided reasonable assurance that the internal control objectives were being met.

Required:

What compensating controls are most likely in place?

3. Physical Security

Avatar Financials, Inc., located on Madison Avenue, New York City, is a company that provides financial advice to individuals and small to mid-sized businesses. Its primary operations are in wealth management and financial advice. Each client has an account where basic personal information is stored on a server within the main office in New York City. The company also keeps the information about the amount of investment of each client on a separate server at its data center in Bethlehem, Pennsylvania. This information includes the total value of the portfolio, type of investments made, the income structure of each client, and associated tax liabilities.

In the last few years, larger commercial banks have started providing such services and are competing for the same set of customers. Avatar, which prides itself in personal consumer relations, is now trying to set up additional services to keep its current customers. It has recently upgraded its Web site, which formerly only allowed clients to update their personal information. Now clients can access information about their investments, income, and tax liabilities that is stored at the data center in Pennsylvania.

As a result of previous dealings, Avatar has been given free access to use the computer room of an older production plant. The company feels believes that this location is secure enough and would keep the data intact from physical intruders. The servers are housed in a room that the production plant used to house its legacy system. The room has detectors for smoke and associated sprinklers. It is enclosed, with no windows, and has specialized temperature-controlled air ducts.

Management has recently started looking at other alternatives to house the server as the plant is going to be shut down. Management has major concerns about the secrecy of the location and the associated measures. It wants to incorporate newer methods of physical data protection. The company's auditors have also expressed a concern that some of the measures at the current location are inadequate and that newer alternatives should be found.

Required:

1. Why are the auditors of Avatar stressing the need to have a better physical environment for the server? If Avatar has proper software controls in place, would that not be enough to secure the information?

2. Name the six essential control features that contribute directly to the security of the computer server environment.

4. Disaster Recovery Plans

The headquarters of Hill Crest Corporation, a private company with $15.5 million in annual sales, is located in California. Hill Crest provides for its 150 clients an online legal software service that includes data storage and administrative activities for law offices. The company has grown rapidly since its inception 3 years ago, and its data processing department has expanded to accommodate this growth. Because Hill Crest's president and sales personnel spend a great deal of time out of the office soliciting new clients, the planning of the IT facilities has been left to the data processing professionals.

Hill Crest recently moved its headquarters into a remodeled warehouse on the outskirts of the city. While remodeling the warehouse, the architects retained much of the original structure, including the wooden-shingled exterior and exposed wooden beams throughout the interior. The minicomputer distributive processing hardware is situated in a large open area with high ceilings and skylights. The openness makes the data processing area accessible to the rest of the staff and encourages a team approach to problem solving. Before occupying the new facility, city inspectors declared the building safe; that is, it had adequate fire extinguishers, sufficient exits, and so on.

In an effort to provide further protection for its large database of client information, Hill Crest instituted a tape backup procedure that automatically backs up the database every Sunday evening, avoiding interruption in the daily operations and procedures. All tapes are then labeled and carefully stored on shelves reserved for this purpose in the data processing department. The departmental operator's manual has instructions on how to use these tapes to restore the database, should the need arise. A list of home phone numbers of the individuals in the data processing department is available in case of an emergency. Hill Crest has recently increased its liability insurance for data loss from $50,000 to $100,000.

This past Saturday, the Hill Crest headquarters building was completely ruined by fire, and the company must now inform its clients that all of their information has been destroyed.

Required:
  a. Describe the computer security weaknesses present at Hill Crest Corporation that made it possible for a disastrous data loss.
  b. List the components that should have been included in the disaster recovery plan at Hill Crest Corporation to ensure computer recovery within 72 hours.
  c. What factors, other than those included in the plan itself, should a company consider when formulating a disaster recovery plan?

5. Separation of Duties

Arcadia Plastics follows the philosophy of transferring employees from job to job within the company. Management believes that job rotation deters employees from feeling that they are stagnating in their jobs and promotes a better understanding of the company. A computer services employee typically works for six months as a data librarian, one year as a systems developer, six months as a database administrator, and one year in systems maintenance. At that point, he or she is assigned to a permanent position.

Required:
Discuss the importance of separation of duties within the information systems department. How can Arcadia Plastics have both job rotation and well-separated duties?

6. DDP Risks

Write an essay discussing the primary risks associated with the distributed processing environment.

7.
Visit SunGard's Web site, http://www.sungard.com, and research its recovery services offered for the following classes: high availability, system recovery, and end-user recovery. Write a report of your findings.

8. End-User Computing
CMA 1287 5-3

The internal audit department of Hastone Manufacturing Company recently concluded a routine examination of the company's computer facilities. The auditor's report identified as a weakness the fact that there had been no coordination by the data processing services department in the purchase of microcomputer systems for the individual departments of Hastone. Among the twelve

microcomputers in the organization, there are three different hardware manufacturers. In addition, there are four to five different software vendors for spreadsheets, word processing, and database applications, along with some networking applications for clusters of microcomputers.

Microcomputers were acquired in the operating departments to allow employees in each department to conduct special analyses. Many of the departments also wanted the capability to download data from the mainframe. Therefore, each operating department had requested guidance and assistance from the data processing services department. Data processing, however, responded that it was understaffed and must devote its full effort to its main priority, the mainframe computer system.

In response to the internal audit report, the director of data processing services, Stan Marten, has issued the following memorandum.

TO: All Employees
FROM: Stan Marten, Director
REFERENCE: Microcomputer Standardization

Policies must be instituted immediately to standardize the acquisition of microcomputers and applications software. The first step is to specify the spreadsheet software that should be used by all personnel. From now on, everyone will use Micromate. All microcomputer hardware should be MS-DOS compatible. During the next month, we will also select the standard software for word processing and database applications. You will use only the user packages that are prescribed by the data processing services department. In the future, any new purchases of microcomputers, hardware, or software must be approved by the director of data processing services.

Several managers of other operating departments have complained about Marten's memorandum. Apparently, before issuing this memorandum, Marten had not consulted with any of the microcomputer users regarding their current and future software needs.

Required:
  a. When acquiring microcomputers for various departments in an organization, describe the factors related to:
     i. Computer hardware that needs to be considered during the initial design and set-up phase of the microcomputer environment.
     ii. Operating procedures and system controls that need to be considered.
  b. Discuss the benefits of having standardized hardware and software for microcomputers in an organization.
  c. Discuss the concerns that the memorandum is likely to create for the microcomputer users at Hastone Manufacturing.

9. End-User Computing
CMA Adapted 688 5-Y6

List the problems inherent in the use, by others, of spreadsheet models developed by users who are not trained in the procedural controls of system design and development.

10. Internal Control and Distributed System
Until a year ago, Dagwood Printing Company had always operated in a centralized computer environment. Now, 75 percent of the office employees have a PC. Users have been able to choose their own software packages, and no documentation of end user–developed applications has been required. Next month, each PC will be linked into a local area network and to the company's mainframe.

Required:

a. Outline a plan of action for Dagwood Printing Company to ensure that the proper controls over hardware, software, data, people, procedures, and documentation are in place.

b. Discuss any exposures the company may face if the devised plan is not implemented.

11. Internal Control Responsibility for Outsourced IT
Explain why managers who outsource their IT function may or may not also outsource responsibility for IT controls. What options are open to auditors regarding expressing an opinion on the adequacy of internal controls?

12. Competing Schools of Thought Regarding Outsourcing
Explain the *core competency* argument for outsourcing and compare/contrast it with *TCE theory*. Why does one theory tend to prevail over the other in making outsourcing decisions?

13. Internal Control and End-User Computing
The National Commercial Bank has fifteen branches and maintains a mainframe computer system at its corporate headquarters. National has recently undergone an examination by the state banking examiners, and the examiners have some concerns about National's computer operations.

During the last few years, each branch has purchased a number of microcomputers to communicate with the mainframe in the emulation mode. Emulation occurs when a microcomputer attaches to a mainframe computer and, with the use of the appropriate software, can act as if it is one of the mainframe terminals. The branch also uses these microcomputers to download information from the mainframe and, in the local mode, manipulate customer data to make banking decisions at the branch level. Each microcomputer is initially supplied with a word processing application package to formulate correspondence to the customers, a spreadsheet package to perform credit and financial loan analyses beyond the basic credit analysis package on the mainframe, and a database management package to formulate customer market and sensitivity information. National's centralized data processing department is responsible only for mainframe operations; microcomputer security is the responsibility of each branch.

Because the bank examiners believe National is at risk, they have advised the bank to review the recommendations suggested in a letter issued by banking regulatory agencies in 2008. This letter emphasizes the risks associated with end-user operations and encourages banking management to establish sound control policies. More specifically, microcomputer end-user operations have outpaced the implementation of adequate controls and have taken processing control out of the centralized environment, introducing vulnerability in new areas of the bank.

The letter also emphasizes that the responsibility for corporate policies identifying management control practices for all areas of information processing activities resides with the board of directors. The existence and adequacy of compliance with these policies and practices will be part of the regular banking examiners' review. The three required control groups for adequate information system security as they relate to National are (1) processing controls, (2) physical and environmental controls, and (3) spreadsheet program development controls.

Required:

For each of the three control groups listed

a. Identify three types of controls for microcomputer end-user operations where National Commercial Bank might be at risk.

b. Recommend a specific control procedure that National should implement for each type of control you identified. Use the following format for your answer.

Control Types	Recommended Procedures

CHAPTER 3

Security Part I: Auditing Operating Systems and Networks

LEARNING OBJECTIVES

After studying this chapter, you should:

- Be able to identify the principal threats to the operating system and the control techniques used to minimize the possibility of actual exposures.

- Be familiar with the principal risks associated with commerce conducted over intranets and the Internet and understand the control techniques used to reduce these risks.

- Be familiar with the risks associated with personal computing systems.

- Recognize the unique exposures that arise in connection with electronic data interchange (EDI) and understand how these exposures can be reduced.

This chapter continues the treatment of general IT controls as defined in the COSO control framework. The focus of the chapter is on Sarbanes-Oxley compliance regarding the security and control of operating systems, communication networks, electronic data exchange, and PC-based accounting system. This chapter examines the risks, controls, audit objectives, and audit procedures that may be performed to satisfy either compliance or attest responsibilities.

AUDITING OPERATING SYSTEMS

The **operating system** is the computer's control program. It allows users and their applications to share and access common computer resources, such as processors, main memory, databases, and printers. If operating system integrity is compromised, controls within individual accounting applications may also be circumvented or neutralized. Because the operating system is common to all users, the larger the computer facility, the greater the scale of potential damage. Thus, with an ever-expanding user community sharing more and more computer resources, operating system security becomes an important internal control issue.

Operating System Objectives

The operating system performs three main tasks. First, it translates high-level languages, such as COBOL, C++, BASIC, and SQL, into the machine-level language that the computer can execute. The language translator modules of the operating system are called **compilers** and **interpreters**. The control implications of language translators are examined in Chapter 5.

Second, the operating system allocates computer resources to users, workgroups, and applications. This includes assigning memory work space (partitions) to applications and authorizing access to terminals, telecommunications links, databases, and printers.

Third, the operating system manages the tasks of job scheduling and multiprogramming. At any point, numerous user applications (jobs) are seeking access to the computer resources under the control of the operating system. Jobs are submitted to the system in three ways: (1) directly by the system operator, (2) from various batch-job queues, and (3) through telecommunications links from remote workstations. To achieve efficient and effective use of finite computer resources, the operating system must schedule job processing according to established priorities and balance the use of resources among the competing applications.

To perform these tasks consistently and reliably, the operating system must achieve five fundamental control objectives:[1]

1. The operating system must protect itself from users. User applications must not be able to gain control of, or damage in any way, the operating system, thus causing it to cease running or destroy data.
2. The operating system must protect users from each other. One user must not be able to access, destroy, or corrupt the data or programs of another user.
3. The operating system must protect users from themselves. A user's application may consist of several modules stored in separate memory locations, each with its own data. One module must not be allowed to destroy or corrupt another module.
4. The operating system must be protected from itself. The operating system is also made up of individual modules. No module should be allowed to destroy or corrupt another module.
5. The operating system must be protected from its environment. In the event of a power failure or other disaster, the operating system should be able to achieve a controlled termination of activities from which it can later recover.

---

1   F. M. Stepczyk, "Requirements for Secure Operating Systems," *Data Security and Data Processing*, vol. 5; Study Results: TRW Systems, Inc. (New York: IBM Corporation, 1974), 25–73.

Operating System Security

Operating system security involves policies, procedures, and controls that determine who can access the operating system, which resources (files, programs, printers) they can use, and what actions they can take. The following security components are found in secure operating systems: log-on procedure, access token, access control list, and discretionary access privileges.

Log-On Procedure

A formal **log-on procedure** is the operating system's first line of defense against unauthorized access. When the user initiates the process, he or she is presented with a dialog box requesting the user's ID and password. The system compares the ID and password to a database of valid users. If the system finds a match, then the log-on attempt is authenticated. If, however, the password or ID is entered incorrectly, the log-on attempt fails and a message is returned to the user. The message should not reveal whether the password or the ID caused the failure. The system should allow the user to reenter the log-on information. After a specified number of attempts (usually no more than five), the system should lock out the user from the system.

Access Token

If the log-on attempt is successful, the operating system creates an **access token** that contains key information about the user, including user ID, password, user group, and privileges granted to the user. The information in the access token is used to approve all actions the user attempts during the session.

Access Control List

An **access control list** is assigned to each IT resource (computer directory, data file, program, or printer), which controls access to the resources. These lists contain information that defines the access privileges for all valid users of the resource. When a user attempts to access a resource, the system compares his or her ID and privileges contained in the access token with those contained in the access control list. If there is a match, the user is granted access.

Discretionary Access Privileges

The central system administrator usually determines who is granted access to specific resources and maintains the access control list. In distributed systems, however, end users may control (own) resources. Resource owners in this setting may be granted **discretionary access privileges**, which allow them to grant access privileges to other users. For example, the controller, who is the owner of the general ledger, may grant read-only privileges to a manager in the budgeting department. The accounts payable manager, however, may be granted both read and write permissions to the ledger. Any attempt the budgeting manager makes to add, delete, or change the general ledger will be denied. Discretionary access control needs to be closely supervised to prevent security breaches resulting from too liberal use.

Threats to Operating System Integrity

Operating system control objectives may not be achieved because of flaws in the operating system that are exploited either accidentally or intentionally. Accidental threats include hardware failures that cause the operating system to crash. Errors in user application programs, which the operating system cannot interpret, also cause operating system failures. Accidental system failures may cause whole segments of memory to be dumped to disks and printers, resulting in the unintentional disclosure of confidential information.

Intentional threats to the operating system are most commonly attempts to illegally access data or violate user privacy for financial gain. However, a growing threat is destructive programs from which there is no apparent gain. These exposures come from three sources:

1. Privileged personnel who abuse their authority. Systems administrators and systems programmers require unlimited access to the operating system to perform maintenance and to recover from system failures. Such individuals may use this authority to access users' programs and data files.
2. Individuals, both internal and external to the organization, who browse the operating system to identify and exploit security flaws.
3. Individuals who intentionally (or accidentally) insert computer viruses or other forms of destructive programs into the operating system.

Operating System Controls and Audit Tests

If operating system integrity is compromised, controls within individual accounting applications that impact financial reporting may also be compromised. For this reason, the design and assessment of operating system security controls are SOX compliance issues. This section presents a variety of control techniques for preserving operating system integrity and describes the associated tests that auditors may conduct. The following areas are examined: access privileges, password control, virus control, and audit trail control.

Controlling Access Privileges

User access privileges are assigned to individuals and to entire workgroups authorized to use the system. Privileges determine which directories, files, applications, and other resources an individual or group may access. They also determine the types of actions that can be taken. Recall that the systems administrator or the owner of the resource may assign privileges. Management should ensure that individuals are not granted privileges that are incompatible with their assigned duties. Consider, for example, a cash receipts clerk who is granted the right to access and make changes to the accounts receivable file.

Overall, the way access privileges are assigned influences system security. Privileges should, therefore, be carefully administered and closely monitored for compliance with organizational policy and principles of internal control.

Audit Objectives Relating to Access Privileges

The auditor's objective is to verify that access privileges are granted in a manner that is consistent with the need to separate incompatible functions and is in accordance with the organization's policy.

Audit Procedures Relating to Access Privileges

To achieve their objectives auditors may perform the following tests of controls:

- Review the organization's policies for separating incompatible functions and ensure that they promote reasonable security.
- Review the privileges of a selection of user groups and individuals to determine if their access rights are appropriate for their job descriptions and positions. The auditor

should verify that individuals are granted access to data and programs based on their need to know.

- Review personnel records to determine whether privileged employees undergo an adequately intensive security clearance check in compliance with company policy.
- Review employee records to determine whether users have formally acknowledged their responsibility to maintain the confidentiality of company data.
- Review the users' permitted log-on times. Permission should be commensurate with the tasks being performed.

Password Control

A **password** is a secret code the user enters to gain access to systems, applications, data files, or a network server. If the user cannot provide the correct password, the operating system should deny access. Although passwords can provide a degree of security, when imposed on nonsecurity-minded users, password procedures can result in end-user behavior that actually circumvents security. The most common forms of contra-security behavior include:

- Forgetting passwords and being locked out of the system.
- Failing to change passwords on a frequent basis.
- The Post-it syndrome, whereby passwords are written down and displayed for others to see.
- Simplistic passwords that a computer criminal easily anticipates.

Reusable Passwords. The most common method of password control is the **reusable password**. The user defines the password to the system once and then reuses it to gain future access. The quality of the security that a reusable password provides depends on the quality of the password itself. If the password pertains to something personal about the user, such as a child's name, pet's name, birth date, or hair color, a computer criminal can often deduce it. Even if the password is derived from nonpersonal data, it may be weak. For example, a string of keystrokes (such as A-S-D-F) or the same letter used multiple times can easily be cracked. Passwords that contain random letters and digits are more difficult to crack, but are also more difficult for the user to remember.

To improve access control, management should require that passwords be changed regularly and disallow weak passwords. Software is available that automatically scans password files and notifies users that their passwords have expired and need to be changed. These systems also use extensive databases of known weak passwords to validate the new password and disallow weak ones. An alternative to the standard reusable password is the one-time password.

One-Time Passwords. The **one-time password** was designed to overcome the aforementioned problems. Under this approach, the user's password changes continuously. This technology employs a credit card–sized smart card that contains a microprocessor programmed with an algorithm that generates, and electronically displays, a new and unique password every 60 seconds. The card works in conjunction with special authentication software located on a mainframe or network server computer. Each user's card is synchronized to the authentication software, so that at any point in time both the smart card and the network software are generating the same password for the same user.

To access the network, the user enters the PIN followed by the current password displayed on the card. The password can be used one time only. If, for example, a computer hacker intercepts the password and PIN during transmission and attempts to use them within the 1-minute time frame, access will be denied. Also, if the smart card should fall into the hands of a computer criminal, access cannot be achieved without the PIN.

Another one-time password technique uses a challenge/response approach to achieve the same end. When the user attempts to log on, the network authentication software issues a six-character code (the challenge) that the card can either scan optically or it can be entered into the card via its built-in keypad. The card's internal algorithm then generates a one-time password (the response) that the user enters through the keyboard of the remote terminal. If the firewall recognizes the current password, access is permitted.

Audit Objectives Relating to Passwords

The auditor's objective here is to ensure that the organization has an adequate and effective password policy for controlling access to the operating system.

Audit Procedures Relating to Passwords

The auditor may achieve this objective by performing the following tests:

- Verify that all users are required to have passwords.
- Verify that new users are instructed in the use of passwords and the importance of password control.
- Review password control procedures to ensure that passwords are changed regularly.
- Review the password file to determine that weak passwords are identified and disallowed. This may involve using software to scan password files for known weak passwords.
- Verify that the password file is encrypted and that the encryption key is properly secured.
- Assess the adequacy of password standards such as length and expiration interval.
- Review the account lockout policy and procedures. Most operating systems allow the system administrator to define the action to be taken after a certain number of failed log-on attempts. The auditor should determine how many failed log-on attempts are allowed before the account is locked. The duration of the lockout also needs to be determined. This could range from a few minutes to a permanent lockout that requires formal reactivation of the account.

Controlling Against Malicious and Destructive Programs

Malicious and destructive programs are responsible for millions of dollars of corporate losses annually. The losses are measured in terms of data corruption and destruction, degraded computer performance, hardware destruction, violations of privacy, and the personnel time devoted to repairing the damage. This class of programs includes viruses, worms, logic bombs, back doors, and Trojan horses. Because these have become popular press terms in recent years, we will not devote space at this point to define them. The appendix to this chapter, however, contains a detailed discussion of this material.

Threats from destructive programs can be substantially reduced through a combination of technology controls and administrative procedures. The following examples are relevant to most operating systems.

- Purchase software only from reputable vendors and accept only those products that are in their original, factory-sealed packages.
- Issue an entity-wide policy pertaining to the use of unauthorized software or illegal (bootleg) copies of copyrighted software.
- Examine all upgrades to vendor software for viruses before they are implemented.
- Inspect all public-domain software for virus infection before using.

- Establish entity-wide procedures for making changes to production programs.
- Establish an educational program to raise user awareness regarding threats from viruses and malicious programs.
- Install all new applications on a stand-alone computer and thoroughly test them with antiviral software prior to implementing them on the mainframe or local area network (LAN) server.
- Routinely make backup copies of key files stored on mainframes, servers, and workstations.
- Wherever possible, limit users to read and execute rights only. This allows users to extract data and run authorized applications, but denies them the ability to write directly to mainframe and server directories.
- Require protocols that explicitly invoke the operating system's log-on procedures to bypass Trojan horses. A typical scenario is one in which a user sits down to a terminal that is already displaying the log-on screen and proceeds to enter his or her ID and password. This, however, may be a Trojan horse rather than the legitimate procedure. Some operating systems allow the user to directly invoke the operating system log-on procedure by entering a key sequence such as CTRL + ALT + DEL. The user then knows that the log-on procedure on the screen is legitimate.
- Use antiviral software (also called vaccines) to examine application and operating system programs for the presence of a virus and remove it from the affected program. Antiviral programs are used to safeguard mainframes, network servers, and personal computers. Most antiviral programs run in the background on the host computer and automatically test all files that are uploaded to the host. The software, however, works only on known viruses. If a virus has been modified slightly (mutated), there is no guarantee that the vaccine will work. Therefore, maintaining a current version of the vaccine is critical.

Audit Objective Relating to Viruses and Other Destructive Programs

The key to computer virus control is prevention through strict adherence to organizational policies and procedures that guard against virus infection. The auditor's objective is to verify that effective management policies and procedures are in place to prevent the introduction and spread of destructive programs, including viruses, worms, back doors, logic bombs, and Trojan horses.

Audit Procedures Relating to Viruses and Other Destructive Programs

- Through interviews, determine that operations personnel have been educated about computer viruses and are aware of the risky computing practices that can introduce and spread viruses and other malicious programs.
- Verify that new software is tested on standalone workstations prior to being implemented on the host or network server.
- Verify that the current version of antiviral software is installed on the server and that upgrades are regularly downloaded to workstations.

System Audit Trail Controls

System audit trails are logs that record activity at the system, application, and user level. Operating systems allow management to select the level of auditing to be recorded in the log. Management needs to decide where to set the threshold between information and irrelevant facts. An effective audit policy will capture all significant events without cluttering the log with trivial activity. Audit trails typically consist of two types of audit logs: (1) detailed logs of individual keystrokes and (2) event-oriented logs.

Keystroke Monitoring.   **Keystroke monitoring** involves recording both the user's keystrokes and the system's responses. This form of log may be used after the fact to reconstruct the details of an event or as a real-time control to prevent unauthorized intrusion. Keystroke monitoring is the computer equivalent of a telephone wiretap. Whereas some situations may justify this level of surveillance, keystroke monitoring may also be regarded as a violation of privacy. Before implementing this type of control, management and auditors should consider the possible legal, ethical, and behavioral implications.

Event Monitoring.   **Event monitoring** summarizes key activities related to system resources. Event logs typically record the IDs of all users accessing the system; the time and duration of a user's session; programs that were executed during a session; and the files, databases, printers, and other resources accessed.

Setting Audit Trail Objectives

Audit trails can be used to support security objectives in three ways: (1) detecting unauthorized access to the system, (2) facilitating the reconstruction of events, and (3) promoting personal accountability.

Detecting Unauthorized Access.   Detecting unauthorized access can occur in real time or after the fact. The primary objective of real-time detection is to protect the system from outsiders attempting to breach system controls. A real-time audit trail can also be used to report changes in system performance that may indicate infestation by a virus or worm. Depending on how much activity is being logged for review, real-time detection can add significantly to operational overhead and degrade performance. After-the-fact detection logs can be stored electronically and reviewed periodically or as needed. When properly designed, they can be used to determine if unauthorized access was accomplished, or attempted and failed.

Reconstructing Events.   Audit trail analysis can be used to reconstruct the steps that led to events such as system failures, or security violations by individuals. Knowledge of the conditions that existed at the time of a system failure can be used to assign responsibility and to avoid similar situations in the future.

Personal Accountability.   Audit trails can be used to monitor user activity at the lowest level of detail. This capability is a preventive control that can influence behavior. Individuals are less likely to violate an organization's security policy when they know that their actions are recorded in an audit log.

A system audit log can also serve as a detective control to assign personal accountability for actions taken such as abuse of authority. For example, consider an accounts receivable clerk with authority to access customer records. The audit log may disclose that the clerk has been printing an inordinate number of records, which may indicate that the clerk is selling customer information in violation of the company's privacy policy.

Implementing a System Audit Trail

The information contained in audit logs is useful to accountants in measuring the potential damage and financial loss associated with application errors, abuse of authority, or unauthorized access by outside intruders. Audit logs, however, can generate data in overwhelming detail. Important information can easily get lost among the superfluous details of daily operation. Thus, poorly designed logs can actually be dysfunctional. Protecting exposures with the potential for material financial loss should drive management's decision as to which users, applications, or operations to monitor, and how much detail to log. As with all controls, the benefits of audit logs must be balanced against the costs of implementing them.

Audit Objectives Relating to System Audit Trails

The auditor's objective is to ensure that the established system audit trail is adequate for preventing and detecting abuses, reconstructing key events that precede systems failures, and planning resource allocation.

Audit Procedures Relating to System Audit Trails

- Most operating systems provide some form of audit manager function to specify the events that are to be audited. The auditor should verify that the audit trail has been activated according to organization policy.
- Many operating systems provide an audit log viewer that allows the auditor to scan the log for unusual activity. These can be reviewed on screen or by archiving the file for subsequent review. The auditor can use general-purpose data extraction tools for accessing archived log files to search for defined conditions such as:
  - Unauthorized or terminated user
  - Periods of inactivity
  - Activity by user, workgroup, or department
  - Log-on and log-off times
  - Failed log-on attempts
  - Access to specific files or applications
- The organization's security group has responsibility for monitoring and reporting security violations. The auditor should select a sample of security violation cases and evaluate their disposition to assess the effectiveness of the security group.

AUDITING NETWORKS

Reliance on networks for business communications poses concern about unauthorized access to confidential information. As LANs become the platform for mission-critical applications and data, proprietary information, customer data, and financial records are at risk. Organizations connected to their customers and business partners via the Internet are particularly exposed. Without adequate protection, firms open their doors to computer hackers, vandals, thieves, and industrial spies both internally and from around the world.

The paradox of networking is that networks exist to provide user access to shared resources, yet the most important objective of any network is to control such access. Hence, for every productivity argument in favor of remote access, there is a security argument against it. Organization management constantly seeks balance between increased access and the associated business risks.

The following section presents various forms of risks that threaten networks. This includes *intranet* risks posed by dishonest employees who have the technical knowledge and position to perpetrate frauds, and *Internet* risks that threaten both consumers and business entities. The material assumes that the reader is familiar with network terms and acronyms. For those who lack this background, the chapter appendix provides an overview of basic network technologies.

Intranet Risks

Intranets consist of small LANs and large WANs that may contain thousands of individual nodes. Intranets are used to connect employees within a single building, between buildings on the same physical campus, and between geographically dispersed locations. Typical intranet activities include e-mail routing, transaction processing between business units, and linking to the outside Internet.

Unauthorized and illegal employee activities internally spawn intranet threats. Their motives for doing harm may be vengeance against the company, the challenge of breaking into unauthorized files, or to profit from selling trade secrets or embezzling assets. The threat from employees (both current and former) is significant because of their intimate knowledge of system controls and/or the lack of controls. Discharged employees, or those who leave under contentious circumstance, raise particular concerns. Trade secrets, operations data, accounting data, and confidential information to which the employee has access are at greatest risk.

Interception of Network Messages

The individual nodes on most intranets are connected to a shared channel across which travel user IDs, passwords, confidential e-mails, and financial data files. The unauthorized interception of this information by a node on the network is called sniffing. The exposure is even greater when the intranet is connected to the Internet. Network administrators routinely use commercially available sniffer software to analyze network traffic and to detect bottlenecks. Sniffer software, however, can also be downloaded from the Internet. In the hands of a computer criminal, sniffer software can be used to intercept and view data sent across a shared intranet channel.

Access to Corporate Databases

Intranets connected to central corporate databases increase the risk that an employee will view, corrupt, change, or copy data. Social Security numbers, customer listings, credit card information, recipes, formulas, and design specifications may be downloaded and sold. Outsiders have bribed employees, who have access privileges to financial accounts, to electronically write off an account receivable or erase an outstanding tax bill. A Computer Security Institute (CSI) study reported that financial fraud losses of this sort averaged $500,000.[2] A previous CSI study found that the average loss from corporate espionage was more than $1 million. Total losses from insider trade secret theft have been estimated to exceed $24 billion per year.

Privileged Employees

We know from Chapter 1 that an organization's internal controls are typically aimed at lower-level employees. According to the CSI study, however, middle managers, who often possess access privileges that allow them to override controls, are most often prosecuted for insider crimes.[3] Information systems employees within the organization are another group empowered with override privileges that may permit access to mission-critical data.

---

2   Association of Certified Fraud Examiners, "2002 Report to the Nation: Occupational Fraud and Abuse," (2002).

3   Financial Executives Institute, "Safety Nets: Secrets of Effective Information Technology Controls, An Executive Report," (June 1997).

Reluctance to Prosecute.   A factor that contributes to computer crime is many organizations' reluctance to prosecute the criminals. According to the CSI study, this situation is improving. In 1996, only 17 percent of the firms that experienced an illegal intrusion reported it to a law enforcement agency. In 2002, 75 percent of such crimes were reported. Of the 25 percent that did not report the intrusions, fear of negative publicity was the most common cited justification for their silence.

Many computer criminals are repeat offenders. Performing background checks on prospective employees can significantly reduce an organization's hiring risk and avoid criminal acts. In the past, employee *backgrounding* was difficult to achieve because former employers, fearing legal action, were reluctant to disclose negative information to prospective employers. A no comment policy prevailed.

The relatively new legal doctrine of negligent hiring liability is changing this. This doctrine effectively requires employers to check into an employee's background. Increasingly, courts are holding employers responsible for criminal acts that employees, both on and off the job, perpetrated if a background check could have prevented crimes. Many states have passed laws that protect a former employer from legal action when providing work-related performance information about a former employee when (1) the inquiry comes from a prospective employer, (2) the information is based on credible facts, and (3) the information is given without malice.

Internet Risks

This section looks at three of the more significant business risks associated with Internet commerce. These are IP spoofing, denial of service attacks, and equipment failure.

IP Spoofing

IP spoofing is a form of masquerading to gain unauthorized access to a Web server and/ or to perpetrate an unlawful act without revealing one's identity. To accomplish this, a perpetrator modifies the IP address of the originating computer to disguise his or her identity. A criminal may use IP spoofing to make a message packet (see Appendix) appear to be coming from a trusted or authorized source and thus slip through control systems designed to accept transmissions from certain (trusted) host computers and block out others. This technique could be used to crack into corporate networks to perpetrate frauds, conduct acts of espionage, or destroy data. For example, a hacker may spoof a manufacturing firm with a false sales order that appears to come from a legitimate customer. If the spoof goes undetected, the manufacturer will incur the costs of producing and delivering a product that was never ordered.

Denial of Service Attack

A **denial of service attacks (Dos)** is an assault on a Web server to prevent it from servicing its legitimate users. Although such attacks can be aimed at any type of Web site, they are particularly devastating to business entities that are prevented from receiving and processing business transactions from their customers. Three common types of Dos attacks are: SYN flood, smurf, and distributed denial of service (DDos).

SYN Flood Attack.   When a user establishes a connection on the Internet through TCP/IP (see Internet protocols in the appendix), a three-way handshake takes place. The connecting server sends an initiation code called a SYN (SYNchronize) packet to the receiving server. The receiving server then acknowledges the request by returning a **SYNchronize–ACKnowledge (SYN-ACK)** packet. Finally, the initiating host machine responds with an ACK packet code. The **SYN flood attack** is accomplished by not sending the final acknowledgment to the server's SYN-ACK response, which causes the server to keep signaling for acknowledgement until the server times out.

The individual or organization perpetrating the SYN flood attack transmits hundreds of SYN packets to the targeted receiver, but never responds with an ACK to complete the connection. As a result, the ports of the receiver's server are clogged with incomplete communication requests that prevent legitimate transactions from being received and processed. Organizations under attack thus may be prevented from receiving Internet messages for days at a time.

If the target organization could identify the server that is launching the attack, a firewall (discussed later) could be programmed to ignore all communication from that site. Such attacks, however, are difficult to prevent because they use IP spoofing to disguise the source of the messages. IP spoofing programs that randomize the source address of the attacker have been written and publicly distributed over the Internet. Therefore, to the receiving site, it appears that the transmissions are coming from all over the Internet.

Smurf Attack.   A **smurf attack** involves three parties: the perpetrator, the intermediary, and the victim. It is accomplished by exploiting an Internet maintenance tool called a **ping**, which is used to test the state of network congestion and determine whether a particular host computer is connected and available on the network. The ping works by sending an echo request message (like a sonar ping) to the host computer and listening for a response message (echo reply). The ping signal is encapsulated in a message packet that also contains the return IP address of the sender. A functioning and available host must return an echo reply message that contains the exact data received in the echo request message packet.

The perpetrator of a smurf attack uses a program to create a ping message packet that contains the forged IP address of the victim's computer (IP spoofing) rather than that of the actual source computer. The ping message is then sent to the intermediary, which is actually an entire subnetwork of computers. By sending the ping to the network's **IP broadcast address**, the perpetrator ensures that each node on the intermediary network receives the echo request automatically. Consequently, each intermediary node sends echo responses to the ping message, which are returned to the victim's IP address, not that of the source computer. The resulting flood echoes can overwhelm the victim's computer and cause network congestion that makes it unusable for legitimate traffic. Figure 3.1 illustrates a smurf attack.

The intermediary in a smurf attack is an unwilling and unaware party. Indeed, the intermediary is also a victim and to some extent suffers the same type of network congestion problems the target victim suffers. One method of defeating smurf attacks is to disable the IP broadcast addressing option at each network firewall and thus eliminate the intermediary's role. In response to this move, however, attackers have developed tools to search for networks that do not disable broadcast addressing. These networks may subsequently be used as intermediaries in smurf attacks. Also, perpetrators have developed tools that enable them to launch smurf attacks simultaneously from multiple intermediary networks for maximum effect on the victim.

Distributed Denial of Service.   A **distributed denial of service (DDos)** attack may take the form of a SYN flood or smurf attack. The distinguishing feature of the DDos is the sheer scope of the event. The perpetrator of a DDos attack may employ a virtual army of so-called **zombie** or bot (robot) computers to launch the attack. Because vast numbers of unsuspecting intermediaries are needed, the attack often involves one or more **Internet relay chat (IRC)** networks as a source of zombies. IRC is a popular interactive service on the Internet that lets thousands of people from around the world engage in real-time communications via their computers.

The problem with IRC networks is that they tend to have poor security. The perpetrator can thus easily access the IRC and upload a malicious program such as a Trojan

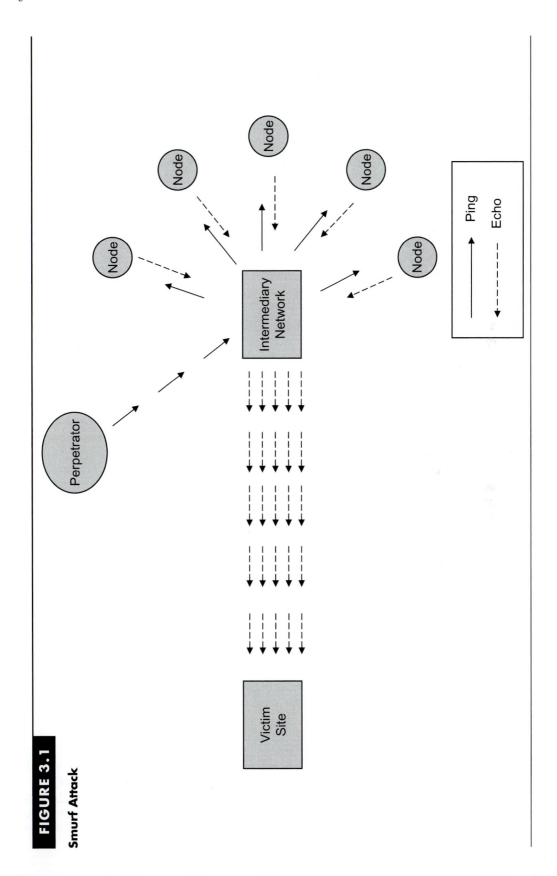

FIGURE 3.1

Smurf Attack

horse (see the appendix for a definition), which contains DDos attack script. This program is subsequently downloaded to the PCs of the many thousands of people who visit the IRC site. The attack program runs in the background on the new zombie computers, which are now under the control of the perpetrator. These collections of compromised computers are known as **botnets**. Figure 3.2 illustrates this technique.

Via the zombie control program, the perpetrator has the power to direct the DDos to specific victims and turn on or off the attack at will. The DDos attack poses a far greater threat to the victim than a traditional SYN flood or smurf attack. For instance, a SYN flood coming from thousands of distributed computers can do far more damage than one from a single computer. Also, a smurf attack coming from a subnetwork of intermediary computers all emanate from the same server. In time, the server can be located and isolated by programming the victim's firewall to ignore transmissions from the attacking site. The DDos attack, on the other hand, literally comes from sites all across the Internet. Thousands of individual attack computers are harder to track down and turn off.

Motivation Behind Dos Attacks.   The motivation behind Dos attacks may originally have been to punish an organization with which the perpetrator had a grievance or simply to gain bragging rights for being able to do it. Today, Dos attacks are also perpetrated for financial gain. Financial institutions, which are particularly dependent on Internet access, have been prime targets. Organized criminals threatening a devastating attack have extorted several institutions, including the Royal Bank of Scotland. The typical scenario is for the perpetrator to launch a short DDos attack (a day or so) to demonstrate what life would be like if the organization were isolated from the Internet. During this time, legitimate customers are unable to access their online accounts and the institution is unable to process many financial transactions. After the attack, the CEO of the organization receives a phone call demanding that a sum of money be deposited in an offshore account, or the attack will resume. Compared to the potential loss in customer confidence, damaged reputation, and lost revenues, the ransom may appear to be a small price to pay.

DDos attacks are relatively easy to execute and can have a devastating effect on the victim. Many experts believe that the best defense against DDos attacks is to implement a layered security program with multiple detection point capability. We revisit this issue later in the chapter to examine methods for dealing DDos attacks.

Risks from Equipment Failure

Network topologies consist of various configurations of (1) communications lines (twisted-pair wires, coaxial cables, microwaves, and fiber optics), (2) hardware components (modems, multiplexers, servers, and front-end processors), and (3) software (protocols and network control systems). In addition to the subversive threats described in the previous sections, network topologies are subject risks from equipment failure. For example, equipment failures in the communications system can disrupt, destroy, or corrupt transmissions between senders and receivers. Equipment failure can also result in the loss of databases and programs stored on network servers.

Controlling Networks

In the following section, we examine various control techniques employed to mitigate the risks outlined in the previous section. We begin by reviewing several controls for dealing with subversive threats including firewalls, deep packet inspection, encryption, and message control techniques. This is followed with the audit objectives and procedures associated with these controls. The section then presents controls, audit objectives, and audit procedures related to threats from equipment failure.

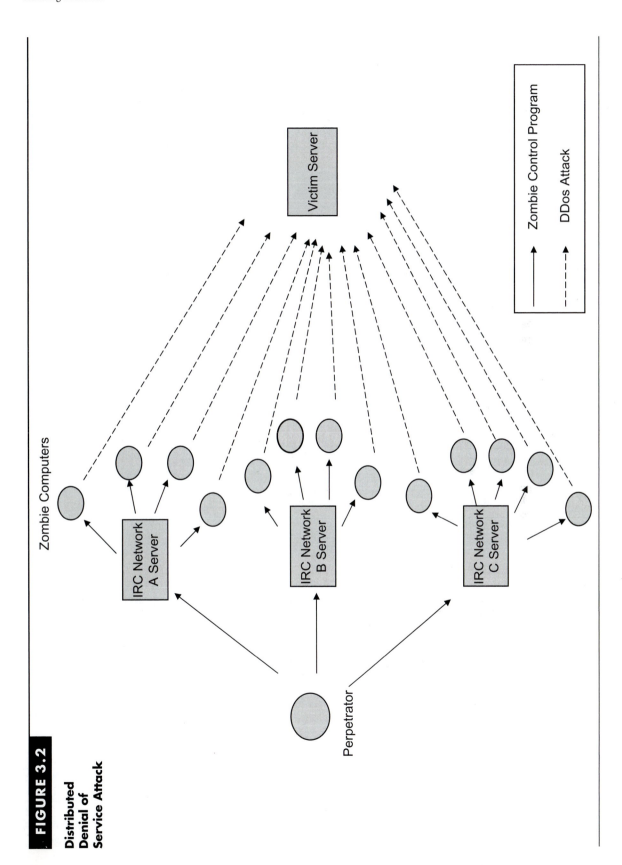

FIGURE 3.2

Distributed Denial of Service Attack

Zombie Computers

Victim Server

Zombie Control Program

DDos Attack

IRC Network A Server

IRC Network B Server

IRC Network C Server

Perpetrator

Controlling Risks from Subversive Threats

Firewalls

Organizations connected to the Internet or other public networks often implement an electronic firewall to insulate their intranet from outside intruders. A **firewall** is a system that enforces access control between two networks. To accomplish this:

- All traffic between the outside network and the organization's intranet must pass through the firewall.
- Only authorized traffic between the organization and the outside, as formal security policy specifies, is allowed to pass through the firewall.
- The firewall must be immune to penetration from both outside and inside the organization.

Firewalls can be used to authenticate an outside user of the network, verify his or her level of access authority, and then direct the user to the program, data, or service requested. In addition to insulating the organization's network from external networks, firewalls can also be used to insulate portions of the organization's intranet from internal access. For example, a LAN controlling access to financial data can be insulated from other internal LANs. Some commercially available firewalls provide a high level of security, whereas others are less secure but more efficient. Firewalls may be grouped into two general types: network-level firewalls and application-level firewalls.

Network-level firewalls provide efficient but low-security access control. This type of firewall consists of a **screening router** that examines the source and destination addresses that are attached to incoming message packets. The firewall accepts or denies access requests based on filtering rules that have been programmed into it. The firewall directs incoming calls to the correct internal receiving node. Network-level firewalls are insecure because they are designed to facilitate the free flow of information rather than restrict it. This method does not explicitly authenticate outside users.

Application-level firewalls provide a higher level of customizable network security, but they add overhead to connectivity. These systems are configured to run security applications called proxies that permit routine services such as e-mail to pass through the firewall, but can perform sophisticated functions such as user authentication for specific tasks. Application-level firewalls also provide comprehensive transmission logging and auditing tools for reporting unauthorized activity.

A high level of firewall security is possible using a dual-homed system. This approach, illustrated in Figure 3.3 has two firewall interfaces. One screens incoming requests from the Internet; the other provides access to the organization's intranet. Direct communication to the Internet is disabled and the two networks are fully isolated. Proxy applications that impose separate log-on procedures perform all access.

Choosing the right firewall involves a trade-off between convenience and security. Ultimately, organization management, in collaboration with internal audit and network professionals, must come to grips with what constitutes acceptable risk. The more security the firewall provides, however, the less convenient it is for authorized users to pass through it to conduct business.

Controlling Denial of Service Attacks

A previous section described three common forms of denial of service attacks: SYN flood attacks, smurf attacks, and distributed denial of service (DDos) attacks. Each of these techniques has a similar effect on the victim. By clogging the Internet ports of the victim's server with fraudulently generated messages, the targeted firm is rendered incapable of processing legitimate transactions and can be completely isolated from the Internet for the duration of the attack.

FIGURE 3.3 **Dual-Homed Firewall**

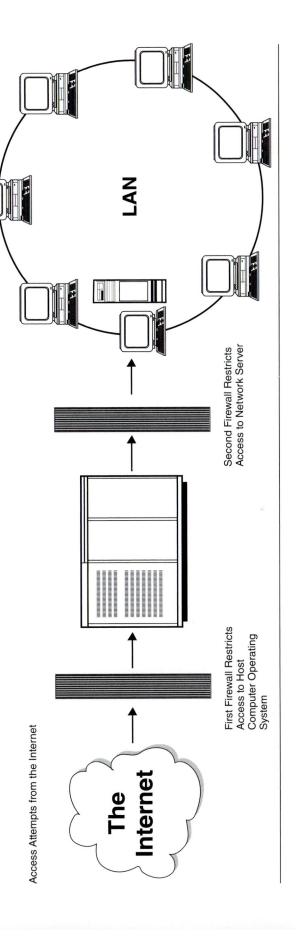

Access Attempts from the Internet

First Firewall Restricts
Access to Host
Computer Operating
System

Second Firewall Restricts
Access to Network Server

LAN

The Internet

In the case of a smurf attack, the targeted organization can program its firewall to ignore all communication from the attacking site, once the attacker's IP address is determined. SYN flood attacks that use IP spoofing to disguise the source, however, are a more serious problem. Although the attack may actually be coming from a single disguised site, the victim's host computer views these transmissions as coming from all over the Internet. IT and network management can take two actions to defeat this sort of attack. First, Internet hosts must embrace a policy of social responsibility by programming their firewalls to block outbound message packets that contain invalid internal IP addresses. This would prevent attackers from hiding their locations from the targeted site and would assure the management of potential intermediary hosts that no undetected attacks could be launched from their sites. This strategy will not, however, prevent attacks from Internet sites that refuse to screen outgoing transmissions. Second, security software is available for the targeted sites that scan for half-open connections. The software looks for SYN packets that have not been followed by an ACK packet. The clogged ports can then be restored to allow legitimate connections to use them.

Distributed denial of service attacks are the most difficult of the three to counter. The victim's site becomes inundated with messages from thousands of zombie sites that are distributed across the Internet. The company is rendered helpless because it cannot effectively block transmissions from so many different locations.

As a countermeasure to DDos attacks, many organizations have invested in **intrusion prevention systems (IPS)** that employ **deep packet inspection (DPI)** to determine when an attack is in progress. DPI uses a variety of analytical and statistical techniques to evaluate the contents of message packets. It searches the individual packets for protocol noncompliance and employs predefined criteria to decide if a packet can proceed to its destination. This is in contrast to the normal packet inspection that simply checks the header portion of a packet to determine its destination. By going deeper and examining the payload or body of the packet, DPI can identify and classify malicious packets based on a database of known attack signatures. Once classified as malicious, the packet can then be blocked and redirected to a security team and/or network reporting agent.

IPS works in line with a firewall at the perimeter of the network to act as a filter that removes malicious packets from the flow before they can affect servers and networks. IPS may also be used behind the firewall to protect specific network segments and servers. This provides additional protection against careless laptop users who have been unknowingly infected with a Trojan horse or worm while working outside the protected network environment. IPS techniques can also be employed to protect an organization from becoming part of a botnet by inspecting outbound packets and blocking malicious traffic before it reaches the Internet.

Encryption
Encryption is the conversion of data into a secret code for storage in databases and transmission over networks. The sender uses an encryption algorithm to convert the original message (called cleartext) into a coded equivalent (called ciphertext). At the receiving end, the ciphertext is decoded (decrypted) back into cleartext.

The earliest encryption method is called the **Caesar cipher**, which Julius Caesar is said to have used to send coded messages to his generals in the field. Like modern-day encryption, the Caesar cipher has two fundamental components: a key and an algorithm.

The **key** is a mathematical value that the sender selects. The **algorithm** is the procedure of shifting each letter in the cleartext message the number of positions that the key value indicates. For example, a key value of +3 would shift each letter three places to the right. This means that the letter A in cleartext would be represented as the letter D in the ciphertext message. The receiver of the ciphertext message reverses the process to decode it and recreates the cleartext, in this case shifting each ciphertext letter three places to the left. Obviously, both the sender and receiver of the message must know the key.

Modern-day encryption algorithms, however, are far more complex, and encryption keys may be up to 128 bits in length. The more bits in the key, the stronger the encryption method. Today, nothing less than 128-bit algorithms are considered truly secure. Two commonly used methods of encryption are **private key** and **public key encryption**.

Private Key Encryption. **Advance encryption standard (AES)** is a 128-bit encryption technique that has become a U.S. government standard for private key encryption. The AES algorithm uses a single key known to both the sender and the receiver of the message. To encode a message, the sender provides the encryption algorithm with the key, which is used to produce a ciphertext message. The message enters the communication channel and is transmitted to the receiver's location, where it is stored. The receiver decodes the message with a decryption program that uses the same key the sender employs. Figure 3.4 illustrates this technique.

Triple-DES encryption is an enhancement to an older encryption technique called the **data encryption standard (DES)**. Triple DES provides considerably improved security over most single encryption techniques. Two forms of triple-DES encryption are EEE3 and EDE3. **EEE3** uses three different keys to encrypt the message three times. **EDE3** uses one

---

FIGURE 3.4 **The Advanced Encryption Standard Technique**

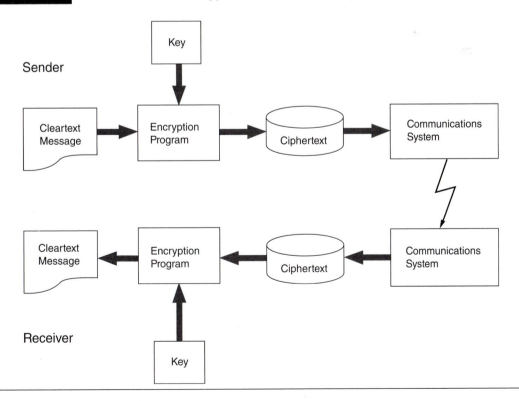

key to encrypt the message. A second key is used to decode it. The resulting message is garbled because the key used for decoding is different from the one that encrypted it. Finally, a third key is used to encrypt the garbled message. The use of multiple keys greatly reduces the chances of breaking the cipher. Triple-DES encryption is thought to be very secure, and major banks use it to transmit transactions. Unfortunately, it is also very slow. The EEE3 and EDE3 techniques are illustrated in Figure 3.5.

All private key techniques have a common problem: the more individuals who need to know the key, the greater the probability of it falling into the wrong hands. If a perpetrator discovers the key, he or she can intercept and decipher coded messages. Therefore, encrypting data that are to be transmitted among large numbers of relative strangers (such as Internet transactions between businesses and customers) requires a different approach. The solution to this problem is public key encryption.

Public Key Encryption.   Public key encryption uses two different keys: one for encoding messages and the other for decoding them. Each recipient has a private key that is kept secret and a public key that is published. The sender of a message uses the receiver's public key to encrypt the message. The receiver then uses his or her private key to decode the message. Users never need to share their private keys to decrypt messages, thus reducing the likelihood that they fall into the hands of a criminal. This approach is illustrated in Figure 3.6.

RSA (Rivest-Shamir-Adleman) is a highly secure public key cryptography method. This method is, however, computationally intensive and much slower than standard DES encryption. Sometimes, both DES and RSA are used together in what is called a **digital envelope**. The actual message is encrypted using DES to provide the fastest decoding. The DES private key needed to decrypt the message is encrypted using RSA and transmitted along with the message. The receiver first decodes the DES key, which is then used to decode the message.

Digital Signatures

A **digital signature** is electronic authentication that cannot be forged. It ensures that the message or document that the sender transmitted was not tampered with after the signature was applied. Figure 3.7 illustrates this process. The sender uses a one-way hashing algorithm to calculate a **digest** of the text message. The digest is a mathematical value calculated from the text content of the message. The digest is then encrypted using the sender's private key to produce the digital signature. Next, the digital signature and the text message are encrypted using the receiver's public key and transmitted to the receiver. At the receiving end, the message is decrypted using the receiver's private key to produce the digital signature (encrypted digest) and the cleartext version of the message. The receiver then uses the sender's public key to decrypt the digital signal to produce the digest. Finally, the receiver recalculates the digest from the cleartext using the original hashing algorithm and compares this to the decoded digest. If the message is authentic, the two digest values will match. If even a single character of the message was changed in transmission, the digest figures will not be equal.

Digital Certificate

The aforementioned process proves that the message received was not tampered with during transmission. It does not prove, however, that the sender is who he or she claims to be. The sender could be an impersonator. Verifying the sender's identity requires a **digital certificate**, which is issued by a trusted third party called a **certification authority (CA)**. A digital certificate is used in conjunction with a public key encryption system to authenticate the sender of a message. The process for certification varies depending on the level of certification desired. It involves establishing one's

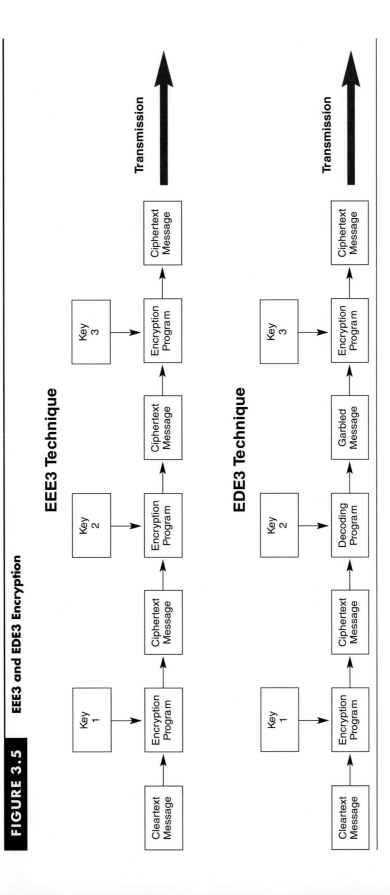

FIGURE 3.5   EEE3 and EDE3 Encryption

EEE3 Technique

EDE3 Technique

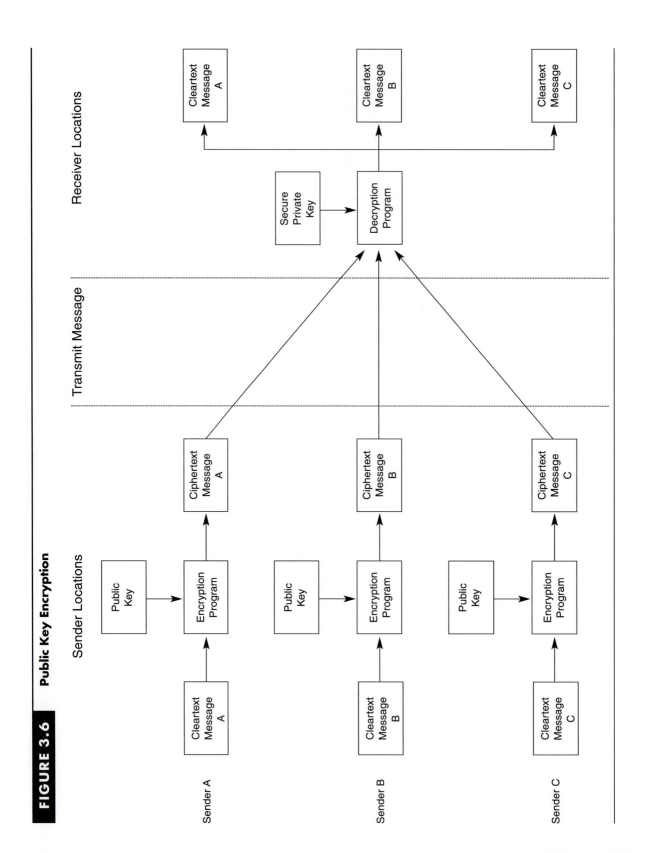

FIGURE 3.6   Public Key Encryption

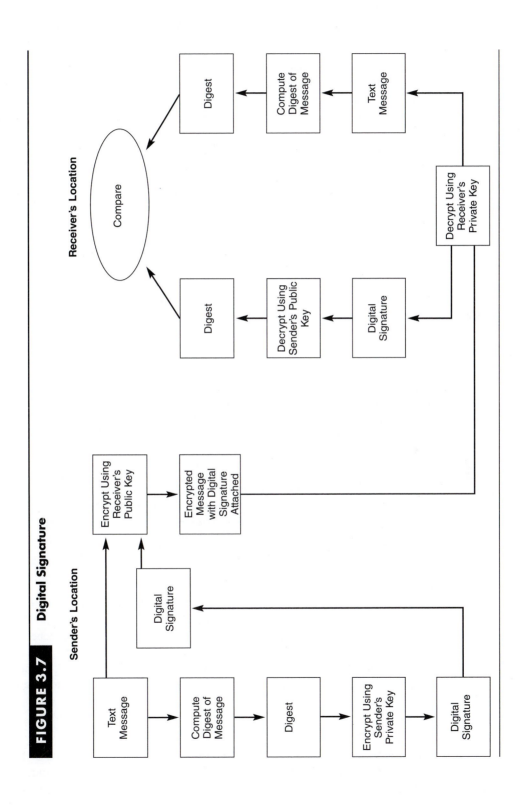

FIGURE 3.7   Digital Signature

identity with formal documents, such as a driver's license, notarization, and finger-prints, and proving one's ownership of the public key. After verifying the owner's identity, the CA creates the certification, which includes the owner's public key and other data that the CA has digitally signed.

The digital certificate is transmitted with the encrypted message to authenticate the sender. The receiver uses the CA's public key, which is widely publicized, to decrypt the sender's public key attached to the message. The sender's public key is then used to de-crypt the message.

Because public key encryption is central to digital authentication, public key man-agement becomes an important internal control issue. **Public key infrastructure (PKI)** constitutes the policies and procedures for administering this activity. A PKI system consists of:

1. A certification authority that issues and revokes digital certificates.
2. A registration authority that verifies the identity of certificate applicants. The pro-cess varies depending on the level of certification desired. It involves establishing one's identity with formal documents, such as a driver's license, notarization, finger-prints, and proving one's ownership of the public key.
3. A certification repository, which is a publicly accessible database that contains cur-rent information about current certificates and a certification revocation list of certi-ficates that have been revoked and the reasons for revocation.

Message Sequence Numbering

An intruder in the communications channel may attempt to delete a message from a stream of messages, change the order of messages received, or duplicate a message. Through **message sequence numbering**, a sequence number is inserted in each message, and any such attempt will become apparent at the receiving end.

Message Transaction Log

An intruder may successfully penetrate the system by trying different password and user ID combinations. Therefore, all incoming and outgoing messages, as well as attempted (failed) access, should be recorded in a **message transaction log**. The log should record the user ID, the time of the access, and the terminal location or telephone number from which the access originated.

Request-Response Technique

An intruder may attempt to prevent or delay the receipt of a message from the sender. When senders and receivers are not in constant contact, the receiver may not know if the communications channel has been interrupted and that messages have been diverted. Using **request-response technique**, a control message from the sender and a response from the receiver are sent at periodic, synchronized intervals. The timing of the messages should follow a random pattern that will be difficult for the intruder to determine and circumvent.

Call-Back Devices

As we have seen, networks can be equipped with security features such as passwords, authentication devices, and encryption. The common weakness to all of these technolo-gies is that they apply the security measure after the criminal has connected to the net-work server. Many believe that the key to security is to keep the intruder off the network to begin with.

A **call-back device** requires the dial-in user to enter a password and be identified. The system then breaks the connection to perform user authentication. If the caller is authorized, the call-back device dials the caller's number to establish a new connection. This restricts access to authorized terminals or telephone numbers and prevents an intruder masquerading as a legitimate user.

Audit Objectives Relating to Subversive Threats

The auditor's objective is to verify the security and integrity of financial transactions by determining that network controls (1) can prevent and detect illegal access both internally and from the Internet, (2) will render useless any data that a perpetrator successfully captures, and (3) are sufficient to preserve the integrity and physical security of data connected to the network.

Audit Procedures Relating to Subversive Threats

To achieve these control objectives, the auditor may perform the following tests of controls:

1. Review the adequacy of the firewall in achieving the proper balance between control and convenience based on the organization's business objectives and potential risks. Criteria for assessing the firewall effectiveness include:
    -   *Flexibility.* The firewall should be flexible enough to accommodate new services as the security needs of the organization change.
    -   *Proxy services.* Adequate proxy applications should be in place to provide explicit user authentication to sensitive services, applications, and data.
    -   *Filtering.* Strong filtering techniques should be designed to deny all services that are not explicitly permitted. In other words, the firewall should specify only those services the user is permitted to access, rather than specifying the services that are denied.
    -   *Segregation of systems.* Systems that do not require public access should be segregated from the Internet.
    -   *Audit tools.* The firewall should provide a thorough set of audit and logging tools that identify and record suspicious activity.
    -   *Probe for weaknesses.* To validate security, the auditor (or a professional security analyst) should periodically probe the firewall for weaknesses just as a computer Internet hacker would do. A number of software products are currently available for identifying security weaknesses.[4]
2. Verify that an intrusion prevention system (IPS) with deep packet inspection (DPI) is in place for organizations that are vulnerable to DDos attacks, such as financial institutions.
3. Review security procedures governing the administration of data encryption keys.
4. Verify the encryption process by transmitting a test message and examining the contents at various points along the channel between the sending and receiving locations.
5. Review the message transaction logs to verify that all messages were received in their proper sequence.
6. Test the operation of the call-back feature by placing an unauthorized call from outside the installation.

---

4   Examples include Security Administrator Tool for Analyzing Networks (SATAN), Internet Security Scanner (ISS), Gabriel, and Courtney.

Controlling Risks from Equipment Failure

Line Errors

The most common problem in data communications is data loss due to **line error**. The bit structure of the message can be corrupted through noise on the communications lines. Noise is made up of random signals that can interfere with the message signal when they reach a certain level. Electric motors, atmospheric conditions, faulty wiring, defective components in equipment, or noise spilling over from an adjacent communications channel may cause these random signals. If not detected, bit structure changes to transmitted data can be catastrophic to the firm. For example, in the case of a database update program, the presence of line errors can result in incorrect transaction values being posted to the accounts. The following two techniques are commonly used to detect and correct such data errors before they are processed.

Echo Check.   The **echo check** involves the receiver of the message returning the message to the sender. The sender compares the returned message with a stored copy of the original. If there is a discrepancy between the returned message and the original, suggesting a transmission error, the message is retransmitted. This technique reduces, by one-half, throughput over communications channels. Using full-duplex channels, which allow both parties to transmit and receive simultaneously, can increase throughput.

Parity Check.   The **parity check** incorporates an extra bit (the parity bit) into the structure of a bit string when it is created or transmitted. Parity can be both vertical and horizontal (longitudinal). Figure 3.8 illustrates both types of parity. Vertical parity adds the parity bit to each character in the message when the characters are originally coded and stored in magnetic form. For example, the number of 1 bits in the bit structure of each character is counted. If the number is even (for instance, there are four 1 bits in a given eight-bit character), the system assigns the parity bit a value of one. If the number of 1 bits is odd, a 0 parity bit is added to the bit structure.

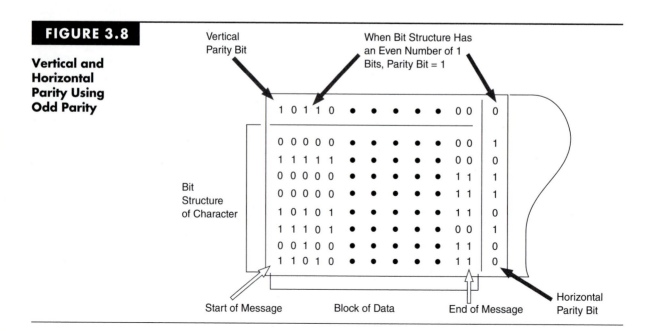

FIGURE 3.8

Vertical and Horizontal Parity Using Odd Parity

The concern is that during transmission, a 1 bit will be converted to a 0 bit or vice versa, thus destroying the bit structure integrity of the character. In other words, the original character is incorrectly presented as a different yet valid character. Errors of this sort, if undetected, could alter financial numbers. A parity check can detect errors at the receiving end. The system again counts the 1 bits, which should always equal an odd number. If a 1 bit is added to or removed from the bit structure during transmission, the number of 1 bits for the character will be even, which would signal an error.

The problem with using vertical parity alone is the possibility that an error will change two bits in the structure simultaneously, thus retaining the parity of the character. In fact, some estimates indicate a 40 to 50 percent chance that line noise will corrupt more than one bit within a character. Using horizontal parity in conjunction with vertical parity reduces this problem. In Figure 3.8, notice the parity bit following each block of characters. The combination of vertical and horizontal parity provides a higher degree of protection from line errors.

Audit Objectives Relating to Equipment Failure
The auditor's objective is to verify the integrity of the electronic commerce transactions by determining that controls are in place to detect and correct message loss due to equipment failure.

Audit Procedures Relating to Equipment Failure
To achieve this control objective, the auditor can select a sample of messages from the transaction log and examine them for garbled content caused by line noise. The auditor should verify that all corrupted messages were successfully retransmitted.

AUDITING ELECTRONIC DATA INTERCHANGE (EDI)

To coordinate sales and production operations and to maintain an uninterrupted flow of raw materials, many organizations enter into a trading partner agreement with their suppliers and customers. This agreement is the foundation for a fully automated business process called **Electronic data interchange (EDI)**. A general definition of EDI is:

> The intercompany exchange of computer-processible business information in standard format.

The definition reveals several important features of EDI. First, EDI is an interorganization endeavor. A firm does not engage in EDI on its own. Second, the information systems of the trading partners automatically process the transaction. In a pure EDI environment, there are no human intermediaries to approve or authorize transactions. Authorizations, mutual obligations, and business practices that apply to transactions are all specified in advance under the trading partner agreement. Third, transaction information is transmitted in a standardized format. This allows firms with different internal systems can exchange information and do business. Figure 3.8 shows an overview of an EDI connection between two companies. Assume that the transaction illustrated in Figure 3.9 is the customer's (Company A) inventory purchase from the supplier (Company B). Company A's purchases system automatically creates an electronic purchase order (PO), which it sends to its EDI translation software. Here, the PO is converted to a standard format electronic message ready for transmission. The message is transmitted to Company B's translation software, where it is converted to the supplier's internal format. Company B's sales order processing system receives the customer order and processes it automatically.

FIGURE 3.9

**Overview
of EDI**

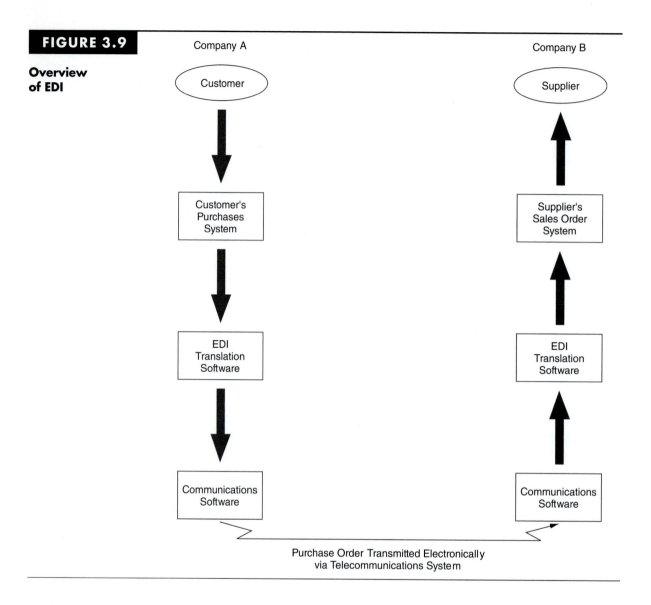

Figure 3.9 shows a direct private communications link between two companies. Many companies, however, choose to use a third-party value added network (VAN) to connect to their trading partners. Figure 3.10 illustrates this arrangement. The originating company transmits its EDI messages to the network rather than directly to the trading partner's computer. The network directs each EDI transmission to its destination and deposits the message in the appropriate electronic mailbox. The messages stay in the mailboxes until the receiving companies' systems retrieve them. VANs can also provide an important degree of control over EDI transactions. We examine EDI control issues later in this section.

EDI Standards

Key to EDI success is the use of a standard format for messaging between dissimilar systems. Over the years, both in the United States and internationally, a number of formats

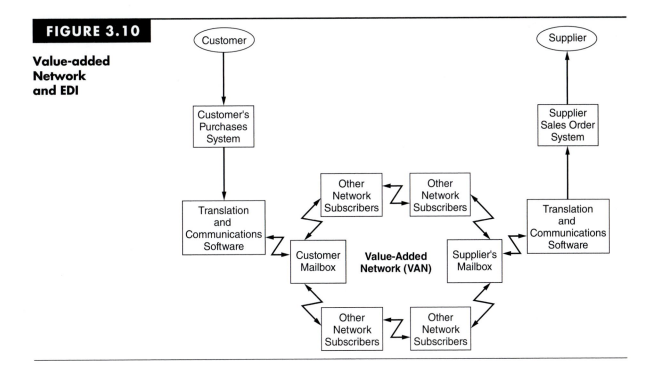

FIGURE 3.10

Value-added Network and EDI

have been proposed. The standard in the United States is the American National Standards Institute (ANSI) X.12 format. The standard used internationally is the EDI for administration, commerce, and transport (EDIFACT) format. Figure 3.11 illustrates the X.12 format.

The X-12 electronic envelope contains the electronic address of the receiver, communications protocols, and control information. A functional group is a collection of transaction sets (electronic documents) for a particular business application, such as a group of sales invoices or purchase orders. The transaction set is composed of data segments and data elements. Figure 3.12 relates these terms to a conventional document. Each data segment is an information category on the document, such as part number, unit price, or vendor name. The data elements are specific items of data related to a segment. In the example in Figure 12.18, these include such items as REX-446, $127.86, and Ozment Supply.

Benefits of EDI

EDI has made considerable inroads in a number of industries, including automotive, groceries, retail, health care, and electronics. The following are some common EDI cost savings that justify the approach.

- *Data keying.* EDI reduces or even eliminates the need for data entry.
- *Error reduction.* Firms using EDI see reductions in data keying errors, human interpretation and classification errors, and filing (lost document) errors.

FIGURE 3.11

The X.12 Format

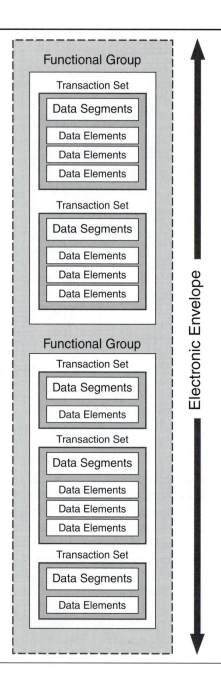

- *Reduction of paper.* The use of electronic envelopes and documents drastically reduces the paper forms in the system.
- *Postage.* Mailed documents are replaced with much cheaper data transmissions.
- *Automated procedures.* EDI automates manual activities associated with purchasing, sales order processing, cash disbursements, and cash receipts.
- *Inventory reduction.* By ordering directly as needed from vendors, EDI reduces the lag time that promotes inventory accumulation.

FIGURE 3.12   Relationship between X.12 Format and a Conventional Source Document

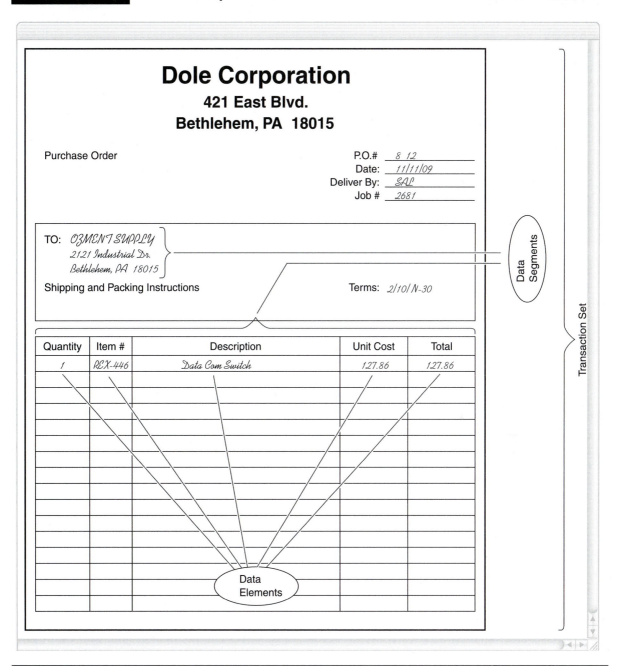

Financial EDI

Using electronic funds transfer (EFT) for cash disbursement and cash receipts processing is more complicated than using EDI for purchasing and selling activities. EFT requires intermediary banks between trading partners. This arrangement is shown in Figure 3.13.

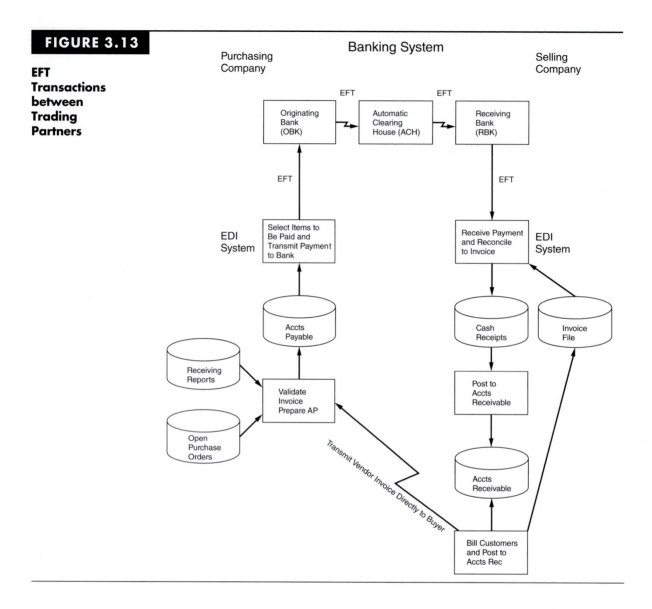

FIGURE 3.13

**EFT
Transactions
between
Trading
Partners**

The buyer's EDI system receives the purchase invoices and automatically approves them for payment. On the payment date, the buyer's system automatically makes an EFT to its originating bank (OBK). The OBK removes funds from the buyer's account and transmits them electronically to the automatic clearinghouse (ACH) bank. The ACH is a central bank that carries accounts for its member banks. The ACH transfers the funds from the OBK to the receiving bank (RBK), which in turn applies the funds to the seller's account.

Transferring funds by EFT poses no special problem. A check can easily be represented within the X.12 format. The problem arises with the remittance advice information that accompanies the check. Remittance advice information is often quite extensive because of complexities in the transaction. The check may be in payment of multiple invoices or only a partial invoice. There may be disputed amounts because of price disagreements, damaged goods, or incomplete deliveries. In traditional systems, modifying the remittance advice and/or attaching a letter explaining the payment resolves these disputes.

Converting remittance information to electronic form can result in very large records. Members of the ACH system are required to accept and process only EFT formats limited to 94 characters of data—a record size sufficient for only very basic messages. Not all banks in the ACH system support the ANSI standard format for remittances, ANSI 820. In such cases, remittance information must be sent to the seller by separate EDI transmission or conventional mail. The seller must then implement separate procedures to match bank and customer EDI transmissions in applying payments to customer accounts.

Recognizing the void between services demanded and those the ACH system supplies, many banks have established themselves as value-added banks (VABs) to compete for this market. A VAB can accept electronic disbursements and remittance advices from its clients in any format. It converts EDI transactions to the ANSI X.12 and 820 formats for electronic processing. In the case of non-EDI transactions, the VAB writes traditional checks to the creditor. The services VABs offer allow their clients to employ a single cash disbursement system that can accommodate both EDI and non-EDI customers.

EDI Controls

The absence of human intervention in the EDI process presents a unique twist to traditional control problems, including ensuring that transactions are authorized and valid, preventing unauthorized access to data files, and maintaining an audit trail of transactions. The following techniques are used in dealing with these issues.

Transaction Authorization and Validation

Both the customer and the supplier must establish that the transaction being processed is to (or from) a valid trading partner and is authorized. This can be accomplished at three points in the process.

1. Some VANs have the capability of validating passwords and user ID codes for the vendor by matching these against a valid customer file. The VAN rejects any unauthorized trading partner transactions before they reach the vendor's system.
2. Before being converted, the translation software can validate the trading partner's ID and password against a validation file in the firm's database.
3. Before processing, the trading partner's application software references the valid customer and vendor files to validate the transaction.

Access Control

To function smoothly, EDI trading partners must permit a degree of access to private data files that would be forbidden in a traditional environment. The trading partner agreement will determine the degree of access control in place. For example, it may permit the customer's system to access the vendor's inventory files to determine if inventories are available. Also, trading partners may agree that the prices on the purchase order will be binding on both parties. The customer must, therefore, periodically access the vendor's price list file to keep pricing information current. Alternatively, the vendor may need access to the customer's price list to update prices.

To guard against unauthorized access, each company must establish valid vendor and customer files. Inquiries against databases can thus be validated, and unauthorized attempts at access can be rejected. User authority tables can also be established, which specify the degree of access a trading partner is allowed. For example, the partner may be authorized to read inventory or pricing data but not change values.

EDI Audit Trail

The absence of source documents in EDI transactions eliminates the traditional audit trail and restricts the ability of accountants to verify the validity, completeness, timing, and accuracy of transactions. One technique for restoring the audit trail is to maintain a control log, which records the transaction's flow through each phase of the EDI system. Figure 3.14 illustrates how this approach may be employed.

As the transaction is received at each stage in the process, an entry is made in the log. In the customer's system, the transaction log can be reconciled to ensure that all transactions the purchases system initiated were correctly translated and communicated. Likewise, in the vendor's system, the control log will establish that the sales order system correctly translated and processed all messages that the communications software received.

FIGURE 3.14

EDI System Using Transaction Control Log for Audit Trail

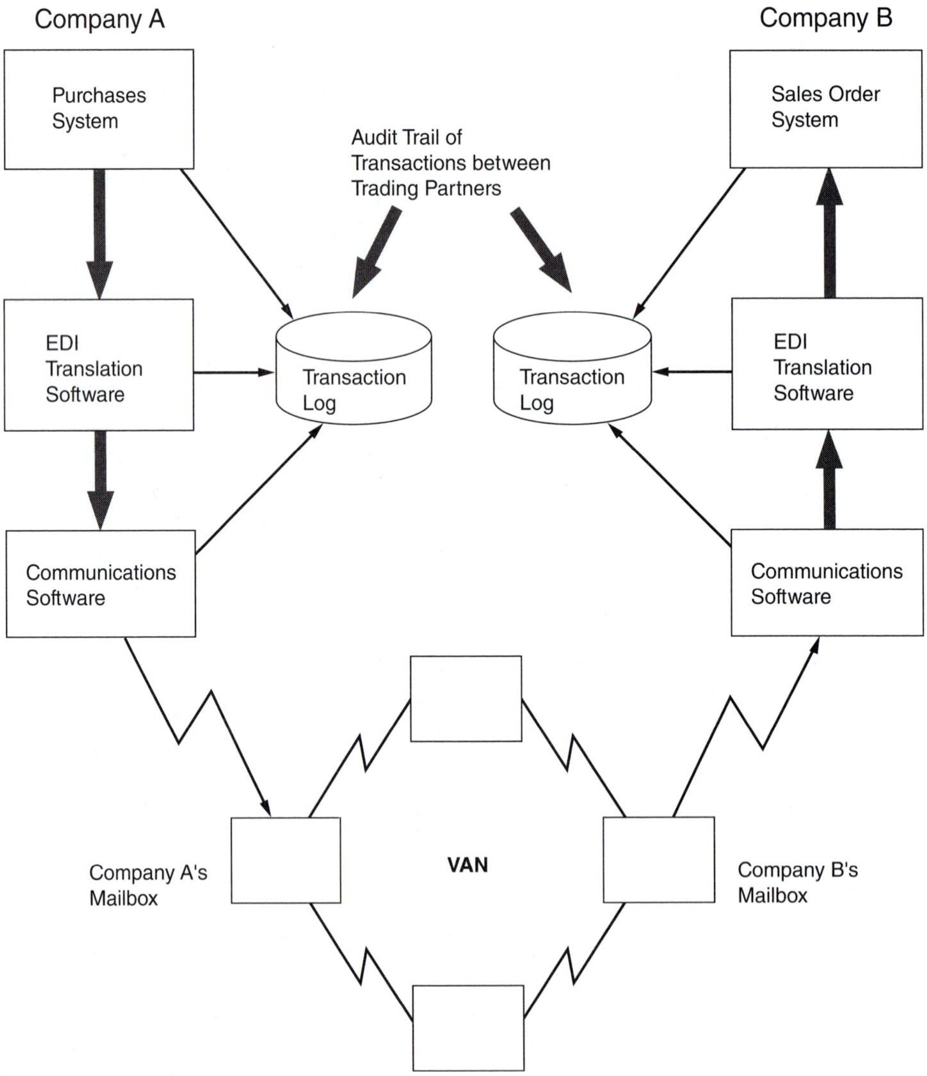

Audit Objectives Relating to EDI

The auditor's objectives are to determine that (1) all EDI transactions are authorized, validated, and in compliance with the trading partner agreement; (2) no unauthorized organizations gain access to database records; (3) authorized trading partners have access only to approved data; and (4) adequate controls are in place to ensure a complete audit trail of all EDI transactions.

Audit Procedures Relating to EDI

To achieve these control objectives, the auditor may perform the following tests of controls.

Tests of Authorization and Validation Controls.   The auditor should establish that trading partner identification codes are verified before transactions are processed. To accomplish this, the auditor should (1) review agreements with the VAN facility to validate transactions and ensure that information regarding valid trading partners is complete and correct, and (2) examine the organization's valid trading partner file for accuracy and completeness.

Tests of Access Controls.   Security over the valid trading partner file and databases is central to the EDI control framework. The auditor can verify control adequacy in the following ways:

1. The auditor should determine that access to the valid vendor or customer file is limited to authorized employees only. The auditor should verify that passwords and authority tables control access to this file and that the data are encrypted.
2. The trading agreement will determine the degree of access a trading partner should have to the firm's database records (such as inventory levels and price lists). The auditor should reconcile the terms of the trading agreement against the trading partner's access privileges stated in the database authority table.
3. The auditor should simulate access by a sample of trading partners and attempt to violate access privileges.

Tests of Audit Trail Controls.   The auditor should verify that the EDI system produces a transaction log that tracks transactions through all stages of processing. By selecting a sample of transactions and tracing these through the process, the auditor can verify that key data values were recorded correctly at each point.

AUDITING PC-BASED ACCOUNTING SYSTEMS

The software market offers hundreds of PC-based accounting systems. In contrast to mainframe and client-server systems that are frequently custom-designed to meet specific user requirements, PC applications tend to be general-purpose systems that serve a wide range of needs. This strategy allows software vendors to mass-produce low-cost and error-free standard products. Not surprisingly, PC accounting systems are popular with smaller firms, which use them to automate and replace manual systems and thus become more efficient and competitive. PC systems have also made inroads with larger companies that have decentralized operations.

Most PC systems are modular in design. Typical business modules include sales order processing and AR, purchases and accounts payable, cash receipts, cash disbursements, general ledger and financial reporting, inventory control, and payroll. Their modular design provides users with some degree of flexibility in tailoring systems to their specific needs. Many vendors target their products to the unique needs of specific industries, such as

FIGURE 3.15

PC Accounting System Modules

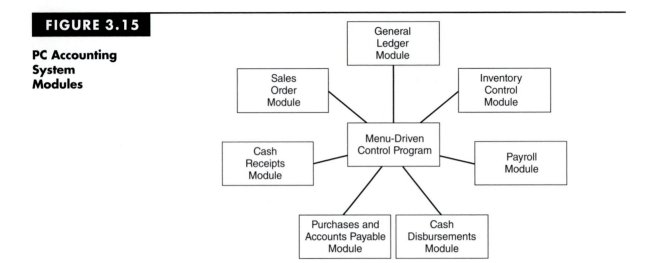

health care, transportation, and food services. By doing so, these firms forgo the advantages of flexibility to achieve a market niche. The modular design technique is illustrated in Figure 3.15.

The central control program provides the user interface to the system. From this control point, the user makes menu selections to invoke application modules as needed. By selecting the sales module, for instance, the user can enter customer orders in real time. At the end of the day, in batch mode, the user can enter cash receipts, purchases, and payroll transactions.

Commercial systems usually have fully integrated modules. This means that data transfers between modules occur automatically. For example, an integrated system will ensure that all transactions captured by the various modules have been balanced and posted to subsidiary and general ledger accounts before the general ledger module produces the financial reports.

PC Systems Risks and Controls

As previously discussed, the computer operating systems and network control techniques in mainframe and distributed environments provide effective system security. PC accounting systems, however, create unique control problems for accountants that arise from inherent weaknesses in their operating systems and the general PC environment. Indeed, the advanced technology and power of modern PC systems stand in sharp contrast to the relatively unsophisticated operational environment in which they exist. Some of the more significant risks and possible control techniques are outlined in the following pages.

Operating System Weaknesses

In contrast to mainframe systems, PCs provide only minimal security for data files and programs contained within them. This control weakness is inherent in the philosophy behind the design of PC operating systems. Intended primarily as single-user systems, they are designed to make computer use easy and to facilitate access, not restrict it. This philosophy, while necessary to promote end-user computing, is often at odds with internal control objectives. The data stored on microcomputers that are shared by multiple users are exposed to unauthorized access, manipulation, and destruction. Once a computer criminal gains access to the user's PC, there may be little or nothing in the way of control to prevent him or her from stealing or manipulating the data stored on the internal hard drive.

Weak Access Control

Security software that provides logon procedures is available for PCs. Most of these programs, however, become active only when the computer is booted from the hard drive. A computer criminal attempting to circumvent the logon procedure may do so by forcing the computer to boot from a CD-ROM, whereby an uncontrolled operating system can be loaded into the computer's memory. Having bypassed the computer's stored operating system and security package, the criminal may have unrestricted access to data and programs on the hard disk drive.

Inadequate Segregation of Duties

Employees in PC environments, particularly those of small companies, may have access to multiple applications that constitute incompatible tasks. For example, a single individual may be responsible for entering all transaction data, including sales orders, cash receipts, invoices, and disbursements. Typically, the general ledger and subsidiary accounts are updated automatically from these input sources. This degree of authority would be similar, in a manual system, to assigning accounts receivable, accounts payable, cash receipts, cash disbursement, and general ledger responsibility to the same person. The exposure is compounded when the operator is also responsible for the development (programming) of the applications that he or she runs. In small-company operations, there may be little that can be done to eliminate these inherent conflicts of duties. However, multilevel password control, discussed next, can reduce the risks.

Multilevel Password Control

Multilevel password control is used to restrict employees who are sharing the same computers to specific directories, programs, and data files. Under this approach, different passwords are used to access different functions. Thus, each employee is required to enter a password to access his or her applications and data. This technique uses stored authorization tables to further limit an individual's access to read-only, data input, data modification, and data deletion capability. Although not a substitute for all manual control techniques, such as employee supervision and management reports that detail transactions and their effects on account balances, multilevel password control can greatly enhance the small organization's control environment.

Risk of Theft

Because of their size, PCs are objects of theft and the portability of laptops places them at the highest risk. Formal policies should be in place to restrict financial and other sensitive data to desktop PCs only. In addition, the organization should provide employee training about appropriate computer usage. This should including stated penalties for stealing or destroying data. Also antitheft security locks can be effective for preventing opportunistic theft, but they will not deter the dedicate thief.

Weak Backup Procedures

Computer failure, usually disk failure, is the primary cause of data loss in PC environments. If the hard drive of a PC fails, recovering the data stored on it may be impossible. To preserve the integrity of mission-critical data and programs, organizations need formal backup procedures. In mainframe and network environments, backup is controlled automatically by the operating system, using specialized software and hardware (database backup is discussed in the next chapter). The responsibility for providing backup in the PC environment, however, falls to the end user. Often, because of lack of computer experience and training, users fail to appreciate the importance of backup procedures until it is too late. Fortunately, inexpensive automated backup systems for PCs are available. For convenience, the backup may be directed to an external hard drive at the user location. Another excellent option is to contract with an online backup service that encrypts and copies the PC-housed data to a secure location. The backup is performed automatically whenever the PC is connected to the Internet.

Risk of Virus Infection

Virus infection is one of most common threats to PC integrity and system availability. Strict adherence to organizational policies and procedures that guard against virus infection is critical to effective virus control. The organization must also ensure that effective antivirus software is installed on the PCs and kept up-to-date.

Audit Objectives Associated with PC Security

Audit objectives for assessing controls in the PC environment include the following:

- Verify that controls are in place to protect data, programs, and computers from unauthorized access, manipulation, destruction, and theft.
- Verify that adequate supervision and operating procedures exist to compensate for lack of segregation between the duties of users, programmers, and operators.
- Verify that backup procedures are in place to prevent data and program loss due to system failures, errors, and so on.
- Verify that systems selection and acquisition procedures produce applications that are high quality, and protected from unauthorized changes.
- Verify that the system is free from viruses and adequately protected to minimize the risk of becoming infected with a virus or similar object.

Audit Procedures Associated with PC Security

- The auditor should observe that PCs are physically anchored to reduce the opportunity of theft.
- The auditor should verify from organizational charts, job descriptions, and observation that programmers of accounting systems do not also operate those systems. In smaller organizational units where functional segregation is impractical, the auditor should verify that there is adequate supervision over these tasks.
- The auditor should confirm that reports of processed transactions, listings of updated accounts, and control totals are prepared, distributed, and reconciled by appropriate management at regular and timely intervals.
- Where appropriate, the auditor should determine that multilevel password control is used to limit access to data and applications and that the access authority granted is consistent with the employees' job descriptions.
- If removable or external hard drives are used, the auditor should verify that the drives are removed and stored in a secure location when not in use.
- By selecting a sample of backup files, the auditor can verify that backup procedures are being followed. By comparing data values and dates on the backup disks to production files, the auditor can assess the frequency and adequacy of backup procedures. If an online backup service is used, the auditor should verify that the contract is current and adequate to meet the organizations needs.
- By selecting a sample of PCs, the auditor should verify that their commercial software packages were purchased from reputable vendors and are legal copies. The

auditor should review the selection and acquisition procedures to ensure that end-user needs were fully considered and that the purchased software satisfies those needs.

- The auditor should review the organization's policy for using antiviral software. This policy may include the following points:

  1. Antiviral software should be installed on all microcomputers and invoked as part of the startup procedure when the computers are turned on. This will ensure that all key sectors of the hard disk are examined before any data are transferred through the network.

  2. All upgrades to vendor software should be checked for viruses before they are implemented.

  3. All public-domain software should be examined for virus infection before it is used.

  4. Current versions of antiviral software should be available to all users. Verify that the most current virus data files are being downloaded regularly, and that the antivirus program is indeed running in the PC's background continuously, and thus able to scan all incoming documents. Corporate versions generally include a "push" update where the software automatically checks the home Web site of the antivirus vendor for new updates each time it is connected to the Internet and the PC is booted.

SUMMARY

This chapter continues the discussion of IT general controls and audit tests begun in Chapter 2. It examined the risks and controls over operating systems, networks, EDI, and PC-based accounting system. The principal threats to the operating system are (1) unauthorized access, (2) intentional or unintentional insertion of viruses, and (3) loss of data due to system malfunctions.

Networks and communication links are susceptible to exposures from both criminal subversion and equipment failure. Subversive threats can be minimized through a variety of security and access control measures including firewalls, IPS, DPI, data encryption, and call-back devices. Equipment failure usually takes the form of line errors, which is noise in communications lines causes. These can be effectively reduced through echo checks and parity checks.

The discussion then turned to EDI, where firms are faced with a variety of exposures that arise in connection with an environment void of human intermediaries to authorize or review transactions. Controls in an EDI environment are achieved primarily through programmed procedures to authorize transactions, limit access to data files, and ensure that transactions the system processes are valid.

The chapter concluded with the risks and controls associated with the PC environment. Three of the most serious exposures are (1) the lack of properly segregated duties, (2) PC-operating systems that do not have the sophistication of mainframes and expose data to unauthorized access, and (3) computer failures and inadequate backup procedures that rely too heavily on human intervention and thus threaten the security of accounting records.

Appendix

Section A: Internet Technologies

The Internet was originally developed for the U.S. military and later became used widely for academic and government research. Over recent years, it has evolved into a worldwide information highway. This growth is attributed to three factors. First, in 1995, national commercial telecommunications companies such as MCI, Sprint, and UUNET took control of the backbone elements of the Internet and have continued to enhance their infrastructures. Large Internet service providers (ISPs) can link into these backbones to connect their subscribers, and smaller ISPs can connect directly to the national backbones or into one of the larger ISPs. Second, online services like CompuServe and America Online connect to the Internet for e-mail, which enables users of different services to communicate with each other. Third, the development of graphics-based Web browsers, such as Microsoft's Internet Explorer, has made accessing the Internet a simple task. The Internet thus became the domain of everyday people with PCs rather than just scientists and computer hackers. As a result, the Web has grown exponentially and continues to grow daily.

Packet Switching

The Internet employs communications technologies based on packet switching. Figure 3.16 illustrates this technique, whereby messages are divided into small packets for transmission. Individual packets of the same message may take different routes to

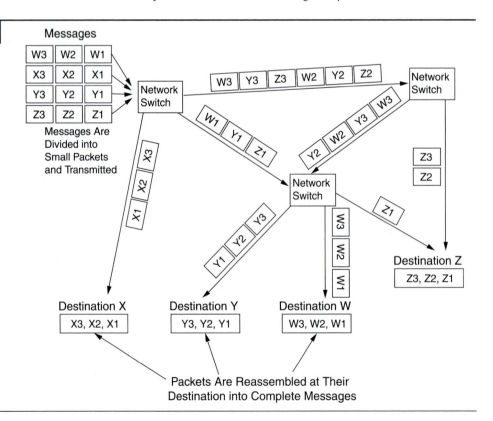

FIGURE 3.16

Message Packet Switching

their destinations. Each packet contains address and sequencing codes so they can be reassembled into the original complete message at the receiving end. The choice of transmission path is determined according to criteria that achieve optimum utilization of the long-distance lines, including the degree of traffic congestion on the line, the shortest path between the end points, and the line status of the path (that is, working, failed, or experiencing errors). Network switches provide a physical connection for the addressed packets only for the duration of the message; the line then becomes available to other users. The first international standard for wide area packet switching networks was X.25, which was defined when all circuits were analog and very susceptible to noise. Subsequent packet technologies, such as frame relay and SMDS (switched multimegabit data service) were designed for today's almost error-free digital lines.

Virtual Private Networks

A virtual private network (VPN) is a private network within a public network. For years, common carriers have built VPNs, which are private from the client's perspective, but physically share backbone trunks with other users. VPNs have been built on X.25 and frame-relay technologies. Today, Internet-based VPNs are of great interest. Maintaining security and privacy in this setting, however, requires encryption and authentication controls that were discussed in the chapter.

Extranets

Another variant on Internet technology is the extranet. This is a password-controlled network for private users rather than the general public. Extranets are used to provide access between trading partner internal databases. Internet sites containing information intended for private consumption frequently use an extranet configuration.

World Wide Web

The World Wide Web (WWW) is an Internet facility that links user sites locally and around the world. In 1989, Tim Berners-Lee of the European Center for Nuclear Research (CERN) in Geneva developed the Web as a means of sharing nuclear research information over the Internet. The fundamental format for the Web is a text document called a Web page that has embedded hypertext markup language (HTML) codes that provide the formatting for the page as well as hypertext links to other pages. The linked pages may be stored on the same server or anywhere in the world. HTML codes are simple alphanumeric characters that can be typed with a text editor or word processor. Most word processors support Web publishing features that allow text documents to be converted to HTML format.

Web pages are maintained at Web sites, which are computer servers that support hypertext transfer protocol (HTTP). The pages are accessed and read via a Web browser such as Internet Explorer. To access a Web site, the user enters the uniform resource locator (URL) address of the target site in the Web browser. When an Internet user visits a Web site, his or her point of entry is typically the site's home page. This HTML document serves as a directory to the site's contents and other pages. Through browsers, the Web provides point-and-click access to the largest collection of online information in the world. The Web has also become a multimedia delivery system that supports audio, video, videoconferencing, and three-dimensional animation. The ease of Web page creation and navigation via browsers have driven the unprecedented growth of the Web. In 1994, there were approximately 500 Web sites in the world; today there are millions.

Internet Addresses

The Internet uses three types of addresses for communications: (1) e-mail addresses, (2) Web site URL addresses, and (3) Internet protocol (IP) addresses of individual computers attached to a network.

E-mail Address.   The format for an e-mail address is USER NAME@DOMAIN NAME. For example, the address of the author of this textbook is jah0@lehigh.edu. There are no spaces between any of the words. The user name (or in this case, the user identification [ID]) is jah0. A domain name is an organization's unique name combined with a top-level domain (TLD) name. In the previous example above, the unique name is lehigh and the TLD is edu. Following are examples of TLD names:

.com	commercial
.net	network provider
.org	nonprofit organization
.edu	education and research
.gov	government
.mil	military agency
.int	international intergovernmental

Outside of the United States, the TLD names consist of the country code, such as .uk for the United Kingdom and .es for Spain. The Internet Ad Hoc Committee (IAHC) has introduced a category called a generic top-level domain (gTLD), which includes the following:

.firm	a business
.store	goods for sale
.web	WWW activities
.arts	culture/entertainment
.rec	recreation/entertainment
.info	information service
.nom	individual/personal

The Internet e-mail addressing system allows the user to send e-mail directly to the mailboxes of users of all major online services, such as America Online and CompuServe.

URL Address.   The URL is the address that defines the path to a facility or file on the Web. URLs are typed into the browser to access Web site home pages and individual Web pages and can be embedded in Web pages to provide hypertext links to other pages. The general format for a URL is protocol prefix, domain name, subdirectory name, and document name. The entire URL is not always needed. For example, to access the South-Western Publishing home page, only the following protocol and domain name are required:

http://www.academic.cengage.com

The protocol prefix is http:// and the domain name is www.academic.cengage.com. From this home page, the user can activate hyperlinks to other pages as desired. The user can go directly to a linked page by providing the complete address and separating the address components with slashes. For example,

http://www.academic.cengage.com/accounting/hall

Subdirectories can be several levels deep. To reference them, each must be separated with a slash. For example, the elements of the following URL for a hypothetical sporting goods company are described below next.

http://www.flyfish.com/equipment/rods/brand_name.html

http://	protocol prefix (most browsers default to HTTP if a prefix is not typed)
www.flyfish.com/	domain name
equipment/	subdirectory name
rods/	subdirectory name
brand_name.html	document name (webWeb page)

IP Address.   Every computer node and host attached to the Internet must have a unique Internet protocol (IP) address. For a message to be sent, the IP addresses of both the sending and the recipient nodes must be provided. Currently, IP addresses are represented by a 32-bit data packet. The general format is four sets of numbers separated by periods. The decomposition of the code into its component parts varies depending on the class to which it is assigned. Class A, class B, and class C coding schemes are used for large, medium, and small networks, respectively. To illustrate the coding technique, the IP address 128.180.94.109 translates into:

128.180	Lehigh University
94	Business Department faculty server
109	A faculty member's office computer (node)

Protocols

The word protocol has been used several times in this section. Let's now take a closer look at the meaning of this term. Protocols are the rules and standards governing the design of hardware and software that permit users of networks, which different vendors have manufactured, to communicate and share data. The general acceptance of protocols within the network community provides both standards and economic incentives for the manufacturers of hardware and software. Products that do not comply with prevailing protocols will have little value to prospective customers.

The data communications industry borrowed the term protocol from the diplomatic community. Diplomatic protocols define the rules by which the representatives of nations communicate and collaborate during social and official functions. These formal rules of conduct are intended to avoid international problems that could arise through the misinterpretation of ambiguous signals passed between diplomatic counterparts. The greatest potential for error naturally exists between nations with vastly dissimilar cultures and conventions for behavior. Establishing a standard of conduct through protocols, which all members of the diplomatic community understand and practice, minimizes the risk of miscommunications between nations of different cultures.

An analogy may be drawn to data communications. A communications network is a community of computer users who also must establish and maintain unambiguous lines of communication. If all network members had homogeneous needs and operated identical systems, this would not be much of a problem; however, networks are characterized by heterogeneous systems components. Typically, network users employ hardware devices (PC, printers, monitors, data storage devices, modems, and so on) and software (user applications, network control programs, and operating systems) that a variety of vendors produce. Passing messages effectively from device to device in such a multivendor environment requires ground rules or protocols.

What Functions Do Protocols Perform?

Protocols serve network functions in several ways. First, they facilitate the physical connection between the network devices. Through protocols, devices are able to identify themselves to other devices as legitimate network entities and initiate (or terminate) a communications session.

Second, protocols synchronize the transfer of data between physical devices. This involves defining the rules for initiating a message, determining the data transfer rate between devices, and acknowledging message receipt.

Third, protocols provide a basis for error checking and measuring network performance. This is done by comparing measured results against expectations. For example, performance measures pertaining to storage device access times, data transmission rates, and modulation frequencies are critical to controlling the network's function. Thus, the identification and correction of errors depends on protocol standards that define acceptable performance.

Fourth, protocols promote compatibility among network devices. To transmit and receive data successfully, the various devices involved in a particular session must conform to a mutually acceptable mode of operation, such as synchronous, asynchronous and duplex, or half-duplex. Without protocols to provide such conformity, messages sent between devices will would be distorted and garbled.

Finally, protocols promote network designs that are flexible, expandable, and cost-effective. Users are free to change and enhance their systems by selecting from the best offerings of a variety of vendors. Manufacturers must, of course, construct these products in accordance with established protocols.

The Layered Approach to Network Protocol

The first networks used several different protocols that emerged in a rather haphazard manner. These protocols often provided poor interfaces between devices that actually resulted in incompatibilities. Also, early protocols were structured and inflexible, thus limiting network growth by making system changes difficult. A change in the architecture at a node on the network could have an unpredictable effect on an unrelated device at another node. Technical problems such as these can translate into unrecorded transactions, destroyed audit trails, and corrupted databases. Out of this situation emerged the contemporary model of layered protocols. The purpose of a layered-protocol model is to create a modular environment that reduces complexity and permits changes to one layer without adversely affecting another.

The data communication community, through the International Standards Organization, has developed a layered set of protocols called the open system interface (OSI). The OSI model provides standards by which the products of different manufacturers can interface with one another in a seamless interconnection at the user level.

Internet Protocols

Transfer control protocol/Internet protocol (TCP/IP) is the basic protocol that permits communication between Internet sites. It was invented by Vinton Cerf and Bob Kahn under contract from the U.S. Department of Defense to network dissimilar systems. This protocol controls how individual packets of data are formatted, transmitted, and received. This is known as a reliable protocol because delivery of all the packets to a destination is guaranteed. If delivery is interrupted by hardware or software failure, the packets are automatically retransmitted.

The TCP portion of the protocol ensures that the total number of data bytes transmitted was received. The IP component provides the routing mechanism. Every server and computer in a TCP/IP network requires an IP address, which is either permanently assigned or dynamically assigned at start-up. The IP part of the TCP/IP protocol contains a network address that is used to route messages to different networks.

Although TCP/IP is the fundamental communications protocol for the Internet, the following are some of the more common protocols that are used for specific tasks.

File Transfer Protocols

File transfer protocol (FTP) is used to transfer text files, programs, spreadsheets, and databases across the Internet. TELNET is a terminal emulation protocol used on TCP/IP-based networks. It allows users to run programs and review data from a remote terminal or computer. TELNET is an inherent part of the TCP/IP communications protocol. While both protocols deal with data transfer, FTP is useful for downloading entire files from the Internet; TELNET is useful for perusing a file of data as if the user were actually at the remote site.

Mail Protocols

Simple network mail protocol (SNMP) is the most popular protocol for transmitting e-mail messages. Other e-mail protocols are post office protocol (POP) and Internet message access protocol (IMAP).

Security Protocols

Secure sockets layer (SSL) is a low-level encryption scheme used to secure transmissions in higher-level HTTP format. Private communications technology (PCT) is a security protocol that provides secure transactions over the Web. PCT encrypts and decrypts a message for transmission. Most Web browsers and servers support PCT and other popular security protocols such as SSL. Secure electronic transmission (SET) is an encryption scheme developed by a consortium of technology firms and banks (Microsoft, IBM, Visa, MasterCard, etc.) to secure credit card transactions. Customers making credit card purchases over the Internet transmit their encrypted credit card number to the merchant, who then transmits the number to the bank. The bank returns an encrypted acknowledgment to the merchant. The customer need not worry about an unscrupulous merchant decrypting the customer's credit card number and misusing the information. Privacy enhanced mail (PEM) is a standard for secure e-mail on the Internet. It supports encryption, digital signatures, and digital certificates as well as both private and public key methods.

Network News Transfer Protocol

Network news transfer protocol (NNTP) is used to connect to Usenet groups on the Internet. Usenet newsreader software supports the NNTP protocol.

HTTP and HTTP-NG

HTTP controls Web browsers that access the Web. When the user clicks on a link to a Web page, a connection is established and the Web page is displayed, then the connection is broken. Hypertext transport protocol–next generation (HTTP-NG) is an enhanced version of the HTTP protocol that maintains the simplicity of HTTP while adding important features such as security and authentication.

HTML

Hypertext markup language (HTML) is the document format used to produce Web pages. HTML defines the page layout, fonts, and graphic elements as well as hypertext links to other documents on the Web. HTML is used to lay out information for display in an appealing manner such as one sees in magazines and newspapers. The ability to lay out text and graphics (including pictures) is important in terms of appeal to users in general. Even more pertinent is HTML's support for hypertext links in text and graphics that enable the reader to virtually jump to another document located anywhere on the World Wide Web.

Section B: Intranet Technologies

Organizations that own or lease networks for internal business use intranets. The following section examines several intranet topologies and techniques for network control.

NETWORK TOPOLOGIES

A **network topology** is the physical arrangement of the components (for example, nodes, servers, communications links, and so on) of the network. In this section, we examine the features of five basic network topologies: star, hierarchical, ring, bus, and client-server. Most networks are a variation on, or combination of, these basic models. However, before proceeding, working definitions are presented for some of the terms that will be used in the following sections.

Local Area Networks and Wide Area Networks

One way of distinguishing between networks is the geographic area that their distributed sites cover. Networks are usually classified as either local area networks (LANs) or wide area networks (WANs). LANs are often confined to a single room in a building, or they may link several buildings within a close geographic area. However, a LAN can cover distances of several miles and connect hundreds of users. The computers connected to a LAN are called nodes.

When networks exceed the geographic limitations of the LAN, they are called WANs. Because of the distances involved and the high cost of telecommunication infrastructure (telephone lines and microwave channels), WANs are often commercial networks (at least in part) that the organization leases. The nodes of a WAN may include microcomputer workstations, minicomputers, mainframes, and LANs. The WAN may be used to link geographically dispersed segments of a single organization or connect multiple organizations in a trading partner arrangement.

Network Interface Cards

The physical connection of workstations to the LAN is achieved through a network interface card (NIC), which fits into one of the expansion slots in the microcomputer. This device provides the electronic circuitry needed for internode communications. The NIC works with the network control program to send and receive messages, programs, and files across the network.

Servers

LAN nodes often share common resources such as programs, data, and printers, which are managed through special-purpose computers called **servers**, as depicted in Figure 3.17. When the server receives requests for resources, the requests are placed in a queue and are processed in sequence.

In a distributed environment, there is often a need to link networks together. For example, users of one LAN may share data with users on a different LAN. Networks

FIGURE 3.17

LAN with File and Print Servers

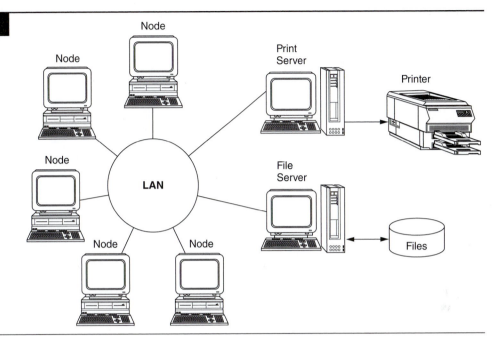

FIGURE 3.18

Bridges and Gateways Linking LANs and WANs

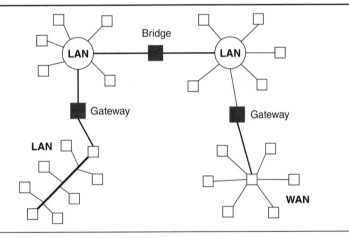

are linked via combinations of hardware and software devices called bridges and gateways. Figure 3.18 illustrates this technique. Bridges provide a means for linking LANs of the same type, for example, an IBM token ring to another IBM token ring. Gateways connect LANs of different types and are also used to link LANs to WANs. With these definitions in mind, we now turn our attention to the five basic network topologies.

Star Topology

The star topology shown in Figure 3.19 describes a network of computers with a large central computer (the host) at the hub that has direct connections to a periphery of smaller computers. Communications between the nodes in the star are managed and controlled from the host site.

FIGURE 3.19

Star Network

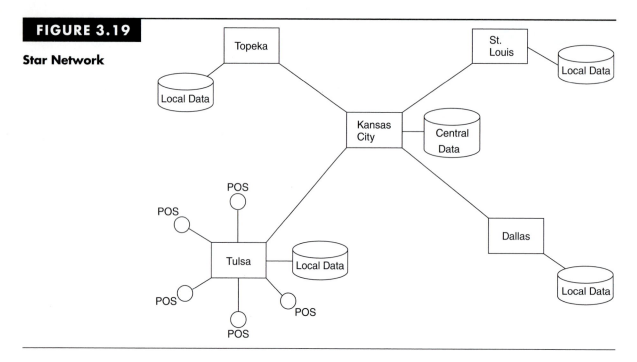

The star topology is often used for a WAN, in which the central computer is a mainframe. The nodes of the star may be microcomputer workstations, minicomputers, mainframes, or a combination. Databases under this approach may be distributed or centralized. A common model is to partition local data to the nodes and centralize the common data. For example, consider a department store chain that issues its own credit cards. Each node represents a store in a different metropolitan area. In Figure 3.19, these are Dallas, St. Louis, Topeka, and Tulsa. The nodes maintain local databases such as records for customers holding credit cards issued in their areas and records of local inventory levels. The central site—Kansas City—maintains data common to the entire regional area, including data for customer billing, accounts receivable maintenance, and overall inventory control. Each local node is itself a LAN, with point-of-sales (POS) terminals connected to a minicomputer at the store.

If one or more nodes in a star network fail, communication between the remaining nodes is still possible through the central site. However, if the central site fails, individual nodes can function locally, but cannot communicate with the other nodes.

Transaction processing in this type of configuration could proceed as follows. Sales are processed in real time at the POS terminals. Local processing includes obtaining credit approval, updating the customer's available credit, updating the inventory records, and recording the transaction in the transaction file (journal). At the end of the business day, the nodes transmit sales and inventory information to the central site in batches. The central site updates the control accounts, prepares customer bills, and determines inventory replenishment for the entire region.

The assumption underlying the star topology is that primary communication will be between the central site and the nodes. However, limited communication between the nodes is possible. For example, assume a customer from Dallas was in Tulsa and made a purchase from the Tulsa store on credit. The Tulsa database would not contain the customer's record, so Tulsa would send the transaction for credit approval to Dallas via Kansas City. Dallas would then return the approved transaction to Tulsa via Kansas City. Inventory and sales journal updates would be performed at Tulsa.

This transaction processing procedure would differ somewhat depending on the database configuration. For example, if local databases are partial replicas of the central database, credit queries could be made directly from Kansas City. However, this would require keeping the central database current with all the nodes.

Hierarchical Topology

A **hierarchical topology** is one in which a host computer is connected to several levels of subordinate, smaller computers in a master–slave relationship. This structure is applicable to firms with many organizational levels that must be controlled from a central location. For example, consider a manufacturing firm with remote plants, warehouses, and sales offices like the one illustrated in Figure 3.20. Sales orders from the local sales departments are transmitted to the regional level, where they are summarized and uploaded to the corporate level. Sales data, combined with inventory and plant capacity data from manufacturing, are used to compute production requirements for the period, which are downloaded to the regional production scheduling system. At this level, production schedules are prepared and distributed to the local production departments. Information about completed production is uploaded from the production departments to the regional level, where production summaries are prepared and transmitted to the corporate level.

Ring Topology

The **ring topology** illustrated in Figure 3.21 eliminates the central site. This is a peer-to-peer arrangement in which all nodes are of equal status; thus, responsibility for managing communications is distributed among the nodes. Every node on the ring has a unique electronic address, which is attached to messages such as an address on an envelope. If Node A wishes to send a message to Node D, then Nodes B and C receive, regenerate, and pass on the message until it arrives at its destination. This is a popular topology for LANs. The peer nodes

FIGURE 3.20   **Hierarchical Topology**

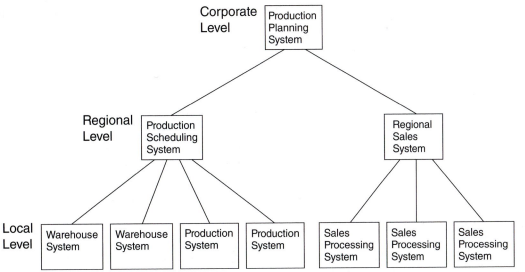

FIGURE 3.21

Ring Topology

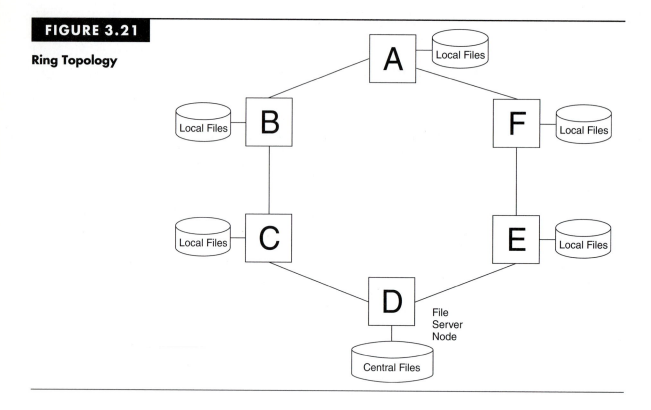

manage private programs and databases locally. However, a file server that is also a node on the network ring can centralize and manage common resources that all nodes share.

The ring topology may also be used for a WAN, in which case the databases may be partitioned rather than centralized. For example, consider a company with widely separated warehouses, each with different suppliers and customers, and each processing its own shipping and receiving transactions. In this case, where there are little common data, it is more efficient to distribute the database than to manage it centrally. However, when one warehouse has insufficient stock to fill an order, it can communicate through the network to locate the items at another warehouse.

Bus Topology

The bus topology illustrated in Figure 3.22 is the most popular LAN topology. It is so named because the nodes are all connected to a common cable—the bus. One or more servers centrally control communications and file transfers between workstations. As with the ring topology, each node on the bus has a unique address, and only one node may transmit at a time. The technique, which has been used for over 2 decades, is simple, reliable, and generally less costly to install than the ring topology.

Client-Server Topology

The term *client-server* is often misused to describe any type of network arrangement. In fact, the client-server topology has specific characteristics that distinguish it from the other topologies. Figure 3.23 illustrates the approach.

FIGURE 3.22

Bus Topology

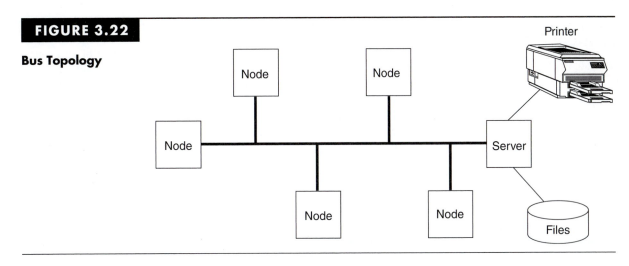

FIGURE 3.23

**Client-Server
Topology**

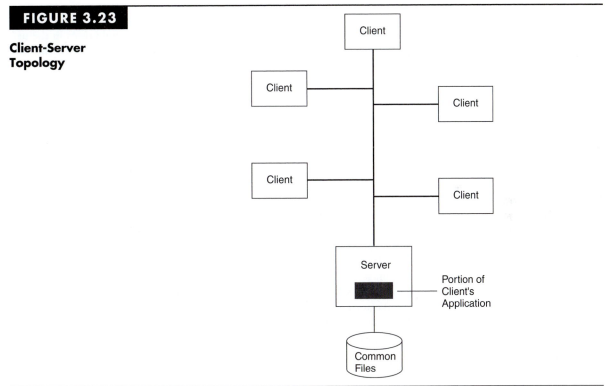

To explain the client-server difference, let's review the features of a traditional distributed data processing system (DDP). DDP can result in considerable data traffic jams. Users competing for access to shared data files experience queues, delays, and lockouts. A factor influencing the severity of this problem is the structure of the database in use. For example, assume that User A requests a single record from a database table located at a central site. To meet this request, the file server at the central site must lock and transmit the entire table to User A. The user's application performs the search for the specific record at the remote site. When the record is updated, the entire file is then transmitted back to the central site.

The client-server model distributes the processing between User A's (client) computer and the central file server. Both computers are part of the network, but each is assigned functions that it performs best. For example, the record-searching portion of an application is placed at the server, and the data-manipulation portion is on the client computer. Thus, only a single record, rather than the entire file, must be locked and sent to the client for processing. After processing, the record is returned to the server, which restores it to the table and removes the lock. This approach reduces traffic and allows more efficient use of shared data. Distributing the record-searching logic of the client's application to the server permits other clients to access different records in the same file simultaneously. The client-server approach can be applied to any topology (for example, ring, star, or bus). Figure 3.23 illustrates the client-server model applied to a bus topology.

NETWORK CONTROL

In this section, we examine methods for controlling communications between the physical devices connected to the network. Network control exists at several points in the network architecture. The majority of network control resides with software in the host computer, but control also resides in servers and terminals at the nodes and in switches located throughout the network. The purpose of network control is to perform the following tasks:

1. Establish a communications session between the sender and the receiver.
2. Manage the flow of data across the network.
3. Detect and resolve data collisions between competing nodes.
4. Detect errors in data that line failure or signal degeneration cause.

Data Collision

To achieve effective network control, there must be an exclusive link or session established between a transmitting and a receiving node. Only one node at a time can transmit a message on a single line. Two or more signals transmitted simultaneously will result in a **data collision**, which destroys both messages. When this happens, the messages must be retransmitted. There are several techniques for managing sessions and controlling data collisions, but most of them are variants of three basic methods: polling, token passing, and carrier sensing.

Polling
Polling is the most popular technique for establishing a communication session in WANs. One site, designated the master, polls the other slave sites to determine if they have data to transmit. If a slave responds in the affirmative, the master site locks the network while the data are transmitted. The remaining sites must wait until they are polled before they can transmit. The polling technique illustrated in Figure 3.24 is well suited to both the star and the hierarchical topologies. There are two primary advantages to polling. First, polling is noncontentious. Because nodes can send data only when the master node requests, two nodes can never access the network at the same time. Data collisions are, therefore, prevented. Second, an organization can set priorities for data communications across the network. Important nodes can be polled more often than less important nodes.

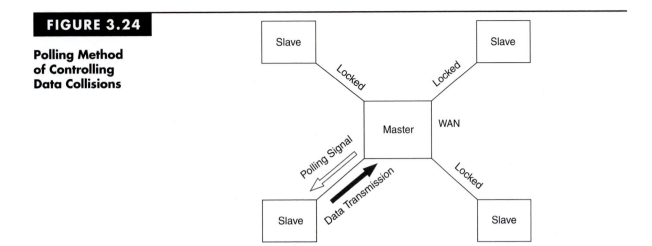

FIGURE 3.24

Polling Method of Controlling Data Collisions

Token Passing

Token passing involves transmitting a special signal—the token—around the network from node to node in a specific sequence. Each node on the network receives the token, regenerates it, and passes it to the next node. Only the node possessing the token is allowed to transmit data.

Token passing can be used with either ring or bus topologies. On a ring topology, the order in which the nodes are physically connected determines the token-passing sequence. With a bus, the sequence is logical, not physical. The token is passed from node to node in a predetermined order to form a logical ring. Token bus and token ring configurations are illustrated in Figure 3.25. Because nodes are permitted to transmit only when they possess the token, the node wishing to send data across the network seizes the token upon receiving it. Holding the token blocks other nodes from transmitting and ensures that no data collisions will occur. After the transmitting node sends its message and receives an acknowledgment signal from the receiving node, it releases the token. The next node in sequence then has the option of either seizing the token and transmitting data or passing the token on to the next node in the circuit.

A major advantage of token passing is its deterministic access method, which avoids data collisions. This is in contrast with the random access approach of carrier sensing (discussed in the next paragraphs). IBM's version of token ring is emerging as an industry standard.

Carrier Sensing

Carrier sensing is a random access technique that detects collisions when they occur. This technique, which is formally labeled carrier-sensed multiple access with collision detection (CSMA/CD), is used with the bus topology. The node wishing to transmit listens to the bus to determine if it is in use. If it senses no transmission in progress (no carrier), the node transmits its message to the receiving node. This approach is not as fail-safe as token passing. Collisions can occur when two or more nodes, unaware of each other's intent to transmit, do so simultaneously when they independently perceive the line to be clear. When this happens, the network server directs each node to wait a unique and random period of time and then retransmit the message. In a busy network, data

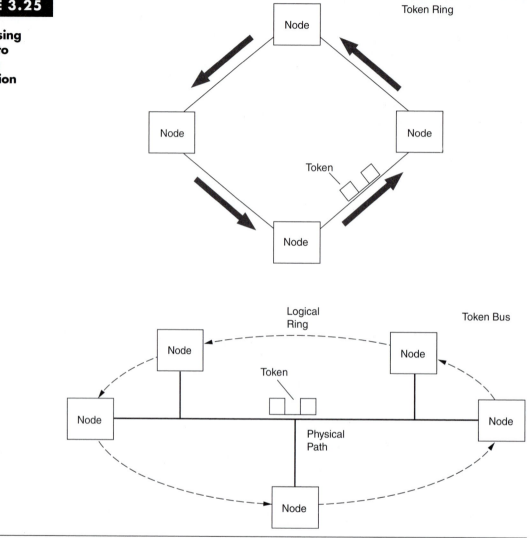

FIGURE 3.25

Token-Passing Approach to Controlling Data Collision

collisions are more likely to occur; thus, it results in delays while the nodes retransmit their messages. Proponents of the token-passing approach point to its collision-avoidance characteristic as a major advantage over the CSMA/CD model.

Ethernet is the best-known LAN software that uses the CSMA/CD standard. Xerox Corporation developed the Ethernet model in the 1970s. In 1980, Digital Equipment Corporation, in a joint venture with Intel Corporation, published the specifications for a LAN based on the Ethernet model. The greatest advantage of Ethernet is that it is established and reliable, and network specialists understand it well. Ethernet also has a number of economic advantages over token ring: (1) the technology, being relatively simple, is well suited to the less costly twisted-pair cabling, whereas token ring works best with more expensive coaxial cable; (2) the network interface cards that Ethernet uses are much less expensive than those used in the token ring topology; and (3) Ethernet uses a bus topology, which is easier to expand.

Section C: Malicious and Destructive Programs

VIRUS

A **virus** is a program (usually destructive) that attaches itself to a legitimate program to penetrate the operating system and destroy application programs, data files, and the operating system itself. An insidious aspect of a virus is its ability to spread throughout the host system and on to other systems before perpetrating its destructive acts. Often a virus will have a built-in counter that will trigger its destructive role only after it has copied itself a specified number of times to other programs and systems. The virus thus grows geometrically, which makes tracing its origin extremely difficult.

Personal computers are a major source of virus penetration. When connected in a network or a mainframe, an infected PC can upload the virus to the host system. Once in the host, the virus can spread throughout the operating system and to other users. Virus programs usually attach themselves to the following types of files:

1. An .EXE or .COM program file
2. An .OVL (overlay) program file
3. The boot sector of a disk
4. A device driver program

Mechanisms for spreading viruses include e-mail attachments, downloading of public-domain programs from the Internet, and using illegal bootleg software. Because of the general lack of control in PC operating systems, microcomputers connected to mainframes pose a serious threat to the mainframe environment as well.

WORM

The term **worm** is used interchangeably with virus. A worm is a software program that virtually burrows into the computer's memory and replicates itself into areas of idle memory. The worm systematically occupies idle memory until the memory is exhausted and the system fails. Technically, worms differ from viruses in that the replicated worm modules remain in contact with the original worm that controls their growth, whereas the replicated virus modules grow independently.

LOGIC BOMB

A logic bomb is a destructive program, such as a virus, that some predetermined event triggers. Often a date (such as Friday the 13th, April Fool's Day, or the 4th of July) will be the logic bomb's trigger. Events of less public prominence, such as the dismissal of an employee, have also triggered these bombs. For example, during the customary 2-week severance period, a terminated programmer may embed a logic bomb in the system that will activate 6 months after his or her departure from the firm.

BACK DOOR

A back door (also called a trap door) is a software program that allows unauthorized access to a system without going through the normal (front door) log-on procedure. Programmers who want to provide themselves with unrestricted access to a system that they are developing for users may create a log-on procedure that will accept either the user's private password or their own secret password, thus creating a back door to the system. The purpose of the back door may be to provide easy access to perform program maintenance, or it may be to perpetrate a fraud or insert a virus into the system.

TROJAN HORSE

A **Trojan horse** is a program whose purpose is to capture IDs and passwords from unsuspecting users. These programs are designed to mimic the normal log-on procedures of the operating system. When the user enters his or her ID and password, the Trojan horse stores a copy of them in a secret file. At some later date, the author of the Trojan horse uses these IDs and passwords to access the system and masquerade as an authorized user.

KEY TERMS

access control list

access token

advance encryption standard (AES)

algorithm

application-level firewall

botnets

Caesar cipher

call-back device

certification authority

compiler

data collision

data encryption standard

deep packet inspection (DPI)

denial of service attacks (Dos)

digest

digital certificate

digital envelope

digital signature

discretionary access privileges

distributed denial of service (DDos)

echo check

EDE3

electronic data interchange (EDI)

EEE3

encryption

event monitoring

firewall

hierarchical topology

internet relay chat (IRC)

interpreter

intranets

intrusion prevention systems (IPS)

IP broadcast address

IP spoofing

key

keystroke monitoring

line error

log-on procedure

message sequence numbering

message transaction log

multilevel password control

network-level firewall

network topology

one-time password

operating system

operating system security

parity check

password

ping

polling

private key

public key encryption

Public key infrastructure (PKI)

request-response technique

reusable password

ring topology

RSA (Rivest-Shamir-Adleman)

screening router

server
smurf attack
SYNchronize–ACKnowledge (SYN-ACK)
SYN flood attack
system audit trails
token passing

triple-DES encryption
trojan horse
virus
worm
zombie

REVIEW QUESTIONS

1. What are the five control objectives of an operating system?
2. What are the three main tasks the operating system performs?
3. What is the purpose of an access control list?
4. What are the four techniques that a virus could use to infect a system?
5. What is an access token?
6. Explain discretionary access privileges.
7. What is event monitoring?
8. What is keystroke monitoring?
9. What is a vaccine and what are its limitations?
10. What are the risks from subversive threats?
11. What are the risks from equipment failure?
12. What is a firewall?
13. Distinguish between network-level and application-level firewalls.
14. What are the most common forms of contra-security behavior?
15. What can be done to defeat a DDos attack?
16. How does public key encryption work?
17. What is a digital envelope?
18. What is a digital signature?
19. Categorize each of the following as either an equipment failure control or an unauthorized access control.
    a. message authentication
    b. parity check
    c. call-back device
    d. echo check
    e. line error
    f. data encryption
    g. request-response technique
20. What is DPI?
21. At what three points in an electronic data interchange transaction and validation process can authorization and validation be accomplished?
22. What is packet switching?
23. What is a VPN?
24. Name the three types of addresses used on the Internet.
25. Describe the elements of an e-mail address.
26. Networks would be inoperable without protocols. Explain their importance and what functions they perform.
27. What is the purpose of the TCP portion of TCP/IP?
28. What does the HTTP do?
29. How do HTTP and HTTP-NG differ?
30. What is a digital certificate? How is it different from a digital signature?
31. What is a certification authority, and what are the implications for the accounting profession?

DISCUSSION QUESTIONS

1. Why is human behavior considered one of the biggest potential threats to operating system integrity?
2. Why would a systems programmer create a back door if he or she has access to the program in his or her day-to-day tasks?
3. Discuss the issues that need to be considered before implementing keystroke monitoring.
4. Explain how an access token and an access control list are used to approve or deny access.
5. Explain how a Trojan horse may be used to penetrate a system.
6. Discuss six ways in which threats from destructive programs can be substantially reduced through a combination of technology controls and administrative procedures.
7. Explain the three ways in which audit trails can be used to support security objectives.
8. Explain how poorly designed audit trail logs can actually be dysfunctional.
9. Many authorities believe that the employer does not prosecute 90 percent of all computer fraud acts. What do you think accounts for this lack of prosecution? Discuss the importance of the establishment

of a formal policy for taking disciplinary (or legal) action against security violations.

10. How can passwords actually circumvent security? What actions can be taken to minimize this?

11. Explain how the one-time password approach works.

12. Explain how smurf attacks and SYN flood attacks can be controlled.

13. Discuss the risks from equipment failure and how they can be controlled.

14. Does every organization that has a LAN need a firewall?

15. Describe three ways in which IPS can be used to protect against DDos attacks.

16. What problem is common to all private key encryption techniques?

17. What is RSA encryption?

18. Explain the triple-DES encryption techniques known as EEE3 and EDE3.

19. Distinguish between a digital signature and a digital certificate.

20. Describe a digest within the context of a digital signature.

21. What is a digital envelope?

22. Why is inadequate segregation of duties a problem in the personal computer environment?

23. Why is the request-response technique important? Discuss the reasons an intruder may wish to prevent or delay the receipt of a message.

24. Discuss how the widespread use of laptop and notebook computers is making data encryption standards more easily penetrable.

25. Discuss the unique control problems EDI creates.

26. "In an EDI system, only the customer needs to verify that the order being placed is from a valid supplier and not vice versa." Do you agree with this statement? Why or why not?

27. Discuss how EDI creates an environment in which sensitive information, such as inventory amounts and price data, is no longer private. What potential dangers exist if the proper controls are not in place? Give an example.

28. What purpose do protocols serve?

29. Explain the purpose of the two elements of TCP/IP.

30. Distinguish between the FTP and TELNET protocols.

31. Distinguish between a network-level firewall and an application-level firewall.

32. What is a certification authority, and what are the implications for the accounting profession?

33. Discuss the key aspects of the following five seal-granting organizations: BBB, TRUSTe, Veri-Sign, Inc., ICSA, and AICPA/CICA WebTrust.

34. Differentiate between a LAN and a WAN. Do you have either or both at your university or college?

MULTIPLE-CHOICE QUESTIONS

1. Sniffer software is
   a. used by malicious Web sites to sniff data from cookies stored on the user's hard drive.
   b. used by network administrators to analyze network traffic.
   c. used by bus topology intranets to sniff for carriers before transmitting a message to avoid data collisions.
   d. an illegal program downloaded from the Web to sniff passwords from the encrypted data of Internet customers.
   e. illegal software for decoding encrypted messages transmitted over a shared intranet channel.

2. An integrated group of programs that supports the applications and facilitates their access to specified resources is called a(n)
   a. operating system.
   b. database management system.
   c. utility system.
   d. facility system.
   e. object system.

3. A user's application may consist of several modules stored in separate memory locations, each with its own data. One module must not be allowed to destroy or corrupt another module. This is an objective of
   a. operating system controls.
   b. data resource controls.
   c. computer center and security controls.
   d. application controls.

4. A program that attaches to another legitimate program but does NOT replicate itself is called a
   a. virus.
   b. worm.
   c. Trojan horse.
   d. logic bomb.

5. Which of the following is NOT a data communications control objective?
   a. maintaining the critical application list
   b. correcting message loss due to equipment failure
   c. preventing illegal access
   d. rendering useless any data that a perpetrator successfully captures

6. Hackers can disguise their message packets to look as if they came from an authorized user and gain access to the host's network using a technique called
   a. spoofing.
   b. IP spooling.
   c. dual-homed.
   d. screening.

7. Transmitting numerous SYN packets to a targeted receiver, but NOT responding to an ACK, is form of
   a. a DES message.
   b. request-response control.
   c. denial of service attack.
   d. call-back device.

8. A message that is contrived to appear to be coming from a trusted or authorized source is called
   a. a denial of service attack.
   b. digital signature forging.
   c. Internet protocol spoofing.
   d. URL masquerading.
   e. a SYN-ACK packet.

9. A DDos attack
   a. is more intensive than a Dos attack because it emanates from single source.
   b. may take the form of either a SYN flood or smurf attack.
   c. is so named because it affects many victims simultaneously, which are distributed across the Internet.
   d. turns the target victim's computers into zombies that are unable to access the Internet.
   e. none of the above is correct.

10. A ping signal is used to initiate
    a. URL masquerading.
    b. digital signature forging.
    c. Internet protocol spoofing.
    d. a smurf attack.
    e. a SYN-ACK packet.

11. A digital signature
    a. is the encrypted mathematical value of the message sender's name.
    b. is derived from the digest of a document that has been encrypted with the sender's private key.
    c. is derived from the digest of a document that has been encrypted with the sender's public key.
    d. is the computed digest of the sender's digital certificate.
    e. allows digital messages to be sent over an analog telephone line.

PROBLEMS

1. **Operating System and Network Control**

   Describe a well-controlled system in terms of access controls for a major insurance company that equips each salesperson (life, property, and investments) with a laptop. Each salesperson must transmit sales data daily to corporate headquarters. Further, the salespeople use their laptops to connect to the company's e-mail system.

2. **Operation System Controls**

   In 2002, Mr. Rollerball started Mighty Mouse, Inc., a small, 75-employee firm that produces and sells wireless keyboards and other devices to vendors through its manufacturing plant in Little Rock, Arkansas. In its first 2 years of business, MM saw a substantial growth in sales and at current capacity was unable to keep up with demand. To compete, MM enlarged its manufacturing facilities. The new facility increased to 250 employees. During this period of expansion, MM has paid little attention to internal control procedures.

   Security

   Recently, systems problems and hardware failures have caused the operating system to crash. Mr. Rollerball was extremely concerned to discover that confidential company information had been printed out a result of these crashes. Also, important digital documents were erased from storage media.

   Malicious programs such as viruses, worms, and Trojan horses have plagued the company and caused significant data corruption. MM has devoted significant funds and time trying to fix the damage caused to its operating system.

   Out of necessity to get the job done, as well as for philosophical reasons, system administrators and programmers have provided users relatively free access to the operating system. Restricting access was found to inhibit business and impede recovery from systems failures. From the outset, an open approach was regarded as an efficient and effective way to ensure that everyone obtained the information they needed to perform their jobs.

Required:

  a. What internal control problems do you find?
  b. How can MM improve internal controls?

3.   Internal Control and Fraud

Charles Hart, an accounts payable clerk, is an hourly employee. He never works a minute past 5 P.M. unless the overtime has been approved. Charles has recently found himself faced with some severe financial difficulties. He has been accessing the system from his home during the evening and setting up an embezzlement scheme. As his boss, what control technique(s) discussed in this chapter could you use to help detect this type of fraud?

4.   Internal Control and Fraud

Stephanie Baskill, an unemployed accounting clerk, lives one block from Cleaver Manufacturing Company. While walking her dog last year, she noticed some ERP manuals in the dumpsters. Curious, she took the manuals home with her. She found that the documentation in the manual was dated 2 months prior, so she thought that the information must be fairly current. Over the next month, Stephanie continued to collect all types of manuals from the dumpster during her dog-walking excursions. Cleaver Manufacturing Company was apparently updating all of its documentation manuals and placing them online. Eventually, Stephanie found manuals about critical inventory reorder formulas, the billing system, the sales order system, the payables system, and the operating system. Stephanie went to the local library and read as much as she could about this particular operating system.

To gain access to the organization, she took a low-profile position as a cleaning woman, giving her access to all areas in the building. While working, Stephanie snooped through offices, watched people who were working late type in their passwords, and guessed passwords. She ultimately printed out lists of user IDs and passwords using a Trojan horse virus, thus obtaining all the necessary passwords to set herself up as a supplier, customer, systems operator, and systems librarian.

As a customer, she ordered enough goods to trigger the automatic inventory procurement system to purchase more raw materials. Then, as a supplier, Stephanie would deliver the goods at the specified price. She then adjusted the transaction logs once the bills were paid to cover her tracks. Stephanie was able to embezzle, on average, $125,000 a month. About 16 months after she began working at Cleaver, the controller saw her at a very expensive French restaurant one evening, driving a Jaguar. He told the internal auditors to keep a close watch on her, and they were able to catch her in the act.

Required:

  a. What weaknesses in the organization's control structure must have existed to permit this type of embezzlement?

  b. What specific control techniques and procedures could have helped prevent or detect this fraud?

5.   Input Controls and Networking

A global manufacturing company has over 100 subsidiaries worldwide reporting to it each month. The reporting units prepare the basic financial statements and other key financial data on prescribed forms, which are e-mailed or faxed to the corporate headquarters. The financial data are then entered into the corporate database from which consolidated statements are prepared for internal planning and decision making.

Current reporting policy requires that the subsidiaries provide the previous month's reports by the tenth working day of each new month. Accounting department staff log and enter the reports into the database. Approximately 15 percent of the reporting units are delinquent in submitting their reports, and 3 to 4 days are required to enter all the data into the database. After the data are loaded into the system, data verification programs are run to check footings, cross-statement consistency, and dollar range limits. Any errors in the data are traced and corrected, and reporting units are notified of all errors via e-mail.

The company has decided to upgrade its computer communications network with a new system that will support more timely receipt of data at corporate headquarters. The systems department at corporate headquarters is responsible for the overall design and implementation of the new system. It will use current computer communications technology and install LANs, PCs, and servers at all reporting units.

The new system will allow clerks at the remote sites to send financial data to the corporate office via the Internet. The required form templates will be downloaded to the remote sites along with the data verification programs. The clerks will enter data into the forms to create a temporary file, which data verification programs will check for errors. All corrections can thus be made before transmitting the data to headquarters. The data would be either transmitted to corporate headquarters immediately or the corporate headquarters computer would retrieve it from disk storage at the remote site as needed. Data used at corporate headquarters would therefore be free from errors and ready for consolidation.

The company's controller is pleased with the prospects of the new system, which should shorten the reporting period by 3 days. He is, however, concerned about security and data integrity during the transmission. He has scheduled a meeting with key personnel from the systems department to discuss these concerns.

Required:

The company could experience data security and integrity problems when transmitting data between the reporting units and corporate headquarters.

a. Identify and explain the data security and integrity problems that could occur.

b. For each problem identified, describe a control procedure that could be employed to minimize or eliminate the problem. Use the following format to present your answer.

Problem Identification and Explanation

Control Procedure and Explanation

6. Preventive Controls

Listed here are five scenarios. For each scenario, discuss the possible damages that can occur. Suggest a preventive control.

a. An intruder taps into a telecommunications device and retrieves the identifying codes and personal identification numbers for ATM cardholders. (The user subsequently codes this information onto a magnetic coding device and places this strip on a piece of cardboard.)

b. Because of occasional noise on a transmission line, electronic messages received are extremely garbled.

c. Because of occasional noise on a transmission line, data being transferred is lost or garbled.

d. An intruder is temporarily delaying important strategic messages over the telecommunications lines.

e. An intruder is altering electronic messages before the user receives them.

7. Operating System Exposures and Controls

Listed here are five scenarios. For each scenario, discuss the potential consequences and give a prevention technique.

a. The systems operator opened a bag of burned microwave popcorn directly under a smoke detector in the computing room where two mainframes, three high-speed printers, and approximately 40 tapes are housed. The extremely sensitive smoke detector triggered the sprinkler system. Three minutes passed before the sprinklers could be turned off.

b. A system programmer intentionally placed an error into a program that causes the operating system to fail and dump certain confidential information to disks and printers.

c. Jane's employer told her she would be laid off in 3 weeks. After 2 weeks, Jane realized that finding another secretarial job was going to be very tough. She became bitter. Her son told her about a virus that had infected his school's computers and that one of his disks had been infected. Jane took the infected disk to work and copied it onto the network server, which is connected to the company's mainframe. One month later, the company realized that some data and application programs had been destroyed.

d. Robert discovered a new sensitivity analysis public-domain program on the Internet. He downloaded the software to his microcomputer at home, then took the application to work and placed it onto his networked personal computer. The program had a virus on it that eventually spread to the company's mainframe.

e. Murray, a trusted employee and a systems engineer, had access to both the computer access control list and user passwords. The firm's competitor recently hired him for twice his salary. After leaving, Murray continued to browse through his old employer's data, such as price lists, customer lists, bids on jobs, and so on. He passed this information on to his new employer.

8. Encryption

The coded message that follows is an encrypted message from Brutus to the Roman Senate. It was produced using the Caesar cipher method, in which each letter is shifted by a fixed number of places (determined by the key value).

OHWV GR MXOLXV RQ PRQGDB PDUFK 48
GUHVV: WRJD FDVXDO (EBRG)

Required:
Determine the key used to produce the coded message and decode it.

9. Security and Control Assessment

Brew Bottle Company (BBC) is in the process of planning a more advanced computer-based information system. Slavish & Moore, LLP, BBC's consulting firm, have recently been provided with an overview of their proposed plan:

The Brew Bottle Company Information System (BBCIS) will be created with the help of its employees so that the system will function effectively. This helps ensure that the end product will perform the tasks that the user wants. System construction will begin with prototyping, computer-aided software engineering (CASE) technology, and Gantt charts. From here, systems professionals and a systems administrator who will work full-time for BBC will create data models of the business process, define conceptual user views, design database tables, and specify system controls. Each user in each department will submit a written description of his or her needs and business problems to the systems professionals. Systems professionals will then perform analysis of feasibility and system design. Each aspect of the system will be properly documented for control reasons; this will help if problems arise in the future stages of development and is essential to long-term system success.

The new systems administrator will determine access privileges, maintain the access control list, and maintain the database authorization table. Anyone requesting access will fill out a petition, which the systems administrator must approve and sign. The administrator will have sole access to the transaction log, which will be used to record all changes made to a file or database. This information will help detect unauthorized access, reconstruct events if needed, and promote personal accountability. The systems administrator will also be responsible for updating virus protection weekly so that viruses planted intentionally or accidentally will not damage the system. One of the most important tasks of the systems administrator will be to copy databases and system documentation for critical applications to tape or disk on a daily basis. These disks and tapes will be stored in a secure location away from the company property.

Employees requiring computer access will be given a user name and password that will be entered when logging on to their computer terminal. A dialog box will appear when the system is turned on and this information will be entered. Correct entry of information will give the user access; if information is entered incorrectly, the user will not be granted access. Furthermore, if a computer terminal is left idle for more than 5 minutes, a password will be needed to regain access. For security reasons, users will be required to change their passwords once every year.

Hardware will be purchased from Bell Computer Company with the advice of in-house systems developers. With the exception of basic applications, user departments will purchase computer software, which will be added to the system.

BBCIS will run off of a computing center located in the company's administration building adjacent to the factory. Access to the computing center will require formal authorization. When entering the room, there will be two security guards. Authorized employees will need to swipe their ID cards to pass though security. Times will be recorded when employees swipe their cards for entrance and exit. The actual room that houses the computer systems will have an advanced air-conditioning and air filtration system to eliminate dust and pollens. There will also be a sprinkler system to minimize damages in case of a fire.

Required:

Based on BBC's plans for the implementation of a new computer system, describe the potential risks and needed controls. Classify these according to the relevant areas of the COSO framework.

10. Encryption

a. Develop a Caesar cipher-type encryption algorithm with a little more complexity in it. For example, the algorithm could alternatively shift the cleartext letters positive and negative by the amount of the key value. Variations on this are limitless.
b. Select a single-digit key.
c. Code a short message using the algorithm and key.
d. Give your instructor the algorithm, key, cleartext, and ciphertext.
e. Optional: Your instructor will randomly redistribute to the class the ciphertext messages completed in part d above. You are to decode the message you receive as an additional assignment.

11. Certification Authority Licensing

Research the current state of certification authority licensing in the United States and Europe. Write a brief report of your findings.

12. Types of Destructive Programs

Required:

Write a report outlining the key features of the following types of destructive programs: virus, worm, logic bomb, back door, and Trojan horse.

13. Controlling Risk from Destructive Programs

Required:

Write an essay discussing the common technology controls and administrative procedures used to reduce threats from destructive programs.

14. Audit Trail Objectives

Required:

Write an essay outlining the following audit trail objectives: (a) detecting unauthorized access to the system, (b) facilitating the reconstruction of events, and (c) promoting personal accountability.

CHAPTER 4

Security Part II: Auditing Database Systems

LEARNING OBJECTIVES

After studying this chapter, you should:

- Understand the operational problems inherent in the flat-file approach to data management that gave rise to the database approach.
- Understand the relationships among the fundamental components of the database concept.
- Recognize the defining characteristics of three database models: hierarchical, network, and relational.
- Understand the operational features and associated risks of deploying centralized, partitioned, and replicated database models in the DDP environment.
- Be familiar with the audit objectives and procedures used to test data management controls.

This chapter continues the treatment of general IT controls as described by the COSO control framework. The focus of the chapter is on Sarbanes-Oxley compliance regarding the security and control of organization databases. The term database is used in a broad context to include two general approaches: the **flat-file model** and the **database model**. The opening section in the chapter describes flat-file data management, which is used in many older (legacy) systems that are still in operation today. Private ownership of data, which characterizes this model, is the root cause of several problems that inhibit data integration. The section then presents a conceptual overview of the database model and illustrates how problems associated with the flat-file model are resolved under this approach. The notions of entity-wide data sharing and centralized control of data lie at the heart of the database philosophy.

The second section describes the key functions and defining features of three common database models: the *hierarchical*, the *network*, and the *relational* models. The three models are presented from the perspective of a centralized IT function. The hierarchical and network models are called *navigational databases* because of their structure and inflexibility. Seen as a marked improvement over flat files, navigational databases were used in the design of many late-era legacy systems. Newer accounting information systems, however, make extensive use of the relational model. This flexible approach presents data in a two-dimensional format that is conceptually more pleasing to end users than complex navigational structures. When properly implemented, the relational model effectively supports entity-wide data integration.

The third section examines the role of database technology in the distributed environment. Distributed data processing (DDP) empowers end users with ownership and control of IT resources, including databases. Since data ownership is contrary to traditional database philosophy, DDP presents an operational dilemma of sorts. This section presents techniques for achieving the goals of DDP while maintaining the principles of data sharing and integration. Three alternative configurations are examined: centralized, replicated, and partitioned databases.

The chapter concludes with a discussion of the control and audit issues related to data management. The risks, audit objectives, and audit procedures relevant to flat files, centralized databases, and distributed databases are presented.

DATA MANAGEMENT APPROACHES

Business organizations follow either or both of two general approaches to data management: the flat-file model and the database model. The differences between the two approaches are both technical and philosophical. The defining features of each are presented below.

The Flat-File Approach

Flat files are data files that contain records with no structured relationships to other files. The flat-file approach is most often associated with so-called **legacy systems**. These are often large mainframe systems that were implemented in the 1970s through the 1980s. Some organizations today still make extensive use of such systems. Eventually, they will be replaced by modern database management systems, but in the meantime, auditors must continue to deal with legacy-system technologies.

The flat-file environment promotes a single-user view approach to data management whereby end users *own* their data files rather than *share* them with other users. Data files are therefore structured, formatted, and arranged to suit the specific needs of the *owner* or primary user of the data. Such structuring, however, may exclude data attributes that are useful to other users, thus preventing successful integration of data across the organization. When multiple users need the same data for different purposes, they must obtain separate data sets structured to their specific needs. Figure 4.1 illustrates how customer sales data might be presented to three different users in a durable goods retailing organization. The accounting function needs customer sales data organized by account number and structured to show outstanding balances. This is used for customer billing, account receivable maintenance, and financial statement preparation. The marketing function needs customer sales history data organized by demographic keys for use in targeting new product promotions and for selling product upgrades. The product service group needs customer sales data organized by products and structured to show scheduled service dates. It will use such information for making after-sales contacts with customers to schedule preventive maintenance and to solicit sales of service agreements.

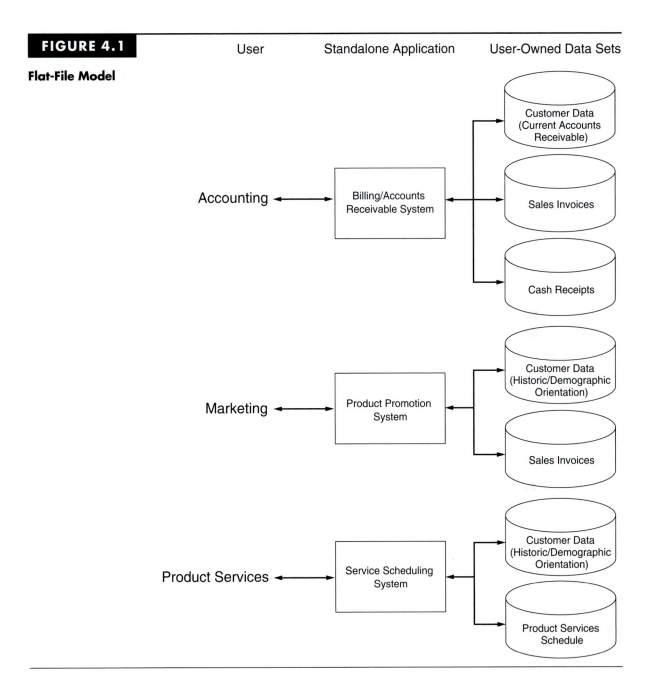

FIGURE 4.1

Flat-File Model

User   Standalone Application   User-Owned Data Sets

This replication of essentially the same data in multiple files is called **data redundancy** and contributes to three significant problems in the flat-file environment: **data storage**, **data updating**, and **currency of information**. These and a fourth problem (not specifically caused by data redundancy) called **task-data dependency** are discussed next.

Data Storage

Efficient data management captures and stores data only once and makes this single source available to all users who need it. In the flat-file environment, this is not possible. To meet the private data needs of diverse users, organizations must incur the costs of both multiple collection and multiple storage procedures. Some commonly used data may be duplicated dozens, hundreds, or even thousands of times within an organization.

Data Updating

Organizations store a great deal of data on master files and reference files that require periodic updating to reflect changes. For example, a change to a customer's name or address must be reflected in the appropriate master files. When users keep separate and exclusive files, each change must be made separately for each user. These redundant updating tasks add significantly to the cost of data management.

Currency of Information

In contrast to the problem of performing multiple updates is the problem of failing to update all the user files that are affected by a change in status. If update information is not properly disseminated, the change will not be reflected in some users' data, resulting in decisions based on outdated information.

Task-Data Dependency

Another problem with the flat-file approach is the user's inability to obtain additional information as his or her needs change: this is known as task-data dependency. In other words, a user's task is limited and decision making ability constrained by the data that he or she possesses and controls. Since users in a flat-file environment act independently, rather than as members of a user community, establishing a mechanism for the formal data sharing is difficult or impossible. Therefore, users in this environment tend to satisfy new information needs by procuring new data files. This takes time, inhibits performance, adds to data redundancy, and drives data management costs even higher.

An organization can overcome the problems associated with flat files by implementing the database approach. The key features of this data management model are discussed next.

The Database Approach

Access to the data resource is controlled by a **database management system (DBMS)**. The DBMS is a special software system that is programmed to know which data elements each user is authorized to access. The user's program sends requests for data to the DBMS, which validates and authorizes access to the database in accordance with the user's level of authority. If the user requests data that he or she is not authorized to access, the request is denied. Clearly, the organization's procedures for assigning user authority are an important control issue for auditors to consider. Figure 4.2 provides an overview of the database environment.

This approach centralizes the organization's data into a common database that is *shared* by other users. With the enterprise's data in a central location, all users have access to the data they need to achieve their respective objectives. Through data sharing, the traditional problems associated with the flat-file approach *may* be overcome.

Elimination of Data Storage Problem

Each data element is stored only once, thereby eliminating data redundancy and reducing data collection and storage costs. For example, in Figure 4.2 only a single occurrence of customer data exists, but this occurrence is shared by accounting, marketing, and product services users. Since no single user or unit owns data, they must be structured in such a way as to be useful to a broad set of users and potential users.

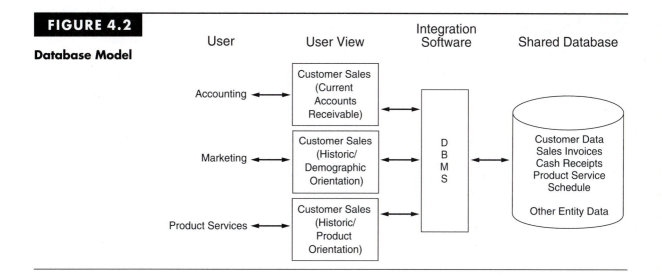

FIGURE 4.2

Database Model

Elimination of Data Update Problem

Because each data element exists in only one place, it requires only a single update procedure. This reduces the time and cost of keeping the database current.

Elimination of Currency Problem

A single change to a database attribute is automatically made available to all users of the attribute. For example, a customer address change entered by the billing clerk is immediately reflected in the marketing and product services views.

Elimination of Task-Data Dependency Problem

The most striking difference between the database model and the flat-file model is the pooling of data into a common database that is shared by all organizational users. With access to the full domain of entity data, changes in user information needs can be satisfied without obtaining additional private data sets. Users are constrained only by the limitations of the data available to the entity and the legitimacy of their need to access them. Therefore the database method eliminates the limited access that flat files, by their nature, dictate to users.

KEY ELEMENTS OF THE DATABASE ENVIRONMENT

This section discusses the key elements of the database environment. These include the database management system (DBMS), users, the database administrator, the physical database, and DBMS models. Figure 4.3 depicts the relationship between several of these elements.

Database Management System

Typical Features

The central element of the database approach depicted in Figure 4.3 is the database management system. The DBMS provides a controlled environment to assist (or prevent)

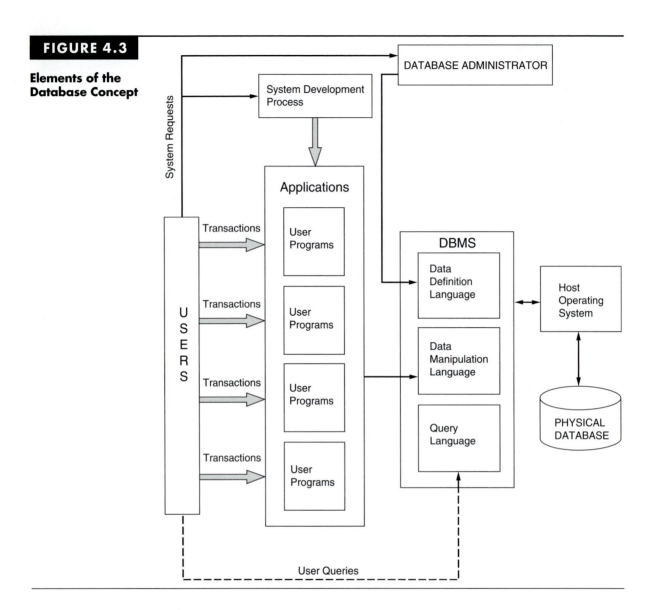

FIGURE 4.3

Elements of the Database Concept

access to the database and to efficiently manage the data resource. Each DBMS is unique in the way it accomplishes these objectives, but some typical features include:

1. *Program development.* The DBMS contains **application development software**. Both programmers and end users may employ this feature to create applications to access the database.
2. *Backup and recovery.* During processing, the DBMS periodically makes backup copies of the physical database. In the event of a disaster (disk failure, program error, or malicious act) that renders the database unusable, the DBMS can recover to an earlier version that is known to be correct. Although some data loss may occur, without the backup and recovery feature the database would be vulnerable to total destruction.
3. *Database usage reporting.* This feature captures statistics on what data are being used, when they are used, and who uses them. This information is used by the database administrator (DBA) to help assign user authorization and maintain the database. We discuss the role of the DBA later in this section.

4. *Database access.* The most important feature of a DBMS is to permit authorized user access, both formal and informal, to the database. Figure 4.3 shows the three software modules that facilitate this task. These are the data definition language, the data manipulation language, and the query language.

Data Definition Language

Data definition language (DDL) is a programming language used to define the database to the DBMS. The DDL identifies the names and the relationship of all data elements, records, and files that constitute the database. This definition has three levels, called *views*: the physical internal view, the conceptual view (schema), and the user view (subschema). Figure 4.4 shows the relationship between these views.

Database Views

Internal View/Physical View. The physical arrangement of records in the database is presented through the **internal view**. This is the lowest level of representation, which is one step removed from the physical database. This internal view describes the structures of data records, the linkages between files, and the physical arrangement and sequence of records in a file. There is only one internal view for the database.

FIGURE 4.4   Overview of DBMS Operation

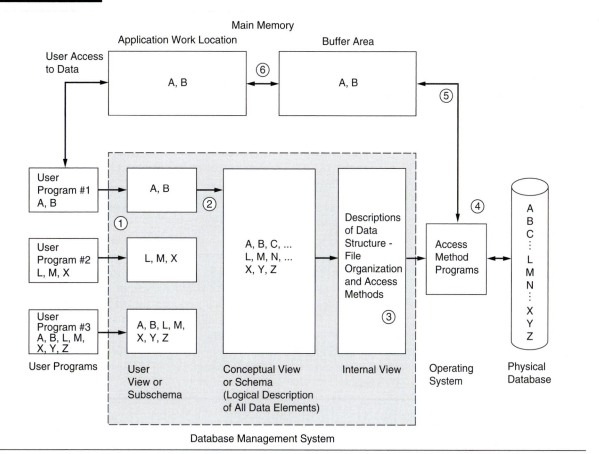

Database Management System

Conceptual View/Logical View (Schema).   The **schema** (or **conceptual view**) describes the entire database. This view represents the database logically and abstractly, rather than the way it is physically stored. There is only one conceptual view for a database.

External View/User View (Subschema).   The **subschema** or **user view**, defines the user's section of the database—the portion that an individual user is authorized to access. To a particular user, the user view is the database. Unlike the internal and conceptual views, there may be many distinct user views. For example, a user in the personnel department may view the database as a collection of employee records and is unaware of the supplier and inventory records seen by the users in the inventory control department.

Users

Formal Access: Application Interfaces

Figure 4.3 shows how users access the database in two ways. First, access is possible by the formal application interfaces. User programs, prepared by systems professionals, send data access requests (calls) to the DBMS, which validates the requests and retrieves the data for processing. Under this mode of access, the presence of the DBMS is transparent to the users. Data processing procedures (both batch and real-time) for transactions such as sales, cash receipts, and purchases are essentially the same as they would be in the flat-file environment.

Data Manipulation Language.   **Data manipulation language (DML)** is the proprietary programming language that a particular DBMS uses to retrieve, process, and store data. Entire user programs may be written in the DML or, alternatively, selected DML commands can be inserted into programs that are written in universal languages, such as JAVA, C++, and even older languages such as COBOL and FORTRAN. Inserting DML commands enables standard programs, which were originally written for the flat-file environment, to be easily converted to work in a database environment. The use of standard language programs also provides the organization with a degree of independence from the DBMS vendor. If the organization decides to switch vendors to one that uses a different DML, it will not need to rewrite all user programs. By replacing the old DML commands with the new commands, user programs can be modified to function in the new environment.

DBMS Operation.   Figure 4.3 illustrates how the DBMS and user applications work together. Let's consider the typical sequence of events that occur while accessing data. The following description is generic and certain technical details are omitted.

1. A user program sends a request for data to the DBMS. The requests are written in a special data manipulation language (discussed later) that is embedded in the user program.
2. The DBMS analyzes the request by matching the called data elements against the user view and the conceptual view. If the data request matches, it is authorized, and processing proceeds to Step 3. If it does not match the views, access is denied.
3. The DBMS determines the data structure parameters from the internal view and passes them to the operating system, which performs the actual data retrieval. Data structure parameters describe the organization and access method for retrieving the requested data. This topic is discussed later.
4. Using the appropriate access method (an operating system utility program), the operating system interacts with the disk storage device to retrieve the data from the physical database.
5. The operating system then stores the data in a main memory buffer area managed by the DBMS.
6. The DBMS transfers the data to the user's work location in main memory. At this point, the user's program is free to access and manipulate the data.

7. When processing is complete, Steps 4, 5, and 6 are reversed to restore the processed data to the database.

Informal Access: Query Language

Definition. The second method of database access is the informal method of queries. A *query* is an ad hoc access methodology for extracting information from a database. Users can access data via direct query, which requires no formal user programs using the DBMS's built-in query facility. This feature allows authorized users to process data independent of professional programmers by providing a "friendly" environment for integrating and retrieving data to produce ad hoc management reports.

SQL. The query capability of the DBMS permits end users and professional programmers to access data in the database directly without the need for conventional programs. IBM's **Structured Query Language (SQL)** (often pronounced *sequel* or S-Q-L), has emerged as the standard query language for both mainframe and microcomputer DBMSs. SQL is a fourth-generation, nonprocedural language (English-like commands) with many commands that allow users to input, retrieve, and modify data easily. The SELECT command is a powerful tool for retrieving data. The example in Figure 4.5 illustrates the use of the SELECT command to produce a user report from a database called *Inventory*.

| **FIGURE 4.5** | **Example of SELECT Command Used to Query an Inventory Database** |

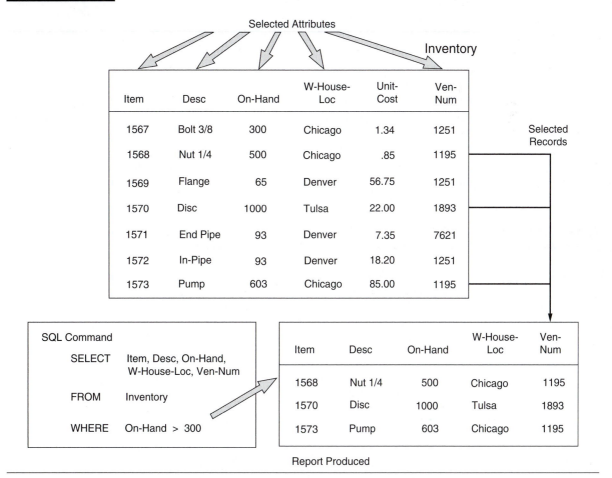

As you can see from this example, SQL is an efficient data processing tool. Although not a natural English language, SQL requires far less training in computer concepts and fewer programming skills than third-generation languages. In fact, the latest generations of query tools require no SQL knowledge at all. Users select data visually by "pointing and clicking" at the desired attributes. This visual user interface then generates the necessary SQL commands automatically. The great advantage of this query feature is that it places ad hoc reporting and data processing capability in the hands of the end user/manager. By reducing reliance on professional programmers, the manager's ability to deal promptly with problems that pop up is greatly improved. The query feature, however, an important control issue. Management must ensure that it is not used to achieve unauthorized access to the database.

The Database Administrator

Refer to Figure 4.3 and note the administrative position of the **database administrator (DBA)**. The DBA is responsible for managing the database resource. The sharing of a common database by multiple users requires organization, coordination, rules, and guidelines to protect the integrity of the database.

In large organizations, the DBA function may consist of an entire department of technical personnel under the database administrator. In smaller organizations, DBA responsibility may be assumed by someone within the computer services group. The duties of the DBA fall into the following areas: database planning; database design; database implementation, operation, and maintenance; and database growth and change. Table 4.1 presents a breakdown of specific tasks within these broad areas.

Organizational Interactions of the DBA

Figure 4.6 shows some of the organizational interfaces of the DBA. Of particular importance is the relationship among the DBA, the end users, and the systems professionals of the organization. Refer again to Figure 4.3 as we examine this relationship.

When information systems needs arise, users send formal requests for computer applications to the systems professionals (programmers) of the organization. The requests are handled through formal systems development procedures; if they have merit, they result

---

TABLE 4.1   ## Functions of the Database Administrator

Database Planning:	**Implementation:**
Develop organization's database strategy	Determine access policy
Define database environment	Implement security controls
Define data requirements	Specify tests procedures
Develop data dictionary	Establish programming standards
Design:	**Operation and Maintenance:**
Logical database (schema)	Evaluate database performance
External users' views (subschemas)	Reorganize database as user needs demand
Internal view of databases	Review standards and procedures
Database controls	
	Change and Growth:
	Plan for change and growth
	Evaluate new technology

in programmed applications. Figure 4.3 shows this relationship as the line from the user block to the systems development block. The user requests also go to the DBA, who evaluates these to determine the user's database needs. Once this is established, the DBA grants the user access authority by programming the user's view (subschema). We see this relationship as the lines between the user and the DBA and between the DBA and DDL module in the DBMS. By keeping database access authority separate from systems development (application programming), the organization is better able to control and protect the database. Intentional and unintentional attempts at unauthorized access are more likely to be discovered when the activities of these two groups are segregated.

The Data Dictionary

Another important function of the DBA is the creation and maintenance of the **data dictionary**. The data dictionary describes every data element in the database. This enables all users (and programmers) to share a common view of the data resource, thus greatly facilitating the analysis of user needs. The data dictionary may be in both paper form and online. Most DBMSs employ special software for managing the data dictionary.

The Physical Database

The fourth major element of the database approach as presented in Figure 4.3 is the **physical database**. This is the lowest level of the database and the only level that exists in physical form. The physical database consists of magnetic spots on metallic coated disks. The other levels of the database (the user view, conceptual view, and internal view) are abstract representations of the physical level.

At the physical level, the database forms a logical collection of records and files that constitute the firm's data resource. This section deals with the data structures used in the

FIGURE 4.6

Organizational Interactions of the Database Administrator

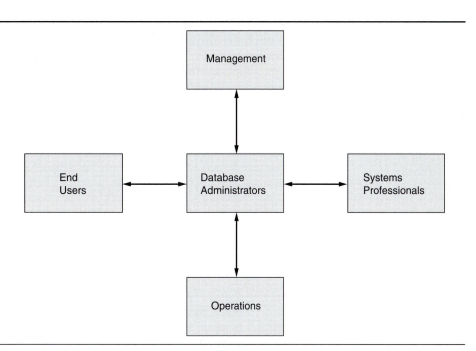

TABLE 4.2	**Typical File Processing Operations**

1. Retrieve a record from the file based on its primary key value.
2. Insert a record into a file.
3. Update a record in the file.
4. Read a complete file of records.
5. Find the next record in a file.
6. Scan a file for records with common secondary keys.
7. Delete a record from a file.

physical database. Table 4.2 contains a list of file processing operations that data structures must support. The efficiency with which the DBMS performs these tasks is a major determinant of its overall success, and depends in great part on how a particular file is structured.

Data Structures

Data structures are the bricks and mortar of the database. The data structure allows records to be located, stored, and retrieved, and enables movement from one record to another. Data structures have two fundamental components: organization and access method.

Data Organization

The **organization** of a file refers to the way records are physically arranged on the secondary storage device. This may be either *sequential* or *random*. The records in sequential files are stored in contiguous locations that occupy a specified area of disk space. Records in random files are stored without regard for their physical relationship to other records of the same file. Random files may have records distributed throughout a disk.

Data Access Methods

The **access method** is the technique used to locate records and to navigate through the database. For our purposes, it is sufficient to deal with access methods at the conceptual level only. However, at a technical level, they exist as computer programs that are provided as part of the operating system. During database processing, the access method program, responding to requests for data from the user's application, locates and retrieves or stores the records. The tasks carried out by the access method are completely transparent to the user's application.

No single structure is best for all processing tasks. Selecting one, therefore, involves a trade-off between desirable features. The criteria that influence the selection of the data structure include

1. Rapid file access and data retrieval
2. Efficient use of disk storage space
3. High throughput for transaction processing
4. Protection from data loss
5. Ease of recovery from system failure
6. Accommodation of file growth

In Chapter 8, we introduce data extraction software for performing substantive tests of details. At that time, we examine a number of data structures used in both flat-file and database environments.

DBMS Models

A data model is an abstract representation of the data about entities, including resources (assets), events (transactions), and agents (personnel or customers, etc.) and their relationships in an organization. The purpose of a data model is to represent entity attributes in a way that is understandable to users.

Each DBMS is based on a particular conceptual model. Three common models are the hierarchical, the network, and the relational models. Because of certain conceptual similarities, we shall examine the hierarchical and network models first. These are termed **navigational models** because of explicit links or paths among their data elements. We shall then review the defining features of the relational model, which is based on implicit linkages between data elements.

Database Terminology

Before introducing these models formally, we need to review some important database terms and concepts:

Data Attribute/Field. A **data attribute** (or **field**) is a single item of data, such as customer's name, account balance, or address.

Entity. An **entity** is a database representation of an individual resource, event, or agent about which we choose to collect data. Entities may be physical (inventories, customers, and employees) or conceptual (sales, accounts receivable, and depreciation expense).

Record Type (Table or File). When we group together the data attributes that logically define an entity, they form a **record type**. For example, the data attributes describing the *sales* event could form the *sales order* record type. Multiple occurrences (more than one) of a particular type of record are physically arranged in tables or files. In other words, a company's sales order record types are physically stored in their Sales Order table, which is part of their corporate database.

Database. A database is the set of record types that an organization needs to support its business processes. Some organizations employ a distributed database approach and create different databases for each of its primary functional areas. Such an organization may have separate databases for marketing, accounting, production, etc. Later in this chapter we review techniques for distributing databases. Other organizations design their systems around a single database. In Chapter 11 we examine enterprise resource planning (ERP) systems that integrate all business functions through a single entity-wide database.

Associations. Record types that constitute a database exist in relation to other record types. This is called an **association**. Three basic record associations are: one-to-one, one-to-many, and many-to-many.

- *One-to-one association.* Figure 4.7(A) shows the **one-to-one (1:1) association**. This means that for every occurrence in Record Type X, there is one (or possibly zero) occurrence in Record Type Y. For example, for every occurrence (employee) in the employee table, there is only one (or zero for new employees) occurrence in the year-to-date earnings table.
- *One-to-many association.* Figure 4.7(B) shows the **one-to-many (1:M) association**. For every occurrence in Record Type X, there are zero, one, or many occurrences in Record Type Y. To illustrate, for every occurrence (customer) in the customer able, there are zero, one, or many sales orders in the sales order table. This means that a particular customer may have purchased goods from the company zero, one or many times during the period under review.

FIGURE 4.7   Record Associations

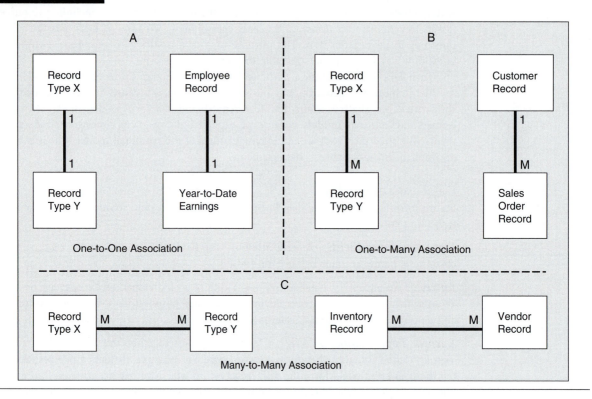

- *Many-to-many association.* Figure 4.7(C) illustrates a **many-to-many (M:M) associ-ation**. For each occurrence of Record Types X and Y, there are zero, one, or many occurrences of Record Types Y and X, respectively. The business relationship be-tween an organization's inventory and its suppliers illustrates the M:M association. Using this example, a particular supplier provides the company with zero (the sup-plier is in the database, but the firm does not buy from the supplier), one, or many inventory items. Similarly, the company may buy a particular inventory item from zero (e.g., the firm makes the item in-house), one, or many different suppliers.

The Hierarchical Model

The earliest database management systems were based on the **hierarchical data model**. This was a popular method of data representation because it reflected, more or less faithfully, many aspects of an organization that are hierarchical in relationship. IBM's **information management system (IMS)** is the most prevalent example of a hier-archical database. It was introduced in 1968 and is still a popular database model over 40 years later. Figure 4.8 presents a data structure diagram showing a portion of a hierarchi-cal database. The hierarchical model is constructed of sets that describe the relationship between two linked files. Each set contains a *parent* and a *child*. Notice that File B, at the second level, is both the child in one set and the parent in another set. Files at the same level with the same parent are called *siblings*. This structure is also called a *tree structure*. The highest level in the tree is the *root* segment, and the lowest file in a particular branch is called a *leaf*.

FIGURE 4.8   Hierarchical Data Model

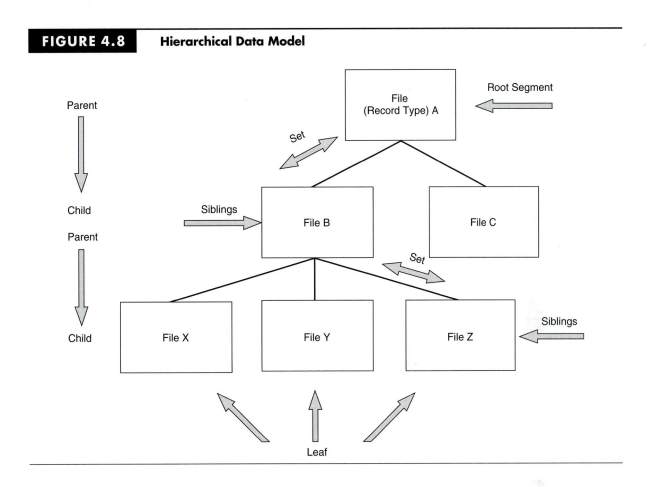

Navigational Databases. The hierarchical data model is called a *navigational database* because traversing the files requires following a predefined path. This is established through explicit linkages (pointers) between related records. The only way to access data at lower levels in the tree is from the root and via the pointers down the navigational path to the desired records. For example, consider the partial database in Figure 4.9. To retrieve an invoice line item record, the DBMS must first access the customer record (the root).

FIGURE 4.9

Portion of a Hierarchical Database

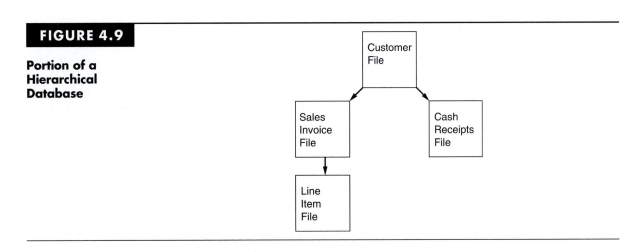

That record contains a pointer to the sales invoice record, which points to the invoice line item record. We examine the steps in this process in more detail later.

Data Integration in the Hierarchical Model.

Figure 4.10 shows the detailed file structures for the partial database in Figure 4.9. Since the purpose of this example is to illustrate the navigational nature of the model, the data content of the records has been simplified.

Assume that a user wishes to retrieve, for inquiry purposes, data pertinent to a particular sales invoice (Number 1921) for customer John Smith (Account Number 1875). The user provides the query application with the primary key (Cust #1875), which searches the *customer* file for a corresponding key value. Upon matching the key, it directly accesses John Smith's record. Notice the customer record contains only summary information. The current balance figure represents the total dollar amount owed ($1,820) by John Smith. This is the difference between the sum of all sales to this customer minus all cash received in payment on account. The supporting details about these transactions are in lower-level sales invoice and cash receipts records.

From a menu, the user selects the option "List Invoices." From this input, the query application reads the pointer value stored in the customer record, which directs it to the specific location (the disk address) where the first invoice for customer John Smith resides. These invoice records are arranged as a linked-list, with each record containing a pointer to the next one in the list. The application will follow each of the pointers and retrieve each record in the list. The sales invoice records contain only summary information pertaining to sales transactions. Additional pointers in these records show the locations of supporting detail records (the specific items sold) in the invoice *line item* file. The application then prompts the user to enter the key value sought (Invoice Number 1921) or select it from a menu. Upon entering this input, the application reads the pointer to the first line item record. Starting with the head (first) record, the application retrieves the entire list of line items for Invoice Number 1921. In this example, there are only two records associated with the invoice—item numbers 9215 and 3914. The sales invoice and line item records are then displayed on the user's computer screen.

Limitations of the Hierarchical Model.

The hierarchical model presents an artificially constrained view of data relationships. Based on the proposition that all business relationships are hierarchical (or can be represented as such), this model does not always reflect reality. The following rules, which govern the hierarchical model, reveal its operating constraints:

1. A parent record may have one or more child records. For example, in Figure 4.9, customer is the parent of both sales invoice and cash receipts.
2. No child record can have more than one parent.

The second rule is often restrictive and limits the usefulness of the hierarchical model. Many firms need a view of data associations that permit multiple parents, such as that represented by Figure 4.11(a). In this example, the sales invoice file has two natural parents: the customer file and the salesperson file. A specific sales order is the product of both the customer's purchase event and a salesperson's selling event. Management, wishing to integrate sales activity with customer service and employee performance evaluation, will need to view sales order records as the logical child of both parents. This relationship, although logical, violates the single parent rule of the hierarchical model. Since complex relationships cannot be depicted, data integration is restricted.

Figure 4.11(b) shows the most common way of resolving this problem. By duplicating the sales invoice file (and the related line item file), we create two separate hierarchical representations. Unfortunately, we achieve this improved functionality at the cost of

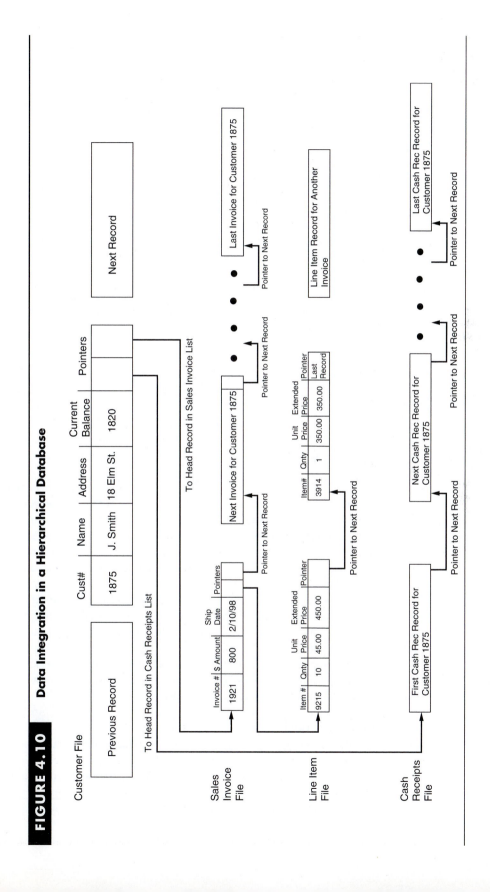

FIGURE 4.10 Data Integration in a Hierarchical Database

FIGURE 4.11

**Multiple Parent
Association**

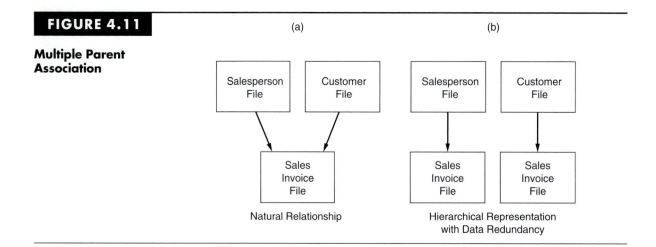

increased data redundancy. The network model, which we examine next, deals with this problem more efficiently.

The Network Model

In the late 1970s, an ANSI committee created the Committee on Development of Applied Symbolic Languages (CODASYL), which formed a database task group to develop standards for database design. CODASYL developed the **network model** for databases. The most popular example of the network model is **IDMS (integrated database management system)**, which Cullinane/Cullinet Software introduced into the commercial market in the 1980s. Although this model has undergone many changes over the years, it is still in use today.

Like the hierarchical model, the network model is a navigational database with explicit linkages between records and files. The distinction is that the network model permits a child record to have multiple parents. For example, referring to Figure 4.12, Invoice Number 1 is the child of Salesperson Number 1 and Customer Number 5. Pointer fields in both parent records explicitly define the path to the invoice (child) record. This invoice record has two links to related (sibling) records. The first is a salesperson (SP) link to Invoice Number 2. This record resulted from a sale by Salesperson Number 1 to Customer Number 6. The second pointer is the customer (C) link to Invoice Number 3. This represents the second sale to Customer Number 5, which was processed this time by Salesperson Number 2. Under this data structure, management can track and report sales information pertaining to customers and sales staff.

The structure can be accessed at either of the root level records (salesperson or customer) by entering the appropriate primary key (SP # or Cust #). Beyond this, the access process is similar to that described for the hierarchical model.

The Relational Model

E. F. Codd originally proposed the principles of the **relational model** in the late 1960s.[1] The formal model has its foundations in relational algebra and set theory, which provide the theoretical basis for most of the data manipulation operations used. The most apparent difference between the relational model and the navigational models is the way in which data associations are represented to the user. The relational model portrays data

---

1   C. J. Date, *An Introduction to Database Systems*, vol. 1, 4th ed. (Reading, MS: Addison-Wesley, 1986), p. 99.

FIGURE 4.12   Linkages in a Network Database

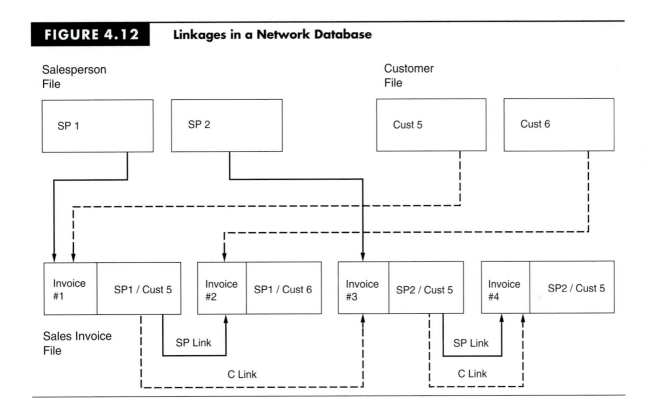

in the form of two-dimensional tables. Figure 4.13 presents an example of a database table called Customer.

Across the top of the table are **attributes** (data fields) forming columns. Intersecting the columns to form rows in the table are **tuples**. A tuple is a normalized array of data that is similar, but not precisely equivalent, to a record in a flat-file system. Properly designed tables possess the following four characteristics:

1. All occurrences at the intersection of a row and a column are a single value. No multiple values (repeating groups) are allowed.
2. The attribute values in any column must all be of the same class.
3. Each column in a given table must be uniquely named. However, different tables may contain columns with the same name.
4. Each row in the table must be unique in at least one attribute. This attribute is the primary key.

The table should be normalized. Each attribute in the row should be dependent on (uniquely defined by) the primary key and independent of the other attributes. In the previous section, we saw how navigational databases use explicit linkages (pointers) between records to establish relationships. The linkages in the relational model are implicit. To illustrate this distinction, compare the file structures of the relational tables in Figure 4.14 with those of the hierarchical example in Figure 4.10. The conceptual relationship between files is the same, but note the absence of explicit pointers in the relational tables.

Relations are formed by an attribute that is common to both tables in the relation. For example, the primary key of the Customer table (Cust #) is also an embedded foreign key in both the Sales Invoice and Cash Receipts tables. Similarly, the primary key in

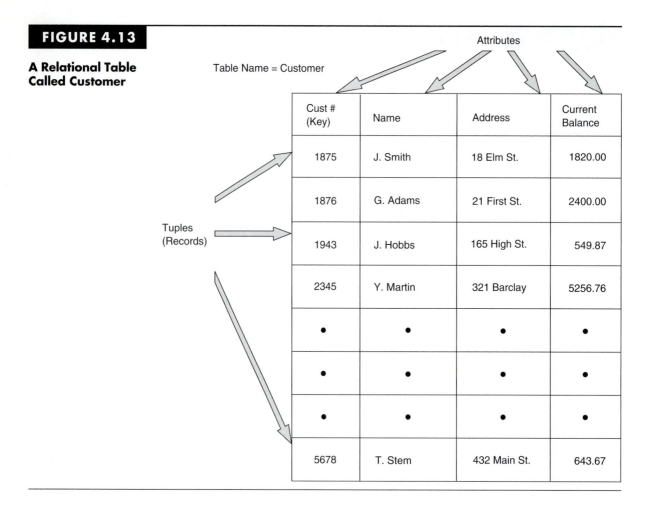

FIGURE 4.13

A Relational Table Called Customer

the Sales Invoice table (Invoice #) is a foreign key in the Line Item table. Note that the Line Item table uses a composite primary key comprising two fields—Invoice # and Item #. Both fields are needed to identify each record in the table uniquely, but only the invoice number portion of the key provides the logical link to the Sales Invoice table.

Linkages between records in related tables are established through logical operations of the DBMS rather than via explicit addressees that are structured into the database. For example, if a user wants to view all the invoices for Customer 1875, the system would search the Sales Invoice table for records with a foreign key value of 1875. We see from Figure 4.14 that there is only one—Invoice 1921. To obtain the line item details for this invoice, a search is made of the Line Item table for records with a foreign key value of 1921. Two records are retrieved.

The degree of the association between two tables determines the method used for assigning foreign keys. Where the association is one-to-one, either table's primary key may be embedded in the other as a foreign key. In one-to-many associations, the primary key on the "one" side is embedded as the foreign key on the "many" side. For example, one customer may have many invoice and cash receipts records. Therefore, the Cust # is embedded in the records of the Sales Invoice and Cash Receipts tables. Similarly, there is a one-to-many association between the Sales Invoice and Line Item tables. Many-to-many associations between tables do not use embedded foreign keys. Instead, a

FIGURE 4.14   Data Integration in the Relational Model

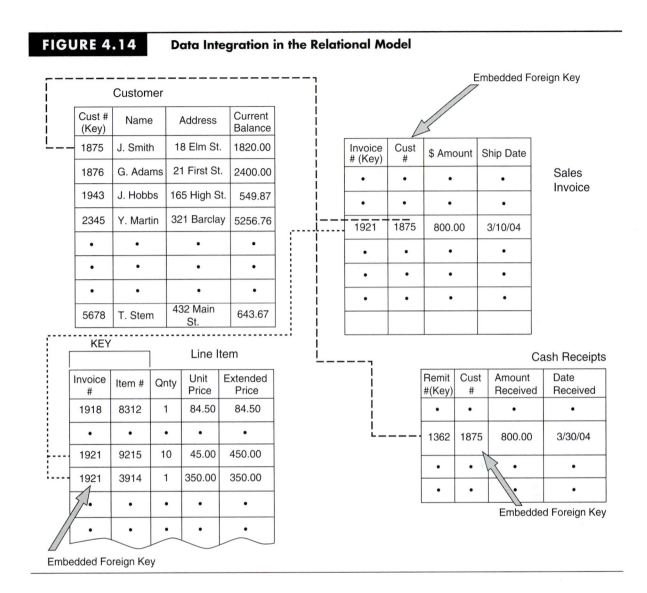

separate link table containing keys for the related tables needs to be created. In Chapter 8, we examine the design of relational tables in more detail.

DATABASES IN A DISTRIBUTED ENVIRONMENT

Chapter 2 presented the concept of distributed data processing (DDP). The physical structure of the organization's data is an important consideration in planning a distributed system. In addressing this issue, the planner has two basic options: the databases can be centralized or they can be distributed. Distributed databases fall into two categories: partitioned databases and replicated databases. This section examines issues, features, and trade-offs that need to be evaluated in deciding the disposition of the database.

Centralized Databases

The first approach involves retaining the data in a central location. Remote IT units send requests for data to the central site, which processes the requests and transmits the data back to the requesting IT unit. The actual processing of the data is performed at the remote IT unit. The central site performs the functions of a file manager that services the data needs of the remote sites. The centralized database approach is illustrated in Figure 4.15. A fundamental objective of the database approach is to maintain data currency. This can be a challenging task in a DDP environment.

Data Currency in a DDP Environment

During data processing, account balances pass through a state of **temporary inconsistency** where their values are incorrectly stated. This occurs during the execution of a transaction. To illustrate, consider the computer logic below for recording the credit sale of $2,000 to customer Jones.

INSTRUCTION		DATABASE VALUES	
		AR-Jones	AR-Control
	START		
1	Read AR-SUB account (Jones)	1500	
2	Read AR-Control account		10000
3	Write AR-SUB account (Jones) + $2000	3500	
4	Write AR-Control account + $2000		12000
	END		

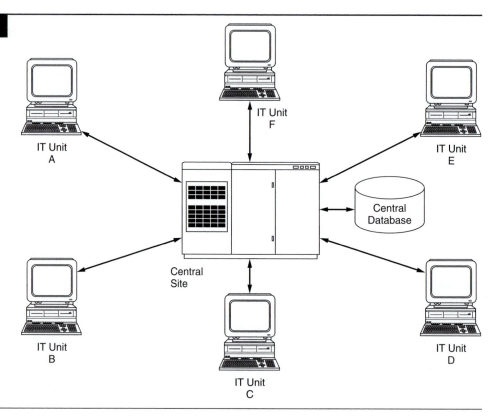

FIGURE 4.15

Centralized Database

IT Unit F

IT Unit A

IT Unit E

Central Site

Central Database

IT Unit B

IT Unit C

IT Unit D

Immediately after the execution of Instruction Number 3, and before the execution of Instruction Number 4, the AR-Control account value is temporarily inconsistent by the sum of $2,000. Only after the completion of the entire transaction is this inconsistency resolved. In a DDP environment, such temporary inconsistencies can result in the corruption of data. To illustrate the potential for damage, let's look at a slightly more complicated example. Using the same computer logic as before, consider the processing of two separate transactions from two remote IT units: Transaction 1 (T1) is the sale of $2,000 on account to customer Jones from IT unit A; Transaction 2 (T2) is the sale of $1,000 on account to customer Smith from IT unit B. The following logic shows the possible interweaving of the two processing tasks and the potential effect on data currency.

INSTRUCTION			DATABASE VALUES		
				Central Site	
IT UNIT A	IT UNIT B		AR-Jones	AR-Smith	AR-Control
T1	T2	START			
1		Read AR-SUB account (Jones)	1500		
	1	Read AR-SUB account (Smith)		3000	
2		Read AR-Control account			10000
3		Write AR-SUB account (Jones) + $2000	3500		
	2	**Read AR-Control account**			10000
4		Write AR-Control account + $2000			12000
	3	Write AR-SUB account (Smith) + $1000		4000	
	4	Write AR-Control account + $1000 END			11000

Notice that IT unit B seized the AR-Control data value of $10,000 when it was in an inconsistent state. By using this value to process its transaction, IT unit B effectively erased Transaction T1, which had been processed by IT unit A. Therefore, instead of $13,000, the new AR-Control balance is misstated at $11,000.

To achieve data currency, simultaneous access to individual data elements by multiple IT units must be prevented. The solution to this problem is to employ a **database lockout**, which is a software control (usually a function of the DBMS) that prevents multiple simultaneous accesses to data. The previous example can be used to illustrate this technique. Immediately upon receiving the access request from IT unit A for AR-Control (T1, Instruction Number 2), the central site DBMS should place a lock on AR-Control to prevent access from other IT units until Transaction T1 is complete. When IT unit B requests AR-Control (T2, Instruction Number 2), it is placed on "wait" status until the lock is removed. When site A's transaction has been posted, IT unit B is granted access to AR-Control and can then complete Transaction T2.

Distributed Databases

Distributed databases can be either partitioned or replicated. We examine both approaches in the following pages.

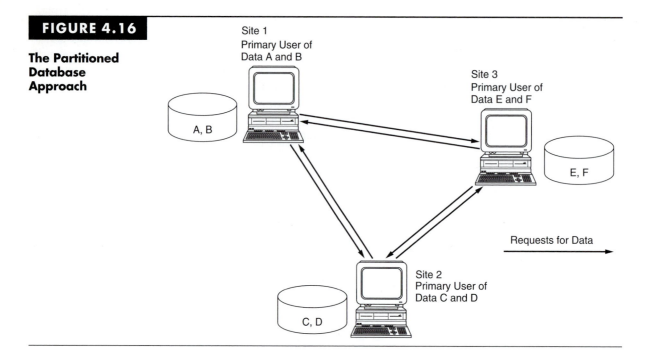

FIGURE 4.16

The Partitioned Database Approach

Partitioned Databases

The **partitioned database approach** splits the central database into segments or partitions that are distributed to their primary users. The advantages of this approach follow:

- Having data stored at local sites increases users' control.
- Transaction processing response time is improved by permitting local access to data and reducing the volume of data that must be transmitted between IT units.
- Partitioned databases can reduce the potential effects of a disaster. By locating data at several sites, the loss of a single IT unit does not eliminate all data processing by the organization.

The partitioned approach, which is illustrated in Figure 4.16, works best for organizations that require minimal data sharing among their distributed IT units. The primary user manages data requests from other sites. To minimize data access from remote users, the organization needs to carefully select the host location. Identifying the optimum host requires an in-depth analysis of user data needs.

The Deadlock Phenomenon. In a distributed environment, it is possible for multiple sites to lock out each other from the database, thus preventing each from processing its transactions. For example, Figure 4.17 illustrates three IT units and their mutual data needs. Notice that Site 1 has requested (and locked) Data A and is waiting for the removal of the lock on Data C to complete its transaction. Site 2 has a lock on C and is waiting for E. Finally, Site 3 has a lock on E and is waiting for A. A deadlock occurs here because there is mutual exclusion to the data resource, and the transactions are in a "wait" state until the locks are removed. This can result in transactions being incompletely processed and the database being corrupted. A **deadlock** is a permanent condition that must be resolved by special software that analyzes each deadlock condition to determine the best solution. Because of the implication for transaction processing, accountants should be aware of the issues pertaining to deadlock resolutions.

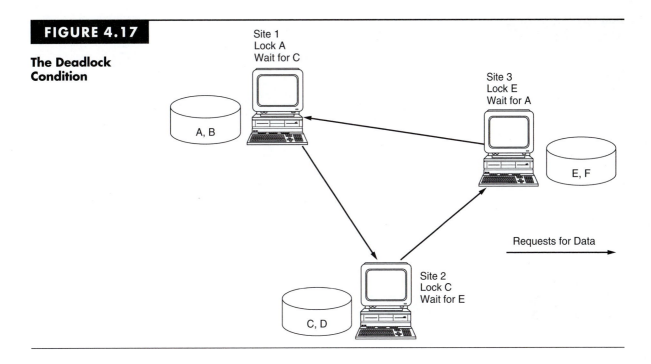

FIGURE 4.17

The Deadlock Condition

Deadlock Resolution.   Resolving a deadlock usually involves terminating one or more transactions to complete processing of the other transactions in the deadlock. The preempted transactions must then be reinitiated. In preempting transactions, the deadlock resolution software attempts to minimize the total cost of breaking the deadlock. Some of the factors that are considered in this decision follow:

- *The resources currently invested in the transaction.* This may be measured by the number of updates that the transaction has already performed and that must be repeated if the transaction is terminated.
- *The transaction's stage of completion.* In general, deadlock resolution software will avoid terminating transactions that are close to completion.
- *The number of deadlocks associated with the transaction.* Because terminating the transaction breaks all deadlock involvement, the software should attempt to terminate transactions that are part of more than one deadlock.

Replicated Databases

Replicated databases are effective in companies where there exists a high degree of data sharing but no primary user. Since common data are replicated at each IT unit site, the data traffic between sites is reduced considerably. Figure 4.18 illustrates the replicated database model.

The primary justification for a replicated database is to support read-only queries. With data replicated at every site, data access for query purposes is ensured, and lockouts and delays due to data traffic are minimized. The problem with this approach is maintaining current versions of the database at each site. Since each IT unit processes only its transactions, common data replicated at each site are affected by different transactions and reflect different values. Using the data from the earlier example, Figure 4.19 illustrates the effect of processing credit sales for Jones at site A and Smith at site B. After the transactions are processed, the value shown for the common AR-Control account is inconsistent ($12,000 at IT unit A and $11,000 at IT unit B) and incorrect at both sites.

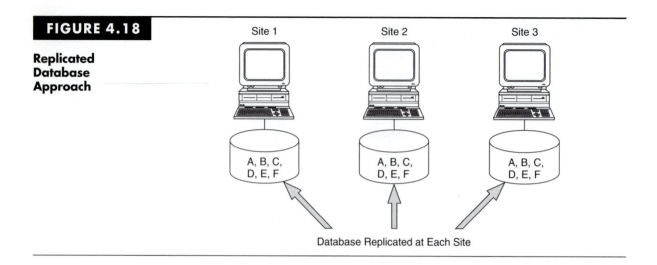

FIGURE 4.18

**Replicated
Database
Approach**

Site 1   Site 2   Site 3

A, B, C,   A, B, C,   A, B, C,
D, E, F   D, E, F   D, E, F

Database Replicated at Each Site

FIGURE 4.19   Replicated Databases Updated Independently

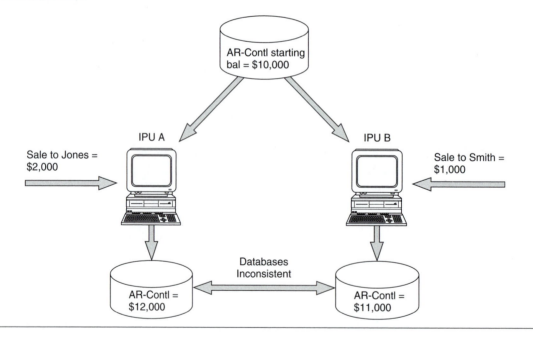

AR-Contl starting
bal = $10,000

IPU A   IPU B

Sale to Jones =   Sale to Smith =
$2,000 $1,000

Databases
Inconsistent

AR-Contl =   AR-Contl =
$12,000 $11,000

Concurrency Control

Database concurrency is the presence of complete and accurate data at all user sites. System designers need to employ methods to ensure that transactions processed at each site are accurately reflected in the databases of all the other sites. Because of the implication for the accuracy of accounting records, the concurrency problem is a matter of concern for auditors. A commonly used method for **concurrency control** is to serialize transactions. This method involves labeling each transaction by two criteria.

First, special software groups transactions into classes to identify potential conflicts. For example, read-only (query) transactions do not conflict with other classes of transactions.

Similarly, accounts payable and accounts receivable transactions are not likely to use the same data and do not conflict. However, multiple sales order transactions involving both read and write operations will potentially conflict.

The second part of the control process is to time-stamp each transaction. A system-wide clock is used to keep all sites, some of which may be in different time zones, on the same logical time. Each time stamp is made unique by incorporating the site's ID number. When transactions are received at each IT unit site, they are examined first by class for potential conflicts. If conflicts exist, the transactions are entered into a serialization schedule. An algorithm is used to schedule updates to the database based on the transaction time stamp and class. This method permits multiple interleaved transactions to be processed at each site with the effect of being executed serially.

Database Distribution Methods and the Accountant

The decision to distribute databases is one that should be entered into thoughtfully. There are many issues and trade-offs to consider. Here are some of the most basic questions to be addressed:

- Should the organization's data be centralized or distributed?
- If data distribution is desirable, should the databases be replicated or partitioned?
- If replicated, should the databases be totally replicated or partially replicated?
- If the database is to be partitioned, how should the data segments be allocated among the sites?

The choices involved in each of these questions impact the organization's ability to maintain data integrity. The preservation of audit trails and the accuracy of accounting records are key concerns. Clearly, these are decisions that the modern auditor should understand and influence intelligently.

CONTROLLING AND AUDITING DATA MANAGEMENT SYSTEMS

Controls over data management systems fall into two general categories: access controls and backup controls. **Access controls** are designed to prevent unauthorized individuals from viewing, retrieving, corrupting, or destroying the entity's data. **Backup controls** ensure that in the event of data loss due to unauthorized access, equipment failure, or physical disaster the organization can recover its database.

Access Controls

Users of flat files maintain exclusive ownership of their data. In spite of the data integration problems associated with this model, it creates an environment in which unauthorized access to data can be effectively controlled. When not in use by the owner, a flat file is closed to other users and may be taken off-line and physically secured in the data library. In contrast, the need to integrate and share data in the database environment means that databases must remain on-line and open to all potential users.

In the shared database environment, access control risks include corruption, theft, misuse, and destruction of data. These threats originate from both unauthorized intruders and authorized users who exceed their access privileges. Several control features are now reviewed.

User Views

The *user view* or subschema is a subset of the total database that defines the user's data domain and provides access to the database. Figure 4.20 illustrates the role of the user

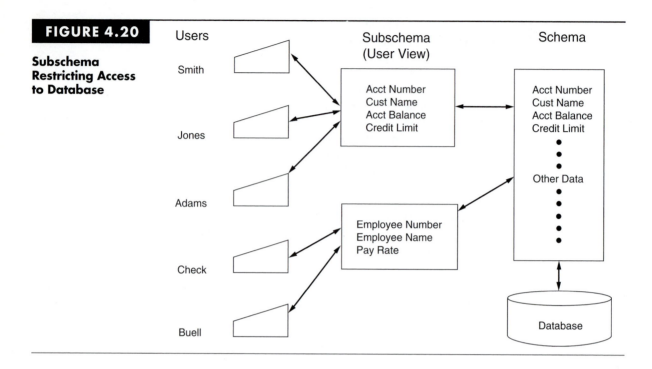

FIGURE 4.20

Subschema Restricting Access to Database

view. In a centralized database environment, the database administrator (DBA) has primary responsibility for user view design but works closely with users and systems designers in this task. Access privileges to the database, as defined in their views, should be commensurate with the users' legitimate needs.

Although user views can restrict user access to a limited set of data, they do not define task privileges such as read, delete, or write. Often, several users may share a single user view but have different authority levels. For example, users Smith, Jones, and Adams in Figure 4.20 all may have access to the same set of data: account number, customer name, account balance, and credit limit. Let's assume that all have read authority, but only Jones has authority to modify and delete the data. Effective access control requires more additional security measures, discussed next.

Database Authorization Table

The **database authorization table** contains rules that limit the actions a user can take. This technique is similar to the access control list used in the operating system. Each user is granted certain privileges that are coded in the authority table, which is used to verify the user's action requests. For example, Figure 4.20 shows that Jones, Smith, and Adams have access to the same data attributes via a common user view, but the authorization table in Table 4.3 shows that only Jones has the authority to modify and delete the data. Each row in the authority table indicates the level of action (read, insert, modify, or delete) that individuals can take based on their entering the correct password.

User-Defined Procedures

A **user-defined procedure** allows the user to create a personal security program or routine to provide more positive user identification than a single password. Thus, in addition to a password, the security procedure asks a series of personal questions (such as the user's mother's maiden name), which only the legitimate user should know.

| TABLE 4.3 | **Database Authorization Table** |

Database Authorization Table

Dept	Accounts Rec			Billings	
User	Jones	Smith	Adams	Check	Buell
Password	Bugs	Dog	Katie	Lucky	Star
Authority:					
Read	Y	Y	Y	Y	Y
Insert	Y	N	Y	Y	N
Modify	Y	N	N	Y	N
Delete	Y	N	N	N	N

Data Encryption

In Chapter 2 we examined the use of encryption for protecting data that are transmitted over communications lines. Database systems also use encryption procedures to protect highly sensitive stored data, such as product formulas, personnel pay rates, password files, and certain financial data thus making it unreadable to an intruder "browsing" the database.

Biometric Devices

The ultimate in user authentication procedures is the use of **biometric devices**, which measure various personal characteristics, such as fingerprints, voice prints, retina prints, or signature characteristics. These user characteristics are digitized and stored permanently in a database security file or on an identification card that the user carries. When an individual attempts to access the database, a special scanning device captures his or her biometric characteristics, which it compares with the profile data stored on file or the ID card. If the data do not match, access is denied. Biometric technology is currently being used to secure ATM cards and credit cards. Because of the distributed nature of modern systems, the degree of remote access to systems, the decline in costs of biometric systems, and the increased effectiveness of biometric systems, biometric devices have a great potential to serve as effective means of access control, especially from remote locations.

Inference Controls

One advantage of the database query capability is that it provides users with summary and statistical data for decision making. For example, managers might ask the following questions:

- What is the total value for inventory items with monthly turnover less than three?
- What is the average charge to patients with hospital stays greater than 8 days?
- What is the total cost of Class II payroll for department XYZ?

Answers to these types of questions are needed routinely for resource management, facility planning, and operations control decisions. Legitimate queries sometimes involve access to confidential data. Thus, individual users may be granted summary and statistical query access to confidential data to which they normally are denied direct access.

To preserve the confidentiality and integrity of the database, **inference controls** should be in place to prevent users from inferring, through query features, specific data

TABLE 4.4	**Payroll Database Containing Confidential Data**

Payroll Database

Empl#	Name	Job Title	Salary	Sex	Other Data	
5439	Jim Jones	Consultant	50,000	Male	•	•
9887	Sam Smith	Lawyer	60,000	Male	•	•
8765	Mary Swindle	Lawyer	65,000	Female	•	•
4462	Bob Haub	Manager	60,000	Male	•	•
7742	Joan Hess	Consultant	50,000	Female	•	•
5532	Ben Huber	Lawyer	62,000	Male	•	•
8332	John Enis	Lawyer	63,000	Male	•	•
9662	Jim Hobbs	Consultant	70,000	Male	•	•
3391	Joe Riley	Manager	75,000	Male	•	•

values that they otherwise are unauthorized to access. Inference controls attempt to prevent three types of compromises to the database.[2]

1. *Positive compromise*—the user determines the specific value of a data item.
2. *Negative compromise*—the user determines that a data item does not have a specific value.
3. *Approximate compromise*—the user is unable to determine the exact value of an item but is able to estimate it with sufficient accuracy to violate the confidentiality of the data.

Let's use the payroll database table presented in Table 4.4 to illustrate how inference techniques are used to compromise a database. The salary field in the table is the confidential data being sought. Assuming that no inference controls are in place, a user wanting to determine the salary of Mary Swindle, a staff lawyer, could make the following queries:

> Q. How many lawyers are female?
> A. One.
> Q. What is the average salary of all who are female and lawyers?
> A. $65,000.

Since she is the only female lawyer, Mary Swindle's salary is explicitly provided by the query system through this statistical feature. This sort of compromise may be prevented by implementing the following inference control rule that places restrictions on the size of the query set to which the system will respond:

> The system will not respond to queries where fewer than two records satisfy the query.

However, a determined and creative user may easily circumvent this control with the following queries:

> Q. What is the total salary for the payroll database?
> A. $555,000.

---

2   R.Weber, *EDP Auditing Conceptual Foundations and Practice*, 2d ed. (New York: McGraw-Hill, 1988), p. 564.

Q. What is the total salary for all not lawyers and not female?
A. $490,000.

Swindle's salary can be calculated in this example by subtracting $490,000 from $555,000. Preventing this compromise requires further restrictions on the query set size. This may be accomplished with the following additional inference control rule:

The system will not respond to queries where greater than $(n - 2)$ records satisfy the query (where n is the number of records in the database).

Under this rule, neither query would have been satisfied.

Audit Objective Relating to Database Access
- Verify that database access authority and privileges are granted to users in accordance with their legitimate needs.

Audit Procedures for Testing Database Access Controls
Responsibility for Authority Tables and Subschemas.   The auditor should verify that database administration (DBA) personnel retain exclusive responsibility for creating authority tables and designing user views. Evidence may come from three sources: (1) by reviewing company policy and job descriptions, which specify these technical responsibilities; (2) by examining programmer authority tables for access privileges to data definition language (DDL) commands; and (3) through personal interviews with programmers and DBA personnel.

Appropriate Access Authority.   The auditor can select a sample of users and verify that their access privileges stored in the authority table are consistent with their job descriptions organizational levels.

Biometric Controls.   The auditor should evaluate the costs and benefits of biometric controls. Generally, these would be most appropriate where highly sensitive data are accessed by a very limited number of users.

Inference Controls.   The auditor should verify that database query controls exist to prevent unauthorized access via inference. The auditor can test controls by simulating access by a sample of users and attempting to retrieve unauthorized data via inference queries.

Encryption Controls.   The auditor should verify that sensitive data, such as passwords, are properly encrypted. Printing the file contents to hard copy can do this.

Backup Controls
Data can be corrupted and destroyed by malicious acts from external hackers, disgruntled employees, disk failure, program errors, fires, floods, and earthquakes. To recover from such disasters, organizations must implement policies, procedures, and techniques that systematically and routinely provide backup copies of critical files.

Backup Controls in the Flat-File Environment
The backup technique employed will depend on the media and the file structure. Sequential files (both tape and disk) use a backup technique called grandparent–parent–child (GPC). This backup technique is an integral part of the master file update process. Direct access files, by contrast, need a separate backup procedure. Both methods are outlined below.

GPC Backup Technique.   Figure 4.21 illustrates the **grandparent–parent–child (GPC)** backup technique that is used in sequential file batch systems. The backup procedure begins when the current master file (the parent) is processed against the transaction

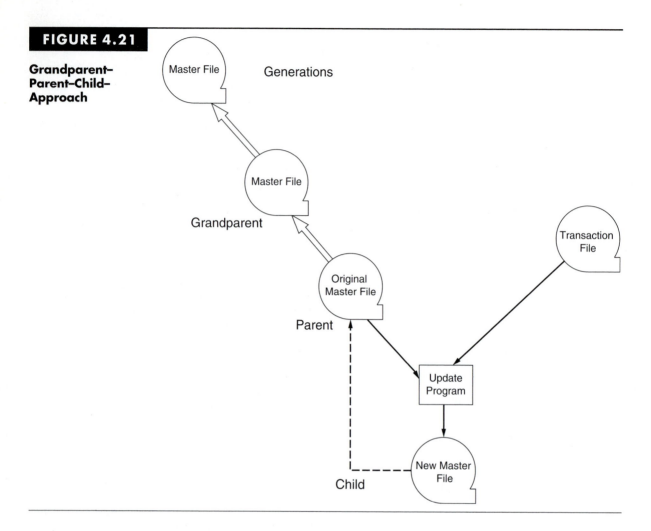

FIGURE 4.21

Grandparent–Parent–Child–Approach

file to produce a new updated master file (the child). With the next batch of transactions, the child becomes the current master file (the parent), and the original parent becomes the backup (grandparent) file. The new master file that emerges from the update process is the child. This procedure is continued with each new batch of transactions, creating generations of backup files. When the desired number of backup copies is reached, the oldest backup file is erased (scratched). If the current master file is destroyed or corrupted, processing the most current backup file against the corresponding transaction file can reproduce it.

The systems designer determines the number of backup master files needed for each application. Two factors influence this decision: (1) the financial significance of the system and (2) the degree of file activity. For example, a master file that is updated several times a day may require 30 or 40 generations of backup, while a file that is updated only once each month may need only four or five backup versions. This decision is important, because certain types of system failures can result in the destruction of large numbers of backup versions within the same family of files.

The author was witness to one system failure that destroyed, through accidental erasure, more than 150 master files in only a few hours. The destruction began when the most current master file (parent) in each application being processed was erased.

Then, one by one, the older generations were systematically scratched. Some systems lost as many as twenty backup copies. In fact, the accounts payable system had only one backup version left when the error was finally detected and stopped. Reconstruction of files after such a disaster requires locating the most current remaining backup version and methodically reprocessing the batches of past transactions until the current version of the master file is reproduced. This will also recreate all the intermediate generations of the master file. When using the GPC approach for financial systems, management and auditors should be involved in determining the needed number of backup files. Insufficient backup can result in the total destruction of accounting records. Most operating systems permit the creation of up to 256 generations for each application.

Direct Access File Backup. Data values in direct access files are changed in place through a process called *destructive replacement*. Therefore, once a data value is changed, the original value is destroyed, leaving only one version (the current version) of the file. To provide backup, direct access files must be copied before being updated. Figure 4.22 illustrates this process.

The timing of the **direct access backup** procedures will depend on the processing method being used. Backup of files in batch systems is usually scheduled prior to the update process. Real-time systems pose a more difficult problem. Since transactions are being processed continuously, the backup procedure takes place at specified intervals throughout the day (for example, every 15 minutes).

If the current version of the master file is destroyed through a disk failure or corrupted by a program error, it can be reconstructed with a special recovery program from the most current backup file. In the case of real-time systems, transactions processed since the last backup and prior to the failure will be lost and will need to be reprocessed to restore the master file to current status.

Off-Site Storage. As an added safeguard, backup files created under both the GPC and direct access approaches should be stored off-site in a secure location. **Off-site storage** was discussed in Chapter 2 in the section dealing with disaster recovery planning.

Audit Objective Relating to Flat-File Backup
- Verify that backup controls in place are effective in protecting data files from physical damage, loss, accidental erasure, and data corruption through system failures and program errors.

Audit Procedures for Testing Flat-File Backup Controls
- *Sequential File (GPC) Backup.* The auditor should select a sample of systems and determine from the system documentation that the number of GPC backup files specified for each system is adequate. If insufficient backup versions exist, recovery from some types of failures may be impossible.
- *Backup Transaction Files.* The auditor should verify through physical observation that transaction files used to reconstruct the master files are also retained. Without corresponding transaction files, reconstruction is impossible.
- *Direct Access File Backup.* The auditor should select a sample of applications and identify the direct access files being updated in each system. From system documentation and through observation, the auditor can verify that each of them was copied to tape or disk before being updated.
- *Off-Site Storage.* The auditor should verify the existence and adequacy of off-site storage. This audit procedure may be performed as part of the review of the disaster recovery plan or computer center operations controls.

FIGURE 4.22

**Backup of Direct
Access Files**

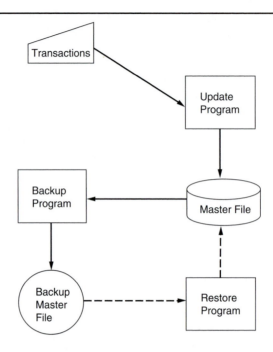

Real-Time Processing System

Real-time systems use timed backup. Transactions processed between backup runs will need to be reprocessed after restoration of the master file.

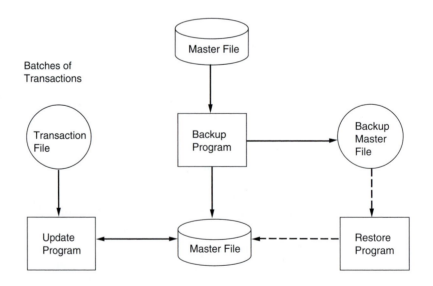

Batch Processing System

In a batch processing system using direct access files, the master file is backed up before the update run.

Backup Controls in the Database Environment

Since data sharing is a fundamental objective of the database approach, this environment is particularly vulnerable to damage from individual users. One unauthorized procedure, one malicious act, or one program error can deprive an entire user community of its information resource. Also, because of data centralization, even minor disasters such as a disk failure can affect many or all users. When such events occur, the organization needs to reconstruct the database to pre-failure status. This can be done only if the database was properly backed up in the first place. Most mainframe DBMSs have a backup and recovery system similar to the one illustrated in Figure 4.23. This system provides four backup and recovery features: database backup, a transaction log, checkpoints, and a recovery module.

Backup. The backup feature makes a periodic backup of the entire database. This is an automatic procedure that should be performed at least once a day. The backup copy should then be stored in a secure remote area.

Transaction Log (Journal). The **transaction log** feature provides an audit trail of all processed transactions. It lists transactions in a transaction log file and records the resulting changes to the database in a separate database change log.

Checkpoint Feature. The **checkpoint** facility suspends all data processing while the system reconciles the transaction log and the database change log against the database. At this point, the system is in a *quiet state*. Checkpoints occur automatically several times an hour. If a failure occurs, it is usually possible to restart the processing from the last checkpoint. Thus, only a few minutes of transaction processing must be repeated.

Recovery Module. The **recovery module** uses the logs and backup files to restart the system after a failure.

FIGURE 4.23

Backup of Direct Access Files

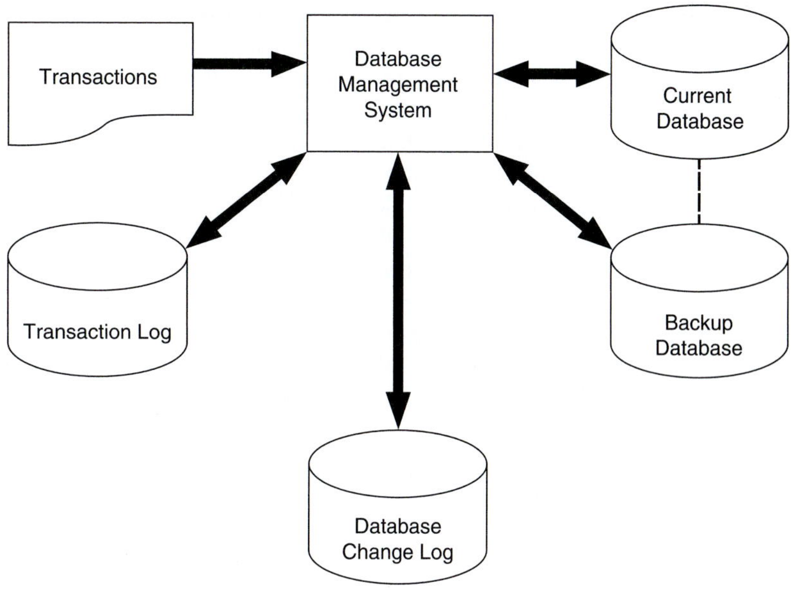

Audit Objective Relating to Database Backup

- Verify that controls over the data resource are sufficient to preserve the integrity and physical security of the database.

Audit Procedures for Testing Database Backup Controls

- The auditor should verify that backup is performed routinely and frequently to facilitate the recovery of lost, destroyed, or corrupted data without excessive reprocessing. Production databases should be copied at regular intervals (perhaps several times an hour). Backup policy should strike a balance between the inconvenience of frequent backup activities and the business disruption caused by excessive reprocessing that is needed to restore the database after a failure.
- The auditor should verify that automatic backup procedures are in place and functioning, and that copies of the database are stored off-site for further security.

SUMMARY

Data management can be divided into two general approaches: the flat-file model and the database model. The chapter began with a description of flat-file data management, which is used in many older (legacy) systems. Private ownership of data characterizes this model and is the cause of several problems that inhibit data integration. A conceptual overview of the database model was used to illustrate how the problems associated with the flat-file model can be resolved through data sharing and centralized control of data.

The second section described the key functions and defining features of three common database models: the hierarchical, the network, and the relational models. The hierarchical and network models are called navigational databases because of their structure and inflexibility. Seen as a marked improvement over flat files, navigational databases were used in the design of many late-era legacy systems that are still in operation today. Newer accounting information systems, however, make extensive use of the relational model. This model presents data in a two-dimensional format that is easy for end users to understand and work with. When properly implemented, the relational model effectively supports entity-wide data integration.

The third section examined the database technology and applications in the distributed environment. Distributed data processing (DDP) empowers end users with ownership and control of IT resources, including databases. This section presented techniques for achieving the goals of DDP while maintaining the principles of data sharing and integration. Three alternative configurations were examined: centralized, replicated, and partitioned databases.

The chapter concluded with a discussion of the control and audit issues related to data management. The risks, audit objectives, and audit procedures relevant to flat files and database systems were presented.

KEY TERMS

access controls
access method
application development software
association
attribute

backup controls
biometric device
checkpoint
conceptual view
concurrency control

currency of information
data attribute (field)
data definition language (DDL)
data dictionary
data manipulation language (DML)
data redundancy
data storage
data structure
data updating
database administrator (DBA)
database authorization table
database lockout
database management system (DBMS)
database model
deadlock
direct access backup
entity
field
flat-file model
grandparent–parent–child (GPC)
hierarchical data model
IDMS (Integrated Database Management System)
inference controls
information management system (IMS)

internal view
legacy systems
many-to-many (M:M) association
navigational models
network model
off-site storage
one-to-many (1:M) association
one-to-one (1:1) association
organization
partitioned database approach
physical database
record type
recovery module
relational model
replicated database
schema (conceptual view)
Structured Query Language (SQL)
subschema (user view)
task-data dependency
temporary inconsistency
transaction log
tuple
user view
user-defined procedure

REVIEW QUESTIONS

1. What is a legacy system?
2. What is the flat-file model?
3. What are the four primary elements of the database approach?
4. What types of problems does data redundancy cause?
5. What flat-file data management problems are solved as a result of using the database concept?
6. What are four ways in which database management systems provide a controlled environment to manage user access and the data resources?
7. Explain the relationship between the three levels of the data definition language. As a user, which level would you be most interested in?
8. What is the internal view of a database?
9. What is SQL?
10. What is DML?
11. What is a data dictionary, and what purpose does it serve?
12. What are the two fundamental components of data structures?
13. What are the criteria that influence the selection of the data structure?
14. What is a data attribute (or field)?
15. Define a data record.
16. What is a record association?
17. What is a database?
18. What is an enterprise database?
19. Discuss and give an example of one-to-one, one-to-many, and many-to-many record associations.
20. Why is a hierarchical database model considered to be a navigational database? What are some limitations of the hierarchical database model?
21. What is a partitioned database, and what are its advantages? Specify any disadvantages.
22. What is a replicated database, and why is concurrency control difficult to manage in this setting?
23. What is time-stamping, and why is it useful?
24. Explain the grandparent–parent–child backup technique. Is it used for sequential files or direct access techniques? Why? How many generations can be backed up?

25. Distinguish between data access and access privileges. Give an example by designing and explaining a database authorization table.
26. What are inference controls? Why are they needed?
27. What are the four basic backup and recovery features necessary in a DBMS? Briefly explain each.
28. What is data encryption?
29. What are biometric devices?
30. What is a user-defined procedure?

DISCUSSION QUESTIONS

1. In the flat-file data management environment, users are said to own their data files. What is meant by this "ownership" concept?
2. Discuss the potential aggravations you might face as a student as a result of your university using a traditional data management environment—that is, different databases for the registrar, library, parking permits, and so on.
3. Discuss why control procedures over access to the database become more crucial under the database concept than in the flat-file data management environment. What role does the DBMS play in helping to control the database environment?
4. What is the relationship between a schema and a subschema?
5. Discuss the two ways in which users can access the database in a database environment.
6. How are special database commands inserted into conventional application programs? Why is this necessary?
7. Why might it be advantageous for an organization to use DML commands written in COBOL versus a proprietary programming language?
8. SQL has been said to place power in the hands of the user. What is meant by this statement?
9. Discuss the importance of the role of the database administrator. Why wasn't such a role necessary in the traditional data management environment? What tasks are performed by the DBA?
10. As users determine new computer application needs, requests must be sent to both the system programmers and the DBA. Why is it important that these two groups perform separate functions, and what are these functions?
11. How can data be centralized in a distributed data processing system?
12. In a distributed data processing system, why can temporary inconsistencies result in permanent damage to accounting records? Explain with an example.
13. Explain the deadlock phenomenon. Discuss how it could occur with a phone-in mail order system that locks the inventory records until the order is complete.
14. Which database method would be most appropriate for ticket sales at thirty different outlets to an assigned seating concert? Why?
15. Why is it risky to allow programmers to create user subschemas and assign access authority to users? What unethical technique do programmers sometimes use when they are not allowed to assign access authority to users?
16. Is access control of greater concern in the flat-file or database file environment?
17. How can passwords actually circumvent security? What actions can be taken to minimize this?
18. Describe the characteristics of properly designed relational tables.
19. In a database environment, individual users may be granted summary and statistical query access to confidential data to which they normally are denied direct access. Describe how security can be preserved through inference controls.
20. Describe the backup and recovery features of centralized DBMSs.

MULTIPLE-CHOICE QUESTIONS

1. The database approach has several unique characteristics not found in traditional (flat-file) systems, specifically file-oriented systems. Which one of the following statements does not apply to the database model?
   a. Database systems have data independence; that is, the data and the programs are maintained separately, except during processing.
   b. Database systems contain a data definition language that helps describe each schema and subschema.
   c. The database administrator is the part of the software package that instructs the operating aspects of the program when data are retrieved.
   d. A primary goal of database systems is to minimize data redundancy.
   e. Database systems increase user interface with the system through increased accessibility and flexibility.

2. One of the first steps in the creation of a relational database is to
   a. integrate accounting and nonfinancial data.
   b. plan for increased secondary storage capacity.
   c. order data-mining software that will facilitate data retrieval.
   d. create a data model of the key entities in the system.
   e. construct the physical user view using SQL.

3. Which of the following is a characteristic of a relational database system?
   a. All data within the system are shared by all users to facilitate integration.
   b. Database processing follows explicit links that are contained within the records.
   c. User views limit access to the database.
   d. Transaction processing and data warehousing systems share a common database.

4. Partitioned databases are most effective when
   a. users in the system need to share common data.
   b. primary users of the data are clearly identifiable.
   c. read-only access is needed at each site.
   d. all of the above.

5. The functions of a database administrator are
   a. database planning, data input preparation, and database design.
   b. data input preparation, database design, and database operation.
   c. database design, database operation, and equipment operations.
   d. database design, database implementation, and database planning.
   e. database operations, database maintenance, and data input preparation.

6. The data attributes that a particular user has permission to access are defined by the
   a. operating system view.
   b. systems design view.
   c. database schema.
   d. user view.
   e. application program.

7. An inventory table in a relational database system contains values for items such as part number, part name, description, color, and quantity. These individual items are called
   a. attributes.
   b. record types.
   c. bytes.
   d. occurrences.

8. Which of the following is a characteristic of a relational database system?
   a. Tables are linked to other related table through pointers.
   b. A parent table may be related to many child tables, but a child table may have only one parent.
   c. Each table must contain an attribute whose value is unique.
   d. Tables in 1:M associations are linked by embedding the primary key of the M side tables into the 1 side table as a foreign key.

9. A database system that has several remote users networked together, but each user site stores a unique portion of the database is called a
   a. replicated data processing network.
   b. partitioned database.
   c. recentralized network.
   d. multidrop data network.
   e. hybrid system.

10. For those instances where individual users may be granted summary and statistical query access to

confidential data to which they normally are denied access, which type of control is *most* suitable?
   a. User-defined procedures
   b. Data encryption
   c. Inference controls
   d. Biometric devices

11. Where are database access permission defined?
   a. Operating system
   b. Database authority table
   c. Database schema
   d. Systems manual
   e. Application programs

12. Database currency is achieved by
   a. implementing partitioned databases at remote sites.
   b. employing data-cleansing techniques.
   c. ensuring that the database is secure from accidental entry.
   d. an external auditor's reconciliation of reports from multiple sites.
   e. a database lockout that prevents multiple simultaneous access.

PROBLEMS

1. **DBMS versus Flat-File Processing**

   The Werner Manufacturing Corporation has a flat-file processing system. The information processing facility is very large. Different applications, such as order processing, production planning, inventory management, accounting systems, payroll, and marketing systems, use separate tape and disk files. The corporation has recently hired a consulting firm to investigate the possibility of switching to a database management system. Prepare a memo to the top management team at Werner explaining the advantages of a DBMS. Also, discuss the necessity of a database administrator and the job functions this person would perform.

2. **Database Design**

   Design a relational database system for a large costume rental store. The store has approximately 3,200 customers each year. It is stocked with over 500 costumes in various sizes. The rental costumes and other items that may be purchased by the customer (e.g., make-up and teeth) are purchased from approximately thirty-five different suppliers. Design the necessary database files. Make sure they are in third normal form, and indicate the necessary linkages.

3. **Database Design**

   Sears Roebuck, the most well-known and oldest mail-order retailer in the country, discontinued its mail-order operations a few years ago. Other mail-order marketers use information systems to trim printing and postage costs of their catalogs. They also want to more effectively target their customers. Explain how an appropriately designed coding system for inventory items incorporated in a database management system with SQL capabilities could allow more cost-efficient and effective mail-order operations. Sketch the necessary database files.

4. **Database Deadlock**

   How is a lockout different from a deadlock? Give an accounting example to illustrate why a database lockout is necessary and how a deadlock can occur. Use actual table names in your example.

5. **System Configuration**

   First State Bank provides full banking services to its customers through
   a. automatic teller machines.
   b. checking and saving accounts.
   c. certificates of deposit.
   d. loans.
   e. electronic payroll.
   f. electronic payment of customers' bills.

   The bank has eleven branch offices that cover a 30-mile radius. The main office maintains a mainframe computer that serves the branch offices. The competitive nature of the banking industry requires that customer satisfaction be considered. Customers want prompt and accurate servicing of transactions. Thus, accuracy and speed are crucial to the success of First State Bank. How would you suggest the databases and data communications facilities be configured for First State Bank?

6. **Database Authorization Table**

   The following information is stored in two relational database files:

   Employee Master File
       Social Security number
       Name
       Address
       Date hired
       Hourly wage rate
       Marital status
       Number of exemptions

Weekly Payroll File
    Social Security number
    Hours worked
    Deductions
    Bonuses

Required:

a. Bogey works in personnel and Bacall works in payroll. Prepare a database authorization table that you think is appropriate for Bogey and Bacall for these two files.
b. Discuss any potential exposure if the right prevention devices are not in place or if Bogey and Bacall collude.

7. Distributed Databases

The XYZ Company is a geographically distributed organization with several sites around the country. Users at these sites need rapid access to common data for read-only purposes. Which distributed database method is best under these circumstances? Explain your reasoning.

8. Distributed Databases

The ABC Company is a geographically distributed organization with several sites around the country. Users at these sites need rapid access to data for transaction processing purposes. The sites are autonomous; they do not share the same customers, products, or suppliers. Which distributed database method is best under these circumstances? Explain your reasoning.

CHAPTER 5

Systems Development and Program Change Activities

LEARNING OBJECTIVES

After studying this chapter, you should:

- Be able to identify the stages in the SDLC.
- Be familiar with common problems that can lead to failure in the systems development process.
- Understand the importance of strategic system planning.
- Have a general understanding of how accountants participate in the SDLC.
- Be able to identify the basic features of both the structured and object-oriented approaches to systems design.
- Be able to identify and discuss the major steps involved in a cost-benefit analysis of proposed information systems.
- Understand the advantages and disadvantages of the commercial software option, and be able to discuss the decision-making process used to select commercial software.
- Understand the purpose of a system walkthrough.
- Be familiar with the different types of system documentation and the purposes they serve.

One of the most valuable assets of the modern business organization is a responsive, user-oriented information system. A well-designed system can increase productivity, reduce inventories, eliminate nonvalue-added activities, improve customer service and management decisions, and coordinate activities throughout the organization.

This chapter concludes our treatment of general control issues as they relate to management and auditor responsibilities under SOX Section 404. It begins by describing the roles of the participants involved in developing an organization's information system, including systems professionals, users, and stakeholders. Then it outlines the key activities that constitute the systems development life cycle (SDLC). These include *systems planning, systems analysis, conceptual design, system selection, detailed design, system implementation, and program change procedures (systems maintenance)*. This multistage procedure is used to guide systems development in many organizations. Finally, it discusses SDLC risks, controls, and audit issues.

PARTICIPANTS IN SYSTEMS DEVELOPMENT

The participants in systems development can be classified into four broad groups: systems professionals, end users, stakeholders, and accountants/auditors.

1. **Systems professionals** are systems analysts, systems engineers, and programmers. These individuals actually build the system. They gather facts about problems with the current system, analyze these facts, and formulate a solution to solve the problems. The product of their efforts is a new system.
2. **End users** are those for whom the system is built. There are many users at all levels in an organization. These include managers, operations personnel, accountants, and internal auditors. In some organizations, it is difficult to find someone who is not a user. During systems development, systems professionals work with the primary users to obtain an understanding of the users' problems and a clear statement of their needs.
3. **Stakeholders** are individuals either within or outside the organization who have an interest in the system but are not end users. These include accountants, internal and external auditors, and the internal steering committee that oversees systems development.
4. **Accountants/Auditors** are those professionals who address the controls, accounting, and auditing issues for systems development. This involvement should include internal auditors and IT auditors. Of course, as discussed in Chapter 1, SOX legislation prohibits external auditors from direct involvement in an audit client's systems development activities.

Why Are Accountants and Auditors Involved with SDLC?

The SDLC process is of interest to accountants and auditors for two reasons. First, the creation of an information system entails significant financial transactions. Conceptually, systems development is like any manufacturing process that produces a complex product through a series of stages. Such transactions must be planned, authorized, scheduled, accounted for, and controlled. Accountants are as concerned with the integrity of this process as they are with any manufacturing process that has financial resource implications. Because of their background, experience, and training, accountants and auditors are experts in financial transactions and thus can provide critical input into the system regarding controls, integrity, timeliness, and a number of other important aspects of financial transactions.

The second and more pressing concern for accountants and auditors is with the nature of the products that emerge from the SDLC. The quality of accounting information rests directly on the SDLC activities that produce accounting information systems (AIS). These systems deliver accounting information to internal and external users. The accountant's responsibility is to ensure that the systems employ proper accounting conventions and rules, and possess adequate controls. Therefore, accountants are greatly concerned with the quality of the process that produces AIS. For example, a sales order system produced by a defective SDLC may suffer from serious control weaknesses that introduce errors into the financial accounting records, or provide opportunities for fraud.

How Are Accountants Involved with the SDLC?

Accountants are involved in systems development in three ways. First, accountants are users. All systems that process financial transactions impact the accounting function in some way. Like all users, accountants must provide a clear picture of their problems and needs to the systems professionals. For example, accountants must specify accounting techniques to be used, internal control requirements (such as audit trails), and special algorithms (such as depreciation models).

Second, accountants participate in systems development as members of the development team. Their involvement often extends beyond the development of strictly AIS applications. Systems that do not process financial transactions directly may still draw from accounting data. The accountant may be consulted to provide advice or to determine if the proposed system constitutes an internal control risk. In all cases, the level of auditor participation is limited by independence issues in professional standards and ethics.

Third, accountants are involved in systems development as auditors. Accounting information systems must be auditable. Some computer audit techniques require special features that need to be designed into the system during the SDLC. We examine such audit tools and their use in Chapters 7 and 8. The auditor has a stake in all systems and should be involved early in their design, especially regarding their auditability, security, and controls.

INFORMATION SYSTEMS ACQUISITION

Organizations usually acquire information systems in two ways: (1) they develop customized systems in-house through formal systems development activities and (2) they purchase commercial systems from software vendors. This section of the text discusses these two alternatives.

In-House Development

Many organizations require systems that are highly tuned to their unique operations. These firms design their own information systems through in-house systems development activities. In-house development requires maintaining a full-time systems staff of analysts and programmers who identify user information needs and satisfy their needs with custom systems.

Commercial Systems

A growing number of systems are purchased from software vendors. Faced with many competing packages, each with unique features and attributes, management must choose the system and the vendor that best serve the needs of the organization. Making the optimal choice requires that this be an informed decision.

Trends in Commercial Software

Four factors have stimulated the growth of the commercial software market: (1) the relatively low cost of general commercial software as compared to customized software; (2) the emergence of industry-specific vendors who target their software to the needs of particular types of businesses; (3) a growing demand from businesses that are too small to afford in-house systems' development staff; and (4) the trend toward downsizing of organizational units and the resulting move toward the distributed data processing environment, which has made the commercial software option more appealing to larger organizations. Indeed, organizations that maintain their own in-house systems' development staff will often purchase commercial software when the need permits. Commercial software packages fall into three basic groups: turnkey systems, backbone systems, and vendor-supported systems.

Types of Commercial Systems

Turnkey Systems. **Turnkey systems** are completely finished and tested systems that are ready for implementation. These are often general-purpose systems or systems customized to a specific industry. Turnkey systems are usually sold only as compiled program modules, and users have limited ability to customize them to their specific needs. Some turnkey systems have software options that allow the user to customize input, output, and some processing through menu choices. Other turnkey system vendors will sell their customers the source code if program changes are desired. For a fee, the user or the vendor can then customize the system by reprogramming the original source code. Some examples of turnkey systems are described next.

General Accounting Systems. **General accounting systems** are designed to serve a wide variety of user needs. By mass-producing a standard system, the vendor is able to reduce the unit cost of these systems to a fraction of in-house development costs. Powerful systems of this sort can be obtained for under $2,000.

To provide as much flexibility as possible, general accounting systems are designed in modules. This allows users to purchase the modules that meet their specific needs. Typical modules include accounts payable, accounts receivable, payroll processing, inventory control, general ledger, financial reporting, and fixed asset.

Special-Purpose Systems. Some software vendors create **special-purpose systems** that target selected segments of the economy. For example, the medical field, the banking industry, and government agencies have unique accounting procedures, rules, and conventions that general-purpose accounting systems do not always accommodate. Software vendors have thus developed standardized systems to deal with industry-specific procedures.

Office Automation Systems. **Office automation systems** are computer systems that improve the productivity of office workers. Examples of office automation systems include word processing packages, database management systems, spreadsheet programs, and desktop publishing systems.

Backbone Systems. **Backbone systems** provide a basic system structure on which to build. Backbone systems come with all the primary processing modules programmed. The vendor designs and programs the user interface to suit the client's needs. Some systems such as Enterprise Resource Planning (ERP) offer a vast array of modules for dealing with almost every conceivable business process, and all are interfaced seamlessly into a single system. By selecting the appropriate modules, the customer can create a highly customized system. Customizing a commercial system, however, is expensive and time consuming. A fully functional ERP system typically takes 18 to 24 months to install and costs anywhere from $10 million to $100 million.

Vendor-Supported Systems. **Vendor-supported systems** are hybrids of custom systems and commercial software. Under this approach, the vendor develops (and maintains) custom systems for its clients. The systems themselves are custom products, but the systems development service is commercially provided. This option is popular in the health care and legal services industries. Since the vendor serves as the organization's in-house systems development staff, the client organization must rely on the vendor to provide custom programming and on-site maintenance of systems. Much of each client's system may be developed from scratch, but by using an object-oriented approach, vendors can produce common modules that can be reused in other client systems. This approach helps to reduce development costs charged to the client firms.

Advantages of Commercial Software

- **Implementation Time.** Custom systems often take a long time to develop. Months or even years may pass before a custom system can be developed through in-house procedures. Unless the organization successfully anticipates future information needs and schedules application development accordingly, it may experience long periods of unsatisfied need. However, commercial software can be implemented almost immediately once a need is recognized. The user does not have to wait.
- **Cost.** A single user must wholly absorb in-house development costs. However, since the cost of commercial software is spread across many users, the unit cost is reduced to a fraction of the cost of a system developed in-house.
- **Reliability.** Most reputable commercial software packages are thoroughly tested before their release to the consumer market. Any system errors not discovered during testing are likely to be uncovered by user organizations shortly after release and corrected. Although no system is certified as being free from errors, commercial software is less likely to have errors than an equivalent in-house system.

Disadvantages of Commercial Software

- **Independence.** Purchasing a vendor-supported system makes the firm dependent on the vendor for maintenance. The user runs the risk that the vendor will cease to support the system or even go out of business. This is perhaps the greatest disadvantage of vendor-supported systems.
- **The need for customized systems.** The prime advantage of in-house development is the ability to produce applications to exact specifications. This advantage also describes a disadvantage of commercial software. Sometimes, the user's needs are unique and complex, and commercially available software is either too general or too inflexible.
- **Maintenance.** Business information systems undergo frequent changes. If the user's needs change, it may be difficult or even impossible to modify commercial software. In-house development, however, provides users with proprietary applications that can be economically maintained.

THE SYSTEMS DEVELOPMENT LIFE CYCLE

Both the in-house development and the commercial package options have advantages and disadvantages. They are not, however, mutually exclusive propositions. A company may satisfy some of its information needs by purchasing commercial software and develop other systems in-house. Both approaches are enhanced by formal procedures that lend structure to the decision-making process. The systems development life cycle described next is generally associated with in-house development, but many of its phases, particularly those involving needs analysis and system specification, can be effectively employed even when the final system is purchased from an outside vendor.

The objectives and sequence of **systems development life cycle (SDLC)** activities are logical and generally accepted by experts in the systems community, and are generally treated as "best practices" for systems development. However, the number and the names of specific stages within this process are matters of some disagreement. Different authorities have proposed SDLC models with as few as 4 and as many as 14 specific activities. From an auditing point of view, the number of actual stages is of no particular importance. We are concerned about the substance and the consistent application of this

FIGURE 5.1 **Systems Development Life Cycle**

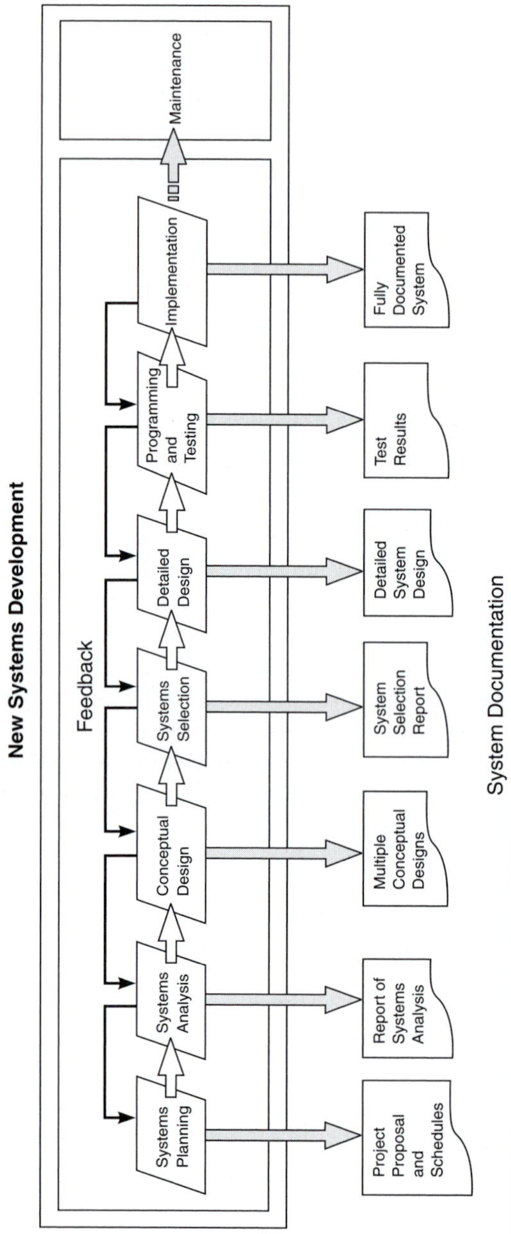

process, however it is defined. The SDLC in Figure 5.1 is an eight-phase process consisting of two major stages: new systems development and maintenance.

The first seven phases of the SDLC describe the activities that all new systems should undergo. **New systems development** involves conceptual steps that can apply to any problem-solving process: identify the problem, understand what needs to be done, consider alternative solutions, select the best solution, and, finally, implement the solution. Each phase in the SDLC produces a set of required documentation that together constitutes a body of audit evidence about the overall quality the SDLC. An eighth step, **systems maintenance**, constitutes the organization's program change procedures; It begins once the seven phases are complete and the system is fully implemented. Each of the SDLC phases is briefly outlined below.

Systems Planning—Phase I

The objective of **systems planning** is to link individual system projects or applications to the strategic objectives of the firm. In fact, the basis for the systems plan is the organization's business plan, which specifies where the firm plans to go and how it will get there. In particular, systems projects are analyzed by using the IT strategic plan, which is developed from and congruent with the organization's business plan. Figure 5.2 presents the relationship between these plans and the strategic objectives of the firm. There must be congruence between the individual projects and the business plan, or the firm may fail to meet its objectives. Effective systems planning provides this goal congruence.

Who Should Do Systems Planning?
Most firms that take systems planning seriously establish a systems steering committee to provide guidance and review the status of system projects. The composition of the **steering committee** may include the chief executive officer, the chief financial officer, the chief information officer, senior management from user areas, the internal auditor, and senior management from computer services. External parties, such as management

---

FIGURE 5.2   **Relationship between Systems Plans and Organizational Objectives**

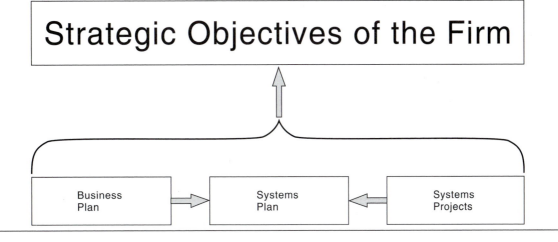

consultants and the firm's external auditors, may also supplement the committee. Typical responsibilities for a steering committee include the following:

- Resolving conflicts that arise from new systems
- Reviewing projects and assigning priorities
- Budgeting funds for systems development
- Reviewing the status of individual projects under development
- Determining at various checkpoints throughout the SDLC whether to continue with the project or terminate it

Systems planning occurs at two levels: strategic systems planning and project planning.

Strategic Systems Planning

Strategic systems planning involves the allocation of systems resources at the macro level. It usually deals with a time frame of 3 to 5 years. This process is similar to budgeting resources for other strategic activities, such as product development, plant expansions, market research, and manufacturing technology.

Technically, strategic systems planning is not part of the SDLC because the SDLC pertains to specific applications. The strategic systems plan is concerned with the allocation of such systems resources as employees (the number of systems professionals to be hired), hardware (the number of workstations, minicomputers, and mainframes to be purchased), software (the funds to be allocated to new systems projects and for systems maintenance), and telecommunications (the funds allocated to networking and EDI). It is important that the strategic plan avoid excessive detail. The plan must allow systems specialists to make informed decisions by considering such relevant factors as price, performance measures, size, security, and control.

Why Perform Strategic Systems Planning?.   Perhaps no aspect of a firm's business activities is as volatile and unpredictable as information systems planning. Who can look 5 years into the future and accurately predict the state of systems technology? Because of this volatility, any long-term plans a firm makes are likely to change. How, therefore, can a firm do strategic systems planning? Why should it?

There are four justifications for strategic systems planning:

1. *A plan that changes constantly is better than no plan at all.* Strategic planning charts the path the firm will follow to reach its information systems goal. Even if it means making many midcourse adjustments, planning is superior to simply wandering in the wilderness.
2. *Strategic planning reduces the crisis component in systems development.* A formal plan is a model for identifying and prioritizing user needs. It allows management to consider the future needs, recognize problems in their early stages, and even anticipate needs before the symptoms of underlying problems emerge. In the absence of a plan, the trigger that stimulates systems development is the recognition of a problem. Often, problems reach a crisis level before they receive attention, which adversely affects the quality of the solution. Strategic planning provides a structured means of separating legitimate needs from desires, and needs versus problems.
3. *Strategic systems planning provides authorization control for the SDLC.* The strategic systems plan lays out authorization rules to ensure that decisions to develop specific systems are congruent with the objectives of the firm. Investing in the wrong systems can be just as damaging to a firm as investing in the wrong plant and equipment.
4. *Cost management.* Historically, systems planning has proven to be a cost-effective means of managing systems projects and application development.

Project Planning

The purpose of **project planning** is to allocate resources to individual applications within the framework of the strategic plan. This involves identifying areas of user needs, preparing proposals, evaluating each proposal's feasibility and contribution to the business plan, prioritizing individual projects, and scheduling the work to be done. The basic purpose of project planning is to allocate scarce resources to specific projects. The product of this phase consists of two formal documents: the project proposal and the project schedule.

The **project proposal** provides management with a basis for deciding whether to proceed with the project. The formal proposal serves two purposes. First, it summarizes the findings of the study conducted to this point into a general recommendation for a new or modified system. This enables management to evaluate the perceived problem along with the proposed system as a feasible solution. Second, the proposal outlines the linkage between the objectives of the proposed system and the business objectives of the firm, especially those outlined in the IT strategic plan. It shows that the proposed new system complements the strategic direction of the firm.

The **project schedule** represents management's commitment to the project. The project schedule is a budget of the time and costs for all the phases of the SDLC. A project team selected from systems professionals, end users, and other specialists such as accountants and internal auditors will complete these phases. The composition of the team and the competence and dedication of its members are critical to the success of the new system.

The Auditor's Role in Systems Planning

Auditors routinely examine the systems planning phase of the SDLC. Planning greatly reduces the risk that an organization has produced unneeded, inefficient, ineffective, and fraudulent systems. Therefore, both internal and external auditors are interested in ensuring that adequate systems planning takes place.

Systems Analysis—Phase II

We now move on to the second phase in the SDLC. **Systems analysis** is actually a two-step process involving first a survey of the current system and then an analysis of the user's needs. A business problem must be fully understood by the systems analyst before he or she can formulate a solution. An incomplete or defective analysis will lead to an incomplete or defective solution. Therefore, systems analysis is the foundation for the rest of the SDLC. The deliverable from this phase is a formal **systems analysis report**, which presents the findings of the analysis and recommendations for the new system.

The Survey Step

Most systems are not developed from scratch. Usually, some form of information system and related procedures are currently in place. The analyst often begins the analysis by determining what elements, if any, of the current system should be preserved as part of the new system. This involves a rather detailed **system survey**. Facts pertaining to preliminary questions about the system are gathered and analyzed. As the analyst obtains a greater depth of understanding of the problem, he or she develops more specific questions for which more facts must be gathered. This process may go on through several iterations. When all the relevant facts have been gathered and analyzed, the analyst arrives at an assessment of the current system. Surveying the current system has both disadvantages and advantages.

Disadvantages of Surveying the Current System

- *Current physical tar pit.* This term is used to describe the tendency on the part of the analyst to be "sucked in" and then "bogged down" by the task of surveying the current dinosaur system.[1]
- *Thinking inside the box.* Some argue that current system surveys stifle new ideas. By studying and modeling the old system, the analyst may develop a constrained notion about how the new system should function. The result is an improved old system rather than a radically new approach.

Advantages of Surveying the Current System

- *Identifying what aspects of the old system should be kept.* Some elements of the system may be functionally sound and can provide the foundation for the new system. By fully understanding the current system, the analyst can identify those aspects worth preserving or modifying for use in the new system.
- *Forcing systems analysts to fully understand the system.* When the new system is implemented, the users must go through a conversion process whereby they formally break away from the old system and move to the new one. The analyst must determine what tasks, procedures, and data will be phased out with the old system and which will continue. To specify these conversion procedures, the analyst must know not only what is to be done by the new system but also what was done by the old one. This requires a thorough understanding of the current system.
- *Isolating the root of problem symptoms.* By surveying the current system, the analyst may determine conclusively the cause of the reported problem symptoms. Perhaps the root problem is not the information system at all; it may be a management or employee problem that can be resolved without redesigning the information system. We may not be able to identify the root cause of the problem if we discard the existing system without any investigation into the symptoms.

Gathering Facts

The survey of the current system is essentially a fact-gathering activity. The facts gathered by the analyst are pieces of data that describe key features, situations, and relationships of the system. System facts fall into the following broad classes.

- **Data sources.** These include external entities, such as customers or vendors, as well as internal sources from other departments.
- **Users.** These include both managers and operations users.
- **Data stores.** Data stores are the files, databases, accounts, and source documents used in the system.
- **Processes.** Processing tasks are manual or computer operations that represent a decision or an action triggered by information.
- **Data flows.** Data flows are represented by the movement of documents and reports between data sources, data stores, processing tasks, and users. Data flows can also be represented in UML diagrams.
- **Controls.** These include both accounting and operational controls and may be manual procedures or computer controls.
- **Transaction volumes.** The analyst must obtain a measure of the transaction volumes for a specified period of time. Many systems are replaced because they have

---

1   This is perhaps the most compelling argument against surveying the current system.

reached their capacity. Understanding the characteristics of a systems transaction volume and its rate of growth are important elements in assessing capacity requirements for the new system.

- **Error rates.** Transaction errors are closely related to transaction volume. As a system reaches capacity, error rates increase to an intolerable level. Although no system is perfect, the analyst must determine the acceptable error tolerances for the new system.
- **Resource costs.** The resources used by the current system include the costs of labor, computer time, materials (such as invoices), and direct overhead. Any resource costs that disappear when the current system is eliminated are called escapable costs. Later, when we perform a cost-benefit analysis, escapable costs will be treated as benefits of the new system.
- **Bottlenecks and redundant operations.** The analyst should note points where data flows come together to form a bottleneck. At peak-load periods, these can result in delays and promote processing errors. Likewise, delays may be caused by redundant operations, such as unnecessary approvals or sign-offs. By identifying these problem areas during the survey phase, the analyst can avoid making the same mistakes in the design of the new system.

Fact-Gathering Techniques

Systems analysts employ several techniques to gather the previously cited facts. Commonly used techniques include observation, task participation, personal interviews, and reviewing key documents.

Observation. Observation involves passively watching the physical procedures of the system. This allows the analyst to determine what gets done, who performs the tasks, when they do them, how they do them, why they do them, and how long they take.

Task Participation. Participation is an extension of observation, whereby the analyst takes an active role in performing the user's work. This allows the analyst to experience first-hand the problems involved in the operation of the current system. For example, the analyst may work on the sales desk taking orders from customers and preparing sales orders. The analyst can determine that documents are improperly designed, that insufficient time exists to perform the required procedures, or that peak-load problems cause bottlenecks and processing errors. With hands-on experience, the analyst can often envision better ways to perform the task.

Personal Interviews. Interviewing is a method of extracting facts about the current system and user perceptions about the requirements for the new system. The instruments used to gather these facts may be open-ended questions or formal questionnaires.

- *Open-ended questions* allow users to elaborate on the problem as they see it and offer suggestions and recommendations. Answers to these questions tend to be difficult to analyze, but they give the analyst a feel for the scope of the problem. The analyst in this type of interview must be a good listener and able to focus on the important facts. Examples of open-ended questions are: "What do you think is the main problem with our sales order system?" and "How could the system be improved?"
- *Questionnaires* are used to ask more specific, detailed questions and to restrict the user's responses. This is a good technique for gathering objective facts about the nature of specific procedures, volumes of transactions processed, sources of data, users of reports, and control issues.

Reviewing Key Documents.   The organization's documents are another source of facts about the system being surveyed. Examples of these include the following:

- Organizational charts
- Job descriptions
- Accounting records
- Charts of accounts
- Policy statements
- Descriptions of procedures
- Financial statements
- Performance reports
- System flowcharts
- Source documents
- Transaction listings
- Budgets
- Forecasts
- Mission statements

Following the fact-gathering phase, the analyst formally documents his or her impressions and understanding of the system. This will take the form of notes, system flowcharts, and data flow diagrams. These documentation techniques are discussed in more detail in Chapter 6.

The Analysis Step

Systems analysis is an intellectual process that is commingled with fact gathering. The analyst is simultaneously analyzing as he or she gathers facts. The mere recognition of a problem presumes some understanding of the norm or desired state. It is therefore difficult to identify where the survey ends and the analysis begins.

Systems Analysis Report

The event that marks the conclusion of the systems analysis phase is the preparation of a formal systems analysis report. This report presents to management or the steering committee the survey findings, the problems identified with the current system, the user's needs, and the requirements of the new system. Figure 5.3 contains a possible format for this report. The primary purpose for conducting a systems analysis is to identify user needs and specify requirements for the new system. The report should set out in detail what the system must do rather than how to do it. The requirements statement within the report establishes an understanding between systems professionals, management, users, and other stakeholders. This document constitutes a formal contract that specifies the objectives and goals of the system. The systems analysis report should establish in clear terms the data sources, users, data files, general processes, data flows, controls, and transaction volume capacity.

The systems analysis report does not specify the detailed design of the proposed system. For example, it does not specify processing methods, storage media, record structures, and other details needed to design the physical system. Rather, the report remains at the objectives level to avoid placing artificial constraints on the conceptual design phase. Several possible designs may serve the user's needs, and the development process must be free to explore all of these.

The Auditor's Role in Systems Analysis

The firm's auditors (both external and internal) are stakeholders in the proposed system. In Chapter 8, we will see how certain CAATTs (such as the embedded audit module and

FIGURE 5.3

FIGURE 5.3

Outline of Main Topics in a Systems Analysis Report

Systems Analysis Report

I. Reasons for System Analysis
   A. Reasons specified in the system project proposal
   B. Changes in reasons since analysis began
   C. Additional reasons

II. Scope of Study
   A. Scope as specified by the project proposal
   B. Changes in scope

III. Problems Identified with Current System
   A. Techniques used for gathering facts
   B. Problems encountered in the fact-gathering process
   C. Analysis of facts

IV. Statement of User Requirements
   A. Specific user needs in key areas, such as:
      1. Output requirements
      2. Transaction volumes
      3. Response time
   B. Nontechnical terms for a broad-based audience, including:
      1. End users
      2. User management
      3. Systems management
      4. Steering committee

V. Resource Implications
   A. Preliminary assessment of economic effect
   B. Is economic feasibility as stated in proposal reasonable?

VI. Recommendations
   A. Continue or drop the project
   B. Any changes to feasibility, strategic impact, or priority of the project as a result of analysis

the integrated test facility) must be designed into the system during the SDLC. Often, advanced audit features cannot be easily added to existing systems. Therefore, the accountant/auditor should be involved in the needs analysis of the proposed system to determine if it is a good candidate for advanced audit features and, if so, which features are best suited for the system.

Conceptual Systems Design—Phase III

The purpose of the **conceptual design** phase is to produce several alternative conceptual systems that satisfy the system requirements identified during systems analysis. By presenting users with a number of plausible alternatives, the systems professional avoids imposing preconceived constraints on the new system. The user will evaluate these conceptual models and settle on the alternatives that appear most plausible and appealing. These alternative designs then go to the systems selection phase of SDLC, where their respective costs and benefits are compared and a single optimum design is chosen.

By keeping systems design conceptual throughout these phases of the SDLC, we minimize the investment of resources in alternative designs that, ultimately, will be rejected. The conceptual system that emerges proceeds to the final phases of the SDLC, where it is designed in detail and implemented.

This section describes two approaches to conceptual systems design: the structured approach and the object-oriented approach. The structured approach develops each new system from scratch from the top down. Object-oriented design (OOD) builds systems from the bottom up through the assembly of reusable modules rather than create each system from scratch. OOD is most often associated with the **iterative approach** to SDLC where small "chunks" or modules cycle through all of the SDLC phases rather rapidly, with a short time frame from beginning to end. Then additional modules are added in some appropriate fashion until the whole system has been developed.

The Structured Design Approach

The **structured design** approach is a disciplined way of designing systems from the top down. It consists of starting with the "big picture" of the proposed system that is gradually decomposed into more and more detail until it is fully understood. Under this approach, the business process under design is usually documented by data flow and structure diagrams. Figure 5.4 shows the use of **data flow diagrams (DFDs)** and a **structure diagram** to depict the top-down decomposition of a hypothetical business process.

We can see from these diagrams how the systems designer follows a top-down approach. The designer starts with an abstract description of the system and, through successive steps, redefines this view to produce a more detailed description. In our example, Process 2.0 in the context diagram is decomposed into an intermediate level DFD. Process 2.3 in the intermediate DFD is further decomposed into an elementary DFD. This decomposition could involve several levels to obtain sufficient details. Let's assume that three levels are sufficient in this case. The final step transforms Process 2.3.3 into a structure diagram that defines the program modules that will constitute the process.

The conceptual design phase should highlight the differences between critical features of competing systems rather than their similarities. Therefore, system designs at this point should be general. The designs should identify all the inputs, outputs, processes, and special features necessary to distinguish one alternative from another. Figure 5.5 presents two alternative conceptual designs for a purchasing system. These designs lack the details needed to implement the system. For instance, they do not include these necessary components:

- Database record structures
- Processing details
- Specific control techniques
- Formats for input screens and source documents
- Output report formats

The designs do, however, possess sufficient detail to demonstrate how the two systems are conceptually different in their functions. To illustrate, let's examine the general features of each system.

Option A is a traditional batch purchasing system. The initial input for the process is the purchase requisition from inventory control. When inventories reach their predetermined reorder points, new inventories are ordered according to their economic order quantity. Transmittal of purchase orders to suppliers takes place once a day via the U.S. mail.

In contrast, Option B employs EDI technology. The trigger to this system is a purchase requisition from production planning. The purchases system determines the quantity and the vendor and then transmits the order online via EDI software to the vendor.

Both alternatives have pros and cons. A benefit of Option A is its simplicity of design, ease of implementation, and lower demand for systems resources than Option B.

Top-Down Decomposition of the Structured Design Approach

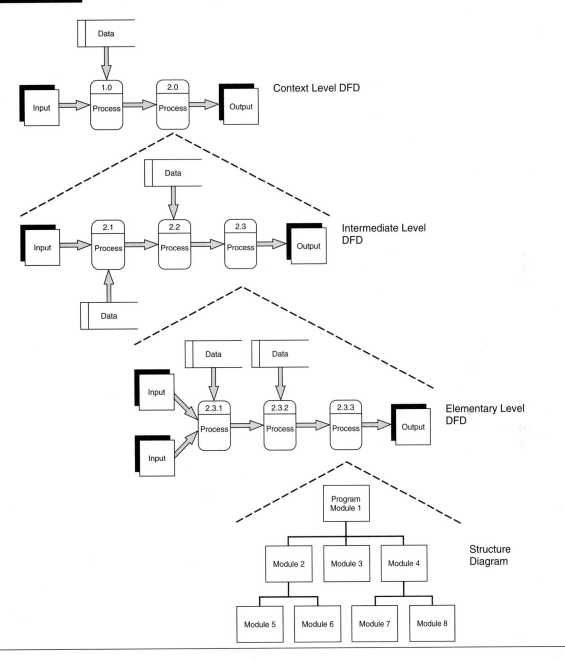

On one hand, a negative aspect of Option A is that it requires the firm to carry inventories. On the other hand, Option B may allow the firm to reduce or even eliminate inventories. This benefit comes at the cost of more expensive and sophisticated system
resources. It is premature, at this point, to attempt to evaluate the relative merits of these
alternatives. This is done formally in the next phase in the SDLC. At this point, system
designers are concerned only with identifying plausible system designs.

FIGURE 5.5   Alternative Conceptual Designs for a Purchasing System

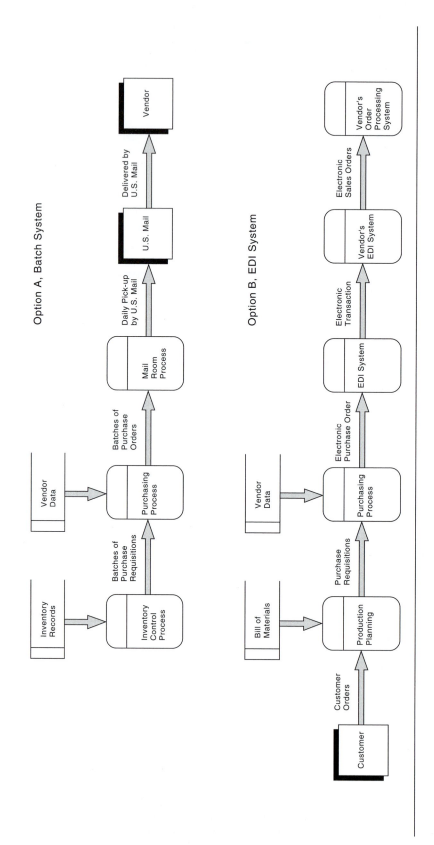

The Object-Oriented Approach

The **object-oriented design (OOD) approach** is to build information systems from reusable standard components or **objects**. This approach may be equated to the process of building an automobile. Car manufacturers do not create each new model from scratch. New models are actually built from standard components that also go into other models. For example, each model of car produced by a particular manufacturer may use the same type of engine, gearbox, alternator, rear axle, radio, and so on. Some of the car's components will be industry-standard products that are used by other manufacturers. Such things as wheels, tires, spark plugs, and headlights fall into this category. In fact, it may be that the only component actually created from scratch for a new car model is the body.

The automobile industry operates in this fashion to stay competitive. By using standard components, car manufacturers minimize production and maintenance costs. At the same time, they can remain responsive to consumer demands for new products and preserve manufacturing flexibility by mixing and matching components according to the customer's specification.

The concept of reusability is *central* to the object-oriented approach to systems design. Once created, standard modules can be used in other systems with similar needs. Ideally, the organization's systems professionals will create a library (inventory) of modules that can be used by other system designers within the firm. The benefits of this approach include reduced time and cost for development, maintenance, and testing and improved user support and flexibility in the development process.

The Auditor's Role in Conceptual Systems Design

The auditor is a stakeholder in all financial systems and, thus, has an interest in the conceptual design stage of the system. The auditability of a system depends in part on its design characteristics. Some computer auditing techniques require systems to be designed with special audit features that are integral to the system. These audit features must be specified at the conceptual design stage.

System Evaluation and Selection—Phase IV

The next phase in the SDLC is the procedure for selecting the one system from the set of alternative conceptual designs that will go to the detailed design phase. The **systems evaluation and selection** phase is an optimization process that seeks to identify the best system. This decision represents a critical juncture in the SDLC. At this point, there is a great deal of uncertainty about the system, and a poor decision here can be disastrous. The purpose of a formal evaluation and selection procedure is to structure this decision-making process and thereby reduce both uncertainty and the risk of making a poor decision. The evaluation and selection process involves two steps:

1. Perform a detailed feasibility study
2. Perform a cost-benefit analysis

Perform a Detailed Feasibility Study

The following discussion outlines five aspects of project feasibility that need to be considered. Each competing project will be assessed in the same manner. By assessing the major constraints on the proposed system, management can evaluate the project's likelihood for success, before committing large amounts of financial and human resources. The acronym TELOS provides guidance for assessing project feasibility. The term stands for technical, economic, legal, operational, and schedule feasibility.

Technical Feasibility.   Technical feasibility is concerned with whether the system can be developed under existing technology or if new technology is needed. As a general proposition, the technology in the marketplace is far ahead of most firms' ability to apply it. Therefore, from an availability viewpoint, technical feasibility is not usually an issue. For most firms, the real issue is their desire and ability to apply available technology. Given that technology is the physical basis for most of the system's design features, this aspect bears heavily on the overall feasibility of the competing system.

Economic Feasibility.   Economic feasibility pertains to the availability of funds to complete the project. At this point, we are concerned with management's financial commitment to this project in view of other competing capital projects under consideration. The level of available economic support directly impacts the operational nature and scope of the proposed system. Later, a cost-benefit analysis is used to identify the best system design for the cost.

Legal Feasibility.   Legal feasibility identifies any conflicts between the conceptual system and the company's ability to discharge its legal responsibilities. In previous chapters, we have studied the need to comply with the control requirement laid down in the Sarbanes-Oxley Act and SAS 109. In addition, many regulations and statutes deal with invasion of privacy and the confidentiality of stored information. The decision maker must be certain the proposed system falls inside all legal boundaries.

Operational Feasibility.   Operational feasibility shows the degree of compatibility between the firm's existing procedures and personnel skills and the operational requirements of the new system. Implementing the new system may require adopting new procedures and retraining operations personnel. The question that must be answered is, can adequate procedural changes be made, sufficient personnel retrained, and new skills obtained to make the system operationally feasible?

Schedule Feasibility.   Schedule feasibility relates to the firm's ability to implement the project within an acceptable time. This feasibility factor impacts both the scope of the project and whether it will be developed in-house or purchased from a software vendor. If the project, as conceptually envisioned, cannot be produced internally by the target date, then its design, its acquisition method, or the target date must be changed.

Perform a Cost–Benefit Analysis

Cost–benefit analysis helps management determine whether (and by how much) the benefits received from a proposed system will outweigh its costs. This technique is frequently used for estimating the expected financial value of business investments. However, in this case, the investment is an information system, and the costs and benefits are more difficult to identify and quantify than those of traditional capital projects. Although imperfect for this setting, cost–benefit analysis is employed because of its simplicity and the absence of a clearly better alternative. In spite of its limitations, cost–benefit analysis, combined with feasibility factors, is a useful tool for comparing competing systems designs.

There are three steps in the application of cost–benefit analysis: identify costs, identify benefits, and compare costs and benefits. We discuss each of these steps below.

Identify Costs.   One method of identifying costs is to divide them into two categories: one-time costs and recurring costs. One-time costs include the initial investment to develop and implement the system. Recurring costs include operating and maintenance costs that recur over the life of the system. Table 5.1 shows a breakdown of typical one-time and recurring costs.

TABLE 5.1	**One-Time and Recurring Costs**

One-Time Costs

Hardware acquisition
Site preparation
Software acquisition
Systems design
Programming and testing
Data conversion from old system to new system
Personnel training

Recurring Costs

Hardware maintenance
Software maintenance contracts
Insurance
Supplies
Personnel

One-time costs include the following:

- *Hardware acquisition.* This cost includes the cost of mainframe, minicomputers, microcomputers, and peripheral equipment, such as tape drives and disk packs. These cost figures can be obtained from the vendor.
- *Site preparation.* This cost involves such frequently overlooked costs as building modifications (e.g., adding air conditioning or making structural changes), equipment installation (which may include the use of heavy equipment), and freight charges. Estimates of these costs can be obtained from the vendor and the subcontractors who do the installation.
- *Software acquisition.* These costs apply to all software purchased for the proposed system, including operating system software (if not bundled with the hardware), network control software, and commercial applications (such as accounting packages). Estimates of these costs can be obtained from vendors.
- *Systems design.* These costs are those incurred by systems professionals performing the planning, analysis, and design functions. Technically, such costs incurred up to this point are "sunk" and irrelevant to the decision. The analyst should estimate only the costs needed to complete the detailed design.
- *Programming and testing.* Programming costs are based on estimates of the personnel hours required to write new programs and modify existing programs for the proposed system. System testing costs involve bringing together all the individual program modules for testing as an entire system. This must be a rigorous exercise if it is to be meaningful. The planning, testing, and analysis of the results may demand many days of involvement from systems professionals, users, and other stakeholders of the system. The experience of the firm in the past is the best basis for estimating these costs.
- *Data conversion.* These costs arise in the transfer of data from one storage medium to another. For example, the accounting records of a manual system must be converted to magnetic form when the system becomes computer-based. This can represent a significant task. The basis for estimating conversion costs is the number and size of the files to be converted.
- *Training.* These costs involve educating users to operate the new system. In-house personnel could do this in an extensive training program provided by an outside organization at a remote site or through on-the-job training. The cost of formal training can be easily obtained. The cost of an in-house training program includes

instruction time, classroom facilities, and lost productivity. This cost is often the first one cut to meet budgets, and such an action can be fatal to systems development (e.g., Hershey's ERP implementation disaster was blamed in part on the drastic reduction in employee training before "going live").[2] Accountants and auditors should be aware of the danger of cutting this important part of systems development.

Recurring costs include the following:

- *Hardware maintenance.* This cost involves the upgrading of the computer (increasing the memory), as well as preventive maintenance and repairs to the computer and peripheral equipment. The organization may enter into a maintenance contract with the vendor to minimize and budget these costs. Estimates for these costs can be obtained from vendors and existing contracts.
- *Software maintenance.* These costs include upgrading and debugging operating systems, purchased applications, and in-house developed applications. Maintenance contracts with software vendors can be used to specify these costs fairly accurately. Estimates of in-house maintenance can be derived from historical data.
- *Insurance.* This cost covers such hazards and disasters as fire, hardware failure, vandalism, and destruction by disgruntled employees.
- *Supplies.* These costs are incurred through routine consumption of such items as paper, magnetic disks, CDs, and general office supplies.
- *Personnel costs.* These are the salaries of individuals who are part of the information system. Some employee costs are direct and easily identifiable, such as the salaries of operations personnel exclusively employed as part of the system under analysis. Some personnel involvement (such as the database administrator and computer room personnel) is common to many systems. Such personnel costs must be allocated on the basis of expected incremental involvement with the system.

Identify Benefits.   The next step in the cost–benefit analysis is to identify the benefits of the system. These may be both tangible and intangible. Table 5.2 lists several types of tangible benefits.

Tangible benefits fall into two categories: those that increase revenue and those that reduce costs. For example, assume a proposed EDI system will allow the organization to reduce inventories and at the same time improve customer service by reducing stockouts. The reduction of inventories is a cost-reducing benefit. The proposed system will use fewer resources (inventories) than the current system. The value of this benefit is the

---

TABLE 5.2   ## Tangible Benefits

Increased Revenues

Increased sales within existing markets
Expansion into other markets

Cost Reduction

Labor reduction
Operating cost reduction (such as supplies and overhead)
Reduced inventories
Less expensive equipment
Reduced equipment maintenance

---

2   ERP systems are discussed in Chapter 11.

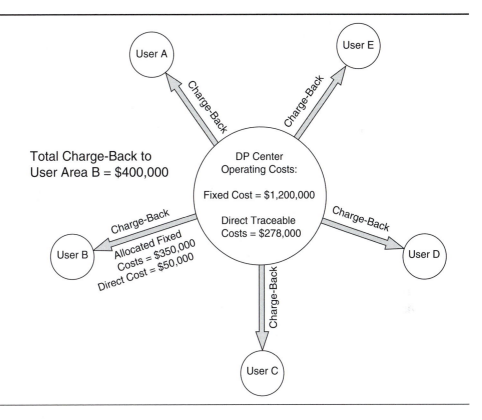

FIGURE 5.6

**DP Center Cost
Charge-Back to
User Areas**

User A

User E

Total Charge-Back to
User Area B = $400,000

Charge-Back

Charge-Back

DP Center
Operating Costs:

Fixed Cost = $1,200,000

Direct Traceable
Costs = $278,000

Charge-Back

Charge-Back

User B

Allocated Fixed
Costs = $350,000
Direct Cost = $50,000

User D

Charge-Back

User C

dollar amount of the carrying costs saved by the annual reduction in inventory. The estimated increase in sales due to better customer service is a revenue-increasing benefit.

When measuring cost savings, it is important to include only escapable costs in the analysis. Escapable costs are directly related to the system, and they cease to exist when the system ceases to exist. Some costs that appear to be escapable to the user are not truly escapable and, if included, can lead to a flawed analysis. For example, data processing centers often "charge back" their operating costs to their user constituency through cost allocations. The charge-back rate they use for this includes both fixed costs (allocated to users) and direct costs created by the activities of individual users. Figure 5.6 illustrates this technique.

Assume the management in User Area B proposes to acquire a computer system and perform its own data processing locally. One benefit of the proposal is the cost savings derived by escaping the charge-back from the current data processing center. Although the user may see this as a $400,000 annual charge, only the direct cost portion ($50,000) is escapable by the organization as a whole. Should the proposal be approved, the remaining $350,000 of the charge-back does not go away. The remaining users of the current system must now absorb this cost.

Table 5.3 lists some common categories of **intangible benefits**. Although intangible benefits are often of overriding importance in information system decisions, they cannot be easily measured and quantified. For example, assume that a proposed point-of-sale system for a department store will reduce the average time to process a customer sales transaction from 11 minutes to 3 minutes. The time saved can be quantified and produces a tangible benefit in the form of an operating cost saving. An intangible benefit is improved customer satisfaction; no one likes to stand in long lines to pay for purchases. But what is the true value of this intangible benefit to the organization? Increased

TABLE 5.3	Intangible Benefits

Increased customer satisfaction
Improved employee satisfaction
More current information
Improved decision making
Faster response to competitor actions
More efficient operations
Better internal and external communications
Improved planning
Operational flexibility
Improved control environment

customer satisfaction may translate into increased sales. More customers will buy at the store—and may be willing to pay slightly more to avoid long checkout lines. But how do we quantify this translation? Assigning a value is often highly subjective.

Systems professionals draw upon many sources in attempting to quantify intangible benefits and manipulate them into financial terms. Some common techniques include customer (and employee) opinion surveys, statistical analysis, expected value techniques, and simulation models. Though systems professionals may succeed in quantifying some of these intangible benefits, more often they must be content to simply state the benefits as precisely as good judgment permits.

Because they defy precise measurement, intangible benefits are sometimes exploited for political reasons. By overstating or understating these benefits, a system may be pushed forward by its proponents or killed by its opponents.

Compare Costs and Benefits.   The last step in the cost–benefit analysis is to compare the costs and benefits identified in the first two steps. The two most common methods used for evaluating information systems are net present value and payback.

Under the **net present value method**, the present value of the costs is deducted from the present value of the benefits over the life of the system. Projects with a positive net present value are economically feasible. When comparing competing projects, the optimal choice is the project with the greatest net present value. Table 5.4 illustrates the net present value method by comparing two competing designs.

The example is based on the following data:

	Design A	Design B
Project completion time	1 year	1 year
Expected useful life of system	5 years	5 years
One-time costs (thousands)	$300	$140
Recurring costs (thousands) incurred in beginning of Years 1 through 5	$45	$55
Annual tangible benefits (thousands) incurred in end of Years 1 through 5	$170	$135

If costs and tangible benefits alone were being considered, then Design A would be selected over Design B. However, the value of intangible benefits, along with the design feasibility scores, must also be factored into the final analysis.

The **payback method** is a variation of break-even analysis. The **break-even point** is reached when total costs equal total benefits. Figure 5.7(A) and 5.7(B) illustrates this approach using the data from the previous example.

TABLE 5.4	Net Present Value Method of Cost–Benefit Analysis				
Year Time	Beginning End Year Outflows	Inflows	Beginning Year Time	End Year Outflows	Inflows
0	$(3,000,000)		0	$(140,000)	
1	(45,000)	170,000	1	(55,000)	135,000
2	(45,000)	170,000	2	(55,000)	135,000
3	(45,000)	170,000	3	(55,000)	135,000
4	(45,000)	170,000	4	(55,000)	135,000
5	(45,000)	170,000	5	(55,000)	135,000
PV Out	$(479,672)		PV Out	$(369,599)	
PV In	$628,428		PV In	$499,089	
NPV	$148,810		NPV	$139,490	
Interest Rate	8.00%				

The total-cost curve consists of the one-time costs plus the present value of the recurring costs over the life of the project. The total benefits curve is the present value of the tangible benefits. The intersection of these lines represents the number of years into the future when the project breaks even, or pays for itself. The shaded area between the benefit curve and the total-cost curve represents the present value of future profits earned by the system.

In choosing an information system, payback speed is often a decisive factor. With brief product life cycles and rapid advances in technology, the effective lives of information systems tend to be short. Using this criterion, Design B, with a payback period of four years, would be selected over Design A, whose payback will take four and one-half years. The length of the payback period often takes precedence over other considerations represented by intangible benefits.

Prepare Systems Selection Report

The deliverable product of the systems selection process is the **systems selection report**. This formal document consists of a revised feasibility study, a cost-benefit analysis, and a list and explanation of intangible benefits for each alternative design. On the basis of this report, the steering committee will select a single system that will go forward to the next phase of the SDLC—detailed design.

The Auditor's Role in Evaluation and Selection

The primary concern for auditors is that the economic feasibility of the proposed system is measured as accurately as possible. Specifically, the auditor should ensure five things:

1. Only escapable costs are used in calculations of cost savings benefits.
2. Reasonable interest rates are used in measuring present values of cash flows.
3. One-time and recurring costs are completely and accurately reported.
4. Realistic useful lives are used in comparing competing projects.
5. Intangible benefits are assigned reasonable financial values.

Errors, omissions, and misrepresentations in the accounting for such items can distort the analysis and may result in a materially flawed decision.

FIGURE 5.7A

Discounted Payback Method of Cash Flow Analysis

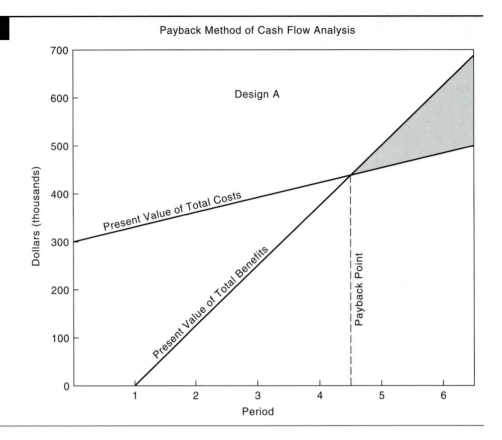

Payback Method of Cash Flow Analysis

FIGURE 5.7B

Discounted Payback Method of Cost–Benefit Analysis

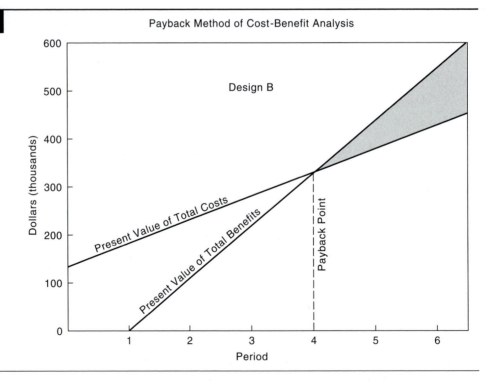

Payback Method of Cost-Benefit Analysis

Detailed Design—Phase V

The purpose of the **detailed design** phase is to produce a detailed description of the proposed system that both satisfies the system requirements identified during systems analysis and is in accordance with the conceptual design. In this phase, all system components (user views, database tables, processes, and controls) are meticulously specified. At the end of this phase, these components are presented formally in a detailed design report. This report constitutes a set of blueprints that specify input screen formats, output report layouts, database structures, and process logic. These completed plans then proceed to the final phase in the SDLC—systems implementation—where the system is physically constructed.

Perform a System Design Walkthrough

After completing the detailed design, the development team usually performs a system design **walkthrough** to ensure that the design is free from conceptual errors that could become programmed into the final system. Many firms have formal, structured walkthroughs conducted by a **quality assurance group**. This group is an independent one made up of programmers, analysts, users, and internal auditors. The job of this group is to simulate the operation of the system to uncover errors, omissions, and ambiguities in the design. Most system errors emanate from poor designs rather than programming mistakes. Detecting and correcting errors in the design phase thus reduces costly reprogramming later.

Review System Documentation

The **detailed design report** documents and describes the system to this point. This report includes the following:

- Designs for all screen inputs and source documents for the system.
- Designs of all screen outputs, reports, and operational documents.
- Normalized data for database tables, specifying all data elements.
- Database structures and diagrams: Entity relationship (ER) diagrams describing the data relations in the system, context diagrams for the overall system, low-level data flow diagrams of specific system processes, structure diagrams for the program modules in the system—including including a pseudocode description of each module.
- An updated data dictionary describing each data element in the database.
- Processing logic (flow charts).

The quality control group scrutinizes these documents, and any errors detected are recorded in a walkthrough report. Depending on the extent of the system errors, the quality assurance group will make a recommendation. The system design will either be accepted without modification, accepted subject to modification of minor errors, or rejected because of material errors.

At this point, a decision is made either to return the system for additional design or to proceed to the next phase—system coding and testing. Assuming the design goes forward, the documents in the design report constitute the blueprints that guide application programmers and the database designers in constructing the physical system.

Application Programming and Testing—Phase VI

Program the Application Software

The next stage of the SDLC is to select a programming language from among the various languages available and suitable to the application. These include *procedural languages* like COBOL, *event-driven languages* like Visual Basic, or *object-oriented programming*

(OOP) languages like Java or C++. This section presents a brief overview of various programming approaches. Systems professionals will make their decision based on the in-house standards, architecture, and user needs.

Procedural Languages.   A **procedural language** requires the programmer to specify the precise order in which the program logic is executed. Procedural languages are often called **third-generation languages (3GLs)**. Examples of 3GLs include COBOL, FORTRAN, C, and PL1. In business (particularly in accounting) applications, COBOL was the dominant language for years. COBOL has great capability for performing highly detailed operations on individual data records and handles large files very efficiently. However, it is an extremely "wordy" language that makes programming a time-consuming task. COBOL has survived as a viable language because many of the "legacy systems" written in the 1970s and 1980s, which were coded in COBOL, are still in operation today. Major retrofits and routine maintenance to these systems need to be coded in COBOL. Upward of 12 billion lines of COBOL code are executed daily in the United States.

Event-Driven Languages.   **Event-driven languages** are no longer procedural. Under this model, the program's code is not executed in a predefined sequence. Instead, external actions or "events" that are initiated by the user dictate the control flow of the program. For example, when the user presses a key, or "clicks" on an icon on the computer screen, the program automatically executes code associated with that event. This is a fundamental shift from the 3GL era. Now, instead of designing applications that execute sequentially from top to bottom in accordance with the way the programmer *thinks* they should function, the user is in control.

Microsoft's Visual Basic is the most popular example of an event-driven language. The syntax of the language is simple yet powerful. Visual Basic is used to create real-time and batch applications that can manipulate flat files or relational databases. It has a screen-painting feature that greatly facilitates the creation of sophisticated *graphical user interfaces (GUI)*.

Object-Oriented Languages.   Central to achieving the benefits of the object oriented approach is developing software in an **object-oriented programming (OOP) language**. The most popular true OOP languages are Java and Smalltalk. However, the learning curve of OOP languages is steep. The time and cost of retooling for OOP is the greatest impediment to the transition process. Most firms are not prepared to discard millions of lines of traditional COBOL code and retrain their programming staffs to implement object-oriented systems. Therefore, a compromise, intended to ease this transition, has been the development of hybrid languages, such as Object COBOL, Object Pascal, and C++.

Programming the System.   Regardless of the programming language used, modern programs should follow a *modular approach*. This technique produces small programs that perform narrowly defined tasks. The following three benefits are associated with modular programming.

1. *Programming efficiency.* Modules can be coded and tested independently, which vastly reduces programming time. A firm can assign several programmers to a single system. Working in parallel, the programmers each design a few modules. These are then assembled into the completed system.
2. *Maintenance efficiency.* Small modules are easier to analyze and change, which reduces the start-up time during program maintenance. Extensive changes can be parceled out to several programmers simultaneously to shorten maintenance time.

3. *Control.* By keeping modules small, they are less likely to contain material errors of fraudulent logic. Since each module is independent of the others, errors are contained within the module.

Test the Application Software

All program modules must be thoroughly tested before they are implemented. There are some proven concepts about testing that should be followed by the system developers, and considered by auditors in conducting audits.

Testing Methodology.   The process itself has structured steps to follow. Figure 5.8 shows a program-testing procedure involving the creation of hypothetical master files and transactions files that are processed by the modules being tested. The results of the tests are then compared against predetermined results to identify programming and logic errors. For example, in testing the logic of the accounts receivable update module illustrated in Figure 5.8, the programmer might create an accounts receivable master file record for John Smith with a current balance of $1,000 and a sales order transaction record for $100. Before performing the update test, the programmer concludes that a new balance of $1,100 should be created. To verify the module's internal logic, the programmer compares the actual results obtained from the run with the predetermined results. This example is a simple one of a program test. Actual testing would be extensive and would involve many transactions that test all aspects of the module's logic.

FIGURE 5.8

**Program–Testing
Procedures**

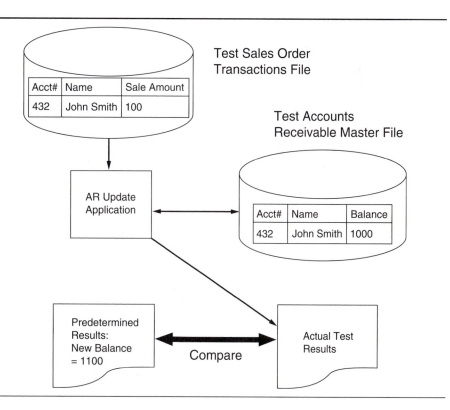

Testing Offline Before Deploying Online.   The first point that is critical in testing is to never underestimate the principle of *testing offline before deploying a system online.* Implementing a system without testing offline is an invitation to disaster. One online e-commerce firm went out of business because it implemented a system online without testing it offline first, and accidentally left a vulnerable Web server open to attacks from crackers. A cracker stole thousands of credit card numbers and eventually the online business failed.

Test Data.   Creating meaningful test data is an extremely time-consuming aspect of program testing. This activity can, however, provide future benefits. As we shall see in Chapter 7, application auditing sometimes involves program testing. To facilitate future testing, test data prepared during the implementation phase should be retained for reuse. This test data will give the auditor a frame of reference for designing and evaluating future audit tests. For example, if a program has undergone no maintenance changes since its original implementation, the test results from the audit should be identical to the original test results. Having a basis for comparison, the auditor can thus quickly verify the integrity of the program code. If changes have occurred, however, the original test data can provide evidence regarding these changes. The auditor can thus focus attention upon those areas. Maintaining test data and its results is also a significant control feature, as future systems development can use the test data and results to test future changes to the application software.

System Implementation—Phase VII

In the **system implementation** phase of the systems development process, database structures are created and populated with data, equipment is purchased and installed, employees are trained, the system is documented, and the new system is installed. The implementation process engages the efforts of designers, programmers, database administrators, users, and accountants. The activities in this phase entail extensive costs and will often consume more personnel-hours than all other preimplementation phases of the SDLC combined.

Testing the Entire System

When all modules have been coded and tested, they must be brought together and tested as a whole. User personnel should direct system-wide testing as a prelude to the formal system implementation. The procedure involves processing hypothetical data through the system. The outputs of the system are then reconciled with predetermined results, and the test is documented to provide evidence of the system's performance. Finally, when those conducting the tests are satisfied with the results, they should then complete a formal acceptance document. This is an explicit acknowledgment by the user that the system in question meets stated requirements. The user acceptance document becomes important in reconciling differences and assigning responsibility during the post-implementation review of the system.

Documenting the System

The system's **documentation** provides the auditor with essential information about how the system works. The documentation requirements of three groups—systems designers and programmers, computer operators, and end users—are of particular importance.

Designer and Programmer Documentation.   Systems designers and programmers need documentation to debug errors and perform maintenance on the system. This group is involved with the system on a highly technical level, which requires both

FIGURE 5.9   **System Designer and Programmer Documentation**

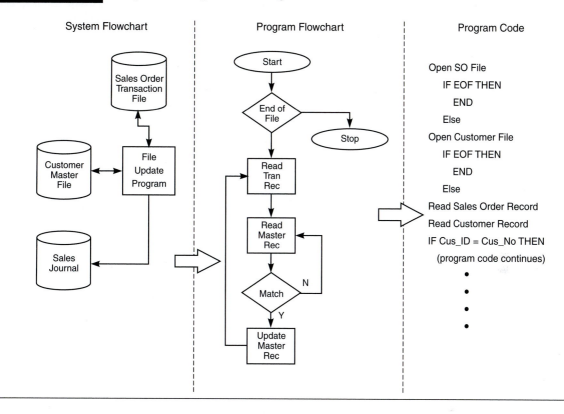

general and detailed information. Some of this is provided through data flow diagrams, entity relation (ER) diagrams, and structure diagrams. In addition, system flowcharts, program flowcharts, and program code listings are important forms of documentation. The *system flowchart* shows the relationship of input files, programs, and output files. However, it does not reveal the logic of individual programs that constitute the system. The *program flowchart* provides a detailed description of the sequential and logical operation of the program. Each program in the system's flowchart is represented by a separate program flowchart, as shown in Figure 5.9. From these, the programmer can visually review and evaluate the program's logic. The program code should itself be documented with comments that describe each major program segment.

Operator Documentation. Computer operators use documentation called a **run manual**, which describes how to run the system. The typical contents of a run manual include

- The name of the system, such as Purchases System
- The run schedule (daily, weekly, time of day, and so on)
- Required hardware devices (tapes, disks, printers, or special hardware)
- File requirements specifying all the transaction (input) files, master files, and output files used in the system
- Run-time instructions describing the error messages that may appear, actions to be taken, and the name and telephone number of the programmer on call, should the system fail
- A list of users who receive the output from the run

For security and control reasons, system flowcharts, logic flowcharts, and program code listings should not be part of the operator documentation. We saw in Chapter 2 that the activities of programmers and operators should be separated. Consistent with this segregation of duties issue, operators should not have access to the details of a system's internal logic.

User Documentation.   Users need documentation describing how to use the system. User tasks include such things as entering input for transactions, making inquiries of account balances, updating accounts, and generating output reports. The nature of user documentation will depend on the user's degree of sophistication with computers and technology. Thus, before designing user documentation, the systems professional must assess and classify the user's skill level. The following is one possible classification scheme:

- **Novices** have little or no experience with computers and are embarrassed to ask questions. Novices also know little about their assigned tasks. User training and documentation for novices must be extensive and detailed.
- **Occasional users** once understood the system but have forgotten some essential commands and procedures. They require less training and documentation than novices.
- **Frequent light users** are familiar with limited aspects of the system. Although functional, they tend not to explore beneath the surface and lack depth of knowledge. This group knows only what it needs to know and requires training and documentation for unfamiliar areas.
- **Frequent power users** understand the existing system and will readily adapt to new systems. They are intolerant of detailed instructions that waste their time. They like to find shortcuts and use macro commands to improve performance. This group requires only abbreviated documentation.

User Handbook.   With these classes in mind, user documentation often takes the form of a **user handbook**, as well as online documentation. The typical user handbook will contain the following items:

- An overview of the system and its major functions
- Instructions for getting started
- Descriptions of procedures with step-by-step visual references
- Examples of input screens and instructions for entering data
- A complete list of error message codes and descriptions
- A reference manual of commands to run the system
- A glossary of key terms
- Service and support information

Online documentation will guide the user interactively in the use of the system. Some commonly found online features include tutorials and help features.

Tutorials.   Online **tutorials** can be used to train the novice or the occasional user. The success of this technique is based on the tutorial's degree of realism. Tutorials should not restrict the user from access to legitimate functions.

Help Features.   Online **help features** range from simple to sophisticated. A simple help feature may be nothing more than an error message displayed on the screen. The user must "walk through" the screens in search of the solution to the problem. More sophisticated help is context-related. When the user makes an error, the system will send the message, "Do you need help?" The help feature analyzes the context of what the user is doing at the time of the error and provides help with that specific function (or command).

Converting the Databases

Database conversion is a critical step in the implementation phase. This is the transfer of data from its current form to the format or medium required by the new system. The degree of conversion depends on the technology leap from the old system to the new one. Some conversion activities are very labor intensive, requiring data to be entered into new databases manually. For example, the move from a manual system to a computer system will require converting files from paper to magnetic disk or tape. In other situations, data transfer may be accomplished by writing special conversion programs. A case in point is changing the file structure of the databases from sequential direct access files. In any case, data conversion is risky and must be carefully controlled. The following precautions should be taken:

1. *Validation.* The old database must be validated before conversion. This requires analyzing each class of data to determine whether it should be reproduced in the new database.
2. *Reconciliation.* After the conversion action, the new database must be reconciled against the original. Sometimes this must be done manually, record by record and field by field. In many instances, this process can be automated by writing a program that will compare the two sets of data.
3. *Backup.* Copies of the original files must be kept as backup against discrepancies in the converted data. If the current files are already in magnetic form, they can be conveniently backed up and stored. However, paper documents can create storage problems. When the user feels confident about the accuracy and completeness of the new databases, he or she may destroy the paper documents.

Converting to the New System

The process of converting from the old system to the new one is called the **cutover**. A system cutover will usually follow one of three approaches: cold turkey, phased, or parallel operation.

Cold Turkey Cutover. Under the **cold turkey cutover** approach (also called the "Big Bang" approach), the firm switches to the new system and simultaneously terminates the old system. When implementing simple systems, this is often the easiest and least costly approach. With more complex systems, it is the riskiest. Cold turkey cutover is akin to skydiving without a reserve parachute. As long as the main parachute functions properly, there is no problem. But things don't always work the way they are supposed to. System errors that were not detected during the walkthrough and testing steps may materialize unexpectedly. Without a backup system, an organization can find itself unable to process transactions and meet its obligations to customers and creditors.

Phased Cutover. Sometimes an entire system cannot, or need not, be cut over at once. The **phased cutover** begins operating the new system in modules. For example, Figure 5.10 shows how we might implement a system, starting with the sales subsystem, followed by the inventory control subsystem, and finally the purchases subsystem.

By phasing in the new system in modules, we reduce the risk of a devastating system failure. However, the phased approach can create incompatibilities between new subsystems and yet-to-be-replaced old subsystems. This problem may be alleviated by implementing special conversion systems that provide temporary interfaces during the cutover period.

Parallel Operation Cutover. **Parallel operation cutover** involves running the old system and the new system simultaneously for a period of time. Figure 5.11 illustrates

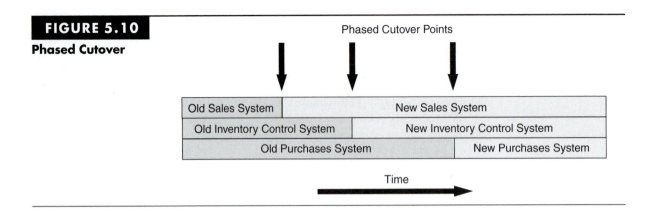

FIGURE 5.10

Phased Cutover

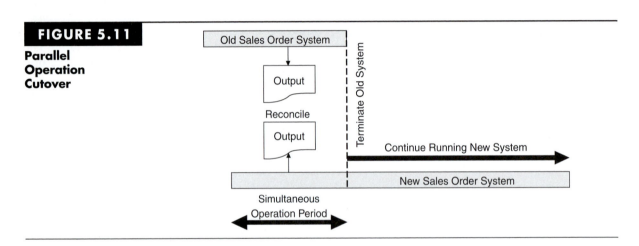

FIGURE 5.11

Parallel Operation Cutover

this approach, which is the most time-consuming and costly of the three. Running two systems in parallel essentially doubles resource consumption. During the cutover period, the two systems consume twice the resources of a single system. This includes twice the source documents, twice the processing time, twice the databases, and twice the output production.

The advantage of parallel cutover is the reduction in risk. By running two systems, the user can reconcile outputs to identify errors and debug errors before running the new system solo. Parallel operation should usually extend for one business cycle, such as one month. This allows the user to reconcile the two outputs at the end of the cycle as a final test of the system's functionality.

The Auditor's Role in System Implementation

External auditors are prohibited by SOX legislation from direct involvement in systems implementation. However, as the preceding discussion has already suggested, the role of internal auditors in the detailed design and implementation phases should be significant. Being a stakeholder in all financial systems, internal auditors should lend their expertise to this process to guide and shape the finished system. Specifically, internal auditors may get involved in the following ways.

Provide Technical Expertise.   The detailed design phase involves precise specifications of procedures, rules, and conventions to be used in the system. In the case of an

AIS, these specifications must comply with GAAP, GAAS, SEC regulations, and IRS codes. Failure to so comply can lead to legal exposure for the firm. For example, choosing the correct depreciation method or asset valuation technique requires a technical background not necessarily possessed by systems professionals. The auditor may provide this expertise to the systems design process.

Specify Documentation Standards. In the implementation phase, the auditor plays a role in specifying system documentation. Since financial systems must periodically be audited, they must be adequately documented. The auditor should actively encourage adherence to effective documentation standards.

Verify Control Adequacy and Compliance with SOX. The AIS applications that emerge from the SDLC must possess adequate controls. In addition, compliance with SOX legislation requires management to certify the existence and effectiveness of those controls. During the implementation process, the internal audit function plays a key role in these verification and compliance activities.

Post-Implementation Review

One of the most important steps in the implementation stage actually takes place some months later in a *post-implementation review*. The review is conducted by an independent team to measure the success of the system and of the process after the dust has settled. Although systems professionals strive to produce systems that are on budget, on time, and meet user needs, this goal is not always attained. The post-implementation review of a newly installed system can provide management with insights into ways to improve the process for future systems. It can also provide auditors (both internal and external) with evidence regarding the adequacy of the SDLC in general and the risks associated with a particular system. The following are examples of valuable post-implementation evidence.

Systems Design Adequacy. The physical features of the system should be reviewed to see if they meet user needs. The reviewer should seek answers to the following types of questions:

- Does the output from the system possess such characteristics of information as relevance, timeliness, completeness, accuracy, and so on?
- Is the output in the format most useful and desired by the user (such as tables, graphs, electronic, hard copy, and so on)?
- Are the databases accurate, complete, and accessible?
- Were data lost, corrupted, or duplicated by the conversion process?
- Are input forms and screens properly designed and meeting user needs?
- Are the users using the system properly?
- Does the processing appear to be correct?
- Can all program modules be accessed and executed properly, or does the user ever get stuck in a loop?
- Is user documentation accurate, complete, and easy to follow?
- Does the system provide the user adequate help and tutorials?

Accuracy of Time, Cost, and Benefit Estimates. The task of estimating time, costs, and benefits for a proposed system is complicated by uncertainty. This is particularly true for large projects involving many activities and long time frames. The more variables in the process, the greater the likelihood for material error in the estimates. History is often the best teacher for decisions of this sort. Therefore, a review of actual performance compared to budgeted amounts provides critical input for future budgeting decisions. From such information, we can learn where mistakes were made and how to avoid them next time. The following questions provide some insight:

- Were actual costs in line with budgeted costs?
- What were the areas of significant departures from budget?
- Were departures from budget controllable (internal) in the short run or noncontrollable (for example, supplier problems)?
- Were estimates of the number of lines of program code accurate?
- Was the degree of rework due to design and coding errors acceptable?
- Are users receiving the expected benefits from the system?
- Were values assigned to tangible and, especially, intangible benefits accurate?

Systems Maintenance—Phase VIII

Once a system is implemented, it enters the final phase in its life cycle. Systems maintenance is a formal process by which application programs undergo changes to accommodate changes in user needs. Some application changes are trivial, such as modifying the system to produce a new report or changing the length of a data field. Maintenance can also be extensive, such as making major changes to an application's logic and the user interface. Depending upon the organization, the systems maintenance period can last 5 years or longer. Systems in highly competitive business environments see much shorter system life spans. When it is no longer feasible for the organization to continue to maintain an aging system, it is scrapped, and a new systems development life cycle begins.

Maintenance represents a significant resource outlay compared to initial development costs. Over a system's life span, as much as 80 to 90 percent of its total cost may be incurred in the maintenance phase. We review the auditing implications of maintenance in the next section.

CONTROLLING AND AUDITING THE SDLC

In this chapter we have reviewed the highly technical and complex processes that constitute the SDLC. Before proceeding, it is useful to place this material in perspective with regard to audit objectives. Simply stated, the purpose of a financial audit is to provide an expert opinion regarding the fair presentation of the financial statements. To render such an opinion, the expert auditor must perform certain audit tests. Naturally, the accuracy of the financial data in the client's databases bears directly on the auditor's opinion. In a CBIS environment, financial data are processed (accessed, stored, and updated) by computer applications. The accuracy and integrity of these programs directly affects the accuracy of the client's financial data. A materially flawed financial application can corrupt financial data, which are then incorrectly reported in the financial statements.

Chapter 7 reviews several techniques for testing application controls. If audit evidence shows that computer applications process data correctly and accurately, the auditor can form the basis for reducing the amount of substantive testing that needs to be performed. Since the client organization could, however, have hundreds of financially significant applications, testing application controls can prove to be a highly technical and time-consuming activity. Auditors, therefore, seek efficient and effective ways to limit the application testing.

The systems development and maintenance process is common to all applications. A properly functioning systems development process ensures that only needed applications are created, that they are properly specified, that they possess adequate controls, and that they are thoroughly tested before being implemented. The systems maintenance process ensures that only legitimate changes are made to applications and that such changes are also tested before being implemented. Together, these processes establish the accuracy of new applications and preserve their integrity throughout the period under review.

If the auditor can verify that these processes are effectively controlled, he or she can limit the extent of application testing that needs to be done. If, however, audit evidence shows SDLC controls to be weak and inconsistently applied, application testing and substantive testing cannot be reduced. In some situations, it may even be necessary to expand the scope of the audit. With this perspective in place, let's now examine the controls, audit objectives, and audit procedures related to these important processes.

Controlling New Systems Development

The first five controllable activities discussed next deal with the authorization, development, and implementation of the original system. The last two controllable activities pertain to systems maintenance procedures.

Systems Authorization Activities

All systems must be properly authorized to ensure their economic justification and feasibility. As with all material transactions, authorizing the development of a new information system should be a formal step in the process. Typically, this requires that each new system request be submitted in writing by users to systems professionals who have both the expertise and authority to evaluate and approve (or reject) the request.

User Specification Activities

Users must be actively involved in the systems development process. Their involvement should not be stifled because the proposed system is technically complex. Regardless of the technology involved, the user can and should provide a detailed written description of the logical needs that must be satisfied by the system. The creation of a user specification document often involves the joint efforts of the user and systems professionals. However, it is most important that this document remain a statement of user needs. It should describe the user's view of the problem, not that of the systems professionals.

Technical Design Activities

The technical design activities translate the user specifications into a set of detailed technical specifications of a system that meets the user's needs. The scope of these activities includes systems analysis, general systems design, feasibility analysis, and detailed systems design. The adequacy of these activities is measured by the quality of the documentation that emerges from each phase. Documentation is both a control and evidence of control and is critical to the system's long-term success. Specific documentation requirements were discussed previously.

Internal Audit Participation

The internal auditor plays an important role in the control of systems development activities, particularly in organizations whose users lack technical expertise. The internal auditor can serve as a liaison between users and the systems professionals to ensure an effective transfer of knowledge. An internal audit group, astute in computer technology and with a solid grasp of the business problems of users, can make a valuable contribution to all aspects of the SDLC process. The auditor should become involved at the inception of the process to make conceptual suggestions regarding system requirements and controls. Auditor involvement should continue throughout all phases of the development process and into the maintenance phase.

User Test and Acceptance Procedures

Just before implementation, the individual modules of the system must be tested as a unified whole. A test team comprising user personnel, systems professionals, and internal audit personnel subjects the system to rigorous testing. Once the test team is satisfied that the system meets its stated requirements, the system is formally accepted by the user department(s).

The formal testing and acceptance of the system by the user is considered by many auditors to be the most important control over the SDLC. This is the last point at which the user can determine that the system adequately meets his or her needs. Although discovering a major flaw at this juncture can be costly, discovering the flaw later, during operation, can be devastating. The user's acceptance of the new system should be formally documented.

Audit Objectives Related to New Systems Development

- Verify that SDLC activities are applied consistently and in accordance with management's policies.
- Determine that the system as originally implemented was free from material errors and fraud.
- Confirm that the system was judged to be necessary and justified at various checkpoints throughout the SDLC.
- Verify that system documentation is sufficiently accurate and complete to facilitate audit and maintenance activities.

Audit Procedures Related to New Systems Development

The auditor should select a sample of completed projects (completed in both the current period and previous periods) and review the documentation for evidence of compliance with SDLC policies. Specific points for review should include determining the following:

- User and computer services management properly authorized the project.
- A preliminary feasibility study showed that the project had merit.
- A detailed analysis of user needs was conducted that resulted in alternative general designs.
- A cost–benefit analysis was conducted using reasonably accurate figures.
- The project's documentation shows that the detailed design was an appropriate and accurate solution to the user's problem.
- Test results show that the system was thoroughly tested at both the individual module and the total system level before implementation. (To confirm these test results, the auditor may decide to retest selected elements of the application.)
- There is a checklist of specific problems detected during the conversion period, along with evidence that they were corrected in the maintenance phase.
- Systems documentation complies with organizational requirements and standards.

The Controlling Systems Maintenance

The last two controllable activities pertain to systems maintenance. Upon implementation, the system enters the maintenance phase of the SDLC. This is the longest period in the SDLC, often spanning several years. It is important to recognize that systems do not remain static throughout this period. Rather, they may undergo substantial changes that constitute a financial outlay many times their original cost. If an application has undergone maintenance (and even if it has not), its integrity may have been compromised since implementation. The auditor's review may, therefore, extend into the maintenance phase to determine that application integrity is still intact.

In this section, we see how uncontrolled program changes can increase a firm's exposure to financial misstatement due to programming errors. Some programming errors are subtle, resulting in the creation and distribution of incorrect information that goes undetected by the user. Other forms of errors are more apparent and result in system failures that can disrupt data processing and even bring operations to a halt. In addition to these exposures, program fraud may take root in an environment of poorly controlled maintenance and can go undetected for years.

Maintenance Authorization, Testing, and Documentation

The benefits achieved from controlling new system development can be quickly lost during system maintenance if control does not continue into that phase. Access to systems for maintenance purposes increases the possibility of systems errors. Logic may be corrupted either by the accidental introduction of errors or intentional acts to defraud. To minimize the potential exposure, all maintenance actions should require, as a minimum, four controls: formal authorization, technical specification of the changes, retesting the system, and updating the documentation. In other words, maintenance activities should be given essentially the same treatment as new development. The extent of the change and its potential impact on the system should govern the degree of control applied. When maintenance causes extensive changes to program logic, additional controls, such as involvement by the internal auditor and the implementation of user test and acceptance procedures, may be necessary.

Source Program Library Controls

In spite of the preceding maintenance procedures, application integrity can be jeopardized by individuals who gain unauthorized access to programs. The remainder of this section deals with control techniques and procedures for preventing and detecting unauthorized access to application programs.

In larger computer systems, application program source code is stored on magnetic disks called the *source program library (SPL)*. Figure 5.12 illustrates the relationship between the SPL and other key components of the operating environment.

To execute a production application, it must first be compiled and linked to create a load module that the computer can process. As a practical matter, load modules are secure and free from the threat of unauthorized modification. Program changes (both authorized maintenance and unauthorized changes) are accomplished by first making changes to the source code stored on the SPL and then recompiling and linking the program to create a new load module that incorporates the changed code. Therefore, the SPL is a sensitive area, which, to preserve application integrity, must be properly controlled.

The Worst-Case Situation: No Controls

Figure 5.12 shows the SPL without controls. This arrangement has the potential to create the following two serious forms of exposure (see the following list).

1. *Access to programs is completely unrestricted.* Programmers and others can access any programs stored in the library, and there is no provision for detecting an unauthorized intrusion.

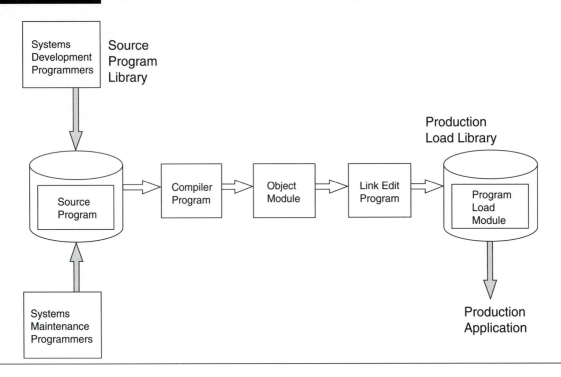

FIGURE 5.12   **Uncontrolled Access to the Source Program Library**

2. *Because of these control weaknesses, programs are subject to unauthorized changes.* Hence, there is no basis for relying on the effectiveness of other controls (maintenance authorization, program testing, and documentation). In other words, with no provision for detecting unauthorized access to the SPL, program integrity cannot be verified.

Control is always in conflict with operational flexibility and efficiency. For these reasons, systems professionals who must work daily within this environment sometimes oppose controlling the SPL. To achieve a mutually acceptable control-flexibility trade-off between the needs of systems professionals and auditors, both must understand the exposures that are created when control features are not employed or are routinely circumvented. In spite of the exposure just described, the no-controls approach is often the choice (perhaps inadvertently) that management makes.

A Controlled SPL Environment
To control the SPL, protective features and procedures must be explicitly addressed, and this requires the implementation of an *SPL management system (SPLMS)*. Figure 5.13 illustrates the use of this technique. The black box surrounding the SPL signifies the SPLMS. This software is used to control four routine but critical functions: (1) storing programs on the SPL, (2) retrieving programs for maintenance purposes, (3) deleting obsolete programs from the library, and (4) documenting program changes to provide an audit trail of the changes.

You may have recognized the similarities between the SPL management system and a database management system. This is a valid analogy, the difference being that SPL software manages program files and DBMSs manage data files. SPLMSs may be supplied

FIGURE 5.13   **Source Program Library under the Control of SPL Management Software**

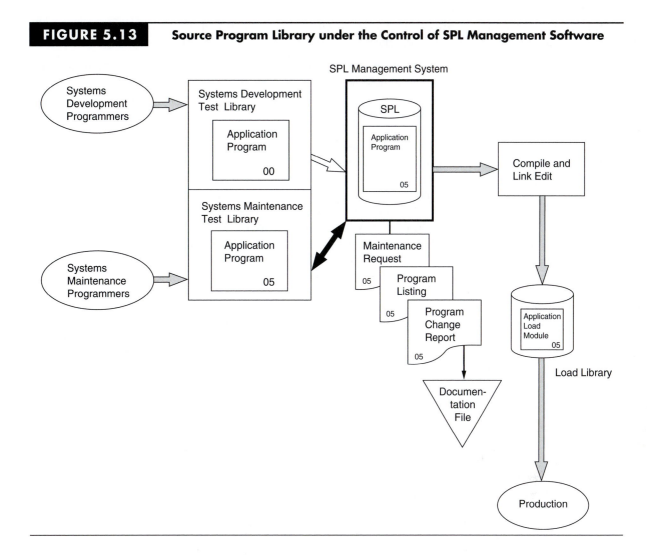

by the computer manufacturer as part of the operating system or may be purchased through software vendors. Some organizations, to provide special control features, develop their own SPL software.

The mere presence of an SPLMS does not guarantee program integrity. Again, we can draw an analogy with the DBMS. To achieve data integrity, the DBMS must be properly used; control does not come automatically, it must be planned. Likewise, an SPL requires specific planning and control techniques to ensure program integrity. The control techniques discussed in the following paragraphs address only the most vulnerable areas and should be considered minimum control.

Password Control.   Assigning passwords provides one form of access control over the SPL. This is similar to password controls used in a DBMS to protect data files. Every financially significant program stored in the SPL can be assigned a separate password. As previously discussed, passwords have drawbacks. When more than one person is authorized to access a program, preserving the secrecy of a shared password is a problem. As more authorized personnel have a need to know the password, the potential for losing control of the password increases. Since responsibility for the secrecy of a shared password lies with the group rather than with an individual, personal accountability is reduced, and individuals within the group may take less care in protecting the password.

Separate Test Libraries.   Figure 5.13 illustrates an improvement on the shared password approach through the creation of separate password-controlled libraries (or directories) for each programmer. Under this concept, programs are copied into the programmer's library for maintenance and testing. Direct access to the production SPL is limited to an authorized librarian who must approve all requests to modify, delete, and copy programs. Further, passwords to access programs can be changed regularly and disclosed only on a need-to-know basis.

A relatively cost-free enhancement to this control feature is the implementation of program naming conventions. The name assigned a program clearly distinguishes it as being either a test or a production program. When a program is copied from the production SPL to the programmer's library, it is given a temporary "test" name. When the program is returned to the SPL, it is renamed with its original production name. This technique greatly reduces the risk of accidentally running an untested version of a program in place of the production program.

Audit Trail and Management Reports.   An important feature of SPL management software is the creation of reports that enhance management control and the audit function. The most useful of these are program modification reports, which describe in detail all program changes (additions and deletions) to each module. These reports should be part of the documentation file of each application to form an audit trail of program changes over the life of the application. During an audit, these reports can be reconciled against program maintenance requests to verify that only changes requested and authorized were actually implemented. For example, if a programmer attempted to use a legitimate maintenance action as an opportunity to commit program fraud, the unauthorized changes to the program code would be presented in the program modification report. These reports can be produced as hard copy and on disk and can be governed by password control, thus limiting access to management and auditors.

Program Version Numbers.   The SPLMS assigns a version number automatically to each program stored on the SPL. When programs are first placed in the libraries (upon implementation), they are assigned a version number of 0. With each modification to the program, the version number is increased by 1. For instance, after five authorized maintenance changes, the production program will be designated version 05, as illustrated in Figure 5.14. This feature, when combined with audit trail reports, provides evidence for identifying unauthorized changes to program modules. An unauthorized change is signaled by a version number on the production load module that cannot be reconciled to the number of authorized changes. For example, if 10 changes were authorized but the production program shows version 12, then one of two possibilities explain this discrepancy: (1) authorized changes occurred that are unsupported by documentation or (2) unauthorized changes were made to the program, which incremented the version numbers.

Controlling Access to Maintenance Commands.   SPL management systems use powerful maintenance commands to alter or eliminate program passwords, alter the program version (modification) number, and temporarily modify a program without generating a record of the modification. There are legitimate technical reasons why systems designers and administrators need these commands. However, if not controlled, maintenance commands open the possibility of unrecorded, and perhaps unauthorized, program modifications. Hence, access to the maintenance commands themselves should be password-controlled, and the authority to use them should be controlled by management or the security group.

FIGURE 5.14   **Auditing SPL Software System**

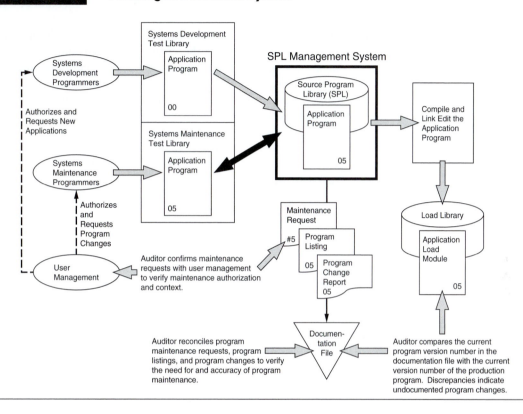

Audit Objectives Related to System Maintenance

- Detect unauthorized program maintenance (which may have resulted in significant processing errors or fraud). Determine that (1) maintenance procedures protect applications from unauthorized changes, (2) applications are free from material errors, and (3) program libraries are protected from unauthorized access.

We will examine each of these objectives in turn, focusing on the tests of controls that are necessary to achieve the objective. The discussion will assume that the organization employs source program library (SPL) software to control program maintenance. It should be noted that without SPL software, it can be difficult to achieve these audit objectives. The procedures described below are illustrated in Figure 5.14.

Audit Procedures Related to System Maintenance

Identify Unauthorized Changes.   To establish that program changes were authorized, the auditor should examine the audit trail of program changes for a sample of applications that have undergone maintenance. The auditor can confirm that authorization procedures were followed by performing the following tests of controls.

- *Reconcile program version numbers.* The permanent file of the application should contain program change authorization documents that correspond to the current version number of the production application. In other words, if the production application is in its tenth version, there should be ten program change authorizations in the permanent file as supporting documentation. Any discrepancies between version numbers and supporting documents may indicate that unauthorized changes were made.

- *Confirm maintenance authorization.* The program maintenance authorization documents should indicate the nature of the change requested and the date of the change. It should also be signed and approved by the appropriate management from both computer services and the user departments. The auditor should confirm the facts contained in the maintenance authorization and verify the authorizing signatures with the managers involved.

Identify Application Errors. The auditor can determine that programs are free from material errors by performing three types of tests of controls: reconciling the source code, reviewing the test results, and retesting the program.

- *Reconcile the source code.* Each application's permanent file should contain the current program listing and listings of all changes made to the application. These documents describe in detail the application's maintenance history. In addition, the nature of the program change should be clearly stated on the program change authorization document. The auditor should select a sample of applications and reconcile each program change with the appropriate authorization documents. The modular approach to systems design (creating applications that comprise many small discrete program modules) greatly facilitates this testing technique. The reduced complexity of these modules enhances the auditor's ability to identify irregularities that indicate errors, omissions, and potentially fraudulent programming code.
- *Review test results.* Every program change should be thoroughly tested before being implemented. Program test procedures should be properly documented by test objectives, test data, and processing results, which support the programmer's decision to implement the change. The auditor should review this record for each significant program change to establish that testing was sufficiently rigorous to identify any errors.
- *Retest the program.* The auditor can retest the application to confirm its integrity. We examine several techniques for application testing in Chapter 7.

Test Access to Libraries. The existence of a secure program library is central to preventing errors and program fraud. One method is to assign library access rights exclusively to individuals who act as librarians. Their function is to retrieve applications from the program libraries for maintenance and to restore the modified programs to the library. In this arrangement, programmers perform program maintenance and testing in their own "private" libraries but do not have direct access to the program library.

The auditor should establish that the program library and private libraries are protected from unauthorized access by performing the following tests of controls.

- *Review programmer authority tables.* The auditor can select a sample of programmers and review their access authority. The programmer's authority table will specify the libraries a programmer may access. These authorizations should be matched against the programmer's maintenance authority to ensure that no irregularities exist.
- *Test authority table.* The auditor should simulate the programmer's access privileges and then violate the authorization rules by attempting to access unauthorized libraries. Any such attempts should be denied by the operating system.

SUMMARY

One of the most valuable assets of the modern business organization is a responsive, user-oriented information system. A well-designed system can increase productivity, reduce inventories, eliminate nonvalue-added activities, improve customer service and management decisions, and coordinate activities throughout the organization.

This chapter examined the purpose, control, and audit of the systems development life cycle. It began by describing the roles of the participants involved in systems development, including systems professionals, users, and stakeholders. Then it outlined the key activities associated with SDLC. This process consists of two primary sets of activities: new systems development and maintenance. The former, which is used to guide the development of information systems in many organizations, includes *systems planning, systems analysis, conceptual design, system selection, detailed design, system programming and testing, and system implementation.* A properly functioning systems development process ensures that only needed applications are created, that they are properly specified, that they possess adequate controls, and that they are thoroughly tested before being implemented. Upon implementation, new systems enter the *systems maintenance* phase, where they remain until they are terminated and ultimately replaced. The systems maintenance process ensures that only legitimate changes are made to applications and that such changes are also tested before being implemented.

The systems development and maintenance process is common to all applications. Together, they establish the accuracy of new applications and preserve their integrity throughout the period under review.

The auditor's objective in testing controls over these processes is to establish application integrity and thus limit the tests of application controls and substantive testing that needs to be done.

KEY TERMS

accountant/auditor
backbone system
break-even point
cold turkey cutover
conceptual design
cutover
database conversion
data flow diagrams (DFDs)
detailed design
detailed design report
documentation
economic feasibility
end user
event-driven language
frequent light user
frequent power user
general accounting system
help features

intangible benefits
iterative approach
legal feasibility
net present value method
new systems development
novice
object-oriented design (OOD) approach
object-oriented programming (OOP) language
object
occasional user
office automation system
operational feasibility
parallel operation cutover
payback method
phased cutover
procedural language
project planning
project proposal

project schedule
quality assurance group
run manual
schedule feasibility
special-purpose system
steering committee
strategic systems planning
structured design
structure diagram
system implementation
system survey
systems analysis
systems analysis report
systems development life cycle (SDLC)

systems evaluation and selection
systems maintenance
systems planning
systems professional
systems selection report
tangible benefits
technical feasibility
third-generation language (3GLs)
turnkey system
tutorial
user handbook
vendor-supported system
walkthrough

REVIEW QUESTIONS

1. Distinguish between systems professionals, end users, and stakeholders.
2. What is the role of the accountant in the SDLC? Why might accountants be called on for input into the development of a nonaccounting information system?
3. What are the three problems that account for most system failures?
4. Why is it often difficult to obtain competent and meaningful user involvement in the SDLC?
5. Who should sit on the systems steering committee? What are their typical responsibilities?
6. Why is strategic systems planning not technically considered to be part of the SDLC?
7. What is strategic systems planning, and why should it be done?
8. What is the purpose of project planning, and what are the various steps?
9. What is the object-oriented design (OOD) approach?
10. What are the broad classes of facts that need to be gathered in the system survey?
11. What are the primary fact-gathering techniques?
12. What are the relative merits and disadvantages of a current systems survey?
13. Distinguish among data sources, data stores, and data flows.
14. What are some of the key documents that may be reviewed in a current systems survey?
15. What is the purpose of a systems analysis, and what type of information should be included in the systems analysis report?

16. What is the primary objective of the conceptual systems design phase?
17. What are two approaches to conceptual systems design?
18. How much design detail is needed in the conceptual design phase?
19. What is an object, and what are its characteristics in the object-oriented approach? Give two examples.
20. What is the auditor's primary role in the conceptual design of the system?
21. Who should be included in the group of independent evaluators performing the detailed feasibility study?
22. What makes the cost–benefit analysis more difficult for information systems than most other investments an organization may make?
23. Classify each of the following as either one-time or recurring costs:
    a. training personnel
    b. initial programming and testing
    c. systems design
    d. hardware costs
    e. software maintenance costs
    f. site preparation
    g. rent for facilities
    h. data conversion from old system to new system
    i. insurance costs
    j. installation of original equipment
    k. hardware upgrades
24. Distinguish between turnkey and backbone systems. Which is more flexible?

25. Discuss the relative merits of in-house programs versus commercially developed software.
26. Why is modular programming preferable to free coding?
27. Why should test data be saved after it has been used?
28. Explain the importance of documentation by the systems programmers.
29. What documents not typically needed by other stakeholders do accountants and auditors need for the new system?

DISCUSSION QUESTIONS

1. Comment on the following statement: "The maintenance stage of the SDLC involves making trivial changes to accommodate changes in user needs."
2. Discuss how rushing the system's requirements stage may delay or even result in the failure of a systems development process. Conversely, discuss how spending too long in this stage may result in "analysis paralysis."
3. Is a good strategic plan detail oriented?
4. Distinguish between a problem and a symptom. Give an example. Are these usually noticed by upper-, middle-, or lower-level managers?
5. What purposes does the systems project proposal serve? How are these evaluated and prioritized? Is the prioritizing process objective or subjective?
6. Most firms underestimate the cost and time requirements of the SDLC by as much as 50 percent. Why do you think this occurs? In what stages do you think the underestimates are most dramatic?
7. A lack of support by top management has led to the downfall of many new systems projects during the implementation phase. Why do you think management support is so important?
8. Many new systems projects grossly underestimate transaction volumes simply because they do not take into account how the new, improved system can actually increase demand. Explain how this can happen and give an example.
9. Compare and contrast the structured design approach and the object-oriented approach. Which do you believe is most beneficial? Why?
10. Do you think legal feasibility is an issue for a system that incorporates the use of machines to sell lottery tickets?
11. Intangible benefits are usually extremely difficult to quantify accurately. Some designers argue that if you understate them, then conservative estimates are produced. Any excess benefits will be greatly welcomed but not required for the new system to be a success. What are the dangers of this viewpoint?
12. If a firm decides early on to go with a special-purpose system, such as SAP, based on the recommendations of the external audit firm, should the SDLC be bypassed?
13. During a test data procedure, why should the developers bother testing "bad" data?
14. If the system is behind schedule and if each program module is tested and no problems are found, is it necessary to test all modules in conjunction with one another? Why or why not?
15. Run manuals for computer operators are similar in theory to the checklists that airplane pilots use for takeoffs and landings. Explain why these are important.
16. Who conducts the post-implementation review? When should it be conducted? If an outside consulting firm were hired to design and implement the new system, or a canned software package were purchased, would a post-implementation review still be useful?
17. Discuss the importance of involving accountants in the detailed design and implementation phases. What tasks should they perform?
18. Discuss the independence issue when audit firms also provide consulting input into the development and selection of new systems.
19. Discuss the various feasibility measures that should be considered. Give an example of each.
20. Discuss three benefits associated with modular programming.

MULTIPLE-CHOICE QUESTIONS

1. All of the following individuals would likely be SDLC participants EXCEPT
   a. accountants.
   b. shareholders.
   c. management.
   d. programmers.
   e. all of the above.

2. Which of the following represents the correct order in problem resolution?
   a. Define the problem, recognize the problem, perform feasibility studies, specify system objectives, and prepare a project proposal.
   b. Recognize the problem, define the problem, perform feasibility studies, specify system objectives, and prepare a project proposal.
   c. Define the problem, recognize the problem, specify system objectives, perform feasibility studies, and prepare a project proposal.
   d. Recognize the problem, define the problem, specify system objectives, perform feasibility studies, and prepare a project proposal.

3. A feasibility study for a new computer system should
   a. consider costs, savings, controls, profit improvement, and other benefits analyzed by application area.
   b. provide the preliminary plan for converting existing manual systems and clerical operations.
   c. provide management with assurance from qualified, independent consultants that the use of a computer system appeared justified.
   d. include a report by the internal audit department that evaluated internal control features for each planned application.

4. Which of the following is the most important factor in planning for a system change?
   a. Having an auditor as a member of the design team.
   b. Using state-of-the-art techniques.
   c. Concentrating on software rather than hardware.
   d. Involving top management and people who use the system.
   e. Selecting a user to lead the design team.

5. In the context of the TELOS acronym, technical feasibility refers to whether
   a. a proposed system is attainable, given the existing technology.
   b. the systems manager can coordinate and control the activities of the systems department.
   c. an adequate computer site exists for the proposed system.
   d. the proposed system will produce economic benefits exceeding its costs.
   e. the system will be used effectively within the operating environment of an organization.

6. Which of the following steps is NOT considered to be part of this systems survey?
   a. Interviews are conducted with operating people and managers.
   b. The complete documentation of the system is obtained and reviewed.
   c. Measures of processing volume are obtained for each operation.
   d. Equipment sold by various computer manufacturers is reviewed in terms of capability, cost, and availability.
   e. Work measurement studies are conducted to determine the time required to complete various tasks or jobs.

7. A systems development approach that starts with broad organizational goals and the types of decisions organizational executives make is called
   a. bottom-up.
   b. network.
   c. top-down.
   d. strategic.
   e. sequential.

8. The TELOS study that determines whether a project can be completed in an acceptable time frame is
   a. a schedule feasibility study.
   b. a time frame feasibility study.
   c. an on-time feasibility study.
   d. an economic completion feasibility study.
   e. a length of contract feasibility study.

9. Which of the following is least likely to be an accountant's role in the SDLC?
   a. user
   b. consultant
   c. auditor
   d. programmer
   e. all of these are likely roles

10. The TELOS acronym is often used for determining the need for system changes. Which of the following types of feasibility studies are elements of TELOS?
   a. legal, environmental, and economic
   b. environmental, operational, and economic
   c. technical, economic, legal, and practical
   d. practical, technical, and operational
   e. technical, operational, and economic

11. What name is given to the time value of money technique that discounts the after-tax cash flows for a project over its life to time period zero using the company's minimum desired rate of return?
   a. net present value method
   b. capital rationing method
   c. payback method
   d. average rate of return method
   e. accounting rate of return method

12. One-time costs of system development include all of the following EXCEPT
   a. site preparation.
   b. hardware maintenance.
   c. programming.
   d. hardware acquisition.
   e. data conversion.

13. Which of the following aspects of a cost-benefit study would have the greatest uncertainty as to its precise value?
   a. the tangible costs
   b. the intangible costs
   c. the tangible benefits
   d. the intangible benefits
   e. none of the above because they are equally precise

14. Which of the following is NOT a one-time cost?
   a. site preparation
   b. insurance
   c. software acquisition
   d. data conversion

15. Which of the following is NOT an advantage of commercial software?
   a. independence
   b. cost

   c. reliability
   d. implementation time
   e. systems design.

16. The technique that recognizes the time value of money by discounting the after-tax cash flows for a project over its life to time period zero using the company's minimum desired rate of return is called the
   a. net present value method.
   b. capital rationing method.
   c. payback method.
   d. average rate of return method.
   e. accounting rate of return method.

17. Fitzgerald Company is planning to acquire a $250,000 computer that will provide increased efficiencies, thereby reducing annual operating costs by $80,000. The computer will be depreciated by the straight-line method over a 5-year life with no salvage value at the end of 5 years. Assuming a 40 percent income tax rate, the machine's payback period is
   a. 3.13 years.
   b. 3.21 years.
   c. 3.68 years.
   d. 4.81 years.
   e. 5.21 years.

18. In conducting a cost–benefit analysis, the estimated category that ordinarily would have the greatest uncertainty as to its precise value is
   a. the tangible costs.
   b. the intangible costs.
   c. the tangible benefits.
   d. the intangible benefits.
   e. none of the above because they are equally precise.

19. At which phase in the SDLC are errors are most costly to correct?
   a. programming
   b. conceptual design
   c. analysis
   d. detailed design
   e. implementation

20. User test and acceptance is part of which phase of the system development life cycle?
   a. implementation
   b. general systems design
   c. program specification and implementation planning
   d. detailed systems design

PROBLEMS

1. Systems Planning

A new systems development project is being planned for the Reindeer Christmas Supplies Company. The invoicing, cash receipts, and accounts payable modules are all going to be updated. The controller, Kris K. Ringle, is a little anxious about this project. The last systems development project that affected his department was not very successful, and the employees in the accounting department did not accept the new system very well at first. He feels that the systems personnel did not interact sufficiently with the users of the systems in the accounting department. Prepare a memo from Ringle to the head of the information systems department, Sandy Klaus. In this memo, provide some suggestions for including the accounting personnel in the systems development project. Give some very persuasive arguments why prototyping would be helpful to the workers in the accounting department.

2. Problem Identification

The need for a new information system may be manifest in various symptoms. In the early stages of a problem, these symptoms seem innocuous and go unrecognized. As the underlying source of the problem grows in severity, so do its symptoms, until they are alarmingly apparent. Classify each of the following as a problem or a symptom. If it is a symptom, give two examples of a possible underlying problem. If it is a problem, give two examples of a possible symptom that may be detected.

a. declining profits
b. defective production process
c. low-quality raw materials
d. shortfall in cash balance
e. declining market share
f. shortage of employees in the accounts payable department
g. shortage of raw material due to a drought in the Midwest
h. inadequately trained workers
i. decreasing customer satisfaction

3. Systems Development and Implementation

Kruger Designs hired a consulting firm 3 months ago to redesign the information system used by the architects. The architects will be able to use state-of-the-art CAD programs to help in designing the products. Further, they will be able to store these designs on a network server where they and other architects may be able to call them back up for future designs with similar components. The consulting firm has been instructed to develop the system without disrupting the architects. In fact, top management believes that the best route is to develop the system and then to "introduce" it to the architects during a training session. Management does not want the architects to spend precious billable hours guessing about the new system or putting work off until the new system is working. Thus, the consultants are operating in a back room under a shroud of secrecy.

Required:
a. Do you think that management is taking the best course of action for the announcement of the new system? Why?
b. Do you approve of the development process? Why?

4. Systems Analysis

Consider the following dialogue between a systems professional, Joe Pugh, and a manager of a department targeted for a new information system, Lars Meyer:

Pugh: The way to go about the analysis is to first examine the old system, such as reviewing key documents and observing the workers perform their tasks. Then we can determine which aspects are working well and which should be preserved.

Meyer: We have been through these types of projects before and what always ends up happening is that we do not get the new system we are promised; we get a modified version of the old system.

Pugh: Well, I can assure you that will not happen this time. We just want a thorough understanding of what is working well and what is not.

Meyer: I would feel much more comfortable if we first started with a list of our requirements. We should spend some time up-front determining exactly what we want the system to do for my department. Then you systems people can come in and determine what portions to salvage if you wish. Just don't constrain us to the old system!

Required:
a. Obviously, these two workers have different views on how the systems analysis phase should be conducted. Comment on whose position you sympathize with the most.
b. What method would you propose they take? Why?

5. Systems Design

Robin Alper, a manager of the credit collections department for ACME Building Supplies, is extremely unhappy with a new system that was installed 3 months ago. Her complaint is that the data flow from the billing and accounts receivable departments are not occurring in the manner originally requested. Further, the updates to the database files are not occurring as frequently as she had envisioned. Thus, the hope that the new system would provide more current and timely information has not materialized. She claims that the systems analysts spent 3 days interviewing her and other workers. During that time, she and the other workers thought they had clearly conveyed their needs. She feels as if their needs were ignored and their time was wasted.

Required:

What went wrong during the systems design process? What suggestions would you make for future projects?

6. Conceptual Design

Prepare two alternative conceptual designs for both an accounts payable system and an accounts receivable system. Discuss the differences in concept between the different designs. From a cost perspective, which is more economical? From a benefits perspective, which is more desirable? Which design would you prefer and why?

7. Systems Design

Robert Hamilton was hired 6 months ago as the controller of a small oil and gas exploration and development company, Gusher, Inc., headquartered in Beaumont, Texas. Before working at Gusher, Hamilton was the controller of a larger petroleum company, Eureka Oil Company, based in Dallas. The joint interest billing and fixed asset accounting systems of Gusher are outdated, and many processing problems and errors have been occurring quite frequently. Hamilton immediately recognized these problems and informed the president, Mr. Barton, that it was crucial to install a new system. Barton concurred and met with Hamilton and Sally Jeffries, the information systems senior manager. Barton instructed Jeffries to make the new system that Hamilton wished to have a top priority in her department. Basically, he told Jeffries to deliver the system to meet Hamilton's needs as soon as possible.

Jeffries left the meeting feeling overwhelmed, since the IS department is currently working on two other very big projects, one for the production department and the other for the geological department. The next day, Hamilton sent a memo to Jeffries indicating the name of a system that he had 100 percent confidence in—Amarillo Software—and he also indicated that he would very much like this system to be purchased as soon as possible. He stated that the system had been used with much success during the past 4 years in his previous job.

When commercial software is purchased, Jeffries typically sends out requests for proposals to at least six different vendors after conducting a careful analysis of the needed requirements. However, due to the air of urgency demonstrated in the meeting with the president and the overworked systems staff, she decided to go along with Hamilton's wishes and sent only one RFP (request for proposal) out, which went to Amarillo Software. Amarillo promptly returned the completed questionnaire. The purchase price ($75,000) was within the budgeted amount. Jeffries contacted the four references provided and was satisfied with their comments. Further, she felt comfortable since the system was for Hamilton, and he had used the system for four years.

The plan was to install the system during the month of July and try it for the August transaction cycle. Problems were encountered, however, during the installation phase. The system processed extremely slowly on the hardware platform owned by Gusher. When Jeffries asked Hamilton how the problem had been dealt with at Eureka, he replied that he did not remember having had such a problem. He called the systems manager from Eureka and discovered that Eureka had a much more powerful mainframe than Gusher. Further investigation revealed that Gusher has more applications running on its mainframe than Eureka did, since Eureka used a two-mainframe distributed processing platform.

Further, the data transfer did not go smoothly. A few data elements being stored in the system were not available as an option in the Amarillo system. Jeffries found that the staff at Amarillo was very friendly when she called, but they could not always identify the problem over the phone. They really needed to come out to the site and investigate. Hamilton was surprised at the delays between requesting an Amarillo consultant to come out and the time in which he or she actually arrived. Amarillo explained that it had to fly a staff member from Dallas to Beaumont for each trip. The system finally began to work somewhat smoothly in January, after a grueling fiscal year-end close in October. Hamilton's staff viewed the project as an unnecessary inconvenience. At one point, two staff accountants threatened to quit. The extra consulting fees amounted to $35,000. Further, the systems department at Gusher spent 500 more hours during the implementation process than it had expected. These additional hours caused other projects to fall behind schedule.

Required:

Discuss what could have been done differently during the design phase. Why were most of the problems encountered? How might a detailed feasibility study have helped?

8. Programming Languages

Describe the basic features of the following three types of programming languages: procedural, event-driven, and object oriented. Give examples of each type of language.

9. **Program Testing**

When program modules have been coded and tested, they must be brought together and tested as a whole. Comment on the importance of testing the entire system.

10. **Database Conversion**

What is database conversion? Why is it a risky activity, and what precautions should be taken?

11. **System Cutover**

Discuss three common approaches to system cutover. Comment on the advantages and disadvantages of each approach.

12. **Audit of Systems Development**

The Balcar Company's auditors are developing an audit plan to review the company's systems development procedures. Their audit objectives are to ensure that

1. The system was judged necessary and justified at various checkpoints throughout the SDLC.
2. Systems development activities are applied consistently and in accordance with management's policies to all systems development projects.
3. The system as originally implemented was free from material errors and fraud.
4. System documentation is sufficiently accurate and complete to facilitate audit and maintenance activities.

The following six controllable activities have been identified as sources of audit evidence for meeting these objectives: systems authorization, user specification, technical design, internal audit participation, program testing, and user testing and acceptance.

Required:
a. Explain the importance of each of the six activities in promoting effective control.
b. Outline the tests of controls that the auditor would perform in meeting audit objectives.

13. **Fact-Gathering Techniques**

Your company, Tractors, Inc., is employing the SDLC for its new information system. You have been chosen as a member of the development team because of your strong accounting background. This background includes a good understanding of both financial and managerial accounting concepts and required data. You also possess a great understanding of internal control activities. You do not, however, fully understand exactly what the internal auditors will need from the system in order to comply with Section 404 of the Sarbanes-Oxley Act. Lay out the fact-gathering techniques you might employ to increase your understanding of this important component of your new system.

14. **Systems Selection**

Your company, Kitchen Works, is employing the SDLC for its new information system. The company is currently performing a number of feasibility studies, including the economic feasibility study. A draft of the economic feasibility study has been presented to you for your review. You have been charged with determining whether only escapable costs have been used, the present value of cash flows is accurate, the one-time and recurring costs are correct, realistic useful lives have been used, and the intangible benefits listed in the study are reasonable. Although you are a member of the development team because of your strong accounting background, you have questions about whether some costs are escapable, the interest rates used to perform present value analysis, and the estimated useful lives that have been used. How might you resolve your questions?

15. **Cost–Benefit Analysis**

Listed in the diagram for Problem 15 are some probability estimates of the costs and benefits associated with two competing projects.
a. Compute the net present value of each alternative. Round the cost projections to the nearest month. Explain what happens to the answer if the probabilities of the recurring costs are incorrect and a more accurate estimate is as follows:

	A		B
.10	$ 75,000	.4	$ 85,000
.55	95,000	.4	100,000
.35	105,000	.2	110,000

b. Repeat step (a) for the payback method.
c. Which method do you think provides the best source of information? Why?

PROBLEM 15: COST-BENEFIT ANALYSIS

Cost of Capital = .14				
	A		**B**	
	Probability	**Amount**	**Probability**	**Amount**
Project completion time	0.5	12 months	0.6	12 months
	0.3	18 months	0.2	18 months
	0.2	24 months	0.1	24 months
Expected useful life	0.6	4 years	0.5	4 years
	0.25	5 years	0.3	5 years
	0.15	6 years	0.2	6 years
One-time costs	0.35	$200,000	0.2	$210,000
	0.4	250,000	0.55	250,000
	0.25	300,000	0.25	260,000
Recurring costs	0.1	$ 75,000	0.4	$ 85,000
	0.55	95,000	0.4	100,000
	0.35	105,000	0.2	110,000
Annual tangible benefits starting with weighted average completion date	0.3	$220,000	0.25	$215,000
	0.5	233,000	0.5	225,000
	0.2	240,000	0.25	235,000

Transaction Processing and Financial Reporting Systems Overview

LEARNING OBJECTIVES

After studying this chapter, you should:

- Understand the broad objectives of the three transaction cycles and the types of transactions processed by each of them.
- Understand the relationship between traditional accounting records and their digital equivalents in computer-based systems.
- Be familiar with the documentation techniques used for representing manual and computer-based systems.
- Understand the technologies used to automate and reengineer accounting information systems.
- Understand the operational features of the general ledger system (GLS) and the financial reporting system (FRS).

The remaining chapters of this book deal with various issues involving AIS applications, including automated procedures, internal controls, audits test, and fraud schemes. As background, this chapter provides an overview of transaction processing systems (TPS) and financial reporting systems (FRS) and presents preliminary topics that are common to all TPS and FRS applications. In subsequent chapters, we will draw heavily from this material as we examine the individual systems in detail.

This chapter is organized into seven major sections. The first is an overview of transaction processing. This section defines the broad objective of the three transaction cycles and specifies the roles of their individual subsystems. The second section describes the relationship among accounting records in forming an audit trail in both manual and computer-based systems. The third section examines documentation techniques used to represent both manual and computer-based systems. The fourth section addresses computer-based systems. It reviews the fundamental features of batch and real-time technologies and their implication for transaction processing. The fifth section examines data coding schemes and their role in transaction processing. The sixth section illustrates the central role of the general ledger as a hub that connects TPS applications and provides input to the FRS. Finally, the chapter outlines imminent changes to the traditional financial reporting process as a result of XBRL (extendable business reporting language) initiatives by the SEC.

AN OVERVIEW OF TRANSACTION PROCESSING

TPS applications process financial transactions. A financial transaction is defined as

> An economic event that affects the assets and equities of the firm, is reflected in its accounts, and is measured in monetary terms.

The most common financial transactions are economic exchanges with external parties. These include the sale of goods or services, the purchase of inventory, the discharge of financial obligations, and the receipt of cash on account from customers. Financial transactions also include certain internal events such as the depreciation of fixed assets; the application of labor, raw materials, and overhead to the production process; and the transfer of inventory from one department to another.

Financial transactions are common business events that occur regularly. For instance, thousands of transactions of a particular type (sales to customers) may occur daily. To deal efficiently with such volume, business firms group similar types of transactions into transaction cycles.

Transaction Cycles

Three transaction cycles process most of the firm's economic activity: the expenditure cycle, the conversion cycle, and the revenue cycle. These cycles exist in all types of businesses—both profit-seeking and not-for-profit types. For instance, every business (1) incurs expenditures in exchange for resources (expenditure cycle), (2) provides value added through its products or services (conversion cycle), and (3) receives revenue from outside sources (revenue cycle). Figure 6.1 shows the relationship of these cycles and the resource flows between them.

The Expenditure Cycle

Business activities begin with the acquisition of materials, property, and labor in exchange for cash—the **expenditure cycle**. Figure 6.1 shows the flow of cash from the organization to the various providers of these resources. Most expenditure transactions are based on a credit relationship between the trading parties. The actual disbursement of cash takes place at some point after the receipt of the goods or services. Days or even weeks may pass between these two events. Thus, from a systems perspective, this transaction has two parts: a physical component (the acquisition of the goods) and a financial component (the cash disbursement to the supplier). A separate subsystem of the cycle processes each component. The major subsystems of the expenditure cycle are those that process purchases/accounts payable, cash disbursements, payroll and fixed asset.

> *Purchases/accounts payable system.* This system recognizes the need to acquire physical inventory (such as raw materials) and places an order with the vendor. When the goods are received, the purchases system records the event by increasing inventory and establishing an account payable to be paid at a later date.

> *Cash disbursements system.* When the obligation created in the purchases system is due, the cash disbursements system authorizes the payment, disburses the funds to the vendor, and records the transaction by reducing the cash and accounts payable accounts.

> *Payroll system.* The payroll system collects labor usage data for each employee, computes the payroll, and disburses paychecks to the employees. Conceptually, payroll is a special-case purchases and cash disbursements system. Because of

FIGURE 6.1   Relationship Between Transaction Cycles

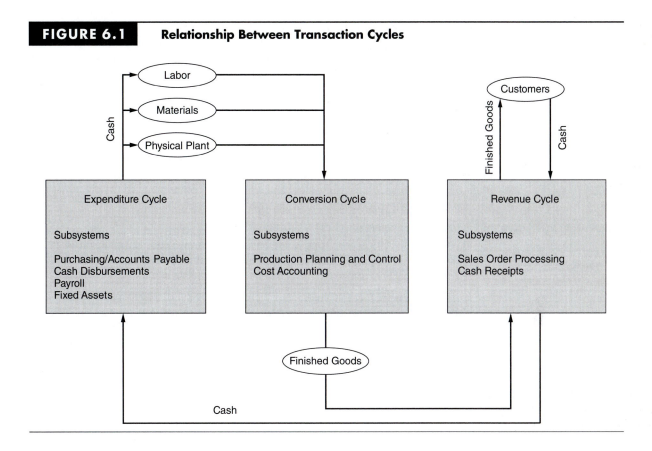

accounting complexities associated with payroll, most firms have a separate system for payroll processing.

Fixed asset system. A firm's fixed asset system processes transactions pertaining to the acquisition, maintenance, and disposal of its fixed assets. These are relatively permanent items that collectively often represent the organization's largest financial investment. Examples of fixed assets include land, buildings, furniture, machinery, and motor vehicles.

The Conversion Cycle

The **conversion cycle** is composed of two major subsystems: the production system and the cost accounting system. The production system involves the planning, scheduling, and control of the physical product through the manufacturing process. This includes determining raw material requirements, authorizing the work to be performed and the release of raw materials into production, and directing the movement of the work-in-process through its various stages of manufacturing. The cost accounting system monitors the flow of cost information related to production. Information this system produces is used for inventory valuation, budgeting, cost control, performance reporting, and management decisions, such as make-or-buy decisions.

Manufacturing firms convert raw materials into finished products through formal conversion cycle operations. The conversion cycle is not usually formal and observable in service and retailing establishments. Nevertheless, these firms still engage in conversion cycle activities that culminate in the development of a salable product or service. These activities include the readying of products and services for market and the allocation of resources such as depreciation, building amortization, and prepaid expenses to the proper accounting period. However, unlike manufacturing firms, merchandising companies do not process these activities through formal conversion cycle subsystems.

The Revenue Cycle

Firms sell their finished goods to customers through the **revenue cycle**, which involves processing cash sales, credit sales, and the receipt of cash following a credit sale. Revenue cycle transactions also have a physical and a financial component, which are processed separately. The primary subsystems of the revenue cycle are outlined below.

> *Sales order processing.* The majority of business sales are made on credit and involve tasks such as preparing sales orders, granting credit, shipping products (or rendering of a service) to the customer, billing customers, and recording the transaction in the accounts (accounts receivable [AR], inventory, expenses, and sales).

> *Cash receipts.* For credit sales, some period of time (days or weeks) passes between the point of sale and the receipt of cash. Cash receipts processing includes collecting cash, depositing cash in the bank, and recording these events in the accounts (AR and cash).

ACCOUNTING RECORDS

Manual Systems

This section describes the purpose of each type of **accounting record** used in transaction cycles. We begin with traditional records used in manual systems (documents, journals, and ledgers) and then examine their magnetic counterparts in computer-based systems.

Documents

A document provides evidence of an economic event and may be used to initiate transaction processing. Some documents are a result of transaction processing. In this section, we discuss three types of documents: source documents, product documents, and turnaround documents.

Source Documents.   Economic events result in some documents being created at the beginning (the source) of the transaction. These are called source documents. **Source documents** are used to capture and formalize transaction data that the transaction cycle needs for processing. Figure 6.2 shows the creation of a source document.

The economic event (the sale) causes the sales clerk to prepare a multipart sales order, which is formal evidence that a sale occurred. Copies of this source document enter the sales system and are used to convey information to various functions, such as billing, shipping, and AR. The information in the sales order triggers specific activities in each of these departments.

Product Documents.   **Product documents** are the result of transaction processing rather than the triggering mechanism for the process. For example, a payroll check to an employee is a product document of the payroll system. Figure 6.3 extends the

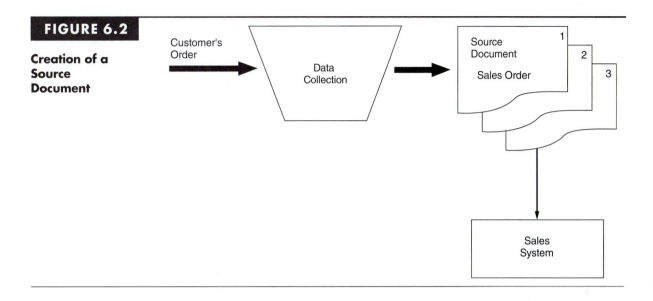

FIGURE 6.2

Creation of a Source Document

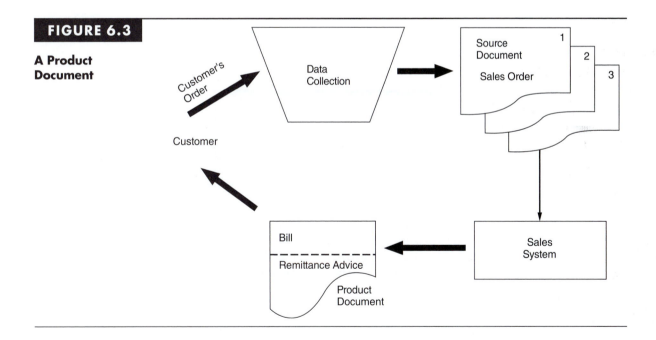

FIGURE 6.3

A Product Document

example in Figure 6.2 to illustrate that the customer's bill is a product document of the sales system. We will study many other examples of product documents in later chapters.

Turnaround Documents. **Turnaround documents** are product documents of one system that become source documents for another system. This is illustrated in Figure 6.4. The customer receives a perforated two-part bill or statement. One portion is the actual bill, and the other portion is the remittance advice. Customers remove the remittance advice

FIGURE 6.4	A Turnaround Document

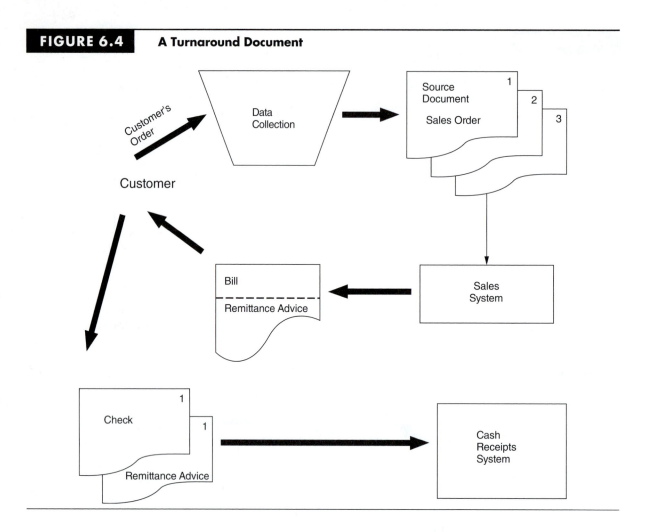

and return it to the company along with their payment (typically a check). A turnaround document contains important information about a customer's account to help the cash receipts system process the payment. One of the problems designers of cash receipts systems face is matching customer payments to the correct customer accounts. Providing this needed information as a product of the sales system ensures accuracy when the cash receipts system processes it.

Journals

A **journal** is a record of a chronological entry. At some point in the transaction process, when all relevant facts about the transaction are known, the event is recorded in a journal in chronological order. Documents are the primary source of data for journals. Figure 6.5 shows a sales order being recorded in the sales journal (see the following discussion on special journals). Each transaction requires a separate journal entry, reflecting the accounts affected and the amounts to be debited and credited. There is often a time lag between initiating a transaction and recording it in the accounts. The journal holds a complete record of transactions and thus provides a means for posting to accounts. There are two primary types of journals: special journals and general journals.

FIGURE 6.5

**Sales Order
Recorded in
Sales Journal**

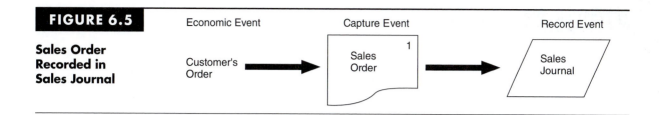

Special Journals.   Special journals are used to record specific classes of transactions that occur in high volume. Such transactions can be grouped together in a special journal and processed more efficiently than a general journal permits. Figure 6.6 shows a special journal for recording sales transactions.

As you can see, the sales journal provides a specialized format for recording only sales transactions. At the end of the processing period (month, week, or day), a clerk posts the amounts in the columns to the ledger accounts indicated (see the discussion of ledgers in this chapter). For example, the total sales will be posted to account number 401. Most organizations use several other special journals, including the cash receipts journal, cash disbursements journal, purchases journal, and the payroll journal.

Register.   The term **register** is often used to denote certain types of special journals. For example, the payroll journal is often called the payroll register. We also use the term *register*, however, to denote a log. For example, a receiving register is a log of all receipts of raw materials or merchandise ordered from vendors. Similarly, a shipping register is a log that records all shipments to customers.

General Journals.   Firms use the general journal to record nonrecurring, infrequent, and dissimilar transactions. For example, we usually record periodic depreciation and closing entries in the general journal. Figure 6.7 shows one page from a general journal.

FIGURE 6.6   **Sales Journal**

Date	Customer	Invoice Num.	Acct. Num.	Post	Debit Acct . Rec. #102	Credit Sales #401
Sept. 1	Hewitt Co.	4523	1120		3300	3300
15	Acme Drilling	8821	1298		6825	6825
Oct. 3	Buell Corp.	22987	1030		4000	4000
10	Check Ltd.	66734	1110		8500	8500

FIGURE 6.7   **General Journal**

	DATE	DESCRIPTION	POST. REF.	DEBIT	CREDIT	
1	Sept. 1, 2010	Depreciation Expense	520	5 0 0 0		1
2		Accumulated Depreciation	210		5 0 0 0	2
3						3
4	Sept. 2, 2010	Insurance Expense	525	1 2 0 0		4
5		Prepaid Insurance	180		1 2 0 0	5
6						6
7	Sept. 3, 2010	Cash	101	1 1 0 0 0		7
8		Capital Stock	310		1 1 0 0 0	8
9						9
10						10
11						11
12						12

Note that the columns are nonspecific, allowing any type of transaction to be recorded. The entries are recorded chronologically.

As a practical matter, most organizations have replaced their general journal with a journal voucher system. A journal voucher is actually a special source document that contains a single journal entry specifying the general ledger accounts that are affected. Journal vouchers are used to record summaries of routine transactions, nonroutine transactions, adjusting entries, and closing entries. The total of journal vouchers processed is equivalent to the general journal.

Ledgers

A **ledger** is a book of accounts that reflects the financial effects of the firm's transactions after they are posted from the various journals. Whereas journals show the chronological effect of business activity, ledgers show activity by account type. A ledger indicates the increases, decreases, and current balance of each account. Organizations use this information to prepare financial statements, support daily operations, and prepare internal reports. Figure 6.8 shows the flow of financial information from the source documents to the journal and into the ledgers.

There are two basic types of ledgers: (1) general ledgers, which contain the firm's account information in the form of highly summarized control accounts, and (2) subsidiary ledgers, which contain the details of the individual accounts that constitute a particular control account.[1]

---

1   Not all control accounts in the general ledger have corresponding subsidiary accounts. Accounts such as sales and cash typically have no supporting details in the form of a subsidiary ledger.

FIGURE 6.8

Flow of Information from the Economic Event to the General Ledger

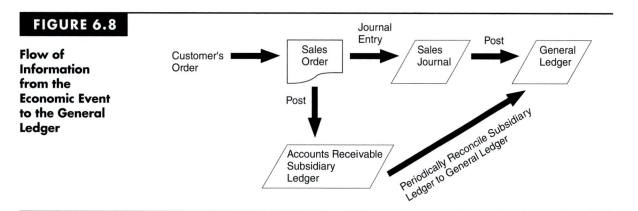

General Ledgers. The general ledger summarizes the activity for each of the organization's accounts. The general ledger department updates these records from journal vouchers prepared from special journals and other sources located throughout the organization. The general ledger presented in Figure 6.9 shows the beginning balances, the changes, and the ending balances as of a particular date for several different accounts.

The general ledger provides a single value for each control account, such as accounts payable, AR, and inventory. This highly summarized information is sufficient for financial reporting, but it is not useful for supporting daily business operations. For example, for financial reporting purposes, the firm's total AR value must be presented as a single figure in the balance sheet. This value is obtained from the AR control account in the general ledger. To actually collect the cash this asset represents, however, the firm must have certain detailed information about the customers that this summary figure does not provide. It must know which customers owe money, how much each customer owes, when the customer last made payment, when the next payment is due, and so on. The AR subsidiary ledger contains these essential details.

Subsidiary Ledgers. Subsidiary ledgers are kept in various accounting departments of the firm, including inventory, accounts payable, payroll, and AR. This separation provides better control and support of operations. Figure 6.10 illustrates that the total of account balances in a subsidiary ledger should equal the balance in the corresponding general ledger control account. Thus, in addition to providing financial statement information, the general ledger is a mechanism for verifying the overall accuracy of accounting data that separate accounting departments have processed. Any event incorrectly recorded in a journal or subsidiary ledger will cause an out-of-balance condition that should be detected during the general ledger update. By periodically reconciling summary balances from subsidiary accounts, journals, and control accounts, the completeness and accuracy of transaction processing can be formally assessed.

The Audit Trail

The accounting records described previously provide an **audit trail** for tracing transactions from source documents to the financial statements. Of the many purposes of the audit trail, most important to accountants is the year-end audit. Although the study of financial auditing falls outside the scope of this text, the following thumbnail sketch of the audit process will demonstrate the importance of the audit trail.

The external auditor periodically evaluates the financial statements of publicly held business organizations on behalf of its stockholders and other interested parties.

FIGURE 6.9A   General Ledger

Cash ACCOUNT NO. 101

DATE		ITEM	POST. REF.	DEBIT	CREDIT	BALANCE DEBIT	BALANCE CREDIT
Sept.	10		S1	3 3 0 0		3 3 0 0	
	15		S1	6 8 2 5		1 0 1 2 5	
Oct.	3		S1	4 0 0 0		1 4 1 2 5	
	10		CD1		2 8 0 0	1 1 3 2 5	

Accounts Receivable ACCOUNT NO. 102

DATE		ITEM	POST. REF.	DEBIT	CREDIT	BALANCE DEBIT	BALANCE CREDIT
Sept.	1		S1	1 4 0 0		1 4 0 0	
	8		S1	2 6 0 5		4 0 0 5	
	15		CR1		1 6 5 0	2 3 5 5	

Accounts Payable ACCOUNT NO. 201

DATE		ITEM	POST. REF.	DEBIT	CREDIT	BALANCE DEBIT	BALANCE CREDIT
Sept.	1		P1		2 0 5 0 0		2 0 5 0 0
	10		CD1	2 8 0 0			1 7 7 0 0

The auditor's responsibility involves, in part, the review of selected accounts and transactions to determine their validity, accuracy, and completeness. Let's assume an auditor wishes to verify the accuracy of a client's AR as published in its annual financial statements. The auditor can trace the AR figure on the balance sheet to the general ledger AR control account. This balance can then be reconciled with the total for the AR subsidiary

| FIGURE 6.9B | General Ledger (Continued) |

Purchases						ACCOUNT NO. 502	
DATE	ITEM	POST. REF.	DEBIT	CREDIT	BALANCE		
					DEBIT	CREDIT	
Sept. 1		P1	2 0 5 0 0		2 0 5 0 0		

| FIGURE 6.10 |

Relationship Between the Subsidiary Ledger and the General Ledger

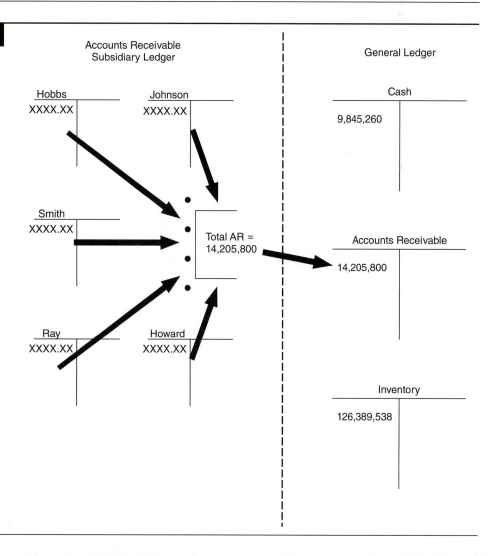

ledger. Rather than examining every transaction that affected the AR account, the auditor will use a sampling technique to examine a representative subset of transactions. Following this approach, the auditor can select a number of accounts from the AR subsidiary ledger and trace these back to the sales journal. From the sales journal, the auditor can identify the specific source documents that initiated the transactions and pull them from the files to verify their validity and accuracy.

The audit of AR often includes a procedure called confirmation. This involves contacting selected customers to determine if the transactions recorded in the accounts actually took place and that customers agree with the recorded balance. Information contained in source documents and subsidiary accounts enable the auditor to identify and locate customers chosen for confirmation. The results from reconciling the AR subsidiary ledger with the control account and from confirming customers' accounts help the auditor form an opinion about the accuracy of AR as reported on the balance sheet. The auditor performs similar tests on all of the client firm's major accounts and transactions to arrive at an overall opinion about the fair presentation of the financial statement. The audit trail plays an important role in this process.

Computer-Based Systems

Types of Files

Audit trails in computer-based systems are less observable than in traditional manual systems, but they still exist. Accounting records in computer-based systems are represented by four different types of magnetic files: master files, transaction files, reference files, and archive files. Figure 6.11 illustrates the relationship of these files in forming an audit trail.

Master File.   A **master file** generally contains account data. The general ledger and subsidiary ledgers are examples of master files. Data values in master files are updated from transactions.

Transaction File.   A **transaction file** is a temporary file of transaction records used to change or update data in a master file. Sales orders, inventory receipts, and cash receipts are examples of transaction files.

Reference File.   A **reference file** stores data that are used as standards for processing transactions. For example, the payroll program may refer to a tax table to calculate the proper amount of withholding taxes for payroll transactions. Other reference files include price lists used for preparing customer invoices, lists of authorized suppliers, employee rosters, and customer credit files for approving credit sales. The reference file in Figure 6.11 is a credit file.

Archive File.   An **archive file** contains records of past transactions that are retained for future reference. These transactions form an important part of the audit trail. Archive files include journals, prior-period payroll information, lists of former employees, records of accounts written off, and prior-period ledgers.

The Digital Audit Trail

Let's walk through the system represented in Figure 6.11 to illustrate how computer files provide an audit trail. We begin with the capture of the economic event. In this example, sales are recorded manually on source documents, just as in the manual system. The next step in this process is to convert the source documents to digital form. This is done in the data-input stage, when the transactions are edited and a transaction file of

FIGURE 6.11   Accounting Records in a Computer-Based System

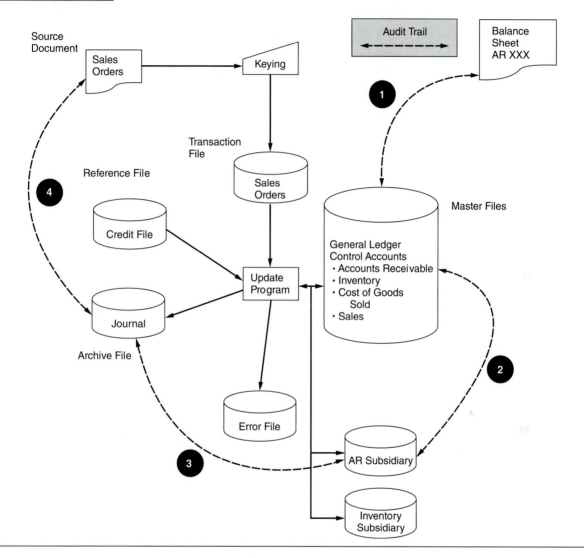

sales orders is produced. Some computer systems do not use physical source documents. Instead, transactions are captured directly on digital media.

The next step is to update the various master file subsidiary and control accounts that the transaction affects. During the update procedure, additional editing of transactions takes place. Some transactions may prove to be in error or invalid for such reasons as incorrect account numbers, insufficient quantities on hand, or customer credit problems. In this example, the system determines the available credit for each customer from the credit file before processing the sale. Any records that are rejected for credit problems are transferred to the error file. The remaining good records are used to update the master files. Only these transactions are added to the archive file that serves as the sales journal. By copying the valid transactions to the journal, the original transaction file is not needed for audit trail purposes. This file can now be erased (scratched) in preparation for the next batch of sales orders.

Like the paper trail, this digital audit trail allows transaction tracing. Again, an auditor attempting to evaluate the accuracy of the AR figure published in the balance sheet could do so via the following steps, which are identified in Figure 6.11.

1. Compare the AR balance in the balance sheet with the master file AR control account balance.
2. Reconcile the AR control figure with the AR subsidiary account total.
3. Select a sample of update entries made to accounts in the AR subsidiary ledger and trace these to transactions in the sales journal (archive file).
4. From these journal entries, identify specific source documents that can be pulled from their files and verified. If necessary, the auditor can confirm the accuracy and propriety of these source documents by contacting the customers in question.

DOCUMENTATION TECHNIQUES

The old saying that a picture is worth a thousand words is very applicable when it comes to documenting systems. A written description of a system can be wordy and difficult to follow. Experience has shown that a visual image can convey vital system information more effectively and efficiently than words. Accountants use system documentation routinely, as both systems designers and auditors. The ability to document systems in graphic form is thus an important skill for accountants to master. Five basic documentation techniques are introduced in this section: data flow diagrams, entity relationship diagrams, system flowcharts, program flowcharts, and record layout diagrams.

Data Flow Diagrams and Entity Relationship Diagrams

Two commonly used systems design and documentation techniques are the entity relationship diagram and the data flow diagram. This section introduces the principal features of these techniques, illustrates their use, and shows how they are related.

Data Flow Diagrams

The **data flow diagram (DFD)** uses symbols to represent the entities, processes, data flows, and data stores that pertain to a system. Figure 6.12 presents the symbol set most commonly used. DFDs are used to represent systems at different levels of detail from very general to highly detailed. A sales order system is illustrated by the intermediate level DFD in Figure 6.13.

Entities in a DFD are external objects at the boundary of the system being modeled. They represent sources of and destinations for data. Entities may be other interacting systems or functions, or they may be external to the organization. Entities should always be labeled as nouns on a DFD, such as *customer* or *supplier.* Data stores represent the accounting records used in each process, and labeled arrows represent the data flows between processes, data stores, and entities.

Processes in the DFD should be labeled with a descriptive verb such as *Ship* Goods, *Update* Records, or *Receive* Customer Order. Process objects should not be represented as nouns like Warehouse, Accounts Receivable Dept., or Sales Dept. The labeled arrows connecting the process objects represent flows of data such as Sales Order, Invoice, or Shipping Notice. Each data flow label should be unique—the same label should not be attached to two different flow lines in the same DFD. When data flow into a process and out again (to another process), they have, in some way, been changed. This is true even if the data have not been physically altered. For example, consider the Approve

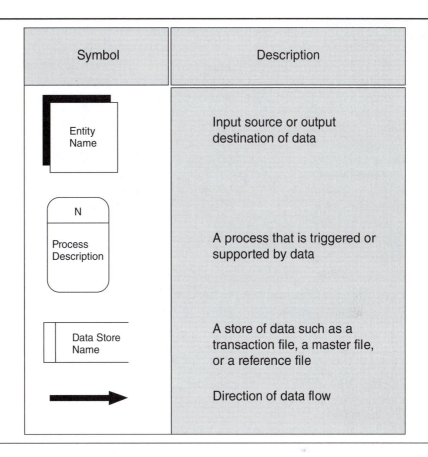

FIGURE 6.12

**Data Flow
Diagram
Symbol Set**

Symbol	Description
Entity Name	Input source or output destination of data
N Process Description	A process that is triggered or supported by data
Data Store Name	A store of data such as a transaction file, a master file, or a reference file
→	Direction of data flow

Sales process in Figure 6.13, where Sales Order is examined for completeness before being processed further. It flows into the process as Sales Order and out of it as Approved Sales Order.

Systems analysts use DFDs extensively to represent the logical elements of the system. This technique does not, however, depict the physical system. In other words, DFDs show what logical tasks are being done, but not how they are done or who (or what) is performing them. For example, the DFD does not show whether the sales approval process is separated physically from the billing process in compliance with internal control objectives.

Entity Relationship Diagrams

An **entity relationship (ER) diagram** is a documentation technique used to represent the relationship between entities. **Entities** are physical resources (automobiles, cash, or inventory), events (ordering inventory, receiving cash, shipping goods), and agents (salesperson, customer, or vendor) about which the organization wishes to capture data. One common use for ER diagrams is to model an organization's database, which we examine in detail in Chapter 8.

Figure 6.14 shows the symbol set used in an ER diagram. The square symbol represents entities in the system. The labeled connecting line represents the nature of the relationship between two entities. The degree of the relationship, called **cardinality**, is the numerical mapping between entity instances. A relationship can be one-to-one (1:1),

FIGURE 6.13   **Data Flow Diagram of Sales Order Processing System**

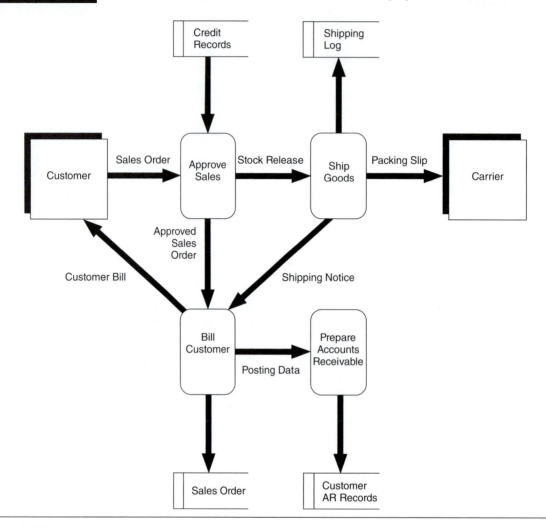

FIGURE 6.14

**Entity
Relationship
Diagram
Symbols**

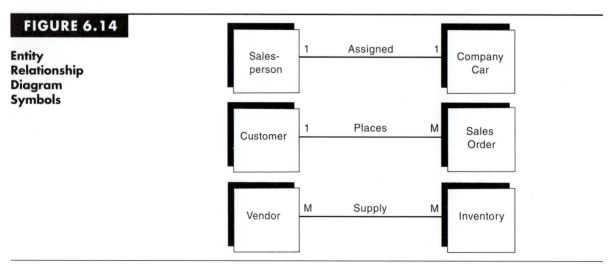

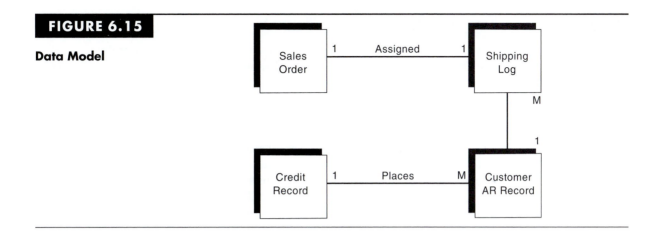

FIGURE 6.15

Data Model

one-to-many (1:M), or many-to-many (M:M).[2] If we think of entities in the ER diagram as files of records, cardinality is the maximum number of records in one file that are related to a single record in the other file and vice versa.

Cardinality reflects normal business rules as well as organizational policy. For instance, the 1:1 cardinality in the first example in Figure 6.14 suggests that each salesperson in the organization is assigned one automobile. If instead the organization's policy were to assign a single automobile to one or more salespersons who share it, this policy would be reflected by a 1:M relationship. Similarly, the M:M relationship between vendor and inventory in Figure 6.14 implies that the organization buys the same type of products from one or more vendors. A company policy to buy particular items from a single vendor would be reflected by a 1:M cardinality.

System designers identify entities and prepare a model of them, similar to the one presented in Figure 6.15. This **data model** is the blueprint for what ultimately will become the physical database. The data model presented in our example is not, however, sufficiently refined to be the plan for a workable database. Constructing a realistic data model is an advanced topic that involves understanding and applying techniques and rules that are beyond the scope of this chapter. We revisit this topic in Chapter 8, where it will be treated in sufficient detail to model and design a practical database.

Relationship Between ER Diagrams and Data Flow Diagrams
DFDs and ER diagrams depict different aspects of the same system, but they are related and can be reconciled. A DFD is a model of system processes, and the ER diagram models the data used in or affected by the system. The two diagrams are related through data; each data store in the DFD represents a corresponding data entity in the ER diagram. Figure 6.15 presents the ER diagram for the DFD in Figure 6.13.

System Flowcharts

A **system flowchart** is the graphical representation of the *physical* relationships among key elements of a system. These elements may include organizational departments, manual activities, computer programs, hard-copy accounting records (documents, journals,

---

2   We will study variants of these three basic cardinalities in Chapter 8 when we examine data modeling in greater detail. At that time, a more precise documentation technique for representing cardinality called crow's foot notation will be introduced.

ledgers, and files), and digital records (reference files, transaction files, archive files, and master files).[3] System flowcharts also describe the type of computer media being employed in the system, such as magnetic tape, magnetic disks, and terminals.

The flowcharting examples in the following sections illustrate techniques for representing both manual and computer-based accounting processes. We begin by documenting manual procedures. We will add computer elements to the system later.

Flowcharting Manual Activities

To demonstrate the flowcharting of manual activities, let's assume that an auditor needs to flowchart a sales order system to evaluate its internal controls and procedures. The auditor will begin by interviewing individuals involved in the sales order process to determine what they do. This information will be captured in a set of written facts similar to those below. Keep in mind that the purpose here is to demonstrate flowcharting. Thus, for clarity, the system facts are intentionally simplistic.

1. A clerk in the sales department receives a hard-copy customer order by mail and manually prepares four hard copies of a sales order.
2. The clerk sends Copy 1 of the sales order the credit department for approval. The other three copies and the original customer order are filed temporarily, pending credit approval.
3. The credit department clerk validates the customer's order against hard-copy credit records kept in the credit department. The clerk signs Copy 1 to signify approval and returns it to the sales clerk.
4. When the sales clerk receives credit approval, he or she files Copy 1 and the customer order in the department. The clerk sends Copy 2 to the warehouse and Copies 3 and 4 to the shipping department.
5. The warehouse clerk picks the products from the shelves, records the transfer in the hard-copy stock records, and sends the products and Copy 2 to the shipping department.
6. The shipping department receives Copy 2 and the goods from the warehouse, attaches Copy 2 as a packing slip, and ships the goods to the customer. Finally, the clerk files Copies 3 and 4 in the shipping department.

Based on these facts, the auditor can create a flowchart of this partial system. It is important to note that flowcharting is as much an art form as it is a technical skill, giving the flowchart author a great deal of license. Nevertheless, the primary objective should be to provide an unambiguous description of the system. With this in mind, certain rules and conventions need to be observed:

1. The flowchart should be labeled to clearly identify the system that it represents.
2. The correct symbols should be used to represent the various entities in the system.
3. All symbols on the flowchart should be labeled.
4. Lines should have arrowheads to clearly show the process flow and sequence of events.
5. If complex processes need additional explanation for clarity, a text description should be included on the flowchart or in an attached document referenced by the flowchart.

---

3   This terminology is a slight departure from the accounting convention that I have followed in earlier editions of this text, in which a distinction is drawn between *document flowcharts* and *system flowcharts*. The term "document flowchart" was coined at a time when systems that exclusively employed manual recording and posting activities, and paper (hard copy) documents, journals, and ledgers were commonplace. Today, few functional systems fall into this category; even basic modern accounting systems incorporate both manual and computer operations. Apart from being obsolete, I have found that the term document flowchart can be misleading for students attempting to master flowcharting. Therefore, in this text we will use the term "system flowchart," or simply "flowchart," for representing the physical accounting system, whether it is manual, computer-based, or has elements of both.

| FIGURE 6.16 | Flowchart Showing Areas of Activity |

| Sales Department | Credit Department | Warehouse | Shipping Department |

Lay out the Physical Areas of Activity. Remember that a flowchart reflects the physical system, which is represented as vertical columns of events and actions separated by lines of demarcation. Generally, each of these areas of activity is a separate column with a heading. From these system facts, we see that there are four distinct areas of activity: sales department, credit department, warehouse, and shipping department. The first step in preparing the flowchart is to lay out these areas of activity and label each of them. This step is illustrated in Figure 6.16.

Transcribe the Written Facts into Visual Format. At this point, we are ready to start visually representing the system facts. The symbols used for this purpose will be selected from the set presented in Figure 6.17. We begin with the first stated fact:

1. *A clerk in the sales department receives a hard-copy customer order by mail and manually prepares four hard copies of a sales order.*

Figure 6.18 illustrates how this fact could be represented. The customer is the source of the order, but is not part of the system. The oval object is typically used to convey a data source or destination that is separate from the system being flowcharted. The

FIGURE 6.17   Symbol Set for Representing Manual Procedures

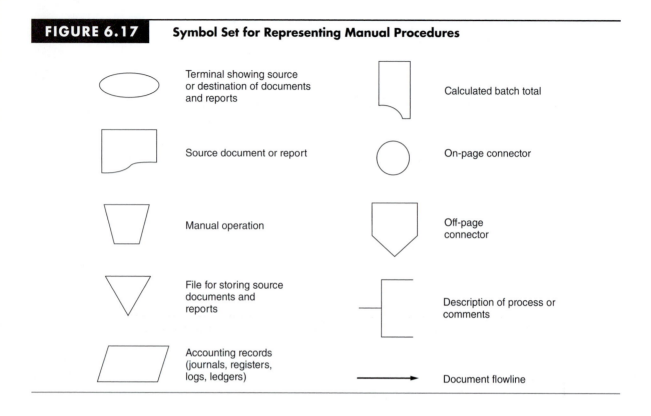

Terminal showing source or destination of documents and reports

Calculated batch total

Source document or report

On-page connector

Manual operation

Off-page connector

File for storing source documents and reports

Description of process or comments

Accounting records (journals, registers, logs, ledgers)

Document flowline

FIGURE 6.18   Flowchart Showing Stated Fact 1 Translated into Visual Symbols

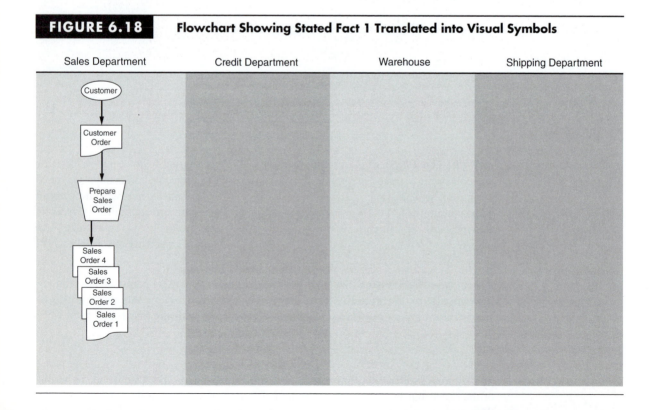

Sales Department   Credit Department   Warehouse   Shipping Department

Customer

Customer Order

Prepare Sales Order

Sales Order 4
Sales Order 3
Sales Order 2
Sales Order 1

document symbol entering the sales department signifies the hard-copy customer order and is labeled accordingly. The bucket-shaped symbol represents a manual process. In this case, the clerk in the sales department prepares four copies of the sales order. Notice that the clerk's task, not the clerk, is depicted. The arrows between the objects show the direction of flow and the sequence of events.

By transcribing each fact in this way, we systematically construct a flowchart. See how the second and third facts restated below add to the flowchart in Figure 6.19.

2. *The clerk sends Copy 1 of the sales order to the credit department for approval. The other three copies and the original customer order are filed temporarily, pending credit approval.*

3. *The credit department clerk validates the customer's order against hard-copy credit records kept in the credit department. The clerk signs Copy 1 to signify approval and returns it to the sales clerk.*

Two new symbols are introduced in this figure. First, the upside-down triangle symbol represents the temporary file mentioned in Fact 2. This is a physical file of paper documents such as a drawer in a filing cabinet or desk. Such files are typically arranged

FIGURE 6.19 **Flowchart Showing Stated Facts 1, 2, and 3 Translated into Visual Symbols**

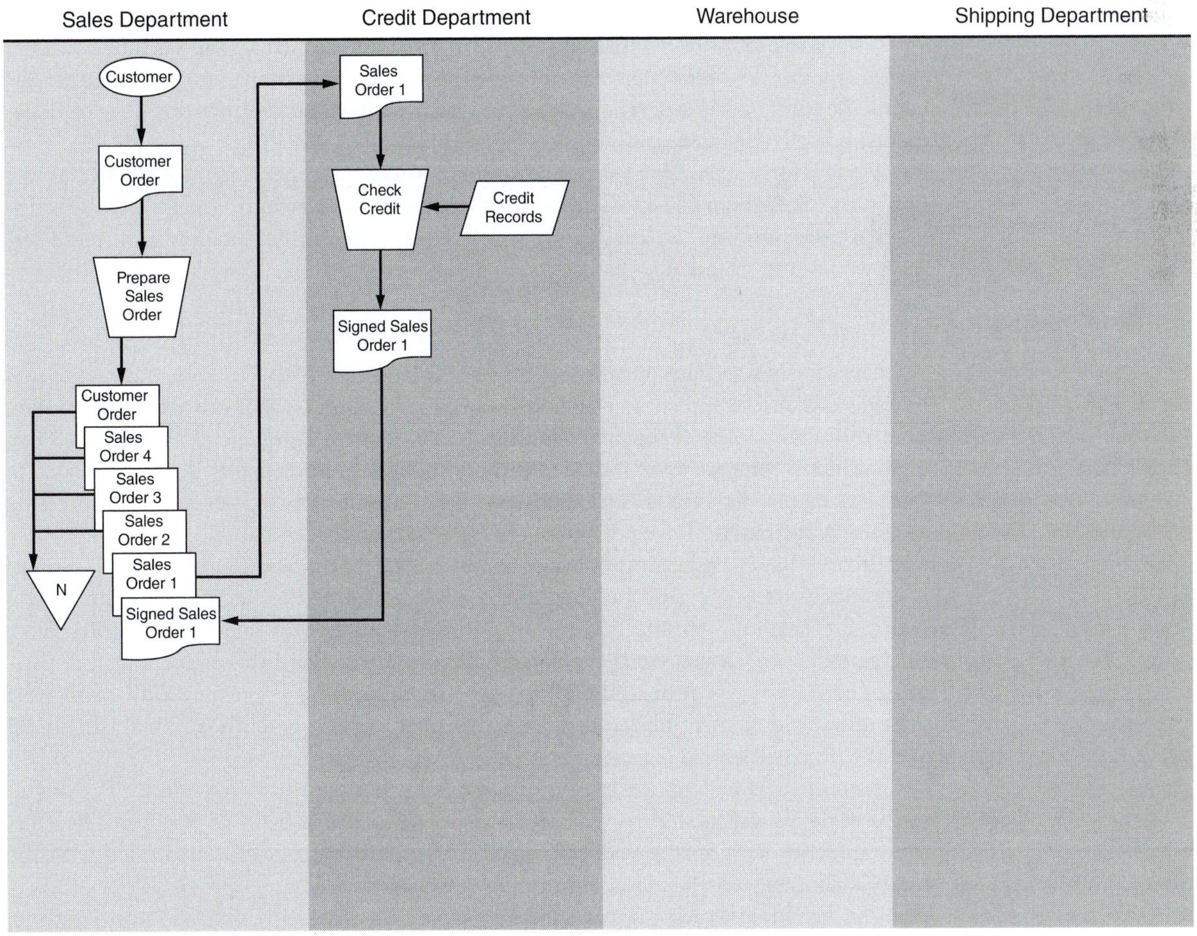

according to a specified order. To signify the filing system used, the file symbol will usually contain an "N" for numeric (invoice number), "C" for chronological (date), or "A" for alphabetical order (customer name). Secondly, the parallelogram shape represents the credit records mentioned in Fact 3. This symbol is used to depict many types of hard-copy accounting records, such as journals, subsidiary ledgers, general ledgers, and shipping logs.

Having laid these foundations, let's now complete the flowchart by depicting the remaining facts.

4. *When the sales clerk receives credit approval, he or she files Copy 1 and the customer order in the department. The clerk sends Copy 2 to the warehouse and Copies 3 and 4 to the shipping department.*
5. *The warehouse clerk picks the products from the shelves, records the transfer in the hard-copy stock records, and sends the products and Copy 2 to the shipping department.*
6. *The shipping department receives Copy 2 and the goods from the warehouse, attaches Copy 2 as a packing slip, and ships the goods to the customer. Finally, the clerk files Copies 3 and 4 in the shipping department.*

The completed flowchart is presented in Figure 6.20. Notice the circular symbol labeled "A." This is an on-page connector used to replace flow lines that otherwise would cause excessive clutter on the page. In this instance, the connector replaces the lines that signify the movement of Copies 3 and 4 from the sales department to the shipping department. Lines should be used whenever possible to promote clarity. Restricted use of connectors, however, can improve the readability of the flowchart.

Notice also that the physical products or goods mentioned in Facts 4 and 5 are not shown on the flowchart. The document (Copy 2) that accompanies and controls the goods, however, is shown. Typically, a system flowchart shows only the flow of documents, not physical assets.

Finally, for visual clarity, system flowcharts show the processing of a single transaction only. You should keep in mind, however, that transactions usually pass through manual procedures in batches (groups). Before exploring documentation techniques further, we need to examine some important issues related to batch processing.

Batch Processing

Batch processing permits the efficient management of a large volume of transactions. A **batch** is a group of similar transactions (such as sales orders) that are accumulated over time and then processed together. Batch processing offers two general advantages. First, organizations improve operational efficiency by grouping together large numbers of transactions into batches and processing them as a unit of work rather than processing each event separately.

Second, batch processing provides control over the transaction process. The accuracy of the process is established by periodically reconciling the batch against the control figure. For example, assume that the total value of a batch of sales orders is $100,000. This number is recorded when the batch is first assembled and then recalculated at various points during its processing. If an error occurs during processing (for example, a sales order is lost), then the recalculated batch total will not equal the original batch total and the problem will be detected.

Both of these advantages have implications for designing batch systems. The first is that economies are derived by making transaction batches as large as possible. The average transaction cost is thus reduced when the processing fixed cost associated with the batch is allocated across a large number of transactions.

The second implication is that finding an error in a very large batch may prove difficult. When a batch is small, error identification is much easier. In designing a batch system, the

FIGURE 6.20 — Flowchart Showing All Stated Facts Translated into Visual Symbols

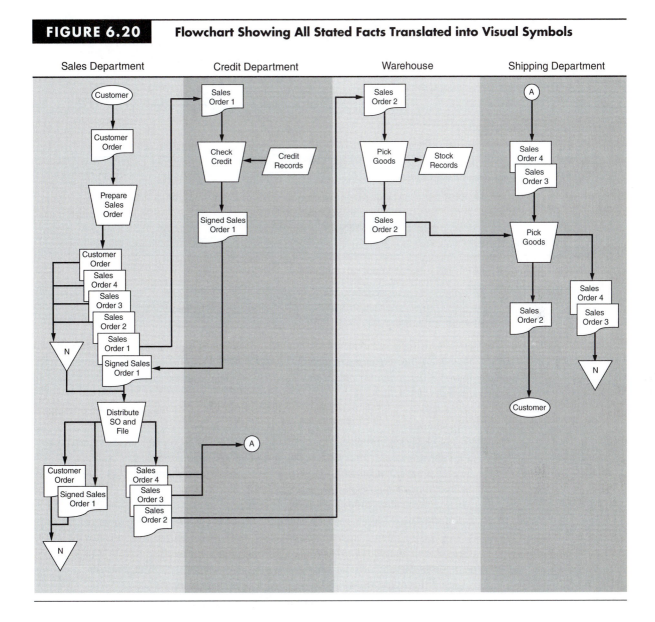

accountant should seek a balance between the economic advantage of large batches and the troubleshooting advantage of small batches. There is no magic number for the size of a batch. This decision is based on a number of operational, business, and economic factors. Among these are the volume of transactions, the competitiveness of the industry, the normal frequency of errors, the financial implications of an undetected error, and the costs of processing. Depending on these factors, a system might be designed to process many small batches throughout the day or an entire day's activity as a single batch.

Flowcharting Computer Processes

We now examine flowcharting techniques to represent a system that employs both manual and computer processes. The symbol set used to construct this system flowchart will come

⬜	Hard copy (source documents and output)	⬜	Terminal input/output device
⬜	Computer process (program run)	➡	Process flow
⬜	Direct access storage device (disk pack)	⬜	Real-time (online) connection
⬜	Magnetic tape (sequential storage device)	⬜	Video display device

from both Figure 6.17 and Figure 6.21. Again, our example is based on a sales order system with the following facts:

1. *A clerk in the sales department receives a customer order by mail and enters the information into a computer terminal that is networked to a centralized computer program in the computer operations department. The original customer order is filed in the sales department.*

    Facts 2, 3, and 4 relate to activities that occur in the computer operations department.

2. *A computer program edits the transactions, checks the customer's credit by referencing a credit history file, and produces a transaction file of sales orders.*

3. *The sales order transaction file is then processed by an update program that posts the transactions to corresponding records in AR and inventory files.*

4. *Finally, the update program produces three hard copies of the sales order. Copy 1 is sent to the warehouse, and Copies 2 and 3 are sent to the shipping department.*

5. *On receipt of Copy 1, the warehouse clerk picks the products from the shelves. Using Copy 1 and the warehouse personal computer (PC), the clerk records the inventory transfer in the digital stock records that are kept on the PC. Next, the clerk sends the physical inventory and Copy 1 to the shipping department.*

6. *The shipping department receives Copy 1 and the goods from the warehouse. The clerk reconciles the goods with Copies 1, 2, and 3 and attaches Copy 1 as a packing slip. Next, the clerk ships the goods (with Copy 1 attached) to the customer. Finally, the clerk records the shipment in the hard-copy shipping log and files Copies 2 and 3 in the shipping department.*

Lay out the Physical Areas of Activity.   The flowcharting process begins by creating a template that depicts the areas of activity similar to the one shown in Figure 6.16. The only differences in this case are that this system has a computer operations department but does not have a credit department.

Transcribe the Written Facts into Visual Format.   As with the manual system example, the next step is to systematically transcribe the written facts into visual objects. Figure 6.22 illustrates how Facts 1, 2, and 3 translate visually.

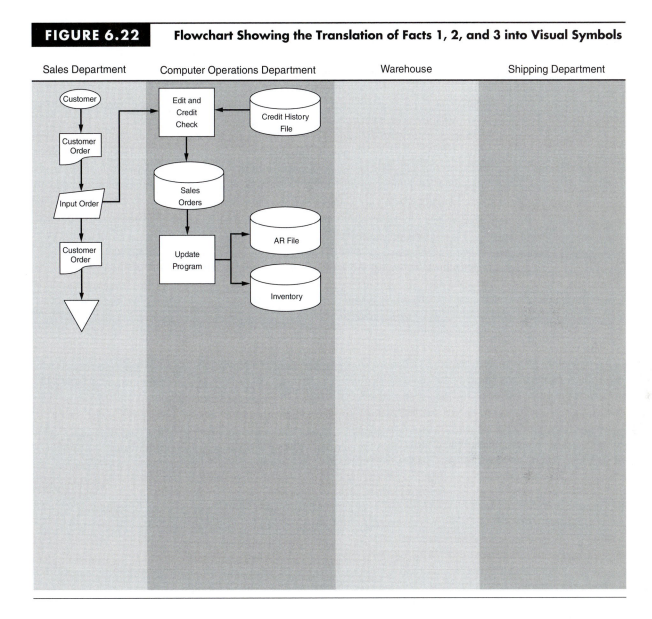

FIGURE 6.22 Flowchart Showing the Translation of Facts 1, 2, and 3 into Visual Symbols

The customer, customer order, and file symbols in this flowchart are the same as in the previous example. The sales clerk's activity, however, is now automated, and the manual process symbol has been replaced with a computer terminal symbol. Also, because this is a data-input operation, the arrowhead on the flowchart line points in the direction of the edit and credit check program. If the terminal was also used to receive output (the facts do not specify such an operation), arrowheads would be on both ends of the line.

Recall that the emphasis in flowcharting is on the physical system. For example, the terminal used by the sales clerk to enter customer orders is physically located in the sales department, but the programs that process the transactions and the files that it uses and updates are stored in a separate computer operations department.

Notice how the flow line points from the credit history file to the edit program. This indicates that the file is read (referenced) but not changed (updated) by the program. In contrast, the interactions between the update program and the AR and inventory files are in the opposite direction. The relevant records in these files have been changed to reflect the transactions. The logic of a file update is explained later in the chapter.

Let's now translate the remaining facts into visual symbols. Fact 4 states that the update program produces three hard-copy documents in the computer operations department, which are then distributed to the warehouse and shipping departments. The translation of this fact is illustrated in Figure 6.23.

Fact 5 states that the warehouse clerk updates the stock records on the department PC and then sends the physical inventory and Copy 1 to the shipping department. Notice on Figure 6.23 how this computer activity is represented. The warehouse PC is a standalone computer system that is not networked into the computer operations department like the terminal in the sales department. The PC, the stock record update program, and the stock records themselves are all physically located in the warehouse.

FIGURE 6.23   Flowchart Showing All Facts Translated into Visual Symbols

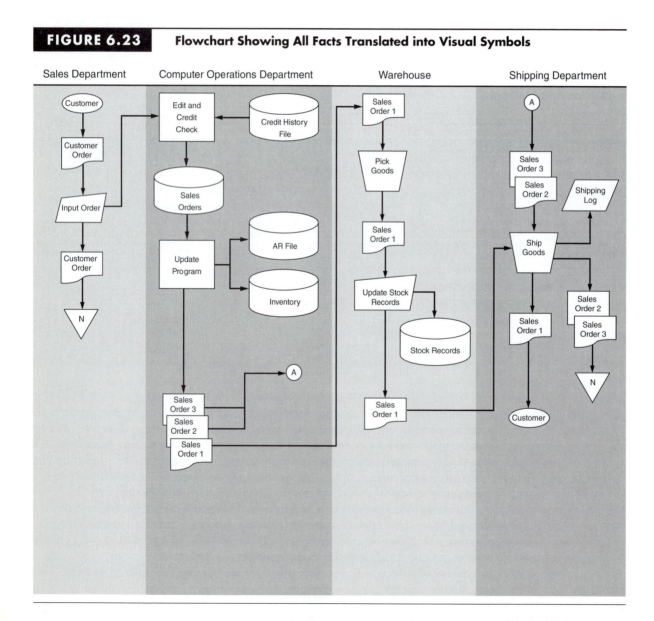

As with manual procedures, when documenting computer operations, the flowchart author must accurately represent the physical arrangement of the system components. As we will see in later chapters, the physical arrangement of system components (both manual and computer) often plays an important role in the auditor's assessment of internal control.

Finally, Fact 6 describes how the shipping department clerk reconciles the goods with the supporting documents, sends the goods and the packing slip to the customer, updates the shipping log, and files two copies of the sales order. This is entirely a manual operation, as evidenced by the symbols in Figure 6.23. Note that the shipping log uses the same symbol that is used for representing journals and ledgers.

Program Flowcharts

The system flowchart in Figure 6.23 shows the relationship between computer programs, the files they use, and the outputs they produce. This high level of documentation, however, does not provide the operational details that are sometimes needed. For example, an auditor wishing to assess the correctness of the edit program's logic cannot do so from the system flowchart. This requires a **program flowchart**. The symbol set used for program flowcharts is presented in Figure 6.24.

Every program represented in a system flowchart should have a supporting program flowchart that describes its logic. Figure 6.25 presents the logic of the edit program shown in Figure 6.26. A separate symbol represents each step of the program's logic, and each symbol represents one or more lines of computer program code. The connector lines between the symbols establish the logical order of execution. Tracing the flowchart downward from the start symbol, we see that the program performs the following logical steps in the order listed:

1. The program retrieves a single record from the unedited transaction file and stores it in memory.
2. The first logical test is to see if the program has reached the end-of-file (EOF) condition for the transaction file. Most file structures use a special record or marker to indicate an EOF condition. When EOF is reached, the edit program will terminate and the next program in the system (in this case, the update program) will be executed. As long as there is a record in the unedited transaction file, the result of the EOF test will be "no" and process control is passed to the next logical step in the edit program.
3. Processing involves a series of tests to identify certain clerical and logical errors. Each test, represented by a decision symbol, evaluates the presence or absence of a condition. For example, an edit test could be to detect the presence of alphabetic data in a field that should contain only numeric data. We examine specific edit and validation tests in Chapter 7.
4. Error-free records are sent to the edited transaction file.

FIGURE 6.24

Program Flowchart Symbols

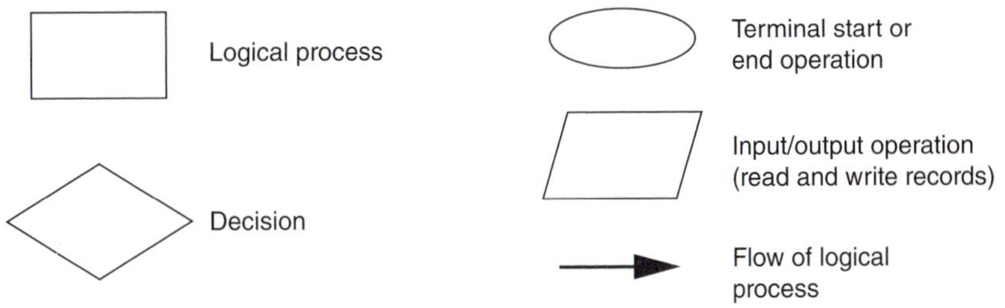

Logical process

Terminal start or end operation

Decision

Input/output operation (read and write records)

Flow of logical process

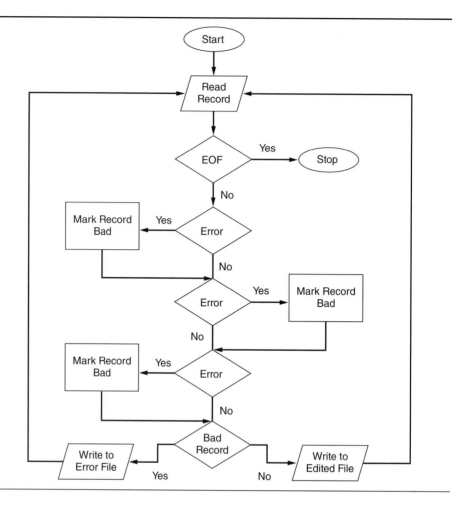

FIGURE 6.25

Program Flowchart for Edit Program

5. Records containing errors are sent to the error file.
6. The program loops back to Step 1, and the process is repeated until the EOF condition is reached.

Accountants sometimes use program flowcharts to verify the correctness of program logic. They compare flowcharts to the actual program code to determine whether the program is actually doing what the documentation describes. Program flowcharts provide essential details for conducting IT audits, which we examine in Chapter 7.

Record Layout Diagrams

Record layout diagrams are used to reveal the internal structure of the records that constitute a file or database table. The layout diagram usually shows the name, data type, and length of each attribute (or field) in the record. Detailed data structure information is needed for such tasks as identifying certain types of system failures, analyzing error reports, and designing tests of computer logic for debugging and auditing purposes. A simpler form of record layout, shown in Figure 6.27, suits our purposes best. This type of layout shows the content of a record. Each data attribute and key field is shown in terms of its name and relative location.

FIGURE 6.26

**System
Flowchart**

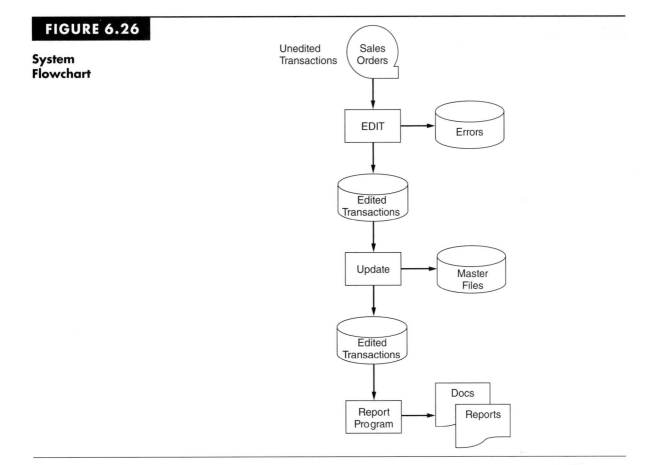

FIGURE 6.27   Record Layout Diagram for Customer File

Customer File

Key						
Customer Number	Customer Name	Street Address	City	State	Zip Code	Credit Limit

COMPUTER-BASED ACCOUNTING SYSTEMS

In this section, we examine alternative computer-based transaction processing models. Computer-based accounting systems fall into two broad classes: batch systems and real-time systems. A number of alternative configurations exist within each of these classes. Systems designers base their configuration choices on a variety of considerations. Table 6.1 summarizes some of the distinguishing characteristics of batch and real-time processing that feature prominently in these decisions.

TABLE 6.1	**Characteristic Differences Between Batch and Real-Time Processing**	
	Data Processing Methods	
Distinguishing Feature	**Batch**	**Real Time**
Information time frame	Lag exists between time when the economic event occurs and when it is recorded.	Processing takes place when the economic event occurs.
Resources	Generally, fewer resources (e.g., hardware, programming, training) are required.	More resources are required than for batch processing.
Operational efficiency	Certain records are processed after the event to avoid operational delays.	All records pertaining to the event are processed immediately.

Differences Between Batch and Real-Time Systems

Information Time Frame

Batch systems assemble transactions into groups for processing. Under this approach, there is always a time lag between the point at which an economic event occurs and the point at which it is reflected in the firm's accounts. The amount of lag depends on the frequency of batch processing. Time lags can range from minutes to weeks. Payroll processing is an example of a typical batch system. The economic events—the application of employee labor—occur continuously throughout the pay period. At the end of the period, the paychecks for all employees are prepared together as a batch.

Real-time systems process transactions individually at the moment the event occurs. Because records are not grouped into batches, there are no time lags between occurrence and recording. An example of real-time processing is an airline reservations system, which processes requests for services from one traveler at a time while he or she waits.

Resources

Generally, batch systems demand fewer organizational resources (such as programming costs, computer time, and user training) than real-time systems. For example, batch systems can use sequential files stored on magnetic tape. Real-time systems use direct access files that require more expensive storage devices, such as magnetic disks. In practice, however, these cost differentials are disappearing. As a result, business organizations typically use magnetic disks for both batch and real-time processing.

The most significant resource differentials are in the areas of systems development (programming) and computer operations. As batch systems are generally simpler than their real-time counterparts, they tend to have shorter development periods and are easier for programmers to maintain. On the other hand, as much as 50 percent of the total programming costs for real-time systems are incurred in designing the user interfaces. Real-time systems must be friendly, forgiving, and easy to work with. Pop-up menus, online tutorials, and special help features require additional programming and add greatly to the cost of the system.

Finally, real-time systems require dedicated processing capacity. Real-time systems must deal with transactions as they occur. Some types of systems must be available 24 hours a day whether they are being used or not. The computer capacity dedicated to such systems cannot be used for other purposes. Thus, implementing a real-time system may require either the purchase of a dedicated computer or an investment in additional computer capacity. In contrast, batch systems use computer capacity only when the program is being run. When the batch job completes processing, the freed capacity can be reallocated to other applications.

Operational Efficiency

Real-time processing in systems that handle large volumes of transactions each day can create operational inefficiencies. A single transaction may affect several different accounts. Some of these accounts, however, may not need to be updated in real time. In fact, the task of doing so takes time that, when multiplied by hundreds or thousands of transactions, can cause significant processing delays. Batch processing of noncritical accounts, however, improves operational efficiency by eliminating unnecessary activities at critical points in the process. This is illustrated with an example later in the chapter.

Efficiency versus Effectiveness

In selecting a data processing mode, the designer must consider the trade-off between efficiency and effectiveness. For example, users of an airline reservations system cannot wait until 100 passengers (an efficient batch size) assemble in the travel agent's office before their transactions are processed. When immediate access to current information is critical to the user's needs, real-time processing is the logical choice. When time lags in information have no detrimental effects on the user's performance and operational efficiencies can be achieved by processing data in batches, batch processing is probably the superior choice.

Alternative Data Processing Approaches

Legacy Systems versus Modern Systems

Not all modern organizations use entirely modern information systems. Some firms employ legacy systems for certain aspects of their data processing. When legacy systems are used to process financially significant transactions, auditors need to know how to evaluate and test them. Legacy systems tend to have the following distinguishing features: they are mainframe-based applications; they tend to be batch oriented; early legacy systems use flat files for data storage, but hierarchical and network databases are often associated with later-era legacy systems. These highly structured and inflexible storage systems are very efficient data processing tools, but promote a single-user environment that discourages information integration within business organizations.

Modern systems tend to be client-server (network)–based and process transactions in real time. Although this is the trend in most organizations, please note that many modern systems are mainframe-based and use batch processing. Unlike their predecessors, modern systems store transactions and master files in relational database tables. A major advantage of database storage is the degree of process integration and data sharing that can be achieved.

The remainder of the section focuses on modern system technologies used for processing accounting transactions. Some systems employ a combination of batch and real-time processing, while others are purely real-time systems. In several chapters that follow, we will examine how these approaches are configured to support specific functions such as sales order processing, purchasing, and payroll.

Updating Master Files from Transactions

Whether batch or real-time processing is being used, updating a master file record involves changing the value of one or more of its variable fields to reflect the effects of a transaction. Figure 6.28 presents record structures for a sales order transaction file and two

---

| FIGURE 6.28 | Record Structures for Sales, Inventory, and Accounts Receivable Files |

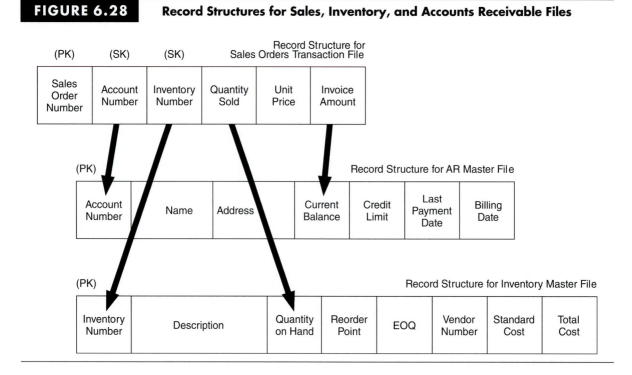

associated master files, AR and inventory. The primary key (PK)—the unique identifier—for the inventory file is INVENTORY NUMBER. The primary key for AR is ACCOUNT NUMBER. Notice that the record structure for the sales order file contains a primary key (SALES ORDER NUMBER) and two secondary key (SK) fields, ACCOUNT NUMBER and INVENTORY NUMBER. These secondary keys are used for locating the corresponding records in the master files. To simplify the example, we assume that each sale is for a single item of inventory. Chapter 8 examines database structures in detail wherein we study the database complexities associated with more realistic business transactions.

The update procedure in this example involves the following steps:

1. A sales order record is read by the system.
2. ACCOUNT NUMBER is used to search the AR master file and retrieve the corresponding AR record.
3. The AR update procedure calculates the new customer balance by adding the value stored in the INVOICE AMOUNT field of the sales order record to the CURRENT BALANCE field value in the AR master record.
4. Next, INVENTORY NUMBER is used to search for the corresponding record in the inventory master file.
5. The inventory update program reduces inventory levels by deducting the QUANTITY SOLD value in a transaction record from the QUANTITY ON HAND field value in the inventory record.
6. A new sales order record is read, and the process is repeated.

Database Backup Procedures

Each record in a database file is assigned a unique disk location or address that is determined by its primary key value. Because only a single valid location exists for each record, updating the record must occur in place. Figure 6.29 shows this technique.

FIGURE 6.29

Destructive Update Approach

Transaction File

Sale = $50

AR Master File

Read $50

Read $100

Update Program

$100 + $50 = $150

Write $150

Current Bal = $100

Record Location A

In this example, an AR record with a $100 current balance is being updated by a $50 sale transaction. The master file record is permanently stored at a disk address designated Location A. The update program reads both the transaction record and the master file record into memory. The receivable is updated to reflect the new current balance of $150 and then returned to Location A. The original current balance, value of $100, is destroyed when replaced by the new value of $150. This technique is called destructive update.

The destructive update approach leaves no backup copy of the original master file. Only the current value is available to the user. To preserve adequate accounting records in case the current master becomes damaged or corrupted, separate backup procedures, such as those shown in Figure 6.30, must be implemented.

Prior to each batch update or periodically (for example, every 15 minutes), the master file being updated is copied to create a backup version of the original file. Should the current master be destroyed after the update process, reconstruction is possible in two stages. First, a special recovery program uses the backup file to create a pre-update version of the master file. Second, the file update process is repeated using the previous batch of transactions to restore the master to its current condition. Because of the potential risk to accounting records, accountants are naturally concerned about the adequacy of all backup procedures. In Chapter 4, we examined several audit issues related to file backup.

FIGURE 6.30

Backup and Recovery Procedures for Database Files

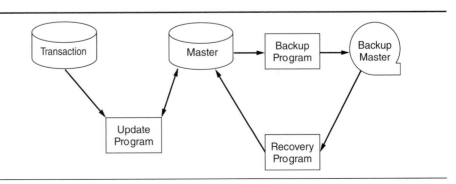

Transaction

Master

Backup Program

Backup Master

Update Program

Recovery Program

Batch Processing Using Real-Time Data Collection

A popular data processing approach, particularly for large operations, is to electronically capture transaction data at the source as they occur. By distributing data input capability to users, certain transaction errors can be prevented or detected and corrected at their source. The result is a transaction file that is free from most of the errors that plague older legacy systems. The transaction file is later processed in batch mode to achieve operational efficiency. Figure 6.31 illustrates this approach with a simplified sales order system such as that used in a department store. Key steps in the process are:

- The sales department clerk captures customer sales data pertaining to the item(s) being purchased and the customer's account.
- The system then checks the customer's credit limit from data in the customer record (account receivable subsidiary file) and updates his or her account balance to reflect the amount of the sale.
- Next, the system updates the quantity-on-hand field in the inventory record (inventory subsidiary file) to reflect the reduction in inventory. This provides up-to-date information to other clerks as to inventory availability.
- A record of the sale is then added to the sales order file (transaction file), which is processed in batch mode at the end of the business day. This batch process records each transaction in the sales journal and updates the affected general ledger accounts.

You may be wondering at this point why the sales journal and general ledger accounts are being processed in batch mode. Why not update them in real time along with the subsidiary accounts? The answer is to achieve operational efficiency. We now examine what that means.

Let's assume that the organization using the sales order system configuration illustrated in Figure 6.31 is large and capable of serving hundreds of customers concurrently. Also assume that 500 sales terminals are distributed throughout its many large departments.

Each customer sale affects the following six accounting records:

- Customer account receivable (Subsidiary—unique)
- Inventory item (Subsidiary—almost unique)
- Inventory control (general ledger—common)
- Account receivable control (general ledger—common)
- Sales (general ledger—common)
- Cost of goods sold (general ledger—common)

To maintain the integrity of accounting data, once a record has been accessed for processing, it is locked by the system and made unavailable to other users until its processing is complete. Using the affected records noted here as an example, consider the implications that this data-locking rule has on the users of the system.

When processing a customer account receivable subsidiary record, the rule has no implications for other users of the system. Each user accesses only his or her unique record. For example, accessing John Smith's account does not prevent Mary Jones from accessing her account. Updating the inventory subsidiary record is almost unique. Because it is possible that both Mary Jones and John Smith are independently purchasing the same item at the same time, Mary Jones may be kept waiting a few seconds until John Smith's transaction releases the lock on the inventory account. This will be a relatively rare event, and any such conflicts will be of little inconvenience to customers. As a general rule, therefore, master file records that are unique to a transaction such as

FIGURE 6.31	Batch Processing with Real-Time Data Collection

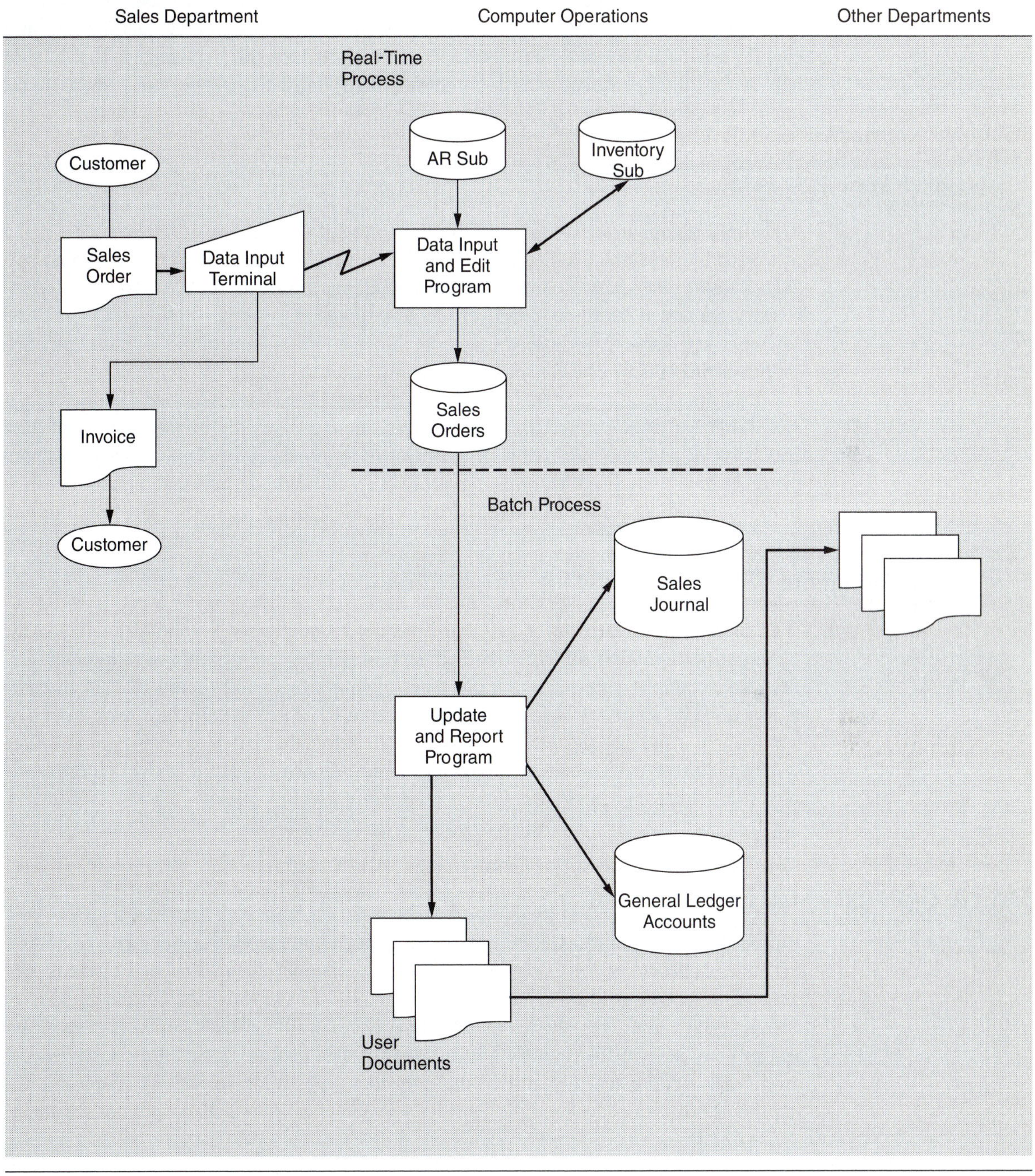

customer accounts and individual inventory records can be updated in real time without causing operational delays.

Updating the records in the general ledger is a different matter. All general ledger accounts previously listed need to be updated by every sales transaction. If the processing of John Smith's transaction begins before that of Mary Jones, then she must wait until all six records have been updated before her transaction can proceed. However, the 20- or 30-second delay brought about by this conflict will probably not inconvenience Mary Jones. This problem becomes manifest as transaction volumes increase. A 20-second delay in each of 500 customer transactions would create operational inefficiency on a chaotic level. Each of the 500 customers must wait until the person ahead of him or her in the queue has completed processing their transaction. The last person in the queue will experience a delay of 500×20 seconds = 2¾ hours.

Real-Time Processing

Real-time systems process the entire transaction as it occurs. For example, a sales order processed by the system in Figure 6.32 can be captured, filled, and shipped the same day. Such a system has many potential benefits, including improved productivity, reduced inventory, increased inventory turnover, decreased lags in customer billing, and enhanced customer satisfaction. Because transaction information is transmitted digitally, physical source documents can be eliminated or greatly reduced.

Real-time processing is well suited to systems that process lower transaction volumes and those that do not share common records. These systems make extensive use of local area network and wide area network technology. Terminals at distributed sites throughout the organization are used for receiving, processing, and sending information about current transactions. These must be linked in a network arrangement so users can communicate.

Controlling the TPS

We will defer our treatment of TPS control issues to later chapters that deal with specific TPS applications. Such controls are, by their very nature, application and technology specific. For example, while it is a basic tenet of internal control theory that all material transactions be authorized, achieving this is accomplished differently in a sales order system than in a purchasing system. Also, manual, automated batch systems, and real-time system require different control techniques to accomplish the same control objective.

DATA CODING SCHEMES

Within the context of transaction processing, data coding involves creating simple numerical or alphabetical codes to represent complex economic phenomena that facilitate efficient data processing. In Figure 6.28, for example, we saw how the secondary keys of transaction file records are linked to the primary keys of master file records. The secondary and primary keys in the example are instances of data coding. In this section, we explore several data coding schemes and examples of their application in AIS. To emphasize the importance of data codes, we first consider a hypothetical system that does not use them.

A System without Codes

Firms process large volumes of transactions that are similar in their basic attributes. For instance, a firm's AR file may contain accounts for several different customers with the same name and similar addresses. To process transactions accurately against the correct accounts, the firm must be able to distinguish one John Smith from another. This task becomes particularly difficult as the number of similar attributes and items in the class increase.

FIGURE 6.32   Real-Time Processing of Sales Orders

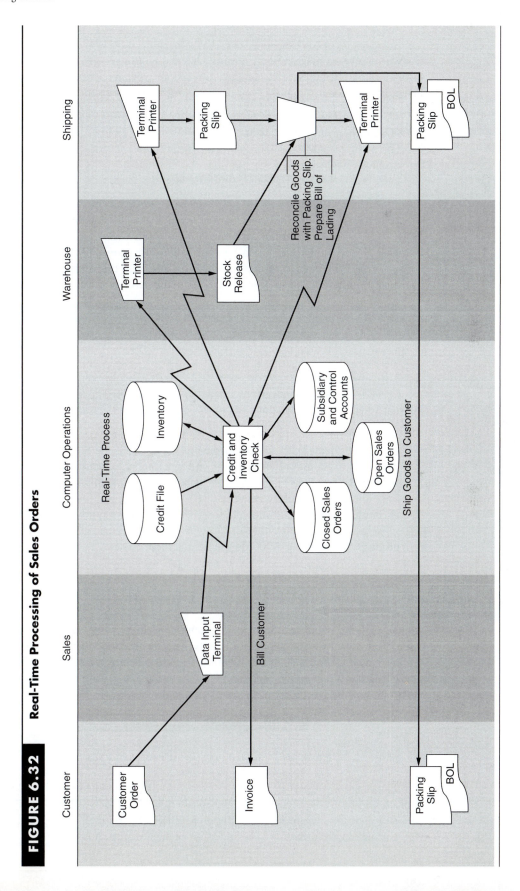

Consider the most elemental item that a machine shop wholesaler firm might carry in its inventory—a machine nut. Assume that the total inventory of nuts has only three distinguishing attributes: size, material, and thread type. As a result, this entire class of inventory must be distinguished on the basis of these three features, as follows:

1. The size attribute ranges from ¼ inch to 1¾ inches in diameter in increments of $\frac{1}{64}$ of an inch, giving 96 nut sizes.
2. For each size subclass, four materials are available: brass, copper, mild steel, and case-hardened steel.
3. Each of these size and material subclasses come in three different threads: fine, standard, and coarse.

Under these assumptions, this class of inventory could contain 1,152 separate items (96 × 4 × 3). The identification of a single item in this class thus requires a description featuring these distinguishing attributes. To illustrate, consider the following journal entry to record the receipt of $1,000 worth of half-inch, case-hardened steel nuts with standard threads supplied by Industrial Parts Manufacturer of Cleveland, Ohio.

	DR	CR
Inventory—nut, ½ inch, case-hardened steel, standard thread	1,000	
AP—Industrial Parts Manufacturer, Cleveland, Ohio		1,000

This uncoded entry takes a great deal of recording space, is time-consuming to record, and is obviously prone to many types of errors. The negative effects of this approach may be seen in many parts of the organization:

1. *Sales staff.* Properly identifying the items sold requires the transcription of large amounts of detail onto source documents. Apart from the time and effort involved, this tends to promote clerical errors and incorrect shipments.
2. *Warehouse personnel.* Locating and picking goods for shipment are impeded and shipping errors will likely result.
3. *Accounting personnel.* Postings to ledger accounts will require searching through the subsidiary files using lengthy descriptions as the key. This will be painfully slow, and postings to the wrong accounts will be common.

A System with Codes

These problems are solved, or at least greatly reduced, by using codes to represent each item in the inventory and supplier accounts. Let's assume the inventory item in our previous example had been assigned the numeric code 896, and the supplier in the accounts payable account is given the code number 321. The coded version of the previous journal entry can now be greatly simplified:

ACCOUNT	DR	CR
896	1,000	
321		1,000

This is not to suggest that detailed information about the inventory and the supplier is of no interest to the organization. Obviously it is! These facts will be kept in reference files and used for such purposes as the preparation of parts lists, catalogs, bills of material, and mailing information. The inclusion of such details, however, would clutter the task of transaction processing and could prove dysfunctional, as this simple example illustrates. Other uses of data coding in AIS are to:

1. Concisely represent large amounts of complex information that would otherwise be unmanageable.
2. Provide a means of accountability over the completeness of the transactions processed.
3. Identify unique transactions and accounts within a file.
4. Support the audit function by providing an effective audit trail.

The following discussion examines some of the more commonly used coding techniques and explores their respective advantages and disadvantages.

Numeric and Alphabetic Coding Schemes

Sequential Codes

As the name implies, **sequential codes** represent items in some sequential order (ascending or descending). A common application of numeric sequential codes is the prenumbering of source documents. At printing, each hard-copy document is given a unique sequential code number. This number becomes the transaction number that allows the system to track each transaction processed and to identify any lost or out-of-sequence documents. Digital documents are similarly assigned a sequential number by the computer when they are created.

Advantages. Sequential coding supports the reconciliation of a batch of transactions, such as sales orders, at the end of processing. If the transaction processing system detects any gaps in the sequence of transaction numbers, it alerts management to the possibility of a missing or misplaced transaction. By tracing the transaction number back through the stages in the process, management can eventually determine the cause and effect of the error. Without sequentially numbered documents, problems of this sort are difficult to detect and resolve.

Disadvantages. Sequential codes carry no information content beyond their order in the sequence. For instance, a sequential code assigned to a raw material inventory item tells us nothing about the attributes of the item (type, size, material, warehouse location, and so on). Also, sequential coding schemes are difficult to change. Inserting a new item at some midpoint requires renumbering the subsequent items in the class accordingly. In applications where record types must be grouped together logically and where additions and deletions occur regularly, this coding scheme is inappropriate.

Block Codes

A numeric **block code** is a variation on sequential coding that partly remedies the disadvantages just described. This approach can be used to represent whole classes of items by restricting each class to a specific range within the coding scheme. A common application of block coding is the construction of a **chart of accounts**.

A well-designed and comprehensive chart of accounts is the basis for the general ledger and is thus critical to a firm's financial and management reporting systems. The more extensive the chart of accounts, the more precisely a firm can classify its transactions and the greater the range of information it can provide to internal and external users. Figure 6.33 presents an example of accounts using block codes.

Notice that each account type is represented by a unique range of codes or blocks. Thus, balance sheet and income statement account classifications and subclassifications can be

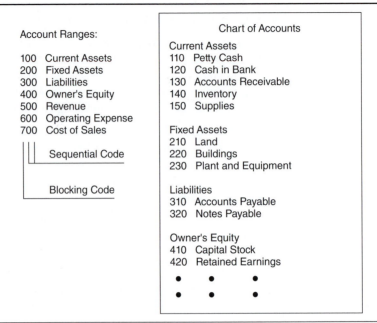

FIGURE 6.33

Chart of Accounts

depicted. In this example, each of the accounts consists of a three-digit code. The first digit is the blocking digit and represents the account classification; for example, current assets, liabilities, or operating expense. The other digits in the code are sequentially assigned.

Advantages.   Block coding allows for the insertion of new codes within a block without having to reorganize the entire coding structure. For example, if advertising expense is account number 626, the first digit indicates that this account is an operating expense. As new types of expense items are incurred and have to be specifically accounted for, they may be added sequentially within the 600 account classification. This three-digit code accommodates 100 individual items (X00 through X99) within each block. Obviously, the more digits in the code range, the more items that can be represented.

Disadvantages.   As with the sequential codes, the information content of the block code is not readily apparent. For instance, account number 626 means nothing until matched against the chart of accounts, which identifies it as advertising expense.

Group Codes

Numeric **group codes** are used to represent complex items or events involving two or more pieces of related data. The code consists of zones or fields that possess specific meaning. For example, a department store chain might code sales order transactions from its branch stores as follows:

Store Number	Dept. Number	Item Number	Salesperson
04	09	476214	99

Advantages.   Group codes have a number of advantages over sequential and block codes.

1. They facilitate the representation of large amounts of diverse data.
2. They allow complex data structures to be represented in a hierarchical form that is logical and more easily remembered by humans.

3. They permit detailed analysis and reporting both within an item class and across different classes of items.

Using the previous example to illustrate, Store Number 04 could represent the Hamilton Mall store in Allentown; Dept. Number 09 represents the sporting goods department; Item Number 476214 is a hockey stick; and Salesperson 99 is Jon Innes. With this level of information, a corporate manager could measure profitability by store, compare the performance of similar departments across all stores, track the movement of specific inventory items, and evaluate sales performance by employees within and between stores.

Disadvantages. Ironically, the primary disadvantage of group coding results from its success as a classification tool. Because group codes can effectively present diverse information, they tend to be overused. Unrelated data may be linked simply because it can be done. This can lead to unnecessarily complex group codes that cannot be easily interpreted. Finally, overuse can increase storage costs, promote clerical errors, and increase processing time and effort.

Alphabetic Codes

Alphabetic codes are used for many of the same purposes as numeric codes. Alphabetic characters may be assigned sequentially (in alphabetical order) or may be used in block and group coding techniques.

Advantages. The capacity to represent large numbers of items is increased dramatically through the use of pure alphabetic codes or alphabetic characters embedded within numeric codes (**alphanumeric codes**). The earlier example of a chart of accounts using a three-digit code with a single blocking digit limits data representation to only 10 blocks of accounts—0 through 9. Using alphabetic characters for blocking, however, increases the number of possible blocks to 26—A through Z. Furthermore, whereas the two-digit sequential portion of that code has the capacity of only 100 items (10^2), a two-position alphabetic code can represent 676 items (26^2). Thus, by using alphabetic codes in the same three-digit coding space, we see a geometric increase in the potential for data representation

$$(10 \text{ blocks} \times 100 \text{ items each}) = 1,000 \text{ items}$$

to

$$(26 \text{ blocks} \times 676 \text{ items each}) = 17,576 \text{ items}$$

Disadvantages. The primary drawbacks with alphabetic coding are (1) as with numeric codes, there is difficulty rationalizing the meaning of codes that have been sequentially assigned; and (2) users tend to have difficulty sorting records that are coded alphabetically.

Mnemonic Codes

Mnemonic codes are alphabetic characters in the form of acronyms and other combinations that convey meaning. For example, a student enrolling in college courses may enter the following course codes on the registration form:

Course Type	Course Number
Acctg	101
Psyc	110
Mgt	270
Mktg	300

This combination of mnemonic and numeric codes conveys a good deal of information about these courses; with a little analysis, we can deduce that Acctg is accounting, Psyc is psychology, Mgt is management, and Mktg is marketing. The sequential number portion of the code indicates the level of each course. Another example of the use of mnemonic codes is assigning state codes in mailing addresses:

Code	Meaning
NY	New York
CA	California
OK	Oklahoma

Advantages.   The mnemonic coding scheme does not require the user to memorize meaning; the code itself conveys a high degree of information about the item that is being represented.

Disadvantages.   Although mnemonic codes are useful for representing classes of items, they have limited ability to represent items within a class. For example, the entire class of accounts receivable could be represented by the mnemonic code AR, but we would quickly exhaust meaningful combinations of alphabetic characters if we attempted to represent the individual accounts that make up this class. These accounts would be represented better by sequential, block, or group coding techniques.

THE GENERAL LEDGER SYSTEM

Figure 6.34 characterizes the general ledger system (GLS) as a hub connected to the other systems of the firm through spokes of information flows. TPS subsystems process various aspects of economic events, which are recorded in their respective special journals and subsidiary accounts. Summaries of these transactions flow into the GLS and become sources of input for the financial reporting system (FRS). Note, however, that information also flows from the FRS as feedback into the GLS. We shall explore this point more thoroughly later. In this section we review key elements of the GLS.

Also, note that the GLS provides data for the management reporting system (MRS). This is the organization's internal, or discretionary, reporting system. Since the MRS does not directly impact the financial reporting process, we give only ancillary treatment to this system.

The Journal Voucher

The source of input to the general ledger is the journal voucher, which is illustrated in Figure 6.35. A journal voucher, which can be used to represent summaries of similar transactions or a single unique transaction, identifies the financial amounts and affected general ledger (GL) accounts. Routine transactions, adjusting entries, and closing entries are all entered into the GL via journal vouchers. Because a responsible manager must approve journal vouchers, they offer a degree of control against unauthorized GL entries.

The GLS Database

The GLS database includes a variety of files. Whereas these will vary from firm to firm, the following examples are representative.

FIGURE 6.34

Relationship of GLS to Other Information Subsystems

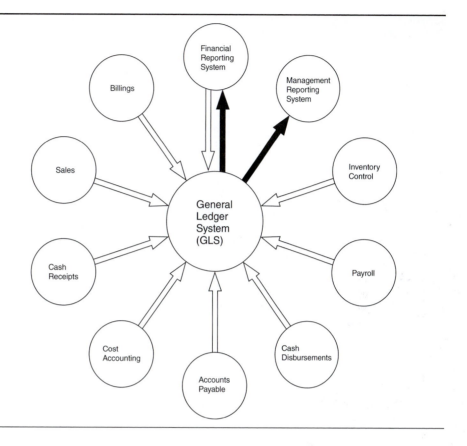

FIGURE 6.35   Journal Voucher Record Layout for a General Ledger Master File

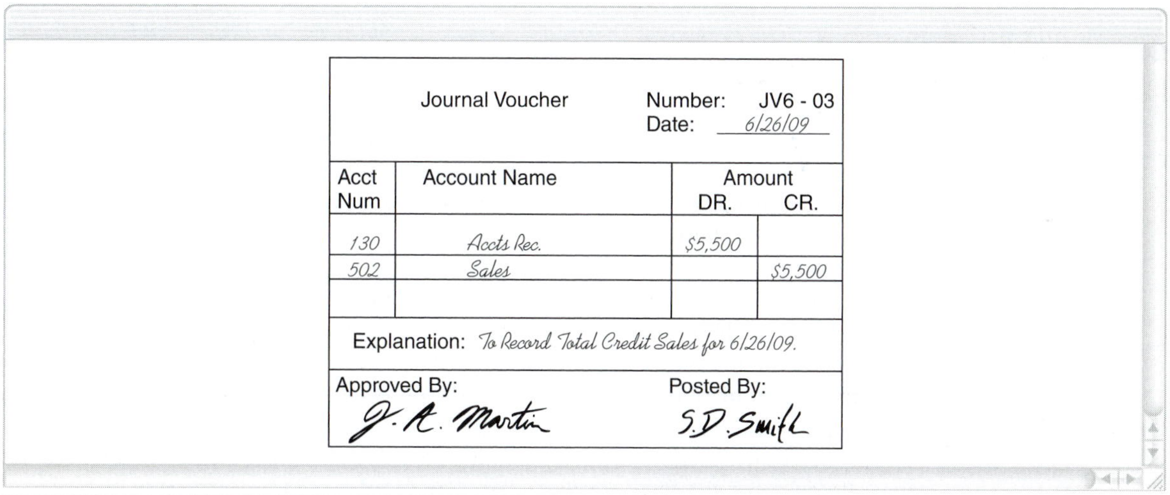

Journal Voucher		Number: JV6 - 03	
		Date: 6/26/09	

Acct Num	Account Name	Amount DR.	Amount CR.
130	Accts Rec.	$5,500	
502	Sales		$5,500

Explanation: To Record Total Credit Sales for 6/26/09.

Approved By:	Posted By:
J. R. Martin	S.D. Smith

FIGURE 6.36

Record Layout
for a General
Ledger Master
File

Account Number	Account Description	Acct Class A = Asset L = Liab R = Rev E = Expense OE = Equity	Normal Balance D = Debit C = Credit	Beginning Balance	Total Debits This Period	Total Credits This Period	Current Balance

The **general ledger master file** is the principle file in the GLS database. This file is based on the organization's published chart of accounts. Each record in the GL master is either a separate GL account (for example, sales) or the control account (such as AR—control) for a corresponding subsidiary ledger in the transaction processing system. Figure 6.36 illustrates the structure of a typical GL master file. The FRS draws upon the GL master to produce the firm's financial statements. The MRS also uses this file to support internal information reporting.

The **general ledger history file** has the same format as the GL master. Its primary purpose is to provide historical financial data for comparative financial reports.

The **journal voucher file** is the total collection of the journal vouchers processed in the current period. This file provides a record of all general ledger transactions and replaces the traditional general journal.

The **journal voucher history file** contains journal vouchers for past periods. This historical information supports management's stewardship responsibility to account for resource utilization. Both the current and historical journal voucher files are important links in the firm's audit trail.

The **responsibility center file** contains the revenues, expenditures, and other resource utilization data for each responsibility center in the organization. The MRS draws upon these data for input in the preparation of responsibility reports for management.

Finally, the **budget master file** contains budgeted amounts for revenues, expenditures, and other resources for responsibility centers. These data, in conjunction with the responsibility center file, are the basis for responsibility accounting.

THE FINANCIAL REPORTING SYSTEM

The law dictates management's responsibility for providing stewardship information to external parties. This reporting obligation is met via the FRS. Much of the information provided takes the form of standard financial statements, tax returns, and documents required by regulatory agencies such as the Securities and Exchange Commission (SEC).

The primary recipients of financial statement information are external users, such as stockholders, creditors, and government agencies. Generally speaking, outside users of information are interested in the performance of the organization as a whole. Therefore, they require information that allows them to observe trends in performance over time and to make comparisons between different organizations. Given the nature of these needs, financial reporting information must be prepared and presented by all organizations in a manner that is generally accepted and understood by external users.

Sophisticated Users with Homogeneous Information Needs

Because the community of external users is vast and their individual information needs may vary, financial statements are targeted at a general audience. They are prepared on the proposition that the audience comprises sophisticated users with relatively homogeneous information needs. In other words, it is assumed that users of financial reports understand the conventions and accounting principles that are applied and that the statements have information content that is useful.

Financial Reporting Procedures

Financial reporting is the final step in the overall accounting process that begins in the transaction cycles. Figure 6.37 presents the FRS in relation to the other information subsystems. The steps illustrated and numbered in the figure are discussed briefly in the following section.

The process begins with a clean slate at the start of a new fiscal year. Only the balance sheet (permanent) accounts are carried forward from the previous year. From this point, the following steps occur:

1. *Capture the transaction.* Within each transaction cycle, transactions are recorded in the appropriate transaction file.
2. *Record in special journal.* Each transaction is entered into the journal. Recall that frequently occurring classes of transactions, such as sales, are captured in special journals. Those that occur infrequently are recorded in the general journal or directly on a journal voucher.
3. *Post to subsidiary ledger.* The details of each transaction are posted to the affected subsidiary accounts.
4. *Post to general ledger.* Periodically, journal vouchers, summarizing the entries made to the special journals and subsidiary ledgers, are prepared and posted to the GL accounts. The frequency of updates to the GL will be determined by the degree of system integration.
5. *Prepare the unadjusted trial balance.* At the end of the accounting period, the ending balance of each account in the GL is placed in a worksheet and evaluated in total for debit–credit equality.
6. *Make adjusting entries.* Adjusting entries are made to the worksheet to correct errors and to reflect unrecorded transactions during the period, such as depreciation.
7. *Journalize and post adjusting entries.* Journal vouchers for the adjusting entries are prepared and posted to the appropriate accounts in the GL.
8. *Prepare the adjusted trial balance.* From the adjusted balances, a trial balance is prepared that contains all the entries that should be reflected in the financial statements.
9. *Prepare the financial statements.* The balance sheet, income statement, and statement of cash flows are prepared using the adjusted trial balance.
10. *Journalize and post the closing entries.* Journal vouchers are prepared for entries that close out the income statement (temporary) accounts and transfer the income or loss to retained earnings. Finally, these entries are posted to the GL.
11. *Prepare the post-closing trial balance.* A trial balance worksheet containing only the balance sheet accounts may now be prepared to indicate the balances being carried forward to the next accounting period.

The periodic nature of financial reporting in most organizations establishes it as a batch process, as illustrated in Figure 6.37. This often is the case for larger organizations with multiple streams of revenue and expense transactions that need to be

FIGURE 6.37   Financial Reporting Process

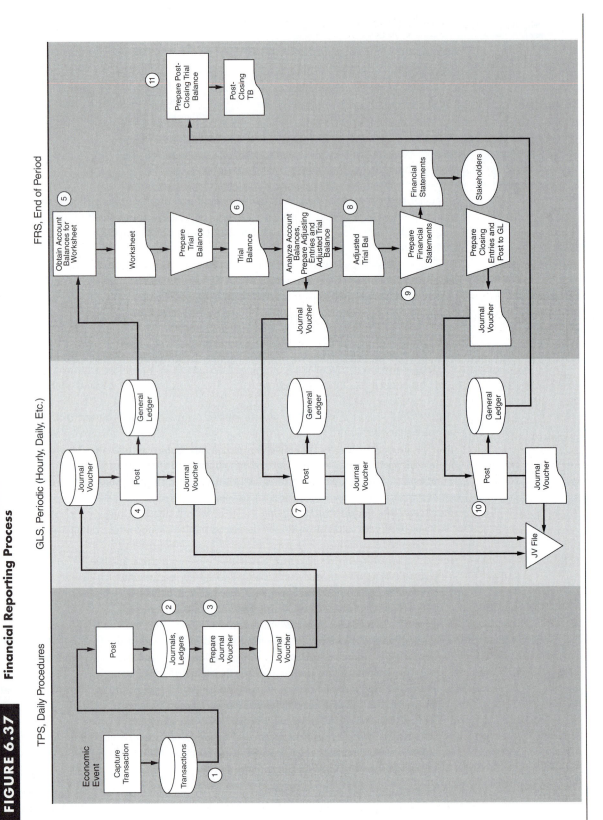

FIGURE 6.38   GL/FRS Using Database Technology

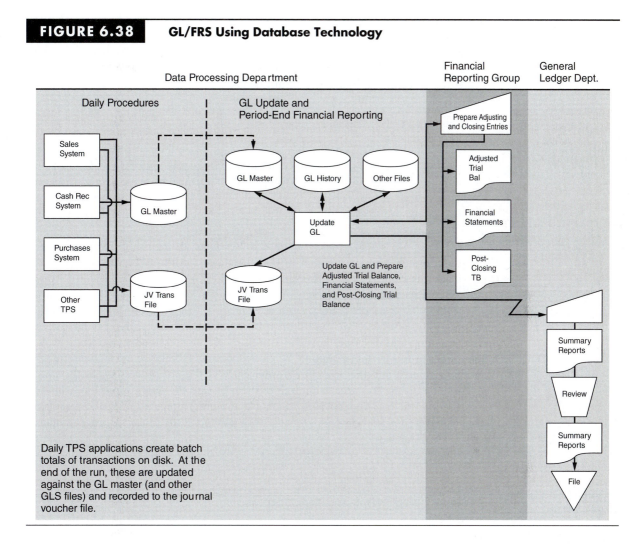

reconciled before being posted to the GL. Many organizations, however, have moved to real-time GL updates and FRSs that produce financial statements on short notice. Figure 6.38 presents an FRS using a combination of batch and real-time computer technology.

XBRL—REENGINEERING FINANCIAL REPORTING

Online reporting of financial data has become a competitive necessity for publicly traded organizations. Currently, most organizations accomplish this by placing their financial statements and other financial reports on their respective Web sites as HTML (hypertext markup language) documents. These documents can then be downloaded by users such as the SEC, financial analysts, and other interested parties. The HTML reports, however, cannot be conveniently processed through IT automation. Performing any analysis on the data contained in the reports requires them to be manually entered into the user's information system.

The solution to this problem is **eXtensible business reporting language (XBRL)**, which is the Internet standard specifically designed for business reporting and information exchange. The objective of XBRL is to facilitate the publication, exchange, and processing of financial and business information. XBRL is a derivative of another Internet standard called **XML (eXtensible markup language)**.

XML

XML is a metalanguage for describing markup languages. The term *extensible* means that any markup language can be created using XML. This includes the creation of markup languages capable of storing data in relational form in which tags (or formatting commands) are mapped to data values. Thus, XML can be used to model the data structure of an organization's internal database.

The examples illustrated in Figure 6.39 serve to distinguish HTML from XML using a bookstore order formatted in both languages.[4] Although essentially the same information is contained in both examples and they look similar in structure, important differences exist between them. Although both examples use tags (words that are bracketed by the symbols < and >) and attributes such as Doe, John, the way in which these tags and attributes are used differs. In the HTML example, the tags have predefined meaning that describes how the attributes will be presented in a document. The book order in this example can only be viewed visually (similar to a FAX) and must be manually entered into the bookstore's order entry system for processing. In the case of the XML order, the tags are customized to the user, and the user's application can read and interpret the tagged data. Thus, the bookstore order prepared in XML presents order attributes in a relational form that can be automatically imported into a bookseller's internal database.

FIGURE 6.39   Comparison of HTML and XML Documents

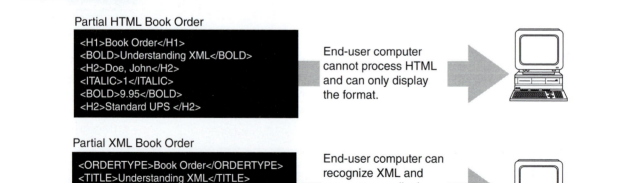

Partial HTML Book Order

```
<H1>Book Order</H1>
<BOLD>Understanding XML</BOLD>
<H2>Doe, John</H2>
<ITALIC>1</ITALIC>
<BOLD>9.95</BOLD>
<H2>Standard UPS </H2>
```

End-user computer cannot process HTML and can only display the format.

Partial XML Book Order

```
<ORDERTYPE>Book Order</ORDERTYPE>
<TITLE>Understanding XML</TITLE>
<AUTHOR>Doe, John</AUTHOR>
<QUANTITY>1</QUANTITY>
<PRICE>9.95</PRICE>
<SHIPPING>Standard UPS </SHIPPING>
```

End-user computer can recognize XML and process accordingly, relieving some of the burden currently placed on web servers.

---

4   http://www.ebusinessforum.gr.

FIGURE 6.40   **Overview of XBRL Reporting Process.**

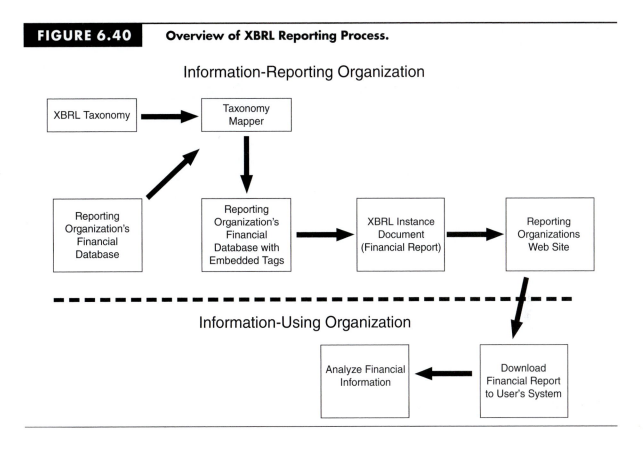

XBRL

Recognizing the potential benefits of XML, the AICPA encouraged research into the creation of an accounting-specific markup language. XBRL is an XML-based language that was designed to provide the financial community with a standardized method for preparing, publishing, and automatically exchanging financial information, including financial statements of publicly held companies. XBRL is typically used for reporting aggregated financial data, but can also be applied to communicating information pertaining to individual transactions. Figure 6.40, presents an overview of the XBRL reporting process, the key elements of which are discussed in the following sections.

The first step in the process is to select an **XBRL taxonomy**. Taxonomies are classification schemes that are compliant with XBRL specifications to accomplish a specific information exchange or reporting objective such as filing with the SEC. In essence, the XBRL taxonomy specifies the data to be included in an exchange or report. The XBRL Standards Committee has created several taxonomies for widespread use. The illustrations in Figures 6.41 through 6.44 are based on XBRL Taxonomy for Financial Reporting for Commercial and Industrial Companies, referred to as CI taxonomy.[5]

The next step is to cross-reference each account in the reporting organization's general ledger to an appropriate XBRL taxonomy element (tag). Figure 6.41 presents part of

---

5   This illustration is based on an example prepared by Charles Hoffman, member of the XBRL Steering Committee Specification Working Group, with assistance from Neal Hannon, XBRL Steering Committee Education co-chair.

FIGURE 6.41	Internal Corporate Database

FullAccount	TrialBalanceDate	Amount	AccountDescription
000-1100-00	5/31/1999	$608,637.31	Cash - Operating Account
000-1101-00	5/31/1999	$8,957.84	Cash in Bank - Canada
000-1102-00	5/31/1999	$18,302.17	Cash in Bank - Australia
000-1103-00	5/31/1999	$6,007.94	Cash in Bank - New Zealand
000-1104-00	5/31/1999	$7,909.80	Cash in Bank - Germany
000-1105-00	5/31/1999	$12,697.77	Cash in Bank - United Kingdom
000-1106-00	5/31/1999	$7,501.90	Cash in Bank - South Africa
000-1107-00	5/31/1999	$6,963.24	Cash in Bank - Singapore
000-1110-00	5/31/1999	$139,080.67	Cash - Payroll
000-1120-00	5/31/1999	$345.32	Cash - Flex Benefits Program
000-1130-00	5/31/1999	$319.54	Petty Cash
000-1140-00	5/31/1999	$16,316.12	Savings
000-1200-00	5/31/1999	$1,740,867.12	Accounts Receivable
000-1205-00	5/31/1999	$3,871.03	Sales Discounts Available
000-1210-00	5/31/1999	($45,963.30)	Allowance for Doubtful Accounts
000-1220-01	5/31/1999	$22,500.00	Credit Card Receivable-American Express
000-1230-00	5/31/1999	$250.00	Interest Receivable
000-1240-00	5/31/1999	$5,000.00	Notes Receivable
000-1260-00	5/31/1999	$250.00	Employee Advances
000-1271-00	5/31/1999	$26,757.58	Accounts Receivable - Canada
000-1272-00	5/31/1999	$11,164.46	Accounts Receivables - Australia
000-1273-00	5/31/1999	$9,381.79	Accounts Receivable - New Zealand
000-1274-00	5/31/1999	$2,716.40	Accounts Receivable - Germany

Record: 1 of 231

a hypothetical company's internal database.[6] This snapshot shows various GL accounts and their values. Currently, these data are organized and labeled according to the reporting company's internal needs and conventions. To make the data useful to outsiders and comparable with other firms, they need to be organized, labeled, and reported in a manner that all XBRL users generally accept. This involves mapping the organization's internal data to XBRL taxonomy elements.

The mapping process is accomplished using a simple tool such as Taxonomy Mapper, pictured in Figure 6.42.[7] Note how the XBRL tag labeled Cash, Cash Equivalents, and Short Term Investments is mapped to the database account labeled Cash in Bank–Canada. Once the mapping process is complete, each database record will contain a stored tag as depicted by the Taxonomy Element field in Figure 6.43.

Data mapping needs to be done only once, but the embedded tags are used whenever the data are placed in XBRL format for dissemination to outsiders. This allows business entities to provide expanded financial information frequently and instantaneously to

---

6   http://www.xbrlsolutions.com.

7   Ibid.

FIGURE 6.42   **GL to Taxonomy Mapper**

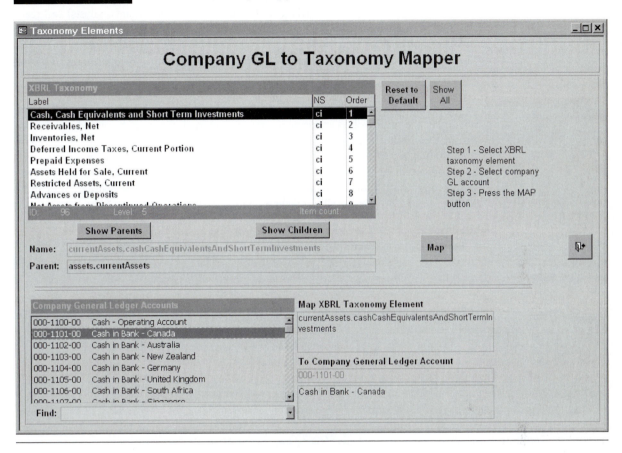

FIGURE 6.43   **Database Structure with XBRL Tag**

FullAccount	TrialBalanceDate	Amount	AccountDescription	TaxonomyElement
000-1100-00	5/31/1999	$608,637.31	Cash - Operating Account	cashAndCashEquivalents.cash
000-1101-00	5/31/1999	$8,957.84	Cash in Bank - Canada	currentAssets.cashCashEquivalentsAndShortTermInvestments
000-1102-00	5/31/1999	$18,302.17	Cash in Bank - Australia	currentAssets.cashCashEquivalentsAndShortTermInvestments
000-1103-00	5/31/1999	$6,007.94	Cash in Bank - New Zealand	currentAssets.cashCashEquivalentsAndShortTermInvestments
000-1104-00	5/31/1999	$7,909.80	Cash in Bank - Germany	currentAssets.cashCashEquivalentsAndShortTermInvestments
000-1105-00	5/31/1999	$12,697.77	Cash in Bank - United Kingdom	currentAssets.cashCashEquivalentsAndShortTermInvestments
000-1106-00	5/31/1999	$7,501.90	Cash in Bank - South Africa	currentAssets.cashCashEquivalentsAndShortTermInvestments
000-1107-00	5/31/1999	$6,963.24	Cash in Bank - Singapore	currentAssets.cashCashEquivalentsAndShortTermInvestments
000-1110-00	5/31/1999	$139,080.67	Cash - Payroll	currentAssets.cashCashEquivalentsAndShortTermInvestments
000-1120-00	5/31/1999	$345.32	Cash - Flex Benefits Program	currentAssets.cashCashEquivalentsAndShortTermInvestments
000-1130-00	5/31/1999	$319.54	Petty Cash	currentAssets.cashCashEquivalentsAndShortTermInvestments
000-1140-00	5/31/1999	$16,316.12	Savings	currentAssets.cashCashEquivalentsAndShortTermInvestments
000-1200-00	5/31/1999	$1,740,867.12	Accounts Receivable	accountsReceivableTradeNet.accountsReceivableTradeGross
000-1205-00	5/31/1999	$3,871.03	Sales Discounts Available	accountsReceivableTradeNet.allowanceForDoubtfulAccounts
000-1210-00	5/31/1999	($45,963.30)	Allowance for Doubtful Accounts	accountsReceivableTradeNet.allowanceForDoubtfulAccounts
000-1220-01	5/31/1999	$22,500.00	Credit Card Receivable-American Express	accountsReceivableTradeNet.allowanceForDoubtfulAccounts
000-1230-00	5/31/1999	$250.00	Interest Receivable	receivablesNet.otherReceivablesNet
000-1240-00	5/31/1999	$5,000.00	Notes Receivable	receivablesNet.notesReceivableNet
000-1260-00	5/31/1999	$250.00	Employee Advances	relatedPartyReceivablesNet.employeeReceivablesNet
000-1271-00	5/31/1999	$26,757.58	Accounts Receivable - Canada	currentAssets.receivablesNet
000-1272-00	5/31/1999	$11,164.46	Accounts Receivables - Australia	currentAssets.receivablesNet

Record: 1 of 231

interested parties. Furthermore, companies that use native-XBRL database technology[8] internally as their primary information storage platform can further speed up the process of reporting. Users of such financial data (for example, investors and analysts) can readily import XBRL documents into internal databases and analysis tools to greatly facilitate their decision-making processes.

From this new database structure, computer programs that recognize and interpret the tags associated with the data attributes can generate **XBRL instance documents** (the actual financial reports). Figure 6.44 presents an example of an instance document.[9]

The XBRL instance document can now be published and made available to users. The document can be placed on an intranet server for internal use; it can be placed on a private extranet for limited dissemination to customers or trading partners; or it can be placed on the Internet for public dissemination. In its current state, the instance document is computer-readable for analysis and processing. To make it more human-readable, HTML layout rules can be provided in a separate style sheet that Web browsers use to present the XBRL information in a visually appealing manner.

FIGURE 6.44	**XBRL Instance Document**

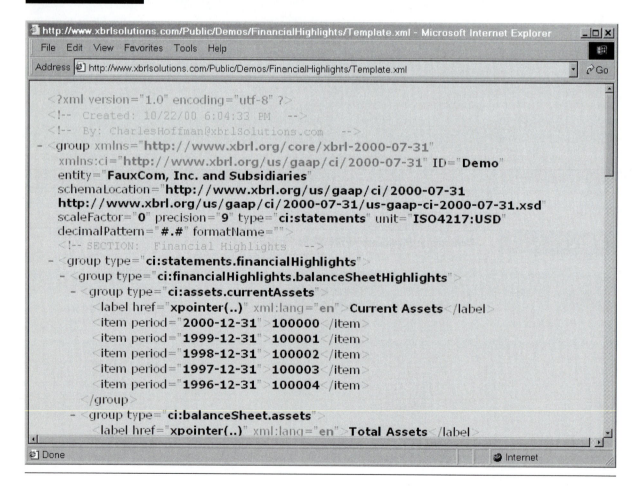

---

8   As opposed to the use of standard databases such as Oracle or Sybase.

9   http://www.xbrlsolutions.com.

The Current State of XBRL Reporting

All members of the financial-reporting community should be aware of XBRL, as it is an important information exchange technology. In the near future, XBRL will likely be the primary vehicle for delivering business reports to investors and regulators. Recent progress toward that end has been substantial both in the United States and internationally. Some of these developments are summarized here.

- Since October 2005, U.S. banking regulators have required quarterly "call reports" to be filed in XBRL. This requirement impacts more than 8,000 banks.
- In April 2005, the SEC began a voluntary financial reporting program that allows registrants to supplement their required filings with exhibits using XBRL.
- In September 2006, the SEC announced its new electronic reporting system to receive XBRL filings. The new system is called IDEA, short for interactive data electronic application.
- In May 2008, the SEC issued rules requiring large publicly held companies to adopt XBRL by December 15 to meet financial reporting requirements.
- Comparable developments to encourage or require XBRL have taken place internationally. Since early 2003, the Tokyo Stock Exchange has accepted XBRL information. In 2007, the Canadian Securities Administrators (CSA) established a voluntary program to help the Canadian marketplace gain practical knowledge in preparing, filing, and using XBRL information. Regulators in China, Spain, the Netherlands, and the United Kingdom are requiring certain companies to use XBRL.

In addition, the use of XBRL will facilitate fulfillment of legal requirements stipulated in the Sarbanes-Oxley Act, which was passed in response to widespread concern and skepticism about financial-reporting standards. In particular, XBRL can play a role in facilitating earlier reporting of financial statements required under SOX legislation.

CONTROLLING THE FRS

SOX legislation requires that management design and implement controls over the financial reporting process. This includes both the FRS and the individual transaction processing systems that feed data into it. For reasons already explained, we need to defer our treatment of TPS controls to later chapters. Here we will examine only the controls that relate to the FRS. The potential risks to the FRS include:

1. A defective audit trail.
2. Unauthorized access to the general ledger.
3. GL accounts that are out of balance with subsidiary accounts.
4. Incorrect GL account balances because of unauthorized or incorrect journal vouchers.

If not controlled, these risks may result in misstated financial statements and other reports, thus misleading users of this information. The potential consequences are litigation, significant financial loss for the firm, and sanctions specified by SOX legislation.

COSO Internal Control Issues

This discussion of FRS physical controls will follow the COSO framework for control activities, which was introduced in Chapter 1.

Transaction Authorization

The journal voucher is the document that authorizes an entry to the general ledger. Journal vouchers have numerous sources, such as the cash receipts processing, sales order processing, and financial reporting group. It is vital to the integrity of the accounting records that the journal vouchers be properly authorized by a responsible manager at the source department.

Segregation of Duties

The general ledger provides verification control for the accounting process. To do so, the task of updating the general ledger must be separate from all accounting and asset custody responsibility within the organization. Therefore, individuals with access authority to GL accounts should not:

1. Have record-keeping responsibility for special journals or subsidiary ledgers.
2. Prepare journal vouchers.
3. Have custody of physical assets.

Notice that in Figure 6.38 transactions are authorized, processed, and posted directly to the general ledger. To compensate for this potential risk, the system should provide end users and GL departments with detailed listings of journal voucher and account activity reports. These documents advise users of the automated actions taken by the system so that errors and unusual events, which warrant investigation, can be identified.

Access Controls

Unauthorized access to the GL accounts can result in errors, fraud, and misrepresentations in financial statements. SOX legislation explicitly addresses this area of risk by requiring organizations to implement controls that limit database access to authorized individuals only. A number of IT general controls designed to serve this purpose were presented in Chapter 4, including properly assigned user views, authorization tables, data encryption and others.

Accounting Records

The audit trail is a record of the path that a transaction takes through the input, processing, and output phases of transaction processing. This involves a network of documents, journals, and ledgers designed to ensure that a transaction can be accurately traced through the system from initiation to final disposition.

An audit trail facilitates error prevention and correction when the data files are conveniently and logically organized. Also, the general ledger and other files that constitute the audit trail should be detailed and rich enough to (1) provide the ability to answer inquiries, for example, from customers or vendors; (2) be able to reconstruct files if they are completely or partially destroyed; (3) provide historical data required by auditors; (4) fulfill government regulations; and (5) provide a means for preventing, detecting, and correcting errors.

Independent Verification

The general ledger function serves as an independent verification step within the accounting information system. The FRS produces two operational reports—journal voucher listing and the GL change report—that provide proof of the accuracy of this process. The **journal voucher listing** provides relevant details about each journal voucher posted to the GL. The **general ledger change report** presents the effects of journal voucher postings to the GL accounts. Figures 6.45 and 6.46 present examples of these reports.

FIGURE 6.45 Journal Voucher Listing

Journal Voucher Listing

Date	JV Num	Description	Account Number	Debit	Credit
6/26/09	JV6 - 01	Cash receipts	10100	109,000	
			20100		50,000
			10600		44,000
			10900		15,000
6/26/09	JV6 - 02	Credit sales	20100	505,000	
			50200		505,000
6/26/09	JV6 - 03	Inventory usage	30300	410,000	
			17100		410,000
•	•	•	•	•	•
•	•	•	•	•	•
•	•	•	•	•	•
6/26/09	JV - 12	Cash disbursements	90310	102,100	
			10100		102,100
				6,230,000	6,230,000

FIGURE 6.46 General Ledger Change Report

General Ledger Change Report

Date	Acct	Description	JV Ref	Balance	Debits	Credits	Net Change	New Balance
6/26/09	10100	Cash receipts	JV6 - 01	1,902,300	109,000			
			JV6 - 12			102,100	6,900	1,909,200
6/26/09	20100	Cash receipts	JV6 - 01	2,505,600		50,000		
		Credit sales	JV6 - 02		505,000		455,000	2,960,600
•	•	•	•	•	•	•	•	•
•	•	•	•	•	•	•	•	•
•	•	•	•	•	•	•	•	•
6/26/09	90310	Cash disburs.	JV6 - 12	703,500	102,100		102,100	805,600
6/26/09	17100	Inven. usage	JV6 - 03	1,600,500		410,000	410,000	2,010,500

Control Totals:

	Debits	Credits
Previous Balance	23,789,300	23,789,300
Total Net Change	6,230,000	6,230,000
Current Balance	30,019,300	30,019,300

Internal Control Implications of XBRL

Although the potential benefits of XBRL and associated Web technologies have been extensively researched, less attention has been given to the potential control implications of using XBRL. There are three areas of specific concern, which are discussed here.

Taxonomy Creation. Taxonomy may be generated incorrectly, which results in an incorrect mapping between data and taxonomy elements that could result in material misrepresentation of financial data. Controls must be designed and put in place to ensure the correct generation of XBRL taxonomies.

Taxonomy Mapping Error. The process of mapping the internal database accounts to the taxonomy tags needs to be controlled. Correctly generated XBRL tags may be incorrectly assigned to internal database accounts resulting in material misrepresentation of financial data.

Validation of Instance Documents. As noted, once the mapping is complete and tags have been stored in the internal database, XBRL instance documents (reports) can be generated. Independent verification procedures need to be established to validate the instance documents to ensure that appropriate taxonomy and tags have been applied before posting to a Web server.

SUMMARY

This chapter began with an overview of transaction processing, showing its vital role as an information provider for financial reporting, internal management reporting, and the support of day-to-day operations. To deal efficiently with large volumes of financial transactions, business organizations group together transactions of similar types into transaction cycles. Three transaction cycles account for most of a firm's economic activity: the revenue cycle, the expenditure cycle, and the conversion cycle. The second section described the relationship among accounting records in both manual and computer-based systems. We saw how both hard-copy and digital documents form an audit trail. The third section of the chapter presented an overview of documentation techniques used to describe the key features of systems. Accountants must be proficient in using documentation tools to perform their professional duties. Five types of documentation are commonly used for this purpose: data flow diagrams, entity relationship diagrams, system flowcharts, program flowcharts, and record layout diagrams. The fourth section presented two computer-based transaction processing systems: (1) batch processing, using real-time data collection; and (2) real-time processing. The section also examined the operational efficiency issues associated with each configuration. The fifth section examined data coding schemes and their role in transaction processing and AIS as a means of coordinating and managing a firm's transactions. In examining the major types of numeric and alphabetic coding schemes, we saw how each has certain advantages and disadvantages. Next the chapter presented the operational features of the GLS and examined the files that constitute a GLS database. Finally, turning to the FRS, we examined how financial information is provided to both external and internal users through a multistep reporting process. The emerging technology of XBRL is changing traditional financial reporting for many organizations. We reviewed the key features of XBRL and considered the internal control implications of this technology.

KEY TERMS

accounting record
alphabetic code
alphanumeric code
archive file
audit trail
batch
batch system
block code
budget master file
cardinality
chart of accounts
conversion cycle
data flow diagram (DFD)
data model
entities
entity relationship (ER) diagram
expenditure cycle
general ledger change report
general ledger master file
group code
journal
journal voucher file

journal voucher history file
journal voucher listing
ledger
master file
mnemonic code
product document
program flowchart
real-time system
record layout diagram
reference file
register
responsibility center file
revenue cycle
sequential code
source document
system flowchart
transaction file
turnaround document
eXtensible business reporting language (XBRL)
XBRL instance document
XBRL taxonomy
eXtensible markup language (XML)

REVIEW QUESTIONS

1. What three transaction cycles exist in all businesses?
2. Name the major subsystems of the expenditure cycle.
3. Identify and distinguish between the physical and financial components of the expenditure cycle.
4. Name the major subsystems of the conversion cycle.
5. Name the major subsystems of the revenue cycle.
6. Name the three types of documents.
7. Name the two types of journals.
8. Distinguish between a general journal and journal vouchers.
9. Name the two types of ledgers.
10. What is an audit trail?
11. What is the confirmation process?
12. Computer-based systems employ four types of files. Name them.
13. Give an example of a record that might comprise each of the four file types found in a computer-based system.
14. What is the purpose of a digital audit trail?
15. Give an example of how cardinality relates to business policy.
16. Distinguish between entity relationship diagrams, data flow diagrams, and system flowcharts.
17. What is meant by cardinality in entity relationship diagrams?
18. For what purpose are entity relationship diagrams used?
19. What is an entity?
20. Distinguish between batch and real-time processing.
21. Distinguish between the sequential file and database approaches to data backup.
22. Is a data flow diagram an effective documentation technique for identifying who or what performs a particular task? Explain.
23. Is a flowchart an effective documentation technique for identifying who or what performs a particular task? Explain.
24. How may batch processing be used to improve operational efficiency?
25. Why might an auditor use a program flowchart?
26. How are system flowcharts and program flowcharts related?

27. What are the distinguishing features of a legacy system?
28. What are the two data processing approaches used in modern systems?
29. How is backup of database files accomplished?
30. What information is provided by a record layout diagram?
31. In one sentence, what does updating a master file record involve?
32. Comment on the following statement: "Legacy systems always use flat-file structures."
33. Explain the technique known as destructive update.
34. What factor influences the decision to employ real-time data collection with batch updating rather that purely real-time processing? Explain.
35. What are the advantages of real-time data processing?
36. What are the advantages of real-time data collection?
37. What are some of the more common uses of data codes in accounting information systems?
38. Compare and contrast the relative advantages and disadvantages of sequential, block, group, alphabetic, and mnemonic codes.
39. What information is contained in a journal voucher?
40. How are journal vouchers used as a control mechanism?
41. What information is contained in the general ledger master file?
42. What is the purpose of the general ledger history file?
43. What is the purpose of a responsibility center file?
44. List the primary users of the FRS and discuss their information needs.
45. Name in order the eleven steps of the financial reporting process?
46. What assumption is made regarding the external users of financial statements?
47. When are adjusting entries made to the worksheet and what is their purpose? When are the corresponding voucher entries made?
48. What tasks should the general ledger clerk not be allowed to do?
49. What does XML stand for?
50. What does XBRL stand for?
51. What is an XBRL taxonomy?
52. What is an XBRL instance document?
53. What is an XBRL tag?

DISCUSSION QUESTIONS

1. Discuss the flow of cash through the transaction cycles. Include in your discussion the relevant subsystems and any time lags that may occur.
2. Explain whether the cost accounting system primarily supports internal or external reporting.
3. Discuss the role of the conversion cycle for service and retailing entities.
4. Can a turnaround document contain information that is subsequently used as a source document? Why or why not?
5. Would the writing down of obsolete inventory be recorded in a special journal or the general journal? Why?
6. Are both registers and special journals necessary?
7. Discuss the relationship between the balance in the accounts payable general ledger control account and what is found in the accounts payable subsidiary ledger.
8. What role does the audit trail play in the task of confirmation?
9. Explain how the magnetic audit trail functions.
10. Are large batch sizes preferable to small batch sizes? Explain.
11. Discuss why an understanding of legacy system technologies is of some importance to auditors.
12. If an organization processes large numbers of transactions that use common data records, what type of system would work best (all else being equal)?
13. If an organization processes transactions that have independent (unique) data needs, what type of system would work best (all else being equal)?
14. Should an auditor wishing to assess the adequacy of separation of functions examine a data flow diagram or a system flowchart? Why?
15. Discuss some of the problems associated with general ledger systems that do not have data coding schemes.
16. For each of the following items, indicate whether a sequential, block, group, alphabetic, or mnemonic code would be most appropriate (you may list multiple methods; give an example and explain why each method is appropriate):
    a. state codes
    b. check number
    c. chart of accounts
    d. inventory item number

e. bin number (inventory warehouse location)
f. sales order number
g. vendor code
h. invoice number
i. customer number

17. Discuss any separation of duties necessary to control against unauthorized entries to the general ledger. What other control procedures regarding the general ledger should be employed?

18. Discuss the various sources of data for the FRS output and how these data are processed into information (output) for the different external users.

19. Explain how erroneous journal vouchers may lead to litigation and significant financial losses for a firm.

20. Ultimately, is the purpose of an audit trail to follow a transaction from its input through its processing and finally to the financial statements or vice versa? Explain your answer.

21. Discuss the benefits that may be realized in switching from a computerized batch processing system to a direct access storage system. Also, discuss any additional control implications.

22. Controls are only as good as the predetermined standard on which they are based. Discuss the preceding comment and give an example.

23. Discuss three audit implications of XBRL.

24. Although HTML and XML documents look very similar, and both use tags, explain how they differ significantly as a financial reporting medium.

MULTIPLE-CHOICE QUESTIONS

1. Which statement is not true?
   a. Business activities begin with the acquisition of materials, property, and labor in exchange for cash.
   b. The conversion cycle includes the task of determining raw materials requirements.
   c. Manufacturing firms have a conversion cycle but retail firms do not.
   d. A payroll check is an example of a product document of the payroll system.
   e. A journal voucher is actually a special source document.

2. A documentation tool that depicts the physical flow of information relating to a particular transaction through an organization is a
   a. system flowchart.
   b. program flowchart.
   c. decision table.
   d. work distribution analysis.
   e. systems survey.

3. Sequential file processing will not permit
   a. data to be edited on a separate computer run.
   b. the use of a database structure.
   c. data to be edited in an offline mode.
   d. batch processing to be initiated from a terminal.
   e. data to be edited on a real-time basis.

4. The production subsystem of the conversion cycle includes all of the following EXCEPT
   a. determining raw materials requirements.
   b. make or buy decisions on component parts.
   c. release of raw materials into production.
   d. scheduling the goods to be produced.

5. Which of the following files is a temporary file?
   a. transaction file
   b. master file
   c. reference file
   d. none of the above

6. A documentation tool used to represent the logical elements of a system is a(n)
   a. programming flowchart.
   b. entity relationship diagram.
   c. system flowchart.
   d. data flow diagram.

7. Which of the following is NOT an advantage of real-time processing files over batch processing?
   a. shorter transaction processing time
   b. reduction of inventory stocks
   c. improved customer service
   d. all are advantages

8. Which of the following is NOT true of a turnaround document?
   a. They may reduce the number of errors made by external parties.
   b. They are commonly used by utility companies (gas, power, water).
   c. They are documents used by internal parties only.
   d. They are both input and output documents.

9. Which of the following is NOT a true statement?
   a. Transactions are recorded on source documents and are posted to journals.

b. Transactions are recorded in journals and are posted to ledgers.

c. Infrequent transactions are recorded in the general journal.

d. Frequent transactions are recorded in special journals.

10. Which of the following is true of the relationship between subsidiary ledgers and general ledger accounts?

a. The two contain different and unrelated data.

b. All general ledger accounts have subsidiaries.

c. The relationship between the two provides an audit trail from the financial statements to the source documents.

d. The total of subsidiary ledger accounts usually exceeds the total in the related general ledger account.

11. Real-time systems might be appropriate for all of the following EXCEPT

a. airline reservations.

b. payroll.

c. point-of-sale transactions.

d. air traffic control systems.

e. all of these applications typically utilize real-time processing.

12. ⬡ is the system flowchart symbol for:

a. on-page connector.

b. off-page connector.

c. home base.

d. manual operation.

e. document.

13. A chart of accounts would best be coded using a(n) _____ coding scheme.

a. alphabetic

b. mnemonic

c. block

d. sequential

14. Which of the following statements is NOT true?

a. Sorting records that are coded alphabetically tends to be more difficult for users than sorting numeric sequences.

b. Mnemonic coding requires the user to memorize codes.

c. Sequential codes carry no information content beyond their order in the sequence.

d. Mnemonic codes are limited in their ability to represent items within a class.

15. A coding scheme in the form of acronyms and other combinations that convey meaning is a(n)

a. sequential code.

b. block code.

c. alphabetic code.

d. mnemonic code.

16. Sequential access means that

a. data are stored on magnetic tape.

b. the address of the location of data is found through the use of either an algorithm or an index.

c. to read any record on the file, all of the preceding records must first be read.

d. each record can be accessed in the same amount of time.

17. Which file has as its primary purpose to provide historical financial data for comparative financial reports?

a. journal voucher history file

b. budget master file

c. responsibility file

d. general ledger history file

18. Which of the following statements is true?

a. Journal vouchers detailing transaction activity flow from various operational departments into the GLS, where they are independently reconciled and posted o the journal voucher history file.

b. Journal vouchers summarizing transaction activity flow from the accounting department into the GLS, where they are independently reconciled and posted to the general ledger accounts.

c. Journal vouchers summarizing transaction activity flow from various operational departments into the GLS, where they are independently reconciled and posted to the general ledger accounts.

d. Journal vouchers summarizing transaction activity flow from various operational departments into the GLS, where they are independently reconciled and posted to the journal voucher history file.

19. Which of the following statements best describes a computer-based GL/FRS?

a. Most firms derive little additional benefit from a real-time FRS.

b. Batch processing is typically not appropriate for transaction processing of GLS.

c. The sequential file approach is an inefficient use of technology.

d. A batch system with direct access files recreates the entire database each time the file is updated.

20. Which of the following is NOT a potential exposure of the FRS?
    a. a defective audit trail
    b. general ledger accounts that are out of balance with subsidiary accounts
    c. unauthorized access to the check register
    d. unauthorized access to the general ledger

21. Which task should the general ledger perform?
    a. update the general ledger
    b. prepare journal vouchers
    c. have custody of physical assets
    d. have record-keeping responsibility for special journals of subsidiary ledgers

PROBLEMS

1. Transaction Cycle Identification

Categorize each of the following activities into the expenditure, conversion, or revenue cycles and identify the applicable subsystem.
a. preparing the weekly payroll for manufacturing personnel
b. releasing raw materials for use in the manufacturing cycle
c. recording the receipt of payment for goods sold
d. recording the order placed by a customer
e. ordering raw materials
f. determining the amount of raw materials to order

2. Types of Files

For each of the following records, indicate the appropriate related file structure: master file, transaction file, reference file, or archive file.
a. customer ledgers
b. purchase orders
c. list of authorized vendors
d. records related to prior pay periods
e. vendor ledgers
f. hours each employee has worked during the current pay period
g. tax tables
h. sales orders that have been processed and recorded

3. System Flowchart

Figure 6.4 illustrates how a customer order is transformed into a source document, a product document, and a turnaround document. Develop a similar flowchart for the process of paying hourly employees. Assume time sheets are used and the payroll department must total the hours. Each hour worked by any employee must be charged to some account (a cost center). Each week, the manager of each cost center receives a report listing the employee's name and the number of hours charged to this center. The manager is required to verify that this information is correct by signing the form and noting any discrepancies, then sending this form back to the payroll department. Any discrepancies noted must be corrected by the payroll department.

4. Entity Relationship Diagram

Shown here is a partial entity relationship diagram of a purchase system. Describe the business rules represented by the cardinalities in the diagram.

Problem 4: Entity Relationship Diagram

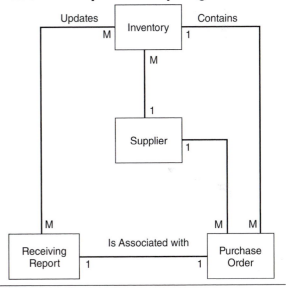

5. Entity Relationship Diagram

Refer to the entity relationship diagram in Problem 4.

Modify the diagram to deal with payments of merchandise purchased. Explain the business rules represented by the cardinalities in the diagram. (You may wish to refer to Chapter 10.)

6. Entity Relationship Diagram

Prepare an entity relationship diagram, in good form, for the expenditure cycle, which consists of both purchasing and cash disbursements. Describe the business rules represented by the cardinalities in the diagrams. (You may wish to refer to Chapter 9.)

7. System Flowchart

Using the diagram for Problem 7 answer the following questions:

a. What do Symbols 1 and 2 represent?
b. What does the operation involving Symbols 3 and 4 depict?
c. What does the operation involving Symbols 4 and 5 depict?
d. What does the operation involving Symbols 6, 8, and 9 depict?

Problem 7: System Flowchart

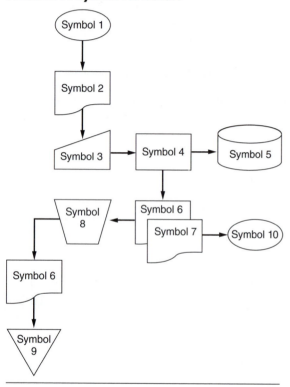

8. System Flowchart

Analyze the system flowchart on for Problem 8 and describe in detail the processes that are occurring.

9. System Flowcharts and Program Flowchart

From the diagram in Problem 8, identify three types of errors that may cause a payroll record to be placed in the error file. Use a program flowchart to illustrate the edit program.

10. Data Flow Diagram

Data flow diagrams employ four different symbols. What are these symbols and what does each symbol represent?

Problem 8: System Flowchart

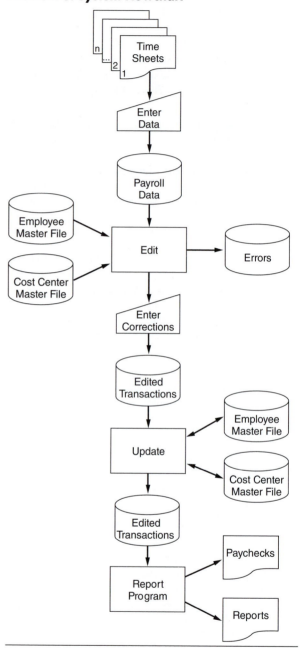

11. Transaction Cycle Relationship

Refer to Figure 6.1, which provides a generic look at relationships between transaction cycles. Modify this figure to reflect the transaction cycles you might find at a dentist's office.

12. System Documentation—Expenditure Cycle (Manual Procedures)

The following describes the expenditure cycle manual procedures for a hypothetical company.

The inventory control clerk examines the inventory records for items that must be replenished and prepares a two-part purchase requisition. Copy 1 of the requisition is sent to the purchasing department and Copy 2 is filed.

Upon receipt of the requisition, the purchasing clerk selects a supplier from the valid vendor file (reference file) and prepares a three-part purchase order. Copy 1 is sent to the supplier, Copy 2 is sent to the accounts payable department where it is filed temporarily, and Copy 3 is filed in the purchases department.

A few days after the supplier ships the order, the goods arrive at the receiving department. They are inspected, and the receiving clerk prepares a three-part receiving report describing the number and quality of the items received. Copy 1 of the receiving report accompanies the goods to the stores, where they are secured. Copy 2 is sent to inventory control, where the clerk posts it to the inventory records and files the document. Copy 3 is sent to the accounts payable department, where it is filed with the purchase order.

A day or two later, the accounts payable clerk receives the supplier's invoice (bill) for the items shipped. The clerk pulls the purchase order and receiving report from the temporary file and compares the quantity ordered, quantity received, and the price charged. After reconciling the three documents, the clerk enters the purchase in the purchases journal and posts the amount owed to the accounts payable subsidiary account.

On the payment due date, the accounts payable clerk posts to the accounts payable subsidiary account to remove the liability and prepares a voucher authorizing payment to the vendor. The voucher is then sent to the cash disbursements clerk. Upon receipt of the voucher, the cash disbursements clerk prepares a check and sends it to the supplier. The clerk records the check in the check register and files a copy of the check in the department filing cabinet.

Required:
Prepare a data flow diagram and a system flowchart of the expenditure cycle procedures previously described.

13. Record Structures for Receipt of Items Ordered

Refer to Figure 6.28 and the discussion about updating master files from transaction files. The discussion presents the record structures for a sales transaction. Prepare a diagram (similar to Figure 6.28) that presents the record structure for the receipt (receiving report) of inventory items ordered. Presume a purchase order file exists and will be updated through information collected via a receiving report. Further, presume the purchase was made on account.

14. System Documentation—Payroll

The following describes the payroll procedures for a hypothetical company.

Every Thursday, the timekeeping clerk sends employee time cards to the payroll department for processing. Based on the hours worked reflected on the time cards, the employee pay rate and withholding information in the employee file, and the tax rate reference file, the payroll clerk calculates gross pay, withholdings, and net pay for each employee. The clerk then manually prepares paychecks for each employee, files hard copies of the paychecks in the payroll department, and posts the earnings to the hard-copy employee records. Finally, the clerk manually prepares a payroll summary and sends it and the paychecks to the cash disbursements department.

The cash disbursements clerk reconciles the payroll summary with the paychecks and manually records the transaction in the hard-copy cash disbursements journal. The clerk then files the payroll summary and sends the paychecks to the treasurer for signing.

The signed checks are then sent to the paymaster, who distributes them to the employees on Friday morning.

Required:
Prepare a data flow diagram and a system flowchart of the payroll procedures previously described.

15. System Documentation—Payroll

Required:
Assuming the payroll system described in Problem 14 uses database files and computer processing procedures, prepare a data flow diagram, an entity relationship diagram, and a systems flowchart.

16. System Documentation—Revenue Cycle Manual and Computer Processes

The following describes the revenue cycle procedures for a hypothetical company.

The sales department clerk receives hard-copy customer orders and manually prepares a six-part hard-copy sales order. Copies of the sales order are distributed to various departments as follows: Copies 1, 2, and 3 go to the shipping department, and Copies 4, 5, and 6 are sent to the billing department where they are temporarily filed by the billing clerk.

Upon receipt of the sales order copies, the shipping clerk picks the goods from the warehouse shelves and ships them to the customer. The clerk sends Copy 1 of the sales order along with the goods to the customer. Copy 2 is sent to the billing department, and Copy 3 is filed in the shipping department.

When the billing clerk receives Copy 2 from the warehouse, she pulls the other copies from the temporary file and completes the documents by adding prices, taxes, and freight charges. Then, using the department PC, the billing clerk records the sale in the digital sales journal, sends Copy 4 (customer bill) to the customer, and sends Copies 5 and 6 to the accounts receivable and inventory control departments, respectively.

Upon receipt of the documents from the billing clerk, the accounts receivable and inventory control clerks post the transactions to the accounts receivable subsidiary and inventory subsidiary ledgers, respectively, using their department PCs. Each clerk then files the respective sales order copies in the department.

On the payment due date, the customer sends a check for the full amount and a copy of the bill (the remittance advice) to the company. These documents are received by the mailroom clerk who distributes them as follows:

1. The check goes to the cash receipts clerk, who manually records it in the hard-copy cash receipts journal and prepares two deposit slips. One deposit slip and the check are sent to the bank; the other deposit slip is filed in the cash receipts department.
2. The remittance advice is sent to the AR clerk, who posts to the digital subsidiary accounts and then files the document.

Required:
Prepare a data flow diagram and a system flowchart of the revenue cycle procedures previously described.

17. System Documentation—Expenditure Cycle (Manual and Computer PROCEDURES)

The following describes the expenditure cycle for a hypothetical company.

The company has a centralized computer system with terminals located in various departments. The terminals are networked to a computer application, and digital accounting records are hosted on a server in the data processing department.

Each day, the computer in the data processing center scans the inventory records, looking for items that must be replenished. For each item below its reorder point, the system creates a digital purchase order and prints two hard copies. A technician in the data center sends the purchase orders to the purchasing department clerk.

Upon receipt of the purchase orders, the purchasing clerk reviews and signs them. He sends Copy 1 to the supplier and files Copy 2 in the purchases department.

A few days later, the supplier ships the order and the goods arrive at the receiving department. The receiving clerk reviews the digital purchase order from his terminal, inspects the goods, creates a digital receiving report record, and prints two hard copies of the receiving report. The clerk sends Copy 1 of the receiving report with the goods to the stores, where they are secured. Copy 2 is filed in the receiving department.

A day or two later, the accounts payable clerk receives a hard-copy supplier's invoice (bill) for the items shipped. The clerk accesses the digital receiving report and purchase order from her terminal. She then reconciles these documents with the suppliers invoice. If all aspects of the order reconcile, the clerk records the purchase in the digital purchases journal and posts the amount owed to the accounts payable subsidiary account from her terminal.

Each day, the computer application in the data processing department automatically scans the accounts payable subsidiary file for items that are due for payment and prints a two-part check. The system closes out the accounts payable record and creates a record in the digital cash disbursements journal. A data processing clerk then sends the check to the cash disbursement department, where it is approved, signed, and distributed to the supplier. The check copy is filed in the CD department.

Required:
Prepare a data flow diagram and a system flowchart of the expenditure cycle procedures previously described.

18. Coding Scheme

Devise a coding scheme using block and sequential codes for the following chart of accounts for Jensen Camera Distributors.

Cash
Accounts Receivable
Office Supplies Inventory
Prepaid Insurance
Inventory
Investments in Marketable Securities
Delivery Truck
Accumulated Depreciation—Delivery Truck
Equipment
Accumulated Depreciation—Equipment
Furniture and Fixtures
Accumulated Depreciation—Furniture and Fixtures
Building
Accumulated Depreciation—Building
Land
Accounts Payable
Wages Payable
Taxes Payable
Notes Payable
Bonds Payable

Common Stock
Paid-In Capital in Excess of Par
Treasury Stock
Retained Earnings
Sales
Sales Returns and Allowances
Dividend Income
Cost of Goods Sold
Wages Expense
Utility Expense
Office Supplies Expense
Insurance Expense
Depreciation Expense
Advertising Expense
Fuel Expense
Interest Expense

19. Coding Scheme

Devise a coding scheme for the warehouse layout shown in Problem 19. Be sure to use an appropriate coding scheme that allows the inventory to be located efficiently from the picking list.

20. Backup and Recovery Procedures for Database Files

Figure 6.30 provides a backup and recovery system for files that are updated using a destructive update approach. Now think about a specific situation that might use this approach. A company creates its sales order transaction file in batches. Once a day, a sales clerk compiles a transaction file by entering data from the previous day's sales orders into the transaction file. When these transactions have all been entered and the transaction file passes editing, the

Problem 19: Coding Scheme

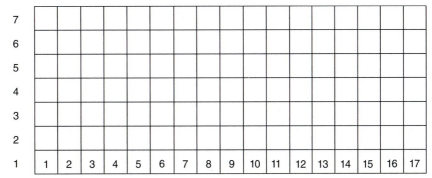

WAREHOUSE LAYOUT

Three warehouse locations—Warehouses 1, 2, and 3
Each warehouse is organized by aisles.

Aisle A

Aisle B

Aisle C

Aisle D

Aisle E

WAREHOUSE LAYOUT

Each aisle is separated into a right and left side, with 7 shelves of goods and 17 partitions, with each storage area called a "bin."

transaction file is used to destructively update both the sales and the accounts receivable master files. Each of these master files is then backed up to a magnetic tape. The magnetic tapes are stored (offline) in a remote location. Now consider what might happen if, in the middle of an update of the sales master file, lightning hit the company's building, resulting in a power failure that caused the computer to corrupt both the transaction file and the master files.

a. Which, if any, files contain noncorrupted data (transaction file, accounts receivable master file, sales master file, or backup master files)?
b. Will a clerk have to reenter any data? If so, what data will have to be reentered?
c. What steps will the company have to take to obtain noncorrupted master files that contain the previous day's sales data?

21. General Ledger System Overview

Draw a diagram depicting the relationship between the general ledger master file, control accounts, subsidiary files, and financial statements.

22. Financial Reporting Process

The following contains the various steps of the financial reporting process. Place these steps in the proper order and indicate whether each step is a function of the TPS, GLS, or FRS.

- Record transaction in special journal
- Make adjusting entries
- Capture the transaction
- Prepare the post-closing trial balance
- Prepare the adjusted trial balance
- Prepare the financial statements
- Journalize and post the adjusting entries
- Post to the subsidiary ledger
- Post to the general ledger
- Journalize and post the closing entries
- Prepare the unadjusted trial balance

23. XBRL

John Ozment, director of special projects and analysis for Ozment's company, is responsible for preparing corporate financial analyses and monthly statements and reviewing and presenting the financial impacts of proposed strategies to upper management. Data for such financial analyses are obtained from operations and financial databases through direct queries of Ozment's department staff. Reports and charts for presentations are then prepared by hand and typed. Multiple copies are prepared and distributed to various users. The pressure on Ozment's group has intensified as demand for more and more current information increases. A solution to this reporting problem must be found.

The systems department wants to develop a proprietary software package to produce the reports automatically.

The project would require the company to make a considerable programming investment. Ozment is concerned about the accuracy, completeness, and currency of data in automatically produced reports. He has heard about a reporting system called XBRL and wonders whether a new system based on this technology would not be more effective and reliable.

Required:
a. Research the current state of XBRL and determine if this technology is appropriate for internal reporting projects such as this.
b. Identify the enhancements to current information and reporting that the company could realize by using XBRL.
c. Discuss any data integrity, internal control, and reporting concerns associated with XBRL.

24. Internal Control

Leslie Epstein, an employee of Bormack Manufacturing Company, prepares journal vouchers for general ledger entries. Because of the large number of voided journal vouchers caused by errors, the journal vouchers are not prenumbered by the printer; rather, Leslie numbers them as she prepares each journal voucher. She does, however, keep a log of all journal vouchers written so that she does not assign the same number to two journal vouchers. Biweekly, Leslie posts the journal vouchers to the general ledger and any necessary subsidiary accounts. Bimonthly, she reconciles the subsidiary accounts to their control accounts in the general ledger and makes sure the general ledger accounts balance.

Required:
Discuss any potential control weaknesses and problems in this scenario.

25. Database GL System

Crystal Corporation processes its journal vouchers using batch procedures similar to the process outlined in Figure 6.37. To improve customer satisfaction, the sales system is going to be converted to a real-time system. Redraw Figure 6.37 to reflect this change in the financial reporting process.

26. Database GL System

The top management team at Olympia, Inc., wishes to have real-time access to the general ledger. Currently the general ledger is updated nightly via a batch processing system, similar to Figure 6.37 in the text. Adjust Figure 6.37 to accommodate this request by top management, assuming that the nightly updates to the general ledger are sufficient.

27. Internal Control

Expand Figure 6.38 to incorporate the journal voucher listing and general ledger change report as control mechanisms. Also discuss the specific controls they impose on the system.

7

Computer-Assisted Audit Tools and Techniques

LEARNING OBJECTIVES

After studying this chapter, you should:

- Be familiar with the classes of transaction input controls used by accounting applications.
- Understand the objectives and techniques used to implement processing controls, including run-to-run, operator intervention, and audit trail controls.
- Understand the methods used to establish effective output controls for both batch and real-time systems.
- Know the difference between black box and white box auditing.
- Be familiar with the key features of the five CAATTs discussed in the chapter.

This chapter examines several issues related to the use of computer-assisted audit tools and techniques (CAATTs) for performing tests of application controls and data extraction. It opens with a description of application controls. These fall into three broad classes: input controls, processing controls, and output controls. The chapter then examines the *black box* and *white box* approaches to testing application controls. The latter approach requires a detailed understanding of the application's logic. Five CAATT approaches used for testing application logic are then examined: the test data method, base case system evaluation, tracing, integrated test facility, and parallel simulation.

APPLICATION CONTROLS

Application controls are programmed procedures designed to deal with potential exposures that threaten specific applications, such as payroll, purchases, and cash disbursements systems. Application controls fall into three broad categories: input controls, processing controls, and output controls.

Input Controls

The data collection component of the information system is responsible for bringing data into the system for processing. **Input controls** at this stage are designed to ensure that these transactions are valid, accurate, and complete. Data input procedures can be either source document-triggered (batch) or direct input (real time).

Source document input requires human involvement and is prone to clerical errors. Some types of errors that are entered on the source documents cannot be detected and corrected during the data input stage. Dealing with these problems may require tracing the transaction back to its source (such as contacting the customer) to correct the mistake. Direct input, on the other hand, employs real-time editing techniques to identify and correct errors immediately, thus significantly reducing the number of errors that enter the system.

Classes of Input Control

For presentation convenience and to provide structure to this discussion, we have divided input controls into the following broad classes:

- Source document controls
- Data coding controls
- Batch controls
- Validation controls
- Input error correction
- Generalized data input systems

These control classes are not mutually exclusive divisions. Some control techniques that we shall examine could fit logically into more than one class.

Source Document Controls.   Careful control must be exercised over physical source documents in systems that use them to initiate transactions. Source document fraud can be used to remove assets from the organization. For example, an individual with access to purchase orders and receiving reports could fabricate a purchase transaction to a non-existent supplier. If these documents are entered into the data processing stream, along with a fabricated vendor's invoice, the system could process these documents as if a legitimate transaction had taken place. In the absence of other compensating controls to detect this type of fraud, the system would create an account payable and subsequently write a check in payment.

To control against this type of exposure, the organization must implement control procedures over source documents to account for each document, as described next:

Use Pre-numbered Source Documents.   Source documents should come prenumbered from the printer with a unique sequential number on each document. Source document numbers permit accurate accounting of document usage and provide an audit trail for tracing transactions through accounting records. We discuss this further in the next section.

Use Source Documents in Sequence.   Source documents should be distributed to the users and used in sequence. This requires that adequate physical security be maintained over the source document inventory at the user site. When not in use, documents should be locked away. At all times, access to source documents should be limited to authorized persons.

Periodically Audit Source Documents.   Reconciling document sequence numbers should identify missing source documents. Periodically, the auditor should compare the numbers of documents used to date with those remaining in inventory plus those voided due to errors. Documents not accounted for should be reported to management.

Data Coding Controls.   Coding controls are checks on the integrity of data codes used in processing. A customer's account number, an inventory item number, and a chart of accounts number are all examples of data codes. Three types of errors can corrupt data codes and cause processing errors: transcription errors, single transposition errors, and multiple transposition errors. **Transcription errors** fall into three classes:

- Addition errors occur when an extra digit or character is added to the code. For example, inventory item number 83276 is recorded as 832766.
- Truncation errors occur when a digit or character is removed from the end of a code. In this type of error, the inventory item above would be recorded as 8327.
- Substitution errors are the replacement of one digit in a code with another. For example, code number 83276 is recorded as 83266.

There are two types of **transposition errors**. *Single transposition errors* occur when two adjacent digits are reversed. For instance, 83276 is recorded as 38276. *Multiple transposition errors* occur when nonadjacent digits are transposed. For example, 83276 is recorded as 87236.

Any of these errors can cause serious problems in data processing if they go undetected. For example, a sales order for customer 732519 that is transposed into 735219 will be posted to the wrong customer's account. A similar error in an inventory item code on a purchase order could result in ordering unneeded inventory and failing to order inventory that is needed. These simple errors can severely disrupt operations.

Check Digits.   One method for detecting data coding errors is a check digit. A **check digit** is a control digit (or digits) added to the code when it is originally assigned that allows the integrity of the code to be established during subsequent processing. The check digit can be located anywhere in the code: as a prefix, a suffix, or embedded someplace in the middle. The simplest form of check digit is to sum the digits in the code and use this sum as the check digit. For example, for the customer account code 5372, the calculated check digit would be

$$5 + 3 + 7 + 2 = 17$$

By dropping the tens column, the check digit 7 is added to the original code to produce the new code 53727. The entire string of digits (including the check digit) becomes the customer account number. During data entry, the system can recalculate the check digit to ensure that the code is correct. This technique will detect only transcription errors. For example, if a substitution error occurred and the above code were entered as 52727, the calculated check digit would be 6 ($5 + 2 + 7 + 2 = 16 = 6$), and the error would be detected. However, this technique would fail to identify transposition errors. For example, transposing the first two digits yields the code 35727, which still sums to 17 and produces the check digit 7. This error would go undetected.

There are many check-digit techniques for dealing with transposition errors. A popular method is modulus 11. Using the code 5372, the steps in this technique are as follows:

1. *Assign weights.* Each digit in the code is multiplied by a different weight. In this case, the weights used are 5, 4, 3, and 2, shown as follows:

Digit		Weight
5	×	5 = 25
3	×	4 = 12
7	×	3 = 21
2	×	2 = 4

2. *Sum the products* (25 + 12 + 21 + 4 = 62).
3. *Divide by the modulus.* We are using modulus 11 in this case, giving 62/11 = 5 with a remainder of 7.
4. *Subtract the remainder from the modulus to obtain the check digit* (11 − 7 = 4 [check digit]).
5. *Add the check digit to the original code to yield the new code*: 53724.

Using this technique to recalculate the check digit during processing, a transposition error in the code will produce a check digit other than 4. For example, if the preceding code were incorrectly entered as 35724, the recalculated check digit would be 6.

When Should Check Digits Be Used?.   The use of check digits introduces storage and processing inefficiencies and therefore should be restricted to essential data, such as primary and secondary key fields. All check digit techniques require one or more additional spaces in the field to accommodate the check digit. In the case of modulus 11, if step three above produces a remainder of 1, the check digit of 10 will require two additional character spaces. If field length is a limitation, one way of handling this problem is to disallow codes that generate the check digit 10. This would restrict the range of available codes by about 9 percent.

Batch Controls.   **Batch controls** are an effective method of managing high volumes of transaction data through a system. The objective of batch control is to reconcile output produced by the system with the input originally entered into the system. This provides assurance that:

- All records in the batch are processed.
- No records are processed more than once.
- An audit trail of transactions is created from input through processing to the output stage of the system.

Batch control is not exclusively an input control technique. Controlling the batch continues through all phases of the system. We are treating this topic here because batch control is initiated at the input stage.

Achieving batch control objectives requires grouping similar types of input transactions (such as sales orders) together in batches and then controlling the batches throughout data processing. Two documents are used to accomplish this task: a batch transmittal sheet and a batch control log. Figure 7.1 shows an example of a batch transmittal sheet. The batch transmittal sheet captures relevant information such as the following about the batch.

- A unique batch number
- A batch date

FIGURE 7.1   **Batch Transmittal Sheet**

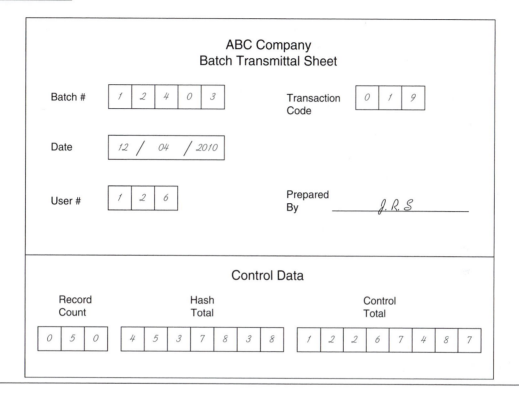

- A transaction code (indicating the type of transactions, such as a sales order or cash receipt)
- The number of records in the batch (record count)
- The total dollar value of a financial field (batch control total)
- The total of a unique nonfinancial field (hash total)

Usually, the batch transmittal sheet is prepared by the user department and is submitted to data control along with the batch of source documents. Sometimes, the data control clerk, acting as a liaison between the users and the data processing department, prepares the transmittal sheet. Figure 7.2 illustrates the batch control process.

The data control clerk receives transactions from users assembled in batches of 40 to 50 records. The clerk assigns each batch a unique number, date-stamps the documents, and calculates (or recalculates) the batch control numbers, such as the total dollar amount of the batch and a hash total (discussed later). The clerk enters the batch control information in the batch control log and submits the batch of documents, along with the transmittal sheet, to the data entry department. Figure 7.3 shows a sample batch control log.

The data entry group codes and enters the transmittal sheet data onto the transaction file, along with the batch of transaction records. The transmittal data may be added as an additional record in the file or placed in the file's internal trailer label. (We will discuss internal labels later in this section.) The transmittal sheet becomes the batch control record and is used to assess the integrity of the batch during processing. For example, the

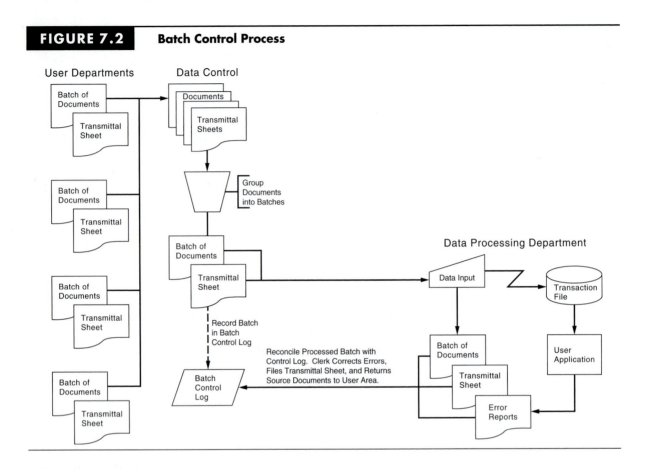

FIGURE 7.2   Batch Control Process

FIGURE 7.3   Batch Control Log

End User							Data Processing					
Batch #	Date	Time	Rec By	Control Total	Hash Total	Record Count	Submitted Date	Time	Returned Date	Time	Error Code	Reconciled By
12 403	12/04/2010	9:05	B.R.	122,674.87	4537838	50	12/04/2010	9:55	12/04/2010	11:05	0	PMR

data entry procedure will recalculate the batch control totals to make sure the batch is in balance. The transmittal record shows a batch of 50 sales order records with a total dollar value of $122,674.87 and a hash total of 4537838. At various points throughout and at the end of processing, these amounts are recalculated and compared to the batch control record. If the procedure recalculates the same amounts, the batch is in balance.

After processing, the output results are sent to the data control clerk for reconciliation and distribution to the user. The clerk updates the batch control log to record that processing of the batch was completed successfully.

Hash Totals.   The term **hash total**, which was used in the preceding discussion, refers to a simple control technique that uses nonfinancial data to keep track of the records in a batch. Any key field, such as a customer's account number, a purchase order number, or an inventory item number, may be used to calculate a hash total. In the following example, the sales order number (SO#) field for an entire batch of sales order records is summed to produce a hash total.

SO#
14327
67345
19983
.
.
.
.
88943
96543
4537838 (hash total)

Let's see how this seemingly meaningless number can be of use. Assume that after this batch of records leaves data control, someone replaced one of the sales orders in the batch with a fictitious record of the same dollar amount. How would the batch control procedures detect this irregularity? Both the record count and the dollar amount control totals would be unaffected by this act. However, unless the perpetrator obtained a source document with exactly the same sales order number (which would be impossible, since they should come uniquely prenumbered from the printer), the hash total calculated by the batch control procedures would not balance. Thus, the irregularity would be detected.

Validation Controls.   Input **validation controls** are intended to detect errors in transaction data before the data are processed. Validation procedures are most effective when they are performed as close to the source of the transaction as possible. However, depending on the type of technology in use, input validation may occur at various points in the system. For example, some validation procedures require making references against the current master file. Systems using real-time processing or batch processing with direct access master files can validate data at the input stage. Figure 7.4(a) and (b) illustrate these techniques.

If the system uses batch processing with sequential files, the transaction records being validated must first be sorted in the same order as the master file. Validating at the data input stage in this case may require considerable additional processing. Therefore, as a practical matter, each processing module prior to updating the master file record performs some validation procedures. This approach is shown in Figure 7.5.

The problem with this technique is that a transaction may be partially processed before data errors are detected. Dealing with a partially complete transaction will require special error-handling procedures. We shall discuss error-handling controls later in this section.

There are three levels of input validation controls:

1. Field interrogation
2. Record interrogation
3. File interrogation

Field Interrogation.   **Field interrogation** involves programmed procedures that examine the characteristics of the data in the field. The following are some common types of field interrogation.

FIGURE 7.4

**Validation during
Data Input**

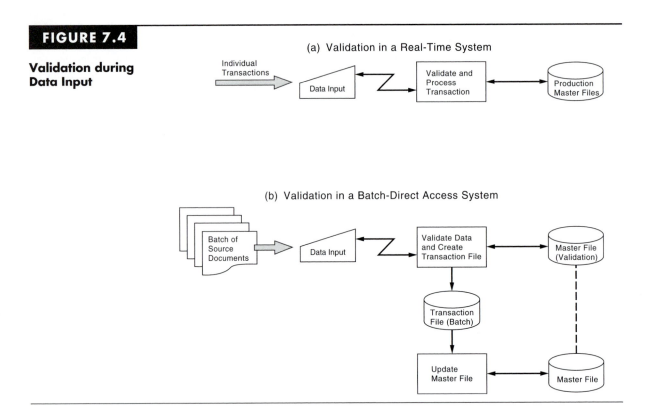

(a) Validation in a Real-Time System

(b) Validation in a Batch-Direct Access System

Missing data checks are used to examine the contents of a field for the presence of blank spaces. Some programming languages are restrictive as to the justification (right or left) of data within the field. If data are not properly justified or if a character is missing (has been replaced with a blank), the value in the field will be improperly processed. In some cases, the presence of blanks in a numeric data field may cause a system failure. When the validation program detects a blank where it expects to see a data value, this will be interpreted as an error.

Numeric-alphabetic data checks determine whether the correct form of data is in a field. For example, a customer's account balance should not contain alphabetic data. As with blanks, alphabetic data in a numeric field may cause serious processing errors.

Zero-value checks are used to verify that certain fields are filled with zeros. Some program languages require that fields used in mathematical operations be initiated with zeros prior to processing. This control may trigger an automatic corrective control to replace the contents of the field with zero if it detects a nonzero value.

Limit checks determine if the value in the field exceeds an authorized limit. For example, assume the firm's policy is that no employee works more than 44 hours per week. The payroll system validation program can interrogate the hours-worked field in the weekly payroll records for values greater than 44.

Range checks assign upper and lower limits to acceptable data values. For example, if the range of pay rates for hourly employees in a firm is between 8 and 20 dollars, all payroll records can be checked to see that this range is not exceeded. The purpose of this control is to detect keystroke errors that shift the decimal point one or more places. It would not detect an error where a correct pay rate of, say, 9 dollars is incorrectly entered as 15 dollars.

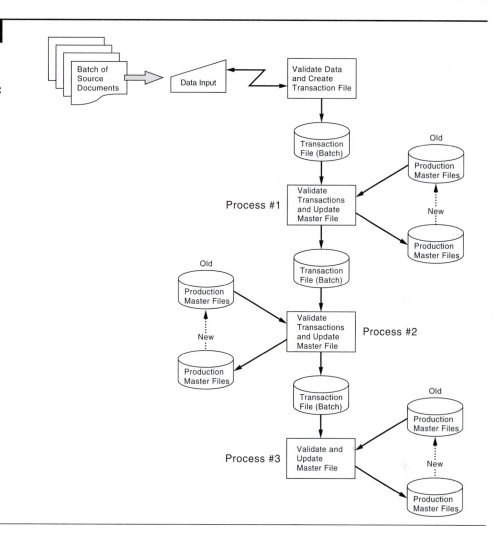

FIGURE 7.5

Validation in Batch Sequential File System (Note: For simplification, the necessary re-sorting of the transaction file between update processes is not shown.)

Validity checks compare actual values in a field against known acceptable values. This control is used to verify such things as transaction codes, state abbreviations, or employee job skill codes. If the value in the field does not match one of the acceptable values, the record is determined to be in error.

This is a frequently used control in cash disbursement systems. One form of cash disbursement fraud involves manipulating the system into making a fraudulent payment to a nonexistent vendor. To prevent this, the firm may establish a list of valid vendors with whom it does business exclusively. Thus, before payment of any trade obligation, the vendor number on the cash disbursement voucher is matched against the valid vendor list by the validation program. If the code does not match, payment is denied, and management reviews the transaction.

Check digit controls identify keystroke errors in key fields by testing the internal validity of the code. We discussed this control technique earlier in the section.

Record Interrogation. **Record interrogation** procedures validate the entire record by examining the interrelationship of its field values. Some typical tests are discussed below.

Reasonableness checks determine if a value in one field, which has already passed a limit check and a range check, is reasonable when considered along with other data fields in the record. For example, an employee's pay rate of 18 dollars per hour falls within an acceptable range. However, this rate is excessive when compared to the employee's job skill code of 693; employees in this skill class never earn more than 12 dollars per hour.

Sign checks are tests to see if the sign of a field is correct for the type of record being processed. For example, in a sales order processing system, the dollar amount field must be positive for sales orders but negative for sales return transactions. This control can determine the correctness of the sign by comparing it with the transaction code field.

Sequence checks are used to determine if a record is out of order. In batch systems that use sequential master files, the transaction files being processed must be sorted in the same order as the primary keys of the corresponding master file. This requirement is critical to the processing logic of the update program. Hence, before each transaction record is processed, its sequence is verified relative to the previous record processed.

File Interrogation.   The purpose of **file interrogation** is to ensure that the correct file is being processed by the system. These controls are particularly important for master files, which contain permanent records of the firm and which, if destroyed or corrupted, are difficult to replace.

Internal label checks verify that the file processed is the one the program is actually calling for. Files stored on magnetic tape are usually kept off-line in a tape library. These files have external labels that identify them (by name and serial number) to the tape librarian and operator. External labeling is typically a manual procedure and, like any manual task, prone to errors. Sometimes, the wrong external label is mistakenly affixed to a file when it is created. Thus, when the file is called for again, the wrong file will be retrieved and placed on the tape drive for processing. Depending on how the file is being used, this may result in its destruction or corruption. To prevent this, the operating system creates an internal header label that is placed at the beginning of the file. An example of a header label is shown in Figure 7.6.

To ensure that the correct file is about to be processed, the system matches the file name and serial number in the header label with the program's file requirements. If the wrong file has been loaded, the system will send the operator a message and suspend processing. It is worth noting that while label checking is generally a standard feature, it is an option that can be overridden by programmers and operators.

Version checks are used to verify that the version of the file being processed is correct. In a grandparent–parent–child approach, many versions of master files and transactions may exist. The version check compares the version number of the files being processed with the program's requirements.

An *expiration date check* prevents a file from being deleted before it expires. In a GPC system, for example, once an adequate number of backup files is created, the oldest backup file is scratched (erased from the disk or tape) to provide space for new files. Figure 7.7 illustrates this procedure.

To protect against destroying an active file by mistake, the system first checks the expiration date contained in the header label (see Figure 7.6). If the retention period has not yet expired, the system will generate an error message and abort the scratch procedure. Expiration date control is an optional measure. The length of the retention period is specified by the programmer and based on the number of backup files that are desired. If the programmer chooses not to specify an expiration date, the control against such accidental deletion is eliminated.

FIGURE 7.6

**Header Label
on Magnetic Tape**

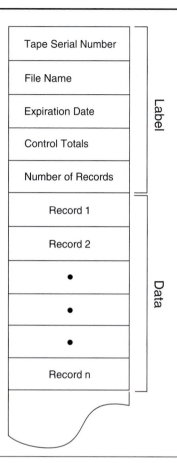

Tape Serial Number

File Name

Expiration Date

Control Totals

Number of Records

Label

Record 1

Record 2

•

•

•

Record n

Data

Input Error Correction. When errors are detected in a batch, they must be corrected and the records resubmitted for reprocessing. This must be a controlled process to ensure that errors are dealt with completely and correctly. There are three common error handling techniques: (1) correct immediately, (2) create an error file, and (3) reject the entire batch.

Correct Immediately. If the system is using the direct data validation approach (refer to 7-4(a) and (b)), error detection and correction can also take place during data entry. Upon detecting a keystroke error or an illogical relationship, the system should halt the data entry procedure until the user corrects the error.

Create an Error File. When delayed validation is being used, such as in batch systems with sequential files, individual errors should be flagged to prevent them from being processed. At the end of the validation procedure, the records flagged as errors are removed from the batch and placed in a temporary error holding file until the errors can be investigated.

Some errors can be detected during data input procedures. However, as was mentioned earlier, the update module performs some validation tests. Thus, error records may be placed on the error file at several different points in the process, as illustrated

FIGURE 7.7   Scratch Tape Approach Using Retention Date

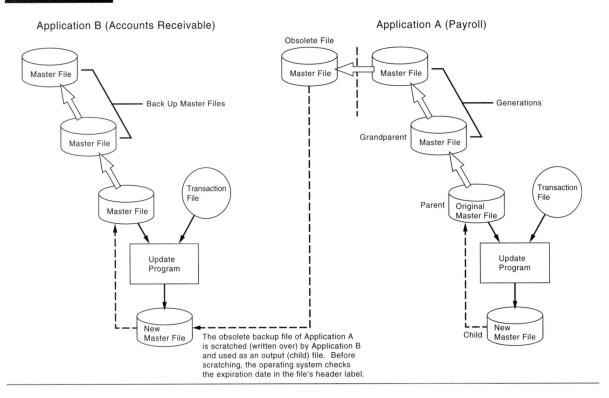

Application B (Accounts Receivable)

Application A (Payroll)

The obsolete backup file of Application A is scratched (written over) by Application B and used as an output (child) file. Before scratching, the operating system checks the expiration date in the file's header label.

by Figure 7.8. At each validation point, the system automatically adjusts the batch control totals to reflect the removal of the error records from the batch. In a separate procedure, an authorized user representative will later make corrections to the error records and resubmit them as a separate batch for reprocessing.

Errors detected during processing require careful handling. These records may already be partially processed. Therefore, simply resubmitting the corrected records to the system via the data input stage may result in processing portions of these transactions twice. There are two methods for dealing with this complexity. The first is to reverse the effects of the partially processed transactions and resubmit the corrected records to the data input stage. The second is to reinsert corrected records to the processing stage in which the error was detected. In either case, batch control procedures (preparing batch control records and logging the batches) apply to the resubmitted data, just as they do for normal batch processing.

Reject the Batch.   Some forms of errors are associated with the entire batch and are not clearly attributable to individual records. An example of this type of error is an imbalance in a batch control total. Assume that the transmittal sheet for a batch of sales orders shows a total sales value of $122,674.87, but the data input procedure calculated a sales total of only $121,454.32. What has caused this? Is the problem a missing or changed record? Or did the data control clerk incorrectly calculate the batch control total? The most effective solution in this case is to cease processing and return the entire batch to data control to evaluate, correct, and resubmit.

FIGURE 7.8

Use of Error File in Batch Sequential File System with Multiple Resubmission Points

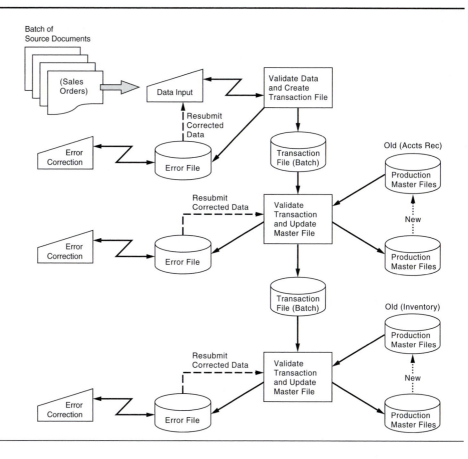

Batch errors are one reason for keeping the size of the batch to a manageable number. Too few records in a batch make batch processing inefficient. Too many records make error detection difficult, create greater business disruption when a batch is rejected, and increase the possibility of mistakes when calculating batch control totals.

Generalized Data Input Systems. To achieve a high degree of control and standardization over input validation procedures, some organizations employ a **generalized data input system (GDIS)**. This technique includes centralized procedures to manage the data input for all of the organization's transaction processing systems. The GDIS approach has three advantages. First, it improves control by having one common system perform all data validation. Second, GDIS ensures that each AIS application applies a consistent standard for data validation. Third, GDIS improves systems development efficiency. Given the high degree of commonality in input validation requirements for AIS applications, a GDIS eliminates the need to recreate redundant routines for each new application. Figure 7.9 shows the primary features of this technique. A GDIS has five major components:[1]

1. Generalized validation module
2. Validated data file

---

1 RonWeber, *EDP Auditing: Conceptual Foundations and Practice*, 2nd ed. (McGraw-Hill, 1988), pp. 424–427.

FIGURE 7.9

Generalized Data Input System

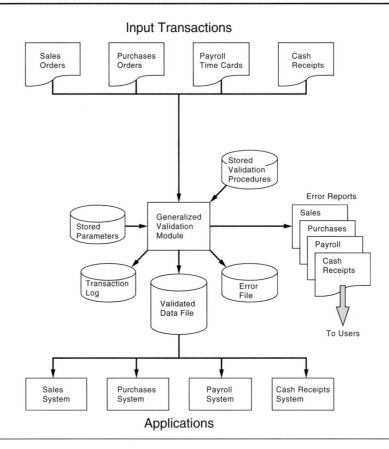

3. Error file
4. Error reports
5. Transaction log

Generalized Validation Module. The **generalized validation module (GVM)** performs standard validation routines that are common to many different applications. These routines are customized to an individual application's needs through parameters that specify the program's specific requirements. For example, the GVM may apply a range check to the HOURLY RATE field of payroll records. The limits of the range are 6 dollars and 15 dollars. The range test is the generalized procedure; the dollar limits are the parameters that customize this procedure. The validation procedures for some applications may be so unique as to defy a general solution. To meet the goals of the generalized data input system, the GVM must be flexible enough to permit special user-defined procedures for unique applications. These procedures are stored, along with generalized procedures, and invoked by the GVM as needed.

- *Validated Data File.* The input data that are validated by the GVM are stored on a **validated data file**. This is a temporary holding file through which validated transactions flow to their respective applications. The file is analogous to a tank of water whose level is constantly changing, as it is filled from the top by the GVM and emptied from the bottom by applications.

- *Error File*. The **error file** in the GDIS plays the same role as a traditional error file. Error records detected during validation are stored in the file, corrected, and then resubmitted to the GVM.
- *Error Reports*. Standardized **error reports** are distributed to users to facilitate error correction. For example, if the HOURLY RATE field in a payroll record fails a range check, the error report will display an error message stating the problem so. The report will also present the contents of the failed record, along with the acceptable range limits taken from the parameters.
- *Transaction Log*. The **transaction log** is a permanent record of all validated transactions. From an accounting records point of view, the transaction log is equivalent to the journal and is an important element in the audit trail. However, only successful transactions (those that will be completely processed) should be entered in the journal. If a transaction is to undergo additional validation testing during the processing phase (which could result in its rejection), it should be entered in the transaction log only after it is completely validated. This issue is discussed further in the next section under Audit Trail Controls.

Processing Controls

After passing through the data input stage, transactions enter the processing stage of the system. **Processing controls** are divided into three categories: run-to-run controls, operator intervention controls, and *Audit Trail Controls*.

Run-to-Run Controls

Previously, we discussed the preparation of batch control figures as an element of input control. **Run-to-run controls** use batch figures to monitor the batch as it moves from one programmed procedure (run) to another. These controls ensure that each run in the system processes the batch correctly and completely. Batch control figures may be contained in either a separate control record created at the data input stage or an internal label. Specific uses of run-to-run control figures are described in the following paragraphs.

Recalculate Control Totals. After each major operation in the process and after each run, dollar amount fields, hash totals, and record counts are accumulated and compared to the corresponding values stored in the control record. If a record in the batch is lost, goes unprocessed, or is processed more than once, this will be revealed by the discrepancies between these figures.

Transaction Codes. The **transaction code** of each record in the batch is compared to the transaction code contained in the control record. This ensures that only the correct type of transaction is being processed.

Sequence Checks. In systems that use sequential master files, the order of the transaction records in the batch is critical to correct and complete processing. As the batch moves through the process, it must be re-sorted in the order of the master file used in each run. The **sequence check** control compares the sequence of each record in the batch with the previous record to ensure that proper sorting took place.

Figure 7.10 illustrates the use of run-to-run controls in a revenue cycle system. This application comprises four runs: (1) data input, (2) accounts receivable update, (3) inventory update, and (4) output. At the end of the accounts receivable run, batch control figures are recalculated and reconciled with the control totals passed from the data input run. These figures are then passed to the inventory update run, where they

FIGURE 7.10

**Run-to-Run
Controls**

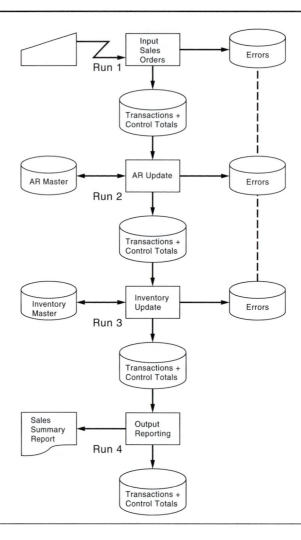

are again recalculated, reconciled, and passed to the output run. Errors detected in each run are flagged and placed in an error file. The run-to-run (batch) control figures are then adjusted to reflect the deletion of these records.

Operator Intervention Controls

Systems sometimes require operator intervention to initiate certain actions, such as entering control totals for a batch of records, providing parameter values for logical operations, and activating a program from a different point when reentering semi-processed error records. Operator intervention increases the potential for human error. Systems that limit operator intervention through **operator intervention controls** are thus less prone to processing errors. Although it may be impossible to eliminate operator involvement completely, parameter values and program start points should, to the extent possible, be derived logically or provided to the system through look-up tables.

Audit Trail Controls

The preservation of an audit trail is an important objective of process control. In an accounting system, every transaction must be traceable through each stage of processing from its economic source to its presentation in financial statements. In an automated environment, the audit trail can become fragmented and difficult to follow. It thus becomes critical that each major operation applied to a transaction be thoroughly documented. The following are examples of techniques used to preserve audit trails in computer based accounting systems.

Transaction Logs.   Every transaction successfully processed by the system should be recorded on a transaction log, which serves as a journal. Figure 7.11 shows this arrangement.

There are two reasons for creating a transaction log. First, the transaction log is a permanent record of transactions. The validated transaction file produced at the data input phase is usually a temporary file. Once processed, the records on this file are erased (scratched) to make room for the next batch of transactions. Second, not all of the records in the validated transaction file may be successfully processed. Some of these records may fail tests in the subsequent processing stages. A transaction log should contain only successful transactions—those that have changed account balances. Unsuccessful transactions should be placed in an error file. The transaction log and error files combined should account for all the transactions in the batch. The validated transaction file may then be scratched with no loss of data.

The system should produce a hard copy transaction listing of all successful transactions. These listings should go to the appropriate users to facilitate reconciliation with input.

Log of Automatic Transactions.   Some transactions are triggered internally by the system. An example of this is when inventory drops below a preset reorder point, and the system automatically processes a purchase order. To maintain an audit trail of these activities, all internally generated transactions must be placed in a transaction log.

Listing of Automatic Transactions.   To maintain control over automatic transactions processed by the system, the responsible end user should receive a detailed listing of all internally generated transactions.

Unique Transaction Identifiers.   Each transaction processed by the system must be uniquely identified with a transaction number. This is the only practical means of tracing

FIGURE 7.11   Transaction Log to Preserve the Audit Trail

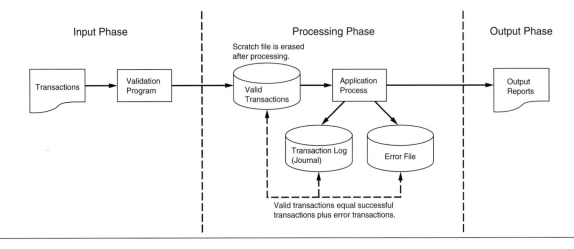

a particular transaction through a database of thousands or even millions of records. In systems that use physical source documents, the unique number printed on the document can be transcribed during data input and used for this purpose. In real-time systems, which do not use source documents, the system should assign each transaction a unique number.

Error Listing.   A listing of all error records should go to the appropriate user to support error correction and resubmission.

Output Controls

Output controls ensure that system output is not lost, misdirected, or corrupted and that privacy is not violated. Exposures of this sort can cause serious disruptions to operations and may result in financial losses to a firm. For example, if the checks produced by a firm's cash disbursements system are lost, misdirected, or destroyed, trade accounts and other bills may go unpaid. This could damage the firm's credit rating and result in lost discounts, interest, or penalty charges. If the privacy of certain types of output is violated, a firm could have its business objectives compromised, or it could even become legally exposed. Examples of privacy exposures include the disclosure of trade secrets, patents pending, marketing research results, and patient medical records.

The type of processing method in use influences the choice of controls employed to protect system output. Generally, batch systems are more susceptible to exposure and require a greater degree of control than real-time systems. In this section, we examine output exposures and controls for both methods.

Controlling Batch Systems Output

Batch systems usually produce output in the form of hard copy, which typically requires the involvement of intermediaries in its production and distribution. Figure 7.12 shows the stages in the output process and serves as the basis for the rest of this section.

The output is removed from the printer by the computer operator, separated into sheets and separated from other reports, reviewed for correctness by the data control clerk, and then sent through interoffice mail to the end user. Each stage in this process is a point of potential exposure where the output could be reviewed, stolen, copied, or misdirected. An additional exposure exists when processing or printing goes wrong and produces output that is unacceptable to the end user. These corrupted or partially damaged reports are often discarded in waste cans. Computer criminals have successfully used such waste to achieve their illicit objectives.

Following, we examine techniques for controlling each phase in the output process. Keep in mind that not all of these techniques will necessarily apply to every item of output produced by the system. As always, controls are employed on a cost–benefit basis that is determined by the sensitivity of the data in the reports.

Output Spooling.   In large-scale data-processing operations, output devices such as line printers can become backlogged with many programs simultaneously demanding these limited resources. This backlog can cause a bottleneck, which adversely affects the throughput of the system. Applications waiting to print output occupy computer memory and block other applications from entering the processing stream. To ease this burden, applications are often designed to direct their output to a magnetic disk file rather than to the printer directly. This is called **output spooling**. Later, when printer resources become available, the output files are printed.

FIGURE 7.12

Stages in the Output Process

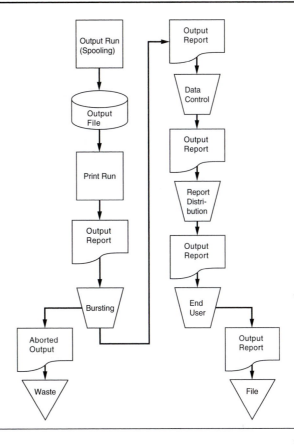

The creation of an output file as an intermediate step in the printing process presents an added exposure. A computer criminal may use this opportunity to perform any of the following unauthorized acts:

- Access the output file and change critical data values (such as dollar amounts on checks). The printer program will then print the corrupted output as if it were produced by the output run. Using this technique, a criminal may effectively circumvent the processing controls designed into the application.
- Access the file and change the number of copies of output to be printed. The extra copies may then be removed without notice during the printing stage.
- Make a copy of the output file to produce illegal output reports.
- Destroy the output file before output printing takes place.

The auditor should be aware of these potential exposures and ensure that proper access and backup procedures are in place to protect output files.

Print Programs. When the printer becomes available, the print run program produces hard copy output from the output file. Print programs are often complex systems that require operator intervention. Four common types of operator actions follow:

1. Pausing the print program to load the correct type of output documents (check stocks, invoices, or other special forms).
2. Entering parameters needed by the print run, such as the number of copies to be printed.

3. Restarting the print run at a prescribed checkpoint after a printer malfunction.
4. Removing printed output from the printer for review and distribution.

Print program controls are designed to deal with two types of exposures presented by this environment: (1) the production of unauthorized copies of output and (2) employee browsing of sensitive data. Some print programs allow the operator to specify more copies of output than the output file calls for, which allows for the possibility of producing unauthorized copies of output. One way to control this is to employ output document controls similar to the source document controls discussed earlier. This is feasible when dealing with prenumbered invoices for billing customers or prenumbered check stock. At the end of the run, the number of copies specified by the output file can be reconciled with the actual number of output documents used. In cases where output documents are not prenumbered, supervision may be the most effective control technique. A security officer can be present during the printing of sensitive output.

To prevent operators from viewing sensitive output, special multipart paper can be used, with the top copy colored black to prevent the print from being read. This type of product, which is illustrated in Figure 7.13, is often used for payroll check printing. The receiver of the check separates the top copy from the body of the check, which contains readable details. An alternative privacy control is to direct the output to a special remote printer that can be closely supervised.

Bursting. When output reports are removed from the printer, they go to the **bursting** stage to have their pages separated and collated. The concern here is that the bursting clerk may make an unauthorized copy of the report, remove a page from the report, or read sensitive information. The primary control against these exposures is supervision. For very sensitive reports, bursting may be performed by the end user.

Waste. Computer output waste represents a potential exposure. It is important to dispose of aborted reports and the carbon copies from multipart paper removed during bursting properly. Computer criminals have been known to sift through trash cans searching for carelessly discarded output that is presumed by others to be of no value. From such trash, computer criminals may obtain a key piece of information about the firm's market research, the credit ratings of its customers, or even trade secrets that they can sell to a competitor. Computer waste is also a source of technical data, such as passwords and authority tables, which a perpetrator may use to access the firm's data files. Passing it through a paper shredder can easily destroy sensitive computer output.

Data Control. In some organizations, the **data control** group is responsible for verifying the accuracy of computer output before it is distributed to the user. Normally, the data control clerk will review the batch control figures for balance; examine the report body for garbled, illegible, and missing data; and record the receipt of the report in data control's batch control log. For reports containing highly sensitive data, the end user may perform these tasks. In this case, the report will bypass the data control group and go directly to the user.

Report Distribution. The primary risks associated with report distribution include reports being lost, stolen, or misdirected in transit to the user. A number of control measures can minimize these exposures. For example, when reports are generated, the name and address of the user should be printed on the report. For multicopy reports, an address file of authorized users should be consulted to identify each recipient of the report. Maintaining adequate access control over this file becomes highly important. If an unauthorized individual were able to add his or her name to the authorized user list, he or she would receive a copy of the report.

FIGURE 7.13   **Multipart Check Stock**

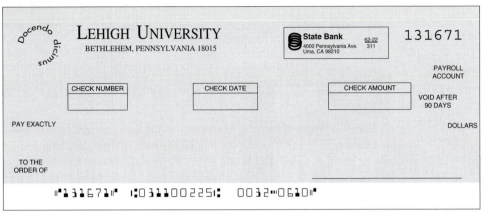

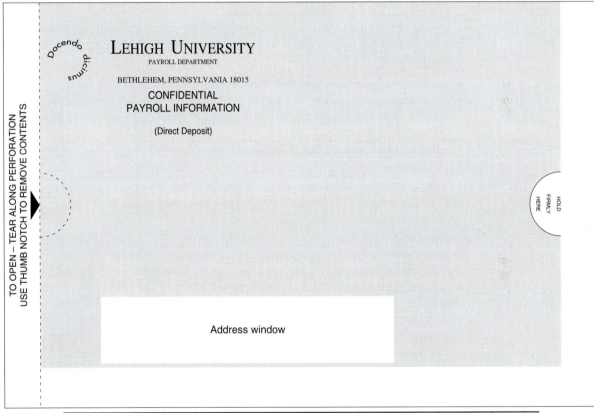

For highly sensitive reports, the following distribution techniques can be used:

- The reports may be placed in a secure mailbox to which only the user has the key.
- The user may be required to appear in person at the distribution center and sign for the report.
- A security officer or special courier may deliver the report to the user.

End User Controls.   Once in the hands of the user, output reports should be reexamined for any errors that may have evaded the data control clerk's review. Users are in a far better position to identify subtle errors in reports that are not disclosed by an imbalance in control totals. Errors detected by the user should be reported to the appropriate computer services management. Such errors may be symptoms of an improper systems design, incorrect procedures, errors inserted by accident during systems maintenance, or unauthorized access to data files or programs.

Once a report has served its purpose, it should be stored in a secure location until its retention period has expired. Factors influencing the length of time a hard copy report is retained include:

- Statutory requirements specified by government agencies, such as the IRS.
- The number of copies of the report in existence. When there are multiple copies, certain of these may be marked for permanent retention, while the remainder can be destroyed after use.
- The existence of magnetic or optical images of reports that can act as permanent backup.

When the retention date has passed, reports should be destroyed in a manner consistent with the sensitivity of their contents. Highly sensitive reports should be shredded.

Controlling Real-Time Systems Output

Real-time systems direct their output to the user's computer screen, terminal, or printer. This method of distribution eliminates the various intermediaries in the journey from the computer center to the user and thus reduces many of the exposures previously discussed. The primary threat to real-time output is the interception, disruption, destruction, or corruption of the output message as it passes along the communications link. This threat comes from two types of exposures: (1) exposures from equipment failure; and (2) exposures from subversive acts, whereby a computer criminal intercepts the output message transmitted between the sender and the receiver. Techniques for controlling communications exposures were discussed previously in Chapter 3.

TESTING COMPUTER APPLICATION CONTROLS

This section examines several techniques for auditing computer applications. Control testing techniques provide information about the accuracy and completeness of an application's processes. These tests follow two general approaches: (1) the black box (around the computer) approach and (2) the white box (through the computer) approach. We first examine the black box approach and then review several white box testing techniques.

Black-Box Approach

Auditors testing with the **black-box approach** do not rely on a detailed knowledge of the application's internal logic. Instead, they seek to understand the functional characteristics

FIGURE 7.14

Auditing Around the Computer— The Black Box Approach

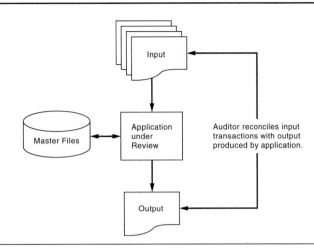

of the application by analyzing flowcharts and interviewing knowledgeable personnel in the client's organization. With an understanding of what the application is supposed to do, the auditor tests the application by reconciling production input transactions processed by the application with output results. The output results are analyzed to verify the application's compliance with its functional requirements. Figure 7.14 illustrates the black box approach.

The advantage of the black-box approach is that the application need not be removed from service and tested directly. This approach is feasible for testing applications that are relatively simple. However, complex applications—those that receive input from many sources, perform a variety of operations, or produce multiple outputs—require a more focused testing approach to provide the auditor with evidence of application integrity.

White-Box Approach

The **white-box approach** relies on an in-depth understanding of the internal logic of the application being tested. The white-box approach includes several techniques for testing application logic directly. These techniques use small numbers of specially created test transactions to verify specific aspects of an application's logic and controls. In this way, auditors are able to conduct precise tests, with known variables, and obtain results that they can compare against objectively calculated results. Some of the more common types of tests of controls include the following:

- **Authenticity tests**, which verify that an individual, a programmed procedure, or a message (such as an EDI transmission) attempting to access a system is authentic. Authenticity controls include user IDs, passwords, valid vendor codes, and authority tables.
- **Accuracy tests**, which ensure that the system processes only data values that conform to specified tolerances. Examples include range tests, field tests, and limit tests.
- **Completeness tests**, which identify missing data within a single record and entire records missing from a batch. The types of tests performed are field tests, record sequence tests, hash totals, and control totals.
- **Redundancy tests**, which determine that an application processes each record only once. Redundancy controls include the reconciliation of batch totals, record counts, hash totals, and financial control totals.

- **Access tests**, which ensure that the application prevents authorized users from unauthorized access to data. Access controls include passwords, authority tables, user-defined procedures, data encryption, and inference controls.
- **Audit trail tests**, which ensure that the application creates an adequate audit trail. This includes evidence that the application records all transactions in a transaction log, posts data values to the appropriate accounts, produces complete **transaction listings**, and generates error files and reports for all exceptions.
- **Rounding error tests**, which verify the correctness of rounding procedures. Rounding errors occur in accounting information when the level of precision used in the calculation is greater than that used in the reporting. For example, interest calculations on bank account balances may have a precision of five decimal places, whereas only two decimal places are needed to report balances. If the remaining three decimal places are simply dropped, the total interest calculated for the total number of accounts may not equal the sum of the individual calculations.

Figure 7.15 shows the logic for handling the rounding error problem. This technique uses an accumulator to keep track of the rounding differences between calculated and reported balances. Note how the sign and the absolute value of the amount in the accumulator determine how the customer account is affected by rounding. To illustrate, the

FIGURE 7.15

Rounding Error Algorithm

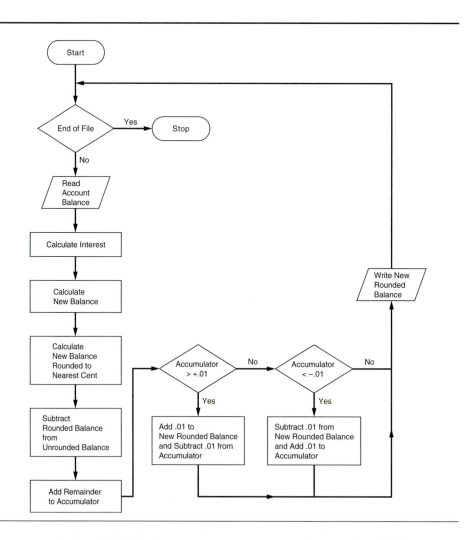

rounding logic is applied in Table 7.1 to three hypothetical bank balances. The interest calculations are based on an interest rate of 5.25 percent.

Failure to properly account for this rounding difference can result in an imbalance between the total (control) interest amount and the sum of the individual interest calculations for each account. Poor accounting for rounding differences can also present an opportunity for fraud.

Rounding programs are particularly susceptible to salami frauds. **Salami frauds** tend to affect a large number of victims, but the harm to each is immaterial. This type of fraud takes its name from the analogy of slicing a large salami (the fraud objective) into many thin pieces. Each victim assumes one of these small pieces and is unaware of being defrauded. For example, a programmer, or someone with access to the preceding

TABLE 7.1	Rounding Logic Risk

Record 1

Beginning accumulator balance	.00861
Beginning account balance	2,741.78
Calculated interest	143.94345
New account balance	2,885.72345
Rounded account balance	2,885.72
Adjusted accumulator balance	.01206 (.00345+.00861)
Ending account balance	**2,885.73 (round up 1 cent)**
Ending accumulator balance	.00206 (.01206 – .01)

Record 2

Beginning accumulator balance	.00206
Beginning account balance	1,893.44
Calculated interest	99.4056
New account balance	1,992.8456
Rounded account balance	1,992.85
Adjusted accumulator balance	–.00646 (.00206 – .0044)
Ending account balance	**1,992,85 (no change)**
Ending accumulator balance	–.00234

Record 3

Beginning accumulator balance	–.00234
Beginning account balance	7,423.34
Calculated interest	389.72535
New account balance	7,813.06535
Rounded account balance	7,813.07
Adjusted accumulator balance	–.00699 (–.00234 –. 00425)
Ending account balance	**7,813.06 (round down 1 cent)**
Ending accumulator balance	.00699

rounding program, can perpetrate a salami fraud by modifying the rounding logic as follows: at the point in the process where the algorithm should increase the customer's account (that is, the accumulator value is > +.01), the program instead adds one cent to another account—the perpetrator's account. Although the absolute amount of each fraud transaction is small, given the thousands of accounts processed, the total amount of the fraud can become significant over time.

Operating system audit trails and audit software can detect excessive file activity. In the case of the salami fraud, there would be thousands of entries into the computer criminal's personal account that may be detected in this way. A clever programmer may disguise this activity by funneling these entries through several intermediate temporary accounts, which are then posted to a smaller number of intermediate accounts and finally to the programmer's personal account. By using many levels of accounts in this way, the activity to any single account is reduced and may go undetected by the audit software. There will be a trail, but it can be complicated. A skilled auditor may also use audit software to detect the existence of unauthorized intermediate accounts used in such a fraud.

COMPUTER-AIDED AUDIT TOOLS AND TECHNIQUES FOR TESTING CONTROLS

To illustrate how application controls are tested, this section describes five CAATT approaches: the test data method, which includes base case system evaluation and tracing, integrated test facility, and parallel simulation.

Test Data Method

The **test data method** is used to establish application integrity by processing specially prepared sets of input data through production applications that are under review. The results of each test are compared to predetermined expectations to obtain an objective evaluation of application logic and control effectiveness. The test data technique is illustrated in Figure 7.16. To perform the test data technique, the auditor must obtain a copy

| **FIGURE 7.16** | **The Test Data Technique** |

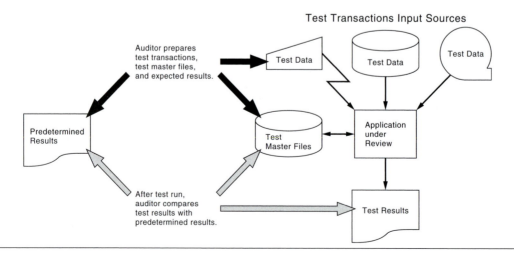

of the current version of the application. In addition, test transaction files and test master files must be created. As illustrated in the figure, test transactions may enter the system from magnetic tape, disk, or via an input terminal. Results from the test run will be in the form of routine output reports, transaction listings, and error reports. In addition, the auditor must review the updated master files to determine that account balances have been correctly updated. The test results are then compared with the auditor's expected results to determine if the application is functioning properly. This comparison may be performed manually or through special computer software.

Figure 7.17 lists selected fields for hypothetical transactions and accounts receivable records prepared by the auditor to test a sales order processing application. The figure also shows an error report of rejected transactions and a listing of the updated accounts receivable master file. Any deviations between the actual results obtained and those expected by the auditor may indicate a logic or control problem.

Creating Test Data

When creating test data, auditors must prepare a complete set of both valid and invalid transactions. If test data are incomplete, auditors might fail to examine critical branches of application logic and error-checking routines. Test transactions should test every possible input error, logical process, and irregularity.

Gaining knowledge of the application's internal logic sufficient to create meaningful test data frequently requires a large investment of time. However, the efficiency of this task can be improved through careful planning during systems development. The auditor should save the test data used to test program modules during the implementation phase of the SDLC for future use. If the application has undergone no maintenance since its initial implementation, current audit test results should equal the test results obtained at implementation. However, if the application has been modified, the auditor can create additional test data that focus on the areas of the program changes.

Base Case System Evaluation

There are several variants of the test data technique. When the set of test data in use is comprehensive, the technique is called the **base case system evaluation (BCSE)**. BCSE tests are conducted with a set of test transactions containing all possible transaction types. These are processed through repeated iterations during systems development testing until consistent and valid results are obtained. These results are the base case. When subsequent changes to the application occur during maintenance, their effects are evaluated by comparing current results with base case results.

Tracing

Another type of the test data technique called **tracing** performs an electronic walk-through of the application's internal logic. The tracing procedure involves three steps:

1. The application under review must undergo a special compilation to activate the trace option.
2. Specific transactions or types of transactions are created as test data.
3. The test data transactions are traced through all processing stages of the program, and a listing is produced of all programmed instructions that were executed during the test.

Implementing tracing requires a detailed understanding of the application's internal logic. Figure 7.18 illustrates the tracing process using a portion of the logic for a payroll application. The example shows records from two payroll files—a transaction record

FIGURE 7.17   Examples of Test Data and Test Results

Test Transaction File

REC #	CUST #	CUSTOMER NAME	PART #	DESCRIPTION	QNTY	UNIT PRICE	TOTAL PRICE
1	231893	Smith, Joe	AX-612	Water Pump	1	20.00	20.00
2	231893	Azar, Atul	J-912	Gear	3	15.00	45.00
3	245851	Jones, Mary	123-LM	Hose	20	20.00	400.00
4	256519	Lang, Tony	Y-771	Spacer	5	2.00	10.00
5	259552	Tuner, Agnes	U-734	Bushing	5	25.00	120.00
6	175995	Hanz, James	EA-74	Seal	1	3.00	3.00
7	267991	Swindle, Joe	EN-12	Rebuilt Engine	1	1,220.00	1,220.00

Original Test AR Master File

CUST #	CUSTOMER NAME	CUSTOMER ADDRESS	CREDIT LIMIT	CURRENT BALANCE
231893	Smith, Joe	1520 S. Maple, City	1,000.00	400.00
256519	Lang, Tony	18 Etwine St., City	5,000.00	850.00
267991	Swindle, Joe	1 Shady Side, City	3,000.00	2,900.00

Updated Test AR Master File

CUST #	CUSTOMER NAME	CUSTOMER ADDRESS	CREDIT LIMIT	CURRENT BALANCE
231893	Smith, Joe	1520 S. Maple, City	1,000.00	420.00
256519	Lang, Tony	18 Etwine St., City	5,000.00	860.00
267991	Swindle, Joe	1 Shady Side, City	3,000.00	2,900.00

Error Report

REC #	CUST #	CUSTOMER NAME	PART #	DESCRIPTION	QNTY	UNIT PRICE	TOTAL PRICE	EXPLANATION OF ERROR
2	231893	Azar, Atul **X**	J-912	Gear	3	15.00	45.00	CUSTOMER NAME does not correspond to CUST # 231893
3	245851 **X**	Jones, Mary	123-LM	Hose	20	20.00	400.00	Check digit error in CUST # field
5	259552	Tuner, Agnes	U-734	Bushing	5	25.00	120.00 **X**	Price extension error
6	175995 **X**	Hanz, James	EA-74	Seal	1	3.00	3.00	Record out of sequence
7	267991	Swindle, Joe	EN-12	Rebuilt Engine	1	1,220.00 **X**	1,220.00 **X**	Credit limit error

showing hours worked and two records from a master file showing pay rates. The trace listing at the bottom of Figure 7.18 identifies the program statements that were executed and the order of execution. Analysis of trace options indicates that Commands 0001 through 0020 were executed. At that point, the application transferred to Command 0060. This occurred because the employee number (the key) of the transaction record did not match the key of the first record in the master file. Then Commands 0010 through 0050 were executed.

FIGURE 7.18

Tracing

Payroll Transaction File

Time Card #	Employee Number	Name	Year	Pay Period	Reg Hrs	OT Hrs
8945	33456	Jones, J.J.	2004	14	40.0	3.0

Payroll Master File

Employee Number	Hourly Rate	YTD Earnings	Dependents	YTD Withhold	YTD FICA
33276	15	12,050	3	3,200	873.62
33456	15	13,100	2	3,600	949.75

Computer Program Logic

```
0001   Read Record from Transaction File
0010   Read Record from Master File
0020   If Employee Number (T) = Employee Number (M)
0030       Wage = (Reg Hrs + (OT Hrs x 1.5) ) x Hourly Rate
0040       Add Wage to YTD Earnings
0050       Go to 0001
0060   Else Go to 0010
```

Trace Listing
0001, 0010, 0020, 0060, 0010, 0020, 0030, 0040, 0050

Advantages of Test Data Techniques

There are three primary advantages of test data techniques. First, they employ through-the-computer testing, thus providing the auditor with explicit evidence concerning application functions. Second, if properly planned, test data runs can be employed with only minimal disruption to the organization's operations. Third, they require only minimal computer expertise on the part of auditors.

Disadvantages of Test Data Techniques

The primary disadvantage of all test data techniques is that auditors must rely on computer services personnel to obtain a copy of the application for test purposes. This entails a risk that computer services may intentionally or accidentally provide the auditor with the wrong version of the application and may reduce the reliability of the audit evidence. In general, audit evidence collected by independent means is more reliable than evidence supplied by the client.

A second disadvantage of these techniques is that they provide a static picture of application integrity at a single point in time. They do not provide a convenient means of gathering evidence about ongoing application functionality. There is no evidence that the application being tested today is functioning as it did during the year under test.

A third disadvantage of test data techniques is their relatively high cost of implementation, which results in audit inefficiency. The auditor may devote considerable time to understanding program logic and creating test data. In the following section, we see how automating testing techniques can resolve these problems.

The Integrated Test Facility

The **integrated test facility (ITF)** approach is an automated technique that enables the auditor to test an application's logic and controls during its normal operation. The ITF is one or more audit modules designed into the application during the systems

FIGURE 7.19

The ITF Technique

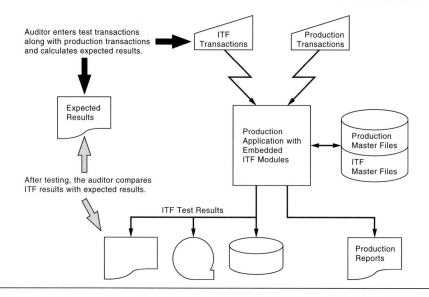

development process. In addition, ITF databases contain "dummy" or test master file records integrated with legitimate records. Some firms create a dummy company to which test transactions are posted. During normal operations, test transactions are merged into the input stream of regular (production) transactions and are processed against the files of the dummy company. Figure 7.19 illustrates the ITF concept.

ITF audit modules are designed to discriminate between ITF transactions and routine production data. This may be accomplished in a number of ways. One of the simplest and most commonly used is to assign a unique range of key values exclusively to ITF transactions. For example, in a sales order processing system, account numbers between 2000 and 2100 can be reserved for ITF transactions and will not be assigned to actual customer accounts. By segregating ITF transactions from legitimate transactions in this way, routine reports produced by the application are not corrupted by ITF test data. Test results are produced separately on storage media or hard copy output and distributed directly to the auditor. Just as with the test data techniques, the auditor analyzes ITF results against expected results.

Advantages of ITF

The ITF technique has two advantages over test data techniques. First, ITF supports ongoing monitoring of controls as required by SAS 78. Second, applications with ITF can be economically tested without disrupting the user's operations and without the intervention of computer services personnel. Thus, ITF improves the efficiency of the audit and increases the reliability of the audit evidence gathered.

Disadvantages of ITF

The primary disadvantage of ITF is the potential for corrupting the data files of the organization with test data. Steps must be taken to ensure that ITF test transactions do not materially affect financial statements by being improperly aggregated with legitimate transactions. This problem is remedied in two ways: (1) adjusting entries may be processed to remove the effects of ITF from general ledger account balances or (2) data files can be scanned by special software that remove the ITF transactions.

Parallel Simulation

Parallel simulation requires the auditor to write a program that simulates key features or processes of the application under review. The simulated application is then used to reprocess transactions that were previously processed by the production application. This technique is illustrated in Figure 7.20. The results obtained from the simulation are reconciled with the results of the original production run to establish a basis for making inferences about the quality of application processes and controls.

Creating a Simulation Program

A simulation program can be written in any programming language. However, because of the one-time nature of this task, it is a candidate for fourth-generation language generators. The steps involved in performing parallel simulation testing are outlined here.

1. The auditor must first gain a thorough understanding of the application under review. Complete and current documentation of the application is required to construct an accurate simulation.
2. The auditor must then identify those processes and controls in the application that are critical to the audit. These are the processes to be simulated.

FIGURE 7.20

Parallel Simulation Technique

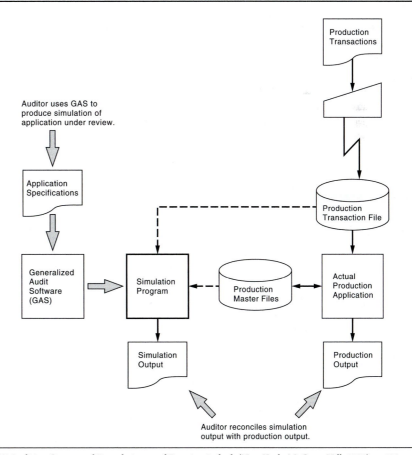

SOURCE: Adapted from R.Weber, *EDP Auditing Conceptual Foundations and Practice*, 2nd ed. (New York: McGraw-Hill, 1988), p. 493.

3. The auditor creates the simulation using a 4GL or **generalized audit software (GAS)**.
4. The auditor runs the simulation program using selected production transactions and master files to produce a set of results.
5. Finally, the auditor evaluates and reconciles the test results with the production results produced in a previous run.

Simulation programs are usually less complex than the production applications they represent. Because simulations contain only the application processes, calculations, and controls relevant to specific audit objectives, the auditor must carefully evaluate differences between test results and production results. Differences in output results occur for two reasons: (1) the inherent crudeness of the simulation program and (2) real deficiencies in the application's processes or controls, which are made apparent by the simulation program.

SUMMARY

This chapter examined issues related to the use of computer-assisted audit tools and techniques (CAATTs) for performing tests of application controls and data extraction. The chapter began by describing three broad classes of application controls: input controls, processing controls, and output controls. Input controls, which govern the gathering and insertion of data into the system, attempt to ensure that all data transactions are valid, accurate, and complete. Processing controls attempt to preserve the integrity of individual records and batches of records within the system and must ensure that an adequate audit trail is preserved. The goal of output controls is to ensure that information produced by the system is not lost, misdirected, or subject to privacy violations. Next, the black box and white box approaches to testing application controls were reviewed. The black box technique involves auditing around the computer. The white box approach requires a detailed understanding of the application's logic. Five types of CAATT that are commonly used for testing application logic were then examined: the test data method, base case system evaluation, tracing, integrated test facility, and parallel simulation.

KEY TERMS

access test	field interrogation
accuracy test	file interrogation
audit trail test	generalized audit software (GAS)
authenticity test	generalized data input system (GDIS)
base case system evaluation (BCSE)	generalized validation module (GVM)
batch controls	hash total
black-box approach	input controls
bursting	integrated test facility (ITF)
check digit	operator intervention controls
completeness test	output controls
data control	output spooling
error file	parallel simulation
error report	processing controls

record interrogation
redundancy test
rounding error test
run-to-run controls
salami fraud
sequence check
test data method
tracing

transaction code
transaction listing
transaction log
transcription error
transposition error
validated data file
validation controls
white-box approach

REVIEW QUESTIONS

1. What are the broad classes of input controls?
2. Explain the importance of source documents and associated control techniques.
3. Give one example of an error that is detected by a check digit control.
4. What are the primary objectives of a batch control?
5. Classify each of the following as a field, record, or file interrogation:
   a. Limit check
   b. Validity check
   c. Version check
   d. Missing data check
   e. Sign check
   f. Expiration date check
   g. Numeric-alphabetic data check
   h. Sequence check
   i. Zero-value check
   j. Header label check
   k. Range check
   l. Reasonableness check
6. Compare the three common error-handling techniques discussed in the text.
7. What are the five major components of a GDIS?
8. What are the three categories of processing controls?
9. If all of the inputs have been validated before processing, then what purpose do run-to-run controls serve?
10. What is the objective of a transaction log?
11. How can spooling present an added exposure?

DISCUSSION QUESTIONS

1. The field calls for an "M" for married or an "S" for single. The entry is a "2." What control will detect this error?
2. The firm allows no more than 10 hours of overtime a week. An employee entered "15" in the field. Which control will detect this error?
3. The password was "CANARY"; the employee entered "CAANARY." Which control will detect this error?
4. The inventory item number was omitted on the purchase order. Which control will detect this error?
5. The order entry system will allow a 10 percent variation in list price. For example, an item with a list price of $1 could be sold for 90 cents or $1.10 without any system interference. The cost of the item is $3 but the cashier entered $2. Which control would detect this error?
6. How does privacy relate to output control?
7. What are some typical problems with passwords?
8. What are the three categories of processing control?
9. Output controls ensure that output is not lost, misdirected, or corrupted and that privacy is not violated. What are some output exposures, or situations where output is at risk?
10. Input validation includes field interrogation that examines the data in individual fields. List four validation tests and indicate what is checked in each.
11. What is record interrogation? Give two examples.

MULTIPLE-CHOICE QUESTIONS

1. CMA 685 5-28

   Routines that use the computer to check the validity and accuracy of transaction data during input are called
   a. operating systems.
   b. edit programs.
   c. compiler programs.
   d. integrated test facilities.
   e. compatibility tests.

2. CMA 686 5-10

   An edit of individual transactions in a direct access file processing system usually
   a. takes place in a separate computer run.
   b. takes place in an online mode as transactions are entered.
   c. takes place during a backup procedure.
   d. is not performed due to time constraints.
   e. is not necessary.

3. CMA Adapted 686 5-13

   An example of an input control is
   a. making sure that output is distributed to the proper people.
   b. monitoring the work of programmers.
   c. collecting accurate statistics of historical transactions while gathering data.
   d. recalculating an amount to ensure its accuracy.
   e. having another person review the design of a business form.

4. A control designed to validate a transaction at the point of data entry is
   a. recalculation of a batch total.
   b. a record count.
   c. a check digit.
   d. checkpoints.
   e. recalculation of a hash total.

5. CMA 687 5-8

   In a manual system, records of current activity are posted from a journal to a ledger. In a computer system, current records from a(n)
   a. table file are updated to a transaction file.
   b. index file are updated to a master file.
   c. transaction file are updated to a master file.
   d. master file are updated to a year-to-date file.
   e. current balance file are updated to an index file.

6. CMA 1287 5-1

   The primary functions of a computerized information system include
   a. input, processing, and output.
   b. input, processing, output, and storage.
   c. input, processing, output, and control.
   d. input, processing, output, storage, and control.
   e. collecting, sorting, summarizing, and reporting.

7. CMA 1287 5-16

   An employee in the receiving department keyed in a shipment from a remote terminal and inadvertently omitted the purchase order number. The best systems control to detect this error would be a
   a. batch total.
   b. completeness test.
   c. sequence check.
   d. reasonableness test.
   e. compatibility test.

8. CMA 1287 5-15

   In an automated payroll processing environment, a department manager substituted the time card for a terminated employee with a time card for a fictitious employee. The fictitious employee had the same pay rate and hours worked as the terminated employee. The best control technique to detect this action using employee identification numbers would be a
   a. batch total.
   b. record count.
   c. hash total.
   d. subsequent check.
   e. financial total.

9. CMA 1287 5-17

   The reporting of accounting information plays a central role in the regulation of business operations. The importance of sound internal control practices is underscored by the Foreign Corrupt Practices Act of 1977, which requires publicly owned U.S. corporations to maintain systems of internal control that meet certain minimum standards. Preventive controls are an integral part of virtually all accounting processing systems, and much of the information generated by the accounting system is used for preventive control purposes. Which one of the following is *not* an essential element of a sound preventive control system?

a. separation of responsibilities for the recording, custodial, and authorization functions

b. sound personnel practices

c. documentation of policies and procedures

d. implementation of state-of-the-art software and hardware

e. physical protection of assets

10. Which of the following is *not* a test for identifying application errors?

a. reconciling the source code

b. reviewing test results

c. retesting the program

d. testing the authority table

11. Which of the following is *not* a common type of white-box test of controls?

a. completeness tests

b. redundancy tests

c. inference tests

d. authenticity tests

12. All of the following are examples of source document control except

a. prenumbering source documents.

b. limiting access to source documents.

c. supervising the bursting of source documents.

d. checking the sequence of numbers to identify missing documents.

13. The correct purchase order number, 123456, was incorrectly recorded as shown in the solutions. All of the following are transcription errors except

a. 1234567

b. 12345

c. 124356

d. 123457

14. Which of the following is correct?

a. Check digits should be used for all data codes.

b. Check digits are always placed at the end of data codes.

c. Check digits do not affect processing efficiency.

d. Check digits are designed to detect transcription errors.

15. Which statement is NOT correct? The goal of batch controls is to ensure that during processing

a. transactions are not omitted.

b. transactions are not added.

c. transactions are processed more than once.

d. an audit trail is created.

16. The data control clerk performs all of the following duties except

a. maintaining the batch control log.

b. computing (or recomputing) batch control data.

c. reconciling the output results to the batch control log.

d. destroying batch control logs when reconciled.

17. An example of a hash total is

a. total payroll checks—$12,315.

b. total number of employees—10.

c. sum of the social security numbers—12,555,437,251.

d. none of the above.

18. Which statement is NOT true? A batch control log

a. is prepared by the user department.

b. records the record count.

c. indicates any error codes.

d. is maintained as a part of the audit trail.

19. Which of the following is an example of a field interrogation?

a. reasonableness check

b. sign check

c. sequence check

d. numeric/alphabetic check

20. Which of the following is an example of record interrogation?

a. sequence check

b. zero value check

c. limit check

d. range check

21. Which input validation check would detect a payment made to a nonexistent vendor?

a. missing data check

b. numeric/alphabetic check

c. range check

d. validity check

22. The employee entered "40" in the "hours worked per day" field. Which check would detect this unintentional error?

a. numeric/alphabetic data check

b. sign check

c. limit check

d. missing data check

23. A specific inventory record indicates that there are twelve items on hand and a customer purchased two of the items. When recording the order, the data entry clerk mistakenly entered twenty items sold. Which check would detect this error?
    a. numeric/alphabetic data check
    b. sign check
    c. sequence check
    d. range check

24. Which check is *not* a file interrogation?
    a. header label
    b. expiration date check
    c. sequence check
    d. version check

25. Which statement is *not* correct?
    a. The purpose of file interrogation is to ensure that the correct file is being processed by the system.
    b. File interrogation checks are particularly important for master files.
    c. Header labels are prepared manually and affixed to the outside of the tape or disk.
    d. An expiration date check prevents a file from being deleted before it expires.

26. A computer operator was in a hurry and accidentally used the wrong master file to process a transaction file. As a result, the accounts receivable master file was erased. Which control would prevent this from happening?
    a. header label check
    b. expiration date check
    c. version check
    d. validity check

27. Which of the following is NOT a component of the generalized data input system?
    a. generalized validation module
    b. validated data file
    c. updated master file
    d. error file

28. Advantages of the generalized data input system include all of the following except
    a. control over quality of data input.
    b. automatic calculation of run-to-run totals.
    c. company-wide standards for data validation.
    d. development of a reusable module for data validation.

29. Run-to-run control totals can be used for all of the following except
    a. to ensure that all data input is validated.
    b. to ensure that only transactions of a similar type are being processed.
    c. to ensure the records are in sequence and are not missing.
    d. to ensure that no transaction is omitted.

30. Methods used to maintain an audit trail in a computerized environment include all of the following except
    a. transaction logs.
    b. unique transaction identifiers.
    c. data encryption.
    d. log of automatic transactions.

31. Risk exposures associated with creating an output file as an intermediate step in the printing process (spooling) include all of the following actions by a computer criminal except
    a. gaining access to the output file and changing critical data values.
    b. using a remote printer and incurring operating inefficiencies.
    c. making a copy of the output file and using the copy to produce illegal output reports.
    d. printing an extra hard copy of the output file.

32. Which statement is NOT correct?
    a. Only successful transactions are recorded on a transaction log.
    b. Unsuccessful transactions are recorded in an error file.
    c. A transaction log is a temporary file.
    d. A hard copy transaction listing is provided to users.

PROBLEMS

1. **Input Validation**

   Identify the types of input validation techniques for the following inputs to the payroll system. Explain the controls provided by each of these techniques.
   a. Operator access number to payroll file
   b. New employee
   c. Employee name
   d. Employee number
   e. Social Security number
   f. Rate per hour or salary
   g. Marital status
   h. Number of dependents

i. Cost center
j. Regular hours worked
k. Overtime hours worked
l. Total employees this payroll period

2. Processing Controls

CMA 691 4-2

Unless adequate controls are implemented, the rapid advance of computer technology can reduce a firm's ability to detect errors and fraud. Therefore, one of the critical responsibilities of the management team in firms where computers are used is the security and control of information service activities.

During the design stage of a system, information system controls are planned to ensure the reliability of data. A well-designed system can prevent both intentional and unintentional alteration or destruction of data. These data controls can be classified as (1) input controls, (2) processing controls, and (3) output controls.

Required:

For each of the three data control categories listed, provide two specific controls and explain how each control contributes to ensuring the reliability of data. Use the following format for your answer.

Control Category	Specific Controls	Contribution to Data Reliability

3. Input Controls and Data Processing

You have been hired by a catalog company to computerize its sales order entry forms. Approximately 60 percent of all orders are received over the telephone, with the remainder either mailed or faxed in. The company wants the phone orders to be input as they are received. The mail and fax orders can be batched together in groups of fifty and submitted for data entry as they become ready. The following information is collected for each order:

- Customer number (if a customer does not have one, one needs to be assigned)
- Customer name
- Address
- Payment method (credit card or money order)
- Credit card number and expiration date (if necessary)
- Items ordered and quantity
- Unit price

Required:

Determine control techniques to make sure that all orders are entered accurately into the system. Also, discuss any differences in control measures between the batch and the real-time processing.

4. Write an essay explaining the following three methods of correcting errors in data entry: immediate correction, creation of an error file, and rejection of the batch.

5. Many techniques can be used to control input data. Write a one-page essay discussing three techniques.

6. The presence of an audit trail is critical to the integrity of the accounting information system. Write a one-page essay discussing three of the techniques used to preserve the audit trail.

7. Write an essay comparing and contrasting the following audit techniques based on costs and benefits:

- test data method
- base case system evaluation
- tracing
- integrated test facility
- parallel simulation

CHAPTER 8

Data Structures and CAATTs for Data Extraction

LEARNING OBJECTIVES

After studying this chapter, you should:

- Understand the components of data structures and how these are used to achieve data-processing operations.

- Be familiar with structures used in flat-file systems, including sequential, indexes, hashing, and pointer structures.

- Be familiar with relational database structures and the principles of normalization.

- Understand the features, advantages, and disadvantages of the embedded audit module approach to data extraction.

- Know the capabilities and primary features of generalized audit software.

- Become familiar with the more commonly used features of ACL.

This chapter examines data structures and the use of CAATTs for data extraction and analysis. The chapter opens with a review of data structures, which constitute the physical and logical arrangement of data in files and databases. Flat-file, navigational database, and relational database structures are examined. Considerable attention is devoted to relational databases, since this is the most common data structure used by modern business organizations. The coverage includes relational concepts, terminology, table-linking techniques, database normalization, and database design procedures.

Understanding how data are organized and accessed is central to using a data extraction CAATT. Auditors make extensive use of these tools in gathering accounting data for testing application controls and in performing substantive tests. In the previous chapter we studied how CAATTs are used to test application controls directly. The data extraction tools discussed in this chapter are used to analyze the data processed by an application rather than the application itself. By analyzing data retrieved from computer files, the auditor can make inferences about the presence and functionality of controls in the application that processed the data.

Another important use of data extraction software is in performing substantive tests. Most audit testing occurs in the substantive-testing phase of the audit. These procedures are called *substantive tests* because they are used for, but not limited to, the following:

- Determining the correct value of inventory.
- Determining the accuracy of prepayments and accruals.
- Confirming accounts receivable with customers.
- Searching for unrecorded liabilities.

CAATTs for data extraction software fall into two general categories: embedded audit modules and general audit software. The chapter describes the features, advantages, and disadvantages of the embedded audit module (EAM) approach. It then outlines typical functions and uses of generalized audit software (GAS). The chapter closes with a review of the key features of ACL (audit command language), the leading product in the GAS market.

DATA STRUCTURES

Data structures have two fundamental components: organization and access method. **Organization** refers to the way records are physically arranged on the secondary storage device. This may be either *sequential* or *random*. The records in sequential files are stored in contiguous locations that occupy a specified area of disk space. Records in random files are stored without regard for their physical relationship to other records of the same file. Random files may have records distributed throughout a disk. The **access method** is the technique used to locate records and to navigate through the database or file. While several specific techniques are used, in general, they can be classified as either direct access or sequential access methods.

Since no single structure is best for all processing tasks, different structures are used for storing different types of accounting data. Selecting a structure, therefore, involves a trade-off between desirable features. The criteria that influence the selection of the data structure are listed in Table 8.1.

In the following section, we examine several data structures. These are divided between flat-file and database systems. In practice, organizations may employ any of these approaches in various combinations for storing their accounting data.

TABLE 8.1	**File Processing Operations**

1. Retrieve a record from the file based on its primary key.
2. Insert a record into a file.
3. Update a record in the file.
4. Read a complete file of records.
5. Find the next record in the file.
6. Scan a file for records with common secondary keys.
7. Delete a record from a file.

Flat-File Structures

Recall from Chapter 4 that the flat-file model describes an environment in which individual data files are not integrated with other files. End users in this environment own their data files rather than share them with other users. Data processing is thus performed by standalone applications rather than integrated systems. The flat-file approach is a single view model that characterizes legacy systems. Data files are structured, formatted, and arranged to suit the specific needs of the owner or primary user. Such structuring, however, may omit or corrupt data attributes that are essential to other users, thus preventing successful integration of systems across the organization.

Sequential Structure

Figure 8.1 illustrates the **sequential structure**, which is typically called the *sequential access method*. Under this arrangement, for example, the record with key value 1875 is placed in the physical storage space immediately following the record with key value 1874. Thus, all records in the file lie in contiguous storage spaces in a specified sequence (ascending or descending) arranged by their primary key.

Sequential files are simple and easy to process. The application starts at the beginning of the file and processes each record in sequence. Of the file-processing operations in Table 8.1, this approach is efficient for Operations 4 and 5, which are, respectively, reading an entire file and finding the next record in the file. Also, when a large portion of the file (perhaps 20 percent or more) is to be processed in one operation, the sequential structure is efficient for record updating (Operation 3 in Table 8.1). An example of this is payroll processing, where 100 percent of the employee records on the payroll file are processed each payroll period. However, when only a small portion of the file (or a single record) is being processed, this approach is not efficient. The sequential structure is not a practical option for the remaining operations listed in Table 8.1. For example, retrieving a single record (Operation 1) from a sequential file requires reading all the records that precede the desired record. On average, this means reading half the file each time a single record is retrieved. The sequential access method does not permit accessing a record directly. Files that require direct access operations need a different data structure. The following data structures address this need.

FIGURE 8.1   Sequential Storage and Access Method

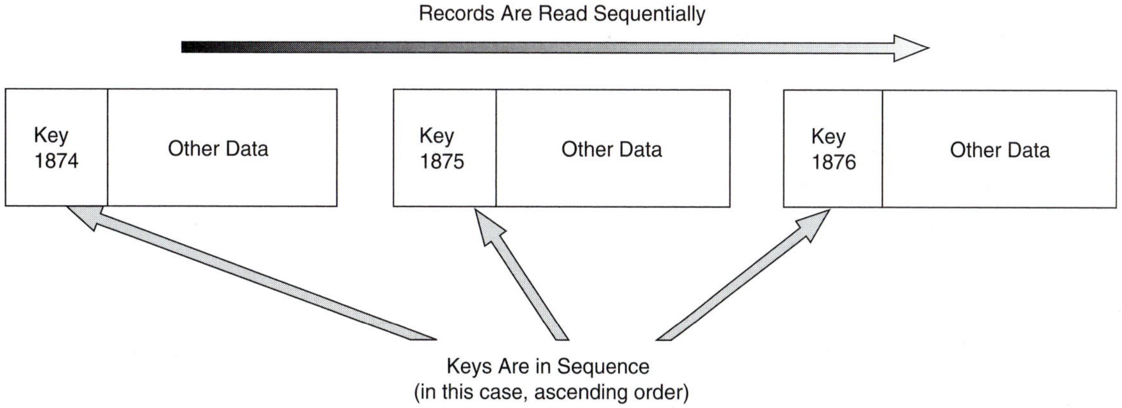

Records Are Read Sequentially

| Key 1874 | Other Data | Key 1875 | Other Data | Key 1876 | Other Data |

Keys Are in Sequence
(in this case, ascending order)

Indexed Structure

An **indexed structure** is so named because, in addition to the actual data file, there exists a separate index that is itself a file of record addresses. This index contains the numeric value of the physical disk storage location (cylinder, surface, and record block) for each record in the associated data file. The data file itself may be organized either sequentially or randomly. Figure 8.2 presents an example of an indexed random file.

Records in an **indexed random file** are dispersed throughout a disk without regard for their physical proximity to other related records. In fact, records belonging to the same file may reside on different disks. A record's physical location is unimportant as long as the operating system software can find it when needed. This locating is accomplished by searching the index for the desired key value, reading the corresponding storage location (address), and then moving the disk read-write head to the address location. When a new record is added to the file, the data management software selects a vacant disk location, stores the record, and adds the new address to the index.

The physical organization of the index itself may be either sequential (by key value) or random. Random indexes are easier to maintain, in terms of adding records, because new key records are simply added to the end of the index without regard to their sequence. Indexes in sequential order are more difficult to maintain because new record keys must be inserted between existing keys. One advantage of a sequential index is that it can be searched rapidly. Because of its logical arrangement, algorithms can be used to speed the search through the index to find a key value. This advantage becomes particularly important for large data files with corresponding large indexes.

FIGURE 8.2   **Indexed Random File Structure**

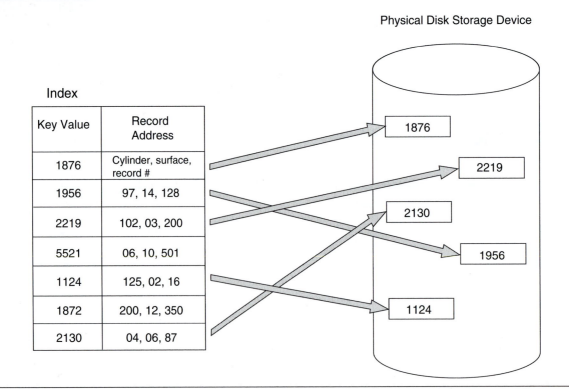

The principal advantage of indexed random files is in operations involving the processing of individual records (Operations 1, 2, 3, and 6 in Table 8.1). Another advantage is their efficient use of disk storage. Records may be placed wherever there is space without concern for maintaining contiguous storage locations. However, random files are not efficient structures for operations that involve processing a large portion of a file. A great deal of access time may be required to access an entire file of records that are randomly dispersed throughout the storage device. Sequential files are more efficient for this purpose.

The **Virtual Storage access method (VSAM)** structure is used for very large files that require routine batch processing and a moderate degree of individual record processing. For instance, the customer file of a public utility company will be processed in batch mode for billing purposes and directly accessed in response to individual customer queries. Because of its sequential organization, the VSAM structure can be searched sequentially for efficient batch processing. Figure 8.3 illustrates how VSAM uses indexes to allow direct access processing.

The VSAM structure is used for files that often occupy several cylinders of contiguous storage on a disk. To find a specific record location, the VSAM file uses a number of indexes that describe in summarized form the contents of each cylinder. For example, in Figure 8.3, we are searching for a record with the key value 2546. The access method goes first to the overall file index, which contains only the highest key value for each cylinder in the file, and determines that Record 2546 is somewhere on Cylinder 99. A quick scan of the surface index for Cylinder 99 reveals that the record is on Surface 3 of Cylinder 99. VSAM indexes do not provide an exact physical address for a single

FIGURE 8.3 **VSAM Used for Direct Access**

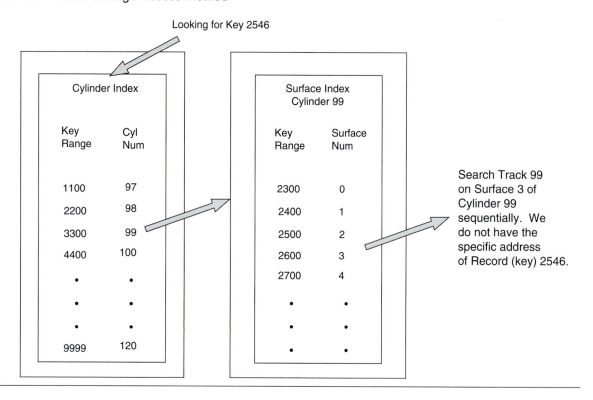

VSAM – Virtual Storage Access Method

record. However, they identify the disk track where the record in question resides. The last step is to search the identified track sequentially to find the record with key value 2546.

The VSAM structure is moderately effective for Operations 1 and 3 in Table 8.1. Because VSAM must read multiple indexes and search the track sequentially, the average access time for a single record is slower than the indexed sequential or indexed random structures. Direct access speed is sacrificed to achieve very efficient performance in Operations 4, 5, and 6.

The greatest disadvantage with the VSAM structure is that it does not perform record insertion operations (Operation 2) efficiently. Because the VSAM file is organized sequentially, inserting a new record into the file requires the physical relocation of all the records located beyond the point of insertion. The indexes that describe this physical arrangement must, therefore, also be updated with each insertion. This is extremely time-consuming and disruptive to operations. One method of dealing with this problem is to store new records in an overflow area that is physically separate from the other data records in the file. Figure 8.4 shows how this is done.

A VSAM file has three physical components: the indexes, the prime data storage area, and the overflow area. Rather than inserting a new record directly into the prime area, the data management software places it in a randomly selected location in the overflow area. It then records the address of the location in a special field (called a *pointer*) in the prime area. Later, when searching for the record, the indexes direct the access method to the track location where the record *should* reside. The pointer at that location reveals the record's *actual* location in the overflow area. Thus, accessing a record may involve searching the indexes, searching the track in the prime data area, and finally

FIGURE 8.4   Inserting a Record into a VSAM File

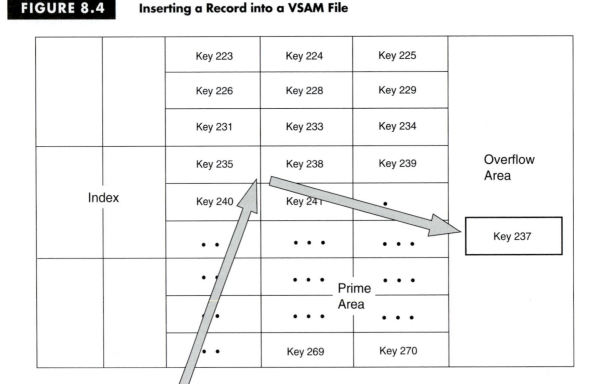

Insert New Record with Key Value = 237

searching the overflow area. This slows data access time for both direct access and batch processing.

Periodically, the VSAM file must be reorganized by integrating the overflow records into the prime area and then reconstructing the indexes. This process involves time, cost, and disruption to operations. Therefore, when a file is highly volatile (records are added or deleted frequently), the maintenance burden associated with the VSAM approach tends to render it impractical. However, for large, stable files that need both direct access and batch processing, the VSAM structure is a popular option.

Hashing Structure

A **hashing structure** employs an algorithm that converts the primary key of a record directly into a storage address. Hashing eliminates the need for a separate index. By calculating the address, rather than reading it from an index, records can be retrieved more quickly. Figure 8.5 illustrates the hashing approach.

This example assumes an inventory file with 100,000 inventory items. The algorithm divides the inventory number (the primary key) into a prime number. Recall that a prime number is one that can be divided only by itself and 1 without leaving a residual value. Therefore, the calculation will always produce a value that can be translated into a storage location. Hence, the residual 6.27215705 becomes Cylinder 272, Surface 15, and Record number 705. The hashing structure uses a random file organization because the process of calculating residuals and converting them into storage locations produces widely dispersed record addresses.

FIGURE 8.5

Hashing Technique with Pointer to Relocate the Collision Record

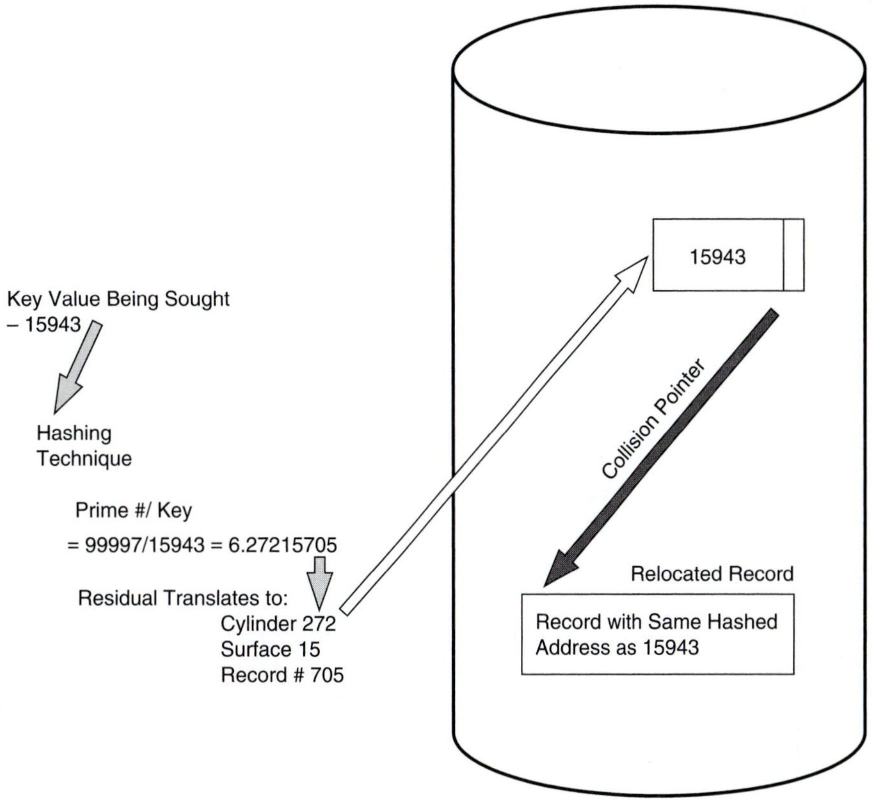

The principal advantage of hashing is access speed. Calculating a record's address is faster than searching for it through an index. This structure is suited to applications that require rapid access to individual records in performing Operations 1, 2, 3, and 6 in Table 8.1.

The hashing structure has two significant disadvantages. First, this technique does not use storage space efficiently. The storage location chosen for a record is a mathematical function of its primary key value. The algorithm will never select some disk locations because they do not correspond to legitimate key values. As much as one-third of the disk pack may be wasted.

The second disadvantage is the reverse of the first. Different record keys may generate the same (or similar) residual, which translates into the same address. This is called a *collision* because two records cannot be stored at the same location. One solution to this problem is to randomly select a location for the second record and place a pointer to it from the first (the calculated) location. This technique is represented by the dark arrow in Figure 8.5.

The collision problem slows down access to records. Locating a record displaced in this manner involves first calculating its theoretical address, searching that location, and then determining the actual address from the pointer contained in the record at that location. This has an additional implication for Operation 7 in Table 8.1—deleting a record from a file. If the first record is deleted from the file, the pointer to the second (collision) record will also be deleted and the address of the second record will be lost. This can be dealt with in two ways: (1) After deleting the first record, the collision record can be physically relocated to its calculated address, which is now vacant; or (2) The first record is marked "deleted" but is left in place to preserve the pointer to the collision record.

Pointer Structures

Figure 8.6 presents the **pointer structure**, which in this example is used to create a *linked-list file*. This approach stores in a field of one record the address (pointer) of a related record. The records in this type of file are spread over the entire disk without concern for their physical proximity with other related records. The pointers provide connections between the records. In this example, Record 124 points to the location of Record 125, Record 125 points to 126, and so on. The last record in the list contains an end-of-file marker.

Pointers may also be used to link records between files. Figure 8.7 shows an accounts receivable record with three pointers. The first pointer links the AR record to the next AR record within the AR file. The second and third pointers link AR records to sales invoice and remittance advice records, respectively. By accessing an accounts receivable record (for example, Customer 4456), we can locate all sales invoices and remittances pertaining to the account. These records may then be displayed on a computer screen or printed for review. The next transaction record (a sale or cash receipt) to be processed will be added to the end of the appropriate linked-list. The address of the record will then be stored in the preceding record to provide future access.

Types of Pointers.   Figure 8.8 shows three types of pointers: physical address, relative address, and logical key pointer. A **physical address pointer** contains the actual disk storage location (cylinder, surface, and record number) needed by the disk controller. This physical address allows the system to access the record directly without obtaining further information. This method has the advantage of speed, since it does not need to be manipulated further to determine a record's location. However, it also has two disadvantages: First, if the related record is moved from one disk location to another, the pointer must be changed. This is a problem when disks are periodically reorganized or

FIGURE 8.6

A Linked-List File

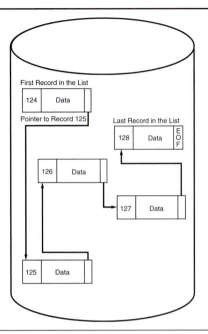

FIGURE 8.7   Pointers within and between Files

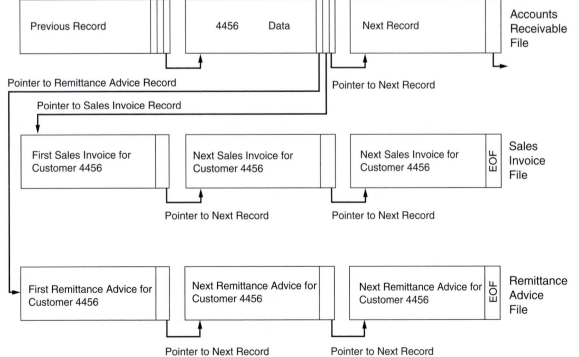

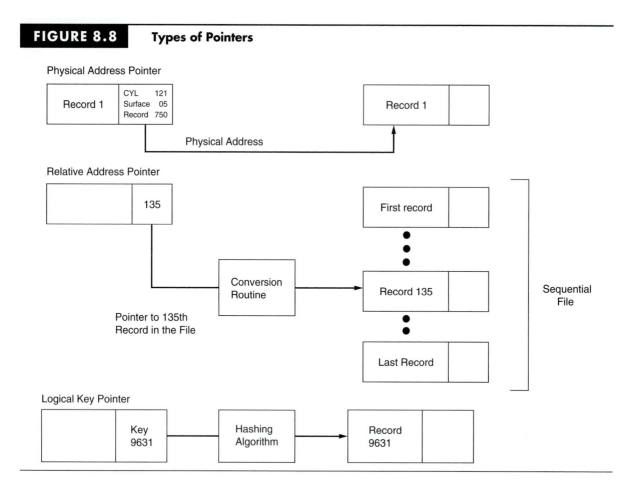

FIGURE 8.8   **Types of Pointers**

copied. Second, the physical pointers bear no logical relationship to the records they identify. If a pointer is lost or destroyed and cannot be recovered, the record it references is also lost.

A **relative address pointer** contains the relative position of a record in the file. For example, the pointer could specify the 135th record in the file. This must be further manipulated to convert it to the actual physical address. The conversion software calculates this by using the physical address of the beginning of the file, the length of each record in the file, and the relative address of the record being sought.

A **logical key pointer** contains the primary key of the related record. This key value is then converted into the record's physical address by a hashing algorithm.

Hierarchical and Network Database Structures

Early hierarchical and network database models employed many of the preceding flat-file techniques as well as new proprietary database structures. A major difference between the two approaches is the degree of process integration and data sharing that can be achieved. Two-dimensional flat files exist as independent data structures that are not linked logically or physically to other files. Database models were designed to support flat-file systems already in place, while allowing the organization to move to new levels of data integration.

By providing linkages between logically related files, a third (depth) dimension is added to better serve multiple-user needs. For example, Figure 8.7 illustrates the use of pointers between files in an example of a simple hierarchical database structure. An example of a complex network database structure is illustrated by Figure 8.9.

Figure 8.9 illustrates a many-to-many association between an inventory file and a vendor file. Each vendor supplies many inventory items and each item is supplied by more than one vendor. Notice that each inventory and vendor record exists only once, but there is a separate link record for each item the vendor supplies and for each supplier of a given inventory item. This arrangement of pointers allows us to find all vendors of a given inventory item and all inventories supplied by each vendor.

Link files may also contain accounting data. For example, the link file in Figure 8.9 shows that the price for Inventory Number 1356 from Vendor Number 1 ($10) is not the same price charged by Vendor Number 3 ($12). Similarly, the delivery time (days-lead time) and discount offered (terms) are different. Transaction characteristics such as these can vary between vendors and even between different items from the same vendor. Data that are unique to the item–vendor associations are stored in the unique link file record, as shown in the figure.

FIGURE 8.9   A Link File in a Many-to-Many Relationship

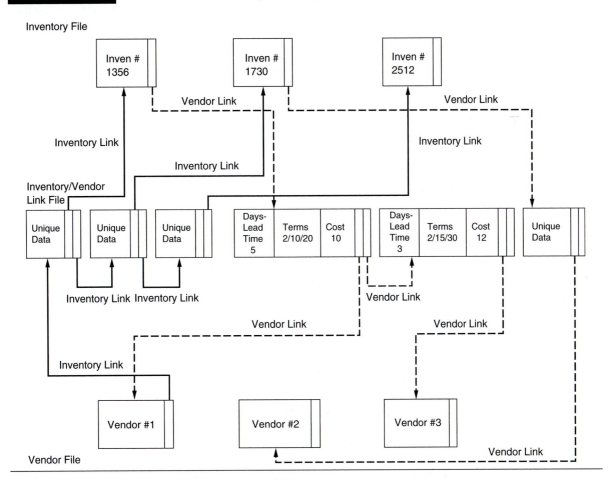

FIGURE 8.10	Indexed Sequential File

Emp Num Index

Key Value	Record Address
101	1
102	2
103	3
104	4
105	5

Employee Table

Emp Num	Name	Address	Skill Code	YTD Earnings
101	L. Smith	15 Main St.	891	15000
102	S. Buell	107 Hill Top	379	10000
103	T. Hill	40 Barclay St.	891	20000
104	M. Green	251 Ule St.	209	19000
105	H. Litt	423 Rauch Ave.	772	18000

YTD Earnings Index

Key Value	Address
20000	3
19000	4
18000	5
15000	1
10000	2

Relational Database Structure, Concepts, and Terminology

The following sections examine the principles that underlie the relational database model and the techniques, rules, and procedures for creating relational tables. You will also see how tables are linked to other tables to permit complex data representations.

Relational databases are based on the **indexed sequential file** structure. This structure, illustrated in Figure 8.10, uses an index in conjunction with a sequential file organization. It facilitates both direct access to individual records and batch processing of the entire file. Multiple indexes can be used to create a cross-reference, called an **inverted list,** which allows even more flexible access to data. Two indexes are shown in Figure 8.10. One contains the employee number (primary key) for uniquely locating records in the file. The second index contains record addresses arranged by year-to-date earnings. Using this nonunique field as a secondary key permits all employee records to be viewed in ascending or descending order according to earnings. Alternatively, individual records with selected earnings balances can be displayed. Indexes may be created for each attribute in the file, allowing data to be viewed from a multitude of perspectives.

Relational Database Theory

E. F. Codd originally proposed the principles of the relational model in the late 1960s.[1] The formal model has its foundations in relational algebra and set theory, which provide the theoretical basis for most of the data manipulation operations used. Accordingly, a system is relational if it:

1. Represents data in the form of two-dimensional tables.
2. Supports the relational algebra functions of restrict, project, and join.

These three algebra functions are explained below:

Restrict: Extracts specified rows from a specified table. This operation, illustrated in Figure 8.11(a), creates a virtual table (one that does not physically exist) that is a subset of the original table.

Project: Extracts specified attributes (columns) from a table to create a virtual table. This is presented in Figure 8.11(b).

---

1 Refer to "Defining Data" under the Index section of ACL's online Help feature for a detailed explanation of this process.

| FIGURE 8.11 | The Relational Algebra Functions Restrict, Project, and Join |

(a) Restrict

(b) Project

(c) Join

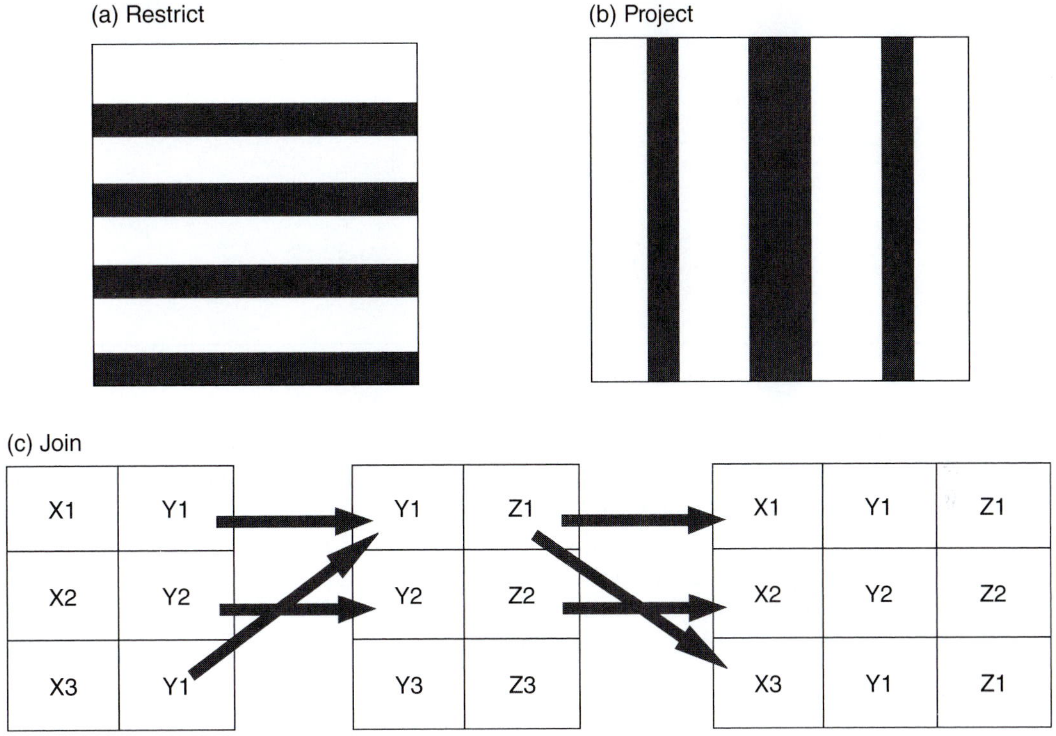

Join: Builds a new physical table from two tables consisting of all concatenated pairs of rows, from each table, as shown in Figure 8.11(c).

Although restrict, project, and join is not the complete set of relational functions, it is a useful subset that satisfies most business information needs.

Relational Database Concepts

In this section, we review basic concepts, terminology, and techniques common to relational database systems. These building blocks are then used later in the chapter to design a small database from scratch.

Entity, Occurrence, and Attributes

An **entity** is anything about which the organization wishes to capture data. Entities may be physical, such as inventories, customers, or employees. They may also be conceptual, such as sales (to a customer), accounts receivable (AR), or accounts payable (AP). Systems designers identify entities and prepare a model of them like the one presented in Figure 8.12. This **data model** is the blueprint for ultimately creating the physical database. The graphical representation used to depict the model is called an **entity relationship (ER) diagram**. As a matter of convention, each entity in a data model is named in the singular noun form, such as "Customer" rather than "Customers." The term **occurrence** is used to describe the number of instances or records that pertain to a specific entity. For example, if an organization has 100 employees, the Employee entity is said

FIGURE 8.12

**Data Model Using
an Entity
Relationship
Diagram**

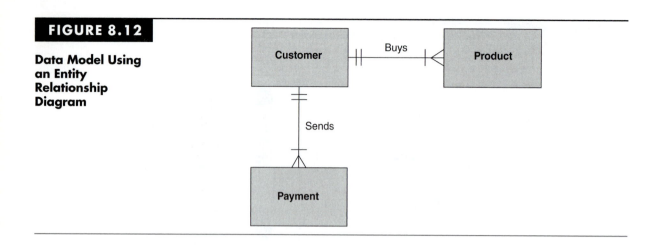

to consist of 100 occurrences. **Attributes** are the data elements that define an entity. For example, an Employee entity may be defined by the following partial set of attributes: Name, Address, Job Skill, Years of Service, and Hourly Rate of Pay. Each occurrence in the Employee entity consists of the same types of attributes, but values of each attribute will vary among occurrences. Because attributes are the logical and relevant characteristics of an entity, they are unique to it. In other words, the same attribute should not be used to define two different entities.

Associations and Cardinality

The labeled line connecting two entities in a data model describes the nature of the **association** between them. This association is represented with a verb, such as ships, requests, or receives. **Cardinality** is the degree of association between two entities. Simply stated, cardinality describes the number of possible occurrences in one table that are associated with a single occurrence in a related table. Four basic forms of cardinality are possible: zero or one (0,1), one and only one (1,1), zero or many (0,M), and one or many (1,M). These are combined to represent logical associations between entities. The value of the upper cardinalities at each end of the association line defines the association. For example, a (0,1) cardinality at one end and a (1,M) cardinality at the other is a (1:M) association. Figure 8.13 presents several examples of entity associations, which are discussed next.

Example 1 (1:1). Assume that a company has 1,000 employees but only 100 of them are sales staff. Assume also that each salesperson is assigned a company car, but nonsales staff are not. Example 1 in Figure 8.13 shows that for every occurrence (record) in the Employee entity, there is a possibility of zero or one occurrence in the Company Car entity.

When determining the cardinality values in an entity association, select a single occurrence (record) of one entity and answer the following question: What are the minimum and maximum number of records that may be associated with the single record that has been selected? For example, selecting an Employee entity record and looking toward the Company Car entity, we see two possible values. If the selected Employee record is that of a salesperson, then he or she is assigned one (and only one) company car. This particular Employee record, therefore, is associated with only one record in the Company Car entity. If, however, the selected Employee record is that of a nonsalesperson, then the individual would be assigned no (zero) car. The Employee record in this case is associated with zero Company Car records. Thus, the minimum cardinality is

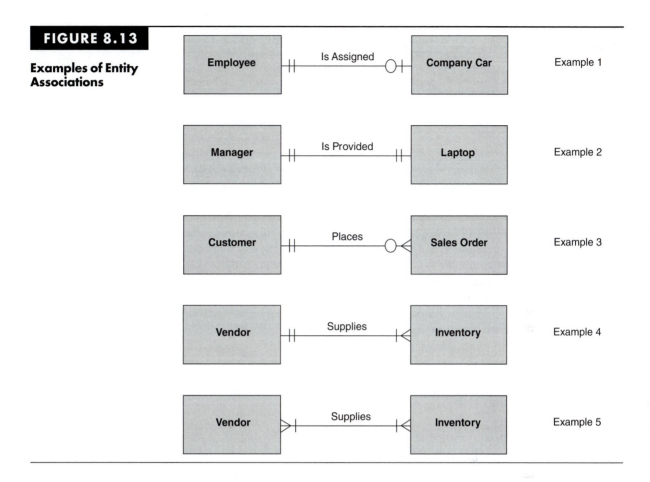

FIGURE 8.13

Examples of Entity Associations

Employee — Is Assigned — Company Car — Example 1

Manager — Is Provided — Laptop — Example 2

Customer — Places — Sales Order — Example 3

Vendor — Supplies — Inventory — Example 4

Vendor — Supplies — Inventory — Example 5

zero and the maximum cardinality is one. A circle and a short line intersecting the line connecting the two entities depict this degree of cardinality. Notice that from the Employee entity perspective, the cardinality is shown at the Company Car end of the association line. Now select a Company Car record and look back at the Employee entity. Because each company car is assigned to only one employee, both the minimum and maximum number of associated records is one. Two short intersecting lines at the Employee end of the association line signify this cardinality.

Example 2 (1:1).   Example 2 illustrates a situation in which each record in one entity is always associated with one (and only one) record in the associated entity. In this case, each company laptop computer is assigned to only one manager, and every manager is assigned only one computer. Two short lines intersecting the connecting line at both ends depict this cardinality.

Example 3 (1:M).   Example 3 presents the relationship between Customer and Sales Order entities. Notice that the minimum number of Sales Order records per Customer record is zero and the maximum is many. This is because in any given period (a year or month) to which the Sales Order entity pertains, a particular customer may have purchased nothing (zero Sales Order records) or purchased several times (many records). From the perspective of the Sales Order entity, however, every record is associated with one and only one customer. The crow's foot symbol (which gives this form of notation its name) depicts the many cardinalities at the Sales Order end of the association line.

Example 4 (1:M).   Example 4 represents a situation in which each specific item of inventory is supplied by one and only one Vendor, and each Vendor supplies one or many different inventory items to the company. Contrast this (1:M) association with Example 5 next.

Example 5 (M:M).   To illustrate the many-to-many association, we again use a Vendor and Inventory relationship in Example 5. This time, however, the company has a policy of purchasing the same types of inventory from multiple suppliers. Management may choose to do this to ensure that they get the best prices or avoid becoming dependent on a single supplier. Under such a policy, each Vendor record is associated with one or many Inventory records, and each Inventory record is associated with one or many Vendors.

Examples 4 and 5 demonstrate how cardinality reflects the business rules in place within an organization. The database designer must obtain a thorough understanding of how the client-company and specific users conduct business to properly design the data model. If the data model is wrong, the resulting database tables will also be wrong. Examples 4 and 5 are both valid but different options and, as we shall see, require different database designs.

Alternative Cardinality Notations.   The cardinality notation technique shown in Figure 8.13 is called "crow's foot." An alternative method is to write the cardinality values on each end of the association line connecting the two entities. Some database designers explicitly show both the upper and lower cardinality values. Some choose a shorthand version that notes only the upper cardinality. For homework assignments, your instructor will advise you of the preferred method to use.

The Physical Database Tables

Physical database tables are constructed from the data model with each entity in the model being transformed into a separate physical table. Across the top of each table are attributes forming columns. Intersecting the columns to form the rows of the table are tuples. A tuple, which Codd gave a precise definition when he first introduced it, corresponds approximately to a record in a flat-file system. In accordance with convention, we will use the term *record* or *occurrence* rather than tuple.

Properly designed tables possess the following four characteristics:

1.   The value of at least one attribute in each occurrence (row) must be unique. This attribute is the **primary key**. The values of the other (nonkey) attributes in the row need not be unique.
2.   All attribute values in any column must be of the same class.
3.   Each column in a given table must be uniquely named. However, different tables may contain columns with the same name.
4.   Tables must conform to the rules of normalization. This means they must be free from structural dependencies including repeating groups, partial dependencies, and transitive dependencies (see this chapter's appendix for a complete discussion).

Linkages between Relational Tables

Logically related tables need to be physically connected to achieve the associations described in the data model. Using **foreign keys** accomplishes this, as illustrated in Figure 8.14. In this example, the foreign keys are embedded in the related table. For instance, the primary key of the Customer table (CUST NUM) is embedded as a foreign key in both the Sales Invoice and Cash Receipts tables. Similarly, the primary key in the Sales Invoice table (INVOICE NUM) is an embedded foreign key in the Line Item table.

Note that the Line Item table uses a composite primary key comprised of INVOICE NUM and ITEM NUM. Both fields are needed to identify each record in the table uniquely, but only the invoice number portion of the key provides the logical link to the Sales Invoice table. Foreign keys are not always embedded like those in Figure 8.14. The nature of the association between the related tables determines the method used for assigning foreign keys. These methods are examined later.

With foreign keys in place, a computer program can be written to navigate among the tables of the database and provide users with the data they need to support their day-to-day tasks and decision-making responsibilities. For example, if a user wants all the invoices for Customer 1875, the program will search the Sales Invoice table for records with a foreign key value of 1875. We see from Figure 8.14 that there is only one such occurrence—invoice number 1921. To obtain the line-item details for this invoice, the program searches the Line Item table for records with a foreign key value of 1921, and two records are retrieved.

FIGURE 8.14   Linkages between Relational Tables

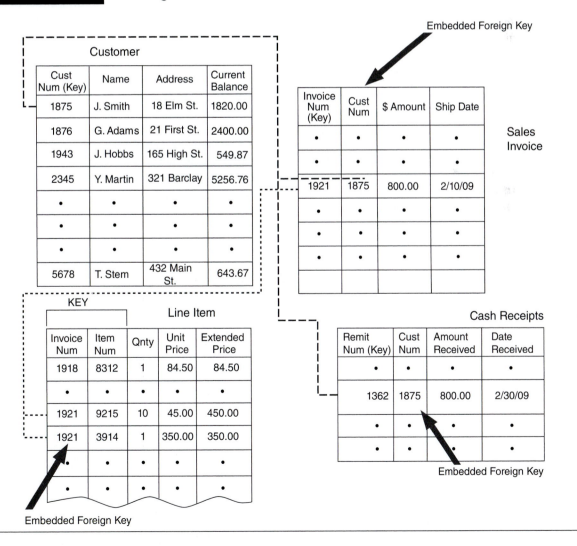

User Views

A **user view** is the set of data that a particular user sees. Examples of user views are computer screens for entering or viewing data, management reports, or source documents such as an invoice. Views may be digital or physical (paper), but in all cases, they derive from underlying database tables. Simple views may be constructed from a single table, while more complex views may require several tables. Furthermore, a single table may contribute data to many different views.

A large organization will have thousands of user views that thousands of individual tables support. The task of identifying all views and translating them into normalized tables is an important responsibility of database designers that has internal control implications. The issues and techniques related to this task are examined next.

Anomalies, Structural Dependencies, and Data Normalization

This section deals with why database tables need to be normalized. In other words, why is it necessary for the organization's database to form an elaborate network of normalized tables linked together like those illustrated in Figure 8.14? Why, instead, can we not simply consolidate the views of one user (or several) into a single common table from which all data needs may be met?

Database Anomalies

The answer to the above questions is that improperly normalized tables can cause DBMS processing problems that restrict, or even deny, users access to the information they need. Such tables exhibit negative operational symptoms called **anomalies**. Specifically, these are the update anomaly, the insertion anomaly, and the deletion anomaly. One or more of these anomalies will exist in tables that are not normalized or are normalized at a low level, such as **first normal form (1NF)** or **second normal form (2NF)**. To be free of anomalies, tables must be normalized to the **third normal form (3NF)** level.

We will demonstrate the negative impact of anomalies with the user view in Figure 8.15. This inventory status report would be used to provide a purchasing agent with information

---

FIGURE 8.15

Inventory Status Report

Ajax Manufacturing Co.
Inventory Status Report

Part Number	Description	Quantity On Hand	Reorder Point	Supplier Number	Name	Address	Telephone
1	Bracket	100	150	22 24 27	Ozment Sup Buell Co. B&R Sup	123 Main St. 2 Broadhead Westgate Mall	555-7895 555-3436 555-7845
2	Gasket	440	450	22 24 28	Ozment Sup Buell Co. Harris Manuf	123 Main St. 2 Broadhead 24 Linden St.	555-7895 555-3436 555-3316
3	Brace	10	10	22 24 28	Ozment Sup Buell Co. Harris Manuf	123 Main St. 2 Broadhead 24 Linden St.	555-7895 555-3436 555-3316
• • •	• • •	• • •	• • •	• • •	• • •	• • •	• • •

about inventory items to be ordered and the various suppliers (vendors) of those items. If this view were to be produced from a single table, it would look similar to the one presented in Figure 8.16. While such a table could indeed store the data to produce the view, it will exhibit the anomalies mentioned above.

Update Anomaly.   The **update anomaly** results from data redundancy in an unnormalized table. To illustrate, notice that Supplier Number 22 provides each of the three inventory items (PART NUM 1, 2, and 3) shown in Figure 8.16. The data attributes pertaining to Supplier Number 22 (NAME, ADDRESS, and TELE NUM) are thus repeated in every record of every inventory item that Supplier Number 22 provides. Any change in the supplier's name, address, or telephone number must be made to each of these records in the table. In the example, this means three different updates. To better appreciate the implications of the update anomaly, consider a more realistic situation where the vendor supplies 10,000 different items of inventory. Any update to an attribute must then be made 10,000 times.

Insertion Anomaly.   To demonstrate the effects of the **insertion anomaly**, assume that a new vendor has entered the marketplace. The organization does not yet purchase from the vendor, but may wish to do so in the future. In the meantime, the organization wants to add the vendor to the database. This is not possible, however, because the primary key for the Inventory table is PART NUM. Because the vendor does not supply the organization with any inventory items, the supplier data cannot be added to the table.

Deletion Anomaly.   The **deletion anomaly** involves the unintentional deletion of data from a table. To illustrate, assume that Supplier Number 27 provides the company with only one item: Part Number 1. If the organization discontinues this item of inventory and deletes it from the table, the data pertaining to Supplier Number 27 will also be deleted. Although the company may wish to retain the supplier's information for future use, the current table design prevents it from doing so.

The presence of the deletion anomaly is less conspicuous, but potentially more serious than the update and insertion anomalies. A flawed database design that prevents the insertion of records or requires the user to perform excessive updates attracts attention

---

FIGURE 8.16   **Unnormalized Database Table**

Inventory Table

Part Num	Description	Quantity On Hand	Reorder Point	Supplier Number	Name	Address	Tele Num
1	Bracket	100	150	22	Ozment Sup	123 Main St.	555-7895
1	Bracket	100	150	24	Buell Co.	2 Broadhead	555-3436
1	Bracket	100	150	27	B&R Sup	Westgate Mall	555-7845
2	Gasket	440	450	22	Ozment Sup	123 Main St.	555-7895
2	Gasket	440	450	24	Buell Co.	2 Broadhead	555-3436
2	Gasket	440	450	28	Harris Manuf	24 Linden St.	555-3316
3	Brace	10	10	22	Ozment Sup	123 Main St.	555-7895
3	Brace	10	10	24	Buell Co.	2 Broadhead	555-3436
3	Brace	10	10	28	Harris Manuf	24 Linden St.	555-3316

Primary Key — Part Num. Nonkey Attributes — Description through Tele Num.

quickly. The deletion anomaly, however, may go undetected, leaving the user unaware of the loss of important data until it is too late. This can result in the unintentional loss of critical accounting records and the destruction of audit trails. Table design, therefore, is not just an operational efficiency issue; it carries internal control significance that accountants need to recognize.

Normalizing Tables

The database anomalies described above are symptoms of structural problems within tables called dependencies. Specifically, these are known as **repeating groups**, **partial dependencies**, and **transitive dependencies**. The normalization process involves identifying and removing structural dependencies from the table(s) under review. (For a full explanation of this process, please review the appendix to this chapter.) The resulting tables will then meet the two conditions below:

1. All nonkey (data) attributes in the table are dependent on (defined by) the primary key.
2. All nonkey attributes are independent of the other nonkey attributes.

In other words, a 3NF table is one in which the primary key of a table wholly and uniquely defines each attribute in the table. Furthermore, none of the table attributes are defined by an attribute other than the primary key. If any attributes violate these conditions, they need to be removed and placed in a separate table and assigned an appropriate key.

Upon examination of Figure 8.16, we see that the primary key PART NUM does not uniquely define the nonkey attributes of SUPPLIER NUMBER, NAME, ADDRESS, and TELE NUM. Instead, each unique primary key value is associated with multiple (repeating group) values for these nonkey attributes. To resolve this structural dependency, the repeating group data must be removed from the Inventory table and placed in a separate table, which we will call Supplier. Figure 8.17 shows the two 3NF tables, Inventory and Supplier, along with a third table called Part/Supplier, which links the two. This linking technique will be explained later.

Normalizing the tables has eliminated the three anomalies. First, the update anomaly is resolved because data about each supplier exist in only one location—the Supplier table. Any change in the data about an individual vendor is made only once, regardless of how many items it supplies. Second, the insert anomaly no longer exists because new vendors can be added to the Supplier table even if they are not currently supplying the organization with inventory. For example, Supplier Number 30 in the table does not supply any inventory items. Finally, the deletion anomaly is eliminated. The decision to delete an inventory item from the database will not result in the unintentional deletion of the supplier data because these data reside independently in different tables.

Linking Normalized Tables

When unnormalized tables are split into multiple 3NF tables, they need to be linked together via foreign keys so the data in them can be related and made accessible to users. The degree of association (joint cardinality) between the resulting tables (that is, 1:1, 1:M, or M:M) determines how the linking occurs. The key-assignment rules for linking tables are discussed next.

Keys in 1:1 Associations.   Where a true 1:1 association exists between tables, either (or both) primary keys may be embedded as foreign keys in the related table. On the other hand, when the lower cardinality value is zero (1:0,1) a more efficient table struc-

FIGURE 8.17   Normalized Database Tables

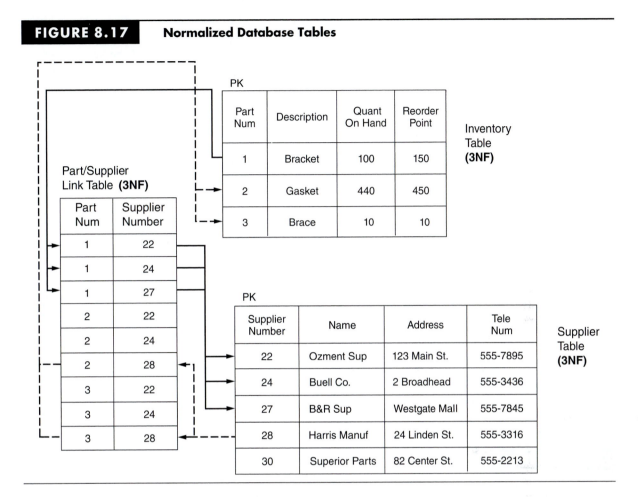

ture can be achieved by placing the one-side (1:) table's primary key in the zero-or-one (:0,1) table as a foreign key. Using the Employee/Company Car example in Figure 8.13, we see the importance of this key-assignment rule. To illustrate, imagine reversing the rule by placing the Company Car (0 side) table's primary key into the Employee (1 side) table. Because most employees are not assigned a company car, most of the foreign keys in the Employee table will have null (blank) values. While this approach would work, it could cause some technical problems during table searches. Correctly applying the key-assignment rule solves this problem because all Company Car records will have an employee assigned and no null values will occur.

Keys in 1:M Associations.   Where a 1:M (or 1:0,M) association exists, the primary key of the 1 side is embedded in the table of the M side. To demonstrate the logic behind this key-assignment rule, consider two alternative business rules for purchasing inventory from suppliers.

> Business Rule 1. Each vendor supplies the firm with three (or fewer) different items of inventory, but each item is supplied by only one vendor.

This unrealistic, but technically possible, business rule describes an upper-bounded 1:M (1:1,3) association between the Supplier and Inventory tables.

To apply this rule, the designer will need to modify the Inventory table structure to include the SUPPLIER NUMBER as illustrated in Figure 8.18. Under this approach, each record in the Inventory table will now contain the value of the key field of the vendor that supplies that item. By contrast, Figure 8.19 shows what the table structure might look like if the designer reversed the key-assignment rule by embedding the PART NUM key in the Supplier table. Notice that the Supplier table now contains three part number fields each linking to an associated record in the Inventory table. Only the links to part numbers 1, 2, and 3 are shown. Although this technique violates the key-assignment rule, it would work. It does so, however, only because the upper limit of the many side of the association is known and is very small (that is, limited to three). How would this table structure look if we assume the following, more realistic business rule?

> Business Rule 2. Each vendor supplies the firm with any number of inventory items, but each item is supplied by only one vendor.

This is a true 1:M association in which the upper limit of the many side of the association is unbounded. For instance, the vendor may supply one item of inventory or 10,000 items. How many fields must we add to the Supplier table structure to accommodate all possible links to the Inventory table? Here we can see the logic behind the 1:M key-assignment rule. The structure in Figure 8.18 still works under this business rule, whereas the technique illustrated in Figure 8.19 does not.

Keys in M:M Associations. To represent the M:M association between tables, a link table needs to be created. The link table has a combined (composite) key consisting of the primary keys of two related tables. Let's now return to the table relationship depicted in

---

FIGURE 8.18

Applying the 1:M Key-Assignment Rule

FIGURE 8.19   **Reversing the 1:M Key-Assignment Rule**

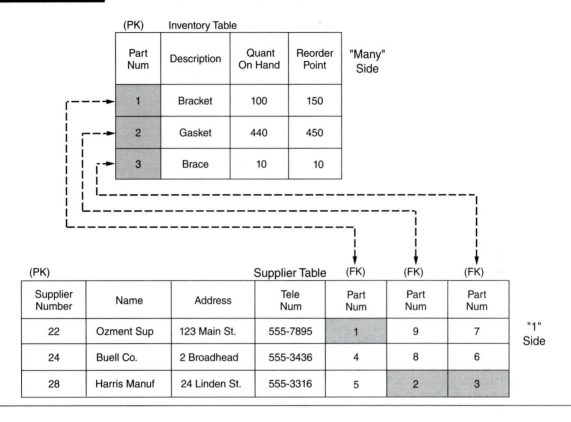

Figure 8.17. These tables illustrate an M:M association that the following business rule describes:

> Business Rule 3. Each vendor supplies the firm with any number of inventory items, and each item may be supplied by any number of vendors.

This business rule is evident by examining the contents of the Inventory Status Report (the user view) in Figure 8.15. Each part number shown has multiple suppliers, and each supplier may supply multiple items. For example, Ozment Supply provides items 1, 2, and 3. Harris Manufacturing also provides items 2 and 3.

An M:M association between tables requires the creation of a separate link table because embedding a foreign key within either table is not possible. The logic in the previous 1:M example that prevented us from embedding the primary key from the many side table of an unbounded association into the table of the one side applies here also. Neither table can donate an embedded foreign key to the other because both are on the many side of the association. The solution, therefore, is to create a new link table containing the key fields of the other two tables.

The link table called Part/Supplier in Figure 8.17 is a table of foreign keys. It contains the primary keys for the records in the Inventory table (PART NUM) and the related Supplier table (SUPPLIER NUMBER). Via the link table, each inventory item can be linked to the corresponding supplier of the item, and each supplier can be linked to the inventory items that it supplies. For example, by searching the Inventory table for PART NUM 1, we see that Suppliers 22, 24, and 27 provide this item. Searching in the opposite direction, SUPPLIER NUMBER 28 provides parts 2 and 3. A separate record in the link table represents each unique occurrence of a supplier/inventory association. For example, if Supplier 24 provides 500 different inventory items, then the link table will contain 500 records to depict these associations.

Auditors and Data Normalization

Database normalization is a technical matter that is usually the responsibility of systems professionals. The subject, however, has implications for internal control that make it the concern of auditors also. For example, the update anomaly can generate conflicting and obsolete database values, the insertion anomaly can result in unrecorded transactions and incomplete audit trails, and the deletion anomaly can cause the loss of accounting records and the destruction of audit trails. Although most auditors will not be responsible for normalizing an organization's databases, they should have an understanding of the process and be able to determine whether a table is properly normalized.

Furthermore, the auditor needs to know how the data are structured before he or she can extract data from tables to perform audit procedures. As we have seen, user views of the data are often very different from their storage structures. For example, the audit task of retrieving data pertaining to a complex user view such as a purchase order will involve identifying and accessing several related tables. These complex relations are illustrated in more detail in the following sections as we examine the steps involved in creating a portion of a corporate relational database.

DESIGNING RELATIONAL DATABASES

Database design is a component of a much larger systems development process that involves extensive analysis of user needs, which was the topic of Chapter 5. Thus, our starting point is one that normally follows considerable preliminary work that has identified in detail the key elements of the system under development. With this backdrop, the focus will be on the following six phases of database design, which are collectively known as **view modeling**:

1. Identify entities.
2. Construct a data model showing entity associations.
3. Add primary keys and attributes to the model.
4. Normalize the data model and add foreign keys.
5. Construct the physical database.
6. Prepare the user views.

Identify Entities

View modeling begins by identifying the primary entities of the business function in question. Recall that entities are things about which the organization wishes to capture data. To demonstrate entity identification, we will analyze the following key features of a simplified purchasing system:

1. The purchasing agent reviews the inventory status report (Figure 8.15) for items that need to be reordered.
2. The agent selects a supplier and prepares an online purchase order.

3. The agent prints a copy of the purchase order (Figure 8.20a) and sends it to the supplier.
4. The supplier ships inventory to the company. Upon its arrival, the receiving clerk inspects the inventory and prepares an online receiving report (Figure 8.20b). The computer system automatically updates the inventory records.

Entities are represented as nouns in a system description. A number of candidate entities can be identified in the previous description: Purchasing Agent, Receiving Clerk, Inventory, Supplier, Inventory Status Report, Purchase Order, and Receiving Report. Not all of these candidates are true entities that need to be modeled in the database. To pass as valid entities, two conditions need to be met:

Condition 1. An entity must consist of two or more occurrences.

Condition 2. An entity must contribute at least one attribute that is not provided through other entities.

We need to test these conditions for each candidate to eliminate any false entities.

Purchasing Agent. Assuming that the organization has only one purchasing agent, then the Purchasing Agent candidate fails Condition 1. If, however, more than one agent exists, Condition 1 is met but Condition 2 may be a problem. If we assume that an Employee table already exists as part of a human resources or payroll system, then basic data about the agent as an employee is captured in that table. We need to determine what data about the agent that is unique to his or her role of order placing needs to be captured. Note that we are not referring to data about the order, but data about the

FIGURE 8.20   Purchase Order and Receiving Report for Purchases System

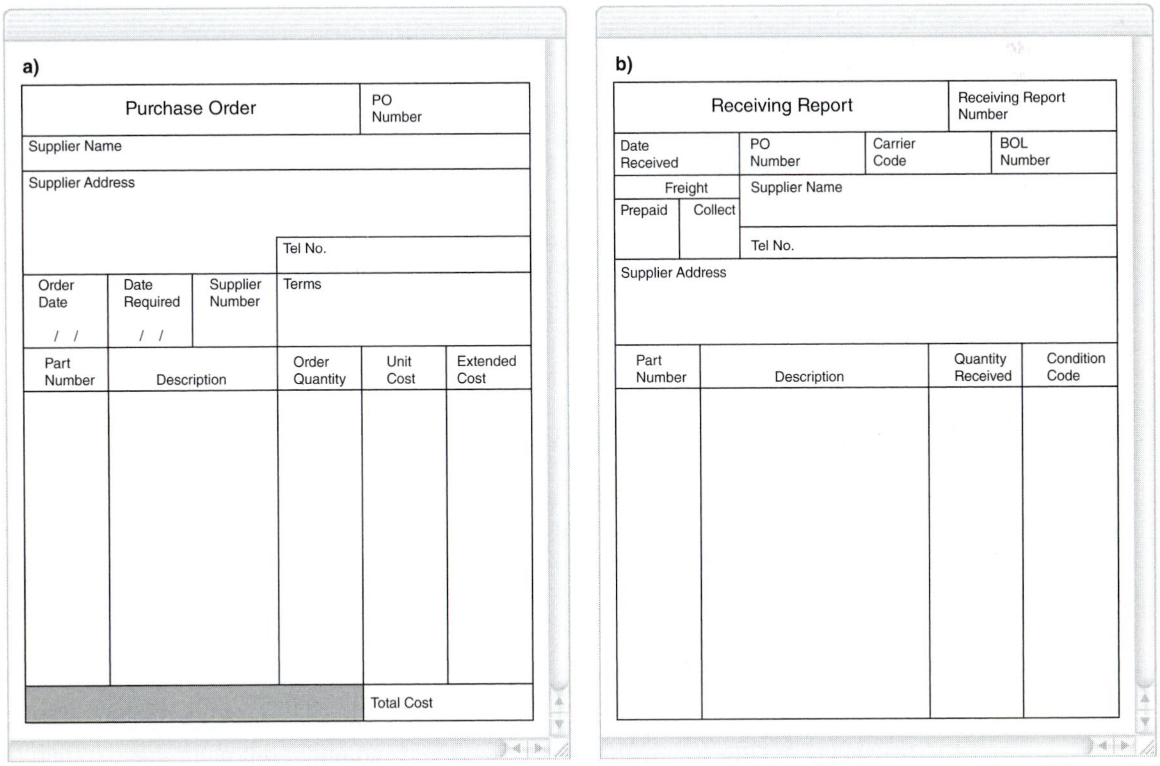

agent. Because we have no information on this point in our brief description of the system, we will assume no agent-specific data are captured. Hence, the Purchasing Agent candidate is not an entity to be modeled.

Receiving Clerk.   The previous argument applies also to the Receiving Clerk entity. We will assume that no clerk-specific data need to be captured that require a dedicated table.

Inventory.   The Inventory entity meets both conditions. The description suggests that the organization holds many items of inventory; thus this entity would contain multiple occurrences. Also, we can logically assume that the attributes that define the Inventory entity are not provided through other tables. The Inventory entity is, therefore, a true entity that will need to be modeled.

Supplier.   The description states that multiple vendors supply inventory; hence the Supplier entity meets the first condition. We can also assume that it meets the second condition since no other entity would logically provide supplier data. The Supplier entity, therefore, will be included in the data model.

Inventory Status Report.   The Inventory Status Report is a user view derived from the Inventory and Supplier entities (see Figure 8.17). While it contains multiple occurrences, it is not an entity because it does not satisfy Condition 2. The view is derived entirely from existing entities and provides no additional data that requires a separate entity. The view will be carefully analyzed, however, to ensure that all the attributes needed for it are included in the existing entities.

Purchase Order.   The Purchase Order entity meets both conditions. Many purchase orders will be processed in a period; thus the entity will have many occurrences. While some purchase order data can be derived from other entities (Inventory and Supplier) in the model, some attributes unique to the purchase event such as order date and order quantity will require a separate entity that needs to be modeled.

Receiving Report.   The Receiving Report meets both conditions. Many receipt events will take place in the period; thus a Receiving Report entity will have multiple occurrences. A Receiving Report entity will contain attributes such as date received and quantity received that are unique to this entity and thus not provided by other entities in the model.

At this point our search has revealed four entities: Inventory, Supplier, Purchase Order, and Receiving Report. These will be used to construct a data model and, ultimately, the physical database tables.

Construct a Data Model Showing Entity Associations

The next step in view modeling is to determine the associations between entities and document them with an ER diagram. Recall that associations represent business rules. Sometimes the rules are obvious and are the same for all organizations. For example, the normal association between a Customer entity and a Sales Order entity is 1:M (or 1:0,M). This signifies that one customer may place many orders during a sales period. The association would never be 1:1. This would mean that the organization restricts each customer to a single sale, which is illogical.

Sometimes the association between entities is not apparent because different rules may apply in different organizations. To reiterate an important point made earlier, the organization's business rules directly impact the structure of the database tables. If the database is to function properly, its designers need to understand the organization's business rules as well as the specific needs of individual users. Figure 8.21 illustrates the entity associations in our example. The underlying business rules are explained next.

1. There is a 0,M:M association between the Purchase Order and Inventory entities. This means that each inventory item may have been ordered many times or never ordered in the current business period. Obviously, every inventory item must have been purchased at least once in the past, so why do we show a 0,M cardinality for the Purchase Order entity? We must keep in mind that transaction entities, such as sales and purchases, are associated with a particular time frame. We will assume that the Purchase Order table for this system will contain records for purchases made in the current period only. Closed purchase orders of past periods will have been removed to an archive table, which is not shown in our example.

2. There is an M:M association between the Inventory and Supplier entities. This means that one or more vendors supply each inventory item, and each of them supplies one or more items of inventory.

3. There is a 1:0,M association between the Supplier and the Purchase Order entities. This means that in the current period, each supplier may have received zero or many purchase orders, but each order goes to only one supplier.

4. There is a 1:1 association between the Purchase Order and Receiving Report entities. A single receiving report record reflects the receipt of goods that are specified on a single purchase order record. Multiple purchase orders are not combined on a single receiving report.

5. The association between the Receiving Report and Inventory entities is 0,M:M. This signifies that within the period, each item of inventory may have been received

FIGURE 8.21

**Data Model
Showing Entity
Associations**

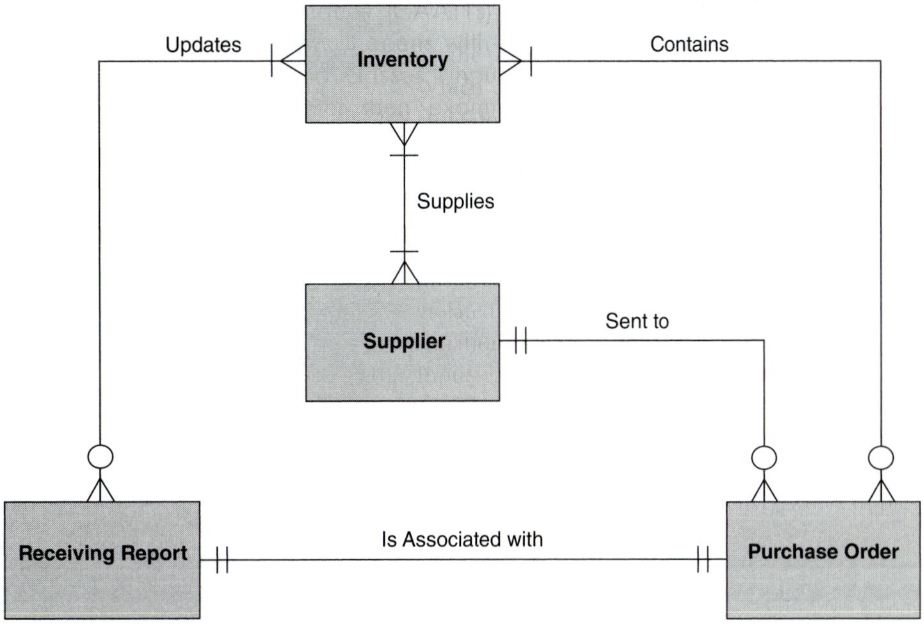

many times or never. Also, each receiving report is associated with at least one and possibly many inventory items.

The many-to-many (M:M and 0,M:M) associations in the data model need to be resolved before the physical databases can be created. We know from previous discussion that these associations signify a missing entity that is needed to link them. We will resolve these problems during the normalization process.

Add Primary Keys and Attributes to the Model

Add Primary Keys.   The next step in the process is to assign primary keys to the entities in the model. The analyst should select a primary key that logically defines the nonkey attributes and uniquely identifies each occurrence in the entity. Sometimes this can be accomplished using a simple sequential code such as an Invoice Number, Check Number, or Purchase Order number. Sequential codes, however, are not always efficient or effective keys. Through careful design of block codes, group codes, alphabetic codes, and mnemonic codes, primary keys can also impart useful information about the nature of the entity. These techniques were discussed in detail in Chapter 6. Figure 8.22 presents the four entities in the model with primary keys assigned.

Add Attributes.   Every attribute in an entity should appear directly or indirectly (a calculated value) in one or more user views. Entity attributes are, therefore, originally derived and modeled from user views. In other words, if stored data are not used in a document, report, or a calculation that is reported in some way, then it serves no purpose and should not be part of the database. The attributes assigned to each entity in Figure 8.23 are derived from the user views of the Purchase Order and Receiving Report illustrated in Figure 8.20 and from the Inventory Status Report that we previously normalized.

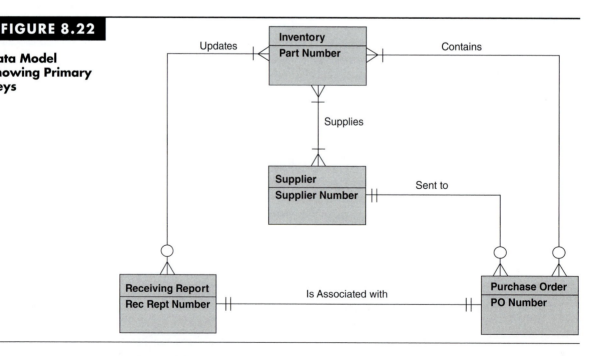

FIGURE 8.22

**Data Model
Showing Primary
Keys**

FIGURE 8.23

**Data Model
Showing Keys
and Attributes**

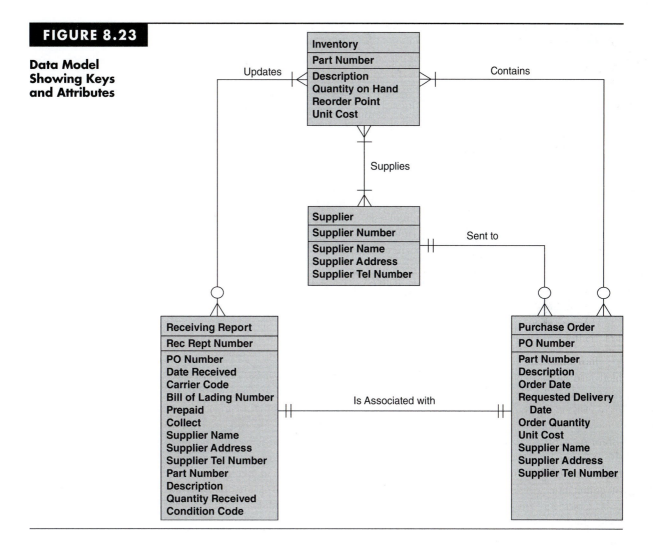

Normalize Data Model and Add Foreign Keys

Figure 8.24 presents a normalized data model. The normalization issues that needed resolution are outlined in the following section:

1. **Repeating Group Data in Purchase Order.** The attributes Part Number, Description, Order Quantity, and Unit Cost are repeating group data. This means that when a particular purchase order contains more than one item (most of the time), then multiple values will need to be captured for these attributes. To resolve this, these repeating group data were removed to a new PO Item Detail entity. The new entity was assigned a primary key that is a composite of Part Number and PO Number. The creation of the new entity also resolved the M:M association between the Purchase Order and Inventory entities by providing a link.

2. **Repeating Group Data in Receiving Report.** The attributes Part Number, Quantity Received, and Condition Code are repeating groups in the Receiving Report entity and were removed to a new entity called Rec Report Item Detail. A COMPOSITE

FIGURE 8.24

**Normalized Data
Model**

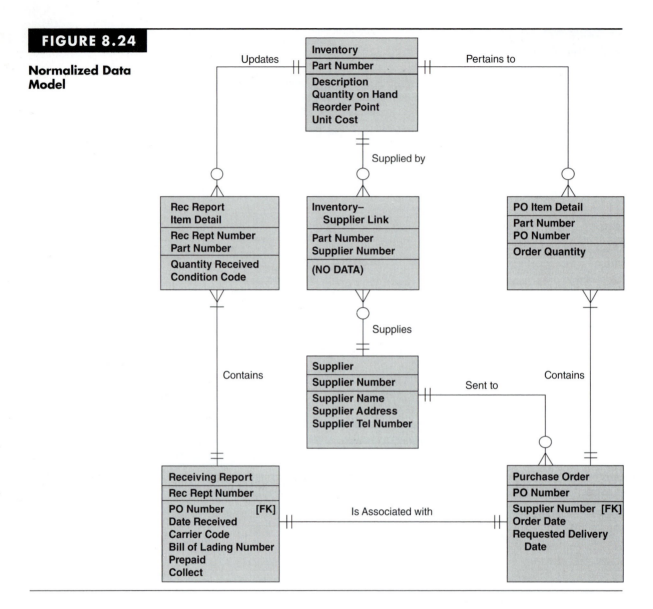

KEY composed of PART NUMBER and REC REPT NUMBER was assigned. As in the previous example, creating this new entity also resolved the M:M association between Receiving Report and Inventory.

3. **Transitive Dependencies.** The Purchase Order and Receiving Report entities contain attributes that are redundant with data in the Inventory and Supplier entities. These redundancies occur because of transitive dependencies (see the Appendix of this chapter) in the Purchase Order and Receiving Report entities and are dropped.

Construct the Physical Database

Figure 8.25 illustrates the 3NF table structures for the database. The primary and foreign keys linking the tables are represented by dotted lines. The following points are worth elaboration.

FIGURE 8.25

Normalized Tables

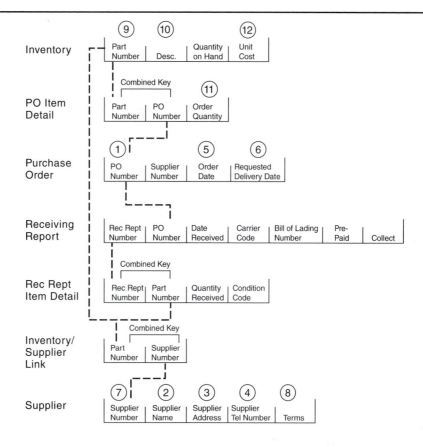

User's View—Purchase Order

Each record in the Rec Report Item Detail table represents an individual item on the receiving report. The table has a combined key comprising REC REPT NUMBER and PART NUMBER. This composite key is needed to uniquely identify the Quantity Received and Condition attributes of each item-detail record. The REC REPT NUMBER portion of the key provides the link to the Receiving Report table that contains general data about the receiving event. The PART NUMBER portion of the key is used to access the Inventory table to facilitate updating the Quantity on Hand field from the Quantity Received field of the Item-Detail record.

The PO Item Detail table uses a composite primary key of PO NUMBER and PART NUMBER to uniquely identify the Order Quantity attribute. The PO NUMBER component of the composite key provides a link to the Purchase Order table. The PART NUMBER element of the key is a link to the Inventory table where Description and Unit Cost data reside.

The next step is to create the physical tables and populate them with data. This is an involved step that must be carefully planned and executed and may take many months in a large installation. Programs will need to be written to transfer organization data currently stored in flat files or legacy databases to the new relational tables. Data currently stored on paper documents may need to be entered into the database tables manually. Once this is done, the physical user views can be produced.

Prepare the User Views

The normalized tables should be rich enough to support the views of all users of the system being modeled. For example, the PO in Figure 8.25, which could be the data entry screen for a purchasing clerk, has been constructed from attributes located in several tables. To illustrate the relationship, the fields in the user view are cross-referenced via circled numbers to the attributes in the supporting tables. Keep in mind that these tables may also provide data for many other views not shown here, such as the receiving report, purchase requisition listing, inventory status report, and vendor purchases activity report.

The query function of a relational DBMS allows the system designer to easily create user views from tables. The designer simply tells the DBMS which tables to use, their primary and foreign keys, and the attributes to select from each table. Older DBMSs require the designer to specify view parameters directly in SQL. Newer systems do this visually. The designer simply points and clicks at the tables and the attributes. From this visual representation, the DBMS generates the SQL commands for the query to produce the view.

The Receiving Report, Purchase Order, and Inventory Status Report views would all be created in this way. To illustrate, the SQL commands needed to produce the inventory status report illustrated in Figure 8.15 are given in the following section.

    SELECT inventory.part-num, description, quant-on-hand, reorder-point,
    EOQ, part-supplier.part-num, part-supplier.supplier-number,
    supplier.supplier-number, name, address, tele-num, FROM inventory,
    part-supplier, supplier

    WHERE inventory.part-num = part-supplier.part-num AND part-supplier.
    supplier-number = supplier.supplier-number AND quant-on hand ≤ reorder-point.

- The SELECT command identifies all of the attributes to be contained in the view. When the same attribute appears in more than one table (for example, PART-NUM), the source table name must also be specified.
- The FROM command identifies the tables used in creating the view.
- The WHERE command specifies how rows in the Inventory, Part-Supplier, and Supplier tables are to be matched to create the view. In this case, the three tables are algebraically joined on the primary keys PART-NUM and SUPPLIER-NUMBER.

- Multiple expressions may be linked with the AND, OR, and NOT operators. In this example, the last expression uses AND to restrict the records to be selected with the logical expression quant-on-hand ≤ reorder-point. Only records whose quantities on hand have fallen to or below their reorder points will be selected for the view. The user will not see the many thousands of other inventory items that have adequate quantities available.

These SQL commands will be saved in a user program called a query. To view the Inventory Status report, the purchasing agent executes the query program. Each time this is done, the query builds a new view with current data from the Inventory and Vendor tables. By providing the user with his or her personal query, rather than permitting access to the underlying base tables, the user is limited to authorized data only.

A report program is used to make the view visually attractive and easy to use. Column headings can be added, fields summed, and averages calculated to produce a hardcopy or computer screen report that resembles the original user report in Figure 8.15. The report program can suppress unnecessary data from the view, such as duplicated fields and the key values in the Inventory/Vendor link table. These keys are necessary to build the view, but are not needed in the actual report.

Global View Integration

The view modeling process described previously pertained to only one business function—the purchases system—and the resulting tables and views constitute only a subschema of the overall database schema. A modern company, however, would need hundreds or thousands of views and associated tables. Combining the data needs of all users into a single schema or enterprise-wide view is called **view integration**. This is a daunting undertaking when creating the entire database from scratch. To facilitate this task, modern Enterprise Resource Planning (ERP) systems (discussed in Chapter 11) come equipped with a core schema, normalized tables, and view templates. These best-practices databases are derived from economic models that identify commonalities among the data needs of different organizations. For example, all organizations that sell products to customers will need an Inventory table, a Customer table, a Supplier table, and so forth. Many of the attributes and keys in these tables are also common to all organizations. Working from a core ERP database, the view modeling process thus becomes one of configuring or tailoring predefined views to accommodate specific user needs. ERP vendors cannot, however, anticipate the information needs of all users in advance. Therefore, new tables and new attributes may need to be added to the core schema. Although configuring the core database in this fashion is far more efficient than working from scratch, the objective is the same. The database designer must produce a set of integrated tables that are free of the update, insert, and deletion anomalies and sufficiently rich to serve the needs of all users.

EMBEDDED AUDIT MODULE

The objective of the **embedded audit module (EAM)**, also known as *continuous auditing*, is to identify important transactions while they are being processed and extract copies of them in real time. An EAM is a specially programmed module embedded in a host application to capture predetermined transaction types for subsequent analysis. The approach is illustrated in Figure 8.26.

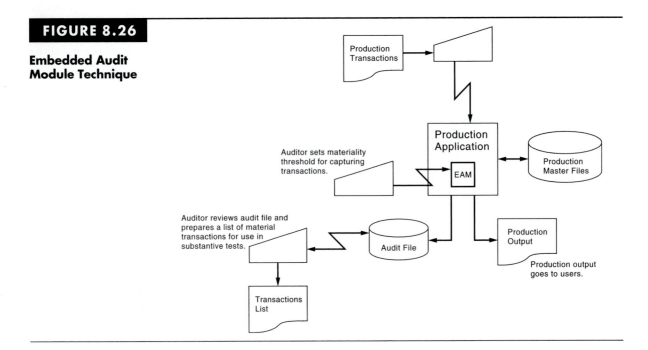

FIGURE 8.26

Embedded Audit Module Technique

As the selected transaction is being processed by the host application, a copy of the transaction is stored in an audit file for subsequent review. The EAM approach allows selected transactions to be captured throughout the audit period. Captured transactions are made available to the auditor in real time, at period end, or at any time during the period, thus significantly reducing the amount of work the auditor must do to identify significant transactions for substantive testing.

To begin data capturing, the auditor specifies to the EAM the parameters and materiality threshold of the transactions set to be captured. For example, let's assume that the auditor establishes a $50,000 materiality threshold for transactions processed by a sales order processing system. Transactions equal to or greater than $50,000 will be copied to the audit file. From this set of transactions, the auditor may select a subset to be used for substantive tests. Transactions that fall below this threshold will be ignored by the EAM.

While primarily a substantive testing technique, EAMs may also be used to monitor controls on an ongoing basis as required by SAS 109. For example, transactions selected by the EAM can be reviewed for proper authorization, completeness and accuracy of processing, and correct posting to accounts.

Disadvantages of EAMs

The EAM approach has two significant disadvantages. The first pertains to operational efficiency and the second is concerned with EAM integrity.

Operational Efficiency

From the user's point of view, EAMs decrease operational performance. The presence of an audit module within the host application may create significant overhead, especially when the amount of testing is extensive. One approach for relieving this burden from the system is to design modules that may be turned on and off by the auditor. Doing so will, of course, reduce the effectiveness of the EAM as an ongoing audit tool.

Verifying EAM Integrity

The EAM approach may not be a viable audit technique in environments with a high level of program maintenance. When host applications undergo frequent changes, the EAMs embedded within the hosts will also require frequent modifications. The integrity concerns raised earlier regarding application maintenance apply equally to EAMs. The integrity of the EAM directly affects the quality of the audit process. Auditors must therefore evaluate the EAM integrity. This evaluation is accomplished in the same way as testing the host application controls.

GENERALIZED AUDIT SOFTWARE

Generalized audit software (GAS) is the most widely used CAATT for IS auditing. GAS allows auditors to access electronically coded data files and perform various operations on their contents. Some of the more common uses for GAS include:

- Footing and balancing entire files or selected data items
- Selecting and reporting detailed data contained in files
- Selecting stratified statistical samples from data files
- Formatting results of tests into reports
- Printing confirmations in either standardized or special wording
- Screening data and selectively including or excluding items
- Comparing multiple files and identifying any differences
- Recalculating data fields

The widespread popularity of GAS is due to four factors: (1) GAS languages are easy to use and require little computer background on the part of the auditor; (2) many GAS products can be used on both mainframe and PC systems; (3) auditors can perform their tests independent of the client's computer service staff; and (4) GAS can be used to audit the data stored in most file structures and formats.

Using GAS to Access Simple Structures

Gaining access to flat-file structures is a relatively simple process, as illustrated in Figure 8.27. In this example, an inventory file is read directly by the GAS, which extracts key information needed for the audit, including the quantity on hand, the dollar value, and the warehouse location of each inventory item. The auditor's task is to verify the existence and value of the inventory by performing a physical count of a representative sample of the inventory on hand. Thus, on the basis of a materiality threshold provided by the auditor, the GAS selects the sample records and prepares a report containing the needed information.

Using GAS to Access Complex Structures

Gaining access to complex structures, such as a hashed file or other form of random file, may pose a problem for the auditor. Not all GAS products on the market may be capable of accessing every type of file structure. If the CAATT in question is unable to deal with

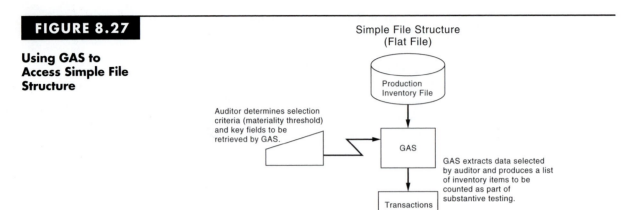

FIGURE 8.27

Using GAS to Access Simple File Structure

Simple File Structure
(Flat File)

Production Inventory File

Auditor determines selection criteria (materiality threshold) and key fields to be retrieved by GAS.

GAS

GAS extracts data selected by auditor and produces a list of inventory items to be counted as part of substantive testing.

Transactions List

FIGURE 8.28

Using GAS to Access Complex File Structure

Complex File Structure

DBMS Utility Program

Database

① Auditor specifies which database records to copy into flat file.

② Database management system produces a flat file of a portion of the database.

Flat File

④ GAS retrieves selected records from the flat file.

GAS

③ Auditor determines the selection criteria used by the GAS.

Transactions List

a complex structure, the auditor may need to appeal to systems professionals to write a special program that will copy the records from their actual structure to a flat-file sequential structure for easy retrieval. Figure 8.28 illustrates this approach.

Most DBMSs have utility features that can be used to reformat complex structures into flat files suitable for this purpose. To illustrate the file flattening process, consider the complex database structure presented in Figure 8.29. The database structure uses pointers to integrate three related files—Customer, Sales Invoice, and Line Item—in a hierarchical arrangement. Extracting audit evidence from a structure of this complexity using GAS may be difficult, if not impossible. A simpler flat-file version of this structure is illustrated in Figure 8.30. The single flat file presents the three record types as a sequential structure that can be easily accessed by GAS.

| FIGURE 8.29 | **Complex Database Structure** |

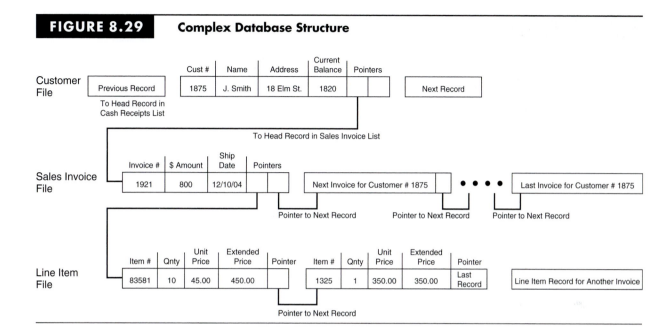

Audit Issues Pertaining to the Creation of Flat Files

The auditor must sometimes rely on computer services personnel to produce a flat file from the complex file structures. There is a risk that data integrity will be compromised by the procedure used to create the flat file. For example, if the auditor's objective is to confirm accounts receivable, certain fraudulent accounts in the complex structure may be intentionally omitted from the flat-file copy that is created. The sample of confirmations drawn from the flat file may therefore be unreliable. Auditors skilled in programming languages may avoid this potential pitfall by writing their own data extraction routines.

ACL SOFTWARE

In the past, public accounting firms developed proprietary versions of GAS, which they used in the audits of their clients. More recently, software companies have serviced this market. Among them, **ACL** (audit command language) is the leader in the industry. ACL was designed as a meta-language for auditors to access data stored in various digital formats and to test them comprehensively. In fact, many of the problems associated with accessing complex data structures have been solved by ACL's Open Database Connectivity (ODBC) interface.

The remainder of the chapter highlights ACL's more commonly used features. In later chapters, these and other features are demonstrated within the context of specific audit procedures, and each chapter contains several assignments designed to provide the student with hands-on ACL experience. The CD that accompanies this textbook contains an educational edition of ACL software, instruction manuals, and sample data files. The assignments used in this book draw upon these resources.

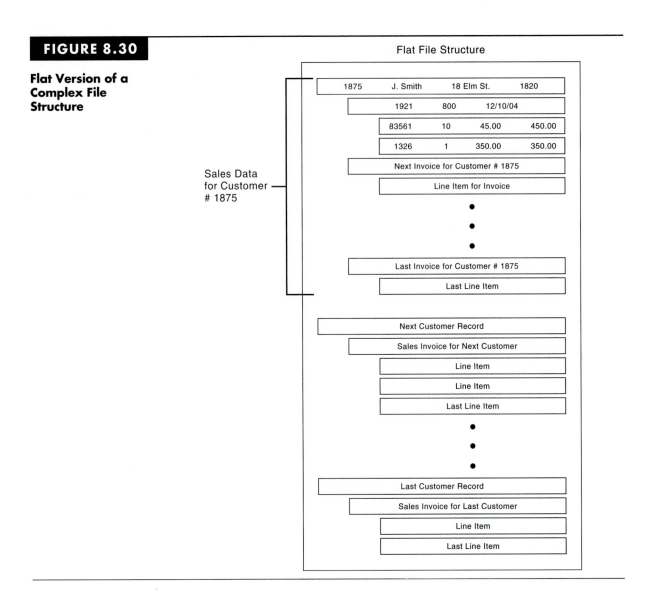

FIGURE 8.30

Flat Version of a Complex File Structure

Data Definition

We have already established that a client's system may store data using a number of flat-file or database structures, including sequential files, VSAM files, linked lists, and relational tables. One of ACL's strengths is the ability to read data stored in most formats. ACL uses the **data definition** feature for this purpose. To create a data definition, the auditor needs to know both where the source file physically resides and its field structure layout. Small files can be imported via text files or spreadsheets. Very large files may need to be accessed directly from the mainframe computer. When this is the case, the auditor must obtain access privileges to the directory in which the file resides. Where possible, however, a copy of the file should be stored in a separate test directory or downloaded to the auditor's PC. This step usually requires the assistance of systems professionals. The auditor should ensure that he or she secures the correct version of the file, that it is complete, and that the file structure documentation is intact. At this point, the auditor is ready to define the file to ACL. Figure 8.31 illustrates ACL's data definition screen.

The data definition screen allows the auditor to define important characteristics of the source file, including overall record length, the name given to each field, the type of data (i.e., numeric or character) contained in each field, and the starting point and length of each field in the file. This definition is stored in a table under a name assigned by the auditor. Since the file in Figure 8.31 contains inventory data, the table shall be named *INVENTORY* for this example. Once the data definition is complete, future access to the table is accomplished simply by selecting *INVENTORY* from ACL's tables folder under the project manager menu. ACL automatically retrieves the file and presents it on screen according to its data definition. For example, Figure 8.32 illustrates the view of the Inventory file after the *INVENTORY.fil* definition is created. As we will see, this view of the data may be changed as needed by the auditor.

FIGURE 8.31   **Data File Definition**

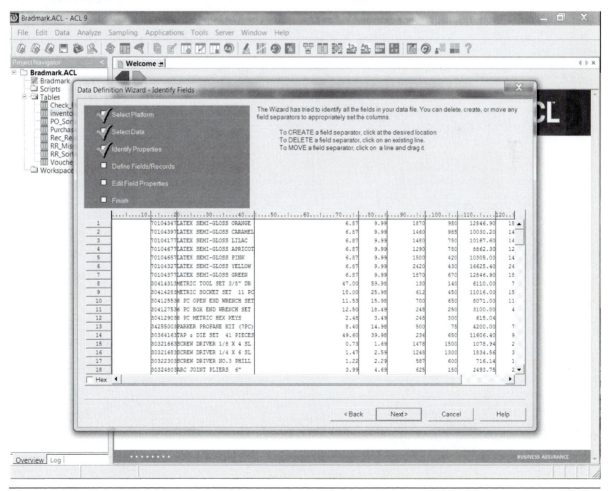

Customizing a View

A view is simply a way of looking at data in a file; auditors seldom need to use all the data contained in a file. ACL allows the auditor to customize the original view created during data definition to one that better meets his or her audit needs. The auditor can create and reformat new views without changing or deleting the data in the underlying file. Only the presentation of the data is affected. For example, the inventory file in Figure 8.32 contains a number of fields that are irrelevant to the audit. Also, the key data of interest to the auditor are not organized in contiguous fields. Instead, they are interspersed with irrelevant data, making review of important data difficult. The auditor can easily delete and/or rearrange the data to facilitate effective usage. Figure 8.33 presents a reorganized view of the inventory data that focuses on critical data elements.

FIGURE 8.32   **View of Inventory Table**

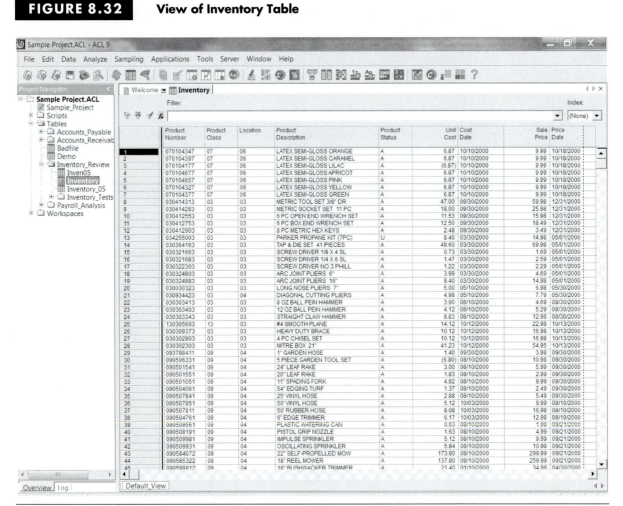

SOURCE: © 2011 ACL Services Ltd.

FIGURE 8.33   Customized View of Inventory Table

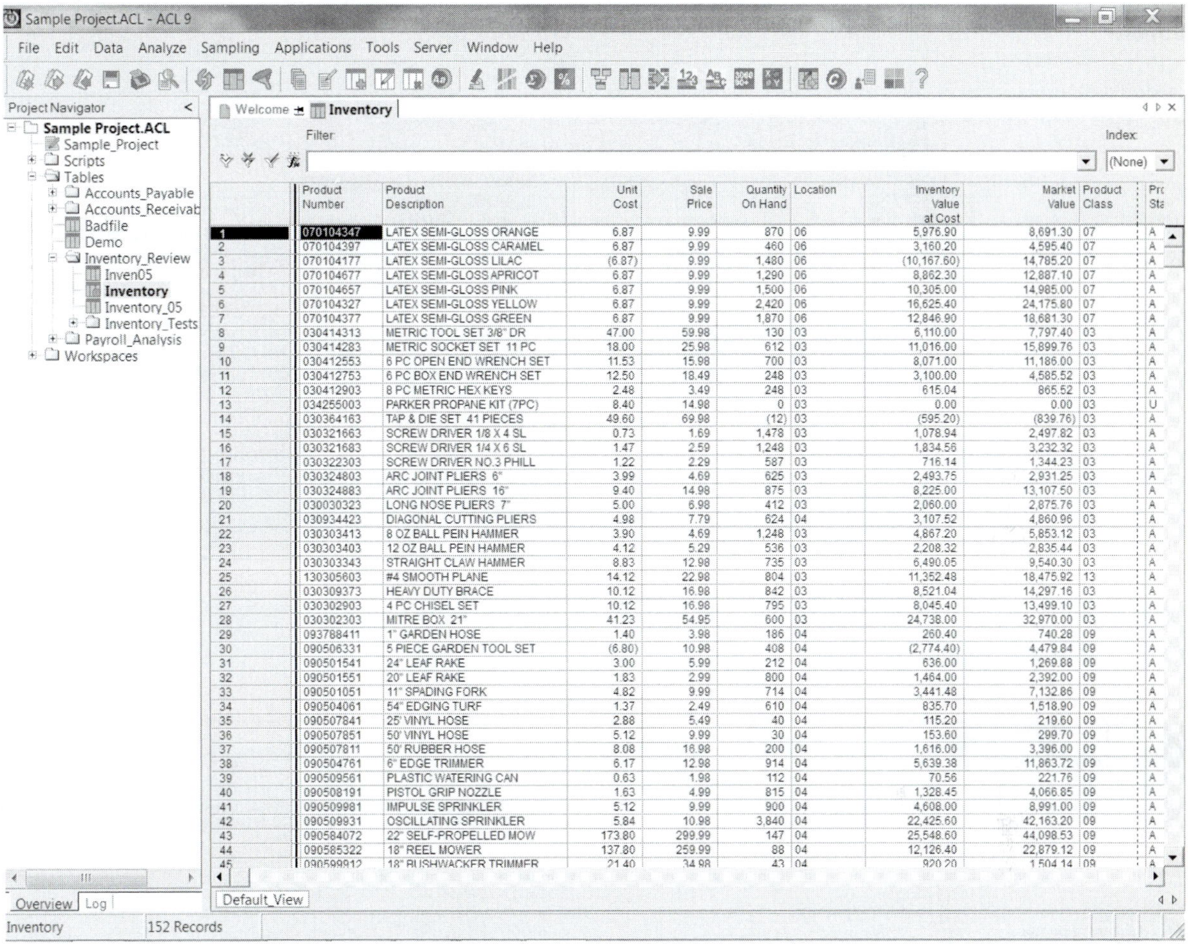

SOURCE: © 2011 ACL Services Ltd.

Filtering Data

ACL provides powerful options for filtering data that support various audit tests. **Filters** are expressions that search for records that meet the filter criteria. ACL's **expression builder** allows the auditor to use logical operators such as AND, OR, <, >, NOT and others to define and test conditions of any complexity and to process only those records that match specific conditions. For example, the auditor can search an inventory file for records with negative or zero quantity on hand. The expression builder screen and the filter needed for this test is illustrated in Figure 8.34.

When the auditor executes this filter procedure, ACL produces a new view of the inventory file (Figure 8.35) containing four records with zero or negative quantity-on-hand levels. This example demonstrates how auditors use ACL to search for anomalies and unusual conditions in accounting files containing thousands of records that defy review by visually scanning their contents.

FIGURE 8.34

Expression Builder

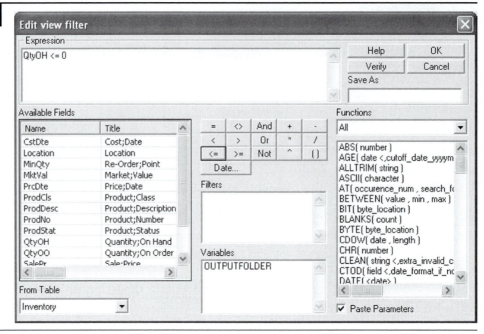

SOURCE: Courtesy ACL Services Ltd.

FIGURE 8.35   View of Filtered Inventory Table

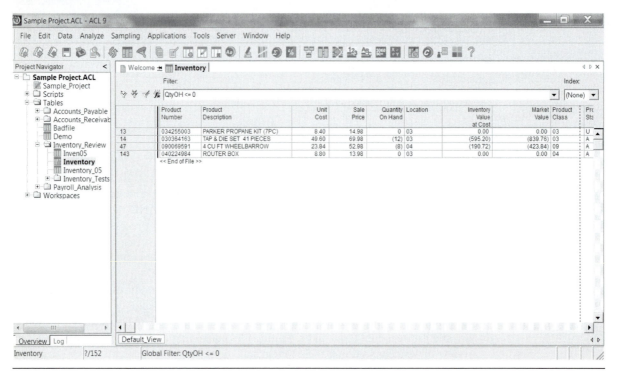

SOURCE: © 2011 ACL Services Ltd.

Stratifying Data

ACL's stratification feature allows the auditor to view the distribution of records that fall into specified strata. Data can be stratified on any numeric field such as sales price, unit cost, quantity sold, and so on. The data are summarized and classified by strata, which can be equal in size (called *intervals*) or vary in size (called *free*). Figure 8.36 illustrates the results of stratifying the inventory table on the unit-cost field. In this example, inventory value is also calculated for each interval.

The stratified report presented in Figure 8.36 shows unit cost data allocated across 10 intervals from $-6.87 to $381.20. The auditor may choose to change the size and number of intervals or examine only a subset of the file. For example, the first two strata show that they contain a disproportionate number of items. The auditor can obtain a clearer picture of the inventory cost structure by increasing the number of intervals or by reducing the upper limit of the range to $71.

Statistical Analysis

ACL offers many sampling methods for statistical analysis. Two of the most frequently used are **record sampling** and **monetary unit sampling (MUS)**. Each method allows random and interval sampling. The choice of methods will depend on the auditor's strategy and the composition of the file being audited. On one hand, when records in a file are fairly evenly distributed across strata, the auditor may want an unbiased sample and will thus choose the record sample approach. Using inventory to illustrate, each record, regardless of the dollar amount of the inventory value field, has an equal chance of being included in the sample. On the other hand, if the file is heavily skewed with large value items, the auditor may select MUS, which will produce a sample that includes all the larger dollar amounts.

FIGURE 8.36

Inventory Table Stratified on Unit Cost

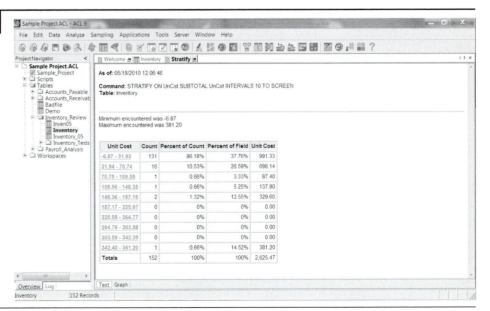

SOURCE: © 2011 ACL Services Ltd.

SUMMARY

This chapter began with a review of data structures, which specify (1) how records are organized in the physical file or database and (2) the access method employed to navigate the file. A number of basic data structures were examined, including sequential, indexed, hashing, and pointers. The chapter also reviewed relational data model in detail. Coverage included relational concepts, terminology, table-linking techniques, database normalization, and database design procedures. The chapter then focused on the use of CAATTs for data extraction and analysis. Data extraction can be performed by embedded audit modules and general audit software. These software tools support two types of audit tests that (1) allow the auditor to make inferences about application control effectiveness, and (2) provide access to data needed for substantive tests. The chapter described the features, advantages, and disadvantages of the embedded audit module (EAM) approach. It then outlined typical functions and uses of generalized audit software (GAS). The chapter closed with a review of the more commonly used features of ACL, the leading commercial GAS product.

Appendix

NORMALIZING TABLES IN A RELATIONAL DATABASE

The database anomalies (described in the chapter) are symptoms of structural problems within tables called dependencies. Specifically, these are known as repeating groups, partial dependencies, and transitive dependencies. The normalization process involves systematically identifying and removing these dependencies from the table(s) under review. Figure 8.37 graphically illustrates the unnormalized table's progression toward 3NF as each type of dependency is resolved. Tables in 3NF will be free of anomalies and will meet two conditions:

1. All nonkey attributes will be wholly and uniquely dependent on (defined by) the primary key.
2. None of the nonkey attributes will be dependent on (defined by) other nonkey attributes.

FIGURE 8.37

Steps in the Normalization Process

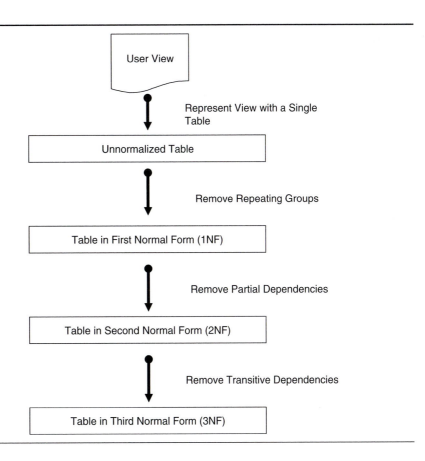

Design the User View

As Illustrated in Figure 8.37, the process begins with a user view such as an output report, a source document, or an input screen. Images of user views may be prepared using a word processor, a graphics package, or simply pencil and paper. At this point, the view is merely a pictorial representation of a set of data the user will eventually have when the project is completed. To demonstrate the normalization process, we will use the customer sales invoice and sample data presented in Figure 8.38. The basic issue here is, can we store all the data needed for this view in a single table that meets the two conditions previously noted?

Represent the View as a Single Table

The next step is to represent the view as a single table that contains all of the view attributes. Figure 8.39 presents a single-table structure containing the sample data from Figure 8.38. Because the table contains customer invoices, invoice number (INVOICE NUM) will serve as a logical primary key. Notice the attributes Ex Price and Total Due have been grayed out in Figure 8.39. The values for these attributes may be either stored or calculated. Because Ex Price is the product of two other attributes (Quantity 3 Unit Price) and Total Due is the sum of all Ex Price values, they both can be calculated from existing stored attributes rather than storing them directly in the database table. To simplify this example, therefore, we will assume that the system will calculate these attributes and they will be ignored from further analysis.

FIGURE 8.38

A User View

SALES INVOICE

Invoice Number: 16459
Order Date: 09/22/2009
Shipped Date: 09/27/2009
Shipped Via: UPS

Customer Number: **1765**
Customer Name: **ABC Associates**
Street Address: **132 Elm St.**
City: **Bethlehem**
State: **PA**
Telephone Number: **610-555-6721**

Prod Num	Description	Quantity	Unit Price	Ex. Price
r234	Bolt cutter	2	$42.50	$85.00
m456	Gear puller	1	$16.50	$16.50
W62	Electric welder	1	$485.00	$485.00
			Total Due	**$586.50**

FIGURE 8.39	Unnormalized Table Supporting User View

PK   Single-Table Structure for Sales Invoice

Invoice Num	Order Date	Shpd Date	Shpd Via	Total Due	Cust Num	Cust Name	Street Address	City	St	Tele Number	Prod Num	Description	Qunty	Unit Price	Ex Price
16459	09/22/09	09/27/09	UPS	586.50	1765	ABC Assoc	132 Elm St	Bethlehem	PA	610-555-6721	r234	Bolt cutter	2	42.50	85.00
16459	09/22/09	09/27/09	UPS	586.50	1765	ABC Assoc	132 Elm St	Bethlehem	PA	610-555-6721	m456	Gear puller	1	16.50	16.50
16459	09/22/09	09/27/09	UPS	586.50	1765	ABC Assoc	132 Elm St	Bethlehem	PA	610-555-6721	W62	Elec welder	1	485.00	485.00

Redundant Data   Repeating Group Data

Now that we have a base table to work from, the next few steps in the normalization process involve identifying and, if necessary, eliminating structural dependencies that exist. If dependencies exist, correcting them will involve splitting the original single-table structure into two or more smaller and independent 3NF tables. Each of the structural dependencies and the techniques for identifying and removing them is outlined in the following sections.

Remove *Repeating Group* Data

The first step in correcting structural dependencies is to determine if the table under review contains repeating groups. Repeating group data is the existence of multiple values for a particular attribute in a specific record. For example, the sales invoice in Figure 8.38 contains multiple values for the attributes PROD NUM, DESCRIPTION, QUANTITY, AND UNIT PRICE (we ignore EX PRICE). These repeating groups represent the transaction details of the invoice. We see repeating group data in many business user views, such as purchase orders, receiving reports, bills of lading, and so on. Relational database theory prohibits the construction of a table in which a single record (a row in the table) represents multiple values for an attribute (a column in the table). To represent repeating group values in a single table, therefore, will require multiple rows as illustrated Figure 8.39. Notice that the invoice attributes, which are common to each occurrence of the repeating group data, will also be represented multiple times. For example, Order Date, Shipped Date, Customer Name, Customer Address, and so on, are recorded along with each unique occurrence of Prod Num, Description, Quantity, and Unit Price. To avoid such data redundancy, the repeating group data need to be removed from the table and placed in a separate table. Figure 8.40 shows the resulting tables. One is called Sales Invoice Table, with INVOICE NUM as the primary key. The second table contains the transaction details for the invoice and is called Line Item Table.

Notice that the primary key of the Line Item Table is a **composite key** comprising two attributes: Invoice Num and Prod Num. Keep in mind that this table will contain the transaction details for our example invoice as well as the transaction details for the invoices for all customers. Relational database theory requires that a table's primary key uniquely identify each record stored in the table. PROD NUM alone cannot do this since

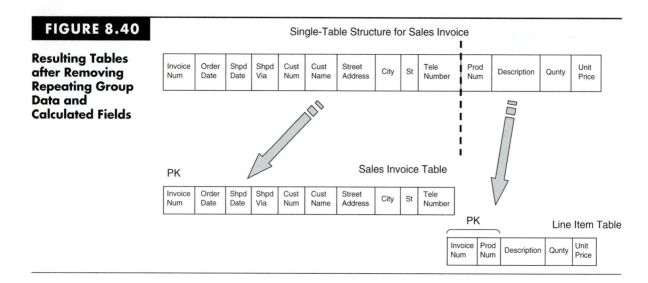

FIGURE 8.40

Resulting Tables after Removing Repeating Group Data and Calculated Fields

a particular product, such as r234 (bolt cutter), may well have been sold to many other customers whose transactions are also in the table. By combining PROD NUM with the INVOICE NUM, however, we can uniquely define each transaction because the table will never contain two occurrences of the same invoice number and product number together.

Remove Partial Dependencies

Next we check to see if the resulting tables contain partial dependencies. A partial dependency occurs when one or more nonkey attributes are dependent on (defined by) only part of the primary key, rather than the whole key. This can occur only in tables that have composite (two or more attribute) primary keys. Because the Sales Invoice Table has a single attribute primary key, we can ignore it in this step of the analysis. This table is already in 2NF. The Line Item Table, however, needs to be examined further. Figure 8.41 illustrates the partial dependencies in it.

In the Line Item Table, INVOICE NUM and PROD NUM together define the quantity sold attribute (Qunty). If we assume, however, that the price charged for r234 is the same for all customers, then the Unit Price attribute is common to all transactions involving product r234. Similarly, the attribute Description is common to all such transactions. These two attributes are not dependent on the Invoice Num component of the composite key. Instead, they are defined by Prod Num and, therefore, only partially rather than wholly dependent on the primary key.

We resolve this by splitting the table into two, as illustrated in Figure 8.41. The resulting Line Item Table is now left with the single nonkey attribute Qunty. Product description and unit price data are placed in a new table called Inventory. Notice that the Inventory table contains additional attributes that do not pertain to this user view. A typical inventory table may contain attributes such as reorder point, quantity on hand, supplier code, warehouse location, and more. This demonstrates how a single table may be used to support many different user views and reminds us that this normalization example pertains to only a small portion of the entire database. We will return to this issue later.

FIGURE 8.41	**Resulting Tables after Removing Partial Dependency**

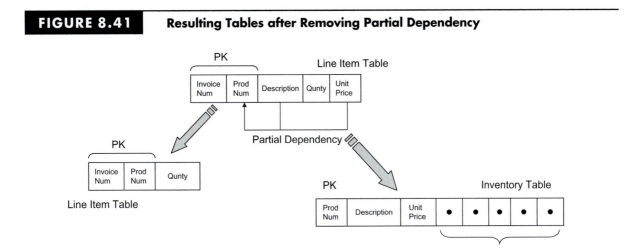

At this point, both of the tables in Figure 8.41 are in 3NF. The Line Item Table's primary key (INVOICE NUM PROD NUM) wholly defines the attribute QUNTY. Similarly, in the Inventory Table, the attributes Description and Unit Price are wholly defined by the primary key PROD NUM.

Remove Transitive Dependencies

The final step in resolving structural dependencies is to remove transitive dependencies. A transitive dependency occurs in a table where nonkey attributes are dependent on another nonkey attribute and independent of the table's primary key. An example of this is illustrated by the Sales Invoice Table in Figure 8.42. The primary key INVOICE NUM uniquely and wholly defines the economic event that the attributes Order Date, Shpd Date, and Shpd Via represent. The key does not, however, uniquely define the customer attributes. The attributes Cust Name, Street Address, and so on, define an entity (Customer) that is independent of the specific transaction captured by a particular invoice record. For example, assume that during the period the firm had sold to a particular customer on ten different occasions. This would result in ten different invoice records stored in the table. Using the current table structure, each of these invoice records would capture the data uniquely related to the respective transaction along with customer data that are common to all ten transactions. Therefore, the primary key does not uniquely define customer attributes in the table. Indeed, they are independent of it.

We resolve this transitive dependency by splitting out the customer data and placing them in a new table called Customer. The logical key for this table is CUST NUM, which was the nonkey attribute in the former table on which the other nonkey customer attributes were dependent. With this dependency resolved, both the revised Sales Invoice Table and the new Customer Table are in 3NF.

Linking the Normalized Tables

At this point, the original single-table structure has been reduced to the four normalized but independent tables presented in Figure 8.43. The tables contain the sample data used in the original single-table structure presented in Figure 8.39. Notice how data

FIGURE 8.42

Resulting Tables after Removing Transitive Dependency

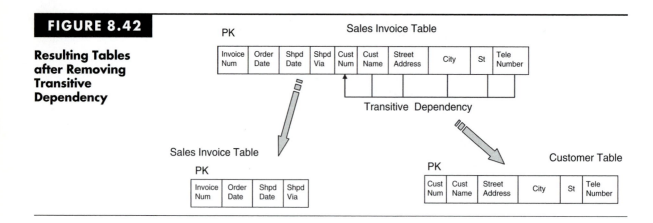

FIGURE 8.43   **Linkages Between Normalized Tables**

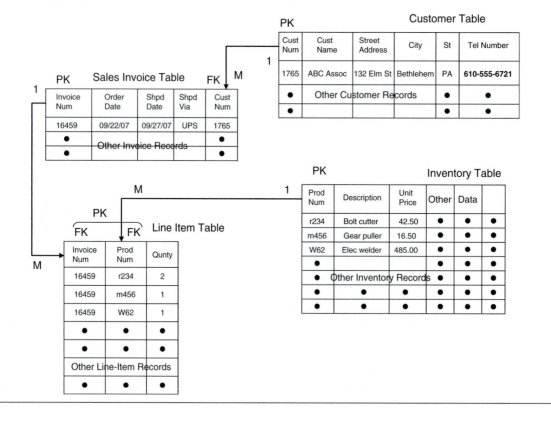

redundancy in the original single-table structure has been eliminated from the more efficient structure represented here. To work together, however, these tables need to be linked via foreign keys. This requires first determining the cardinality (degree of association) between the tables and then assigning foreign keys.

Determine Cardinality

In our example, the cardinality between the four tables is one-to-many (1:M), as explained below.

1. Each customer (Customer Table) may be associated with one or many sales events (Sales Invoice Table), but each invoice is for a single customer.
2. Each Sales Invoice record is associated with one or more Line-Item records, but each Line Item is associated with only one Sales Invoice.
3. Each Inventory record is associated with one or more Line Items (a particular product has been sold many times to many customers) but each Line-Item record represents only one inventory item.

Assign Foreign Keys

Rules assigning foreign keys are explained in detail in the chapter. When linking in a 1:M relation as depicted in Figure 8.43, the rule is to take the primary key from the table on the 1 side of the relation and embed it as a foreign key in the table of the M side. Notice that in the relations between the Line Item Table, the Invoice Table, and the Inventory Table, this is already the case because of the Line Item Table's composite key. The Sales Invoice Table, however, needs to be modified to include CUST NUM as the FOREIGN KEY, which links it to the Customer Table.

Producing the User View from the Normalized Tables

After these tables have been created within the DBMS, they will be populated with data from several sources. For example, customer services will add customers' data to the Customer Table, inventory control will enter product values into the Inventory Table, and the Sales Invoice and Line Item tables will be populated by sales transactions data from the Sales Order process. The following steps describe how the batch process might produce the actual invoices.

1. A computer program reads the Sales Invoice Table. We will assume that the first record read is invoice number 16459 (our sample record). The record attributes are stored in memory.
2. The program then reads the foreign key CUST NUM and searches the Customer Table for a record with the primary key value 1765. The customer record attributes are then stored in memory.
3. The computer program then reads the primary key INVOICE NUM and searches the Line Item Table for all occurrences of records whose INVOICE NUM Component of the primary key has a value of 16459. It locates three such records and stores them in memory.
4. The program next reads the PROD NUM Component of the three Line-Item records and one by one searches the Inventory File for each occurrence. The DESCRIPTION and UNIT PRICE attributes of each located record is stored in memory.
5. The program then calculates the EX PRICE Attribute for each item and sums these to obtain the TOTAL DUE Attribute.
6. At this point, all the attributes needed to produce the original user view are in memory. They are formatted and sent to printing.
7. The computer then clears memory, reads the next record from the Invoice Table, and repeats the steps above until all invoices have been processed.

KEY TERMS

access method	logical key pointer
ACL	monetary unit sampling (MUS)
anomalies	occurrence
cardinality	organization
composite key	partial dependency
data model	physical address pointer
data structures	pointer structure
deletion anomaly	primary key
embedded audit module (EAM)	record sampling
expression builder	relative address pointer
filter	repeating group
first normal form (1NF)	second normal form (2NF)
foreign key	sequential structure
generalized audit software (GAS)	third normal form (3NF)
hashing structure	transitive dependency
indexed random file	update anomaly
indexed sequential file	user view
indexed structure	view integration
insertion anomaly	view modeling
inverted list	virtual storage access method (VSAM)

REVIEW QUESTIONS

1. What are the two fundamental components of data structures?
2. What are the criteria that influence the selection of the data structure?
3. What are the advantages and disadvantages of using a sequential data structure? Give an example of each.
4. What are the advantages and disadvantages of using an indexed random file structure? An indexed sequential file structure?
5. What are the three physical components of an VSAM file? Explain how a record is searched through these components.
6. What is a pointer? Discuss the three commonly used types of pointers and their relative merits.
7. What are some limitations of the hierarchical database model?
8. Discuss and give an example of one-to-one, one-to-many, and many-to-many record associations.
9. Why is a hierarchical database model considered to be a navigational database?
10. Explain how a separate linking file works in a network model.
11. What is an embedded audit module?
12. Explain what GAS is and why it is so popular with larger public accounting firms. Discuss the independence issue related to GAS.
13. Discuss and give an example of the following types of associations: (1:0,1), (1:1), (1:M), and (M:M).
14. Distinguish between association and cardinality.
15. Explain how a separate linking table works in a many-to-many association.
16. What are the four characteristics of properly designed relational database tables?
17. What do the relational features restrict, project, and join mean?
18. What are the conditions for third normal form (3NF)?
19. Explain how the SELECT and WHERE commands help a user to view the necessary data from multiple database files (tables).
20. What is a data model?
21. How can a poorly designed database result in unintentional loss of critical records?
22. What is a user view?

23. Does a user view always require multiple tables to support it? Explain.
24. What two conditions must valid entities meet?
25. Can two different entities have the same defining attributes? Explain.

DISCUSSION QUESTIONS

1. Explain how a hashing structure works and why it is quicker than using an index. Give an example. If it is so much faster, why isn't it used exclusively?
2. Explain how an embedded audit module works and why auditors may choose not to use it.
3. Explain the term *navigational data models*. Contrast the hierarchical model and the network model.
4. Explain the three types of anomalies associated with database tables that have not been normalized.
5. Contrast embedded audit modules with generalized audit software.
6. Describe a specific accounting application that could make use of an VSAM file.
7. Explain why auditors should be familiar with the principle of data normalization.
8. How is a user view different from a database table?
9. Explain what the term *third normal form* (3NF) means.
10. Why is a separate link table required when an M:M association exits between related tables?
11. In a relational database environment, certain accounting records (for example, journals, subsidiary ledgers, and event general ledger accounts) may not exist. How is this possible?
12. Explain how to link tables in a 1:1 association. Why may this be different in a 1:0,1 association?
13. Discuss the accounting implications of the update, insertion, and deletion anomalies associated with improperly normalized tables.
14. Give three examples that illustrate how cardinality reflects an organization's underlying business rules.
15. Explain the following three types of pointers: physical address pointer, relative address pointer, and logical key pointer.
16. Explain why GAS technology is popular with most auditors.
17. Explain the risk associated with using GAS to access complex file structures.
18. Explain the purpose of the input file definition feature of ACL.
19. Assume that an auditor is reviewing a file containing twenty-five fields of data, only five of which are relevant to the auditor's objective. Explain how ACL can help in this situation.
20. Explain the purpose of ACL's filter capability.
21. Distinguish between record sampling and monetary unit sampling (MUS).

MULTIPLE-CHOICE QUESTIONS

1. CIA 1186 III-33
   In an inventory system on a database management system, one stored record contains part number, part name, part color, and part weight. These individual items are called
   a. fields.
   b. stored files.
   c. bytes.
   d. occurrences.
2. CIA 586 III-31
   The use of pointers can save time when sequentially updating a
   a. master file.
   b. database management system.
   c. batch file.
   d. random file.
3. It is appropriate to use a sequential file structure when
   a. records are routinely inserted.
   b. a large portion of the file will be processed in one operation.
   c. records need to be scanned using secondary keys.
   d. single records need to be retrieved.
4. Which statement is *not* correct?
   a. The sequential file structure is appropriate for payroll records.
   b. An advantage of a sequential index is that it can be searched rapidly.

c. The index sequential access method performs record insertion operations efficiently.

d. The principal advantage of the hashing structure is speed of access.

5. Which of the following statements is *not* true?
   a. Indexed random files are dispersed throughout the storage device without regard for physical proximity with related records.
   b. Indexed random files use disk storage space efficiently.
   c. Indexed random files are efficient when processing a large portion of a file at one time.
   d. Indexed random files are easy to maintain in terms of adding records.

6. Which statement is *not* correct? The indexed sequential access method
   a. is used for very large files that need both direct access and batch processing.
   b. may use an overflow area for records.
   c. provides an exact physical address for each record.
   d. is appropriate for files that require few insertions or deletions.

7. Which statement is true about a hashing structure?
   a. The same address could be calculated for two records.
   b. Storage space is used efficiently.
   c. Records cannot be accessed rapidly.
   d. A separate index is required.

8. In a hashing structure,
   a. two records can be stored at the same address.
   b. pointers are used to indicate the location of all records.
   c. pointers are used to indicate the location of a record with the same address as another record.
   d. all locations on the disk are used for record storage.

9. Pointers can be used for all of the following except
   a. to locate the subschema address of the record.
   b. to locate the physical address of the record.
   c. to locate the relative address of the record.
   d. to locate the logical key of the record.

10. An advantage of a physical address pointer is that
    a. it points directly to the actual disk storage location.
    b. it is easily recovered if it is inadvertently lost.

c. it remains unchanged when disks are reorganized.

d. all of the above are advantages of the physical address pointer.

11. Pointers are used
    a. to link records within a file.
    b. to link records between files.
    c. to identify records stored in overflow.
    d. all of the above.

12. In a hierarchical model,
    a. links between related records are implicit.
    b. the way to access data is by following a predefined data path.
    c. an owner (parent) record may own just one member (child) record.
    d. a member (child) record may have more than one owner (parent).

13. In a network model,
    a. there is one predefined path to a particular record.
    b. many-to-many relationships are supported in a simple network.
    c. management can track and report information by one criterion only.
    d. link files are used to connect records in different files.

14. Which term is *not* associated with the relational database model?
    a. tuple
    b. attribute
    c. collision
    d. relation

15. In the relational database model,
    a. relationships are explicit.
    b. the user perceives that files are linked using pointers.
    c. data are represented on two-dimensional tables.
    d. data are represented as a tree structure.

16. In the relational database model, all of the following are true except
    a. data are presented to users as tables.
    b. data can be extracted from specified rows from specified tables.
    c. a new table can be built by joining two tables.
    d. only one-to-many relationships can be supported.

17. In a relational database,
    a. the user's view of the physical database is the same as the physical database.
    b. users perceive that they are manipulating a single table.

c. a virtual table exists in the form of rows and columns of a table stored on the disk.

d. a programming language (COBOL) is used to create a user's view of the database.

18. The update anomaly in unnormalized databases
    a. occurs because of data redundancy.
    b. complicates adding records to the database.
    c. may result in the loss of important data.
    d. often results in excessive record insertions.

19. The most serious problem with unnormalized databases is the
    a. update anomaly.
    b. insertion anomaly.
    c. deletion anomaly.
    d. none of the above.

20. The deletion anomaly in unnormalized databases
    a. is easily detected by users.
    b. may result in the loss of important data.
    c. complicates adding records to the database.
    d. requires the user to perform excessive updates.

21. The data attributes that a particular user has permission to access are defined by the
    a. operating system view.
    b. systems design view.
    c. database schema.
    d. user view.
    e. application program.

22. Database entities
    a. may contain zero or many occurrences.
    b. are represented as verbs in an ER diagram.
    c. may represent both physical assets and intangible phenomena.
    d. are often defined by common attributes that also define other entities.
    e. are unique to a specific user view.

23. A transitive dependency
    a. is a database condition that is resolved through special monitoring software.

b. is a name given to one of the three anomalies that result from unnormalized database tables.

c. can exist only in a table with a composite primary key.

d. cannot exist in tables that are normalized at the 2NF level.

e. is none of the above.

24. A partial dependency
    a. is the result of simultaneous user requests for the same data in a partitioned database environment.
    b. is a name given to one of the three anomalies that result from unnormalized database tables.
    c. can exist only in a table with a composite primary key.
    d. may exist in tables that are normalized at the 2NF level.
    e. is none of the above.

25. Repeating group data
    a. is a form of data redundancy common to replicated databases in a distributed database environment.
    b. is a name given to one of the three anomalies that result from unnormalized database tables.
    c. can exist only in a table with a composite primary key.
    d. cannot exist in tables that are normalized at the 2NF level.
    e. is none of the above.

26. The database model most likely to be used in the development of a modern (not legacy) system is
    a. hierarchical.
    b. structured.
    c. relational.
    d. network.
    e. navigational.

PROBLEMS

1. Access Methods

For each of the following file processing operations, indicate whether a sequential file, indexed random file, indexed sequential access method (VSAM), hashing, or pointer structure works the best. You may choose as many as you wish for each step. Also indicate which would perform the least optimally.

a. Retrieve a record from the file based on its primary key value.

b. Update a record in the file.

c. Read a complete file of records.

d. Find the next record in a file.

e. Insert a record into a file.

f. Delete a record from a file.

g. Scan a file for records with secondary keys.

2. File Organization

For the following situations, indicate the most appropriate type of file organization. Explain your choice.

a. A local utility company has 80,000 residential customers and 10,000 commercial customers. The monthly billings are staggered throughout the month and, as a result, the cash receipts are fairly uniform throughout the month. For 99 percent of all accounts, one check per month is received. These receipts are recorded in a batch file, and the customer account records are updated biweekly. In a typical month, customer inquiries are received at the rate of about twenty per day.

b. A national credit card agency has 12 million customer accounts. On average, 30 million purchases and 700,000 receipts of payments are processed per day. Additionally, the customer support hot line provides information to approximately 150,000 credit card holders and 30,000 merchants per day.

c. An airline reservation system assumes that the traveler knows the departing city. From that point, fares and flight times are examined based on the destination. Once a flight is identified as being acceptable to the traveler, then the availability is checked and, if necessary, a seat is reserved. The volume of transactions exceeds one-half million per day.

d. A library system stocks more than 2 million books and has 30,000 patrons. Each patron is allowed to check out five books. On average, there are 1.3 copies of each title in the library. Over 3,000 books are checked out each day, with approximately the same amount being returned daily. The check-outs are posted immediately, as well as any returns of overdue books by patrons who wish to pay their fines.

3. Structured Query Language

The vice president of finance has noticed in the aging of the accounts receivable that the amount of overdue accounts is substantially higher than anticipated. He wants to investigate this problem. To do so, he requires a report of overdue accounts containing the attributes shown in the top half of the of Problem 3 table on the next page. The bottom half of the table contains the data fields and relevant files in the relational database system. Further, he wants to alert the salespeople of any customers not paying their bills on time. Using the SQL commands given in this chapter, write the code necessary to generate a report of overdue accounts that are greater than $5,000 and more than 30 days due. Each customer has an assigned salesperson.

4. Virtual Storage Access Method

Using the index provided explain, step-by-step, how the Key 12987 would be found using the virtual storage access method. Once a surface on a cylinder is located,

what is the average number of records that must be searched?

CYLINDER INDEX		SURFACE INDEX CYLINDER	
Key Range	**Cylinder Number**	**Key Range**	**Surface Number**
2,000	44	12,250	0
4,000	45	12,500	1
6,000	46	12,750	2
8,000	47	13,000	3
10,000	48	13,250	4
12,000	49	13,500	5
14,000	50	14,750	6
16,000	51	15,000	7
18,000	52		
20,000	53		

5. Hashing Algorithm

The systems programmer uses a hashing algorithm to determine storage addresses. The hashing structure is 9,997/key. The resulting number is then used to locate the record. The first two digits after the decimal point represent the cylinder number, while the second two digits represent the surface number. The fifth, sixth, and seventh digits after the decimal point represent the record number. This algorithm results in a unique address 99 percent of the time. What happens the remainder of the time when the results of the algorithm are not unique? Explain in detail the storage process when Key=3 is processed first, Key=2307 at a later date, and shortly thereafter Key=39.

6. Normalization of Data

On the next page is a table of data for a library. Normalize these data into the third normal form, preparing it for use in a relational database environment. The library's computer is programmed to compute the due date to be 14 days after the check-out date. Document the steps necessary to normalize the data similar to the procedures found in the chapter. Add foreign keys and show how the databases are related.

7. Normalization of Data

On page 388 is a table of data for a veterinary practice. Normalize this data into the third normal form, preparing it for use in a relational database environment. Indicate the primary keys and embedded foreign keys in the tables.

Problem 3: Structured Query Language

Report Attributes

Salesperson Name, Salesperson Branch Office, Customer Number, Customer Name, Amount Overdue, Last Purchase Date, Goods Delivered?, Amount of Last Sales Order, Amount of Last Payment, Date of Last Payment

FILES AVAILABLE:

Salesperson Table	Customer Table	Sales Order Table
Salesperson Name	Customer Number	Sales Order Number
Salesperson Number	Customer Name	Customer Number
Commission Rate	Customer Address 1	Order Date
Rank	Customer Address 2	Amount
Branch	Salesperson Number	Delivery Date
Date of Hire	Last Sales Order Number	
	Year to Date Purchases	
	Account Balance	
	Overdue Balance	
	Amount of Last Payment	
	Date of Last Payment	

Problem 6: Normalization of Data

Student ID Number	Student First Name	Student Last Name	Number of Books Out	Book Call No	Book Title	Date Out	Due Date
678-98-4567	Amy	Baker	3	hf351.j6	Avalanches	09-02-04	09-16-04
678-98-4567	Amy	Baker	4	hf878.k3	Tornadoes	09-02-04	09-16-04
244-23-2348	Ramesh	Sunder	1	i835.123	Politics	09-02-04	09-16-04
398-34-8793	James	Talley	3	k987.d98	Sports	09-02-04	09-16-04
398-34-8793	James	Talley	4	d879.39	Legal Rights	09-02-04	09-16-04
678-98-4567	Amy	Baker	4	p987.t87	Earthquakes	09-03-04	09-17-04
244-23-2348	Ramesh	Sunder	1	q875.i76	Past Heroes	09-03-04	09-17-04

8. **Normalization of Data**

Prepare the base tables, in third normal form, needed to produce the user view on page 389.

9. **Normalization of Data**

Prepare the base tables, in third normal form, needed to produce the user view on page 389.

10. **Exposure Identification and Plan of Action**

As the manager of the external audit team, you realize that the embedded audit module writes only "material" invoices to the audit file for the accounts receivable confirmation process. You are immediately concerned that the accounts receivable account may be substantially overstated this year and for the prior years in which this EAM was used.

Required:

Explain why you are concerned since all "material" invoices are candidates for confirmation by the customer. Outline a plan for determining if the accounts receivable are overstated.

11. Generalized Audit Software

CMA 1290 4-Y7

The internal audit department of Sachem Manufacturing Company is considering buying computer software that will aid in the auditing process. Sachem's financial and manufacturing control systems are completely automated on a large mainframe computer. Melinda Robinson, the director of internal audit, believes that Sachem should acquire computer audit software to assist in the financial and procedure audits that her department conducts. The types of software packages that Robinson is considering are described below.

- A generalized audit software package that assists in basic audit work, such as the retrieval of live data from large computer files. The department would review this information using conventional audit investigation techniques. More specifically, the department could perform criteria selection, sampling, basic computations for quantitative analysis, record handling, graphical analysis, and the printing of output (confirmations).

- An integrated test facility package that uses, monitors, and controls dummy test data through existing programs and checks the existence and adequacy of program data entry controls and processing controls.

- A control flowcharting package that provides a graphical presentation of the data flow of information through a system, pinpointing control strengths and weaknesses.

- A program (parallel) simulation and modeling package that uses actual data to conduct the same systemized process by using a different computer-logic program developed by the auditor. The package can also be used to seek answers to difficult audit problems (involving many comparisons and computations) within statistically acceptable confidence limits.

Required:

a. Without regard to any specific computer audit software, explain to the internal auditor the general advantages of using computer audit software to assist with audits.

b. Describe the audit purpose facilitated and the procedural steps to be followed by the internal auditor to use a(n)
   i. generalized audit software package.
   ii. integrated test facility package.
   iii. control flowcharting package.
   iv. program (parallel) simulation and modeling package.

Problem 7: Normalization of Data

Patient ID Number	Patient Name	Owner ID Number	Owner Last Name	Owner First Name	Address1	Address2	Date	Animal Code	Animal Description	Service Code	Service Description	Charge
417	Beau	Magel	Magee	Elaine	23 Elm St	Houston, TX	01/04/05	GR	Golden Retriever	238	Rabies Shot	15.00
417	Beau	Magel	Magee	Elaine	23 Elm St	Houston, TX	01/04/05	GR	Golden Retriever	148	Flea Dip	25.00
417	Beau	Magel	Magee	Elaine	23 Elm St	Houston, TX	01/04/05	GR	Golden Retriever	337	Bloodwork II	20.00
632	Liugi	Cacil	Caciolo	Tony	8 Oak St	Houston, TX	01/09/05	DN	Dalmation	238	Rabies Shot	15.00
632	Luigi	Cacil	Caciolo	Tony	8 Oak St	Houston, TX	01/09/05	DN	Dalmation	500	Kennel—medium	9.00
632	Luigi	Cacil	Caciolo	Tony	8 Oak St	Houston, TX	01/24/05	DN	Dalmation	500	Kennel—medium	9.00
632	Luigi	Cacil	Caciolo	Tony	8 Oak St	Houston, TX	02/01/05	DN	Dalmation	148	Flea Dip	25.00
168	Astro	Jetsl	Jetson	George	3 Air Rd	Sprockley, TX	02/02/05	MX	Canine—mixed	368	Ear Cleaning	17.00

Problem 8: Normalization of Data

USER VIEW									
Part#	Description	QOH	Reorder Point	EOQ	Unit Cost	Ven #	Ven Name	Ven Address	Tel
132	Bolt	100	50	1000	1.50	987	ABC Co.	654 Elm St	555 5498
143	Screw	59	10	100	1.75	987	ABC Co.	654 Elm St	555 5498
760	Nut	80	20	500	2.00	742	XYZ Co.	510 Smit	555 8921
982	Nail	100	50	800	1.00	987	ABC Co.	654 Elm St	555 5498

Problem 9: Normalization of Data

USER VIEW									
Part#	Description	QOH	Reorder Point	EOQ	Unit Cost	Ven #	Ven Name	Ven Address	Tel
132	Bolt	100	50	1000	1.50	987	ABC Co.	654 Elm St	555 5498
					1.55	750	RST Co.	3415 8th St	555 3421
					1.45	742	XYZ Co.	510 Smit	555 8921
982	Nail	100	50	800	1.00	987	ABC Co.	654 Elm St	555 5498
					1.10	742	XYZ Co.	510 Smit	555 8921
					1.00	549	LMN Co.	18 Oak St.	555 9987

12. Exposure Identification and Plan of Action

Two years ago an external auditing firm supervised the programming of embedded audit modules for Previts Office Equipment Company. During the audit process this year, the external auditors requested that a transaction log of all transactions be copied to the audit file. The external auditors noticed large gaps in dates and times for transactions being copied to the audit file. When they inquired about this, they were informed that increased processing of transactions had been burdening the mainframe system and that operators frequently had to turn off the EAM to allow the processing of important transactions in a timely fashion. In addition, much maintenance had been performed during the past year on the application programs.

Required:

Outline any potential exposures and determine the courses of action the external auditors should use to proceed.

13. Normalization of Data

Prepare the 3NF base tables needed to produce the sales report view shown in the diagram for Problem 13.

14. Normalization of Data—Purchase Order

Acme Plywood Company uses the purchase order shown in the diagram for Problem 14.

Acme business rules:

1. Each vendor may supply many items; an item is supplied by only one vendor.
2. A purchase order may list many items; an item may be listed on many purchase orders.
3. An employee may complete several purchase orders, but only one employee may fill out an individual PO.

Prepare the 3FN base tables needed to produce this purchase order.

15. Table Linking

Solve this problem per the text within the diagram for Problem 15.

16. Defining Entities and Data Modeling— Payroll

Employees at the Sagerod Manufacturing Company record their hours worked on paper time cards that are inserted into a time clock machine at the beginning

Problem 13: Normalization of Data

Sales Report

Customer Number: 19321
Customer Name : Jon Smith
Address   : 520 Main St., City

Invoice Num	Date	Invoice Total	Part Num	Quantity	Unit Price	Ext'd Price
12390	11/11/09	$850	2	5	$20	$100
			1	10	50	500
			3	25	10	250
12912	11/21/09	$300	4	10	$30	$300

Customer Total: $1,150

           **   *   ***   *   ***   *   ***   *   ***   *   ***   *   **   *

Customer Number: 19322
Customer Name : Mary Smith
Address   : 2289 Elm St., City

Invoice Num	Date	Invoice Total	Part Num	Quantity	Unit Price	Ext'd Price
12421	11/13/09	$1,000	6	10	$20	$200
			1	2	50	100
			5	7	100	700
12901	11/20/09	$500	4	10	$30	$300
			2	10	20	200

Customer Total: $1,500

           **   *   ***   *   ***   *   ***   *   ***   *   ***   *   **   *

Next Customer
   •
   •
   •
Next Customer

---

and end of each shift. On Fridays, the supervisor collects the time cards, reviews and signs them, and sends them to the payroll clerk. The clerk calculates the pay for each employee and updates the employee earnings file. This involves adding a new record for each employee in the pay period that reflects the employee's gross pay, tax deductions, and other withholdings for the period. The clerk then prepares a paycheck for each employee and records them in the check register. The check register and corresponding paychecks reflect each employee's net earnings for the period. Based on these records, the clerk prepares a payroll summary, which is sent with the paychecks to the cash disbursements clerk. The clerk reviews the payroll **summary**, updates the cash disbursements journal to record the total payroll, and prepares a check for the total payroll, which is deposited into the **payroll imprest account**. The clerk then signs the paychecks and distributes them to the employees.

Required:

Assume that this manual system is to be automated using a relational database system. Perform the following tasks.

Problem 14: Normalization of Data

Purchase Order

Acme Plywood Co.
1234 West Ave.
Somewhere, OH 00000

P.O. #
Date: __/__/__

Vendor: _____

_____

_____

Ship Via: _____   Please refer to this P.O. number on all correspondence.

Prepared by: _____

Item #	Description	Quantity	Cost	Extension

You may need to make assumptions about how certain automated activities will be performed.

a. List all candidate entities in the procedures described.

b. Identify the valid entities and explain why the rejected entities should not be modeled.

c. Create a data model of the process showing entity associations.

17. Defining Entities and Data Modeling— Purchases Procedures

The business rules that constitute the purchases system for the Safe Buy Grocery Stores chain are similar at all the store locations. The purchase manager at each location is responsible for selecting his or her local suppliers. If the manager needs a product, he or she chooses a supplier. Each store follows the steps described here.

1. The purchasing function begins with sales representatives from suppliers periodically observing the shelves and displays at each location and recognizing the need to restock inventory. Inventory declines by direct sales to the customers or by spoilage of perishable goods. In addition, the supplier's sales representatives review obsolescence reports that the purchase manager prepares. These reports identify slow-moving and dated products that are deemed unsalable at a particular location. These products are returned to the supplier and replaced with more successful products. The sales representatives prepare a hard-copy purchase requisition and meet with the purchase managers of the individual store locations. Together, the sales representative and the purchase manager create a purchase order defining the products, the quantity, and the delivery date.

2. At the intended delivery date, Safe Buy Grocery Stores receive the goods from the suppliers. Goods received are unloaded from the delivery trucks and stocked on the shelves and displays by part-time employees.

3. The unloading personnel create a receiving report. Each day a receiving report summary is prepared and sent to the purchase managers for review.

4. The supplier subsequently submits an invoice to the AP department clerk, who creates an invoice record. The clerk reconciles the invoice against the receiving report and purchase order and then creates a payment obligation to be paid at a future date, depending on the terms of trade.

5. On the due date, a check is automatically prepared and sent to the supplier, and the payment is recorded in the check register. At the end of each day, a payment summary is sent to the purchase managers for review.

Problem 15: Table Linking

Several related tables with their primary keys (PK) are shown below. Place the foreign key(s) in the tables to link them according to the associations shown (e.g., 1:M and M:M). Create any new table(s) that may be needed.

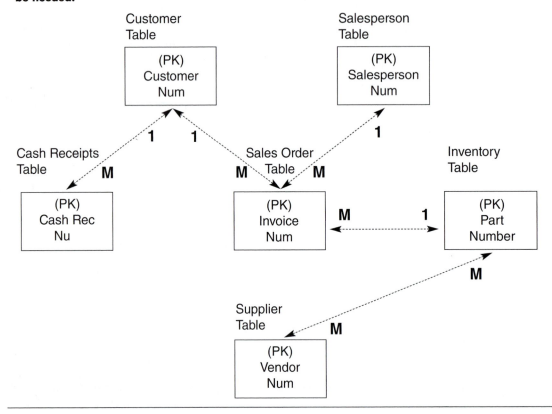

Required:

Assume that the manual system described is to be automated using a relational database system. Perform the following tasks. You may need to make assumptions about how certain automated activities will be performed.

a. List all candidate entities in the procedures described.

b. Identify the valid entities and explain why the rejected entities should not be modeled.

c. Create a data model of the process showing entity associations.

d. Create a fully attributed model by adding primary keys, foreign keys, and data attributes. Normalize the model.

18. Defining Entities and Data Modeling—Fixed Asset Procedures

The business rules that constitute the fixed asset procedures for the Safe Buy Grocery Stores chain are similar at all the store locations. The store manager at each location is responsible for identifying needed

fixed assets and for selecting the vendor. Freezers, refrigerators, delivery vans, and store shelving are examples of fixed asset purchases. Once the need has been identified, each store follows the procedures described next.

The manager creates a purchase order, which is sent to the supplier. The supplier delivers the asset to the receiving clerk, who prepares a receiving report. Each week the fixed asset department clerk reviews the fixed asset receiving report summary and creates a fixed asset inventory record for each receipt. The fixed asset clerk maintains the inventory records and depreciation schedules. The vendor subsequently submits an invoice to the AP department clerk, who creates an invoice record. The clerk reconciles the invoice against the receiving report and purchase order and then creates a payment obligation to be paid at a future date, depending on the terms of trade. On the due date, a check is automatically prepared and sent to the vendor, and the payment is recorded in the check register. At the end of each day, a payment summary is sent to the AP manager for review.

Required:

Assume that the manual system described is to be automated using a relational database system. Perform the following tasks. You may need to make assumptions about how certain automated activities will be performed.

a. List all candidate entities in the procedures described.

b. Identify the valid entities and explain why the rejected entities should not be modeled.

c. Create a data model of the process showing entity associations.

d. Create a fully attributed model by adding primary keys, foreign keys, and data attributes. Normalize the model.

19. Defining Entities and Data Modeling—Sales Order Procedures

Sales Procedures

Customer Lotus Tea Importer Company places an order with a sales representative by phone or fax. The sales department employee then transcribes the customer order into a standard sales order format and produces the following documents: three copies of sales orders, a stock release document, a shipping notice, and a packing slip. The accounting department receives a copy of the sales order, the warehouse receives the stock release and a copy of the sales order, and the shipping department receives a shipping notice and packing slip. The sales clerk files a copy of the sales order in the department.

Upon receipt of the sales order, the accounting department clerk prepares a customer invoice by adding prices to the sales order, which she obtains from the official price list. She then sends the invoice to the customer. Using data from the sales order the clerk then records the sale in the sales journal and in the AR subsidiary ledger. At the end of the day the clerk prepares a sales journal voucher, which she sends to the general ledger department for posting to the sales and AR control accounts.

The warehouse receives a copy of the sales order and stock release document. A warehouse employee picks the product and sends it to the shipping department along with the stock release document. A warehouse clerk then updates the inventory records to reflect the reduction of inventory on hand. At the end of the day the clerk prepares a hard-copy inventory account summary and sends it to the general ledger department for posting to the inventory control and cost of goods sold accounts.

Upon receipt of the stock release document from the warehouse, the shipping clerk prepares the two

copies of a bill of lading. The BOLs and the packing slip are sent with the product to the carrier. The clerk then files the stock release in the department.

Cash Receipts Procedure

The mail room has five employees who open mail and sort the checks from the remittance advices. The remittance advices are sent to the accounting department where the accounting clerk updates the customer AR subsidiary ledger to reflect the reduction in accounts receivable. At the end of the day, the clerk prepares an account summery and sends it to the general ledger department for posting.

The mail room clerk sends the checks to the cash receipts department, where a clerk endorses each check with the words "For Deposit Only." Next, the clerk records the cash receipts in the cash receipts journal. Finally, the clerk prepares a deposit slip and sends it and the checks to the bank.

Required:

Assume that the manual system described is to be automated using a relational database system. Perform the following tasks. You may need to make assumptions about how certain automated activities will be performed.

a. List all candidate entities in the procedures described.

b. Identify the valid entities and explain why the rejected entities should not be modeled.

c. Create a data model of the process showing entity associations.

d. Create a fully attributed model by adding primary keys, foreign keys, and data attributes. Normalize the model.

20. Defining Entities and Data Modeling— Business Rules

Given the following business rules, construct an ER diagram so each rule is captured for the database. Presume each rule is to be treated individually. Construct an ER diagram for each rule.

a. A retail sales company prepares sales orders for its customers' purchases. A customer can make many purchases, but a sales order is written for a single customer.

b. A retail sales company orders inventory using a purchase order. An inventory item may be ordered many times, and a purchase order may be created for more than one inventory item.

c. A company that sells antique cars prepares a sales order for each car sold. The inventory for this company consists of unique automobiles, and only one of these automobiles may be listed on a sales order.

d. A grocery store identifies returning customers via a plastic card that the clerk scans at the time of each purchase. The purpose of this card is to track inventory and to maintain a database of customers and their purchases. Obviously, a customer may purchase an unlimited number of items from the grocery store. Items are unique only by a UPC code, and each UPC code may be associated with many different customers.

    e. A video rental store uniquely identifies each of its inventory items so customers can rent a movie and return the movie via a drop box, and the store can identify which copy of the movie was rented and returned. A customer is allowed to rent up to six movies at a time, but a copy of a movie can only be rented by one customer at a time.

21. Comprehensive Case

(Prepared by Katie Daley and Gail Freeston, Lehigh University)

    D&F is a distributor of CDs and cassettes that offers benefits such as discount prices and an introductory offer of ten CDs or cassettes for a penny (not including the shipping and handling costs). Its primary target customers are college students; its main marketing strategy is constant deals to club members. The company's main competitors in the industry are BMG and Columbia House; both offer similar promotions.

    D&F started in 1993 with an office in Harrisburg, Pennsylvania, initially targeting college students in the surrounding area. The company realized there was a high demand for discounted music merchandise and the convenience of mail delivery within universities. After its second year, with a constant increase in customer orders, D&F relocated to Philadelphia, where it was located near more colleges and universities. The move has had a positive effect on net profits and demand, supporting the decision to continue the growth of the company. D&F recently expanded its facility to be able to fulfill a higher demand for its services. Its customer base ranges from areas as close as Villanova University to as far as Boston College. As of 2007, there were 103 employees. Their prior year's gross sales were $125 million.

    D&F's market share is on the rise, but is not yet comparable to the magnitude of BMG and Columbia House. However, the corporation's goals for the upcoming years include establishing itself as an industry player through increased customer satisfaction and loyalty. D&F is also considering the installation of a new information-processing system. This system will reengineer their current business functions by reducing loopholes in their internal control problems.

    D&F receives CDs and cassettes from various wholesale suppliers and music store chains, totaling 32 suppliers nationwide. The office has its own warehouse, stores its own merchandise, and is responsible for replenishing the inventory. D&F has had no substantial problems in the past with their suppliers. On the other hand, it has encountered problems with excess inventory, stock-outs, and discrepancies with inventory records.

Revenue Cycle

Becoming a member of D&F Music Club involves calling the toll-free number and speaking with a sales representative, who establishes a new customer account. A customer's account record contains his or her name, address, phone number, previous orders he or she made with the company, and a sequentially assigned unique customer account number.

    Customers place orders by phone with a sales representative, who prepares a sales order record. John, in the billing department, reviews the sales orders, adds prices and shipping charges, and prints a copy (invoice) that is sent to the customer. John then adds a record to the sales journal to record the sale.

    Chris, a warehouse employee, verifies the information on the sales order, picks the goods, prints the packing slip, and updates the inventory subsidiary ledger. Chris prepares the bill of lading for the carrier. The goods are then shipped.

    Sandy in AR updates the customer accounts and general ledger control accounts. When customers make a payment on account, they send both the remittance advice (that was attached to the invoice) and a check with their account number on it. Scott, a mail room clerk, opens all the cash receipts. He separates the check and remittance advice and prepares a remittance list, which, along with the checks, is sent to the cash receipts department.

    Laura, the cash receipts clerk, reconciles the checks with the remittance, updates the customer's account and the general ledger, and then deposits the checks in the bank. She sends the deposit slip to Sandy in the accounting department.

    Upon receiving the bank receipt, Sandy files it and updates the cash receipts journal to record the amount deposited. Upon the receipt of the CDs or cassettes ordered, the customer has a 15-day trial period. If, at the end of that period, he or she sends a payment, it is understood that the goods have been accepted. If, on the other hand, the customer is dissatisfied with the product for any reason, he or she can return it to D&F Music Club at no charge. However, to return the CD or cassette, the customer must call the company to obtain an authorization number. When the goods arrive, Chris prepares the return record and updates the inventory subsidiary ledger. Printed copies of the return record are sent to John and Sandy. John reviews the return record and updates the sales journal. Sandy credits the customer's account and updates the general ledger to reverse the transaction.

Expenditure Cycle

The purchases system and the cash disbursements system comprise D&F Music Club's expenditure cycle. The three departments within the purchasing system are the warehouse, purchasing, and accounting. The purchasing function begins in the warehouse, which stores the inventory of CDs and cassettes. Jim, the warehouse manager, compares inventory records with the various demand forecasts of each week, which the market research analyst teams provide, to determine the necessary orders to make. At the end of the week, Jim prepares the purchase requisition record.

Sara, the purchasing clerk, reviews the purchase requisitions, selects the suppliers, and prepares the purchase orders. Copies of the purchase orders are sent to the supplier and accounting.

When the shipment arrives, Chris, the warehouse clerk, working from a blind copy of the purchase order, counts and inspects the goods for damage. He then prepares a receiving report and updates the inventory records.

Upon receipt of the supplier's invoice, Diana, the accounting clerk, compares it to the respective purchase order and receiving report. If the invoice is accurate, Diana creates an AP record, sets a due date to be paid, and updates general ledger accounts.

On the due date, Evan, the cash disbursements clerk, closes the AP record, cuts a check, and sends it to the supplier. He then updates the check register and the general ledger.

Required:

Assume that the manual system described is to be automated using a relational database system. Perform the following tasks. You may need to make assumptions about how certain automated activities will be performed.

a. List all candidate entities in the procedures described.
b. Identify the valid entities and explain why the rejected entities should not be modeled.
c. Create a data model of the processes showing entity associations.
d. Create a fully attributed model by adding primary keys, foreign keys, and data attributes. Normalize the model.
e. Prepare a data flow diagram of the system showing the data stores.

22. ACL Exercise—Overview of ACL

Load the ACL student edition onto your computer and download the ACL Getting Started manual (ACLStart.pdf). Read the manual and complete the exercises.

9

Auditing the Revenue Cycle

LEARNING OBJECTIVES

After studying this chapter, you should:

- Understand the operational tasks associated with the revenue cycle under different levels of technology.
- Understand audit objectives related to the revenue cycle.
- Be familiar with revenue cycle control issues related to alternative technologies.
- Recognize the relationship between revenue cycle audit objectives, controls, and tests of controls.
- Understand the nature of substantive tests in achieving revenue cycle audit objectives.
- Be familiar with common features and functions of ACL that are used to perform substantive tests.

This chapter examines audit procedures associated with the revenue cycle. The chapter is divided into three main sections. It begins with a review of alternative technologies used in both legacy and modern systems. The focus is on the key operational tasks performed under each technological environment. The second section discusses the revenue cycle audit objectives, controls, and tests of controls that an auditor would perform to gather evidence needed to limit the scope, timing, and extent of substantive tests. The last section describes revenue cycle substantive tests in relation to audit objectives. Specific procedures based on ACL software are illustrated.

REVENUE CYCLE ACTIVITIES AND TECHNOLOGIES

This chapter assumes that the reader is familiar with the general procedures that constitute the revenue cycle and with the key accounting records and documents employed in revenue cycle transaction processing. Those who need to review this body of material should turn to the appendix at this point, where it is presented in detail.

This section examines alternative information technologies used to support revenue cycle activities. The first of these is a sales order system that employs batch processing and uses sequential files for storing accounting records. This is an example of an early legacy-type system. This approach characterizes the era of data ownership in which files were designed exclusively for the use of a single user. Data sharing is difficult, if not impossible, in this setting and results in a great deal of data redundancy and data obsolescence. Although archaic, such systems are still used because they continue to add value for organizations. For years, the anticipation was that legacy systems would be replaced before the end of the twentieth century to avoid highly publicized Y2K problems. Instead, many organizations opted to commit significant resources to repair and modify these systems for the next millennium. Once the investments were made, the pressure to replace legacy systems was reduced. Odds favor the likelihood that auditors will be dealing with these technologies for some time to come.

Second, we review the operational features of a cash receipts system that employs batch processing and uses direct access files. This configuration is found in both modern systems and late-era legacy systems. The direct access file approach offers operational advantages over sequential file processing and permits limited data sharing.

The final example depicts a modern real-time sales order and cash receipts system that uses database technology. Modern systems design embraces **reengineering** to radically reshape business processes and workflow. The objective of reengineering is to reduce business-processing costs by identifying and eliminating non-value-added tasks. This process involves replacing some traditional procedures with procedures that are innovative and sometimes very different from those that previously existed.

You should recognize that space limitations prohibit a review of all possible configurations of processing technologies, techniques, and file structures. The objective, instead, is to present examples of fundamentally different approaches that are typically found in practice and examine their control and audit implications.

Batch Processing Using Sequential Files—Manual Procedures

Figure 9.1 illustrates an automated sales order system that uses batch processing and sequential files. In this basic system, order taking, credit checking, warehousing, and shipping are performed manually. Computer programs process the accounting records. The following discussion outlines the key features of the system.

Obtaining and Recording the Customers' Orders

The sales process begins in the sales department with the receipt of a **customer order** indicating the type and quantity of merchandise being requested. At this point, the customer order is not in a standard format and may not be a physical document. Orders may arrive by mail, by telephone, or from a field representative who visited the customer's place of business. When the customer is also a business entity, the order is usually a copy of the customer's purchase order.

The primary objective of this step is to ensure that relevant data about the transaction are transcribed into a standard format that can be processed by the selling entity's system. The document prepared in this procedure is the **sales order**.

The sales order captures such vital information as the name and address of the customer; the customer's account number; the name, number, and description of the items sold; the quantities and unit prices of each item sold; and other financial information such as taxes, discounts, and freight charges. In manual systems, multiple copies of sales orders are produced to serve different purposes. The number of copies created will vary from system to system, depending on the operations to be supported. The hypothetical system in Figure 9.1 uses sales order copies for credit authorizations, packing slips, stock

FIGURE 9.1 **Batch Processing with Sequential Files**

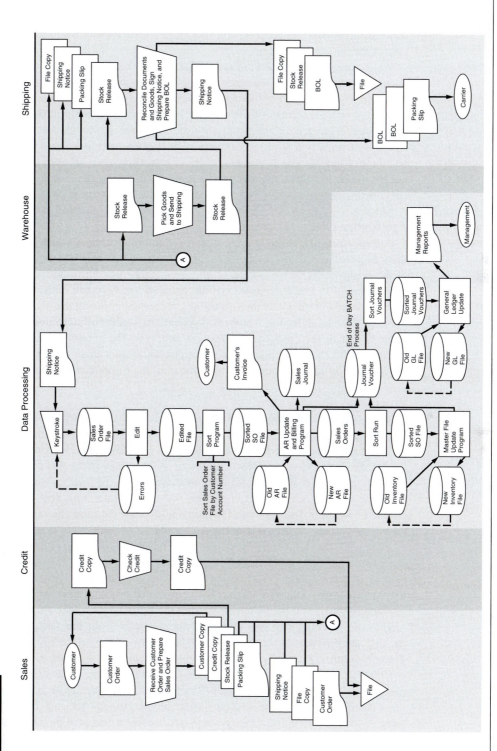

release documents, and shipping notices. Customer invoicing and ledger posting are performed by the computer system. In an actual system, the various sales order copies would be numbered or color-coded to signify their purpose and distribution. Copies that are used for more than one purpose, and that go to several locations, sometimes have routing information printed on them.

After preparing the sales order, the sales clerk files one copy of it in the **customer open order file** for future reference. Filling the order and getting the product to the customer may take days or even weeks. Customers frequently contact their suppliers by telephone to check the status of their orders. To facilitate customer inquiries, the open order file is often organized alphabetically by customer name. Although customer name is not an efficient primary key for accessing data, it is often used as a secondary key to cross-reference orders because customers do not always know their account numbers and may not have copies of their invoices handy. In these situations, the customer file enables the clerk to find the sales order and respond to the customer's questions.

Approving Credit

The next step in the revenue cycle is transaction authorization, which involves verifying the customer's creditworthiness. The circumstances of the sale will determine the nature of the credit check. For example, a seller may perform a full financial investigation on new customers to establish a line of credit. However, once a credit limit is set, credit checking on subsequent sales may involve nothing more than ensuring that the current sale does not exceed the limit. In our hypothetical system, the **credit authorization** copy of the sales order is sent to the credit department for approval. The returned approval triggers the release of the other sales order copies simultaneously to various departments. The credit copy is filed in the customer open order file until the transaction is completed.

Processing Shipping Orders

The sales department sends the **stock release** (also called the **picking ticket**) copy of the sales order to the warehouse. This document identifies the items of inventory that must be located and picked from the warehouse shelves. It also provides formal authorization for the warehouse clerk to release custody of the specified assets. After picking the stock, the clerk initials the stock release copy to indicate that the order is complete and accurate. Any out-of-stock items are noted on the stock release copy. One copy of the stock release travels with the goods to the shipping department, and the other is filed in the warehouse to provide a record of the transaction.

The clerk then adjusts the stock records to reflect the reduction in inventory. The stock records are *not* the formal accounting records for these assets. Assigning the warehouse clerk asset custody and record-keeping responsibility would violate internal control. Updating the inventory accounting records is an automated procedure that is described later.

Before the arrival of the goods and the stock release copy, the shipping department receives the **packing slip** and **shipping notice** copies from the sales department. The packing slip travels with the goods to the customer to describe the contents of the order. These are either placed inside the shipping container or attached to the outside in a special plastic pouch. The shipping notice informs the billing department that the customer's order has been filled and shipped. This document contains such pertinent facts as the date of shipment, items and quantities shipped, the carrier, and freight charges. In some systems, the shipping notice is a separate document prepared by the shipping clerk.

Upon receiving the goods from the warehouse, the shipping clerk reconciles the physical items with the stock release documents, the packing slip, and the shipping notice to verify the correctness of the order. This control is important because it is the last opportunity to detect errors before shipment. The shipping clerk packages the goods, attaches the packing slip to the container, completes the shipping notice, and prepares a **bill of lading**.

The shipping clerk transfers custody of the goods, the packing slip, and two copies of the bill of lading to the carrier, then performs the following tasks:

1. Records the shipment in the shipping log.
2. Sends the stock release document and the shipping notice to the billing department as proof of shipment.
3. Files one copy each of the bill of lading and the shipping document.

Batch Processing Using Sequential Files—Automated Procedures

In the last section, we noted that order taking, credit checking, warehousing, and shipping are manual operations as illustrated in Figure 9.1. The figure also illustrates a fifth operation—data processing. This is an automated operation and is discussed in this section in greater detail. The computer system described here is an example of a *legacy* system that employs the sequential file structure for its accounting records. Both tapes and disks can be used as the physical storage medium for such systems. However, the use of tapes has declined considerably in recent years. For day-to-day operations, tapes are inefficient because they must be physically mounted on a tape drive and then dismounted when the job ends. This approach is labor intensive and expensive. The constant decline in the cost of disk storage in recent years has eliminated the economic advantage once associated with tapes. Most organizations that still use sequential files store them on disks that are permanently connected (online) to the computer system and require no human intervention. The operational features of sequential files described earlier are the same for both tape and disk media. Today, tapes are used primarily as backup devices and for storing archive data. For these purposes, they provide an efficient and effective storage medium for a large system.

Keypunch/Data Entry

The process begins with the arrival of batches of shipping notices from the shipping department. These documents are copies of the sales orders that contain accurate information about the number of units shipped and information about the carrier. The data processing (DP) clerk converts the shipping notices to magnetic media to produce a transaction file of sales orders. Typically, this process is continual. Throughout the day, the DP clerks receive and convert batches of shipping notices to magnetic media. The resulting transaction file will thus contain many separate batches of sales orders. **Batch control totals** are calculated for each batch on the file.

Edit Run

Periodically, the batch sales order system is executed. Depending on the volume of transaction and computer resource constraints, the process may take place only once or several times each day. The edit program is the first run in the batch process. This program validates transactions by testing each record for the existence of clerical or logical errors. Typical tests include field checks, limit tests, range tests, and price times quantity extensions. Recall from Chapter 7 that detected errors are removed from the batch and copied to a separate error file. Later, these are corrected by an authorized person and resubmitted for processing with the next day's business. The edit program recalculates the batch control totals to reflect changes due to the removal of error records. The "clean" transaction file is then passed to the next run in the process.

Sort Run

At this point, the sales order file is in no useful sequence. To process a sequential transaction file, it must be placed in the same sequence as the master file that it is updating. Since the first master file to be updated in the systems is accounts receivable, the sort run physically arranges the sales order transaction file sequentially by Account Number, which is one of its secondary keys.

AR Update and Billing Run

The AR update program posts to accounts receivable by sequentially matching the Account Number key in each sales order record with the corresponding record in the AR-SUB master file. This procedure creates a new AR-SUB master file that incorporates all the changes to the customer accounts that are affected by transaction records. The original AR-SUB master file remains complete and unchanged by the process. The creation of a new and separate master file is a characteristic of sequential file processing. A side benefit of this is the automatic creation of a backup version of the file being updated. Figure 9.2 illustrates this method with some sample records.

Each sales transaction record processed is added to the sales journal file. At the end of the run, these are summarized and an entry is made to the journal voucher file to reflect total sales and total increases to accounts receivable.

To spread the billing task evenly over the month, some firms employ **cycle billing** of their customers. The update program searches the billing date field in the AR-SUB master file for those customers to be billed on that day of the month and prepares statements for the selected accounts. The statements are then mailed to the customer.

Sort and Inventory Update Runs

The procedures for the second sort and inventory update runs are similar to those just described. The sort program sorts the sales order file on the other secondary key— Inventory Number. The inventory update program reduces the Quantity-on-Hand field in the affected inventory records by the Quantity Sold field in each sales order record. A new inventory master file is created in the process. Figure 9.3 illustrates the process.

In addition, the program compares values of the Quantity-on-Hand and the Reorder Point fields to identify inventory items that need to be replenished. This information is sent to the purchasing department. Finally, a journal voucher is prepared to reflect cost of goods sold and the reduction in inventory.

General Ledger Update Run

Under the sequential file approach, the general ledger master file is not updated after each batch of transactions. To do so would result in the recreation of the entire general ledger every time a batch of transactions (such as sales orders, cash receipts, purchases, and cash disbursements) is processed. Firms using sequential files typically employ separate end-of-day procedures to update the general ledger accounts. This technique is depicted in Figure 9.1.

At the end of the day, the general ledger system accesses the journal voucher file. This file contains journal vouchers reflecting all of the day's transactions processed by the organization. The journal vouchers are sorted by general ledger account number and posted to general ledger in a single run, and a new general ledger is created.

The end-of-day procedures will also generate a number of management reports. These may include sales summaries, inventory status reports, transaction listings, journal voucher listings, and budget and performance reports. Quality management reports play

FIGURE 9.2 Update of Accounts Receivable from Sales Orders

Sales Order Transaction File

PK	SK								
Order #	Acct Num	Inven Num	Order Date	Ship Date	Carrier Code	Shipping Charges	Qnty Sold	Unit Price	Invoice Amount
3	1	17	12/22	12/24	011	10	25	10	250
1	4	14	12/22	12/24	011	5	10	2	20
2	7	16	12/22	12/24	011	20	100	5	500

Transaction file sorted by secondary key to primary key of master file

Original Account Receivable Master File

Update Fields

PK						
ACCT NUM	Address	Current Balance	Credit Limit	Last Payment Date	Billing Date
1	123 Elm St., City	350	1000	12/8/04	1
2	35 Main S.	600	1500	12/12/04	1
3	510 Barclay Dr. Beth.	1000	1500	12/5/04	1
4	26 Taylo Rd. Alltn.	100	2000	12/16/04	8
5	4 High St., Naz.	800	1000	12/9/04	1
6	850 1st, Beth.	700	2000	12/7/04	8
7	78 Market Alltn.	150	2000	12/17/04	15

New Account Receivable Master File

ACCT NUM	Address	Current Balance	Credit Limit	Last Payment Date	Billing Date
1	123 Elm St., City	600	1000	12/8/04	1
2	35 Main S.	600	1500	12/12/04	1
3	510 Barclay Dr. Beth.	1000	1500	12/5/04	1
4	26 Taylo Rd. Alltn.	120	2000	12/16/04	8
5	4 High St., Naz.	800	1000	12/9/04	1
6	850 1st, Beth.	700	2000	12/7/04	8
7	78 Market Alltn.	650	2000	12/17/04	15

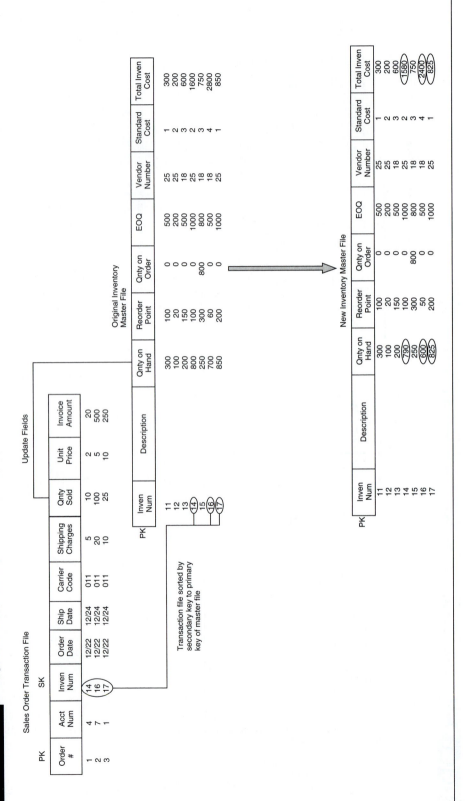

FIGURE 9.3   Update of Inventory from Sales Order

a key role in helping management monitor operations to ensure that controls are in place and functioning properly.

Batch Cash Receipts System with Direct Access Files

Cash receipts procedures are natural batch systems. Unlike sales transactions, which tend to occur continuously throughout the day, cash receipts are discrete events. Checks and remittance advices arrive from the postal service in batches. Likewise, the deposit of cash receipts in the bank usually happens as a single event at the end of the business day. Because of these characteristics, many firms see no significant benefit from investing in costly real-time cash procedures.

The cash receipts system in Figure 9.4 uses direct access files and batch processing. The technology employed in this example is used to automate traditional procedures. The following discussion outlines the main points of this system.

Mailroom

The mailroom separates the checks and remittance advices and prepares a remittance list. These checks and a copy of the remittance list are sent to the cash receipts department. The remittance advices and a copy of the remittance list go to the AR department.

Cash Receipts Department

The cash receipts clerk reconciles the checks and the remittance list and prepares the deposit slips. Via terminal, the clerk creates a journal voucher record of total cash received. The clerk files the remittance list and one copy of the deposit slip. At the end of the day, the clerk deposits the cash in the bank.

Accounts Receivable (AR) Department

The AR clerk receives and reconciles the remittance advices and remittance list. Via terminal, the clerk creates the cash receipts transaction file based on the individual remittance advices. The clerk then files the remittance advices and the remittance list.

Data Processing Department

At the end of the day, the batch program reconciles the journal voucher with the transaction file of cash receipts, and updates the AR-SUB and the general ledger control accounts (AR-Control and Cash). This process employs the direct access method described earlier. Finally, the system produces a transaction listing that the AR clerk will reconcile against the remittance list.

Real-Time Sales Order Entry and Cash Receipts

Figure 9.5 illustrates a reengineered sales order system. Interactive computer terminals now replace many of the manual procedures and physical documents. This system provides real-time input and output with batch updating of only some of the master files.

Order Entry Procedures

Sales Procedures. Under real-time processing, sales clerks receiving orders from customers process each transaction separately as it is received. Using a computer terminal

FIGURE 9.4   Computer-Based Cash Receipts System

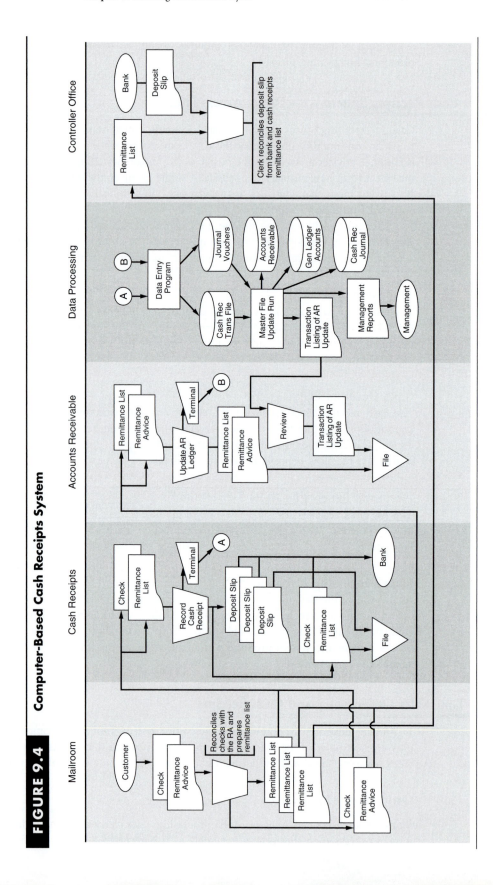

FIGURE 9.5   Real-Time Sales Order Entry and Cash Receipts

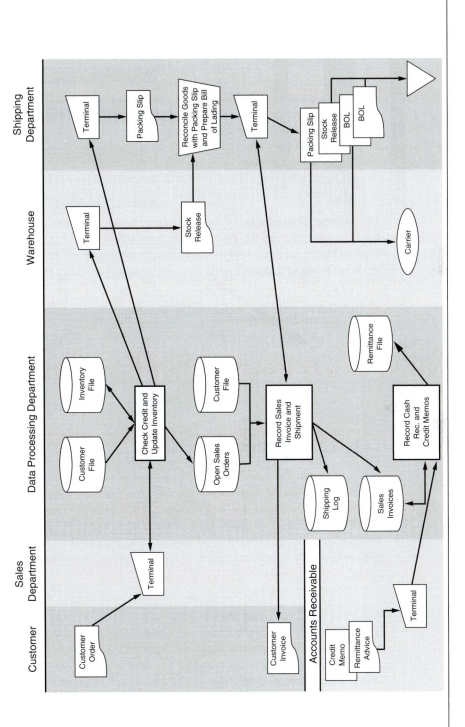

connected to an edit/inquiry program, the clerk performs the following tasks in real-time mode:

1. Perform a credit check online by accessing the customer credit file. This file contains information such as the customer's credit limit, current balance, date of last payment, and current credit status. Based on programmed criteria, the customer's request for credit is approved or denied.
2. If credit is approved, the clerk then accesses the inventory master file and checks the availability of the inventory. The system reduces inventory by the quantities of items sold to present an accurate and current picture of inventory on hand and available for sale.
3. The system automatically transmits an electronic stock release record to the warehouse and a shipping notice to the shipping department, and records the sale in the open sales order file. This is a temporary holding file for sales orders until they are shipped and can then be billed.

Warehouse Procedures. The warehouse clerk's terminal immediately produces a hard copy printout of the electronically transmitted stock release document. The clerk then picks the goods and sends them, along with a copy of the stock release document, to the shipping department.

Shipping and Billing. The shipping clerk reconciles the goods, the stock release document, and the hard copy packing slip produced on the terminal. The clerk then selects a carrier and prepares the goods for shipment. From a terminal, the clerk transmits a shipping notice containing invoice, date, and carrier information to create a shipping log record of the event. The transaction record is removed from the open sales order file and added to the sales invoice file. Finally, drawing from data in the customer file, the system automatically prepares the customer's bill.

Cash Receipts Procedures

In open invoice systems, such as this, each invoice is billed and paid individually. Cash from customers may be received and processed as just described or may be sent directly to a bank lock-box. In either case, the remittance advices (and credit memos to reflect returns and allowances) are sent to the AR department where the clerk enters them into the system via a terminal. Each remittance record is assigned a unique remittance number and is added to the remittance file. Placing the remittance number and the current date in the respective fields then closes the corresponding open invoice record.

Features of Real-Time Processing

This system is a departure from traditional accounting. A central feature of the system is the use of an **events database**. Traditional accounting records may not exist per se. For instance, in this example the sales invoice file replaces the sales journal and AR-SUB ledger. Total sales is the sum of *all* invoices for the period. Summing the *open* sales invoices (those not closed by cash receipts or credit memos) provides accounts receivable information. In theory, such a system does not even need a general ledger because sales, sales returns, accounts receivable-control, and cost of goods sold can all be derived from the invoices in the events database. Most organizations, however, prefer to maintain a separate general ledger file for efficiency and as a cross check of processing accuracy.

Reengineered sales order processes can significantly reduce operating costs and improve efficiency. Four advantages make this approach an attractive option for many organizations:

1. *Real-time processing greatly shortens the cash cycle of the firm.* Lags inherent in traditional systems can cause delays of several days between taking an order and billing the customer. A real-time system with remote terminals reduces or eliminates these lags. An order received in the morning may be shipped by early afternoon, thus permitting same-day billing of the customer.

2. *Real-time processing can give a firm a competitive advantage in the marketplace.* By maintaining current inventory information, sales staff can determine immediately whether inventories are available. In contrast, batch systems do not provide salespeople with current information. As a result, a portion of the order must sometimes be back-ordered, causing customer dissatisfaction. Current information provided through real-time processing enhances the firm's ability to maximize customer service, which translates to increased sales.

3. *Manual procedures tend to produce clerical errors, such as incorrect account numbers, invalid inventory numbers, and price–quantity extension miscalculations.* These errors may go undetected in batch systems until the source documents reach data processing, by which time the damage may already be done. For example, the firm may find that it has shipped goods to the wrong address, shipped the wrong goods, or promised goods to a customer at the wrong price. Real-time editing permits the identification of many kinds of errors when they occur and greatly improves the efficiency and the effectiveness of operations.

4. *Real-time processing reduces the amount of paper documents in a system.* Hard copy documents are expensive to produce and clutter the system. The permanent storage of these documents can become a financial and operational burden. Documents in electronic format are efficient, effective, and adequate for most audit trail purposes.

Point-of-Sale (POS) Systems

The revenue cycle systems that we have examined so far are used by organizations that extend credit to their customers. Obviously, this approach is not valid for all types of business enterprises. For example, grocery stores do not usually function in this way; they exchange goods directly for cash in a transaction that is consummated at the point of sale.

POS systems like the one shown in Figure 9.6 are used extensively in grocery stores, department stores, and other types of retail organizations. In this example, only cash, checks, and bank credit card sales are valid. The organization maintains no customer accounts receivable and inventory is kept on the store's shelves, not in a separate warehouse. The customers personally pick the items they wish to buy and carry them to the checkout location, where the transaction begins.

Daily Procedures

First, the checkout clerk scans the **universal product code (UPC)** label on the items being purchased with a laser light scanner. The scanner, which is the primary input device of the POS system, may be handheld or mounted on the checkout table. The POS system is connected online to the inventory file from which it retrieves product price data and displays this on the clerk's terminal. The inventory quantity on hand is reduced in real time to reflect the items sold. As items fall to minimum levels, they are automatically reordered.

FIGURE 9.6   **Point-of-Sale System**

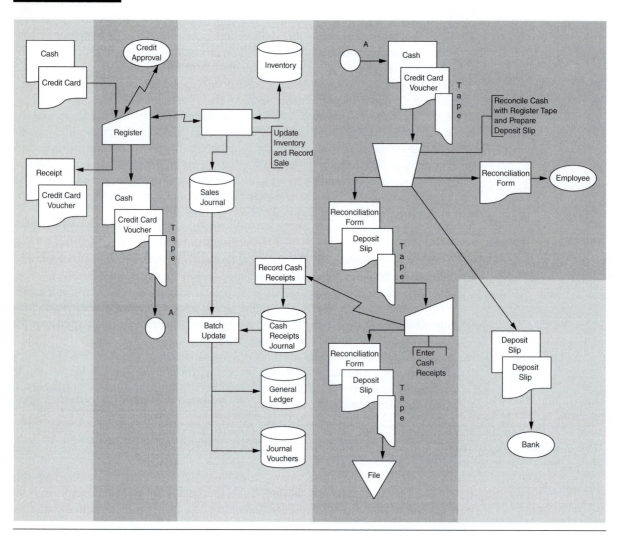

When all the UPCs are scanned, the system automatically calculates taxes, discounts, and the total for the transaction. In the case of credit card transactions, the sales clerk obtains transaction approval from the credit card issuer via an online connection. When the approval is returned, the clerk prepares a credit card voucher for the amount of the sale, which the customer signs. The clerk gives the customer one copy of the voucher and secures a second copy in the cash drawer of the register. For cash sales, the customer renders cash for the full amount of the sale, which the clerk secures in the cash drawer.

The clerk enters the transaction into the POS system via the register's keypad, and a record of the sale is added to the sales journal in real time. The record contains the following key data: date, time, terminal number, total amount of sale, cash or credit card sale, cost of items sold, sales tax, and discounts taken. The sale is also recorded on a two-part paper tape. One copy is given to the customer as a receipt; the other is secured internally within the register and the clerk cannot access it. This internal tape is later used to close out the register when the clerk's shift is over.

At the end of the clerk's shift, a supervisor unlocks the register and retrieves the internal tape. The cash drawer is removed and replaced with a new cash drawer containing a known amount of start-up cash (float) for the next clerk. The supervisor and the clerk whose shift has ended take the cash drawer to the cash room (treasury), where the contents are reconciled against the internal tape. The cash drawer should contain cash and credit card vouchers equal to the amount recorded on the tape.

Often, small discrepancies will exist because of errors in making change for customers. Organizational policy will specify how cash discrepancies are handled. Some organizations require sales clerks to cover all cash shortages via payroll deductions. Other organizations establish a materiality threshold. Cash shortages within the threshold are recorded but not deducted from the employee's pay. Excess shortages, however, should be reviewed for possible disciplinary action.

When the contents of the cash drawer have been reconciled, the cash receipts clerk prepares a cash reconciliation form and gives one copy to the sales clerk as a receipt for cash remitted and records cash received and cash short/over in the cash receipts journal. The clerk files the credit card vouchers and secures the cash in the safe for deposit in the bank at the end of the day.

End-of-day Procedures

At the end of the day, the cash receipts clerk prepares a three-part deposit slip for the total amount of the cash received. One copy is filed and the other two accompany the cash to the bank. Because cash is involved, armed guards are often used to escort the funds to the bank repository. Finally, a batch program summarizes the sales and cash receipts journals, prepares a journal voucher, and posts to the general ledger accounts as follows:

	DR	CR
Cash	XXXX.XX	
Cash Over/Short	XX.XX	
Accounts Receivable (credit card)	XXX.XX	
Cost of Goods Sold	XXX.XX	
Sales		XXXX.XX
Inventory		XXX.XX

The accounting entry above may vary among businesses. Some companies will treat credit card sales as cash. Others will maintain an AR until the credit card issuer transfers the funds into their account.

REVENUE CYCLE AUDIT OBJECTIVES, CONTROLS, AND TESTS OF CONTROLS

Chapter 1 introduced the concept of audit objectives for transactions and account balances that are derived from management assertions about financial statement presentations. The assertions are existence or occurrence, completeness, accuracy, rights and

TABLE 9.1	Relationship between Management Assertions and Revenue Cycle Audit Objectives

Management Assertions	Revenue Cycle Audit Objectives
Existence or Occurrence	Verify that the accounts receivable balance represents amounts actually owed to the organization at the balance sheet date.
	Establish that revenue from sales transactions represent goods shipped and services rendered during the period covered by the financial statements.
Completeness	Determine that all amounts owed to the organization at the balance sheet date are reflected in accounts receivable. Verify that all sales for shipped goods, all services rendered, and all returns and allowances for the period are reflected in the financial statements.
Accuracy	Verify that revenue transactions are accurately computed and based on current prices and correct quantities.
	Ensure that the AR subsidiary ledger, the Sales Invoice file, and the Remittance file are mathematically correct and agree with general ledger accounts.
Rights and Obligations	Determine that the organization has a legal right to recorded accounts receivable. Customer accounts that have been sold or factored have been removed from the accounts receivable balance.
Valuation or Allocation	Determine that the accounts receivable balance states its net realizable value.
	Establish that the allocation for uncollectible accounts is appropriate.
Presentation and Disclosure	Verify accounts receivable and revenues reported for the period are properly described and classified in the financial statements.

obligations, valuation or allocation and presentation and disclosure. Table 9.1 shows how these translate to specific revenue cycle audit objectives.[1]

Achieving these audit objectives requires designing audit procedures to gather evidence that either corroborates or refutes the management assertions. Generally, this process involves a combination of tests of controls and substantive tests of details. The specific controls we address here are based on the more-extensive discussion of application controls issues contained in Chapter 7. The discussion in this section presumes that the reader is familiar with that material. Recall that computer application controls fall into three broad categories: input controls, process controls, and output controls. Within this framework, we examine application controls, tests of controls, and the audit objectives

---

1   Adapted from *Montgomery's Auditing,* 12th ed. (New York: Coopers & Lybrand, L.L.P., 1998), p. 18.

to which they relate. Substantive tests and their relationship to audit objectives are considered later in the chapter.

Input Controls

Input controls are designed to ensure that transactions are valid, accurate, and complete. Control techniques vary considerably between batch and real-time systems. The following input controls relate to revenue cycle operations.

Credit Authorization Procedures

The purpose of the credit check is to establish the creditworthiness of the customer. Only customer transactions that meet the organization's credit standards are valid and should be processed further. In batch systems with manual credit authorization procedures, the credit department (or credit manager) is responsible for implementing the firm's credit policies. In POS systems, the authorization process involves validating credit card charges and establishing that the customer is the valid user of the card. After receiving online approval from the credit card company, the clerk should match the customer's signature on the sales voucher with the one on the credit card.

When credit checks are computerized, the organization's credit policy is implemented through decision rules that have been programmed into the system. For routine transactions, this typically involves determining if the current transaction plus the customer's current account receivable balance exceeds a preestablished credit limit. If the credit limit is exceeded by the transaction, it should be rejected by the program and passed to an exception file, where it can be reviewed by management. The credit manager will decide either to disapprove the sale or to extend the credit limit consistent with the manager's authority.

Testing Credit Procedures

Failure to apply credit policy correctly and consistently has implications for the adequacy of the organization's allowance for uncollectible accounts. The following tests provide evidence pertaining to the *valuation/allocation* audit objectives and, to a lesser extent, the *accuracy* objective.

The auditor needs, therefore, to determine that effective procedures exist to establish appropriate customer credit limits; communicate this information adequately to the credit policy decision makers; review credit policy periodically and revise it as necessary; and monitor adherence to current credit policy.

The auditor can verify the correctness of programmed decision rules by using either the *test data* or *integrated test facility (ITF)* approaches to directly test their functionality. This testing is easily accomplished by creating several dummy customer accounts with various lines of credit and then processing test transactions that will exceed some of the credit limits. The auditor can then analyze the rejected transactions to determine if the computer application correctly applied the credit policy.

The integrity of reference data is an important element in testing credit policy controls. A correctly functioning computer application cannot successfully apply credit policy if customer credit limits are excessively high or can be changed by unauthorized personnel. The auditor needs to verify that authority for making line-of-credit changes is limited to authorized credit department personnel. Performing substantive tests of detail to identify customers with excessive credit limits can do this. Substantive tests traditionally follow tests of controls because the results of tests of controls are used to determine the nature, timing, and extent of the substantive tests. In this case, however, substantive tests may be the most efficient way to verify if credit policy is being properly applied.

Data Validation Controls

Input validation controls are intended to detect transcription errors in transaction data before they are processed. Since errors detected early are less likely to infiltrate the accounting records, validation procedures are most effective when they are performed as close to the source of the transaction as possible. In the batch system depicted in Figure 9.1, data validation occurs only after the goods have been shipped. Extensive error logs, error correction, and transaction resubmission procedures characterize such systems. By contrast, validity tests performed in real time and POS systems can deal with most errors as they occur. This approach also minimizes human data entry and thus reduces the risk of data entry errors. For example, when the clerk enters the customer's account number, the system automatically retrieves his or her name and mailing address. When the clerk enters the product number and quantity sold, the data entry system automatically retrieves the product description and price, and then calculates the extended price plus tax and shipping charges.

Chapter 7 presented a number of general types of validation tests. Examples that are relevant to the revenue cycle include the following:

- *Missing data checks* are used to examine the contents of a field for the presence of blank spaces. Missing product numbers, missing customer account numbers, or incomplete mailing or billing addresses will cause the transaction to be rejected. When the validation program detects a blank where it expects to see a data value, this will be interpreted as an error.
- *Numeric-alphabetic data checks* determine whether the correct form of data is in a field. For example, an invoice total should not contain alphabetic data. As with blanks, alphabetic data in a numeric field may cause serious processing errors.
- *Limit checks* determine if the value in the field exceeds an authorized limit. For example, an organization may allow its sales personnel to negotiate prices with customers up to a maximum discount percentage. The order entry validation program can interrogate the discount field in the sales order records for values that exceed the threshold.
- *Range checks* assign upper and lower limits to acceptable data values. For example, the actual sales price charged for a product can be compared to a range of acceptable prices. The purpose of this control is to detect keystroke errors that shift the decimal point one or more places.
- *Validity checks* compare actual values in a field against known acceptable values. This control is used to verify such things as product codes, shipping company codes, and state abbreviations in customer addresses. If the value in the field does not match one of the acceptable values, the record is determined to be in error.
- *Check digit* controls identify keystroke errors in key fields by testing their internal validity. This check is often used to control data entry errors that would otherwise cause the wrong customer's account to be charged for a transaction.

Testing Validation Controls

Data entry errors that slip through edit programs undetected can cause recorded accounts receivable and revenue amounts to be materially misstated. The audit procedures described here provide evidence about the *accuracy* assertion.

The central audit issue is whether the validation programs in the data editing system are functioning correctly and have continued to function as intended throughout the period. Testing the logic of a validation program, however, represents a significant undertaking. The auditor may decide to rely on the quality of other controls to provide the assurance needed to reduce substantive testing. For example, after reviewing systems development and maintenance controls, the auditor may determine that controls over original program design and testing and subsequent changes to programs are effective. This evidence permits the auditor to assess the risk of material program errors at a low level and thus reduce the substantive tests related to the audit objective of accuracy.

If controls over systems development and maintenance are weak, however, the auditor may decide that testing the data editing controls would be more efficient than performing extensive substantive tests of details. In such a case, ITF or the test data approach would enable the auditor to perform explicit tests of the logic. This type of testing would require the auditor to gain a familiarity with all of the validation procedures in place. The auditor would need to create a comprehensive set of test transactions that include both valid and erroneous data values that fall within and outside of the test parameters. An analysis of the test results will show the auditor which types of errors, if any, can pass undetected by the validation program. This evidence will help the auditor determine the nature, timing, and extent of subsequent substantive tests.

In addition to direct testing of program logic, the auditor can achieve some degree of assurance by reviewing error listings and error logs. These documents provide evidence of the effectiveness of the data entry process, the types and volume of errors encountered, and the manner in which the errors are corrected and reentered into the system. Error listings and logs do not, however, provide evidence of undetected errors. An analysis of error conditions not present in the listing can be used to guide the auditor in designing substantive tests to perform. For example, assume that the error listing of the sales invoice file contains no price limit errors. On the one hand, this situation might simply mean that sales personnel strictly adhere to pricing guidelines. On the other hand, it may mean that the validation program does not test for this type of error. To determine whether material price discrepancies exist in the sales invoice file, the auditor can perform substantive tests that compare the actual price charged with the suggested retail price.

Batch Controls

Batch controls are used to manage high volumes of transaction data through a system. The objective of batch control is to reconcile output produced by the system with the input originally entered into the system. While initiated at the data input stage, batch control continues through all phases of data processing. For example, in the revenue cycle sales invoices are gathered together and enter the system at data entry. After each subsequent processing stage in the system, the batch is reviewed for completeness. An important element of batch control is the batch transmittal sheet, which captures relevant information about the batch, such as the following:

- A unique batch number
- A batch date
- A transaction code (indicating the type of transactions, such as a sales order or cash receipt)
- The number of records in the batch (record count)
- The total dollar value of a financial field (batch control total)
- The total of a unique nonfinancial field (hash total)

The information contained in the transmittal sheet is entered as a separate control record that the system uses to verify the integrity of the batch. The task of reconciling processing with the control record provides assurance that:

- All sales invoices and cash receipts records that were entered into the system were processed.
- No invoices or cash receipts were processed more than once.
- All invoices and cash receipts entered into the system are accounted for as either successfully processed or rejected because of errors.

Testing Batch Controls.   The failure of batch controls to function properly can result in records being lost or processed multiple times. Tests of batch controls provide the auditor with evidence relating to the management assertions of *completeness* and *accuracy*.

Testing batch controls involves reviewing transmittal records of batches processed throughout the period and reconciling them to the batch control log. The auditor needs to investigate out-of-balance conditions to determine the cause. For example, assume that a batch's transmittal record shows 100 sales invoices with a total dollar value of $182,674.87 were entered into the system, but the completed batch log shows that only 96 records were processed with a batch total of $172,834.60. What caused this? Is the problem due to lost or changed invoices? Did the data entry clerk incorrectly calculate the batch control totals? Were error records rejected in processing and removed from the batch? Were rejected records corrected and resubmitted for processing?

The auditor should be able to obtain answers to these questions by reviewing and reconciling transaction listings, error logs, and logs of resubmitted records. Gathering such evidence, however, could involve scanning literally thousands of transactions. In modern systems, batch control logs are stored online in text files that can be read by word processing and spreadsheet programs. Modern audit software such as ACL is capable of searching log files for out-of-balance conditions.

Batch control totals, such as those on the batch transmittal sheet, are also a valuable tool in doing IT audits and fraud audits. For example, it is typical in IT audits to download a copy of the database or sets of data files from a real-time, online system to a microcomputer for analysis and audit procedures by the auditor. One technique for assuring that the data being downloaded are the same data as those being analyzed and tested is to perform batch controls on the live system, which will then be used as control totals for the data loaded on a separate system. Thus, throughout the audit processes, the auditor can be assured that the data are the same (i.e., they have integrity) by checking totals of the test data against the control totals obtained from the live system. This process is particularly helpful to auditors who use generalized audit software, such as ACL. Batch controls can serve as one means of obtaining "custody of evidence" in a fraud audit. Securing the data, obtaining batch controls, and then running tests that can be used as forensic evidence can be an effective process for fraud audits. ACL commands such as PROFILE, TOTAL, and COUNT will provide the kind of information necessary to adequately develop a set of batch controls. See Figure 9.7 for a screen shot of ACL using the AR table, and Figure 9.8 to see the results in the log file of running PROFILE, TOTAL, and COUNT on AR.

Process Controls
Process controls include computerized procedures for file updating and restricting access to data. Depending on the level of computer technology in place, process controls may also include physical manual tasks. We begin by examining three control techniques related to file updating. Access and physical controls are then examined.

FIGURE 9.7

**ACL View of an
AR Table**

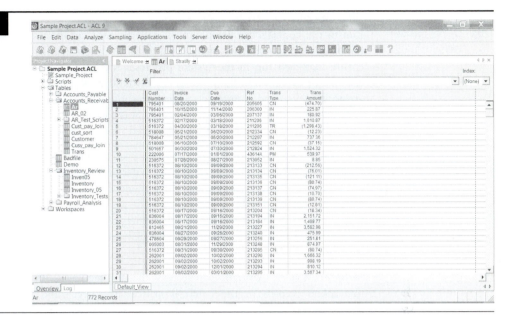

FIGURE 9.8

**ACL Screen of
Command Log
Results**

Command: PROFILE FIELDS amount
Table: ar

Field Name	Total Value	Absolute Value	Minimum	Maximum
Trans Amount	468,880.69	585,674.41	-3,582.98	5,549.19

Command: TOTAL FIELDS amount
Table: ar

amount	468,880.69

Command: COUNT
Table: ar

772 records counted

File Update Controls

Run-to-run controls use batch control data discussed in the previous section to monitor the batch as it moves from one programmed procedure (run) to another. These controls ensure that each run in the system processes the batch correctly and completely. After each major operation in the process, key fields such as invoice amount and record counts are accumulated and compared to the corresponding values stored in the control record. A discrepancy may indicate that a record was lost in processing, a record in the batch went unprocessed, or a record was processed more than once.

Transaction Code Controls. Revenue cycle systems are often designed to process multiple record types. For example, the order entry application may process both sales orders and returns and allowances transactions. The actual tasks performed by the application are determined by a transaction code assigned to each record. Errors in transaction codes, or in the program logic that interprets them, can cause incorrect processing of transactions and may result in materially misstated sales and accounts receivable balances.

Sequence Check Control. In systems that use sequential master files, the order of the transaction records in the batch is critical to correct and complete processing. As the batch moves through the process, it must be re-sorted in the order of the master file used in each run. An out-of-sequence sales order record in a batch may prevent the remaining downstream records from being processed. A more serious problem can occur when the sequencing error is not detected and the downstream records are processed against the wrong customer accounts. A sequence check control should be in place to compare the sequence of each record in the batch with the previous record to ensure that proper sorting took place. Out-of-sequence records should be rejected and resubmitted for subsequent processing to allow the other records in the batch to be properly processed.

Testing File Update Controls. The failure of file update controls to function properly can result in records going unprocessed, being processed incorrectly (i.e., returns are treated as sales), or being posted to the wrong customer's account. Tests of file update controls provide the auditor with evidence relating to the assertions of *existence*, *completeness*, and *accuracy*.

We examined the audit procedures for reviewing batch controls previously as part of the discussion of input controls. Testing run-to-run controls is a logical extension of these procedures and needs no further explanation. Tests of transaction codes and sequence checks can be performed using ITF or the tests–data approach. The auditor should create test data that contain records with incorrect transaction codes and records that are out of sequence in the batch and verify that each was handled correctly. Implicit in this test is verifying the mathematical correctness of the computer operation. For example, consider a sales order for five units of product valued at $100. Assume that before the transaction is processed, the current value of the customer's account is $1,000 and the inventory in question shows 250 units on hand. After processing, this transaction should increase the customer balance to $1,100 and reduce the inventory to 245 units.

The efficient use of logic-testing CAATTs like ITF requires careful planning. By determining in advance the input and process controls to be tested, a single audit procedure can be devised that performs all tests in one operation. For example, a single test designed to examine credit authorization controls, transaction code controls, and the mathematical accuracy of the update program can provide evidence that supports multiple audit objectives.

Access Controls

Access controls prevent and detect unauthorized and illegal access to the firm's assets. Inventories and cash are the physical assets of the revenue cycle. Traditional techniques used to limit access to these assets include the following:

- Using warehouse security, such as fences, alarms, and guards
- Depositing cash daily in the bank
- Using a safe or night deposit box for cash
- Locking cash drawers and safes in the cash receipts department

Controlling access to accounting records is no less important. An individual with unrestricted access to data can manipulate the physical assets of the firm and cause financial statements to be materially misstated. Accounting files stored on magnetic media are particularly vulnerable to unauthorized access, whether its cause is accidental, an act of malice by a disgruntled employee, or an attempt at fraud. The following are examples of risks specific to the revenue cycle:

1. An individual with access to the AR subsidiary ledger could remove his or her account (or someone else's) from the books. With no record of the account, the firm would not send the customer monthly statements.
2. Access to blank sales orders may enable an unauthorized individual to trigger the shipment of a product.
3. An individual with access to both cash and accounting records could remove cash from the firm and cover the act by adjusting the cash account.
4. An individual with access to physical inventory and inventory records could steal products and adjust the records to cover the theft.

Testing Access Controls. Access control is at the heart of accounting information integrity. In the absence of controls, invoices can be deleted, added, or falsified. Individual account balances can be erased, or the entire AR file can be destroyed. Evidence gathered about the effectiveness of access controls tests the management assertions of *existence, completeness, accuracy, valuation and allocation, right and obligations*, and *presentation and disclosure*.

Computer access controls are both system-wide and application-specific. Access control over revenue cycle applications depends on effectively controlling access to the operating systems, the networks, and the databases with which they interact. The control techniques discussed in previous chapters—including passwords, data encryption, firewalls, and user views—apply also in preventing unauthorized access to revenue cycle processes. The auditors will typically test these controls as part of their review of general controls.

Physical Controls

Segregation of Duties. Proper segregation of duties ensures that no single individual or department processes a transaction in its entirety. The number of employees in the organization and the volume of transactions being processed will influence how tasks are divided. In general, the following three rules apply:

- **Rule 1.** Transaction authorization should be separate from transaction processing. For example, within the revenue cycle, the credit department is segregated from the rest of the process, so that the formal authorization of material transactions is an independent event. The importance of this separation is clear when one considers the potential conflict in objectives between the individual salesperson and the organization. Often, sales staff compensation is based on their sales levels. To achieve their personal objective of maximizing sales volume, sales personnel may not always consider the creditworthiness of the prospective customer. The credit department, acting as an independent authorization group, detects risky customers and discourages poor and irresponsible sales decisions.

- **Rule 2.** Asset custody should be separate from the record-keeping task. In the sales-order processing system, the inventory warehouse clerk with custody of the physical assets should not also maintain the inventory records. Similarly, the cash receipts clerk (with custody of cash) should not record accounts receivable.
- **Rule 3.** The organization should be so structured that the perpetration of a fraud requires collusion between two or more individuals. The record-keeping functions must be carefully divided. Specifically, the subsidiary ledgers (AR and inventory), the journals (sales and cash receipts), and the general ledger should be separately maintained. An individual with total record-keeping responsibility, in collusion with someone with asset custody, is in a position to perpetrate fraud. By separating these tasks, collusion must involve more people, which increases the risk of detection and is, therefore, less likely to occur.

Supervision.   Some firms have too few employees to achieve an adequate separation of functions and must rely on supervision as a compensating control. By closely supervising employees who perform potentially incompatible functions, a firm can compensate for the exposure inherent in a system.

Supervision can also provide control in systems that are properly segregated. For example, the mailroom is a point of exposure for any firm. The individual who opens the mail has access both to cash (the asset) and to the remittance advice (the record of the transaction). A dishonest employee may use this opportunity to steal the check, cash it, and destroy the remittance advice, thus leaving no evidence of the transaction. Ultimately, this sort of fraud will come to light when the customer receives another bill and, in response, produces the canceled check. However, by the time the firm gets to the bottom of this problem, the perpetrator may have committed the crime many times over and left the organization. Detecting crimes after the fact accomplishes little. Prevention is the best solution. The deterrent effect of supervision can provide an effective preventive control.

Independent Verification.   The purpose of independent verification is to review the work performed by others at key junctures in the process to identify and correct errors. Following are two examples in the revenue cycle:

1. The shipping department verifies that the goods sent from the warehouse are correct in type and quantity. Before the goods are sent to the customer, the stock release document and the packing slip are reconciled to identify discrepancies.
2. The billing department reconciles the shipping notice with the sales invoice to ensure that customers are billed only for the items and quantities that were actually shipped.

Testing Physical Controls.   Inadequate segregation of duties and the lack of effective supervision and independent verification can result in fraud and material errors. The exposure issues here are similar to the access control issues discussed earlier. Inappropriate access privileges are often associated with incompatible duties. Similarly, the purpose of collusion is to achieve unauthorized access to assets as well as the information needed to conceal the crime. In the absence of supervision and independent verification activities, errors and fraud may go undetected.

The auditor's review of job descriptions and organizational charts, and by observing physical processes, should disclose the more egregious examples of incompatible tasks, such as one individual opening the mail, depositing the check, and recording receipts in the customer accounts. Covert relationships that lead to collusion may not be apparent from an organizational chart. For example, married employees (or those otherwise related) who work in incompatible areas go unnoticed. The auditor should verify that the organization has rules for appropriately dealing with nepotism issues.

Many tasks that are normally segregated in manual systems are consolidated in the data-processing function of computer-based systems. Computer programs in the revenue cycle perform inventory control, accounts receivable, billing, and general ledger tasks. In this situation, the auditor's concern should focus on the integrity of the computer programs that perform these tasks. The following questions need answers: Is the logic of the computer program correct? Has anyone tampered with the application since it was last tested? Have changes been made to the program that could have caused an undisclosed error?

Answers to these questions come from the auditor's review of systems development and maintenance controls and by reviewing organizational structure. Recall from earlier chapters that duties pertaining to the design, maintenance, and operation of computer programs need to be separated. Programmers who write the original computer programs should not be responsible for making program changes. Also, individuals who operate the computer system should not be involved in systems design, programming, or maintenance activities. Personal relationships (i.e., marriage) between individuals in these incompatible areas may require further investigation.

Output Controls

Output controls are designed to ensure that information is not lost, misdirected, or corrupted and that system processes function as intended. For example, managers receive daily summaries of sales orders placed by customers, goods shipped, and cash received, and use such data to monitor the status of their operations. Output control can be designed to identify potential problems. For example, an exception report derived from the customer open order file listing end-of-day open sales orders can identify orders placed but not shipped. Such a report can help management assess the operational performance of the shipping process.

Reconciling the general ledger is an output control that can detect certain types of transaction processing errors. For example, the total of all credit sales recorded by billing should equal the total increases posted to the AR subsidiary accounts. A sales transaction that is entered in the journal but not posted to the customer's account would be detected by an imbalance in the general ledger. The specific cause of an out-of-balance condition could not be determined at this point, but the error would be noted. Finding the error may require examining all the transactions processed during the period. This could be time consuming. For this reason, rather than summarizing an entire day's transactions in a single batch, entities often group transactions into small batches of 50 to 100 items. This facilitates reconciling balances by isolating a problem to a specific batch.

Another important element of output control is the maintenance of an audit trail. To resolve transaction processing errors, each detected error needs to be traced to its source. It is not sufficient to know that 100 transactions entered the system and only 99 came out. Details of transaction processing produced at intermediate points can provide an audit trail that reflects activity through every stage of operations. The following are examples of audit trail output controls.

Accounts Receivable Change Report

This is a summary report that shows the overall change to accounts receivable from sales orders and cash receipts. These numbers should reconcile with total sales, total cash receipts (on account), and the general ledger.

Transaction Logs

Every transaction successfully processed by the system should be recorded on a transaction log, which serves as a journal. A transaction log serves two purposes. First, the transaction log is a permanent record of valid transactions. The original transaction file produced at the data input phase is usually only a temporary file. Once processed, the records on this file are erased (scratched) to make room for the next batch of transactions. Second, not all of the records in the temporary transaction file will always be successfully processed. Some of these records may fail validity tests and will be rejected. A transaction log should contain only successful transactions. Rejected transactions should be placed in an error file. The transaction log and error files combined should account for all the transactions in the batch. The validated transaction file may then be scratched with no loss of data.

Transaction Listings

The system should produce a (hard copy) transaction listing of all successful transactions. These listings should go to the appropriate users to facilitate reconciliation with input. For example, a listing of cash receipts processed will go to the controller to be used for a bank reconciliation.

Log of Automatic Transactions

Some transactions are triggered internally by the system. For example, EDI sales orders are accepted and processed without human authorization. To maintain an audit trail of these activities, all internally generated transactions must be placed in a transaction log, and a listing of these transactions should be sent to the appropriate manager.

Unique Transaction Identifiers

Each transaction processed by the system must be uniquely identified with a transaction number. This control is the only practical means of tracing a particular transaction through a database of thousands or even millions of records. In systems that use physical source documents, the unique number printed on the document can be transcribed during data input and used for this purpose. In real-time systems, which do not use source documents, each transaction should be assigned a unique number by the system.

Error Listing

A listing of all error records should go to the appropriate user to support error correction and resubmission.

Testing Output Controls

The absence of adequate output controls has adverse implications for operational efficiency and financial reporting. Evidence gathered through tests of output controls relates to the *completeness* and *accuracy* assertions.

Testing output controls involves reviewing summary reports for accuracy, completeness, timeliness, and relevance to the decisions that they are intended to support. In addition, the auditor should trace sample transactions through audit trail reports, including transaction listings, error logs, and logs of resubmitted records. Gathering such evidence, however, may involve sorting through thousands of transactions.

In modern systems, audit trails are usually stored online in text files. Data extraction software such as ACL can be used to search log files for specific records to verify the completeness and accuracy of output reports. Alternatively, the auditor can test output controls directly using ITF. A well-designed ITF system will permit the auditor to produce a batch of sample transactions, including some error records, and trace them through all phases of processing, error detection, and output reporting.

SUBSTANTIVE TESTS OF REVENUE CYCLE ACCOUNTS

This section deals with the substantive tests that an auditor may perform to achieve audit objectives related to the revenue cycle. The strategy used in determining the nature, timing, and extent of substantive tests derives from the auditor's assessment of inherent risk, unmitigated control risk, materiality considerations, and the need to conduct the audit in an efficient manner.

Revenue Cycle Risks and Audit Concerns

In general, the auditor's concerns in the revenue cycle pertain to the potential for overstatement of revenues and accounts receivable rather than their understatement. Overstatement of accounts can result from material errors in the processing of normal transactions that occur throughout the year. In addition, the auditor should focus attention on large and unusual transactions at or near period-end. Examples of specific issues that give rise to these concerns include these following:

- Recognizing revenues from sales transactions that did not occur
- Recognizing sales revenues before they are realized (i.e., billing customers for items still being manufactured at period-end)
- Failing to recognize period-end cutoff points, thus allowing reported sales revenues for the current period to be inflated by post-period transactions
- Underestimating the allowance for doubtful accounts, thus overstating the realizable value of accounts receivable
- Shipping unsolicited products to customers in one period that are returned in a subsequent period
- Billing sales to the customer that are held by the seller (Special terms associated with such transactions may require no payment for a lengthy period of time.)

In resolving these concerns, the auditor will seek evidence by performing a combination of tests of internal controls and substantive tests. Tests of controls include testing both general controls (discussed in Chapters 2 through 7) and application controls specifically related to revenue cycle procedures. Various application control techniques were examined in Chapter 7. For example, the auditor may use an integrated test facility (ITF) to test the accuracy of sales transaction postings to the AR file. Although positive results from such a test may enable the auditor to reduce the degree of substantive testing needed to gain assurance about the mathematical accuracy of account processing, they offer no assurance about the collectability of those accounts receivable. Similarly, ITF can be used to test the credit-limit logic of the edit program to provide assurance that the organization's credit policy is being properly implemented. This test, however, provides no evidence that proper cutoff procedures were followed in calculating the total value of accounts receivable.

From these examples, we see that in addition to tests of controls, the auditor must perform substantive tests to achieve audit objectives. The remainder of this chapter deals with audit objectives related to the revenue cycle and the substantive tests most commonly performed. Keep in mind that the quality of internal controls bears on the nature and extent of substantive tests determined by the auditor to be necessary. Normally, not all of the tests described will be performed.

Understanding Data

The following tests involve accessing and extracting data from accounting files for analysis. To do this, the auditor needs to understand the systems and controls that produced the data, as well as the physical characteristics of the files that contain them. Much of this chapter has been devoted to explaining alternative revenue cycle configurations and their control implications. The previous chapter described several common file structures and their audit implications. The discussion that follows presumes that the auditor is using ACL for performing the audit tests. Before we proceed, however, we need to review a few salient points regarding file preparation.

First, the auditor must verify that he or she is working with the correct version of the file to be analyzed. To do so the auditor must understand the file backup procedures and, whenever possible, work with the original files. Second, ACL can read most sequential files and relational database tables directly, but esoteric and/or complex file structures may require "flattening" before they can be analyzed. This process may involve additional procedures and special programs to produce a copy of the original file in a format that ACL can accept. If the client organization's systems personnel perform the flattening process, the auditor must verify that the correct version of the original file was used and that all relevant records from the original were transferred to the copy for analysis.

The discussion that follows presumes that any joining of tables or file copying necessary to produce test data was done so under adequate controls to preserve data integrity. These files may reside on either a mainframe or a PC. The audit tests described next are applicable to both environments. The focus is on explaining the logic underlying various substantive tests and on illustrating the functionality of ACL in achieving audit objectives. The audit procedures described are based on the file structure in Figure 9.9. These structures indicate the primary keys (PK), the relevant data fields, and foreign keys (FK) that permit logical linkages between files. A description of each file follows.

Customer File

The Customer master file contains address and credit information about customers. The Credit Limit value is used to validate sales transactions. If the sum of the customer's outstanding account balance and the amount of current sales transaction exceeds the pre-established credit limit, then the transaction is rejected.

Sales Invoice File and Cash Receipts File

Sales Invoice file, along with the Line Item file, captures sales transaction data for the period. The Sales invoice file contains summary data for each invoice. When an order is shipped to a customer, a record is added to the file. Summing Invoice Amount for all records in the file yields total sales (sale journal) for the period. When customer cash payments are received, they are matched to the open invoice record, which is then closed by placing the current date in the Closed Date field. At that time a record is added

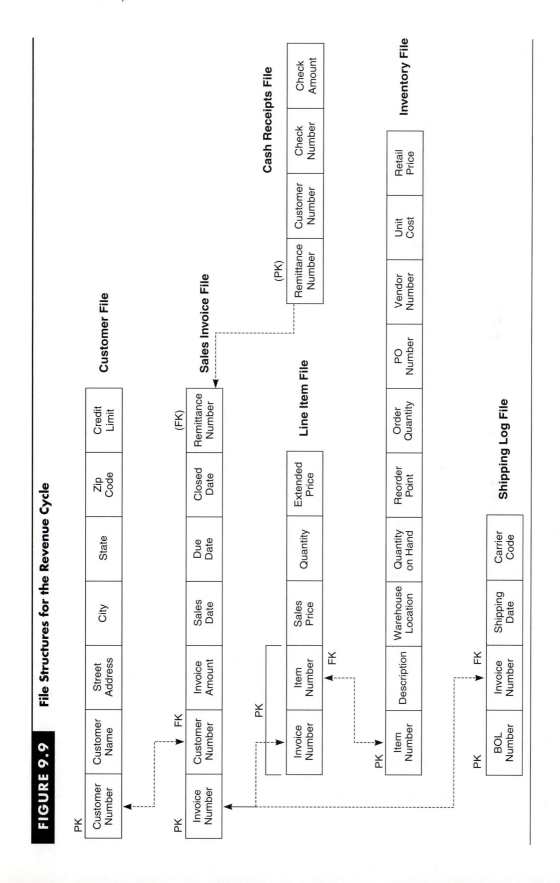

FIGURE 9.9 **File Structures for the Revenue Cycle**

to the **Cash Receipts File**. The Remittance Number, which is the primary key of the cash receipt record, is added to the invoice record as a foreign key. The accounts receivable balance for a particular customer is calculated by summing the Invoice Amount fields for all of the customer's open invoices (those with no value in the Closed Date field). Total accounts receivable for financial reporting purposes are the sum of all the open invoice records in the file.

Line Item File

The Line Item file contains a record of every product sold. Since a single transaction can involve one or more products, each record in the Sales Invoice file is associated with (linked to) one or more records in this file. Notice that the file contains a primary key comprised of two fields—Invoice Number and Item Number. Both fields are needed to uniquely define each record in the file. They also provide links to related records in the Sales Invoice and Inventory files. Although financial reporting of sales and accounts receivable information requires only the data contained in the Sales Invoice file, the Line Item file is needed for operational tasks such as billing, customer service, marketing, and auditing. For example, sales details in the file allow marketing to evaluate the demand for its products. These data also provide audit evidence needed to corroborate the accuracy of price times quantity calculations that are summarized in the **sales invoices**.

Inventory File

The Inventory file contains quantity, price, supplier, and warehouse location data for each item of inventory. When products are sold, the Quantity on Hand field in the associated records is reduced by the value of the Quantity field in the Line Item record. The Quantity on Hand field is increased by inventory receipts from suppliers. This activity is discussed in the next chapter.

Shipping Log File

The shipping log is a record of all sales orders shipped to customers. The primary key of the file is the bill of lading (BOL) number. The data in this file are useful for verifying that all sales reflected in the Sales Invoice file were shipped in the period under review. As an efficiency tool, these data can also be used to determine if customer orders are being shipped in a timely manner.

File Preparation Procedures

The data contained in the files shown in Figure 9.9 provide evidence that may either corroborate or refute audit objectives. Most of the tests described in the following section involve using ACL to access and extract data from these files. For a detailed explanation of ACL commands, review the instruction manual that accompanies the ACL software and consult ACL's online Help feature.

   As a preliminary step in using ACL, each file needs to be defined in terms of its physical location and its structure. Through a series of easy-to-use pop-up menus, ACL's Data Definition Wizard allows the auditor to specify the name of the file, specify its location (on the mainframe or PC) and define the file's structure in terms of the length of each field and the data type contained in each field (i.e., numeric, character, or date). When the file definition is completed, it is saved under a unique name assigned by the auditor. All future file access is accomplished by simply selecting the file definition from an ACL menu. ACL automatically locates the file and presents it on screen, where the auditor can review and manipulate its contents.

Sometimes the actual contents of a data field are different from what they are supposed to be. For example, a numeric field in one or more records may contain alphabetic data because of a program error or a clerical mistake. Also, a field may contain corrupted data because of an error in the file-flattening process. Whatever the cause, prior to performing any substantive tests on a new file, it is important to validate its contents. Invalid data will distort the test results and may cause a system failure. ACL's *Verify* command analyzes the data fields in the selected file to ensure that their contents are consistent with the field type in the file definition. Any validity errors detected by ACL need to be traced to their source and resolved. The auditor may also find batch control totals to be an effective means of verifying data integrity. For purposes of discussion, we will assume that the files used in all tests described hereafter have been properly defined and verified.

Testing the Accuracy and Completeness Assertions

The audit procedures described in this section provide evidence relating to management assertions of *accuracy* and *completeness*. Auditors often precede substantive tests of details with an **analytical review** of account balances. In the case of the revenue cycle, an analytical review will provide the auditor with an overall perspective for trends in sales, cash receipts, sales returns, and accounts receivable. Analytical procedures do not necessarily require computer technology. For example, the auditor may compare reported sales for the quarter with those for the same period in previous years. Ratio analysis may be used to compare total sales to cost of goods sold, sales to accounts receivable, and allowance for doubtful accounts to accounts receivable. Significant variations in account balances over time, or unusual ratios, may signify financial statement misrepresentations. However, analytical procedures can provide assurance that transactions and accounts are reasonably stated and complete and may thus permit the auditor to reduce substantive tests of details on these accounts.

A medium- to large-sized organization's sales and accounts receivable data may constitute thousands or perhaps millions of records. Substantive tests of details of such volumes of data cannot be effectively accomplished using manual techniques. The following examples of substantive tests that can be performed using ACL are based on the file structures depicted in Figure 9.9.

Review Sales Invoices for Unusual Trends and Exceptions

A useful audit procedure for identifying potential audit risks involves scanning data files for unusual transactions and account balances. For example, scanning accounts receivable for excessively large balances may indicate that the organization's credit policy is being improperly applied. Credit balances in accounts receivable may suggest unusual sales return activity or errors in the application of cash receipts to customer accounts. The auditor can use ACL's *Stratify* feature to identify such anomalies as shown in the table below. The stratify function groups data into predetermined intervals and counts the number of records that fall into each interval. Using data similar to the sample data illustrated in the table below, the stratify function will produce the report for the Sales Invoice File presented in Figure 9.10.

Invoice Number	Customer Number	Invoice Sales Amount	Due Date	Closed Date	Remittance Date
214088	065003	13.08	12/04/10	12/14/10	12/11/10
611243					
214114	065003	9.76	12/04/10	12/14/10	
214129	065003	116.72	12/04/10	12/14/10	
214121	165006	29.40	12/04/10	12/14/10	12/12/10
613457					
214185	165009	9.17	12/04/10	12/14/10	12/23/10
614476					
213309	376005	–931.55	12/04/10	12/14/10	
213355	376005	–374.71	12/04/10	12/14/10	

FIGURE 9.10

Stratification of Sales Invoice File

As of: 06/10/2010 10:27:33

Command: STRATIFY ON amount MINIMUM -1000 MAXIMUM 5549.19 INTERVALS 10 TO SCREEN
Table: ar

Minimum encountered was -3,582.98
Maximum encountered was 5,549.19

Trans Amount	Count	Percent of Count	Percent of Field	Trans Amount
<-1,000.00	20	2.59%	-6.81%	-31,928.54
-1,000.00 - -345.09	29	3.76%	-3.7%	-17,355.17
-345.08 - 309.83	216	27.98%	0.48%	2,250.97
309.84 - 964.75	308	39.9%	40.23%	188,622.25
964.76 - 1,619.67	129	16.71%	33.99%	159,371.25
1,619.68 - 2,274.59	42	5.44%	16.81%	78,824.30
2,274.60 - 2,929.51	12	1.55%	6.58%	30,835.20
2,929.52 - 3,584.43	11	1.42%	7.64%	35,840.18
3,584.44 - 4,239.35	2	0.26%	1.6%	7,490.28
4,239.36 - 4,894.27	1	0.13%	0.94%	4,426.14
4,894.28 - 5,549.19	2	0.26%	2.24%	10,503.83
Totals	772	100%	100%	468,880.69

The report groups the Invoice Amount field into ten intervals based upon the upper and lower limits of the data in the field. Analysis of the results allows the auditor to identify unusual trends and exceptions. For example:

- The minimum invoice amount was –$3,582.98 and the maximum was $5,549.19.
- Forty-nine items constitute $49,283 of negative sales.
- Fifty-three percent of the sales are between $310 and $1,620.
- Only two items were sales over $4,894.

The auditor can use other ACL features to seek answers to questions raised by the preceding analysis. For example, since this is a Sales Invoice file, it should normally contain only positive numbers. Negative numbers may have been inserted into the records in a number of ways. For example, they could be the result of a defective computer program, unintentional clerical errors, an effort to reverse the effects of erroneous sales transactions, or a fraudulent attempt to reduce a customer's accounts receivable balance. Although the auditor cannot specifically identify from the stratification which records are causing the anomalies, the potential problem has been flagged. The auditor will probably want to pursue this matter further, but to do so will require more detailed information.

ACL provides a *filter capability* that can be used to select or ignore specific records from an entire file. Using this feature, the auditor can select from the Sales Invoice file only those records with negative invoice amounts. The resulting view of the file is much smaller and provides the auditor with the details needed to investigate these anomalies. Sample records from the filtered file are listed below. With knowledge of specific customer account numbers, invoice numbers, and sales dates, the questionable items can be traced to their sources for resolution.

Invoice Number	Customer Number	Invoice Sales Amount	Due Date	Closed Date	Remittance Date
213309	376005	–931.55	12/04/10	12/14/10	
213355	376005	–374.71	12/04/10	12/14/10	
212297	784647	–537.36	12/04/10	12/14/10	
214389	262001	–300.39	12/10/10	12/20/10	
214390	641464	–46.77	12/10/10	12/20/10	
214391	222006	–62.15	12/10/10	12/20/10	
213699	878035	–378.45	12/07/10	12/20/10	
213700	878035	–742.75	12/07/10	12/20/10	

Review Sales Invoice and Shipping Log Files for Missing and Duplicate Items

Searching for missing and/or duplicate transactions is another important test that helps the auditor corroborate or refute the completeness and accuracy assertions. Duplicate and missing transactions in the revenue cycle may be evidence of over- or understated sales and accounts receivable. Duplicate sales invoice records may indicate a computer program error that materially overstates sales and accounts receivable. On one hand, a missing sales invoice may point to an unrecorded sale that was shipped but not billed, thus understating these accounts. On the other hand, it may indicate nothing more than an invoice that was issued and voided because of a clerical error.

| **TABLE 9.2** | **Duplicates and Gaps on Invoice Number** |

As of: 06/10/2004 10:59:15

Command: GAPS ON ref DUPLICATES TO SCREEN PRESORT
Table: ar

0 sequence errors detected
243 gaps and/or duplicates detected

Duplicates:

Record Number	Ref No
5	13452X
10	211206
12	212297
13	212297
17	212824
31	213227
34	213248
48	213309
55	213328
61	213355
73	213392
75	213398
81	213418
85	213423

Gaps Found Between:

Ref No
10,000 - 12,284
12,284 - 13,065
13,065 - 13,452
13,452 - 205,605
205,605 - 206,300
206,300 - 207,137
207,137 - 211,206
211,206 - 212,297
212,297 - 212,334
212,334 - 212,592
212,592 - 212,824
212,824 - 213,052

ACL is capable of testing a designated field for out-of-sequence records, gaps in sequence numbers, and duplicate values for the entire file. Using this feature, the auditor can scan the Invoice Number field of all records in the Sales Invoice file. The ACL system would return an on-screen report similar to Table 9.2.

The partial report shows that 243 records in the Sales Invoice file are either duplicated or missing. In resolving this issue, the auditor will need to interview management and employees involved in the process and seek answers to the following types of questions:

- Are procedures in place to document and approve voided invoices?
- How are gaps in sales invoices communicated to management?
- What physical controls exist over access to sales invoice source documents?
- Are batch totals used to control total transactions during data processing?
- Are transaction listings reconciled and reviewed by management?

Tests for missing and duplicate documents can also be performed on the Shipping Log file. Consider the sample data in the table below, which is based on the file structure in Figure 9.9.

BOL Number	Invoice Number	Shipping Date	Carrier Code
50449	214088	11/29/10	538
50450	214090	11/29/10	530
50451	214089	11/30/10	531
50452	214087	11/30/10	532
50453	214092	12/14/10	533
50455	214093	12/10/10	523

In this example, the auditor would test the Invoice Number field for gaps and duplicate records. A duplicate record may indicate that the same product was shipped to the customer twice. If we presume that the customer was billed only once, then the organization has forfeited the revenue from the second shipment. Missing invoices may denote that some customer orders are not shipped at all. Depending on the circumstances, sales and accounts receivable may be overstated.

Here is an example of how a single test procedure can support more than one audit objective. Invoices missing from the shipping log provide evidence that also tests the *existence or occurrence* assertion. The auditor seeks assurance that sales revenue is recognized only when appropriate criteria are met. In most organizations, this means that sales are recognized only when the products are shipped. The auditor should review the shipping log for the following period to determine if the missing invoice numbers are recorded there. If so, this would indicate that the merchandise was shipped after the cut-off period. It may be necessary to adjust the sales and accounts receivable balances accordingly.

Review Line Item and Inventory Files for Sales Price Accuracy

Evidence from testing the product prices charged to customers supports the audit objective of *accuracy*. Sometimes sales personnel are given limited authority to negotiate prices with customers. Significant discrepancies between the suggested retail price and the price actually charged, however, may indicate incompetence, clerical errors, or sales personnel exceeding their authority. A retail outlet such as a department store will usually establish a nonnegotiable pricing policy. Sales prices are calculated automatically by the point-of-sale system to eliminate salesperson intervention and clerical errors. Pricing inconsistency in such a setting may indicate a computer program error or the use of obsolete pricing data.

Traditionally, auditors would verify pricing accuracy by comparing sales prices on the invoices with the published price list. But because of the physical effort involved with this approach, it could be done only on a sample basis. Therefore, out of thousands of sales records, perhaps only one or two hundred would be tested. ACL allows the auditor to compare the prices charged on every invoice in the file for the period under review. Based on the file structures for the Line Item and Inventory files presented in Figure 9.9, we can illustrate this procedure using the sample data on the next page.

LINE ITEM FILE

Invoice Number	Item Number	Sales Price	Quantity	Extended Price
214297	030303413	4.69	20	93.88
214297	030303403	5.29	10	52.90
214297	030303343	12.98	2	25.96
214298	130305603	16.00	5	80.00
214298	030302303	44.95	12	539.40

INVENTORY FILE

Item Number	Description	Ware-house Location	Quantity on Hand	Reorder Point	Order Quantity	PO Number	Unit Cost	Retail Price	Vendor Number
030303413	8 oz. Ball Peen Hammer	03	1,248	510	1,500		3.90	4.69	10879
030303403	12 oz. Ball Peen Hammer	03	536	550	1,200	111104	4.12	5.29	12248
030303343	Straight Claw Hammer	03	735	550	1,600		8.83	12.98	10951
130305603	#4 Smooth Plane	03	804	800	2,000	107427	14.12	22.98	10879
030309373	Heavy Duty Brace	03	842	900	1,200	108123	10.12	16.98	10951
030302903	4 pc. Chisel Set	03	795	620	1,200		10.12	16.98	13411
030302303	Mitre Box 21″	03	600	650	1,200	129124	41.23	54.95	11182

This procedure involves a few simple steps. First, notice that the actual sales price charged is stored in the Sales Price field in the Line Item file. The suggested retail price for each product is the Retail Price field in the Inventory file. In addition, the two files have Item Number as a common field. This field is the key field on which the two files are related. Using this common field, the objective of the test is to match each record in the Line Item file with the corresponding record in the Inventory file. We can compare the Sales Price and Retail Price fields for constancy. Significant discrepancies can then be identified and investigated. The actual steps in this test are described next.

First, both files need to be ordered according to their common key. Item number is the primary key of the inventory master file, and we will assume that this file is already in the proper sequence. Since the Line Item file contains the details of the Invoice file, it is probably organized by Invoice Number at this time. It is therefore necessary to sort this file on the Item Number field to place it in the same order as the Inventory file. This process involves simply opening the file and invoking ACL's *Sort* feature.

The next step is to combine the two files to create a third. ACL accomplishes this with its *Join* feature. The auditor has several options when joining files. The one most relevant to this test is to create a third file that consists only of matched records. In other words, the new file will contain only the Line Item and Inventory records whose value for the Item Number field match. Any Inventory records that are not matched with a Line Item record will not be part of the new file.

ACL's *Join* feature permits the auditor to specify the fields from the two input files that are to be passed to the new output file. Usually, it is neither necessary nor desirable to include all fields from both of the original files. In this example, the fields needed from the Line Item file to verify pricing accuracy are Invoice Number, Item Number, and Sales Price; from the Inventory file, the fields are Description and Retail Price. The file structure of the new file and some sample records are presented in the table below.

Invoice Number	Item Number	Description	Sales Price	Retail Price
214297	030303413	8 OZ. BALL PEEN HAMMER	4.69	4.69
214297	030303403	12 OZ. BALL PEEN HAMMER	5.29	5.29
214297	030303343	STRAIGHT CLAW HAMMER	12.98	12.98
214298	130305603	#4 SMOOTH PLANE	16.00	22.98
214298	030302303	MITRE BOX 21"	44.95	54.95

At this point, the resulting file may still be very large. Scanning the file visually for price differences could be time-consuming and ineffective. Here again is an application for a *filter*. Through a series of pop-up menus, the auditor can easily create a filter that will ignore all records in which Sales Price and Retail Price are equal. The resulting file will thus contain only price discrepancies. Using other ACL features, the auditor can calculate the total price variance and make a determination as to its materiality. If material, this issue would need to be pursued with management.

Testing for Unmatched Records

A variation on the preceding test can be used to address some related issues. By selecting a different join option, the auditor can produce a new file of only unmatched records. There are two possible causes for unmatched records. The first is because the value of the Item Number field in the Line Item record is incorrect and does not match an Inventory record. Since the operational assumption is that the inventory master file is correct, then any Line Item records in the unmatched file are errors. The presence (or absence) of such errors is evidence that refutes or corroborates the accuracy assertion.

The second source of unmatched records is the Inventory file. The presence of Inventory records in the unmatched file means that there were no corresponding records in the Line Item file. This result is not an error; it means that these products did not sell during the period. After adjusting for any seasonal influences on sales, such evidence may refute the valuation assertion. The auditor may require that the inventory be written down to reflect its market value.

Testing the Existence Assertion

One of the most widely performed tests of existence is the **confirmation of accounts receivable**. This test involves direct written contact between the auditors and the client's customers to confirm account balances and transactions. *Statement on Auditing Standards No. 67* (SAS 67), *The Confirmation Process*, states that auditors should request confirmations of accounts receivable except in the following three situations: (1) accounts receivable are immaterial; (2) based on a review of internal controls, the auditor has assessed control risk to be low; or (3) the confirmation process will be ineffective.

This last point is worthy of further explanation. Because of the way some organizations account for their liabilities, they may be unable to respond to requests for confirmation. For example, government agencies and large industrial organizations often use an **open-invoice system** for liabilities. Under this approach, invoices are recorded individually rather than being summarized or grouped by creditor. In this environment, no accounts payable subsidiary ledger exists. Each invoice is paid (closed) as it comes due. For financial reporting purposes, total accounts payable is calculated simply by summing the open (unpaid) invoices. Determining the liability due to a particular creditor, which may consist of multiple open invoices, is not such a simple task. The auditor should not assume that an organization using this approach would invest the time needed to respond to the confirmation request. Under such circumstances, the confirmation process would be ineffective.

In the discussion that follows, we assume that accounts receivable are material and that the auditor has decided to request confirmations from the client's customers. The confirmation process involves three stages: selecting the accounts to confirm, preparing confirmation requests, and evaluating the responses.

Selecting Accounts to Confirm

Given the file structures used in our example, selecting accounts receivable for confirmation involves processing data that are contained in both the Customer and the Sales Invoice files. Each customer record is associated with one or more sales invoice records. Recall from a previous discussion that the accounts receivable balance for a particular customer is calculated by summing the open sales invoices (those with no values in the Closed Date and Remittance Number fields) for the customer. Once cash is received in payment of an invoice, it is closed by placing the payment date and the cash receipt number in the respective fields. Thus, the Sales Invoice file provides the financial information needed for the confirmation requests, and the customer mailing information is contained in the Customer file. Obtaining a set of accounts for confirmation requires three steps: consolidate the invoices by customer, join the data from the two files, and select a sample of accounts from the joined file.

Consolidate Invoices. The first step in the process is to consolidate all the open invoices for each customer. Using the sample data presented in Table 9.3, ACL's *Classify* command allows the auditor to set a filter to select only the open sales invoices (those

---

TABLE 9.3   ## Sales Invoice File

Invoice Number	Customer Number	Invoice Amount	Sales Date	Due Due	Closed Date	Remittance Number
212209	376005	931.55	12/04/10	12/14/10		
212255	376005	377.71	12/04/10	12/14/10		
212297	784647	537.36	12/04/10	12/14/10		
214088	065003	13.08	12/04/10	12/14/10	12/11/01	611243
214389	262001	300.39	12/10/10	12/20/10		
214100	641464	46.77	12/10/10	12/20/10		
214114	065003	9.76	12/04/10	12/14/10		
214129	262001	116.72	12/04/10	12/14/10		
214121	165006	29.40	12/04/10	12/14/10	12/12/01	613457
214185	165009	9.17	12/04/10	12/14/10	12/23/01	614476

with blanks in the Remittance Number field) and to summarize the Invoice Amount field for each record based on the Customer Number. The summarized records are then passed to a new file called Classified Invoices, presented in Table 9.4.

Join the Files.   The next step in the confirmation process is to join the Classified Invoices file and the Customer file (illustrated in Table 9.5 with sample data) to produce another new file called Accounts Receivable, which is presented in Table 9.6. Recall that when using ACL's *Join* feature both files must be ordered on the same key. This requires first sorting the Classified Invoices file by Customer Number to place it in the same

---

TABLE 9.4   Classified Invoices File

Customer Number	Invoice Amount
376005	1,279.26
784647	537.36
262001	417.11
641464	46.77
065003	9.76

TABLE 9.5   Customer File Structure with Sample Data

Customer Number	Customer Name	Street Address	City	State	Zip Code	Credit Limit
065003	Accel Enterprises	1000 Strayer Rd.	Brookline	MA	02167	72,000
262001	Connecticut Corp.	600 Paragon Dr.	Brooklyn	NY	11201	80,000
376005	Bully Industries	8 West Street	Las Vegas	NV	89109	53,000
641464	First Healthcare	88 State St.	Austin	TX	78752	28,000
784647	Salt Bank of Amer.	401 N. Broadway	Bentonville	AR	72712	27,000

TABLE 9.6   Accounts Receivable File Structure

Customer Number	Customer Name	Street Address	City	State	Zip Code	Invoice Amount
065003	Accel Enterprises	1000 Strayer Rd.	Brookline	MA	02167	9.76
262001	Connecticut Corp.	600 Paragon Dr.	Brooklyn	NY	11201	417.11
376005	Bully Industries	8 West Street	Las Vegas	NV	89109	1,279.26
641464	First Healthcare	88 State St.	Austin	TX	78752	46.77
784647	Salt Bank of Amer.	401 N. Broadway	Bentonville	AR	72712	537.36

sequence as the Customer master file. As noted previously, the *Join* feature allows the auditor to select only relevant fields from each of the input files when creating the new file. In this example, Credit Limit, which is not needed for preparing the confirmations, has been dropped from the new Accounts Receivable file structure.

Select a Sample of Accounts. In a moderate- to large-sized organization, the Accounts Receivable file may contain thousands of records. Rather than confirming all of these accounts, the auditor will probably choose to select a sample of records. To assist the auditor in this task, ACL's *Sample* feature offers two basic sampling methods: *random (record) sampling* and *monetary unit sampling (MUS)*. The choice of methods will depend on the auditor's strategy and the composition of the Accounts Receivable file. If the account balances are fairly evenly distributed, the auditor may want an unbiased sample and will thus choose the random sample approach. Under this method, each record, regardless of the size of the accounts receivable balance, has an equal chance of being included in the sample. If, on the other hand, the file is heavily skewed with large customer account balances, the auditor may select MUS, which will produce a sample biased toward the larger dollar amounts.

ACL's *Size* command helps the auditor calculate sample size and sampling intervals based on the auditor's desired confidence level, the size of the population being sampled, and the assessed materiality threshold. These parameters are entered into ACL to draw a physical sample from the Accounts Receivable file that is sent to a new output file called AR-Sample. The structure of this file is the same as the Accounts Receivable file, but it contains far fewer records. For example, from the several thousand records in the accounts receivable population, perhaps only 150 records are selected for the sample.

Preparing Confirmation Requests

The next stage in the confirmation process involves preparing confirmation requests that contain the information captured in the AR-Sample file. The requests, which usually take the form of letters, are drafted and administered by the auditor, but are written in the client entity's name. A sample confirmation letter is presented in Figure 9.11.

FIGURE 9.11

Confirmation Letter

CLIENT LETTERHEAD
(CLIENT NAME AND ADDRESS)

(Name and Address of Client's Customer)

To whom it may concern:

In accordance with the request from our external auditors, we ask that you confirm your outstanding account balance with our organization. Our records indicate that your account balances as of **(end-of-period date)** amounted to **($ amount)**.

If your records agree with this balance, please indicate by signing in the space provided below and return this letter directly to our auditors using the enclosed envelope. Your prompt compliance with this request is greatly appreciated.

If the amount indicated is not in agreement with your records, inform the auditors directly using the enclosed envelope. In your response, please show the amount owed according to your records and include full details of the discrepancy.

Sincerely,
(Name of Entity)

The amount stated above is correct: **(Customer Name)**

The letter shown in Figure 9.11 is an example of a **positive confirmation**. Recipients are asked to respond whether their records agree or disagree with the amount stated. Positive confirmations are particularly useful when the auditor suspects that a large number of accounts may be in dispute. They are also used when confirming unusual or large balances or when a large proportion of total accounts receivable arises from a small number of significant customers.

A problem with positive confirmations is poor response rate. Customers who do not dispute the amount shown in the confirmation letter may not respond. The auditor cannot assume, however, that lack of response means agreement. To obtain the highest response rate possible, second and even third requests may need to be sent to nonrespondents.

Negative confirmations request the recipients to respond only if they disagree with the amount shown in the letter. This technique is used primarily when accounts receivable consist of a large number of low-value balances and the control risk of misstatement is considered to be low. The sample size for this type of test is typically large and may include the entire population. Evidence from nonreturned negative confirmations selected from a large population provides indirect evidence to support the auditor's expectation that accounts receivable are not materially misstated.

Responses to negative confirmations, particularly if they are widespread in a large population, may indicate a potential problem. Since the negative confirmations approach does not prove that the intended recipients actually received and reviewed the confirmation letters, evidence of individual misstatements provided by returned responses cannot be projected to the entire population. In other words, responses to negative confirmations cannot be used as a basis for determining the total dollar amount of the misstatement in the account. Such evidence can be used, however, to reinforce the auditor's prior expectation that the account balance may be materially misstated and that additional testing of details is needed to determine the nature and amount of the misstatement.

Once the auditor decides upon the nature and the wording of the confirmation letter, he or she can create it using a word processor. ACL's *Export* feature can greatly facilitate the physical task of inserting the relevant financial data for each customer into the individual letters. Using this option, the auditor can produce a text version of the AR-Sample file that can be integrated with the confirmation letter text using the mail/merge feature of a word processing package such as Microsoft Word or WordPerfect. This facility greatly reduces the clerical effort traditionally associated with confirmation activities.

Evaluating and Controlling Responses

Maintaining control over the confirmation process is critical to its integrity. Evidence provided through confirmations is less reliable when contact between the auditor and the debtor is disrupted by client intervention. The auditor should take all reasonable steps to ensure the following procedures are observed:

- The auditor should retain custody of the confirmation letters until they are mailed.
- The confirmation letters, together with self-addressed stamped envelopes, should be addressed to the auditor, rather than the client organization.
- The confirmation request should be mailed by the auditor. If client mailroom personnel participate in the process, they should be adequately supervised.

When responses are returned to the auditor, discrepancies in the amount owed should be investigated. The auditor should evaluate exceptions to determine if they represent isolated instances or signify a larger potential problem. For example, frequent complaints by debtors that the client is slow to record cash payments may indicate misappropriations of cash and the lapping of accounts receivable. Lapping is discussed in Chapter 12.

Nonresponses to positive confirmations also need to be investigated. SAS 67 requires auditors to use alternative procedures to resolve this issue. A commonly used procedure is to review the following period's closed invoices to determine if the accounts were actually paid. Since it is unlikely that a customer will pay an account that is not owed, subsequent cash payments provide good evidence of the *existence*, *accuracy*, and *valuation* objectives.

Testing the Valuation/Allocation Assertion

The auditor's objective regarding proper valuation and allocation is to corroborate or refute that accounts receivable are stated at net realizable value. This objective rests on the reasonableness of the allowance for doubtful accounts, which is derived from aged accounts receivable balances. To achieve this objective, the auditor needs to review the accounts receivable aging process to determine that the allowance for doubtful accounts is adequate.

Aging Accounts Receivable

As accounts age, the probability that they will ultimately be collected is decreased. Hence, as a general rule, the larger the number of older accounts that are included in an organization's AR file, the larger the allowance for doubtful accounts needs to be to reflect the risk. Historical trends in collection success also play an important part in estimating the bad debt losses for the period. A key issue for auditors to resolve, therefore, is whether the allowance calculated by the client is consistent with the composition of their organization's AR portfolio and with prior years. In addition, the auditor needs to determine that the allowance is consistent with current economic conditions. For example, an organization entering into a period of economic decline may experience an increased percentage of bad debts relative to prior, more prosperous, years. Under such circumstances, a larger portion of past-due accounts may need to be included in the allowance calculation than had previously been the case. As a starting point in an attempt to gain assurance on these issues, the auditor may decide to recalculate the aging schedule.

The following describes ACL's Accounts Receivable Aging feature using the Sales Invoice file presented in Table 9.3. The key data fields used in calculation are Invoice Amount and Due Date. The system compares the Due Date in the record with a specified cutoff date to produce aged summaries of the Invoice Amount data. The default intervals used are 30, 60, 90, and 120 days past due. These, however, can be changed to any values that better suit the auditor's needs.

Keep in mind that the Sales Invoice file contains all sales invoices for the period. Only the open sales invoices (those with blanks in the Remittance Number field) as of the cutoff date should be considered in the calculation. By filtering on the Remittance Number field, ACL will ignore all closed invoices. Upon executing the Age command, a report similar to Table 9.7 will be produced.

The aging report provides a clear picture of the accounts receivable composition. The total balance of accounts receivable outstanding at the end of the audit period is $468,880.69. As of the cutoff date, $217,113.27 of the outstanding balance is not past due. However, 17 invoices are between 90 and 120 days past due, and 13 invoices are over 120 days past due. The auditor should review past-due balances with the credit manager to obtain information for basing an opinion on their collectability. The

TABLE 9.7	**Aging of Accounts Receivable Produced with ACL**

As of: 06/10/2004 11:28:00

Command: AGE ON due CUTOFF 20031231 INTERVAL 0,30,60,90,120,10000 TO SCREEN
Table: ar

Minimum encountered was -124
Maximum encountered was 834

Days	Count	Percent of Count	Percent of Field	Trans Amount
≤0	255	33.03%	46.3%	217,113.27
0 - 29	259	33.55%	38.66%	181,252.50
30 - 59	170	22.02%	11.66%	54,676.94
60 - 89	58	7.51%	1.81%	8,496.10
90 - 119	17	2.2%	1.52%	7,137.88
120 - 10,000	13	1.68%	0.04%	204.00
Totals	772	100%	100%	468,880.69

auditor's objective is not to assess the collectability of each account, but to determine that the methods used by the credit manager to estimate the allowance for doubtful accounts is adequate and that the overall allowance is reasonable.

SUMMARY

This chapter examined audit procedures associated with the revenue cycle. The chapter began with a review of alternative technologies used in both legacy and modern systems. The emphasis was on key operational tasks under alternative technologies. The second main section of the chapter presented revenue cycle audit objectives and controls. In this section, we examined the tests of controls that an auditor may perform. Evidence gathered from tests of controls contributes to audit objectives and may permit the auditor to limit the scope, timing, and extent of substantive tests. The last section described the use of ACL in performing the more common substantive tests. The tests were presented in relation to the management assertions that they were designed to corroborate or refute.

Appendix

OVERVIEW OF REVENUE CYCLE ACTIVITIES AND DOCUMENTS

In this appendix, we examine the revenue cycle conceptually. Using data flow diagrams (DFDs) as a guide, we will trace the sequence of activities through three processes that constitute the revenue cycle for most retail, wholesale, and manufacturing organizations. These are sales order procedures, sales return procedures, and cash receipts procedures. Service companies such as hospitals, insurance companies, and banks would use different industry-specific methods.

This discussion is intended to be technology-neutral. In other words, the tasks described may be performed manually or by computer. The focus is on what (conceptually) needs to be done, not how (physically) it is accomplished. At various stages in the processes we will examine specific documents, journals, and ledgers as they are encountered. Again, this review is technology-neutral. These documents and files may be physical (hard copy) or digital (computer-generated). In the main text, we examine examples of physical computer based systems.

Sales Order Procedures

Sales order procedures include the tasks involved in receiving and processing a customer order, filling the order and shipping products to the customer, billing the customer at the proper time, and correctly accounting for the transaction. The relationships between these tasks are presented with the DFD in Figure 9.12 and described in the following section.

Receive Order. The sales process begins with the receipt of a **customer order** indicating the type and quantity of merchandise desired. At this point, the customer order is not in a standard format and may or may not be a physical document. Orders may arrive by mail, by telephone, or from a field representative who visited the customer. When the customer is also a business entity, the order is often a copy of the customer's purchase order. A purchase order is an expenditure cycle document, which is discussed in Chapter 10.

Because the customer order is not in the standard format that the seller's order processing system needs, the first task is to transcribe it into a formal **sales order,** an example of which is presented in Figure 9.13.

The sales order captures vital information such as the customer's name, address, and account number; the name, number, and description of the items sold; and the quantities and unit prices of each item sold. At this point, financial information such as taxes, discounts, and freight charges may or may not be included. After creating the sales order, a copy of it is placed in the **customer open order file** for future reference. The task of filling an order and getting the product to the customer may take days or even weeks. During this period, customers may contact their suppliers to check the status of their orders. The customer record in the open order file is updated each time the status of the order changes such as credit approval, on back-order, and shipment. The open

FIGURE 9.12 DFD of Sales Order Processing System

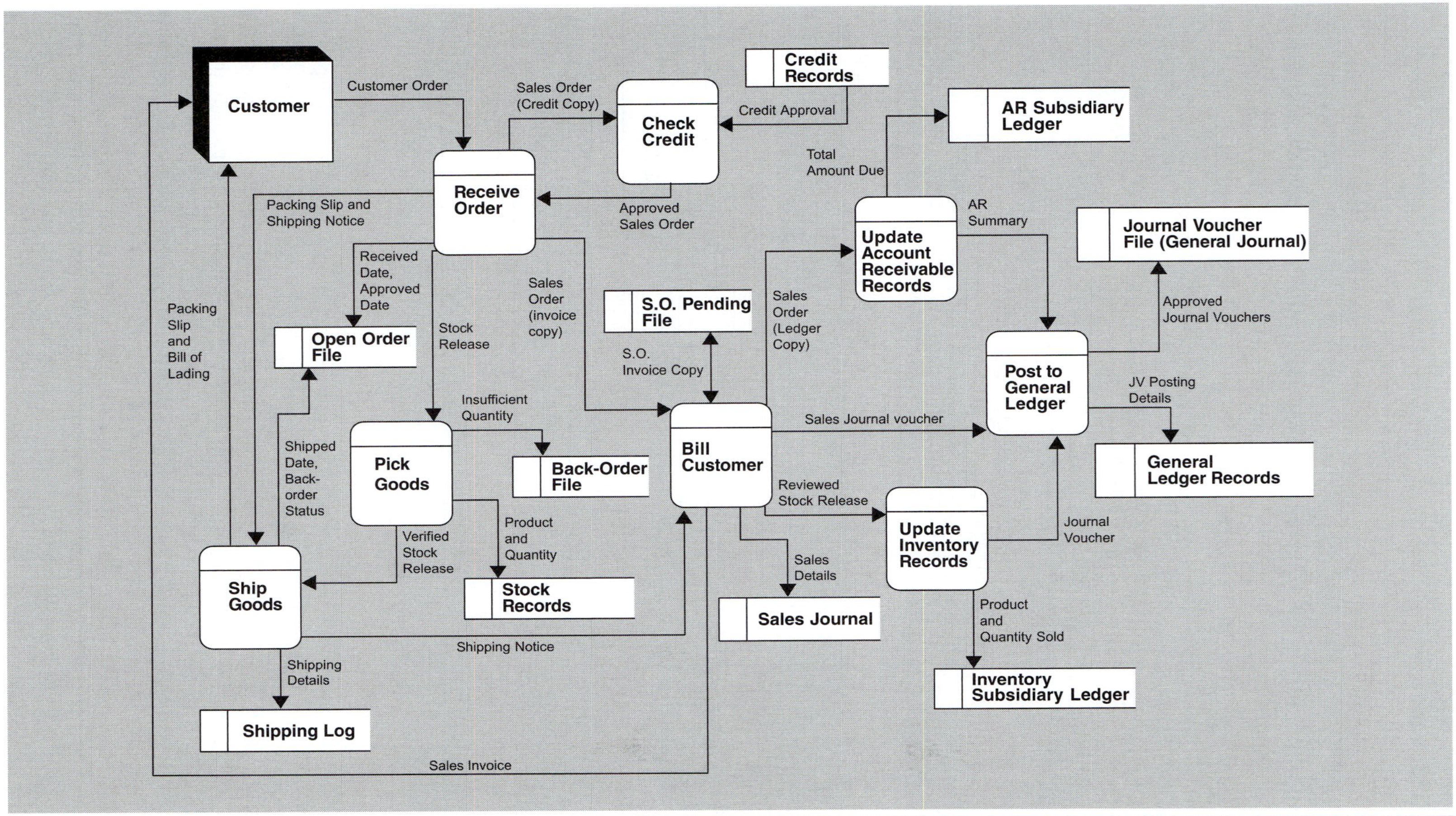

FIGURE 9.13

Sales Order

CREDIT SALE INVOICE

MONTEREY PENINSULA CO-OP
527 River Road
Chicago, IL 60612
(312) 555-0407

INVOICE NUMBER _____

SOLD TO
FIRM NAME _____
ATTENTION OF _____
ADDRESS_____
CITY_____
STATE _____ ZIP _____

INVOICE DATE _____
PREPARED BY _____
CREDIT TERMS_____

CUSTOMER PURCHASE ORDER
NUMBER_____
DATE_____
SIGNED BY _____

SHIPMENT DATE _____
SHIPPED VIA _____
B.O.L. NO. _____

QUANTITY ORDERED	PRODUCT NUMBER	DESCRIPTION	QUANTITY SHIPPED	UNIT PRICE	TOTAL
		TOTAL SALE			
		CUSTOMER ACCT. NO.			
		VERIFICATION			

order file thus enables customer service employees to respond promptly and accurately to customer questions.

Check Credit. Before processing the order further, the customer's creditworthiness needs to be established. The circumstances of the sale will determine the nature and degree of the credit check. For example, new customers may undergo a full financial investigation to establish a line of credit. Once a credit limit is set, however, credit checking on subsequent sales may be limited to ensuring that the customer has a history of paying his or her bills and that the current sale does not exceed the preestablished limit.

The credit approval process is an authorization control and should be performed as a function separate from the sales activity. In our conceptual system, the receive-order task sends the **sales order (credit copy)** to the check-credit task for approval. The returned **approved sales order** then triggers the continuation of the sales process by releasing sales order information simultaneously to various tasks. Several documents mentioned in the following sections, such as the stock release, packing slip, shipping notice, and sales invoice, are simply special-purpose copies of the sales order and are not illustrated separately.

Pick Goods.   The receive order activity forwards the **stock release** document (also called the picking ticket) to the pick goods function, in the warehouse. This document identifies the items of inventory that must be located and picked from the warehouse shelves. It also provides formal authorization for warehouse personnel to release the specified items. After picking the stock, the order is verified for accuracy and the goods and **verified stock release** document are sent to the ship goods task. If inventory levels are insufficient to fill the order, a warehouse employee adjusts the verified stock release to reflect the amount actually going to the customer. The employee then prepares a **back-order** record, which stays on file until the inventories arrive from the supplier (not shown in Figure 9.14). Back-ordered items are shipped before new sales are processed.

Finally, the warehouse employee adjusts the **stock records** to reflect the reduction in inventory. These stock records are not the formal accounting records for controlling inventory assets. They are used for warehouse management purposes only. Assigning asset custody and accounting record-keeping responsibility to the warehouse clerk would violate a key principle of internal control. The inventory control function, discussed later, maintains the formal accounting inventory records.

Ship Goods.   Before the arrival of the goods and the verified stock release document, the shipping department receives the **packing slip** and **shipping notice** from the receive order function. The packing slip will ultimately travel with the goods to the customer to describe the contents of the order. The shipping notice will later be forwarded to the billing function as evidence that the customer's order was filled and shipped. This document conveys pertinent new facts such as the date of shipment, the items and quantities actually shipped, the name of the carrier, and freight charges. In some systems, the shipping notice is a separate document prepared within the shipping function.

Upon receiving the goods from the warehouse, the shipping clerk reconciles the physical items with the stock release, the packing slip, and the shipping notice to verify that the order is correct. The ship goods function thus serves as an important independent verification control point and is the last opportunity to detect errors before shipment. The shipping clerk packages the goods, attaches the packing slip, completes the shipping notice, and prepares a **bill of lading**. The bill of lading, as shown in Figure 9.14, is a formal contract between the seller and the shipping company (carrier) to transport the goods to the customer. This document establishes legal ownership and responsibility for assets in transit. Once the goods are transferred to the carrier, the shipping clerk records the shipment in the shipping log, forwards the shipping notice and the stock release to the bill-customer function as proof of shipment, and updates the customer's open order file.

Bill Customer.   The shipment of goods marks the completion of the economic event and the point at which the customer should be billed. Billing before shipment encourages inaccurate record keeping and inefficient operations. When the customer order is originally prepared, some details such as inventory availability, prices, and shipping charges may not be known with certainty. In the case of back-orders, for example, suppliers do not typically bill customers for out-of-stock items. Billing for goods not shipped causes

FIGURE 9.14

Bill of Lading

UNIFORM STRAIGHT BILL OF LADING — Domestic

Monterey Peninsula Co-Op
527 River Road
Chicago, IL 60612
(312) 555-0407

Document No._____

Shipper No._____

Carrier No._____

TO:

Date_____

Consignee _____

Street _____

City/State _____

Zip Code _____

_____
(Name of Carrier)

Route:			Vehicle		
No. Shipping Units	Kind of packaging, description of articles, special marks and exceptions		Weight	Rate	Charges

TOTAL CHARGES $

The agreed or declared value of the property is hereby specifically stated by the shipper to be not exceeding: $ _____ per_____	IF WITHOUT RECOURSE: The carrier shall not make delivery of this shipment without payment of freight _____ (Signature of Consignor)

FREIGHT CHARGES
  Check appropriate box:
    [ ] Freight prepaid
    [ ] Collect
    [ ] Bill to shipper
	Signature below signifies that the goods described above are in apparent good order, except as noted. Shipper hereby certifies that he is familiar with all the bill of lading terms and agrees with them.

SHIPPER Monterey Peninsula Co-op	CARRIER
PER	PER DATE

(This bill of lading is to be signed
by the shipper and agent of the
carrier issuing same.)
CONSIGNEE

confusion, damages relations with customers, and requires additional work to make adjustments to the accounting records.

To prevent such problems, the billing function awaits notification from shipping before it bills. Figure 9.12 shows that upon credit approval, the bill-customer function receives the **sales order (invoice copy)** from the receive order task. This document is placed in an **S.O. pending file** until receipt of the shipping notice, which describes the products that were actually shipped to the customer. Upon arrival, the items shipped are reconciled with those ordered and unit prices, taxes, and freight charges are added to the invoice copy of the sales order. The completed **sales invoice** is the customer's bill, which formally depicts the charges to the customer. In addition, the billing function performs the following record-keeping-related tasks:

- Records the sale in the sales journal.
- Forwards the ledger copy of the sales order to the "update accounts receivable" task.
- Sends the stock release document to the update inventory records task.

The **sales journal** is a special journal used for recording completed sales transactions. The details of sales invoices are entered in the journal individually. At the end of the period, these entries are summarized into a **sales journal voucher**, which is sent to the general ledger task for posting to the following accounts:

	DR	CR
Accounts Receivable—Control	XXXX.XX	
Sales		XXXX.XX

Figure 9.15 illustrates a **journal voucher**. Each journal voucher represents a general journal entry and indicates the general ledger accounts affected. Summaries of transactions, adjusting entries, and closing entries are all entered into the general ledger via this method. When properly approved, journal vouchers are an effective control against unauthorized entries to the general ledger. The journal voucher system eliminates the need for a formal general journal, which is replaced by a **journal voucher file**.

Update Inventory Records. The inventory control function updates **inventory subsidiary ledger** accounts from information contained in the stock release document. In a

FIGURE 9.15

Journal Voucher

Journal Voucher		Number: JV6-03	
		Date: 10/7/2009	
Account Number	Account Name	Amount DR.	CR.
20100	Accounts Receivable	5,000	
50200	Sales		5,000
Explanation: to record total credit sales for 10/7/2009			
Approved by: JRM		Posted by: MJJ	

FIGURE 9.16   Inventory Subsidiary Ledger

Perpetual Inventory Record – Item # 86329

Item Description	Date	Units Received	Units Sold	Qnty On Hand	Reorder Point	EOQ	Qnty On Order	Purch Order #	Vendor Number	Standard Cost	Total Inven. Cost
3" Pulley	9/15			50	950	200	1,000	—	—	—	2	1,900
	9/18			300	650							1,300
	9/20			100	550							1,100
	9/27			300	250							500
	10/1			100	150	200	1,000	1,000	87310	851	2	300
	10/7	1,000			1,150			—				2,300

perpetual inventory system, every inventory item has its own record in the ledger containing, at a minimum, the data depicted in Figure 9.16. Each stock release document reduces the quantity on hand of one or more inventory accounts. Periodically, the financial value of the total reduction in inventory is summarized in a journal voucher and sent to the general ledger function for posting to the following accounts:

	DR	CR
Cost of Goods Sold	XXX.XX	
Inventory—Control		XXX.XX

Update Accounts Receivable.   Customer records in the **accounts receivable (AR) subsidiary ledger** are updated from information the sales order (**ledger copy**) provides. Every customer has an account record in the AR subsidiary ledger containing, at minimum, the following data: customer name; customer address; current balance; available credit; transaction dates; invoice numbers; and credits for payments, returns, and allowances. Figure 9.17 presents an example of an AR subsidiary ledger record.

FIGURE 9.17

Accounts Receivable Subsidiary Ledger

Name: Howard Supply   Account Number 1435
Address: 121 Maple St.
              Winona, NY 18017

Date	Explanation	Invoice Number	Payment (CR)	Sale (DR)	Account Balance	Credit Limit	Available Credit
9/27	3" Pulley (300 Units)	92131		600.00	600.00	1000.00	400.00
10/7			600.00		0.00		1000.00

Periodically, the individual account balances are summarized in a report that is sent to the general ledger. The purpose for this is discussed next.

Post to General Ledger. By the close of the transaction processing period, the general ledger function has received journal vouchers from the billing and inventory control tasks and an account summary from the AR function. This information set serves two purposes. First, the general ledger uses the journal vouchers to post to the following control accounts:

	DR	CR
Accounts Receivable Control	XXXX.XX	
Cost of Goods Sold	XXX.XX	
Inventory Control		XXX.XX
Sales		XXXX.XX

Because general ledger accounts are used to prepare financial statements, they contain only summary figures (no supporting detail) and require only summary posting information. Second, this information supports an important independent verification control. The AR summary, which the AR function independently provides, is used to verify the accuracy of the journal vouchers from billing. The AR summary figures should equal the total debits to AR reflected in the journal vouchers for the transaction period. By reconciling these figures, the general ledger function can detect many types of errors. We examine this point more fully in a later section dealing with revenue cycle controls.

Sales Return Procedures

An organization can expect that a certain percentage of its sales will be returned. This occurs for a number of reasons, some of which may be:

- The company shipped the customer the wrong merchandise.
- The goods were defective.
- The product was damaged in shipment.
- The buyer refused delivery because the seller shipped the goods too late or they were delayed in transit.

When a return is necessary, the buyer requests credit for the unwanted products. This involves reversing the previous transaction in the sales order procedure. Using the DFD in Figure 9.18, let's now review the procedures for approving and processing returned items.

Prepare Return Slip. When items are returned, the receiving department employee counts, inspects, and prepares a **return slip** describing the items. The goods, along with a copy of the return slip, go to the warehouse to be restocked. The employee then sends the second copy of the return slip to the sales function to prepare a credit memo.

Prepare Credit Memo. Upon receipt of the return slip, the sales employee prepares a **credit memo**. This document is the authorization for the customer to receive credit for the merchandise returned. Note that the credit memo illustrated in Figure 9.19, is similar

FIGURE 9.18   **DFD of Sales Return Procedures**

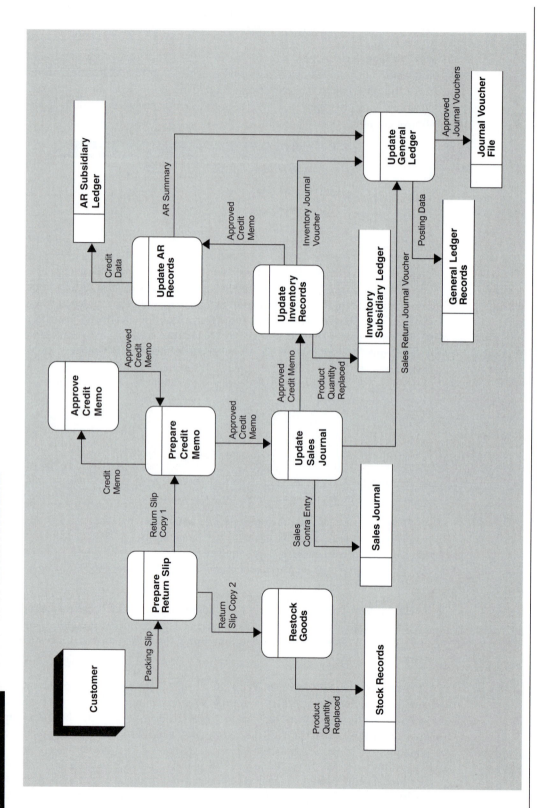

FIGURE 9.19   **Credit Memo**

Credit Memo

Monterey Peninsula Co-Op
527 River Road
Chicago, IL 60612
(312) 555-0407

Customer
Invoice # _____

Received from _____   Reason for Return

Address _____

City _____

State _____ Zip _____

Product Number	Description	Quantity Returned	Unit Price	Total
Approved By:			Total Credit	

in appearance to a sales order. Some systems may actually use a copy of the sales order marked credit memo.

In cases in which specific authorization is required (that is, the amount of the return or circumstances surrounding the return exceed the sales employee's general authority to approve), the credit memo goes to the credit manager for approval. However, if the clerk has sufficient general authority to approve the return, the credit memo is sent directly to the billing function, where the customer sales transaction is reversed.

Approve Credit Memo.   The credit manager evaluates the circumstances of the return and makes a judgment to grant (or disapprove) credit. The manager then returns the **approved credit memo** to the sales department.

Update Sales Journal.   Upon receipt of the approved credit memo, the transaction is recorded in the sales journal as a contra entry. The credit memo is then forwarded to the inventory control function for posting. At the end of the period, total sales returns are summarized in a journal voucher and sent to the general ledger department.

Update Inventory and AR Records.   The inventory control function adjusts the inventory records and forwards the credit memo to AR, where the customer's account is also adjusted. Periodically, inventory control sends a journal voucher summarizing the total value of inventory returns to the general ledger update task. Similarly, accounts receivable submits an AR account summary to the general ledger function.

Update General Ledger.   Upon receipt of the journal voucher and account summary information, the general ledger function reconciles the figures and posts to the following control accounts:

	DR	CR
Inventory—Control	XXXX.XX	
Sales Returns and Allowances	XXX.XX	
Cost of Goods Sold		XXX.XX
Accounts Receivable—Control		XXXX.XX

Cash Receipts Procedures

The sales order procedure described a credit transaction that resulted in the establishment of an account receivable. Payment on the account is due at some future date, which the terms of trade determine. Cash receipts procedures apply to this future event. They involve receiving and securing the cash; depositing the cash in the bank; matching the payment with the customer and adjusting the correct account; and properly accounting for and reconciling the financial details of the transaction. The DFD in Figure 9.20 shows the relationship between these tasks. They are described in detail in the following section.

Open Mail and Prepare Remittance Advice.   A mail room employee opens envelopes containing customers' payments and **remittance advices**. Remittance advices (see Figure 9.21) contain information needed to service individual customers' accounts. This includes payment date, account number, amount paid, and customer check number. Only the portion above the perforated line is the remittance advice, which the customer removes and returns with the payment. In some systems, the lower portion of the document is a customer statement that the billing department sends out periodically. In other cases, this could be the original customer invoice, which was described in the sales order procedures.

The remittance advice is most apparent in firms that process large volumes of cash receipts daily. For example, processing a check from John Smith with no supporting details would require a time-consuming and costly search through perhaps thousands of records to find the correct John Smith. This task is greatly simplified when the customer provides necessary account number and posting information. Because of the possibility of transcription errors and omissions, however, sellers do not rely on their customers to provide this information directly on their checks. Errors are avoided and operational efficiency is greatly improved when using remittance advices.

Mail room personnel route the checks and remittance advices to an administrative clerk who endorses the checks "For Deposit Only" and reconciles the amount on each remittance advice with the corresponding check. The clerk then records each check on a form called a **remittance list** (or cash prelist), where all cash received is logged. In this example, the clerk prepares three copies of the remittance list. The original copy is sent

FIGURE 9.20 DFD of Cash Receipts Procedure

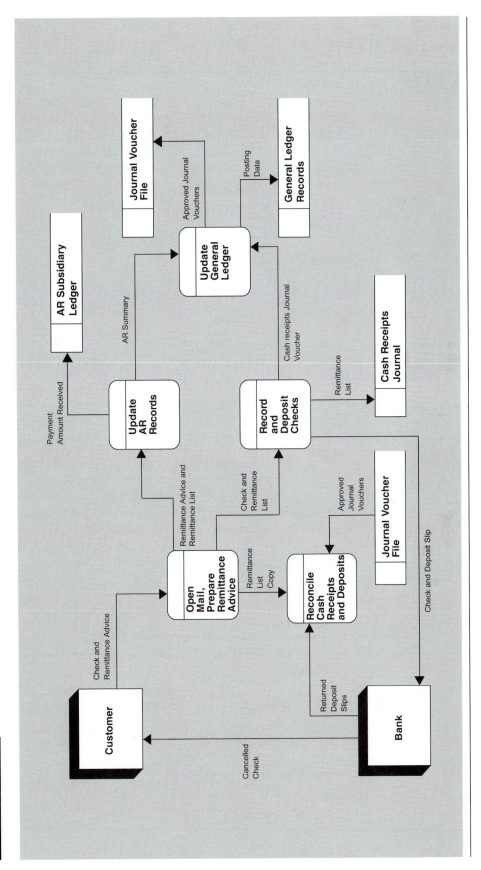

FIGURE 9.21   **Remittance Advice**

Send To: Monterey Peninsula Co-Op   Page: 1
                        527 River Road
                        Chicago, IL 60612
                        (312) 555-0407

Remittance Advice:

Date	Customer No.	Amount Pd.	Check No.
10/4/09	811901	125.00	2002

Please return the upper portion with your payment — Thank You

To: John Smith
       R.D. #2, Box 312
       Prunedale, CA 09278–5704

Due Date	Customer No.	Amount Due
10/10/09	811901	125.00

Date	Invoice Number	Description	Amount Due	
9/28/09	6112115	Cleaning Supplies	125.00	

Thank you for giving Monterey Peninsula the opportunity to serve you

Previous Bal.	300.00
Payments	300.00
Sales	125.00
Late Fees	—
Tax	—
Ending Bal.	125.00

FIGURE 9.22	**Cash Receipts Journal**

Cash Receipts Journal

Date	Account	Post Ref	Check #	Cash Acct. # 101 (Debit)	Sales Discounts Acct. # 430 (Debit)	Accounts Receivable Acct. # 102	Sales Acct. # 401 Credit	Sundry Accounts Debit (Credit)
9/3	Capital Stock	301	2150	14,000				14,000
9/5	Ogment Supply	✓	6712	2,970	30	3,000		
9/9	Marvin Co.		3491	1,000			1,000	

with the checks to the record and deposit checks function. The second copy goes with the remittance advices to the update AR function. The third goes to a reconciliation task.

Record and Deposit Checks. A cash receipts employee verifies the accuracy and completeness of the checks against the prelist. Any checks possibly lost or misdirected between the mail room and this function are thus identified. After reconciling the prelist to the checks, the employee records the check in the **cash receipts journal**. All cash receipts transactions, including cash sales, miscellaneous cash receipts, and cash received on account, are recorded in the cash receipts journal. Figure 9.22 illustrates this with an example of each type of transaction. Notice that each check received from a customer is listed as a separate line item.

Next, the clerk prepares a bank **deposit slip** showing the amount of the day's receipts and forwards this along with the checks to the bank. Upon deposit of the funds, the bank teller validates the deposit slip and returns it to the company for reconciliation. At the end of the day, the cash receipts employee summarizes the journal entries and sends the following journal voucher entry to the general ledger function.

	DR	CR
Cash	XXXX.XX	
Accounts Receivable Control		XXXX.XX

Update Accounts Receivable. The remittance advices are used to post to the customers' accounts in the AR subsidiary ledger. Periodically, the changes in account balances are summarized and forwarded to the general ledger function.

Update General Ledger. Upon receipt of the journal voucher and the account summary, the general ledger function reconciles the figures, posts to the cash and AR control accounts, and files the journal voucher.

Reconcile Cash Receipts and Deposits.   Periodically (weekly or monthly), a clerk from the **controller's** office (or an employee not involved with the cash receipts procedures) reconciles cash receipts by comparing the following documents: (1) a copy of the prelist, (2) deposit slips received from the bank, and (3) related journal vouchers.

KEY TERMS

accounts receivable (AR) subsidiary ledger
analytical review
batch control totals
bill of lading
confirmation of accounts receivable
controller
credit authorization
credit memo
customer open order file
customer order
cycle billing
events database
inventory subsidiary ledger
ledger copy

negative confirmation
open-invoice system
packing slip
positive confirmation
reengineering
remittance advices
remittance list
return slip
sales invoice
sales invoice file
sales journal voucher
sales order
shipping notice
stock release (picking ticket)

REVIEW QUESTIONS

1. What document initiates the sales process?
2. Distinguish between a packing slip, a shipping notice, and a bill of lading.
3. What are three input controls?
4. What are the three rules that ensure that no single employee or department processes a transaction in its entirety?
5. What is automation, and why is it used?
6. What is the objective of reengineering?
7. Distinguish between an edit run, sort run, and update run.
8. How is the record's primary key critical in preserving the audit trail?
9. What are the advantages of real-time processing?
10. Why does billing receive a copy of the sales order when the order is approved but does not bill until the goods are shipped?
11. How do tests of controls relate to substantive tests?
12. In a manual system, after which event in the sales process should the customer be billed?
13. What is a bill of lading?
14. What document initiates the billing process?
15. Where in the cash receipts process does supervision play an important role?
16. List the revenue cycle audit objectives derived from the "existence or occurrence" management assertion.
17. List the revenue cycle audit objectives derived from the "completeness" management assertion.
18. List the revenue cycle audit objectives derived from the "accuracy" management assertion.

DISCUSSION QUESTIONS

1. Distinguish between the sales, billing, and AR departments. Why can't the sales or AR departments prepare the bills?
2. Explain the risks associated with mailroom procedures.
3. How could an employee embezzle funds by issuing an unauthorized sales credit memo if the appropriate segregation of duties and authorization controls were not in place?
4. What task can the AR department engage in to verify that all checks sent by the customers have been appropriately deposited and recorded?
5. Why is access control over revenue cycle documents just as important as the physical control devices over cash and inventory?
6. For a batch processing system using sequential files, describe the intermediate and permanent files that are created after the edit run has successfully been completed when processing the sales order file and updating the accounts receivable and inventory master files.
7. Why has the use of magnetic tapes as a storage medium declined in recent years? What are their primary uses currently?
8. Discuss both the tangible and intangible benefits of real-time processing.
9. Distinguish between positive and negative confirmations.
10. What is the purpose of analytical reviews in the audit of revenue cycle accounts?
11. Explain the open-invoice system. What effect might it have on confirmation responses?
12. What financial statement misrepresentations may result from an inconsistently applied credit policy? Be specific.
13. Give three examples of access control in a POS system.
14. What makes POS systems different from revenue cycles of manufacturing firms?
15. Is a POS system that uses bar coding and a laser light scanner foolproof against inaccurate updates? Discuss.

MULTIPLE-CHOICE QUESTIONS

1. Which document is *not* prepared by the sales department?
   a. packing slip
   b. shipping notice
   c. bill of lading
   d. stock release
2. Which document triggers the update of the inventory subsidiary ledger?
   a. bill of lading
   b. stock release
   c. sales order
   d. shipping notice
3. Which function should *not* be performed by the billing department?
   a. recording the sales in the sales journal
   b. sending the ledger copy of the sales order to accounts receivable
   c. sending the stock release document and the shipping notice to the billing department as proof of shipment
   d. sending the stock release document to inventory control
4. When will a credit check approval most likely require specific authorization by the credit department?
   a. when verifying that the current transaction does not exceed the customer's credit limit
   b. when verifying that the current transaction is with a valid customer
   c. when a valid customer places a materially large order
   d. when a valid customer returns goods
5. Which type of control is considered to be a compensating control?
   a. segregation of duties
   b. access control
   c. supervision
   d. accounting records
6. Which of the following is *not* an output control?
   a. The shipping department verifies that the goods sent from the warehouse are correct in type and quantity.
   b. General ledger clerks reconcile journal vouchers that were independently prepared in various departments.

c. The sales clerk uses pre-numbered sales orders.

d. The billing department reconciles the shipping notice with the sales invoice to ensure that customers are billed only for the quantities shipped.

7. Which function or department below records the decrease in inventory due to a sale?
   a. warehouse
   b. sales department
   c. billing department
   d. inventory control

8. Which situation indicates a weak internal control structure?
   a. the AR clerk authorizes the write off of bad debts
   b. the record-keeping clerk maintains both AR and AP subsidiary ledgers

c. the inventory control clerk authorizes inventory purchases

d. the AR clerk prepares customer statements every month

9. The bill of lading is prepared by the
   a. sales clerk.
   b. warehouse clerk.
   c. shipping clerk.
   d. billing clerk.

10. Which of following functions should be segregated?
    a. opening the mail and recording cash receipts in the journal
    b. authorizing credit and determining reorder quantities
    c. shipping goods and preparing the bill of lading
    d. providing information on inventory levels and reconciling the bank statement

PROBLEMS

1. Process Description
Describe the procedures, documents, and departments involved when insufficient inventory is available to fill a customer's approved order.

2. Process Description
Refer to Figure 9.1 and explain where the batch totals come from and which accounts in the general ledger are affected by the end-of-day batch process.

3. Flowchart Analysis
Use the flowchart for Problem 3 to answer these questions:
   a. What accounting document is represented by symbol A?
   b. What is an appropriate name for the department labeled B?
   c. What would be an appropriate description for process C?
   d. What is the location represented by symbol D?
   e. What accounting record is represented by symbol E?
   f. What is an appropriate name for the department labeled H?
   g. What device is represented by symbol F?
   h. What device is represented by symbol G?
   i. What accounting record is represented by symbol G?

4. Internal Control Evaluation
Identify the control weaknesses depicted in the flowchart for Problem 4.

5. Segregation of Functions
Which, if any, of the following situations represent improper segregation of functions?

a. The billing department prepares the customers' invoices, and the AR department posts to the customers' accounts.

b. The sales department approves sales credit memos as the result of product returns, and subsequent adjustments to the customer accounts are performed by the AR department.

c. The shipping department ships goods that have been retrieved from stock by warehouse personnel.

d. The general accounting department posts to the general ledger accounts after receiving journal vouchers that are prepared by the billing department.

6. Internal Controls
CMA 688 5-2

Jem Clothes, Inc., is a twenty-five-store chain concentrated in the Northeast that sells ready-to-wear clothes for young men and women. Each store has a full-time manager and an assistant manager, both of whom are paid a salary. The cashiers and sales personnel are typically young people working part-time who are paid an hourly wage plus a commission based on sales volume. The Problem 6 flowchart depicts the flow of a sales transaction through the organization of a typical store. The company uses unsophisticated cash registers with four-part sales invoices to record each transaction. These sales invoices are used regardless of the payment type (cash, check, or bank card).

On the sales floor, the salesperson manually records his or her employee number and the transaction (clothes, class, description, quantity, and unit price),

Problem 3: Flowchart Analysis

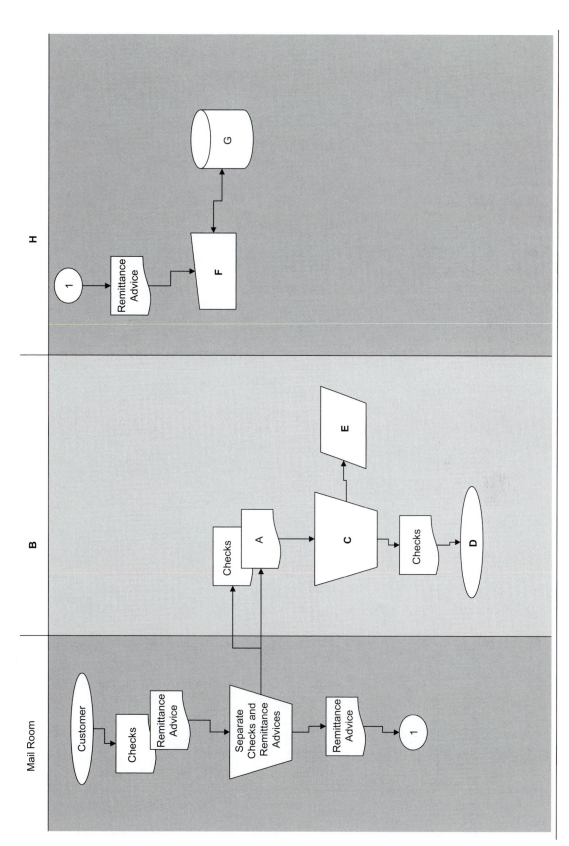

Problem 4: Internal Control Evaluation

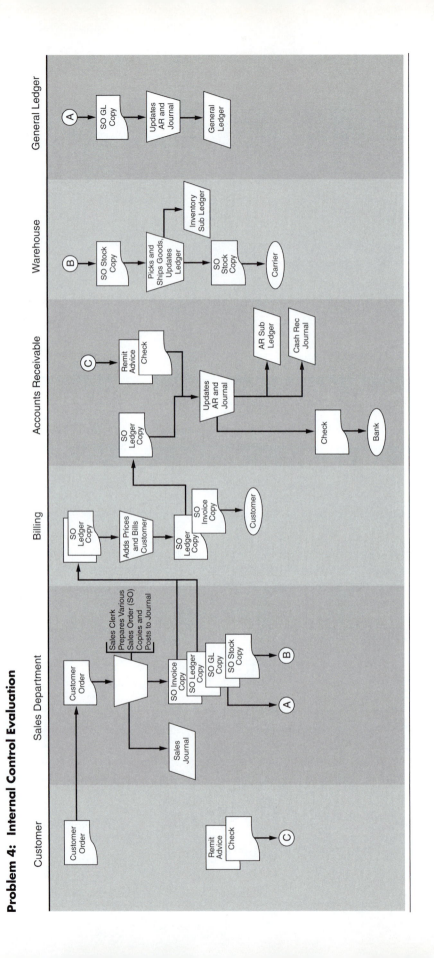

Problem 6: Internal Controls

totals the sales invoice, calculates the discount when appropriate, calculates the sales tax, and prepares the grand total. The salesperson then gives the sales invoice to the cashier, retaining one copy in the sales book.

The cashier reviews the invoice and inputs the sale. The cash register mechanically validates the invoice by automatically assigning a consecutive number to the transaction. The cashier is also responsible for getting credit approval on charge sales and approving sales paid by check. The cashier gives one copy of the invoice to the customer and retains the second copy as a store copy and the third for a bank card, if a deposit is needed. Returns are handled in exactly the reverse manner, with the cashier issuing a return slip.

At the end of each day, the cashier sequentially orders the sales invoices and takes cash register totals for cash, bank card, and check sales, and cash and bank card returns. These totals are reconciled by the assistant manager to the cash register tapes, the total of the consecutively numbered sales invoices, and the return slips. The assistant manager prepares a daily reconciliation report for the store manager's review.

Cash, check, and bank card sales are reviewed by the manager, who then prepares the daily bank deposit (bank card sales invoices are included in the deposit). The manager makes the deposit at the bank and files the validated deposit slip.

The cash register tapes, sales invoices, and return slips are then forwarded daily to the central data processing department at corporate headquarters for processing. The data processing department returns a weekly sales and commission activity report to the manager for review.

Required:
a. Identify six strengths in the Jem Clothes system for controlling sales transactions.
b. For each strength identified, explain what problem(s) Jem Clothes has avoided by incorporating the strength in the system for controlling sales transactions.
Use the following format in preparing your answer.

1. *Strength*   2. *Problem(s) Avoided*

7.   Stewardship
Identify which department has stewardship over the following journals, ledgers, and files:
a. Customer open order file
b. Sales journal
c. Journal voucher file
d. Cash receipts journal
e. Inventory subsidiary ledger
f. AR subsidiary ledger
g. Sales history file
h. Shipping report file
i. Credit memo file
j. Sales order file
k. Closed sales order file

8.   Control Weaknesses
For the past 11 years, Elaine Wright has been an employee of the Star-Bright Electrical Supply store. Elaine is a very diligent employee who rarely calls in sick and takes her vacation days staggered throughout the year so that no one else gets bogged down with her tasks for more than one day. Star-Bright is a small store that employs only four people other than the owner. The owner and one of the employees help customers with their electrical needs. One of the employees handles all receiving, stocking, and shipping of merchandise. Another employee handles the purchasing, payroll, general ledger, inventory, and accounts payable functions. Elaine handles all of the point-of-sale cash receipts and prepares the daily deposits for the business. Furthermore, Elaine opens the mail and deposits all cash receipts (about 30 percent of the total daily cash receipts). Elaine also keeps the AR records and bills the customers who purchase on credit.

Required:
a. Point out any control weaknesses you see in the above scenario.
b. List some recommendations to remedy any weaknesses you have found working under the constraint that no additional employees can be hired.

9.   Internal Control
Iris Plant owns and operates three floral shops in Magnolia, Texas. The accounting functions have been performed manually. Each of the shops has a manager who oversees the cash receipts and purchasing functions for the shop. All bills are sent to the central shop and are paid by a clerk who also prepares payroll checks and maintains the general journal. Iris is seriously considering switching to a computerized system. With so many information systems packages on the market, Iris is overwhelmed.

Required:
    Advise Iris as to which business modules you think her organization could find beneficial. Discuss advantages, disadvantages, and internal control issues.

Problem 11: Data Processing

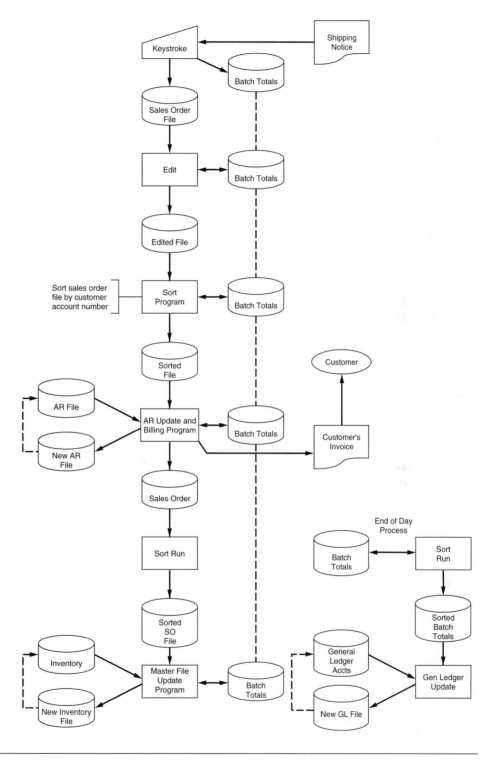

10. Internal Control

You are investing your money and opening a fast-food Mexican restaurant that accepts only cash for payments. You plan on periodically issuing coupons through the mail and in local newspapers. You are particularly interested in access controls over inventory and cash.

Required:

Design a carefully controlled system and draw a document flowchart to represent it. Identify and discuss the key control issues.

11. Data Processing

The computer processing portion of a sales order system is represented by the Problem 11 flowchart on the following page. Answer the following questions:

Required:

a. What type of data processing system is this? Explain, and be specific.

b. The auditor suggests that this system can be greatly simplified by changing to direct access files. Explain the major operational changes that would occur in the system if this were done.

c. The auditor warns of control implications from this change that must be considered. Explain the nature of the control implications.

d. Sketch a flowchart (the computerized portion only) of the proposed new system. Use correct symbols and label the diagram.

12. System Configuration

The flowchart for Problem 12 represents the computer processing portion of a sales order system. Answer the following questions.

a. What type of data processing system is this? Explain, and be specific.

b. The marketing manager suggests that this system can be greatly improved by processing all files in real time. Explain the major operational changes that would occur in the system if this were done.

c. The auditor warns of operational efficiency implications from this change that must be considered. Explain the nature of these implications.

d. Sketch a flowchart of the proposed new system. Use correct symbols and label the diagram.

Problem 12: System Configuration

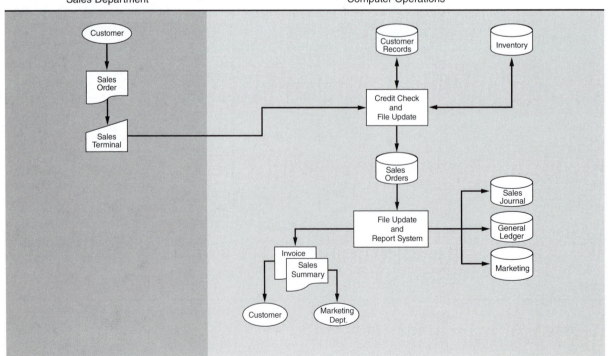

INTERNAL CONTROL CASES

1. Smith's Market (Small Business POS Accounting System)

In 1989, Robert Smith opened a small fruit and vegetable market in Bethlehem, Pennsylvania. Originally, Smith sold only produce grown on his family farm and orchard. As the market's popularity grew, however, he added bread, canned goods, fresh meats, and a limited supply of frozen goods. Today, Smith's Market is a full-range farmers' market with a strong local customer base. Indeed, the market's reputation for low prices and high quality draws customers from other Pennsylvania cities and even from the neighboring state of New Jersey. Currently Smith's Market has forty employees. These include sales staff, shelf stockers, farm laborers, shift supervisors, and clerical staff. Recently Smith has noticed a decline in profits and sales, while his purchases of products for resale have continued to rise. Although the company does not prepare audited financial statements, Robert Smith has commissioned your public accounting firm to assess his company's sales procedures and controls. Smith's Market revenue cycle procedures are described in the following paragraphs:

Customers push their shopping carts to the checkout register where a clerk processes the sale. The market has four registers, but they are not dedicated to specific sales clerks because the clerks play many rolls in the day-to-day operations. In addition to checking out customers, sales clerks will stock shelves, unload delivery trucks, or perform other tasks as demand in various areas rises and falls throughout the day. This fluid work demand makes the assignment of clerks to specific registers impractical.

At the beginning of the shift, the shift supervisor collects four cash register drawers from the treasury clerk in an office in the back of the market. The drawers contain $100 each in small bills (known as float) to enable the clerks to make change. The supervisor signs a log indicating that he has taken custody of the float and places the drawers into the respective cash registers.

Sales to customers are for cash, check, or credit card only. Credit card sales are performed in the usual way. The clerk swipes the card and obtains online approval from the card issuer at the time of sale. The customer then signs the credit card voucher, which the clerk places in a special compartment of the cash register drawer. The customer receives a receipt for the purchase and a copy of the credit card voucher.

For payments by check, the clerk requires the customer to present a valid driver's license. The license number is added to the check and the check is matched against a "black" list of customers who have previously passed bad checks. If the customer is not on the list, the check is accepted for payment and placed in the cash register drawer. The clerk then gives the customer a receipt.

The majority of sales are for cash. The clerk receives the cash from the customer, makes change, and issues a receipt for the purchase.

At the end of the shift, the supervisor returns the cash register drawers containing the cash, checks, and credit cards receipts to the treasury clerk and signs a log that he has handed in the cash drawers. The clerk later counts the cash and credit card sales. Using a standalone PC, he records the total sales amounts in the sales journal and the general Ledger Sales and Cash accounts. The Treasury clerk then prepares a deposit slip and delivers the cash, checks, and credit card vouchers to the local branch of the bank two blocks away from the market.

Required:

  a. Create a data flow diagram of the current system.
  b. Create a system flowchart of the existing system.
  c. Analyze the internal control weaknesses in the system. Model your response according to the six categories of physical control activities specified in COSO.

2. Spice Is Right Imports (Standalone PC-Based Accounting System)

Spice Is Right was established in 1990 in Boston, where it began importing exotic spices and cooking sauces from India and China. The company distributes these specialty foods to ethnic food shops, cafés, and restaurants across the country. In addition to its Boston headquarters and warehouse, the company has a distribution center in Elizabeth, New Jersey. Spice Is Right currently employs over 100 people, has dozens of suppliers, and trades in hundreds of ethnic and exotic foods from all over the world.

Recently Spice Is Right has been receiving complaints from customers and suppliers about billing, shipping, and payment errors. Management believes that these complaints stem, in part, from an antiquated computer system. Spice's current information system includes manual procedures supported by independent (nonnetworked) PCs in each department, which cannot communicate with each other. Document flows between the departments is entirely in hard-copy form. The following is a description of its revenue cycle at the Boston headquarters office.

Sales Procedures

Spice Is Right's revenue cycle begins when a customer places an order with a sales representative by phone or fax. A sales department employee enters the customer order into a standard sales order format using a word processor installed on a PC to produces six documents: three copies of sales orders, a stock release, a shipping notice, and a packing slip. The accounting department receives a copy of the sales order, the warehouse receives the stock release and a copy of the sales order, and the shipping department receives a shipping notice and packing slip. The sales clerk files a copy of the sales order in the department.

Upon receipt of the sales order, the accounting department clerk manually prepares an invoice and sends it to the customer. Using data from the sales order, the clerk then enters the sale in the department PC and records the sale in the sales journal and in the AR subsidiary ledger. At the end of the day, the clerk prepares a hard-copy sales journal voucher, which is sent to the general ledger department.

The warehouse receives a copy of the sales order and stock release. A warehouse employee picks the product and sends it to the shipping department, along with the stock release. A warehouse clerk updates the inventory records on the warehouse PC and files sales order in the warehouse. At the end of the day, the clerk prepares a hard-copy AR account summary and sends it to the general ledger department.

The shipping department receives a shipping notice and packing slip from the sales department. The shipping notice is filed. Upon receipt of the stock release, the shipping clerk prepares the two copies of a bill of lading using a word processor. The bills of lading and the packing slip are sent with the product to the carrier. The clerk then files the stock release in the department.

The general ledger clerk posts the journal voucher and inventory summary to the general ledger, which is stored on the department PC; the clerk then files these documents in the general ledger department.

Cash Receipts Procedure

The mailroom has five employees who open and sort all mail. Each employee has two bins, one for remittance advices and one for checks. Before separating the two documents and putting them in their respective bins, the clerks reconcile the amounts on the checks and remittance advices.

The remittance advices are sent to the accounting department, where a clerk records each remittance advice on a remittance list. The remittance list is then sent to the cash receipts department. Using the remittance advices, the accounting clerk updates the customer accounts receivable on the department PC and files the advice in the department. At the end of the day the clerk prepares an account summery on the PC. A hard copy of the summary is sent to the general ledger department.

The mailroom clerk sends the checks to the cash receipts department, where a clerk endorses each check with the words "For Deposit Only." Next, the clerk reconciles the checks with the remittance list and records the cash receipts in the cash receipts journal on the department PC. Finally, the clerk prepares a deposit slip and sends it and the checks to the bank.

The general ledger posts the AR summary to general ledger and files it in the general ledger department.

Required:

a. Create a data flow diagram of the current system.
b. Create a system flowchart of the existing system.
c. Identify the internal control weaknesses in the system. Use the six categories of physical control activities specified in COSO for your analysis.
d. Prepare a system flowchart of a redesigned computer-based system that resolves the control weaknesses that you identified in "c" above.

3. ABE Plumbing, Inc. (Centralized Small Business Accounting System)

ABE Plumbing, Inc., opened its doors in 1979 as a wholesale supplier of plumbing equipment, tools, and parts to hardware stores, home-improvement centers, and professional plumbers in the Allentown–Bethlehem–Easton metropolitan area. Over the years, the company has expanded its operations to serve customers across the nation and now employs over 200 people as technical representatives, buyers, warehouse workers, and sales and office staff. Most recently, ABE has experienced fierce competition from the large online discount stores such as Harbor Freight and Northern Supply. In addition, the company is suffering from operational inefficiencies related to its archaic information system. ABE's revenue cycle procedures are described in the following paragraphs:

Revenue Cycle

ABE's sales department consists of seventeen full-time and part-time employees. They receive orders via traditional mail, e-mail, telephone, and the occasional walk-in. Because ABE is a wholesaler, the vast majority of its business is conducted on a credit basis. The process begins in the sales department, where the sales clerk enters the customer's order into the centralized computer sales order system. The computer and file server is housed in ABE's small data processing department.

If the customer has done business with ABE in the past, his or her data are already on file. If the customer is a first-time buyer, however, the clerk creates a new record in the customer file. The system then creates a record of the transaction in the open sales order file. When the order is entered, an electronic copy of it is sent to the customer's e-mail address as confirmation.

A clerk in the warehouse department periodically reviews the open sales order file from a terminal and prints two copies of a stock release document for each new sale, which he uses to pick the items sold from the shelves. The warehouse clerk sends one copy of the stock release to the sales department and the second copy, along with the goods, to the shipping department. The warehouse clerk then updates the inventory subsidiary file to reflect the items and quantities shipped. Upon receipt of the stock release document, the sales clerk accesses the open sales order file from a terminal, closes the sales order, and files the stock release document in the sales department. The sales order system automatically posts these transactions to the sales, inventory control, and cost-of-goods sold accounts in the general ledger file.

Upon receipt of the goods and the stock release, the shipping department clerk prepares the goods for shipment to the customer. The clerk prepares three copies of the bill of lading. Two of these go with the goods to the carrier and the third, along with the stock release document, is filed in the shipping department.

The billing department clerk reviews the closed sales orders from a terminal and prepares two copies of the sales invoice. One copy is mailed to the customer and the other is filed in the billing department. The clerk then creates a new record in the account receivable subsidiary file. The sales order system automatically updates the account receivable control account in the general ledger file.

ABE has hired your public accounting firm to review is sales order procedures for internal control compliance and to make recommendations for changes.

Required:
    a. Create a data flow diagram of the current system.
    b. Create a system flowchart of the existing system.
    c. Analyze the internal control weaknesses in the system. Model your response according to the six categories of physical control activities specified in the COSO control model.
    d. Prepare a system flowchart of a redesigned computer-based system that resolves the control weaknesses that you identified.

4. Walker Books, Inc. (Manual System with Minimal PC Support)

(Prepared by Matt Wisser, Lehigh University)

Company Background

Walker Books, Inc., is the fastest-growing book distributor in the United States. Established in 1981 in Palo Alto, California, Walker Books was originally a side project of founder and current president Curtis Walker, who at the time was employed by a local law firm. Because reading was much more than just a hobby of his, he decided to use some of his savings to buy an abandoned restaurant and convert it into a neighborhood bookstore, mainly selling used books that were donated and obtained from flea markets. When the doors first opened, Walker's wife, Lauren, was the only employee during the week and Curtis worked weekends. At the end of the first fiscal year, Walker Books had grossed $20,000 in sales.

As the years passed, Curtis Walker quit the law firm and began concentrating fully on his bookstore. He hired more employees, more books were traded in, and sales increased annually. During the mid-1990s, however, Walker was faced with two problems: many large, upscale bookstores were being built in the area, and the use of the Internet for finding and ordering books was becoming cheaper and more popular for current customers. In 1995, Walker's sales started to decline. Deciding to take a risk because of the new-found competition, he closed his doors to the neighborhood, invested more money to expand the current property, and transformed his company from simply selling used books to being a distributor of new books. His business model was to obtain books from publishers at a discount, store them in his warehouse, and resell them to large bookstore chains.

Walker Books, Inc., has rapidly become one of the largest book distributors in the country. Although it is still at its original location in Palo Alto, California, it distributes books to all 50 states and, because of that, now sees gross sales of about $105,000,000 per year. When Mr. Walker is asked about his fondest memory, he always responds that he will never forget how the little bookstore, with two employees, has expanded to now have more than 145 employees.

Under his current business model, all of Walker's customers are large-chain bookstores who themselves net many millions of dollars in revenue per year. Some of these customers, however, are now experiencing problems with Walker Books that threaten their business relationship: books are ordered but not sent, Walker's poor inventory management causes stock-outs, and Walker is commonly unable to provide legitimate documentation of transactions.

One potential source of these problems rests with Walker's antiquated accounting system, which is a combination of manual procedures supported by standalone PC work stations. These computers are not networked and cannot share data between departments. All interdepartmental communication takes place through hard-copy documents.

You have been hired as an independent expert to express an opinion on the appropriateness of Walker

Books' business processes and internal controls. The revenue cycle is described below:

Revenue Cycle
Sales Order Processing System

The sales order process begins when a customer calls in his or her order to an experienced sales representative, who then manually transcribes the necessary customer information, ISBN, and quantity and type of books requested onto a formal customer order document. Because of recent problems the company has had with uncollectable accounts, Walker Books has set up a computer terminal in the department so the sales representative can check the customer's credit with an online credit bureau. If the credit rating falls below the sales representative's expectations, the transaction is disallowed; if the sales representative concludes, however, that the credit rating is acceptable, he proceeds to manually prepare five hard copies of the sales order.

Once prepared, one copy of the sales order is sent to the warehouse to be used as the stock release. Another copy of the sales order, the shipping notice, is sent to the shipping department. Two of the copies (invoice and ledger copies) are sent to the billing department, and the final copy of the sales order is stapled to the corresponding customer order, which is then filed in the sales department. Once the documents are sent to their designated locations, the sales representative manually updates the hard-copy sales journal to record the transaction. At the end of the day, the sales representative manually prepares a hard-copy journal voucher and sends it to the general ledger department.

When the warehouse clerk receives the stock release copy, he reviews the document for clerical accuracy. He then manually records the appropriate decrease in inventory in the hard-copy inventory subsidiary records that are maintained in the warehouse. Once recorded, he picks the goods and sends them and the stock release document to the shipping department. At the end of day, the warehouse clerk prepares a hard-copy account summary that he sends to the general ledger department.

The shipping clerk receives the shipping notice from the sales department and the stock release and goods from the warehouse. The clerk reconciles the documents with the books being shipped and, if all is correct, creates a digital bill of lading record using the shipping department personal computer. The computer automatically prints out a hard copy packing slip and bill of lading, which accompany the goods to the carrier. The shipping notice is then sent to the billing department and the stock release is filed in the shipping department.

The billing department clerk receives the customer invoice and ledger copy of the sales order from the sales department and the shipping notice from the shipping department. The billing clerk then adds prices and other charges to the invoice, which she sends to the customer. The clerk files the shipping notice in the department and sends the ledger copy to the AR department.

The clerk in the AR department receives ledger copy of the sales order and uses it to manually update the hard-copy AR subsidiary ledger. The clerk then files the ledger copy in the department. At the end of day, the AR clerk prepares an account summary and sends it to the general ledger department.

Upon the receipt of the journal vouchers and the AR summary, the general ledger department clerk reconciles the documents and updates the appropriate control accounts in the digital general ledger via his computer terminal. The documents are then filed in the department.

Cash Receipts System

The cash receipts process begins in the mail room, which is staffed with many employees who have the responsibility of receiving and opening both routine mail (catalogs, advertisements) and mail containing customer payments. Each mail clerk opens the envelope and separates the check and remittance advice. The clerk reconciles the two and then manually adds each receipt to a common remittance list. When all customer payments have been so processed, the finished remittance lists and the associated checks are sent to the cash receipts department. The remittance advices are sent to the AR department.

The cash receipts clerk receives the checks and the remittance list, which he reconciles. At that time he endorses each check "For Deposit Only" and manually records it in the hard-copy cash receipts journal. He then sends the signed checks and remittance list to the AR department. At the end of day the clerk manually prepares a journal voucher summarizing the cash receipts and sends it to the general ledger department.

The AR clerk receives the remittance advices, the checks, and the remittance list. He reconciles them and manually posts the amounts received to the customer accounts in the hard-copy AR subsidiary ledger. The clerk files the remittance advices and the remittance list in the department. He next prepares a deposit slip and sends it, along with the checks, to the bank. Finally, the clerk manually prepares a hard-copy account summary, which he sends to the general ledger department.

The general ledger department receives the account summary and the journal voucher from the AR department and cash receipts, respectively. The clerk reviews the two documents and updates the control accounts in the digital general ledger via the department personal computer. Finally, the clerk files the account summary and journal voucher in the department.

Required:

  a. Create a data flow diagram of the current system.
  b. Create a system flowchart of the existing system.
  c. Analyze the internal control weaknesses in the system. Model your response according to the six categories of physical control activities specified in COSO.
  d. Prepare a system flowchart of a redesigned computer-based system that resolves the control weaknesses you identified.

5. A&V Safety, Inc. (Manual and Stand Alone Computer Processing)

(Prepared by Adam Johnson and Aneesh Varma, Lehigh University)

A&V Safety, Inc., is a growing company specializing in the sales of safety equipment to commercial entities. It currently employs 200 full-time employees, all of whom work out of its headquarters in San Diego, California. During the summer, the company expands to include about ten summer interns who are delegated smaller jobs and other errands. A&V currently competes with Office Safety, Inc., and X-Safe, who lead the industry. Suppliers for A&V include Halotron Extinguishers, Kadelite, and Exit Signs, Inc. A&V attempts to maintain inventory levels sufficient to service two weeks of sales. This level has shown to avoid stock-outs, and the excess inventory is held in a warehouse in a suburb of San Diego.

A&V has a legacy accounting system that employs a combination of manual procedures supported by standalone PCs in the various departments. Recently it has experienced business inefficiencies that have been linked to their antiquated accounting system. You have been retained by A&V management to review its procedures for compliance with the Sarbanes-Oxley Act and to provide recommendations for improvement. The A&V expenditure cycle is presented in the following paragraphs.

Revenue Cycle

A&V Safety, Inc., has one sales department at its headquarters in San Diego. Sales representatives visit current and potential clients in sales districts and all customer orders go through a sales representative. The orders are faxed, mailed, or delivered in person to the sales department by the representative at the end of each day.

In the sales department a sales clerk receives the orders and manually prepares a three-part hard-copy sales order. The clerk sends one sales order copy to the billing department, the stock release copy to the warehouse, and the packing slip copy to the shipping department. The original customer order is filed in the sales department.

Upon receipt of the sales order, the billing clerk records the sale in the digital sales journal using the department PC. The clerk then prints a hard-copy invoice, which is sent to the customer. Next, the clerk sends the sales order to the AR department for further processing. At the end of the day, the clerk prints a hard-copy sales journal voucher from the PC and sends it to the general ledger.

The warehousing clerk uses the stock release copy to pick the goods from the shelves and then updates the digital inventory subsidiary ledger using the warehouse PC. Next, the clerk sends the good and the stock release to the shipping department. At the end of the business day, the clerk prints an inventory summary from the PC and sends it to the general ledger department.

The shipping clerk reconciles the packing slip sent from the sales department with the stock release and goods received from the warehouse. If all is correct, the clerk manually prepares a hard copy bill of lading. He then attaches the packing slip and bill of lading to the goods, which go to the carrier for delivery to the customer. Finally, the clerk files the stock release in the department.

The accounts payable clerk receives the sales order from the billing department and uses it to update the digital AR subledger from the department PC. The sales order is then filed in the department. At the end of the day the clerk prints an AR summary from the PC and sends it to the general ledger department.

Customer payments come into the mail room where mail clerks open the envelopes and send the checks and remittance advices to the accounts payable department. The AR clerk reconciles the remittance advice with the check and updates the customer's account in the digital AR subsidiary ledger. The clerk then files the remittance advices in the department and sends the checks to the cash receipts department. As previously mentioned, at the end of the day, the AR clerk prints a hard-copy AR summary from the department personal computer and sends it to the general ledger department.

The cash receipt clerk receives the checks and records the payments in the digital cash receipts journal. The clerk then manually prepares a hard-copy deposit slip and sends the checks and deposit slip to the bank. At the end of the day, the clerk prints a cash receipt journal voucher from the department PC and sends it to the general ledger department.

The general ledger clerk receives the sales journal voucher, cash receipts journal voucher, the AR summary, and the inventory summary. The clerk reconciles these documents and posts to the appropriate control accounts in the digital general ledger from the department PC. Finally, the general ledger clerk files the summaries and journal vouchers in the department.

Required:

   a. Create a data flow diagram of the current system.

   b. Create a system flowchart of the existing system.

   c. Identify the internal control weaknesses in the system. Model your response according to the six categories of physical control activities specified in COSO.

   d. Prepare a system flowchart of a redesigned computer-based system that resolves the control weaknesses you identified.

6. Premier Sports Memorabilia (Networks Computer System with Manual Procedures)

(Prepared by Chris Polchinski, Lehigh University)

Premier Sports Memorabilia is a medium-sized, rapidly growing online and catalogue-based retailer centered in Brooklyn, New York. The company was founded in 1990 and specializes in providing its customers with authentic yet affordable sports memorabilia from their favorite players and teams, past and present. Traditionally, the company's customers were located in the northeast region of the United States. Recently, however, Premier launched a successful an ad campaign to expand its customer base. This has increased sales, which has in turn placed a strain on the organization's operational resources. The company currently employs 205 employees, who are spread out among its three warehouses and two offices in the tri-state area.

The firm purchases from large number of manufacturers and memorabilia dealers around the country and is always looking for additional contacts that have new or rare items to offer.

The company has a computer network installed, which, until recently, has served it well. The firm is now, however, experiencing operational inefficiencies and accounting errors. Your firm has been hired to evaluate Premier's business processes and internal controls. The revenue cycle is described in the following paragraphs.

Revenue Cycle Procedures

Premier's revenue process is initiated when a customer places an order either online, by mail, or through a telephone representative. The order is then manually entered into the computer system for mail or telephone orders, while online orders are automatically entered upon arrival. When the customer order is entered, the system automatically performs an online credit check. If credit is approved, the sales process continues. If credit is denied, the process ends and the customer is notified of the automatic rejection.

For approved order, the clerk manually prepares four hard copies of each sales order. One copy is entered into the terminal in the sales department and filed. The approved sale is automatically posted to the digital sales journal. A second copy is sent to the billing department, where it is further processed. A third copy is sent to the warehouse. A final copy is sent to the customer as a receipt stating that the order has been received and processed.

At the warehouse, the sales order is used as a stock release, authorizing a warehouse clerk to physically pick the requested items from the shelves. The clerk then manually prepares a bill of lading and packing slip, which accompany the goods to the carrier. The warehouse clerk then accesses the computer terminal and creates a digital shipping notice for the billing department. Finally, the clerk files the stock release hard copy in the warehouse.

From a terminal, the billing department clerk reconciles the hard-copy sales order and the digital shipping notice and prints two hard copies of an invoice. One copy is sent to the customer as a bill and the other is sent to the AR department. The clerk then files the sales order copy in the department.

Upon receipt of the hard-copy invoice, the AR clerk creates a digital record in the AR subsidiary ledger from his terminal. The clerk then files the invoice copy in the department.

Customer payments and remittance advices come into the mailroom. The clerk separates the documents and sends the remittance advice to AR and the checks to the cash receipts department.

Upon receipt of the remittance advice, the AR clerk accesses the customer's account in the AR subsidiary ledger from a terminal and adjusts the balance accordingly. The clerk files the remittance advices in the department.

The cash receipts clerk receives the checks and posts them to the cash receipts journal from her terminal. The clerk then manually prepares a hard-copy deposit slip and sends it with the cash to the bank.

Finally, at the end of each day, the system prepares batch totals of all sales and cash receipts transactions and posts them automatically to the control accounts in the digital general ledger.

Required:

   a. Create a data flow diagram of the current system.

   b. Create a system flowchart of the existing system.

   c. Analyze the internal control weaknesses in the system. Model your response according to the six categories of physical control activities specified in COSO.

    d. Prepare a system flowchart of a redesigned computer-based system that resolves the control weaknesses you identified.

7. Bait 'n Reel Superstore (Combination of Networked Computers and Manual System)

(Prepared by Matt Wisser, Lehigh University)

Bait 'n Reel was established in 1983 by Jamie Roberts, an avid fisherman and environmentalist. Growing up in Pennsylvania's Pocono Mountains region, Roberts was lucky enough to have a large lake right down the road, where he found himself fishing throughout the year. Unfortunately, he had to drive more than 15 miles to purchase his fishing supplies, such as lines, hooks, and bait. Throughout his early adulthood, Roberts frequently overheard other fishermen expressing their displeasure at not having a local fishing store to serve their needs. Roberts vowed to himself that he would open his own store if he could ever save up enough money.

By 1983, he had sufficient funds and the opportunity arose when a local grocery store went up for sale. He bought the building and converted it into the "Bait 'n Reel" fishing store. His early business involved cash-only transactions with local fishermen. By the mid-1990s, however, the building had expanded into a superstore that sold a wide range of sporting products and camping gear. People from all over the county shopped at Bait 'n Reel as Roberts increased his advertising efforts, emphasizing his ability to provide excellent service and a wide range of products. Roberts moved away from a cash-only business and began offering store credit cards to consumers. He also became a regional wholesaler to many smaller sporting goods stores.

With the help of a friend, Roberts installed a computer network. Although these computers helped automate the company's business processes and facilitated the sharing of data between departments, much interdepartmental communication continued to be via hard-copy documents.

Revenue increased sharply during the four years after the implementation of the computer system. In spite of this, Roberts had some questions about the quality of processes, as many of the subsidiary accounts did not match the general ledger control accounts. This didn't prove to be a material problem, however, until recently, when the computers began listing supplies on hand that were not actually on the shelves. This created problems as customers became frustrated by stock-outs. Roberts knew something was wrong, but he couldn't put his finger on it.

You have been hired by Roberts to evaluate Bait 'n Reel's processes and internal controls and make recommendations for improvement. Bait 'n Reel's revenue cycle relating to the credit based wholesale portion of the business is described in the following paragraphs.

Revenue Cycle
Sales Order Processing Procedures

Wholesale customer orders are mailed or faxed to the sales department. When the order is received, the sales clerk checks the customer's creditworthiness from a computer terminal. After the customer's credit is verified, the clerk keys in the sales orders into his computer terminal. A digital copy of the order is distributed to the warehouse and the shipping department terminals for further processing. The computer system automatically records the sale in the sales journal. Finally, the clerk files the hard copy of the customer order in the sales department.

Prompted by receipt of the digital sales order, the warehouse manager prints out two copies of it: the stock release and a shipping notice. Using the stock release copy, the warehouse clerk picks the selected goods from the shelves. The goods, accompanied by both documents, are sent to the shipping department. The manager then updates the inventory subsidiary ledger and the general ledger his computer terminal.

Once the shipping clerk receives the goods, the stock release, and the shipping notice, he matches them to the corresponding digital sales order from his terminal. Assuming everything matches, he prints out three hard copies of the bill of lading and a packing slip. Two of the bill of lading copies and the packing slip are sent, along with the goods, to the carrier. The stock release copy and the shipping notice are sent to the AR department. The third bill of lading copy is filed in the shipping department.

When the AR clerk receives the stock release and shipping notice, he manually creates a hard-copy invoice, which is immediately mailed to the customer. After mailing the invoice, the clerk goes to his terminal and updates the AR subsidiary ledger and general ledger from the information on the stock release. After the records are updated, the clerk files the stock release and shipping notice in the AR department.

Cash Receipts Procedures

Customer payments come directly to the general mailroom along with other mail items. The mail clerk sorts through the mail, opens the customer payment envelope, removes the customer's check and remittance advice, and reconciles the two documents. To control the checks and remittance advices, the clerk manually prepares two hard copies of a remittance list. He sends one copy to the AR department along with the corresponding remittance advices. The other copy of the remittance list accompanies the checks to the cash receipts department.

Once the checks and remittance list arrive in the cash receipts department, the treasurer reconciles the documents, signs the check, and manually prepares three hard copies of the deposit slip. He then updates the cash receipts journal and the general ledger on his computer terminal. Next, the treasurer sends checks and two copies of the deposit slip to the bank. Finally, he files the third copy of the deposit slip and the remittance in the department.

When the AR clerk receives the remittance list and remittance advices from the mail room, he reconciles the two documents. Then, from his terminal, he updates the AR subsidiary ledger and the general ledger. Finally, the two documents are filed in the department.

Required:

a. Create a data flow diagram of the current system.
b. Create a system flowchart of the existing system.
c. Analyze the internal control weaknesses in the system. Model your response according to the six categories of physical control activities specified in COSO.
d. Prepare a system flowchart of a redesigned computer-based system that resolves the control weaknesses you identified.

8. Green Mountain Coffee Roasters, Inc. (Manual Procedures and Stand-alone PCs)

(Prepared by Ronica Sharma, Lehigh University)

Green Mountain Coffee Roasters, Inc., was founded in 1981 as a small café in Waitsfield, Vermont, roasting and serving premium coffee on the premises. Green Mountain blends and distributes coffee to a variety of customers, including cafés, delis, and restaurants, and currently has about 6,700 customer accounts reaching states across the nation. As the company has grown, several beverages have been added to its product line, including signature blends, light and heavy roasts, decaffeinated coffee and teas, and herbal teas. Green Mountain Coffee Roasters, Inc., has been publicly traded since 1993.

Green Mountain Coffee has a warehouse and manufacturing plant located in Wilton, Vermont, where it presently employees 250 full-time and part-time workers. The company receives its beans in bulk from a select group of distributors located across the world, with their largest supplier being Columbia Beans Co. Green Mountain Coffee also sells accessories that complement its products, including mugs, thermoses, and coffee containers that it purchases from its supplier, Coffee Lovers, Inc. In addition, Green Mountain purchases paper products such as coffee bags, coffee cups, and stirrers, which it distributes to their customers.

Green Mountain's accounting system consists of manual procedures supported by standalone PCs located in various departments. Because these computers are not networked, they cannot share data digitally, and all interdepartmental communication is through hard-copy documents.

Green Mountain is a new audit client for your CPA firm. As manager on the assignment, you are examining its internal controls. The revenue cycle is described in the following paragraphs.

Sales Order System

The sales process begins when a customer sends a customer order to the sales clerk, who does a credit check by manually reviewing the hard-copy customer sales history records. From the approved customer order, the sales clerk then manually prepares several hard copies of a sales order, including a customer copy, a stock release, two file copies, a packing slip, an invoice, and a ledger copy. The invoice, ledger copy, and a file copy are sent to the billing department. The second file copy and the stock release are sent to Sara in the warehouse. The packing slip is sent to the shipping department. The clerk files the approved customer order in the department.

The billing department clerk reviews the source documents that she received from sales and adds prices to the invoice. Using the department PC, the clerk then enters the billing information into the computer to record the sale in the sales journal. The invoice is mailed to the customer, the ledger copy is sent to the AR clerk in the accounting department, and the file copy is filed in the billing department. At the end of day, a journal voucher is printed from the PC and sent to Vic, the general ledger clerk.

Sara in the warehouse uses the stock release and file copies to pick the goods from the shelf. She files the file copy in the warehouse. Guided by the information on the stock release copy, she then updates the digital inventory subsidiary ledger from the warehouse personal computer. Next, she sends the stock release copy, along with the goods, to the shipping department. At the end of the day, Sara prepares a journal voucher from the PC and sends it to the general ledger clerk.

The shipping clerk reconciles the stock release copy with the packing slip from sales. He then manually prepares a hard-copy bill of lading and records the shipment into the hard-copy shipping log. The bill of lading, packing slip, and goods are sent to the carrier and the stock release copy is filed in the shipping department.

In the accounting department, relevant information taken from the ledger copy (sent from billing) is entered into the computer to update the AR records. A summary (end of day) is sent to Vic. The ledger copy is then filed in the accounting department. Vic reconciles the AR summary with the journal vouchers and then updates the digital general ledger prom the department PC. All documents are then filed.

Cash Receipts System

The mailroom clerk receives the checks and remittance advices from the customer. He reconciles the checks with the remittance advices and prepares two copies of a remittance list. The checks and a remittance list are then sent to John, in the AR department. John uses a PC to process the cash receipts, update the cash receipts journal, and prepare a journal voucher and three deposit slips. The journal voucher is sent to Vic, the general ledger clerk. The checks and two deposit slips are sent to the bank to be deposited into Green Mountain Coffee's account. The third deposit slip and the remittance list are filed. The second remittance list and the remittance advices are sent to Mary, another AR clerk, who, using the same PC, updates the AR subsidiary ledger and prepares an account summary, which is sent to

Vic. The remittance list and the remittance advice are then filed. Vic uses the journal voucher and the account summary to update the general ledger. These two documents are then filed.

Required:

a. Create a data flow diagram of the current system.
b. Create a system flowchart of the existing system.
c. Analyze the internal control weaknesses in the system. Model your response according to the six categories of physical control activities specified in COSO.
d. Prepare a system flowchart of a redesigned computer-based system that resolves the control weaknesses you identified.

ACL Assignments

The **AR** and **Customer** files used for the following assignments are located in the *sampleproject.acl* that accompanies ACL. The AR file is actually an invoice file that contains several related records as designated by the Trans Type field:

IN = Sales invoice
PM = Payment from customer
CN = Credit note (credit memo)
TR = Transfer (write-off)

Sales invoices should be represented by positive Trans Amount values, while the other transaction types are negative.

Some of the following assignments employ the ACL's *Relation* and *Join* features. For detailed information on the use of these and other commands, consult ACL's online Help feature.

1. Open the **AR** file, *Profile* the data, and *Stratify* on the Trans Amount field. Print the Last Results window and write an analysis providing possible explanations for the results obtained.

2. Open the **AR** file, stratify the file on the Trans Amount field, and use the expression builder to create filters that limit the strata to

   (a) sales invoice transactions only.
   (b) credit note (memo) transactions only.
   (c) payment transactions only.
   (d) transfer (write-off) transactions.

3. Open the **AR** file and use the expression builder to create a filter that screens for invalid transaction types. Print the results and comment.

4. Using the *Relation* feature, create a view from data in both the **AR** and **Customer** files that shows customer details (**name** and **street address**) for payment transactions with abnormal (positive) amount values. Print the view and comment on the results.

5. Using the *Join* feature create a view from data in both the **AR** and **Customer** files that show customer details (**name** and **address**) for payment transactions with abnormal (positive) amount values. Print the view and comment on the results.

6. The following Assignments are located in the **ACL Tutorial** folder in the Student Resources section of this textbook's Web site.

7. Tutorial 1 relates to the following commands: TOTAL, PROFILE, STATISTICS, SAMPLE, SEQUENCE, SORT, DUPLICATES, GAPS.

8. Tutorial 4 relates to the following commands: AGE, JOIN, MERGE.

9. Tutorial 5 relates to the following commands: TOTAL, COUNT, EXTRACT, EXPORT, SORT, INDEX.

10. Bradmark Comprehensive Case

Required:

Access the Bradmark ACL Case in the Student Resource section of textbook's Web site. Your instructor will tell you which questions to answer.

CHAPTER 10

Auditing the Expenditure Cycle

LEARNING OBJECTIVES

After studying this chapter, you should:

- Understand the primary tasks associated with the expenditure cycle under different levels of technology.
- Understand audit objectives related to the expenditure cycle.
- Be familiar with expenditure cycle control issues related to alternative technologies.
- Recognize the relationship between expenditure cycle audit objectives, controls, and tests of controls.
- Understand the nature of substantive tests in achieving expenditure cycle audit objectives.
- Be familiar with common features and functions of ACL that are used to perform substantive tests.

This chapter examines audit procedures associated with the expenditure cycle. This chapter is divided into three main sections. It begins with a review of computer technologies used in both legacy and modern systems. The focus is on the way that key operational tasks are performed under different technological environments. The second section discusses the expenditure cycle audit objectives, controls, and tests of controls that an auditor would normally perform to gather the evidence needed to limit the scope, timing, and extent of substantive tests. The last section describes substantive tests in relation to expenditure cycle audit objectives that can be performed using ACL software.

EXPENDITURE CYCLE ACTIVITIES AND TECHNOLOGIES

This chapter assumes that the reader is familiar with the general procedures that constitute the expenditure cycle and with the key accounting records and documents employed in expenditure cycle transaction processing. Those who need to review this body of material should turn to the appendix at this point, where it is presented in detail.

This section examines alternative information technologies used to support expenditure cycle activities. The first of these is a purchases and cash disbursements system that employs batch processing and uses sequential files for storing accounting data. This type of system is an example of an early legacy system. This approach characterizes the era of data ownership in which files were designed exclusively for the use of a single user. Data sharing is virtually impossible in this setting and results in a great deal of data redundancy and data obsolescence. Second, we review the operational features of a modern system that employs real-time processing and uses direct access files or databases. The final example depicts a modern payroll system that uses real-time processing and database technology.

You should recognize that space limitations prohibit a review of all possible configurations of processing technologies, techniques, and file structures. The objective, instead, is to present examples of fundamentally different approaches that are typically found in practice and examine their control and audit implications.

Purchases and Cash Disbursement Procedures Using Batch Processing Technology

Many of the manual functions in the batch system presented in Figure 10.1 are the same as those found in manual purchase systems. The principal difference is that the routine accounting tasks are automated. The following section describes the sequence of events as they occur in this system.

Data Processing Department: Step 1

The purchasing process begins in the data processing department, where the inventory control function is performed. The revenue cycle (in retailing firms) or the conversion cycle (in manufacturing firms) actually initiates this activity. When inventories are reduced by sales to customers or usage in production, the system determines if the affected items in the **inventory subsidiary file** have fallen to their reorder points.[1] If so, a record is created in the open requisition file. Each record in the open requisition file defines a separate inventory item to be replenished. The record contains the inventory item number, a description of the item, the quantity to be ordered, the standard unit price, and the vendor number of the primary supplier. The information needed to create the requisition record is selected from the inventory subsidiary record. The inventory subsidiary record is then flagged "On Order" to prevent the item from being ordered again before it arrives.

At the end of the day, the system sorts the open requisition file by vendor number and consolidates multiple items from the same vendor in to a single requisition. Next, vendor mailing information is retrieved from the valid vendor file to produce purchase requisition documents. Copies of these documents go to manual procedures in the purchasing and accounts payable (AP) departments.

Purchasing Department. Upon receipt of the purchase requisition, the purchasing department prepares a five-part purchase order. Copies go to the vendors, accounts payable, receiving, data processing, and the purchasing department's own file.

The system in Figure 10.1 employs manual procedures to control the ordering process. A computer program identifies inventory requirements and prepares traditional purchase requisitions, thus allowing the purchasing agent to verify the purchase transaction before placing the order. Some firms use this technique to reduce the risk of placing unnecessary

---

1   This may be batch or real time, depending on the revenue and conversion cycle systems that interface with the expenditure cycle. The raw materials and finished goods inventory files link these three transaction cycles together. The design of one system influences the others. For example, if sales processing (revenue cycle) reduces inventories in real time, the system will naturally identify inventory requirements in real time also. This is true even if the purchases system is batch oriented.

FIGURE 10.1 Batch Purchases System

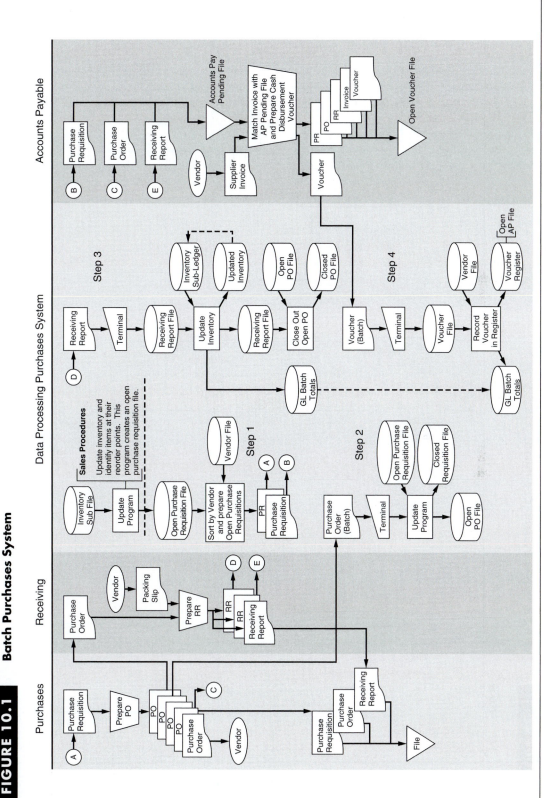

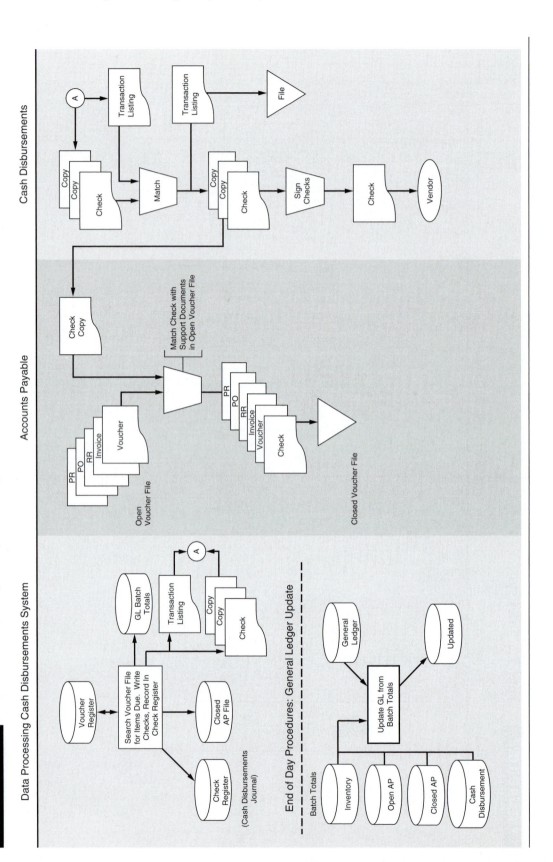

FIGURE 10.1   **Batch Purchases System (Continued)**

orders with vendors due to a computer error. However, such manual intervention creates delays in the ordering process. If sufficient computer controls are in place to prevent or detect purchasing errors, then more efficient ordering procedures can be implemented.

Before continuing with our example, we need to discuss alternative approaches for authorizing and ordering inventories. Figure 10.2 illustrates three different methods. In *alternative one*, the system advances the procedures shown in Figure 10.1 one-step further. This system prepares the purchase order documents and sends them to the purchasing department for review and signing. The purchasing agent then mails the approved purchase orders to the vendors and distributes copies to other internal users.

The system shown in *alternative two* expedites the ordering process by distributing the purchase orders directly to the vendors and internal users, thus bypassing the purchasing department completely. This system produces a transaction list of items ordered for the purchasing agent's review.

Alternative three represents a reengineering system that uses *electronic data interchange (EDI)*. This method produces no physical documents (purchase orders or sales orders). Instead, the computer systems of both the buying and selling companies are connected via a special telecommunications link. The buyer and seller are parties in a trading partner arrangement in which the entire ordering process is automated and unimpeded by human intervention.

In each of the three alternatives, the authorization and the ordering steps in the process are consolidated and performed by the computer system. Purchase requisition documents serve no purpose in such systems and are not produced. However, requisition records may still exist on magnetic disk or tape to provide an audit trail.

Data Processing Department: Step 2
Returning to Figure 10.1, the purchase order is used to create an open purchase order record and to transfer the corresponding record(s) in the open purchase requisition file to the closed purchase requisition file.

Receiving Department
When the goods arrive from vendors, the receiving clerk prepares a receiving report. Copies go to purchasing, accounts payable, and data processing.

Data Processing Department: Step 3
The data processing department runs a batch job (Step 3) that updates the inventory subsidiary file from the receiving reports and removes the "On Order" flag from the inventory records. The system calculates batch totals of inventory receipts for the general ledger update procedure and then closes the corresponding records in the open purchase order file to the closed purchase order file.

Accounts Payable. When the accounts payable clerk receives the supplier's invoice, he or she reconciles it with the supporting documents that were previously placed in the accounts payable pending file. The clerk then prepares a voucher, files it in the open voucher file, and sends a copy of the voucher to data processing.

Data Processing Department: Step 4
A batch program validates the voucher records against the valid vendor file, adds them to the voucher register (or open AP subsidiary file), and prepares batch totals for posting to the AP control account in the general ledger.

FIGURE 10.2   Alternative Inventory Ordering Procedures

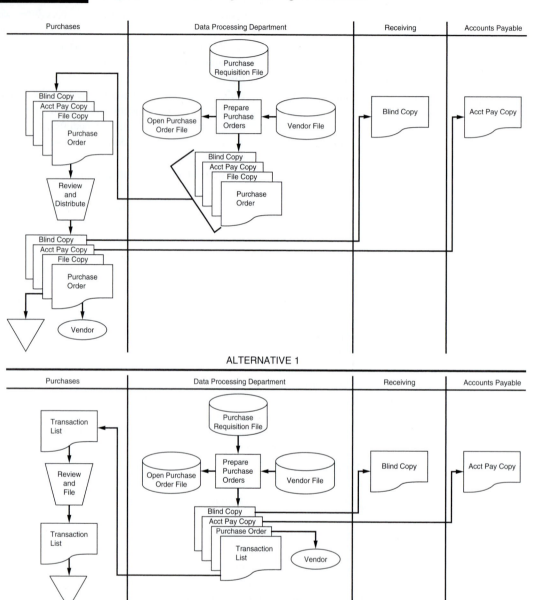

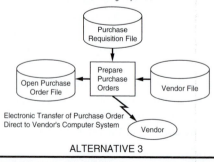

Cash Disbursement: Data Processing Department.   Each day, the system scans the Due Date field of the voucher register for items due. Checks are printed for these items, and each check is recorded in the check register (cash disbursements journal). The check number is recorded in the voucher register to close the voucher and transfer the items to the closed AP file. The checks, along with a transaction listing, are sent to the cash disbursements department. Finally, batch totals of closed accounts payable and cash disbursements are prepared for the general ledger update procedure.

At the end of the day, batch totals of open (unpaid) and closed (paid) accounts payable, inventory increases, and cash disbursements are posted to the accounts payable control, inventory control, and cash accounts in the general ledger. The totals of closed accounts payable and cash disbursements should balance.

Cash Disbursement: Cash Disbursements Department

The cash disbursements clerk reconciles the checks with the transaction listing and submits the negotiable portion of the checks to management for signing. The checks are then mailed to the suppliers. One copy of each check goes to accounts payable, and the other copy is filed in cash disbursements along with the transaction listing.

Cash Disbursement: Accounts Payable.   Upon receipt of the check copies, the accounts payable clerk matches them with open vouchers and transfers these closed items to the closed voucher file. The expenditure cycle process concludes with this step.

Reengineering the Purchases/Cash Disbursement System

The automated system just described simply replicates many of the procedures in a manual system. In particular, the accounts payable task of reconciling supporting documents with supplier invoices is labor intensive and costly. The following example shows how reengineering this process can produce considerable savings.

The Ford Motor Company employed more than 500 clerks in its North American accounts payable department. Analysis of the function showed that a large part of Ford's accounts payable clerks' time was devoted to reconciling discrepancies between supplier invoices, receiving reports, and purchase orders. The first step in solving the problem was to bring about fundamental changes in the business environment. Ford initiated trading partner agreements with suppliers in which they agreed in advance to terms of trade such as price, quantities to be shipped, discounts, and lead times. With these sources of discrepancy eliminated, Ford reengineered the workflow to take advantage of the new environment. The flowchart in Figure 10.3 depicts key features of a reengineered system.

Data Processing

The following tasks are performed automatically:

1. The inventory file is searched for items that have fallen to their reorder point.
2. A record is entered in the purchase requisition file for each item to be replenished.
3. Requisitions are then consolidated according to vendor number.
4. Vendor mailing information is retrieved from the valid vendor file.
5. Purchase orders are prepared and sent to the vendor. Alternatively, these may be transmitted using EDI technology.
6. A record of each transaction is added to the open purchase order file.
7. A transaction listing of purchase orders is sent to the purchasing department for review.

| FIGURE 10.3 | **Reengineered Purchases/Cash Disbursement System** |

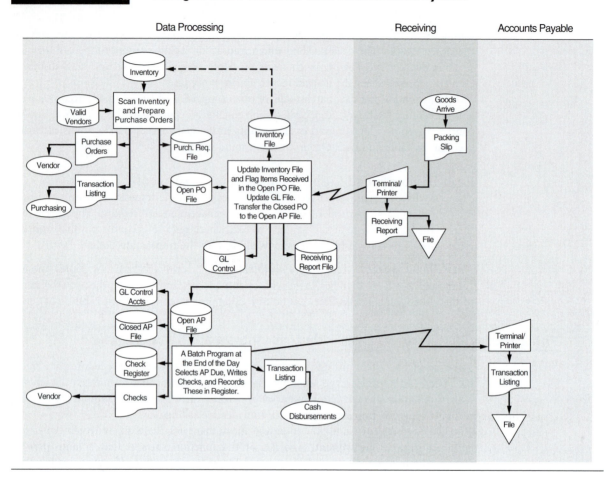

Receiving Department

When the goods arrive, the receiving clerk accesses the open purchase order file in real time by entering the purchase order number taken from the packing slip. The receiving screen, illustrated in Figure 10.4, then prompts the clerk to enter the quantities received for each item on the purchase order.

Data Processing

The following tasks are performed automatically by the system:

1. Quantities of items received are matched against the open purchase order record, and a "Y" value is placed in a logical field to indicate the receipt of inventories.
2. A record is added to the receiving report file.
3. The inventory subsidiary records are updated to reflect the receipt of the inventory items.
4. The general ledger inventory control account is updated.
5. The record is removed from the open purchase order file and added to the open AP file, and a due date for payment is established.

FIGURE 10.4

Receiving Screen

DATE: 12/15/04 PURCH. ORDER # 567 CLERK ID MD

ITEM #	QTY RECVD	QTY ORDER	Discrepancy
		Displays after Qty Recvd has been entered	
45-709	50	55	5

MANUAL ENTRY =

Each day, the Due Date fields of the accounts payable records are checked for items due to be paid. The following procedures are performed for the selected items:

1. Checks are printed, signed, and distributed to the mailroom for mailing to vendors. EDI vendors receive payment electronically.
2. The payments are recorded in the check register file.
3. Items paid are transferred from the open accounts payable file to the closed AP file.
4. The general ledger accounts payable and cash accounts are updated.
5. Reports detailing these transactions are transmitted via terminal to the accounts payable and cash disbursements departments for management review and filing.

Since the financial information about purchases is known in advance from the trading partner agreement, the **vendor's invoice** provides no critical information that cannot be derived from the receiving report. By eliminating this source of potential discrepancy, Ford was able to eliminate the task of reconciling vendor invoices with the supporting documents for the majority of purchase transactions. As a result of its reengineering effort, the company was able to reduce its accounts payable staff from 500 to 125.

Control Implications

The technology control issues (i.e., those pertaining to the use of sequential files versus direct access files) are general in nature. The points made in the last chapter apply to the expenditure cycle also. Therefore, let's examine only the issues specific to this cycle by focusing on the differences between an automated versus a reengineered system.

The Automated System

Improved Inventory Control. The greatest advantage of the automated (batch) system over its manual counterpart is its improved ability to manage inventory needs. Inventory requirements are detected as they arise and are processed automatically. As a result, the risks of accumulating excessive inventory or of running out of stock are reduced. However, with this advantage comes a control concern. Authorization rules governing purchase transactions are consolidated within a computer program. Program errors or flawed inventory models can cause firms to be suddenly inundated with inventories or desperately short of stock. Therefore, it is extremely important to monitor automated decisions. A well-controlled system will provide management with adequate summary reports on inventory purchases, inventory turnover, spoilage, and slow-moving items.

Better Cash Management.   This type of system promotes effective cash management by scanning the voucher file daily for items due, thus avoiding early payments and missed due dates. In addition, by writing checks automatically, the firm reduces labor cost, saves processing time, and promotes accuracy.

As a control against unauthorized payments, comparing the vendor number on the voucher with a valid vendor file validates all entries in the voucher file. If the vendor number is not on file, the record is presumed to be invalid and is diverted to an error file for management review.

In this system, a manager in the cash disbursements department physically signs the checks, thus providing control over the disbursement of cash. However, many computer systems automate check signing with special printing equipment, which is more efficient when check volume is high, but relinquishes some control. To offset this exposure, firms often set a materiality threshold for check writing. Checks for amounts below the threshold are signed automatically, and an authorized manager or the treasurer signs those above the threshold.

Less Time Lag.   A lag exists between the arrival of goods in the receiving department and recording inventory receipts in the inventory file. Depending on the type of sales order system in place, this lag may affect sales negatively. Because of this time lag, sales clerks will not know the current status of inventory, and sales may be lost.

Better Purchasing Time Management.   In this hypothetical batch system, the purchasing department is directly involved with all purchase decisions. For many firms, this creates additional work that extends the time lag in the ordering process. A vast number of routine purchases could be automated. By freeing purchasing agents from routine work, such as preparing purchase orders and mailing them to the vendors, attention can be focused on problem orders (such as special items or those in short supply), and the purchasing staff can be reduced.

Reduction of Paper Documents.   The basic batch system is laden with paper documents. All operations departments create documents, which are sent to data processing and which data processing must then convert to magnetic media. A number of costs are associated with paper documents, since the paper must be purchased and the documents filed, stored, handled by internal mail carriers, and converted by data processing personnel. Organizations with high volumes of transactions benefit considerably from reducing or eliminating paper documents in their systems.

The Reengineered System

This system addresses many of the operational weaknesses found in the basic batch system. Specifically, the improvements in this system are that (1) it uses real-time procedures and direct-access files to shorten the lag time in recordkeeping; (2) it eliminates routine manual procedures through automation; and (3) it achieves a significant reduction in paper documents by using electronic communications between departments and by storing records on direct-access media. These operational improvements, however, carry control implications.

Segregation of Duties.   This system removes the fundamental separation between authorization and transaction processing. Here, computer programs authorize and process purchase orders and authorize and issue checks to vendors. To compensate for this exposure, the system needs to provide management with detailed transaction listings and summary reports. These documents describe the automated actions taken by the system and allow management to spot errors and any unusual events that warrant investigation.

Accounting Records and Access Controls. This system maintains accounting records exclusively on magnetic disks. To preserve the integrity of these records, the organization must implement controls that limit access to the disks. Unauthorized access to magnetic records carries the same consequences as access to source documents, journals, and ledgers in a manual environment. Organizations can employ a number of physical and software techniques to provide adequate access control. However, keep in mind that some techniques are costly, and management must justify these costs against their expected benefits.

Overview of Payroll Procedures

Payroll processing is actually a special expenditure system. In theory, payroll checks could be processed through the regular accounts payable and cash disbursements system. However, as a practical matter, this approach would have a number of drawbacks:

- *General expenditure procedures that apply to all vendors will not apply to employees.* Payroll procedures differ greatly among classes of employees. For example, different procedures are used for hourly employees, salaried employees, piece workers, and commissioned employees. Also, payroll processing requires special accounting procedures for employee deductions and withholdings for taxes. Cash disbursements for trade accounts do not require special processing. Therefore, general expenditure systems are not designed to deal with these complications.
- *Writing checks to employees requires special controls.* It is easier to conceal payroll fraud when payroll checks are combined with trade account checks.
- *General expenditure procedures are designed to accommodate a relatively smooth flow of transactions.* Business enterprises are constantly purchasing inventories and disbursing funds to vendors. Naturally, they design systems to deal adequately with their normal level of transaction activity. Payroll activities are discrete rather than continuous. Disbursements to employees occur weekly, biweekly, or monthly. To periodically impose this processing burden on the general system may have an overwhelming peak-load effect.

Because payroll systems run infrequently (weekly or monthly), they are often well suited to batch processing and sequential files. Figure 10.5 shows a flowchart for such a system. The data processing department receives the personnel action forms and time cards, which it converts to sequential files. Batch computer programs perform the detailed record-keeping, check-writing, and general ledger functions.

Control Implications

The strengths and weaknesses of this system are similar to those in the batch system for general expenditures discussed earlier. This system promotes accounting accuracy and reduces check-writing errors. Beyond this, it does not significantly enhance operational efficiency; however, for many types of organizations, this level of technology is adequate.

Reengineering the Payroll System

For moderate-sized and large organizations, payroll processing is often integrated within the **human resource management (HRM) system.** The HRM system captures and processes a wide range of personnel-related data, including employee benefits, labor resource planning, employee relations, employee skills, personnel actions (pay rates, deductions, and so on), as well as payroll. HRM systems must support real-time access to personnel files for purposes of direct inquires and recording changes in employee status as they occur. Figure 10.6 illustrates a payroll system as part of an HRM system.

FIGURE 10.5   Batch Payroll System with Sequential Files

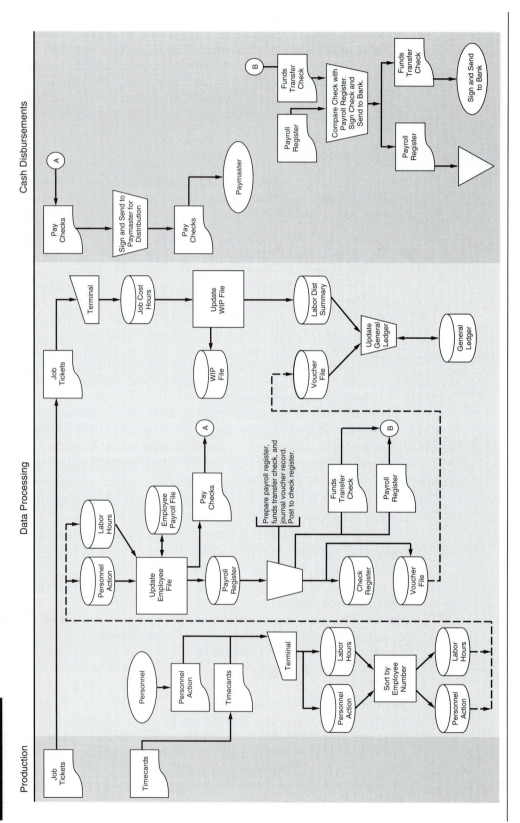

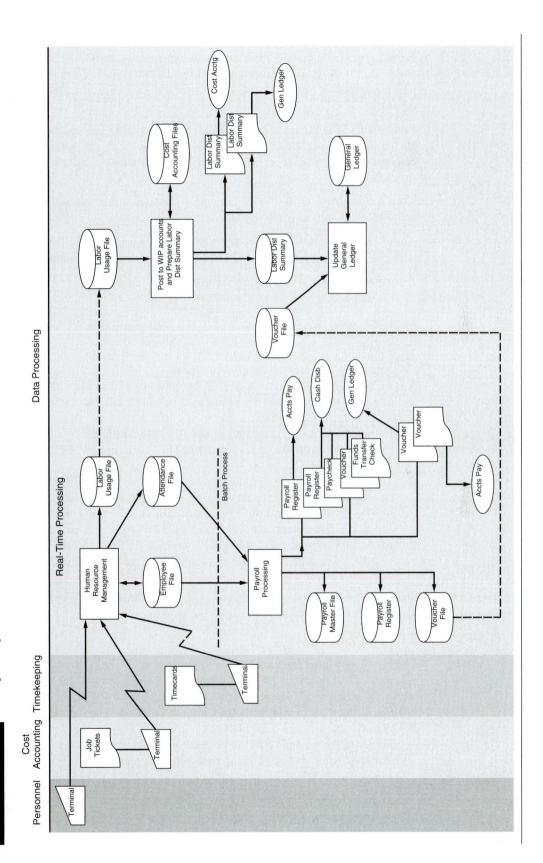

FIGURE 10.6   Payroll System with Real-Time Elements

This system differs from the simple automated system described previously in the following ways: (1) operations departments transmit transactions to data processing via terminals, (2) direct access files are used for data storage, and (3) many processes are now performed in real time. We discuss the key operating features of this system as follows:

Personnel.   The personnel department makes changes to the employee file in real time via terminals. These changes include additions of new employees, deletions of terminated employees, changes in dependents, changes in withholding, and changes in job status (pay rate).

Cost Accounting.   The cost accounting department enters job cost data (real time or daily) to create the **labor usage file.**

Timekeeping.   Upon receipt of the approved timecards from the supervisor at the end of the week, the timekeeping department creates the current **attendance file.**

Data Processing.   At the end of the work period, the following tasks are performed in a batch process:

1. Labor costs are distributed to various work-in-process, overhead, and expense accounts.
2. An online labor distribution summary file is created. Copies of the file go to the cost accounting and general ledger departments.
3. An online payroll register is created from the attendance file and the **employee file.** Copies of the files go to the accounts payable and cash disbursements departments.
4. The employee records file is updated.
5. Payroll checks are prepared and signed. They are sent to the treasurer for review and reconciliation with the payroll register. The paychecks are then distributed to the employees.[2]
6. The disbursement voucher file is updated and a check is prepared for the funds transfer to the payroll imprest account.[3] The check and a hard copy of the disbursement voucher go to cash disbursements. One copy of the voucher goes to the general ledger department, and the final copy goes to accounts payable.
7. At the end of processing, the system retrieves the labor distribution summary file and the disbursements voucher file and updates the general ledger file.

EXPENDITURE CYCLE AUDIT OBJECTIVES, CONTROLS, AND TESTS OF CONTROLS

Chapter 1 introduced the concept of audit objectives derived from general management assertions about financial statement presentation. The assertions are existence or occurrence, completeness, accuracy, rights and obligations, valuation or allocation, and presentation and disclosure. Table 10.1 shows how these translate to specific expenditure cycle audit objectives.

Achieving these audit objectives requires designing audit procedures to gather evidence that either corroborates or refutes management assertions. As we saw in the

2   For added internal control, many companies encourage their employees to have their checks directly deposited in their bank accounts.

3   An imprest account is established at a specified, predetermined amount of the total payroll. When all paychecks clear, the account balance is 0.

TABLE 10.1	Relationship Between Management Assertions and Expenditure Cycle Audit Objectives

Management Assertions	Expenditure Cycle Audit Objectives
Existence or Occurrence	Verify that the accounts payable balance represents amounts actually owed by the organization at the balance sheet date. Establish that purchases transactions represent goods and services actually received during the period covered by the financial statements. Determine that payroll transactions represent wages for services actually performed during the period covered by the financial statements.
Completeness	Determine that accounts payable represent all amounts owed by the organization for purchases of goods and services as of the balance sheet date. Ensure that the financial statements reflect all goods and services received by the organization, less returns, for the period covered. Verify that the financial statements reflect all wages for services performed during the period covered.
Accuracy	Establish that purchases transactions are accurately computed and based on correct prices and correct quantities. Ensure that the accounts payable subsidiary ledger is mathematically correct and agrees with the general ledger accounts. Verify that payroll amounts are based on correct pay rates and hours worked and are accurately computed.
Rights and Obligations	Establish that the accounts payable and accrued payroll recorded at the balance sheet date are legal obligations of the organization.
Valuation or Allocation	Verify that accounts payable are stated at correct amounts owed.
Presentation and Disclosure	Ensure that accounts payable, accrued payroll, and expenses reported for the period are properly described and classified in the financial statements.

last chapter, this often involves a combination of tests of controls and substantive tests of details. The specific controls addressed here are based on the application controls framework presented in Chapter 7, which classifies controls into three broad categories: input controls, process controls, and output controls. Within this framework, we examine application controls, tests of controls, and the audit objectives to which they relate. Substantive tests and their relationship to management assertions and corresponding audit objectives are considered later in the chapter.

Input Controls

Input controls are designed to ensure that transactions are valid, accurate, and complete. Control techniques vary considerably between batch and real-time systems. The following input controls relate to expenditure cycle operations.

Data Validation Controls
Input validation controls are intended to detect transcription errors in transaction data before they are processed. Since errors detected early are less likely to infiltrate the

accounting records, validation procedures are most effective when they are performed as close to the source of the transaction as possible. In the batch purchases system depicted in Figure 10.1, validation of purchase orders occurs only after they have been sent to the vendor. Because of inevitable transcription errors that occur in preparation of source documents, such systems are characterized by the need for extensive error correction and transaction resubmission procedures. On the other hand, the real-time input of timecard data illustrated in Figure 10.6 can identify and resolve most errors as they occur. This approach also minimizes human data entry and thus reduces the risk of data entry errors. For example, when the clerk enters the employee number, the system automatically retrieves his or her name, mailing address, pay rate, and other relevant data from the employee file.

Chapter 7 presented a number of general types of validation tests. Examples that are relevant to the expenditure cycle are reviewed in the following paragraphs.

Missing data checks are used to examine the contents of a field for the presence of blank spaces. An employee number missing from an attendance record, the quantity-received value missing from a receiving report, or an incomplete mailing address in a purchase order record will cause the transaction to be rejected. When the validation program detects a blank where it expects to see a data value, this situation will be interpreted as an error.

Numeric-alphabetic data checks determine whether the correct form of data is in a field. For example, the quantity field in a purchase order should not contain alphabetic data. As with blanks, alphabetic data in a numeric field may cause serious processing errors.

Limit checks determine if the value in the field exceeds an authorized limit. For example, if the firm has a policy that no employee works more than 44 hours per week, the payroll system validation program can interrogate the hours-worked field in the weekly payroll records for values greater than 44.

Range checks assign upper and lower limits to acceptable data values. This technique can be used to control orders placed with vendors. For example, a range of 500 to 1,000 units can be set as the normal order quantity for a particular class of product. A range check is also useful for controlling payroll transactions. If the range of pay rates for hourly employees in a firm is between $8 and $20, all payroll records can be checked to see that this range is not exceeded. The purpose of this control is to detect keystroke errors that shift the decimal point one or more places. It would not detect an error where a correct pay rate of, say, $9 is incorrectly entered as $15.

Validity checks compare actual values in a field against known acceptable values. This control is used to verify such things as state abbreviations or employee job skill codes. If the value in the field does not match one of the acceptable values, the record is determined to be in error.

Check digit controls identify keystroke errors in key fields by testing their internal validity. A check digit could be used to verify a vendor number on a purchase order record.

Testing Validation Controls

Data entry errors that slip through edit programs undetected can cause recorded accounts payable and expense amounts to be materially misstated. The following audit procedures provide evidence about the accuracy assertion.

The central audit issue is whether the validation programs in the data editing system are functioning correctly and have functioned as intended throughout the period. Testing the logic of a validation program, however, represents a significant undertaking. The auditor may decide to rely on the quality of other controls to provide the assurance needed to reduce substantive testing. For example, after reviewing systems development and maintenance controls, the auditor may determine that controls over original program design and testing and subsequent changes to programs are effective. This evidence permits the auditor to assess the risk of material program errors at a low level and thus reduce the substantive tests related to the audit objective of accuracy.

If controls over systems development and maintenance are weak, however, the auditor may decide that testing data editing controls will be more efficient than performing extensive substantive tests of details. In such a case, ITF or the test data approach can enable the auditor to perform explicit tests of the validation logic. This testing would require the auditor to gain a familiarity with all of the validation procedures in place. The auditor would need to create a comprehensive set of test transactions that include both valid and erroneous data values that fall within and outside of the test parameters. An analysis of the test results will show the auditor which types of errors, if any, can pass undetected by the validation program. This evidence will help the auditor determine the nature, timing, and extent of subsequent substantive tests.

In addition to direct testing of program logic, the auditor can achieve some degree of assurance by reviewing error listings and error logs. These documents provide evidence of the effectiveness of the data entry process, the types and volume of errors encountered, and the manner in which the errors are corrected and reentered into the system. Recall from the last chapter that error listings and logs do not provide evidence of undetected errors. An analysis of error conditions not present in the listing can, however, guide the auditor in designing substantive tests to perform. For example, assume that the error listing of the purchase order file contains no order-quantity range errors. This fact may simply mean that data entry personnel are skilled and no transcription errors of that sort occurred. On the other hand, it may mean that the validation program does not test for this type of error. To determine whether material order-quantity discrepancies existed, the auditor can perform substantive tests that compare the actual quantity ordered on purchase orders with the order-quantity data stored in the inventory records.

Batch Controls

Batch controls are used to manage high volumes of transaction data through a system. The objective of batch control is to reconcile output produced by the system with the input originally entered into the system. Batch control is initiated at the data input stage and continues through all phases of data processing. For example, a batch of supplier invoices enters the system at the data entry stage; after each subsequent processing stage, the batch is reviewed for completeness.

The information contained in the transmittal sheet is entered as a separate control record that the system uses to verify the integrity of the batch. Periodic reconciliation between the data in the transmittal record and actual processing results provides assurance of the following:

- All invoices that were entered into the system were processed.
- No invoices were processed and paid more than once.
- All invoices entered into the system are accounted for as either successfully processed or rejected because of errors.

Testing Batch Controls

The failure of batch controls to function properly can result in records being lost or processed multiple times. Tests of batch controls provide the auditor with evidence relating to the assertions of *completeness* and *accuracy*.

Testing batch controls involves reviewing transmittal records of batches processed throughout the period and reconciling them to the batch control log. The auditor needs to investigate out-of-balance conditions to determine their cause. For example, assume that the transmittal record for a batch of supplier invoices shows that 100 records with an invoice total of $285,458.86 entered the system. The completed batch log, however, shows that 101 records were processed with a batch total of $288,312.50. What caused this anomaly? Did the system process one record twice due to a programming error? Was an extra record entered into the system during processing? Did the data entry clerk incorrectly calculate the batch control totals? By reviewing and reconciling transaction listings and error logs, the auditor should be able to obtain answers to these questions.

Purchases Authorization Controls

Purchases authorization actually occurs in the revenue cycle when goods are sold to customers. At that time, the system compares the quantity-on-hand with the reorder point to determine if the inventory needs to be reordered. If so, a purchases requisition for the standard order quantity is created and the item is flagged "On Order" to prevent subsequent orders from being placed. In the expenditure cycle, the purchase requisition file is sorted by vendor number and purchases orders are then prepared.

Testing Purchases Authorization Controls

Incorrectly functioning purchase authorization controls can cause unnecessary and incorrect orders to be placed with vendors. The following tests of controls provide evidence pertaining to the *accuracy* and *valuation* assertions.

Since purchase requisitions are internally generated, they should be free from clerical errors and do not need validating. However, computer logic errors in this procedure can cause negative operational and financial consequences that may go undetected. Two concerns are of particular importance. First, the auditor needs to verify that the correct order quantity is used when a requisition is created. Errors in programming logic (or data entry) may cause an intended order quantity of 1,000 to be recorded as 100 or 10,000. This sort of error can result in unanticipated stock-outs, excessive ordering costs, or overinvestment in inventory. Second, the auditor should verify that the inventory record is flagged "On Order" when a requisition is first prepared. Failure to do so will result in overinvestment in inventory due to multiple orders being placed for the same item. Testing these controls using CAATTs involves creating test inventory records and sales transactions that reduce the inventory items below their reorder point. The resulting purchase requisitions and inventory records can then be examined for evidence of properly functioning controls.

Employee Authorization

The personnel department prepares and submits personnel action forms to the payroll department. These documents are used to effect changes in hourly pay rates, payroll deductions, and job classification. They also identify employees who are authorized to receive a paycheck. This information plays an important role in preventing errors and payroll fraud. A common form of fraud is to submit timecards on behalf of employees who are not employed by the firm. To prevent this kind of fraud, someone in the payroll department should be designated to compare timecards with the list of authorized employees sent from personnel. Another common fraud is to create checks for "ghost" employees. The authorization of employees should be done in such a way as to help prevent this kind of fraud.

When employee authorization procedures are computerized, the payroll program matches each attendance record with a corresponding record in the current personnel action file. Any attendance records that do not match should be rejected and investigated by management.

Testing Employee Authorization Procedures

Failure to implement employee authorization procedures can result in payroll distributions to unauthorized individuals. The following tests of controls provide evidence pertaining to the *existence, accuracy, valuation,* and *rights and obligation* assertions.

The auditor needs to determine that effective procedures exist in the personnel department to identify current employees, communicate their status completely and correctly to the payroll function, and monitor adherence to employee authorization procedures. Using either the test data or integrated test facility (ITF) approaches, the auditor can assess the correctness of programmed procedures that validate employee authenticity. This testing involves creating a dummy authorized employee file and a corresponding attendance file containing both records that match and some that do not. The auditor can analyze the processing results to determine if the payroll application correctly identified and rejected the invalid transactions.

The integrity of standing data is an important consideration in the preceding test. A correctly functioning payroll application cannot successfully validate payroll transactions if the authorized employee file is itself invalid. The auditor can obtain assurance that the file has integrity when the following controls exist: access to the authorized employee file is password controlled; additions to and deletions from the file are restricted to authorized individuals in the personnel department; and the employee records stored on the file are encrypted.

Process Controls

Process controls include computerized procedures for updating files and restricting access to data. Depending on the level of computer technology in place, process controls may also include physical controls associated with manual activities. We begin by examining three control techniques related to file updating. Access and physical controls are examined later.

File Update Controls

Run-to-run controls use batch control data discussed in the previous section to monitor the batch as it moves from one programmed procedure (run) to another. These controls ensure that each run in the system processes the batch correctly and completely. After each major operation, key fields such as invoice amount and record counts are accumulated and compared to the corresponding values stored in the transmittal record. A discrepancy may indicate that a record was lost in processing, a record in the batch went unprocessed, or a record was processed more than once.

Sequence Check Control.   In systems that use sequential master files (mostly legacy systems), the order of the transaction records in the batch is critical to correct and complete processing. As the batch moves through the process, it must be re-sorted in the order of the master file used in each run. An out-of-sequence supplier's invoice record in a batch will prevent other downstream records from being processed. In more serious cases, the downstream records may be processed against the wrong suppliers' accounts. A sequence check control needs to be in place to compare the sequence of each record in the batch with the previous record to ensure that proper sorting took place. Out-of-sequence records should be rejected and resubmitted, thus allowing the other records in the batch to be processed.

Liability Validation Control.   An important control in purchases/accounts payable systems is the validation of the liability prior to making payment. The process involves reconciling supporting documents including the purchase order, receiving report, and supplier's invoice. When these documents agree as to the items and quantities ordered and received, and the prices charged match the expected prices, then a liability (account payable) should be recognized and recorded. At a future date, cash will be disbursed to pay the liability.

In business environments where discrepancies in prices charged and quantities received are commonplace, the validation process is difficult to automate. Programmed decision rules must be implemented to accept less-than-perfect matches between supporting documents. For example, the system may be designed to accept invoice prices that are within five percent of expected prices. Discrepancies in the items and quantities ordered and received, however, are more difficult to resolve. Dealing with these problems often requires reordering inventory and/or making adjustments to accounts payable records. In this type of business setting, many organizations employ manual procedures for reconciling supporting documents and validating the liability.

Trading partner relationships (such as the Ford example described earlier) stabilize the business environment and permit organizations to depart from traditional accounting procedures. Because prices, quantities, and product quality are guaranteed by the trading partner agreement, the liability validation process can be greatly simplified and automated. For example, matching the receiving report to the original purchase order is all that is necessary to establish the liability.

Valid Vendor File.   The **valid vendor file** is similar to the authorized employee file discussed earlier. This file consists of a list of vendors with whom the organization normally does business. Fraudulent transactions in the expenditure cycle often culminate in a payment to someone posing as a legitimate vendor. Before payment, the recipient of the cash disbursement should be validated against the valid vendor file. Any record that does not match should be rejected and investigated by management.

Testing File Update Controls.   Failure of file update controls to function properly can result in transactions (1) not being processed (liabilities are not recognized and recorded), (2) being processed incorrectly (i.e., payments are approved for unauthorized recipients), or (3) being posted to the wrong supplier's account. Tests of file update controls provide the auditor with evidence relating to the management assertions of *existence, completeness, rights and obligations,* and *accuracy.*

Tests of sequence checks can be performed using either ITF or the test data approach. The auditor should create test data that contain records that are out of sequence in the batch and verify that each was handled correctly. In addition, the auditor needs to verify the mathematical correctness of the procedure. For example, a receiving report record of 1,000 units of product costing $10,000 should increase the quantity-on-hand of that inventory item by 1,000 units and increase its total carrying value by $10,000. Similarly, a payroll record of $1,000 updating an employee's year-to-date earnings record of $10,000 should produce a new balance of $11,000.

Testing the liability validation logic requires understanding the decision rule for matching supporting documents. By creating test purchase orders, receiving reports, and supplier invoices, the auditor can verify whether decision rules are being correctly applied. Similarly, the ITF and test data methods can be used to test the effectiveness of valid vendor control. This testing involves creating a reference file of valid vendors and a file of supplier invoices (accounts payable) to be paid. Invoice records with vendor numbers that do not match a valid vendor record should be rejected by the program and passed to an error file for management review.

The efficient use of logic-testing CAATTs such as ITF requires determining in advance the input and process controls to be tested. A single audit procedure can be devised that performs many or all of the needed tests. For example, when testing payroll, a single transaction that tests employee authorization controls, sequence checks, and mathematical accuracy can provide evidence that supports multiple audit objectives.

Access Controls

Access controls prevent and detect unauthorized and illegal access to the firm's assets. Inventories and cash are the physical assets of the expenditure cycle. Traditional techniques used to limit access to these assets include:

- Warehouse security, such as fences, alarms, and guards.
- Moving assets promptly from the receiving dock to the warehouse.
- Paying employees by check rather than cash.

Controlling access to accounting records is no less important. An individual with unrestricted access to data can manipulate the physical assets of the firm and cause financial statements to be materially misstated. Accounting files stored on magnetic media are particularly vulnerable to unauthorized access, whether its cause is accidental, an act of malice by a disgruntled employee, or an attempt at fraud. The following are examples of risks specific to the expenditure cycle:

1. An individual with access to the AP subsidiary ledger (and supporting documents) could add his or her account (or someone else's) to the file. Once recognized by the system as a legitimate liability, the account will be paid even though no purchase transaction transpired.
2. Access to employee attendance cards may enable an unauthorized individual to trigger an unauthorized paycheck.
3. An individual with access to both cash and accounts payable records could remove cash from the firm and record the act as a legitimate disbursement.
4. An individual with access to physical inventory and inventory records can steal products and adjust the records to cover the theft.

Testing Access Controls

Access control lies at the heart of accounting information integrity. In the absence of adequate controls, supplier invoices can be deleted, added, or falsified. Individual payroll account balances can be erased or the entire accounts payable file can be destroyed. Evidence gathered about the effectiveness of access controls tests the management assertions of *existence, completeness, accuracy, valuation and allocation, rights and obligations*, and *presentation and disclosure*.

Since payments to false vendors carries such potential for material loss, the auditor is concerned about the integrity of the valid vendor file. By gaining access to the file, a computer criminal can place his or her name on it and masquerade as an authorized vendor. The auditor should therefore assess the adequacy of access controls protecting the file. These include password controls, restricting access to authorized managers, and using data encryption to prevent the file contents from being read or changed.

As discussed in previous chapters, computer access controls are both system-wide and application-specific. Access control includes controlling access to the operating systems, the networks, and the databases with which all applications interact. The auditors will typically test these controls as part of their review of general controls.

Physical Controls

Physical controls include manual activities and human actions to initiate computer procedures to safeguard the assets of the organization. The relevant physical controls for the purchases and payroll systems follow.

Purchases System Controls

- *Segregation of inventory control from the warehouse.* The primary assets at risk in the expenditure cycle are inventory and cash. Warehouse clerks responsible for asset custody should not be given responsibility for maintaining inventory records. Otherwise, inventory could be removed from the warehouse and the accounting records adjusted to conceal the event.

- *Segregation of the general ledger and accounts payable from cash disbursements.* An individual with the combined responsibilities of writing checks, posting to the cash account, and maintaining accounts payable could perpetrate fraud against the firm. An individual with such access could withdraw cash and then adjust the cash account accordingly to hide the transaction. Also, he or she could establish fraudulent accounts payable (to an associate in a nonexistent vendor company) and then write checks to discharge the phony obligations. By segregating these functions, the organization's management can greatly reduce this exposure.

- *Supervision of receiving department.* Large quantities of valuable assets flow through the receiving department on their way to the warehouse. Close supervision here reduces the chances of two types of exposure: failure to properly inspect the assets and the theft of assets.

  - *Inspection of assets.* When goods arrive from the supplier, receiving clerks must inspect items for proper quantities and condition (damage, spoilage, and so on). For this reason, the receiving clerk receives a blind copy of the original purchase order from purchasing. A blind purchase order has all the relevant information about the goods being received except for the quantities and prices. To obtain the information on quantities, which is needed for the receiving report, the receiving personnel are forced to physically count and inspect the goods. If receiving clerks were provided with quantity information through formal documentation (i.e., the purchase order), they may be tempted to transfer this information to the receiving report without performing a physical count. Inspecting and counting the items received protects the firm from incomplete orders and damaged goods. Supervision is critical at this point to ensure that the clerks properly carry out these important duties. Incoming goods are accompanied by a packing slip containing quantity information that could be used to circumvent the inspection process. A supervisor should take custody of the packing slip while receiving clerks count and inspect the goods.

  - *Theft of assets.* Receiving departments are sometimes hectic and cluttered during busy periods. In this environment, incoming inventories are exposed to theft until they are securely placed in the warehouse. Improper inspection procedures coupled with inadequate supervision can create a situation that is conducive to the theft of inventories in transit.

- *Reconciliation of supporting documents.* The accounts payable department plays a vital role in controlling the disbursement of cash to vendors. Copies of supporting documents flow into this department for review and comparison. Each document contains unique facts about the purchase transaction, which the accounts payable clerk needs to verify before the obligation is recognized.

  - *The purchase order,* which shows that the purchasing agent ordered only the needed inventories from a valid vendor.[4]

---

4   Firms often establish a list of valid vendors with whom they do regular business. Purchasing agents must acquire inventories only from valid vendors. This technique deters certain types of fraud, such as an agent buying from suppliers with whom he or she has a relationship (a relative or friend) or buying at excessive prices from vendors in exchange for a kickback or bribe.

- *The receiving report*, which is evidence of the physical receipt of the goods, their condition, and the quantities received. The reconciliation of this document with the purchase order signifies the point of realization of the obligation.
- *The supplier's invoice*, which provides the financial information needed to record this obligation as an account payable. The accounts payable clerk verifies that the prices on the invoice are reasonable (in compliance with organizational policy) compared with the expected prices stated on the purchase order.

Payroll System Controls

- *Verification of timecards.* The **timecard** is the formal record of daily attendance. Each day at the beginning of the shift, employees place their timecards in a special clock that records arrival. They clock out for their lunch period and at the end of the shift. Before sending timecards to payroll, the supervisor must verify their accuracy and sign them.
- *Supervision.* Sometimes an employee will clock in for another worker who is late or absent. Supervisors should observe the clocking process and reconcile the timecards with actual attendance.
- *Paymaster.* The use of an independent **paymaster** to distribute checks (rather than the normal supervisor) helps verify the existence of the employees. This control is useful in uncovering a fraud whereby the supervisor is pretending to distribute paychecks to nonexistent employees.
- *Payroll imprest account.* Employee paychecks are drawn on a special **payroll imprest account** at the bank, which is used only for payroll clearing. Funds must be transferred from the general cash account to this imprest account before the paychecks can be cashed. The amount of the funds transfer is determined from the payroll register, which is reviewed for correctness and approved by accounts payable. The imprest account technique physically limits the organization's exposure. Individual checks that exceed the imprest amount will not clear. This result will expose the existence of checks written in error (duplicates) or created through fraudulent activities.

Testing Physical Controls

Inadequate segregation of duties and lack of supervision can result in fraud and errors that can cause financial statements to be materially misstated. The exposure issues here are similar to the access control issues discussed earlier. Granting inappropriate access privileges is often due to assigning incompatible duties to an individual. Similarly, the purpose of collusion is to achieve unauthorized access to assets as well as the information needed to conceal the crime. Evidence gathered by reviewing the segregation of duties can be used to test *all* of the management assertions outlined in Table 10.1.

The auditor's review of organizational structure should disclose the more egregious examples of incompatible tasks, such as one individual opening and approving time-cards, authorizing employee payments, and receiving and distributing the paychecks. Covert relationships that may lead to collusion may not be apparent from an organizational chart. For example, married employees (or those otherwise related) who work in incompatible areas may go unnoticed. The auditor should determine whether the organization has an effective policy for dealing with nepotism.

Many tasks that are normally segregated in manual systems are consolidated in the data processing function of computer-based systems. Computer programs in the expenditure cycle authorize purchases, place orders, update inventory records, approve payments to vendors, and write the checks. In automated environments, the auditor's concern should focus on the integrity of the computer programs that perform these tasks. The following questions need to be answered: Is the logic of the computer program correct? Has anyone tampered with the application since it was last tested? Have changes been made to the program that could have caused an undisclosed error? Are there adequate formal procedures (i.e., supervision) to compensate for the lack of segregation of duties? These formal procedures could be reports, especially error reports, sent directly to the supervisor.

Answers to these questions come from the auditor's review of systems development and maintenance controls and by reviewing organizational structure. Recall from earlier chapters that duties pertaining to the design, maintenance, and operation of computer programs need to be separated. Programmers who write the original computer programs should not be responsible for making program changes. Also, individuals who operate the computer system should not perform systems design, programming, or maintenance activities. Personal relationships (i.e., marriage) between individuals in these incompatible areas may require further investigation.

Output Controls

Output controls are designed to ensure that information is not lost, misdirected, or corrupted and that system processes function as intended. For example, daily summaries of cash disbursements to vendors and inventory receipts should go to managers to report the status of their operations. Output control can be designed to identify operational and internal control problems. For example, an exception report derived from the Suppliers Invoice (accounts payable) file listing past-due liabilities can identify discounts lost and help management assess the operational performance of the accounts payable process. Output, however, is not limited to end-of-day reporting. System output is also needed at intermediate junctures where processing accuracy can be reviewed and verified and errors can be detected quickly and corrected.

Reconciling the general ledger can detect certain types of transaction processing errors. For example, the total of all reductions to accounts payable should equal the total cash disbursements to vendors. A cash disbursement that is entered in the journal but not posted to the vendor's account would be detected by an imbalance in the general ledger. The specific cause of an out-of-balance condition may not be apparent at this point, but the error would be noted. Finding the error may require examining all the transactions processed during the period and could be time consuming. For this reason, rather than summarizing an entire day's transactions in a single batch, entities often group transactions into small batches of 50 to 100 items. This process facilitates reconciling balances by isolating a problem to a specific batch.

Another important element of output control is the maintenance of an audit trail. Details of transaction processing produced at intermediate points can provide an audit trail that reflects activity through every stage of operations. The following are examples of audit trail output controls.

Accounts Payable Change Report
This document is a summary report that shows the overall change to accounts payable. These figures should reconcile with total vendor invoices received, total cash disbursements, and the general ledger.

Transaction Logs
Every transaction successfully processed by the system should be recorded on a **transaction log,** which serves as a journal. Transactions rejected because of input errors should be placed in an error file, corrected, and resubmitted. The transaction log and error files together thus account for all economic activity.

Transaction Listing

The system should produce a (hard copy) **transaction listing** of all successful transactions. Listings should go to the appropriate users to facilitate reconciliation with input. For example, a listing of cash disbursements processed will go to the controller to be used for the bank reconciliation.

Log of Automatic Transactions

Some transactions are triggered internally by the system. For example, EDI purchase orders are initiated and processed without human authorization. To maintain an audit trail of these activities, all internally generated transactions must be placed in a transaction log, and a listing of these transactions should be sent to the appropriate manager for review.

Unique Transaction Identifiers

Each transaction processed by the system must be uniquely identified with a transaction number. This feature is the only practical means of tracing a particular transaction through a database of thousands or even millions of records. In systems that use physical purchase orders, the unique number printed on the document can be transcribed during data input and used for this purpose. In real-time systems that do not use source documents, each purchase order should be assigned a unique number by the system.

Error Listing

A listing of all error records should go to the appropriate user to support error correction and resubmission.

Testing Output Controls

The absence of adequate output controls has adverse implications for operational efficiency and financial reporting. Evidence gathered through tests of output controls relates to the *completeness* and *accuracy* assertions.

Testing output controls involves reviewing summary reports for accuracy, completeness, timeliness, and relevance to the decision that they are intended to support. In addition, the auditor should trace sample transactions through audit trail reports, including transaction listings, error logs, and logs of resubmitted records. Gathering such evidence, however, may involve sorting through thousands of transactions.

In modern systems, audit trails are usually stored online as text files that can be read by word processing and spreadsheet programs. Data extraction CAATTs such as ACL are capable of searching log files for specific records to verify completeness and accuracy of the output reports. Alternatively, the auditor can test output controls directly using ITF. A well-designed ITF system will permit the auditor to produce a batch of sample transactions, including some error records, and trace them through all phases of processing, error detection, and output reporting.

SUBSTANTIVE TESTS OF EXPENDITURE CYCLE ACCOUNTS

This section deals with the substantive tests that an auditor may perform to achieve audit objectives related to the expenditure cycle. The strategy used in determining the nature, timing, and extent of substantive tests derives from the auditor's assessment of inherent risk, unmitigated control risk, materiality considerations, and the need to conduct the audit in an efficient manner.

Expenditure Cycle Risks and Audit Concerns

Taking the most narrow attest-function view, external auditors are concerned primarily with the potential for understatement of liabilities and related expenses. Reported balances usually consist of items that have been reviewed, validated, and acknowledged by management. Attempts to improve financial statement presentation may involve actions to suppress the recognition and reporting of valid liabilities related to the period under review. Substantive tests of expenditure cycle accounts are therefore directed toward gathering evidence of understatement and omission of material items rather than their overstatement. Broader operational audit concerns, however, include process efficiency, fraud, and losses due to errors. Within this context, overstatement of liabilities and related expenses are also important.

In resolving these concerns, the auditor will seek evidence by performing a combination of tests of internal controls and substantive tests. Tests of controls include testing both general controls (discussed in Chapters 2 through 5 and application controls specifically related to the expenditure cycle). Various application control-testing techniques were examined in Chapter 7 and specific tests related to the expenditure cycle were described in this chapter. In addition to tests of controls, the auditor must perform substantive tests to achieve audit objectives. The remainder of this chapter deals with audit objectives related to expenditure cycle accounts and the substantive tests most commonly performed. Keep in mind that the quality of internal controls bears on the nature and extent of substantive tests determined by the auditor to be necessary. Ordinarily, not all of the following tests will be performed.

Understanding Data

The substantive tests described in this section involve extracting data from accounting files for analysis. To do this task, the auditor needs to understand the systems and controls that produced the data as well as the physical characteristics of the files that contain them. Much of this chapter was devoted to explaining various expenditure cycle configurations and their control implications. Chapter 8 described several common file structures and their audit implications. The discussion that follows presumes that the auditor is using ACL for performing the audit tests. Before we proceed, however, we need to review a few salient points regarding file preparation.

First, the auditor must verify that he or she is working with the correct version of the file to be analyzed. To do so, the auditor must understand the file backup procedures and, whenever possible, work with the original files. Second, ACL can read most sequential files and relational database tables directly, but esoteric and/or complex file structures may require "flattening" before they can be analyzed. This process may involve additional procedures and special programs to produce a copy of the original file in a format that ACL can accept. If the organization's systems personnel perform the flattening process, the auditor must verify that the correct version of the original file was used and that all relevant records from the original were transferred to the copy for analysis.

The discussion that follows presumes that any file copying necessary to produce test data was performed under adequate controls to preserve data integrity. Furthermore, the tests described are applicable to both mainframe and PC environments. The focus of this material is on explaining the logic underlying various substantive tests and on illustrating the functionality of ACL in achieving audit objectives. The audit procedures described are based on the file structure in Figure 10.7. These structures indicate the key data and logical linkages between files. A description of each file follows.

FIGURE 10.7   File Structures for the Expenditure Cycle

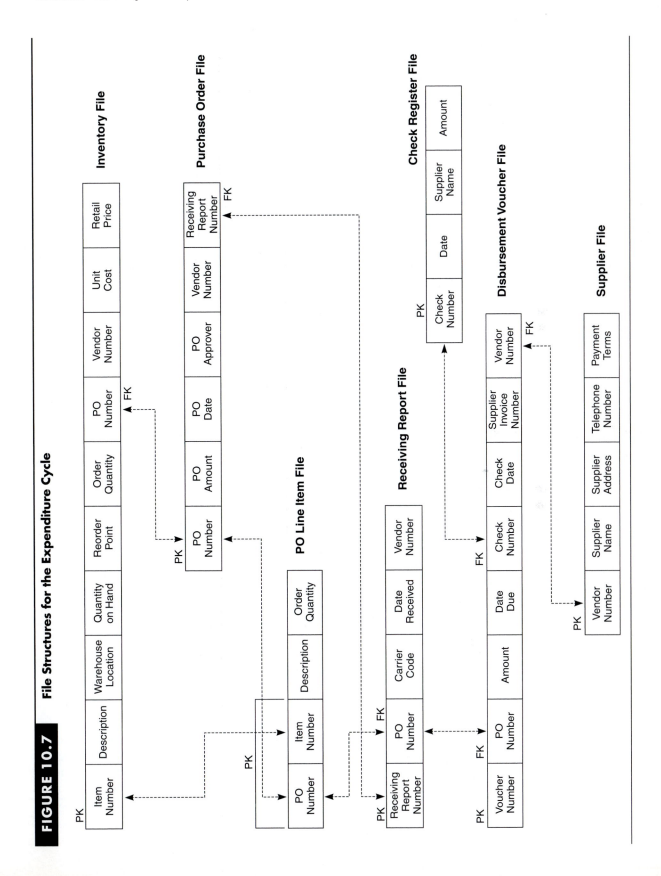

Inventory File

The Inventory file contains quantity, price, supplier, and warehouse location data for each item of product inventory. The purchasing process begins with a review of the inventory records to identify inventory items that need to be ordered. In a retail organization, this step is performed when sales of finished goods to customers are recorded in the inventory records. In this case, the purchasing process involves replenishing the finished goods inventory. Purchasing systems of manufacturing firms replenish raw materials inventory as these items are used in the production process. In either case, when inventory items are sold or used in production, the Quantity-on-Hand field is reduced accordingly by a computer application. With each inventory reduction, the system tests for a "reorder" condition, which occurs when the quantity-on-hand falls below the reorder point. At that time, the system prepares a purchase order, which is sent to the vendor, and adds a record to the Purchase Order file. The quantity-on-hand value will remain below the reorder-point until the inventory is received from the supplier. This process may take days or even weeks. To signify that the item is on order and to prevent it from being reordered each time the computer application detects the same reorder condition, a computer-generated purchase order number is placed in the PO-Number field of the inventory record. Normally, this field is blank.

Purchase Order File

This file contains records of purchases placed with suppliers. The record remains open until the inventory arrives. Placing the receiving report number in the dedicated field closes the record.

Purchase Order Line Item File

The Line Item file contains a record of every item ordered. Since a single transaction can involve one or more products, each record in the Purchase Order file is associated with (linked to) one or more records in this file. Notice that the file contains a composite primary key—Purchase Order Number and Item Number. Both of these attributes are needed to uniquely define each record in the file. They also provide links to related records in the Purchase Order and Inventory files.

Receiving Report File

When the ordered items arrive from the supplier, they are counted and inspected, and receiving documents are prepared. Via terminal, the receiving clerk enters information about the items received. The system automatically performs the following tasks: (1) increases the Quantity-on-Hand field in the inventory record(s); (2) removes the reorder condition by resetting the PO-Number field to its normal blank state; (3) creates a receiving report record of the event; and (4) closes the purchase order record by placing the receiving report number in the designated field.

Disbursement Voucher File and Check Register File

For most companies, discrepancies between amounts ordered, received, and billed are legitimate concerns that must be resolved before payment to the vendor is approved. Because of its complexity, this reconciliation is often a manual process that is triggered by receipt of the supplier's invoice. The accounts payable clerk reviews the supporting records in the Purchase Order and Receiving Report files and compares them to the invoice. If the items, quantities, and prices match, then a record is added to the

Disbursement Voucher File. Based on the supplier's terms of trade and the company's payment policy, the payment due date is determined and placed in the disbursement voucher record.

Each payment day, the Cash Disbursement application selects the items due to be paid and adds a record to the Check Register File for each payment. It flags the items *paid* in the respective disbursement voucher records by entering the current date and the system-assigned Check Number (foreign key) into the appropriate fields. The system then cuts the checks that are mailed to the suppliers. The Disbursement Voucher file provides two important pieces of information for the auditor: (1) it is a record of the timing and amount of vendor invoices received; and (2) at any point in time, the open items (unpaid vouchers) in the file constitute the company's outstanding accounts payable balance.

File Preparation Procedures

The data contained in the preceding files provide evidence that may either corroborate or refute audit objectives. Most of the tests described in the following section involve using ACL to access and extract data from these files. Recall from the previous chapter that each file needs to be defined in terms of its physical location and its structure. Through a series of easy-to-use pop-up menus, the auditor specifies the name of the file and where it resides on the mainframe or PC. ACL then prompts the auditor to define the file's structure in terms of the length of each field and the data type contained in each field (i.e., numeric, character, or date). When the data definition is completed, it is saved under a unique name assigned by the auditor. All future file access is accomplished by simply selecting the data definition from an ACL menu. ACL automatically locates the file and presents it on screen, where the auditor can review and manipulate its contents. Figure 10.8 shows a sample ACL data definition screen.

Sometimes the contents of a data field are different from what they are supposed to be. For example, a numeric field in one or more records may contain alphabetic data because of a program error or a clerical mistake. Also, a field may contain corrupted data because of an error in the file-flattening process. Whatever the cause, prior to performing any substantive tests on a new file, it is important that the auditor validate its contents. Invalid data will distort the test results and may cause a system failure. ACL's *Verify* command analyzes the data fields in the selected file to ensure that their contents are consistent with the field type in the file definition. Any validity errors detected by ACL need to be traced to their source and resolved. For purposes of discussion, we will assume that the files used in all tests described hereafter have been properly defined and verified. Figure 10.9 shows the ACL Verify command box.

Testing the Accuracy and Completeness Assertions

The audit procedures described in this section provide evidence relating to management assertions of *accuracy* and *completeness*. We saw in the last chapter that auditors often precede substantive tests of details with an *analytical review* of account balances. Analytical procedures can identify relationships between accounts and risks that are not otherwise apparent. In the case of the expenditure cycle, an analytical review can provide the auditor with an overall perspective for trends in accounts payable and related expenses. Current expenses may be compared to historical expenses and management budgets. For example, the auditor may compare current payroll expenses for the

FIGURE 10.8   ACL Data Definition Screen

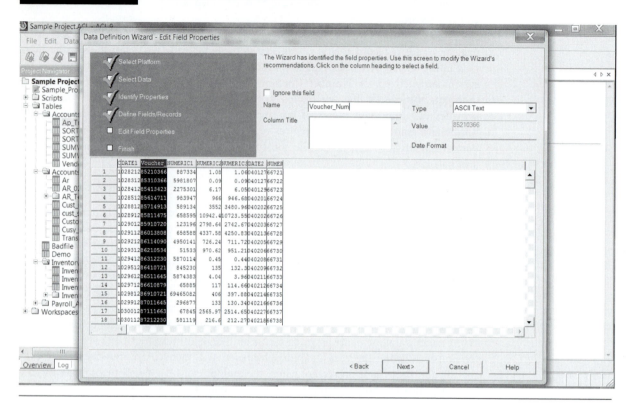

quarter with those for the same period in previous years. Unusual trends or variances should be noted and examined for cause. On the one hand, analytical procedures may indicate trends, even in adequately controlled organizations, that lead the auditor to extend substantive tests. On the other hand, they can provide assurance that transactions and accounts are reasonably stated and complete and may thus permit the auditor to reduce substantive testing.

A medium- to large-sized organization's expenses and accounts payable data may constitute thousands or perhaps millions of records. Unlike analytical procedures, which can be performed without CAATTs, substantive tests of details of such volumes of data cannot be effectively accomplished without using CAATTs. The following substantive tests that can be performed using ACL are based on the file structures depicted in Figure 10.7.

Review Disbursement Vouchers for Unusual Trends and Exceptions

A useful audit procedure for identifying potential audit risks involves scanning data files for unusual transactions and account balances. For example, scanning accounts payable for excessively large balances may indicate abnormal dependency on a particular supplier. However, a high number of vendors with small balances may indicate the need to consolidate business activity. Various corporate surveys have estimated the cost of processing a purchase order at between $50 and $125. Restricting the number of vendors with whom the organization does business can reduce this expense.

FIGURE 10.9   **ACL Verify Command Box**

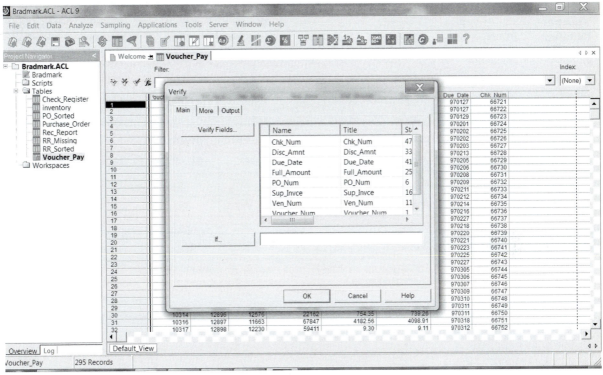

The auditor can use ACL's *Stratify* and *Classify* features to identify various characteristics and anomalies associated with accounts payable procedures. Both of these functions are used to group data into predetermined intervals, count the number of records that fall into each interval, and accumulate a financial value for each interval. The stratify function groups financial data into specific strata. Using data similar to those in Table 10.2, we demonstrate its use for stratifying disbursement vouchers by accumulating the Amount field for each strata. The classify function forms strata based on nonfinancial (and nonnumeric) data. In our example, this feature is used to group the vouchers by vendor number. In this case also, the Amount field is accumulated. The results of the two procedures are presented in Figure 10.10 and Figure 10.11, respectively.

The first report gives the auditor an overall perspective for the nature of the purchasing process. Notice that 91 percent of the total number of disbursement vouchers constitutes only 15 percent of the business volume for the period. The second report shows the business activity associated with individual vendors. Over 40 percent of the organization's purchases are from a single vendor, while most of the other vendors receive only a small percentage of the total business. These findings may reflect a natural business phenomenon, or they may signify potential risks.

Excessive purchases from a single supplier may reflect an unusual business dependency that may prove harmful to the firm if the supplier raises prices or cannot deliver on schedule. This situation may also signify a fraudulent relationship involving kickbacks to purchasing agents or other management.

TABLE 10.2		Disbursement Voucher Sample Data					

Voucher Number	PO Number	Amount	Due Date	Check Number	Check Date	Supplier Invoice Number	Vendor Number
12655	12923	158.32	12/21/09	6484	01/02/04	1223467	28788
512973	12958	1,802.63	01/15/10	6537	01/09/04	67783pl	15545
511810	12960	10,815.75	01/12/10	6567	01/09/04	88746pl	15545
1064	12998	4,427.99	01/15/10	6571	01/09/04	667223	28847
1060	13002	117,667.60	01/03/10	6611	01/09/04	844001	28847
77696	13006	150.95	12/04/09	6641	01/09/04	po2298	1564485

FIGURE 10.10	

Stratified Disbursement Voucher Data

As of: 06/09/2010 14:53:14

Command: STRATIFY ON Full_Amount MINIMUM -7000 MAXIMUM 120000 INTERVALS 10 TO SCREEN
Table: DisbVoucher

Minimum encountered was -584.22
Maximum encountered was 110,035.04

Full_Amount	Count	Percent of Count	Percent of Field	Full_Amount
-7,000.00 - 5,699.99	268	90.85%	15.25%	164,962.05
5,700.00 - 18,399.99	14	4.75%	11.68%	126,341.70
18,400.00 - 31,099.99	0	0%	0%	0.00
31,100.00 - 43,799.99	3	1.02%	10.35%	111,997.56
43,800.00 - 56,499.99	3	1.02%	12.71%	137,496.48
56,500.00 - 69,199.99	3	1.02%	17.31%	187,256.91
69,200.00 - 81,899.99	2	0.68%	14.38%	155,598.63
81,900.00 - 94,599.99	1	0.34%	8.14%	88,051.68
94,600.00 - 107,299.99	0	0%	0%	0.00
107,300.00 - 120,000.00	1	0.34%	10.17%	110,035.04
Totals	295	100%	100%	1,081,740.05

The large number of small volume suppliers is evidence of a highly inefficient purchasing process. Management may consider reducing the number of suppliers and increasing the size of their order quantities to reduce the number of orders placed. This situation may also be a signal to the auditor that a valid vendor approach to purchasing is *not* in use. It is unlikely that an organization would add vendors to the file for control purposes unless they expect significant levels of business.

FIGURE 10.11	As of: 06/09/2010 14:40:31

Disbursement Voucher Data Classified on Vendor Number

Command: CLASSIFY ON Ven_Num SUBTOTAL Full_Amount TO SCREEN
Table: DisbVoucher

Ven_Num	Count	Percent of Count	Percent of Field	Full_Amount
10001	12	4.07%	0.78%	8,441.85
10025	3	1.02%	0%	40.23
10101	1	0.34%	0.01%	120.33
10134	1	0.34%	-0.01%	-54.57
10366	48	16.27%	40.79%	441,293.98
10559	4	1.36%	0.61%	6,548.21
10656	2	0.68%	0.03%	357.54
10787	7	2.37%	0.27%	2,950.73
10879	13	4.41%	0.65%	7,008.51
10951	6	2.03%	0.01%	108.59
11009	1	0.34%	0.01%	72.72
11182	6	2.03%	0.18%	1,964.99
11213	1	0.34%	0%	11.53
11247	7	2.37%	7.27%	78,608.55
11435	4	1.36%	0.06%	651.10
11475	5	1.69%	1.49%	16,091.94
11645	12	4.07%	0.19%	2,068.54
11663	18	6.1%	11.19%	121,010.48
11837	7	2.37%	0.04%	458.52

Reviewing for Accurate Invoice Prices

Comparing prices on supplier invoices to original purchase order prices provides evidence for testing the management assertion of *accuracy*. Significant discrepancies between expected prices and the prices actually charged may be due to clerical errors, failure to review supporting documents before authorizing payment, or accounts payable personnel exceeding their authority in dealing with price discrepancies.

Traditionally, auditors verify pricing accuracy by comparing invoice prices with the purchase orders on a sample basis only. Of the thousands of invoices processed during the period, perhaps only one or two hundred can be tested manually. ACL allows the

TABLE 10.3	Purchase Order File				
PO Number	**PO Amount**	**PO Date**	**PO Approver**	**Vendor Number**	**Rec. Rpt Number**
12821	493.05	12/16/09	Controller	25152	10134
12838	138.95	01/24/10	PurchMgr	25152	10101
12848	14,463.75	01/10/10	Controller	28847	10787
12891	2,845.57	01/30/10	Controller	28847	11663
12894	252.54	12/06/09	PurchMgr	28529	11922
12946	238.65	12/13/09	PurchMgr	28529	11475
12958	1,802.63	12/16/09	Controller	15545	11668

auditor to compare the prices charged on every invoice in the file for the period under review. The test will involve the Disbursement Voucher file and the Purchase Order file, which is illustrated with some sample data in Table 10.3.

Testing pricing accuracy involves matching records from the two files using ACL's *Join* feature. This can be accomplished in a few simple steps. First, recall from Chapter 9 that both files being joined need to be ordered on a common key. In this example, PO Number is a common secondary key. Reorganizing both files on this field requires opening each file separately, invoking ACL's sort function, specifying the sort field, and designating the file name to receive the sorted output. The results of this process will be two new files ordered in the same sequence.

The next step is to combine the two files to create a third output file. The auditor achieves this with the *Join* command. Several options are available when joining files. The relevant option in this case is to create an output file that consists only of matched records from the two files. ACL's *Join* feature permits the auditor to specify the fields from the two input files that are to be passed to the new output file. Usually, it is neither necessary nor desirable to include all fields from both of the original files. In this example, the fields needed from the Purchase Order file to verify pricing accuracy are PO Number and PO Amount; from the Disbursement Voucher file the fields are Voucher Number, Amount, Check Number, and Vendor Number. The file structure of the new combined PO/Disbursement file with some sample records is presented in Table 10.4.

TABLE 10.4	Combined PO/Disbursement File				
PO Number	**PO Amount**	**Voucher Number**	**Amount**	**Check Number**	**Vendor Number**
12821	493.05	121655	493.05	6484	25152
12838	138.95	512973	138.95	6537	25152
12848	14,463.75	511810	14,463.75	6537	28847
12891	2,845.57	105436	2,845.57	6541	28847
12894	252.54	102360	252.54	6544	28529
12946	238.65	776756	238.65	6555	28529
12958	1,802.63	514760	1,802.63	6652	15545

FIGURE 10.12   ACL's Expression Builder

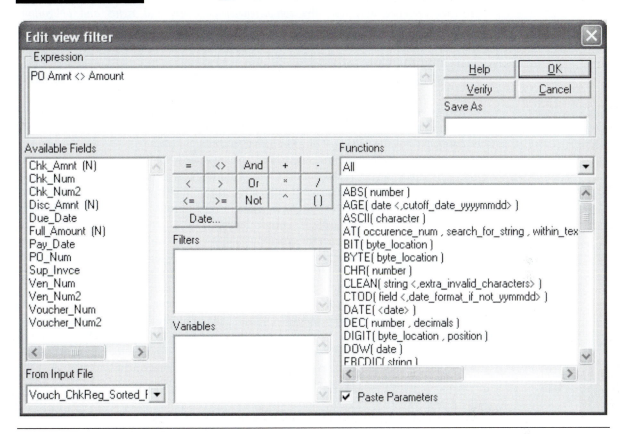

At this point, the resulting file may be quite large. Scanning the file visually for price differences can be time consuming and ineffective. Here again is an application for a *filter*. Using ACL's *Expression Builder* feature, the auditor can easily create a filter that will select only records where PO Amount and Amount are not equal. The resulting file will thus contain only records with price discrepancies. Using other ACL features, the auditor can calculate the total price variance and make a determination as to its materiality. If material, the matter should be pursued with management. Figure 10.12, presents ACL's Expression Builder window.

Testing the Completeness, Existence, and Rights and Obligations Assertions

Inventories received from valid suppliers in response to authorized purchase orders constitute liabilities. In most systems, however, the trigger that causes the liability to be recognized and recorded as an account payable (in our example, a disbursement voucher) is the receipt of the supplier's invoice, which often lags the receipt of the merchandise. Normally, the time lag between liability realization and recognition does not impact financial reporting. At period-end closing, however, it becomes an issue requiring special attention. Items of inventory received at the end of the audit period, whose related invoice is not received until early into the following period, may not be included as an accounts payable. Management should have procedures for identifying invoices received in a subsequent period that relate to the audit period and adjusting the liabilities accordingly. The search for unrecorded liabilities described in the following paragraphs provides evidence that tests the *completeness*, *existence*, and *rights and obligations* assertions.

Searching for Unrecorded Liabilities

The search for unrecorded liabilities involves the Disbursement Voucher and Receiving Report files, illustrated without data in Table 10.5. Each record of an inventory receipt contained in the Inventory Report File for the period should match a corresponding record in the Disbursement Voucher file. Again, using the *Join* feature, the two files can be compared for the existence of mismatched records.

As in the previous example, the two files being joined need to be ordered on a common key, which, again, is PO Number. Since the Disbursement Voucher file was previously sorted on this key, that sorted output file can be used for this test also. Therefore, only the Receiving Report file needs to be reorganized. The next step is to join the two files to create a combined output file. This time, however, the output option is different from the previous example. The relevant option in this case is to create an output file that consists only of *unmatched* records from the *primary* file. Remember, the auditor is attempting through this test to identify receiving report records that have not been recorded as liabilities. The primary file in this instance is the Receiving Report file, and the Disbursement Voucher file is the secondary file. In choosing this option, all the inventory receipts that were correctly recorded as liabilities will be ignored by the *Join* process. Only the unmatched receiving report records will be contained in the new output file. The structure of the file is the same as the Receiving Report file in Table 10.5. If the output file contains any records, the auditor needs to review this information with management to determine if the appropriate adjustments were made to the accounts payable balance.

Searching for Unauthorized Disbursement Vouchers

A variation on the preceding test can be used to address questions pertaining to overstated accounts payable. By selecting the Disbursement Vouchers file as the primary file and the Receiving Report file as the secondary file, the preceding test will produce a file of vouchers for which the organization has no record of inventory receipts. This might indicate that payments are approved solely on the basis of receiving a supplier's invoice rather than also verifying that inventories were ordered and actually received. Unsupported disbursement vouchers may signify an attempt at fraud or a poor control environment in which multiple payments are made for the same purchase. The latter situation is now examined further.

| **TABLE 10.5** | **Disbursement Voucher and Receiving Report Files** |

Disbursement Voucher File

Voucher Number	PO Number	Amount	Due Date	Check Number	Check Date	Invoice Number	Vendor Number

Receiving Report File

Rec.Rpt Number	PO Number	Carrier Code	Date Received	Vendor Number

Review for Multiple Checks to Vendors

Corporate losses from multiple payments to vendors for the same merchandise have been estimated to be in the hundreds of millions of dollars per year. Malfunctioning computer programs, data entry errors, and the failure of authorization controls are usually the basis for duplicate payments. Occasionally, however, they are the result of dishonest vendors who attempt to circumvent internal controls by sending two supplier invoices with different invoice numbers for the same purchase. Sometimes they send multiple copies of the same invoice or simply add a letter behind one of the invoice numbers to differentiate them. The auditor can test for duplicate records in a large file by employing ACL's *Duplicate* feature. This technique is demonstrated below using the Disbursement Voucher file in Table 10.5.

Various fields or combination of fields may be used to test for duplicate records. The auditor, however, needs to understand the relationship between the files to draw meaningful conclusions from the test results. For instance, in our example each disbursement voucher is issued in payment of a single supplier's invoice, and each supplier invoice relates to a single purchase order. Recognizing this relationship, the auditor can conclude that the same PO Number value should not normally exist in two or more records in the Disbursement Voucher file. A search for duplicate records in the file produces the report in Figure 10.13.

The report indicates that two records (voucher numbers 10392 and 10393) have the same purchase order number. The cause of this situation will require further examination in consultation with the appropriate management. The explanation may simply be that vouchers were created in error, voided, and resubmitted. However, the results may signify that, on two occasions, checks were issued for the same merchandise. This anomaly may be due to a computer error or an internal control problem in the voucher approval process, or it could be a result of fraud.

Auditing Payroll and Related Accounts

Testing accrued payroll and related accounts for completeness and accuracy consist primarily of analytical procedures and reviews of cash disbursements made in the

FIGURE 10.13

Duplicate Records Report

As of: 06/09/2010 13:28:45

Command: DUPLICATES ON PO_Num OTHER Voucher_Num TO SCREEN PRESORT
Table: Voucher_Pay

0 sequence errors detected
1 gap or duplicate detected

Duplicates:

PO_Num	Voucher_Num
12977	10392
12977	10393

following period. The auditor should test the mathematical accuracy of payroll summaries and trace totals to the payroll records and to the general ledger accounts. The average salary per employee in the current period can be compared to the previous year's averages. ACL's *Stratify* feature can help the auditor detect unusual trends and abnormal balances in the payroll file. Substantive tests of details, however, are normally not performed on payroll expense accounts unless analytical procedures or severe weaknesses in internal controls indicate the need for additional testing.

SUMMARY

This chapter examined audit procedures associated with the expenditure cycle. It began with a review of alternative technologies used in both legacy and modern systems. The focus was on the key operational tasks that constitute the purchases, cash disbursement, and payroll procedures. The second section explained expenditure cycle audit objectives, controls, and tests of controls that an auditor normally performs. Evidence from such procedures is used to determine the nature, timing, and extent of substantive tests. The last section described substantive tests in relation to expenditure cycle assertions based upon ACL software applications.

Appendix

Overview of Purchases and Cash Disbursements Activities

In this section of the appendix we examine the expenditure cycle conceptually. Using data flow diagrams (DFDs) as a guide, we will trace the sequence of activities through two of the processes that constitute the expenditure cycle for most retail, wholesale, and manufacturing organizations. These are purchases processing and cash disbursements procedures. Payroll procedures are presented in the next section of the appendix.

This discussion is intended to be technology-neutral. The tasks described here may be performed manually or by computer. At this point our focus is on what (conceptually) needs to be done, not how (physically) it is accomplished. At various stages in the processes, we will examine specific documents, journals, and ledgers as they are encountered. Again, this review is technology-neutral. These documents and files may be physical (hard copy) or digital (computer generated). In the main body of the chapter we examine examples of physical systems.

Purchases Processing Procedures

Purchases procedures include the tasks involved in identifying inventory needs, placing the order, receiving the inventory, and recognizing the liability. The relationships between these tasks are presented with the DFD in Figure 10.14. In general, these procedures apply to both manufacturing and retailing firms. A major difference between the two business types lies in the way purchases are authorized. Manufacturing firms purchase raw materials for production, and their purchasing decisions are authorized by the production planning and control function. Merchandising firms purchase finished goods for resale. The inventory control function provides the purchase authorization for this type of firm.

Monitor Inventory Records. Firms deplete their inventories by transferring raw materials into the production process (the conversion cycle) and by selling finished goods to customers (revenue cycle). Our illustration assumes the latter case, in which inventory control monitors and records finished goods inventory levels. When inventories drop to a predetermined reorder point, a **purchase requisition** is prepared and sent to the prepare purchase order function to initiate the purchase process. Figure 10.15 presents an example of a purchase requisition.

Although procedures will vary from firm to firm; typically a separate purchase requisition will be prepared for each inventory item as the need is recognized. This can result in multiple purchase requisitions for a given vendor. These purchase requisitions need to be combined into a single purchase order (discussed next), which is then sent to the vendor. In this type of system, each purchase order will be associated with one or more purchase requisitions.

Prepare Purchase Order. The Prepare Purchase Order function receives the purchase requisitions that are sorted by vendor if necessary. Next, a **purchase order (PO)** is prepared for each vendor, as illustrated in Figure 10.16. A copy of the PO is sent to the

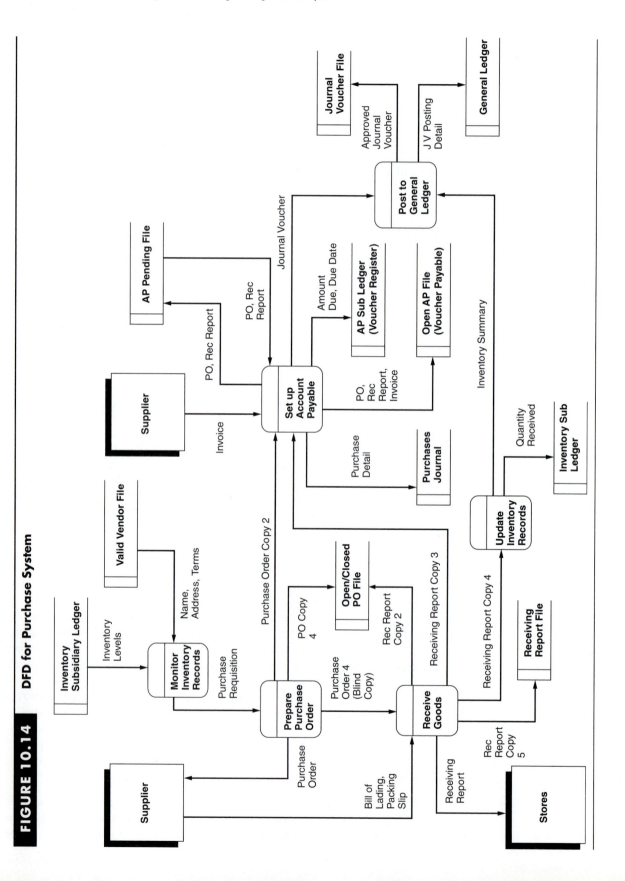

FIGURE 10.14   DFD for Purchase System

FIGURE 10.15   **Purchase Requisition**

Hampshire Supply Co.				No. 89631
Purchase Requisition				

Suggested Vendor — *Jones and Harper Co.*
1620 North Main St.
Bethlehem PA 18017

Date Prepared		Date Needed	
8/15/2009		*9/1/2009*	

Part No.	Quantity	Description	Unit Price	Extended Price
86329	*200*	*Engine Block Core Plug*	*$1.10*	*$220*

Prepared By: *RBJ*	Approved By: *THJ*	Total Amount *$220.00*	Vendor Account *4001*

vendor. In addition, a copy is sent to the set up accounts payable (AP) function for filing temporarily in the AP pending file, and a blind copy is sent to the receive goods function, where it is held until the inventories arrive. The last copy is filed in the **open/closed purchase order file.**

To make the purchasing process efficient, the inventory control function will supply much of the routine ordering information that the purchasing department needs directly from the inventory and **valid vendor** files. This information includes the name and address of the primary supplier, the economic order quantity (EOQ) of the item, and the standard or expected unit cost of the item. This allows the purchasing department to devote its efforts to meeting scarce, expensive, or unusual inventory needs. To obtain the best prices and terms on special items, the purchasing department may need to prepare detailed product specifications and request bids from competing vendors. Dealing with routine purchases as efficiently as good control permits is desirable in all organizations. The valid vendor file contributes to both control and efficiency by listing only those vendors approved to do business with the organization. This reference helps to reduce certain vendor fraud schemes discussed in Chapter 12.

Receive Goods.   Most firms encounter a time lag (sometimes a significant one) between placing the order and receiving the inventory. During this time, the copies of the PO reside in temporary files in various departments. Note that no economic event has yet occurred. At this point, the firm has received no inventories and incurred no financial obligation. Hence, there is no basis for making a formal entry into any accounting

FIGURE 10.16	Purchase Order

Hampshire Supply Co.
Purchase Order

No. 23591

Please show the above number on all shipping documents and invoices.

To : Jones and Harper Co.
1620 North Main St.
Bethlehem PA 18017

Vendor Number	Date Ordered		Date Needed	Purchasing Agent	Terms
4001		8/15/09	9/1/09	J. Buell	2/10, n/30

Purchase Req. No.	Part No.	Quantity	Description	Unit Price	Extended Price
89631	86329	200	Engine Block Core Plug	$ 1.10	$220.00
89834	20671	100	Brake Shoes	9.50	950.00
89851	45218	10	Spring Compressors	33.00	330.00

Prepared By :	BKG	Approved By :	RMS	Total Amount	$1,500.00

record. However, firms often make memo entries of pending inventory receipts and associated obligations.

The next event in the expenditure cycle is the receipt of the inventory. Goods arriving from the vendor are reconciled with the blind copy of the PO. The **blind copy**, illustrated in Figure 10.17, contains no quantity or price information about the products being received. The purpose of the blind copy is to force the receiving clerk to count and inspect inventories prior to completing the receiving report. At times, receiving docks are very busy and receiving staff are under pressure to unload the delivery trucks and sign the bills of lading so the truck drivers can go on their way. If receiving clerks are only provided quantity information, they may be tempted to accept deliveries on the basis of this information alone, rather than verify the quantity and condition of the goods. Shipments that are short or contain damaged or incorrect items must be detected before the firm accepts and places the goods in inventory. The blind copy is an important device in reducing this exposure.

Upon completion of the physical count and inspection, the receiving clerk prepares a **receiving report** stating the quantity and condition of the inventories. Figure 10.18 contains an example of a receiving report. One copy of the receiving report accompanies the physical inventories to either the raw materials storeroom or finished goods warehouse for safekeeping. Another copy is filed in the open/closed PO file to close out the purchase order. A third copy of the receiving report is sent to the AP department, where it is filed in the **AP pending file**. A fourth copy of the receiving report is sent to inventory control for updating the inventory records. Finally, a copy of the receiving report is placed in the **receiving report file**.

FIGURE 10.17   **Blind Copy Purchase Order**

Hampshire Supply Co.
Purchase Order

No. 23591

Please show the above number on all shipping documents and invoices.

To : Jones and Harper Co.
1620 North Main St.
Bethlehem PA 18017

Vendor Number	Date Ordered		Date Needed	Purchasing Agent	Terms
4001		8/15/09	9/1/09	J. Buell	2/10, n/30

Purchase Req. No.	Part No.	Quantity	Description	Unit Price	Extended Price
89631	86329		Engine Block Core Plug		
89834	20671		Brake Shoes		
89851	45218		Spring Compressors		

Prepared By :	Approved By :	Total Amount
BKG	RMS	

FIGURE 10.18   **Receiving Report**

Hampshire Supply Co.
Receiving Report

No. 62311

Vendor	Jones and Harper Co.	Shipped Via :	Vendor
Purchase Order No.	23591	Date Received	9/1/09

Part No.	Quantity	Description	Condition
86329	200	Engine Block Core Plug	Good
20671	100	Brake Shoes	Good
45218	10	Spring Compressors	Ear on one unit bent

Received By:	Inspected By:	Delivered To:
RTS	LEW	DYT

FIGURE 10.19 Inventory Subsidiary Ledger Using Standard Cost

HAMPSHIRE MACHINE CO.

Perpetual Inventory Record—Item #86329

Item Description	Units Received	Units Sold	Qnty on Hand	Reorder Point	Qnty on Order	EOC	Vendor Number	Standard Cost	Total Inven. Cost
Engine Block Core Plug	200		200	30		200	4001	1.10	220
		30	170						187
		20	150						165

Update Inventory Records. Depending on the inventory valuation method in place, the inventory control procedures may vary somewhat among firms. Organizations that use a **standard cost system** carry their inventories at a predetermined standard value regardless of the price actually paid to the vendor. Figure 10.19 presents a copy of a standard cost inventory ledger.

Posting to a standard cost inventory ledger requires only information about the quantities received. Because the receiving report contains quantity information, it serves this purpose. Updating an **actual cost inventory ledger** requires additional financial information, such as a copy of the supplier's invoice when it arrives.

Set Up Accounts Payable. During the course of this transaction, the set up AP function has received and temporarily filed copies of the PO and receiving report. The organization has received inventories from the vendor and has incurred (realized) an obligation to pay for the goods.

At this point in the process, however, the firm has not received the **supplier's invoice**[5] containing the financial information needed to record the transaction. The firm will thus defer recording (recognizing) the liability until the invoice arrives. This common situation creates a slight lag (a few days) in the recording process, during which time the firm's liabilities are technically understated. As a practical matter, this misstatement is a problem only at period-end when the firm prepares financial statements. To close the books, the accountant will need to estimate the value of the obligation until the invoice arrives. If the estimate is materially incorrect, an adjusting entry must be made to correct the error. Because the receipt of the invoice typically triggers AP procedures, accountants need to be aware that unrecorded liabilities may exist at period-end closing.

When the invoice arrives, the AP clerk reconciles the financial information with the receiving report and PO in the pending file. This is called a three-way match, which verifies that what was ordered was received and is fairly priced. Once the reconciliation is complete, the transaction is recorded in the purchases journal and posted to the

---

5   Note that the supplier's invoice in the buyer's expenditure cycle is the sales invoice of the supplier's revenue cycle.

supplier's account in the **AP subsidiary ledger**. Figure 10.20 shows the relationship between these accounting records.

Recall that the inventory valuation method will determine how inventory control will have recorded the receipt of inventories. If the firm is using the actual cost method, the AP clerk would send a copy of the supplier's invoice to inventory control. If standard costing is used, this step is not necessary.

After recording the liability, the AP clerk transfers all source documents (PO, receiving report, and invoice) to the **open AP file**. Typically, this file is organized by payment due date and scanned daily to ensure that debts are paid on the last possible date without missing due dates and losing discounts. We examine cash disbursements procedures later in this section. Finally, the AP clerk summarizes the entries in the purchases journal for the period (or batch) and prepares a journal voucher for the general ledger function (see Figure 10.20). Assuming the organization uses the perpetual inventory method, the journal entry will be:

	DR	CR
Inventory—Control	6,800.00	
Accounts Payable—Control		6,800.00

If the periodic inventory method is used, the entry will be:

	DR	CR
Purchases	6,800.00	
Accounts Payable—Control		6,800.00

Vouchers Payable System

Rather than using the AP procedures described in the previous section, many firms use a **vouchers payable system**. Under this system, the AP department uses **cash disbursement vouchers** and maintains a voucher register. After the AP clerk performs the three-way match, he or she prepares a cash disbursement voucher to approve payment. Vouchers provide improved control over cash disbursements and allow firms to consolidate several payments to the same supplier on a single voucher, thus reducing the number of checks written. Figure 10.21 shows an example of a cash disbursement voucher.

Each voucher is recorded in the **voucher register**, as illustrated in Figure 10.22. The voucher register reflects the AP liability of the firm. The sum of the unpaid vouchers in the register (those with no check numbers and paid dates) is the firm's total AP balance. The AP clerk files the cash disbursement voucher, along with supporting source documents, in the **vouchers payable file.** This file is equivalent to the open AP file discussed earlier and also is organized by due date. The DFD in Figure 10.14 illustrates both liability recognition methods.

Post to General Ledger. The general ledger function receives a journal voucher from the AP department and an account summary from inventory control. The general ledger function posts from the journal voucher to the inventory and AP control accounts and reconciles the inventory control account and the inventory subsidiary summary. The approved journal vouchers are then posted to the journal voucher file. With this step, the purchases phase of the expenditure cycle is completed.

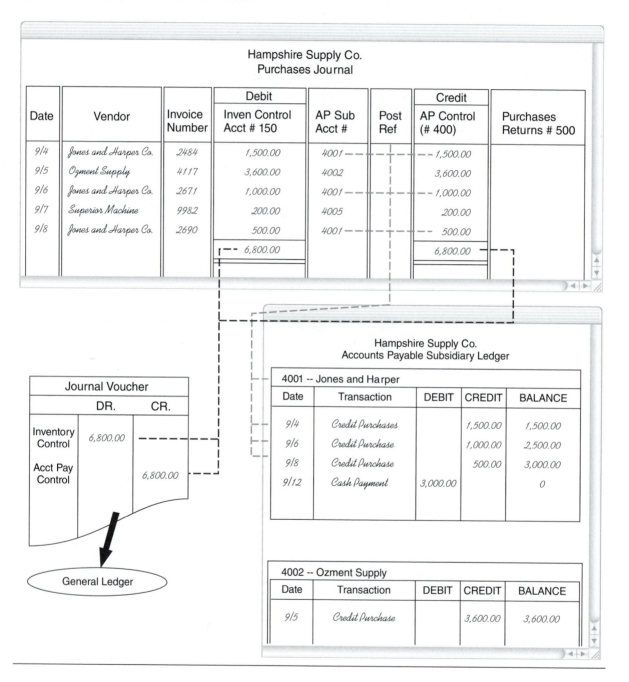

FIGURE 10.21 **Cash Disbursement Voucher**

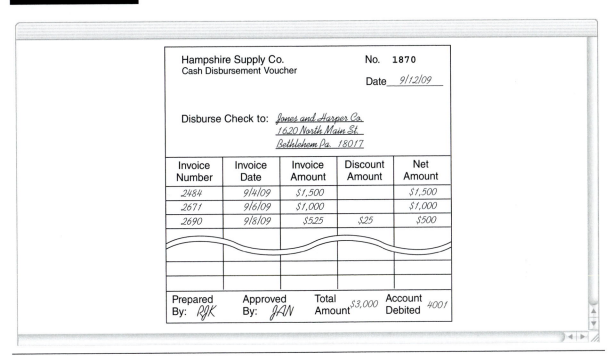

FIGURE 10.22 **Voucher Register**

		Paid								Misc. Debits	
Date	Voucher No.	Check No.	Date	Voucher Payable (Credit)	Merchandise Debit	Supplies Debit	Selling Expense Debit	Administrative Expense Debit	Fixed Assets Debit	Acct. No.	Amount
9/12/09	1870	104	9/14	3,000	3,000						
9/13/09	1871			3,600		3,600					
9/14/09	1872	105	9/15	500			500				

The Cash Disbursements Systems

The cash disbursements system processes the payment of obligations created in the purchases system. The principal objective of this system is to ensure that only valid creditors receive payment and that amounts paid are timely and correct. If the system makes payments early, the firm forgoes interest income that it could have earned on the funds. If obligations are paid late, however, the firm will lose purchase discounts or may damage its credit standing. Figure 10.23 presents a DFD conceptually depicting the information flows and key tasks of the cash disbursements system.

Identify Liabilities Due.   The cash disbursements process begins in the AP department by identifying items that have come due. Each day, the AP function reviews the open AP file (or vouchers payable file) for such items and sends payment approval in the form of a voucher packet (the voucher and/or supporting documents) to the cash disbursements department.

Prepare Cash Disbursement.   The cash disbursements clerk receives the voucher packet and reviews the documents for completeness and clerical accuracy. For each disbursement, the clerk prepares a check and records the check number, dollar amount, voucher number, and other pertinent data in the **check register**, which is also called the **cash disbursements journal.** Figure 10.24 shows an example of a check register.

Depending on the organization's materiality threshold, the check may require additional approval by the cash disbursements department manager or treasurer (not shown in Figure 5-10). The negotiable portion of the check is mailed to the supplier, and a copy of it is attached to the voucher packet as proof of payment. The clerk marks the documents in the voucher packets paid and returns them to the AP clerk. Finally, the cash

---

FIGURE 10.23   **DFD for Cash Disbursements System**

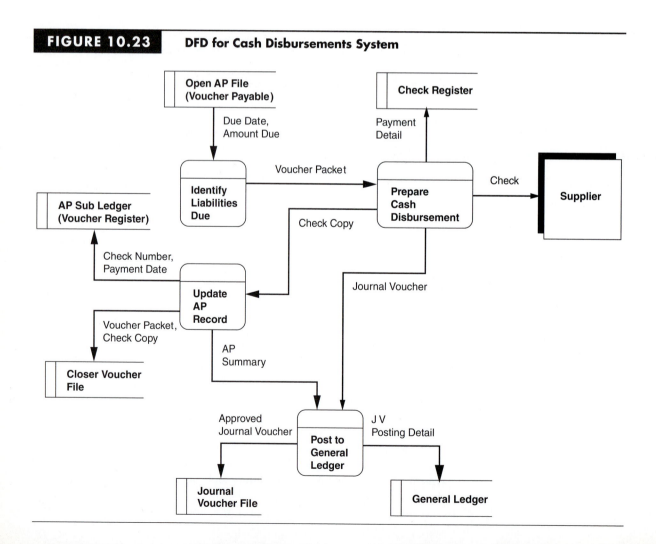

FIGURE 10.24	Cash Disbursements Journal (Check Register)

Cash Disbursements Journal

Date	Check No.	Voucher No.	Description	Credit		GL / Subsidiary Account Debited	Posted	Vouch Pay 401	Freight-in 516	Op Expen 509	Other	Posted
				Cash	Purch. Disc.							
9/4/09	101	1867	Martin Motors	500		Auto					500	✓
9/4/09	102	1868	Pen Power	100		Utility	✓			100		
9/12/09	103	1869	Acme Auto	500		Purchases					500	✓
9/14/09	104	1870	Jones and Harper	3,000				3,000				

disbursements clerk summarizes the entries made to the check register and sends a journal voucher with the following journal entry to the general ledger department:

	DR	CR
Accounts Payable	XXXX.XX	
Cash		XXXX.XX

Update AP Record. Upon receipt of the voucher packet, the AP clerk removes the liability by debiting the AP subsidiary account or by recording the check number and payment date in the voucher register. The voucher packet is filed in the closed voucher file, and an account summary is prepared and sent to the general ledger function.

Post to General Ledger. The general ledger function receives the journal voucher from cash disbursements and the account summary from AP. The voucher shows the total reductions in the firm's obligations and cash account as a result of payments to suppliers. These numbers are reconciled with the AP summary, and the AP control and cash accounts in the general ledger are updated accordingly. The approved journal voucher is then filed. This concludes the cash disbursements procedures.

Overview of Payroll Activities

Specific payroll procedures vary among firms and industries. To illustrate the key features, however, Figure 10.25 presents a data flow diagram (DFD) of a manufacturing firm's payroll system. The functions presented in the DFD are described in the following paragraphs.

Personnel Department

The personnel department prepares and submits **personnel action forms** to the prepare payroll function. These documents identify employees authorized to receive a paycheck and are used to reflect changes in hourly pay rates, payroll deductions, and job classification. Figure 10.26 shows a personnel action form used to advise payroll of an increase in an employee's salary.

FIGURE 10.25   **DFD of Payroll Procedures**

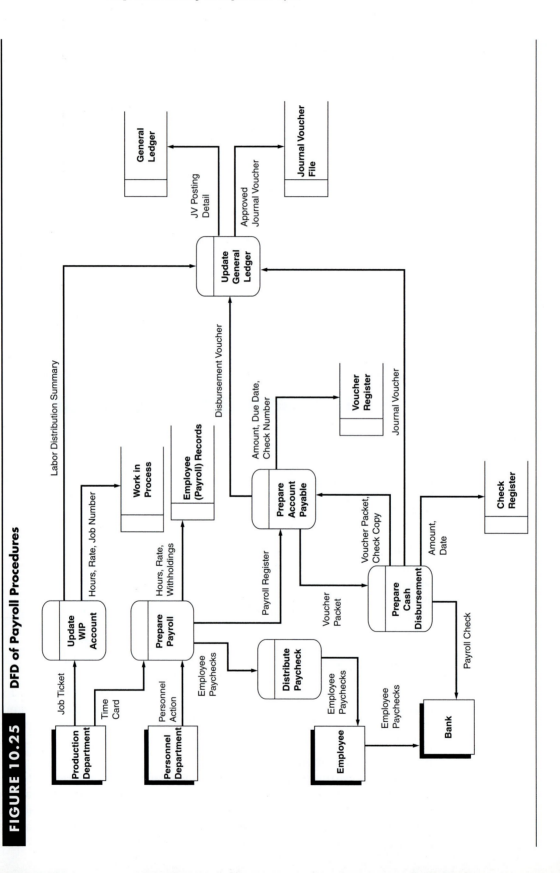

Production Department

Production employees prepare two types of time records: job tickets and time cards. **Job tickets** capture the time that individual workers spend on each production job. Cost accounting uses these documents to allocate direct labor charges to work-in-process (WIP) accounts. **Time cards** capture the time the employee is at work. These are sent to the prepare payroll function for calculating the amount of the employee's paycheck. Figure 10.27 illustrates a job ticket, and Figure 10.28 illustrates a time card.

Each day at the beginning of the shift, employees place their time cards in a special clock that records the time. Typically, they clock out for lunch and at the end of the shift. This time card is the formal record of daily attendance. At the end of the week, the supervisor reviews, signs, and sends the time cards to the payroll department.

Update WIP Account

After cost accounting allocates labor costs to the WIP accounts, the charges are summarized in a **labor distribution summary** and forwarded to the general ledger function.

Prepare Payroll

The payroll department receives pay rate and withholding data from the personnel department and hours-worked data from the production department. A clerk in payroll then performs the following tasks.

1. Prepares the payroll register (Figure 10.29) showing gross pay, deductions, overtime pay, and net pay.
2. Enters the above information into the employee payroll records (Figure 10.30).
3. Prepares employee paychecks (Figure 10.31).
4. Sends the paychecks to the distribute paycheck function.
5. Files the time cards, personnel action form, and copy of the payroll register (not shown).

Distribute Paycheck

A form of payroll fraud involves submitting time cards for nonexistent employees. To prevent this, many companies use a paymaster to distribute the paychecks to employees. This individual is independent of the payroll process—not involved in payroll authorization or preparation tasks. If a valid employee does not claim a paycheck, the paymaster returns the check to payroll. The reason the check went unclaimed can then be investigated.

Prepare Accounts Payable

The accounts payable (AP) clerk reviews the payroll register for correctness and prepares copies of a cash disbursement voucher for the amount of the payroll. The clerk records the voucher in the voucher register and submits the voucher packet (voucher and payroll register) to cash disbursements. A copy of the disbursement voucher is sent to the general ledger function.

Prepare Cash Disbursement

Upon receipt of the voucher packet, the cash disbursements function prepares a single check for the entire amount of the payroll and deposits it in the payroll imprest account. The employee paychecks are drawn on this account, which is used only for payroll. Funds must be transferred from the general cash account to this imprest account before the paychecks can be cashed. The clerk sends a copy of the check along with the disbursement voucher and the payroll register to the AP department, where they are filed (not shown). Finally, a journal voucher is prepared and sent to the general ledger function.

FIGURE 10.26   **Personnel Action Form**

Salary Increase Recommendation

Based on the attached appraisal form, the following recommendation is made for:

Name:	*Jane Doe*
Position:	*Accounting Clerk*
Social Security Number:	*111 – 22 – 3333*

Current Salary:	*23,520.00*
Current Bonus Level:	*00%*
Last Increase Date:	*08/22/08*
Next Increase Date:	*08/22/09*

Current Performance Rating:
(from attached appraisal)   *good*

Salary Increase Guidelines:

Outstanding:	6–9%	9–12 months
Superior:	4–6%	12 months
Good:	3–4%	12–15 months
Provisional:	0%	Review again in 90 days.

In view of the Current Performance and the Salary Increase Guidelines, I recommend the following salary treatment:

Percentage Increase:	*4* %
New Salary:	$ *24,460*
Effective Date:	*8* / *22* / *09*

Promotions:
In the case of a promotion, a standard 5% increase for the promotion and a prorated merit increase (based on time since last merit increase) are appropriate. The next increase will be considered from the date of promotion.

Other Considerations:
In some situations, it is possible to advance a salary beyond the above guidelines as an exception, with the President's approval. Some typical situations are, but are not limited to, equity adjustment and job reevaluation. If such is the case here, please provide justification below:

Approvals: *J. R. Johnson*   Supervisor
                            H. M. Morris   Director of Personnel

Exception approval if needed: *N/A*   President

Update General Ledger

The general ledger function receives the labor distribution summary from cost accounting, the disbursement voucher from AP, and the journal voucher from cash disbursements. With this information, the general ledger clerk makes the following accounting entries:

FROM THE LABOR DISTRIBUTION SUMMARY

	DR	CR
Work-in-Process (Direct Labor)	XXX.XX	
Factory Overhead (Indirect Labor)	XXX.XX	
Wages Payable		XXX.XX

FROM DISBURSEMENT VOUCHER

	DR	CR
Wages Payable	XXX.XX	
Cash		XXX.XX
Federal Income Tax Withholdings Payable		XXX.XX
State Income Tax Withholdings Payable		XXX.XX
FICA Income Tax Withholdings Payable		XXX.XX
Group Insurance Premiums Payable		XXX.XX
Pension Fund Withholdings Payable		XXX.XX
Union Dues Payable		XXX.XX

The debits and credits from these entries must equal. If they do not, there is an error in the calculation of either labor distribution charges or payroll. When the equality has been verified, the clerk files the voucher and labor distribution summary.

FIGURE 10.27 **Job Ticket**

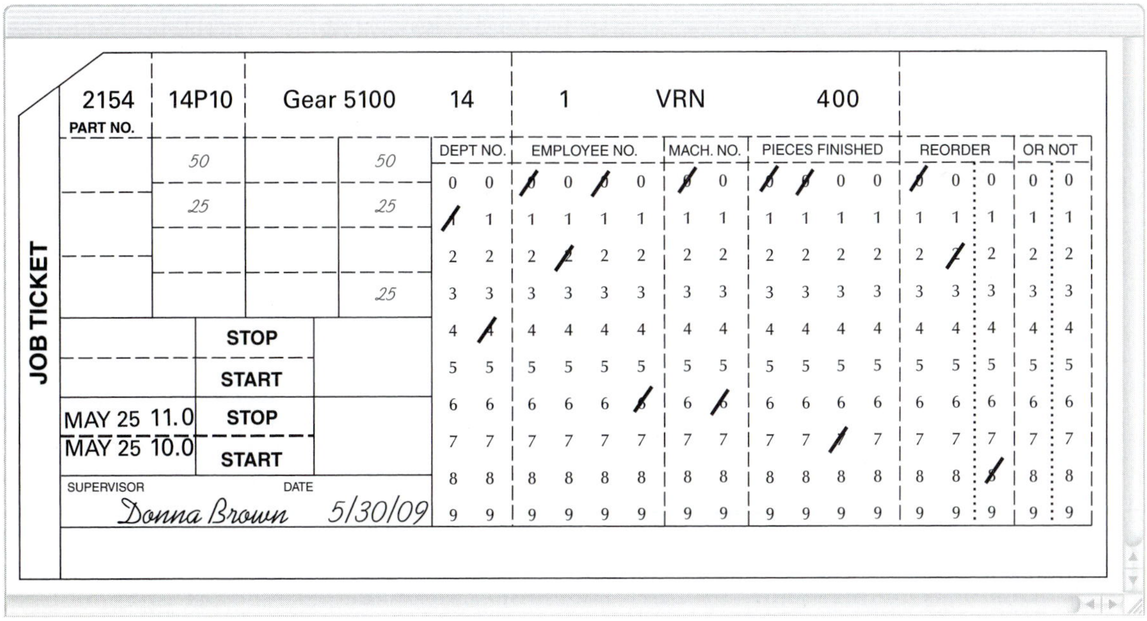

FIGURE 10.28   **Time Card**

No.	447–32–4773			Pay End	June 15, 2009	
Name	Joe Smith			Signature	JAM	

			Out	In	M	8:02
		SUNDAY	In	Out	M	12:40
			Out	In	M	13:34
			In	Out	M	17:05
			Out	In	TU	8:00
		SATURDAY	In	Out	TU	11:06
			Out	In		
			In	Out		
			Out	In	W	8:15
		FRIDAY	In	Out	W	12:35
			Out	In	W	13:04
			In	Out	W	17:06
			Out	In	TH	12:02
		THURSDAY	In	Out	TH	16:02
			Out	In	TH	16:08
			In	Out	TH	21:08
			Out	In	FR	8:14
		WEDNESDAY	In	Out	FR	11:45
			Out	In	FR	12:42
			In	Out	FR	17:32
			Out	In	SA	9:08
		TUESDAY	In	Out	SA	12:00
			Out	In		
			In	Out		
			Out	In		
		MONDAY	In	Out		
			Out	In		
			In	Out		

SECOND WEEK	FIRST WEEK

K14-32

FIGURE 10.29   **Payroll Register**

H͖C HAMPSHIRE SUPPLY COMPANY

Payroll register for period ending   10/31/09
Checks: All
Employee(s): All

Check# 5000   Paid to Emp# CAS : CASEY, SUE

PAY	Hours	Rate	Gross	DEDUCTIONS	
Regular	173.33		1,000.00	SD SDI	9.00
Overtime			0.00	HL INSUR	100.00
Sick			0.00	SV SAVINGS	100.00
Holiday			0.00		0.00
Vacation			0.00	Fed. withholding	16.25
			0.00	Addl. fed. withholding	0.00
				State withholding	21.77
Totals	173.33		1,000.00	Social Security	62.00
				Medicare	14.50
Days worked 21				NET PAY	676.48

Check# 5001   Paid to Emp# JON : JONES, JESSICA

PAY	Hours	Rate	Gross	DEDUCTIONS	
Regular	173.33	15.00	2,599.95	SD SDI	23.40
Overtime		30.00	0.00	HL INSUR	100.00
Sick		15.00	0.00	SV SAVINGS	260.00
Holiday		45.00	0.00		0.00
Vacation		15.00	0.00	Fed. withholding	256.24
			0.00	Addl. fed. withholding	0.00
				State withholding	116.98
Totals	173.33		2,599.95	Social Security	161.20
				Medicare	37.70
Days worked 21				NET PAY	1,644.43

Check# 5002   Paid to Emp # ROB : ROBERTS, WILLIAM

PAY	Hours	Rate	Gross	DEDUCTIONS	
Regular	173.33	15.00	2,599.95	SD SDI	23.40
Overtime		30.00	0.00	HL INSUR	100.00
Sick		15.00	0.00	SV SAVINGS	260.00
Holiday		45.00	0.00		0.00
Vacation		15.00	0.00	Fed. withholding	396.07
			0.00	Addl. fed. withholding	0.00
				State withholding	208.04
Totals	173.33		2,599.95	Social Security	161.20
				Medicare	37.70
Days worked 21				NET PAY	1,413.54

FIGURE 10.30   **Employee Payroll Record**

H₂C HAMPSHIRE SUPPLY COMPANY

Employee pay and earnings information

Period Ending   10/31/09

Emp# : JON   SS# : 682–63–0897   JESSICA JONES

Rate: 15.00/hour

Addl   FITW/check: 0.00

Normal deduction(s)			Amount
Ded 1 SD	%	0.9000	0.00
Ded 2 HL	%	0.0000	100.00
Ded 3 SV	%	10.0000	0.00
Ded 4	%	0.0000	0.00

Earnings:	– Quarter to date –		— Year to date —	
	Hours	Amount	Hours	Amount
Regular	173.3	2,599.95	173.3	2,599.95
Overtime	0.0	0.00	0.0	0.00
Sick	0.0	0.00	0.0	0.00
Vacation	0.0	0.00	0.0	0.00
Holiday	0.0	0.00	0.0	0.00
	0.0	0.00	0.0	0.00
Withholding:				
FIT		256.24		256.24
SIT		116.98		116.98
Social Security		161.20		161.20
Medicare		37.70		37.70
Deductions:				
SDI		23.40		23.40
HEALTH INSUR		100.00		100.00
SAVINGS		260.00		260.00
		0.00		0.00

FIGURE 10.31 **Employee Paycheck**

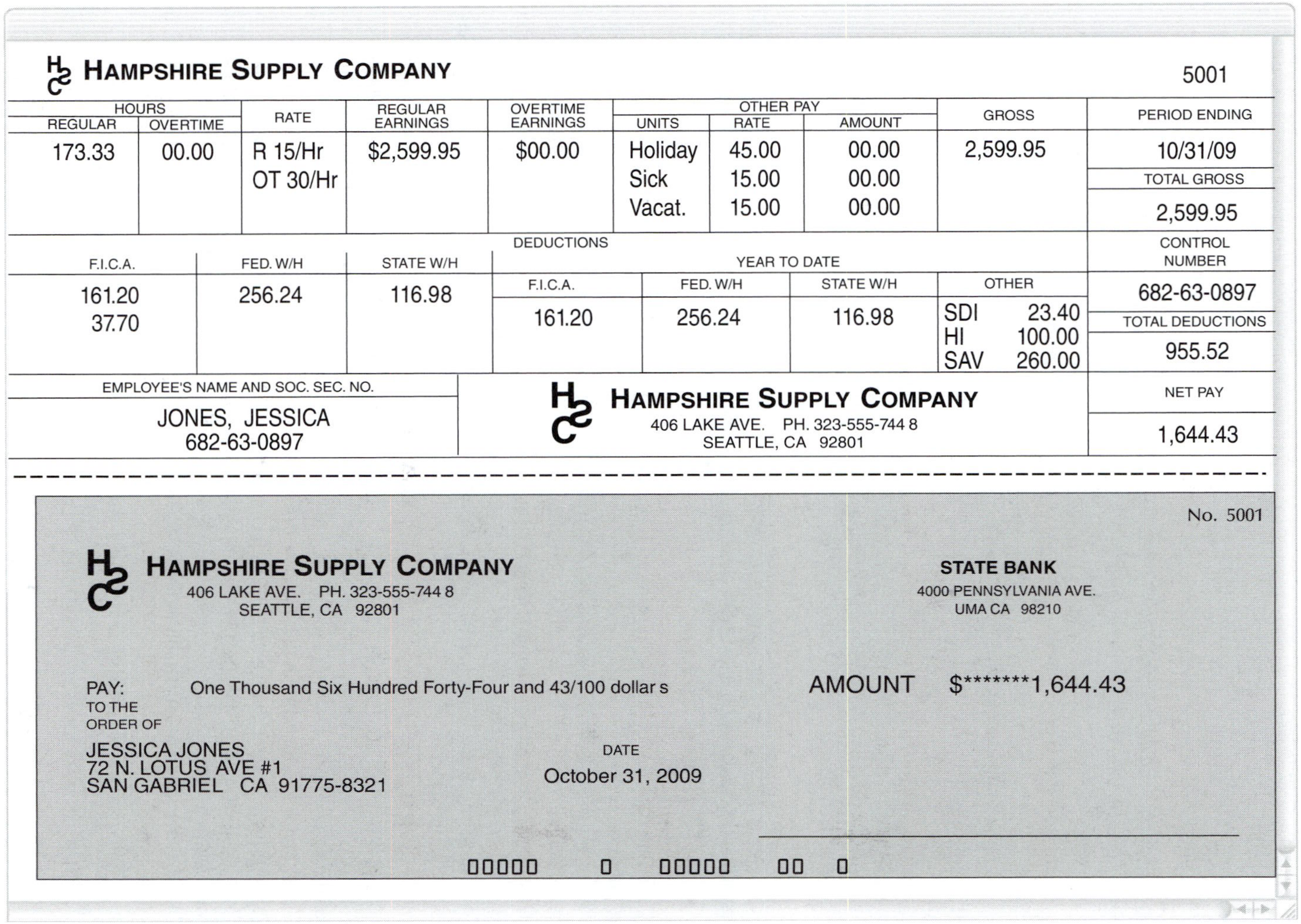

HAMPSHIRE SUPPLY COMPANY — 5001

HOURS REGULAR	HOURS OVERTIME	RATE	REGULAR EARNINGS	OVERTIME EARNINGS	OTHER PAY UNITS	OTHER PAY RATE	OTHER PAY AMOUNT	GROSS	PERIOD ENDING
173.33	00.00	R 15/Hr OT 30/Hr	$2,599.95	$00.00	Holiday Sick Vacat.	45.00 15.00 15.00	00.00 00.00 00.00	2,599.95	10/31/09 TOTAL GROSS 2,599.95

DEDUCTIONS

F.I.C.A.	FED. W/H	STATE W/H	YEAR TO DATE F.I.C.A.	YEAR TO DATE FED. W/H	YEAR TO DATE STATE W/H	YEAR TO DATE OTHER	CONTROL NUMBER
161.20 37.70	256.24	116.98	161.20	256.24	116.98	SDI 23.40 HI 100.00 SAV 260.00	682-63-0897 TOTAL DEDUCTIONS 955.52

EMPLOYEE'S NAME AND SOC. SEC. NO.		NET PAY
JONES, JESSICA 682-63-0897	HAMPSHIRE SUPPLY COMPANY 406 LAKE AVE. PH. 323-555-744 8 SEATTLE, CA 92801	1,644.43

No. 5001

HAMPSHIRE SUPPLY COMPANY
406 LAKE AVE. PH. 323-555-744 8
SEATTLE, CA 92801

STATE BANK
4000 PENNSYLVANIA AVE.
UMA CA 98210

PAY: One Thousand Six Hundred Forty-Four and 43/100 dollar s

AMOUNT $*******1,644.43

TO THE ORDER OF
JESSICA JONES
72 N. LOTUS AVE #1
SAN GABRIEL CA 91775-8321

DATE
October 31, 2009

00000 0 00000 00 0

KEY TERMS

actual cost inventory ledger
AP pending file
AP subsidiary ledger
attendance file
blind copy
cash disbursements journal
cash disbursement vouchers
check register
disbursement voucher file
employee file
human resource management (HRM) system
inventory subsidiary file
Job tickets
labor distribution summary
labor usage file
open AP file
paymaster

payroll imprest account
personnel action forms
purchase order (PO)
purchase requisition
receiving report
receiving report file
standard cost system
supplier's (vendor's) invoice
Time cards
transaction listing
transaction log
valid vendor file
vendor's invoice
vouchers payable file
vouchers payable system
voucher register

REVIEW QUESTIONS

1. Differentiate between a purchase requisition and a purchase order.
2. What purpose does a purchasing department serve?
3. Distinguish between an accounts payable file and a vouchers payable file.
4. What are the three logical steps of the cash disbursements system?
5. What general ledger journal entries are triggered by the purchases system?
6. What two types of exposure can close supervision of the receiving department reduce?
7. What steps of independent verification does the general ledger department perform?
8. What is (are) the purpose(s) of maintaining a valid vendor file?
9. What is the purpose of the blind copy of a purchase order?
10. Give one advantage of using a vouchers payable system.

11. How do computerized purchasing systems help to reduce the risk of purchasing bottlenecks?
12. Which document is used by cost accounting to allocate direct labor charges to work-in-process?
13. Which department authorizes changes in employee pay rates?
14. Why should the employee's supervisor not distribute paychecks?
15. Why should employee paychecks be drawn against a special checking account?
16. Why should employees clocking on and off the job be supervised?
17. What is a personnel action form?
18. What tasks does a payroll clerk perform upon receipt of hours-worked data from the production department?
19. What documents constitute the audit trail for payroll?

DISCUSSION QUESTIONS

1. What is the importance of the job ticket? Illustrate the flow of this document and its information from inception to impact on the financial statements.
2. What documents support the payment of an invoice? Discuss where these documents originate and the resulting control implications.
3. Discuss the time lags between realizing and recognizing economic events in the purchase and payroll systems. What is the accounting profession's view on this matter as it pertains to these two systems?
4. Discuss the importance of supervision controls in the receiving department and the reasons behind blind fields on the receiving report, such as quantity and price.
5. How does the procedure for determining inventory requirements differ between a basic batch processing system and batch processing with real-time data input of sales and receipts of inventory?
6. What advantages are achieved in choosing:
   a. a basic batch computer system over a manual system?
   b. a batch system with real-time data input over a basic batch system?
7. Discuss the major control implications of batch systems with real-time data input. What compensating procedures are available?
8. Discuss some specific examples of how information systems can reduce time lags that positively affect an organization.
9. Discuss some service industries that may require their workers to use job tickets.
10. Payroll is often used as a good example of batch processing using sequential files. Explain why.

MULTIPLE-CHOICE QUESTIONS

1. Which document helps to ensure that the receiving clerks actually count the number of goods received?
   a. packing list
   b. blind copy of purchase order
   c. shipping notice
   d. invoice
2. When the goods are received and the receiving report has been prepared, which ledger may be updated?
   a. standard cost inventory ledger
   b. inventory subsidiary ledger
   c. general ledger
   d. accounts payable subsidiary ledger
3. Which statement is *not* correct for an expenditure system with proper internal controls?
   a. Cash disbursements maintain the check register.
   b. Accounts payable maintains the accounts payable subsidiary ledger.
   c. Accounts payable is responsible for paying invoices.
   d. Accounts payable is responsible for authorizing invoices.
4. Which duties should be segregated?
   a. matching purchase requisitions, receiving reports, and invoices and authorizing payment
   b. authorizing payment and maintaining the check register
   c. writing checks and maintaining the check register
   d. authorizing payment and maintaining the accounts payable subsidiary ledger
5. Which documents would an auditor most likely choose to examine closely in order to ascertain that all expenditures incurred during the accounting period have been recorded as a liability?
   a. invoices
   b. purchase orders
   c. purchase requisitions
   d. receiving reports
6. Which task must still require human intervention in an automated purchases/cash disbursements system?
   a. determination of inventory requirements
   b. preparation of a purchase order
   c. preparation of a receiving report
   d. preparation of a check register

7. In a well-designed internal control structure, two tasks that should be performed by different persons are
   a. preparation of purchase orders and authorization of monthly payroll.
   b. preparation of bank reconciliations and recording of cash disbursements.
   c. distribution of payroll checks and approval of credit sales.
   d. posting of amounts from both the cash receipts journal and cash disbursements journal to the general ledger.
   e. posting of amounts from the cash receipts journal to the general ledger and distribution of payroll checks.

8. Which one of the following situations represents a strength in the internal control for purchasing and accounts payable?
   a. Prenumbered receiving reports are issued randomly.
   b. Invoices are approved for payment by the purchasing department.
   c. Unmatched receiving reports are reviewed on an annual basis.
   d. Vendors' invoices are matched against purchase orders and receiving reports before a liability is recorded.
   e. The purchasing department reconciles the accounts payable subsidiary vendor ledger with the general ledger control account.

9. Which of the following tasks should the cash disbursement clerk NOT perform?
   a. review the supporting documents for completeness and accuracy
   b. prepare checks
   c. approve the liability
   d. mark the supporting documents paid

10. Which of the following is true?
    a. The cash disbursement function is part of accounts payable.
    b. Cash disbursements is an independent accounting function.
    c. Cash disbursements is a treasury function.
    d. The cash disbursement function is part of the general ledger department.

11. The document that captures the total amount of time that individual workers spend on each production job is called a

    a. time card.
    b. job ticket.
    c. personnel action form.
    d. labor distribution form.

12. An important reconciliation in the payroll system is when
    a. the general ledger department compares the labor distribution summary from cost accounting to the disbursement voucher from accounts payable.
    b. the personnel department compares the number of employees authorized to receive a paycheck to the number of paychecks prepared.
    c. the production department compares the number of hours reported on job tickets to the number of hours reported on time cards.
    d. the payroll department compares the labor distribution summary to the hours reported on time cards.

13. Which internal control is not an important part of the payroll system?
    a. supervisors verify the accuracy of employee time cards
    b. paychecks are distributed by an independent paymaster
    c. the accounts payable department verifies the accuracy of the payroll register before transferring payroll funds to the general checking account
    d. the general ledger department reconciles the labor distribution summary and the payroll disbursement voucher

14. The department responsible for approving pay rate changes is
    a. payroll
    b. treasurer
    c. personnel
    d. cash disbursements

15. Which function should distribute paychecks?
    a. personnel
    b. timekeeping
    c. paymaster
    d. payroll

PROBLEMS

1. Payroll Fraud

John Smith worked in the stockyard of a large building supply company. One day he unexpectedly and without notice left for California, never to return. His foreman seized the opportunity to continue to submit timecards for John to the payroll department. Each week, as part of his normal duties, the foreman received the employee paychecks from payroll and distributed them to the workers on his shift. Since John Smith was not present to collect his paycheck, the foreman forged John's name and cashed it.

Required:
Describe two control techniques to prevent or detect this fraud scheme.

2. Payroll Controls

Refer to the Problem 2 flowchart in the next column.

Required:
a. What risks are associated with the payroll procedures depicted in the flowchart?
b. Discuss two control techniques that will reduce or eliminate the risks.

Problem 2: Payroll Controls

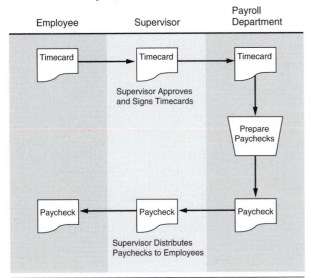

3. Payroll Controls

Sherman Company employs 400 production, maintenance, and janitorial workers in eight separate departments. In addition to supervising operations, the supervisors of the departments are responsible for recruiting, hiring, and firing workers within their areas of responsibility. The organization attracts casual labor and experiences a 20 to 30 percent turnover rate in employees per year. A portion of Sherman Company's payroll procedures are as follows:

Employees clock on and off the job each day to record their attendance on timecards. Each department has its own clock machine that is located in an unattended room away from the main production area. Each week, the supervisors gather the timecards, review them for accuracy, and sign and submit them to the payroll department for processing. In addition, the supervisors submit personnel action forms to reflect newly hired and terminated employees. From these documents, the payroll clerk prepares payroll checks and updates the employee records. The supervisor of the payroll department signs the paychecks and sends them to the department supervisors for distribution to the employees. A payroll register is sent to accounts payable for approval. Based on this approval, the cash disbursements clerk transfers funds into a payroll clearing account.

Required:
Discuss the risks for payroll fraud in the Sherman Company payroll system. What controls would you implement to reduce the risks? Use the COSO framework of control activities to organize your response.

4. Flowchart Analysis

Examine the Problem 4 diagram and indicate any incorrect initiation and/or transfer of documentation. What problems could this cause?

5. Accounting Records and Files

Indicate which department—accounts payable, cash disbursements, data processing, purchasing, inventory, or receiving—has ownership over the following files and registers:
a. Open Purchase Order file
b. Purchase Requisition file
c. Open Purchase Requisition file
d. Closed Purchase Requisition file
e. Inventory file
f. Closed Purchase Order file
g. Valid Vendor file
h. Voucher register
i. Open Vouchers Payable file
j. Receiving Report file
k. Closed Voucher file
l. Check register (cash disbursements journal)

Problem 4: Flowchart Analysis

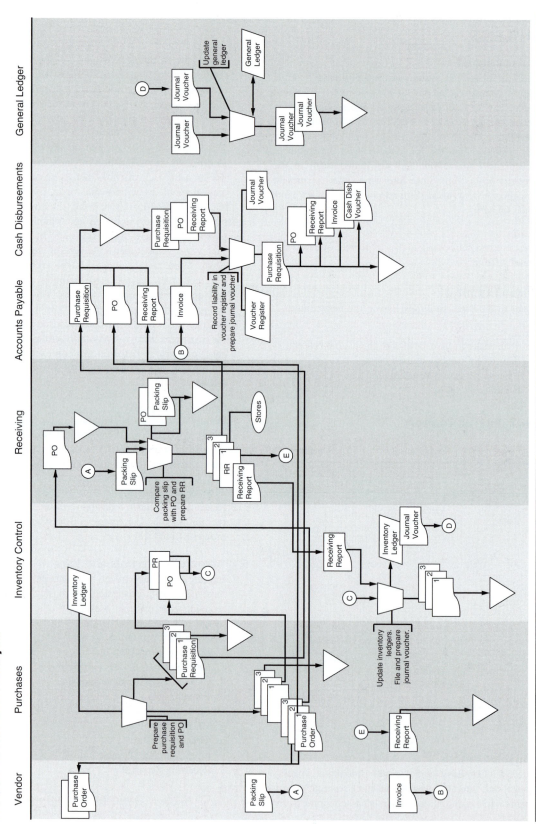

6. Source Documents Identification

Refer to the Problem 6 figure that shows typical expenditure cycle files and attributes. Explain, in detail, the process by which these data are obtained and used in the requisition, purchase, and payment to inventory.

7. Internal Control

Using the Problem 7 flowchart of a purchases system, identify six major control weaknesses in the system. Discuss and classify each weakness in accordance with the COSO framework.

8. Purchase Discounts Lost

Estimate the money that could be saved by the accounts payable and cash disbursements departments if a basic batch processing system were implemented. Assume that the clerical workers cost the firm $12 per hour, that 13,000 vouchers are prepared, and that 5,000 checks are written per year. Assume that total cash disbursements to vendors amount to $5 million per year. Due to sloppy bookkeeping, the current system takes advantage of only about 25 percent of the discounts offered by vendors for timely payments. The average discount is 2 percent if payment is made within 10 days. Payments are currently made on about the 15th day after the invoice is received. Make your own assumptions (and state them) regarding how long specific tasks will take. Also discuss any intangible benefits of the system. (Don't worry about excessive paper documentation costs.)

9. Data Processing Output

Using the information provided in Problem 8, discuss all transaction listings and summary reports that would be necessary for a batch system with real-time input of data.

10. Internal Control

Discuss any control weaknesses found in the Problem 10 flowchart. Recommend any necessary changes.

Problem 6: Source Documents Identification

Inven Num	Description	Qnty on Hand	Reorder Point	Qnty On Order★	EOQ	Vendor Number	Standard Cost	Total Inven. Cost	Inventory Master File

Pur Req Number	Inven Num	Qnty on Order	Vendor Number	Unit Standard Cost	Purchase Requisition File

Vendor Number	Address	Terms of Trade	Date of Last Order	Lead Time	Vendor File

PO Num	Pur Req Number	Inven Num	Qnty on Order	Vendor Number	Address	Standard Cost	Expected Invoice Amount	Rec Flag	Inven Flag	Open (and Closed) Purchase Order File

Voucher Number	Check Num	Invoice Num	Invoice Amount	Acct Cr	Acct DR	Vendor Number	Open Date	Due Date	Close Date

Voucher Register (Open AP File)

★A value in this field is a "flag" to the system not to order item a second time. When inventories are received, the flag is removed by changing this value to zero.

Problem 7: Internal Control

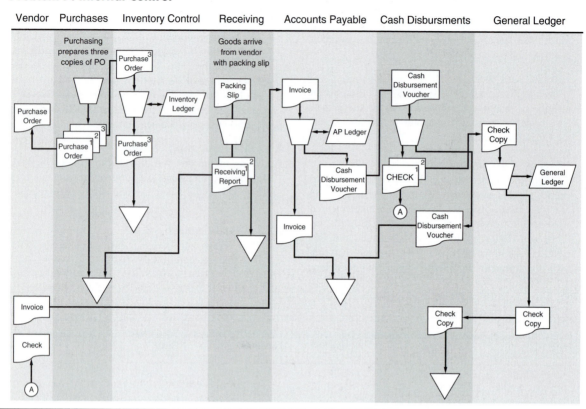

11. Internal Control

CMA 1288 5-3

Lexsteel is a leading manufacturer of steel furniture. Although the company has manufacturing plants and distribution facilities throughout the United States, the purchasing, accounting, and treasury functions are centralized at corporate headquarters.

While discussing the management letter with the external auditors, Ray Lansdown, controller of Lexsteel, became aware of potential problems with the accounts payable system. The auditors had to perform additional audit procedures to attest to the validity of accounts payable and cutoff procedures. The auditors have recommended that a detailed systems study be made of the current procedures. Such a study would not only assess the exposure of the company to potential embezzlement and fraud, but would also identify ways to improve management controls.

Lansdown has assigned the study task to Dolores Smith, a relatively new accountant in the department. Because Smith could not find adequate documentation of the accounts payable procedures, she interviewed those employees involved and constructed a flowchart of the current system (see Problem 11 flowchart). A description of the current procedures follows.

Computer Resources Available

The host computer mainframe is located at corporate headquarters with interactive, remote job-entry terminals at each branch location. In general, data entry occurs at the source and is transmitted to an integrated database maintained on the host computer. Data transmission is made between the branch offices and the host computer over leased telephone lines. The software allows flexibility for managing user access and editing data input.

Procedures for Purchasing Raw Materials

Production orders and appropriate bills of materials are generated by the host computer at corporate headquarters. Based on these bills of materials, purchase orders for raw materials are generated by the centralized purchasing function and mailed directly to the vendors. Each purchase order instructs the vendor to ship the materials directly to the appropriate manufacturing plant. Assuming that the necessary purchase orders have been issued, the manufacturing plants proceed with the production orders received from corporate headquarters.

Problem 10: Internal Control

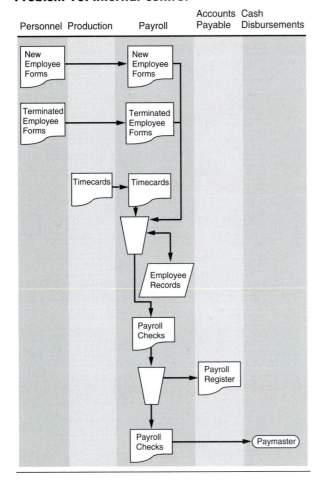

When goods are received, the manufacturing plant examines and verifies the count with the packing slip and transmits the receiving data to accounts payable at corporate headquarters. In the event that raw material deliveries fall behind production, each branch manager is given the authority to order materials and issue emergency purchase orders directly to the vendors. Data about the emergency orders and verification of materials receipt are transmitted via computer to accounts payable at corporate headquarters. Because the company employs a computerized perpetual inventory system, physical counts of raw materials are deemed not to be cost effective and are not performed.

Accounts Payable Procedures

Vendor invoices are mailed directly to corporate headquarters and entered by accounts payable personnel when received; this often occurs before the receiving data are transmitted from the branch offices. The final day of the invoice term for payment is entered as the payment due date. This due date must often be calculated by the data entry person using information listed on the invoice.

Once a week, invoices due the following week are printed in chronological entry order on a payment listing, and the corresponding checks are drawn. The checks and the payment listing are sent to the treasurer's office for signature and mailing to the payee. The check number is printed by the computer and displayed on the check, and the payment listing is validated as the checks are signed. After the checks are mailed, the payment listing is returned to accounts payable for filing. When there is insufficient cash to pay all the invoices, certain checks and the payment listing are retained by the treasurer until all checks can be paid. When the remaining checks are mailed, the listing is then returned to accounts payable. Often, weekly check mailings include a few checks from the previous week, but rarely are there more than two weekly listings involved.

When accounts payable receives the payment listing back from the treasurer's office, the expenses are distributed, coded, and posted to the appropriate plant or cost center accounts. Weekly summary performance reports are processed by accounts payable for each cost center and branch location reflecting all data entry to that point.

Required:
  a. Identify and discuss three areas where Lexsteel Corporation may be exposed to fraud or embezzlement due to weaknesses in the procedures described, and recommend improvements to correct these weaknesses.
  b. Describe three areas where management information could be distorted due to weaknesses in the procedures, and recommend improvements to correct these weaknesses.
  c. Identify three strengths in the procedures described and explain why they are strengths.

12. Human Resource Data Management

In a payroll system with real-time processing of human resource management data, control issues become very important. List some items in this system that could be very sensitive or controversial. Also describe what types of data must be carefully guarded to ensure that they are not altered. Discuss some control procedures that might be put into place to guard against unwanted changes to employees' records.

13. Unrecorded Liabilities

You are auditing the financial statements of a New York City company that buys a product from a manufacturer in Los Angeles. The buyer closes its books on June 30. Assume the following details:

Terms of trade: FOB shipping point
June 10, buyer sends purchase order to seller

Problem 11: Internal Control

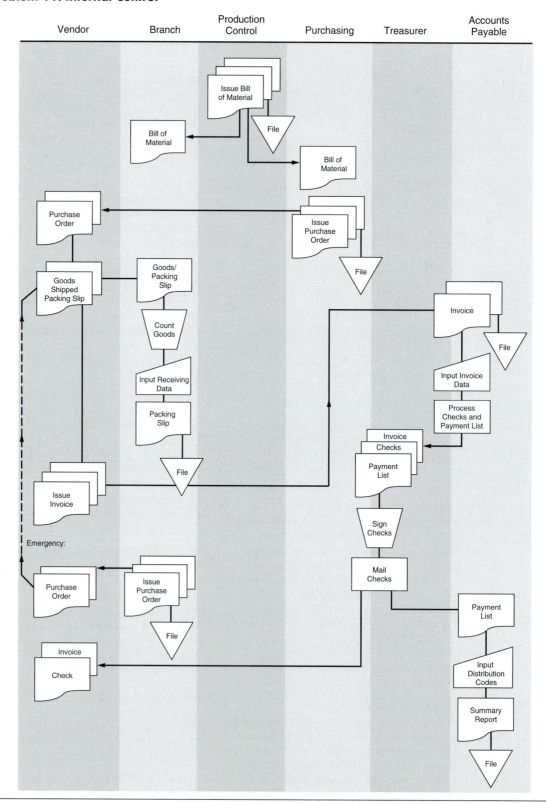

June 15, seller ships goods
July 5, buyer receives goods
July 10, buyer receives seller's invoice

Required:

a. Could this transaction have resulted in an unrecorded liability in the buyer's financial statements?

b. If yes, what documents provide audit trail evidence of the liability?

c. On what date did the buyer realize the liability?

d. On what date did the buyer recognize the liability?
New assumption:
Terms of trade: FOB destination

e. Could this transaction have resulted in an unrecorded liability in the buyer's financial statements?

f. If yes, what documents provide audit trail evidence of the liability?

g. On what date did the buyer realize the liability?

h. On what date did the buyer recognize the liability?

14. Inventory Ordering Alternatives

Refer to Figure 10.2 in the text, which illustrates three alternative methods of ordering inventory.

Required:

a. Distinguish between a purchase requisition and a purchase order.

b. Discuss the primary advantage of alternative two over alternative one. Be specific.

c. Under what circumstances can you envision management using alternative one rather than alternative two?

15. Payroll Flowchart Analysis

Discuss the risks depicted by the payroll system flowchart for Problem 15. Describe the internal control improvements to the system that are needed to reduce these risks.

Problem 15: Payroll Flowchart Analysis

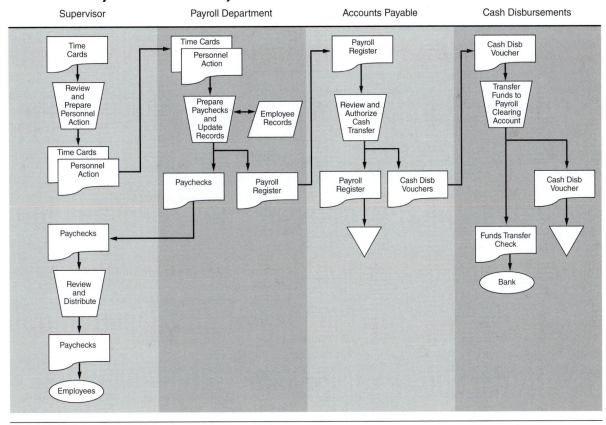

INTERNAL CONTROL CASES

1. Smith's Market (Small Business Cash Sales Accounting System)

In 1989, Robert Smith opened a small fruit and vegetable market in Bethlehem, Pennsylvania. Originally Smith sold only produce grown on his family farm and orchard. As the market's popularity grew, however, he added bread, canned goods, fresh meats, and a limited supply of frozen goods. Today, Smith's Market is a full-range farmers' market with a strong local customer base. Indeed, the market's reputation for low prices and high quality draws customers from other Pennsylvania cities and even from the neighboring state of New Jersey. Smith's currently has forty employees, including sales staff, shelf stockers, farm laborers, shift supervisors, and clerical staff. Recently Smith has noticed a decline in profits and sales, while his purchases of products for resale have continued to rise. Although the company does not prepare audited financial statements, Robert Smith has commissioned your public accounting firm to assess his company's sales procedures and internal controls. Smith's Market expenditure cycle procedures are described below:

Expenditure Cycle

The expenditure cycle begins in the warehouse adjacent to the market where Smith's keeps its inventory of nonperishable goods, such as canned goods and paper products. It also maintains a one-day inventory of produce and other perishable products in the warehouse where it can quickly restock the shelves when necessary. At the close of business each evening, the warehouse clerk reviews the market shelves for items that need to be replenished. The clerk restocks the shelves and adjusts the digital stock records accordingly from the warehouse PC. At this time, the clerk takes note of what needs to be reordered from the suppliers and prints purchase orders from the PC. Depending upon the nature of the product and the urgency of the need, the clerk either mails the purchase order to the supplier or orders by phone. Phone orders are followed up by faxing the purchase order to the supplier.

When the goods arrive from the vendor, the warehouse clerk reviews the packing slip, restocks the warehouse shelves, and updates the stock records from the PC. At the end of the day, the clerk prepares a hard-copy purchases summary from the PC and sends it to the treasury clerk for posting to general ledger.

The vendor's invoice is sent to the accounting clerk. She examines it for correctness and files it in a temporary file until it is due to be paid. The clerk reviews the temporary file daily, looking for invoices to be paid. Using the accounting department PC, the clerk prints a check and records it in the digital check register. She then files the invoice and mails the check to the supplier. At the end of the day, she prints a hard-copy journal voucher from the PC, which summarizes the day's cash disbursements, and sends it to the treasury clerk for posting to the general ledger.

Using the department PC, the treasury clerk posts the journal voucher and purchases summary information to the appropriate general ledger accounts.

Required:
   a. Create a data flow diagram of the current system.
   b. Create a system flowchart of the current system.
   c. Analyze the internal control weaknesses in the system. Model your response according to the six categories of physical control activities specified in the COSO internal control model.

2. Spice is Right Imports (Standalone PC-based Accounting System)

Spice Is Right was established in 1990 in Boston, where it began importing exotic spices and cooking sauces from India and China. The company distributes these specialty foods to ethnic food shops, cafes, and restaurants across the country. In addition to its Boston headquarters and warehouse, the company has a distribution center in Elizabeth, New Jersey. Spice Is Right currently employs over 100 people, has dozens of suppliers, and trades in hundreds of ethnic and exotic foods from all over the world.

Recently, Spice Is Right has been receiving complaints from customers and suppliers about billing, shipping, and payment errors. Management believes that these complaints stem, in part, from an antiquated computer system. Spice's current information system includes manual procedures supported by independent (nonnetworked) PCs in each department, which cannot communicate with each other. Document flows between the departments is entirely in hard-copy form. The following is a description of its expenditure cycle at the Boston headquarters office.

Purchasing Process
The purchasing agent monitors the inventory levels by reviewing the inventory subsidiary ledger from his department computer. He decides which items need to be replenished and selects a supplier. He then enters this information into the computer terminal to create a digital purchase order. The computer terminal generates three hard copies of the purchase order. The

purchasing agent sends one copy to the supplier, one copy to the AP department, where it is filed temporarily, and files the third copy in the purchasing department.

When the goods are received, the receiving department inspects and verifies them using the packing slip, which is attached to the goods. The receiving clerk manually prepares two hard copies of a receiving report. One copy accompanies the goods to the warehouse for storage. The receiving clerk sends the second copy to the purchasing agent, who uses it to update the inventory subsidiary ledger and close the open purchase order. The purchase agent then files the receiving report in the department.

Accounts Payable and Cash Disbursements Procedures

The accounts payable clerk receives the supplier's invoice and reconciles it with the purchase order in the temporary file. From her computer terminal, the clerk records the purchase in the purchases journal and records the liability by creating a cash disbursement voucher. The clerk then updates the inventory control and accounts payable control accounts in the general ledger. The purchases order and invoice are then filed in the department.

Each day, the clerk visually searches the cash disbursements voucher file from her terminal for open invoices that are due to be paid. From her computer terminal, the clerk prepares the check and records it in the check register. The negotiable portion of the check is mailed to the vendor, and a check copy is filed. The clerk then closes the voucher register and updates the accounts payable control and cash accounts in the general ledger.

Required:

  a. Create a data flow diagram of the current system.
  b. Create a system flowchart of the existing system.
  c. Analyze the internal control weaknesses in the system. Model your response according to the six categories of physical control activities specified in the COSO internal control model.
  d. Prepare a system flowchart of a redesigned computer-based system that resolves the control weaknesses you identified.

3. ABE Plumbing, Inc. (Centralized Small Business Accounting System)

ABE Plumbing, Inc., opened its doors in 1979 as a wholesale supplier of plumbing equipment, tools, and parts to hardware stores, home-improvement centers, and professional plumbers in the Allentown–Bethlehem–Easton metropolitan area. Over the years, the company has expanded its operations to serve customer across the nation and now employs over 200 people as technical representatives, buyers, warehouse workers, and sales and office staff. Most recently, ABE has experienced fierce competition from the large online discount stores such as Harbor Freight and Northern Supply. In addition, the company is suffering from operational inefficiencies related to its archaic information system. ABE's expenditure cycle procedures are described in the following paragraphs.

Expenditure Cycle

ABE uses a centralized accounting system for managing inventory purchases and recording transactions. The system is almost entirely paperless. Each department has a computer terminal that is networked to the "Purchases/Accounts Payable System" that is run from a small data processing department. All accounting records are maintained on centralized computer files that are stored on a file server in the data processing department.

Purchasing

The process begins in the purchasing department. Each morning, the purchasing agent reviews the inventory levels from his department terminal and searches for items that have fallen to their reorder points and need to be replenished. The purchasing agent then selects the vendors and creates digital purchase orders in the purchase order file. He then prints two hard copies of each purchase order and sends them to the respective vendors.

Receiving

When the items are received, the receiving department clerk reconciles the goods with the attached packing slip and the digital purchase order, which he accesses from his computer terminal. The clerk then creates a digital receiving report, stating the condition of the materials received. The system automatically closes the purchase order previously created by the purchasing agent. In addition, the receiving clerk prints a hard copy of the receiving report, which he sends with the inventory to the warehouse where the items are stored.

Warehouse

Upon receipt of the inventory, the warehouse clerk reconciles the items with the receiving report and updates the inventory subsidiary ledger. The accounting system automatically and immediately updates the inventory control account in the general ledger.

Accounts Payable

Once the accounts payable clerk receives the vendor's invoice, she reconciles it with the purchase order and receiving report from her terminal. The clerk then creates a digital cash disbursement voucher record and sets a due date for payment. The system automatically updates the AP control account in the general ledger. Daily, the AP clerk reviews the open cash disbursement voucher records from her terminal looking for items that need to be paid. The clerk then creates a record for the payment in the digital check register and closes the open cash disbursement voucher. Finally, the clerk prints a hard copy of the check and sends it to the vendor. The system automatically updates the AP and cash general ledger accounts.

Required:

    a. Create a data flow diagram of the current system.

    b. Create a system flowchart of the existing system.

    c. Identify the internal control weaknesses in the system. Model your response according to the six categories of physical control activities specified in the COSO internal control model.

    d. Prepare a system flowchart of a redesigned computer-based system that resolves the control weaknesses you identified.

4. Walker Books, Inc. (Manual System with Minimal PC Support)

(Prepared by Matt Wisser, Lehigh University)

Company Background

Walker Books, Inc., is one of the fastest-growing book distributor in the United States. Established in 1981 in Palo Alto, California, Walker Books was originally a side project of founder and current president Curtis Walker, who at the time was employed by a local law firm. Because reading was much more than just a hobby of his, he decided to use some of his savings to buy an abandoned restaurant and convert it into a neighborhood bookstore, mainly selling used books that were donated and obtained from flea markets. When the doors first opened, Walker's wife, Lauren, was the only employee during the week and Curtis worked weekends. At the end of the first fiscal year, Walker Books had grossed $20,000 in sales.

As the years passed, Curtis Walker quit the law firm and began concentrating fully on his bookstore. He hired more employees, more books were traded in, and sales increased annually. During the mid-1990s, however, Walker was faced with two problems: many large, upscale bookstores were being built in the area, and the use of the Internet for finding and ordering books was becoming cheaper and more popular for current customers. In 1995, Walker's sales started to decline. Deciding to take a risk because of the new-found competition, he closed his doors to the neighborhood, invested more money to expand the current property, and transformed his company from simply selling used books to being a distributor of new

books. His business model was to obtain books from publishers at a discount, store them in his warehouse, and resell them to large bookstore chains.

Walker Books, Inc., has rapidly become one of the largest book distributors in the country. Although it is still at its original location in Palo Alto, California, it distributes books to all 50 states and, because of that, now sees gross sales of about $105,000,000 per year. When Mr. Walker is asked about his fondest memory, he always responds that he will never forget how the little bookstore, with two employees, has expanded to now have more than 145 employees.

Under his current business model, all of Walker's customers are large-chain bookstores who themselves net many millions of dollars in revenue per year. Some of these customers, however, are now experiencing problems with Walker Books that threaten their business relationship: books are ordered but not sent, Walker's poor inventory management causes stockouts, and Walker is commonly unable to provide legitimate documentation of transactions.

One potential source of these problems rests with Walker's antiquated accounting system, which is a combination of manual procedures supported by standalone PC work stations. These computers are not networked and cannot share data between departments. All interdepartmental communication takes place through hard-copy documents.

You have been hired as an independent expert to express an opinion on the appropriateness of Walker Books' business processes and internal controls. The expenditure cycle is described below:

Expenditure Cycle

Purchases System

The purchases process begins with the purchasing agent, who monitors the levels of books available via a computer terminal that lists current inventory. Upon noticing deficiencies in inventory levels, the agent manually generates four hard copies of a purchase order: one is sent to AP, one is sent to the vendor, one is sent to the receiving department, and the last is filed within the department.

Vendors will generally ship the products within five business days of the order. When goods arrive in the receiving department, the corresponding packing slip always accompanies them. The receiving department clerk unloads the goods and then reconciles the packing slip with the purchase order. After unloading the goods, the clerk manually prepares three hard copies of the receiving report. One copy goes with the goods to the warehouse, another is sent to the purchasing department, and the final copy is filed in the receiving department. In the warehouse, the copy is simply filed once the goods are stored on the shelves. In the purchasing department, the clerk receives this copy of the receiving report and files it with the purchase order.

When the AP department receives the purchase order, it is temporarily filed until the respective invoice arrives from the vendor. Upon receipt of the invoice, the AP clerk removes the purchase order from the temporary file and reconciles the two documents. The clerk then manually records the liability in the hard copy AP subsidiary ledger. Finally, the clerk files the purchase order and invoice in the open AP file in the department. At the end of the day, the clerk prepares a hard-copy journal voucher and sends it to the general ledger department.

Once the general ledger department receives the journal voucher, the clerk examines it for any obvious errors and then enters the relevant data into the department PC to update the appropriate digital general ledger accounts.

Cash Disbursements System

The AP clerk periodically reviews the open AP file for liabilities that are due. To maximize returns on invested cash, yet still take advantage of vendor discounts, the clerk will pull the invoice two days before its applicable due date. Upon finding an open accounts payable file in need of payment, the clerk manually prepares a check for the amount due as per the invoice. The hard copy AP ledger is also updated by the AP clerk. The check number, dollar amount, and other pertinent data are manually recorded in the hard-copy check register. The check is then sent to the cash disbursements department. Finally, the invoice is discarded, as it no longer has any relevant information that hasn't already been recorded elsewhere.

When the cash disbursements clerk receives the unsigned check, she examines it to ensure that no one has tampered with any of the information and that no errors have been made. Because she is familiar with all of the vendors with whom Walker deals, she can identify any false vendors or any payment amounts that seem excessive. Assuming everything appears in order, she signs the check using a signature block that displays the name of the assistant treasurer, Tyler Matthews. Only Matthews' signature can validate a vendor check. The cash disbursements clerk then photocopies the check for audit trail purposes.

Once the check is signed, it is sent directly to the supplier. The photocopy of the check is marked as paid and then filed in the cash disbursements department. The clerk then creates a journal voucher, which is sent to the general ledger department. Once the general ledger department receives the journal voucher, the clerk examines it for any obvious errors and then enters the relevant data into the department

PC to update the appropriate digital general ledger accounts.

Required:

a. Create a data flow diagram of the current system.
b. Create a system flowchart of the existing system.
c. Analyze the internal control weaknesses in the system. Model your response according to the six categories of physical control activities specified in the COSO internal control framework.
d. Prepare a system flowchart of a redesigned computer-based system that resolves the control weaknesses you identified.

5. A&V Safety, Inc. (Manual and Standalone Computer Processing)

(Prepared by Adam Johnson and Aneesh Varma, Lehigh University)

A&V Safety, Inc., is a growing company specializing in the sales of safety equipment to commercial entities. It currently employs 200 full-time employees all of whom work out of its headquarters in San Diego, California. During the summer, the company expands to include about ten summer interns who are delegated smaller jobs and other errands. A&V currently competes with Office Safety, Inc., and X-Safe, who leads the industry. Suppliers for A&V include Halotron Extinguishers, Kadelite, and Exit Signs, Inc. A&V attempts to maintain inventory levels sufficient to service two weeks of sales. This level has shown to avoid stockouts, and the excess inventory is held in a warehouse in a suburb of San Diego.

A&V has a legacy accounting system that employs a combination of manual procedures supported by standalone PCs in the various departments. Recently it has experienced business inefficiencies that have been linked to its antiquated accounting system. You have been retained by A&V management to review its procedures for compliance with the Sarbanes-Oxley Act and to provide recommendations for improvement. The A&V expenditure cycle is presented in the following paragraphs.

Expenditure Cycle

The company purchases safety devices such as fire extinguishers, exit signs, and sensors from many different suppliers. When the quantity-on-hand of a particular product falls to a low level, the warehouse clerk selects a vendor and manually prepares three hard copies of a purchase order. The clerk sends one copy of the purchase order to the vendor, one copy to the general ledger department, and the third to the receiving department to be used to verify the goods when they arrive. When the goods arrive from the vendor, they first go to the receiving department. The receiving clerk matches the packing slip in the shipment to the purchase order that the warehouse clerk had previously sent. After comparing the quantities and products on the packing slip to those specified on the purchase order, the receiving clerk signs the purchase order and sends it to the accounting department. The receiving clerk then manually prepares a hard-copy receiving report, which he sends with the goods to the warehouse. From his department PC, the warehouse clerk uses the receiving report to update the inventory subsidiary ledger to reflect the receipt of the goods.

Subsequently, the accounting department's AP clerk receives the supplier's invoice, which she matches and reconciles to the previously received purchase order from the receiving clerk. From her department PC, the AP clerk then updates the digital accounts payable subsidiary ledger to reflect the new liability and records the event in the digital purchases journal.

Cash Disbursements Procedures

The AP clerk in the accounting department reviews the liabilities that are due by searching the AP subsidiary ledger from the department PC. The clerk then prints out a hard-copy cash disbursement voucher for each item due for payment. The clerk then sends cash disbursements voucher to the cash disbursements department for payment. At the end of the day, the clerk prints a hard-copy AP summary from the department PC and sends it to the general ledger department.

From his department PC, the cash disbursement clerk uses the cash disbursement voucher to record the payment in the digital check register and then pints a three-part check. The clerk signs the negotiable portion of the check and sends it to the vendor. One check copy is filed in the department and the clerk sends the second check copy, along with the original cash disbursement voucher, to the accounting department AP clerk. At the end of the day, the clerk prints a hard-copy summary of the check register and sends it to the general ledger department.

From the accounting department PC, the AP clerk uses the check copy and cash disbursement voucher to record the payment in the digital check register and to close out the liability in the digital AP subsidiary ledger. The clerk then files the hard-copy cash disbursement voucher and check copy in the department.

From the department PC, the general ledger clerk posts the summaries received from the accounting and cash disbursement departments to the appropriate general ledger accounts. The clerk files the hard copy summaries in the general ledger department.

Required:

a. Create a data flow diagram of the current system.
b. Create a system flowchart of the existing system.

c. Analyze the internal control weaknesses in the system. Model your response according to the six categories of physical control activities specified in the COSO internal control framework.
d. Prepare a system flowchart of a redesigned computer-based system that resolves the control weaknesses you identified.

6. Premier Sports Memorabilia (Networks Computer System with Manual Procedures)

(Prepared by Chris Polchinski, Lehigh University)
Premier Sports Memorabilia is a medium-sized, rapidly growing online and catalogue-based retailer centered in Brooklyn, New York. The company was founded in 1990 and specializes in providing its customers with authentic yet affordable sports memorabilia from their favorite players and teams, past and present. Traditionally, the company's customers were located in the northeast region of the United States. Recently, however, Premier launched a successful an ad campaign to expand its customer base. This has increased sales, which has in turn placed a strain on the organization's operational resources. The company currently employs 205 employees, who are spread out among its three warehouses and two offices in the tristate area.

The firm purchases from a large number of manufacturers and memorabilia dealers around the country and is always looking for additional contacts who have new or rare items to offer.

The company has a computer network installed, which, until recently, has served it well. The firm is now, however, experiencing operational inefficiencies and accounting errors. Your firm has been hired to evaluate Premier's business processes and internal controls. The expenditure cycle is described in the following paragraphs.

Purchase System Procedures

Premier's purchase transactions are initiated when its inventory levels for a certain item falls below the designated reorder point. This is electronically monitored through Premier's inventory requisition system, which is directly linked to the inventory file. Once an item falls below the reorder point, an open requisition record is automatically created. A valid vendor file is used both to retrieve stored vendor information and to check that items are being ordered through a preapproved vendor with which the company has done business in the past. Digital purchase requisitions are made available to the clerks in the inventory control department and the purchasing department via the computer terminal.

When the purchasing department clerk views the digital requisition, she prepares and prints five hard copies of the purchase order. One copy is filed in the department. A second copy is sent to the receiving department. A third copy is sent to the AP department. A fourth copy is sent to the inventory control department. A final copy is sent to the vendor as placement of the order.

Upon receiving the purchase order, the inventory control clerk uses a terminal to access the open requisition file and closes the record. In addition, the program automatically creates a digital pending open purchase record.

Shortly after receiving the purchase order, the vendor will send out both the goods and a packing slip to Premier's receiving department. After the receiving clerk has both the purchase order and the packing slip, he physically inspects the condition of the goods and checks that both the type and quantity received are correct. Upon completion of the inspection, the clerk manually creates three hard copies of a receiving report. One copy is filed in the department. The second copy is sent to AP for reconciliation. The third copy is sent to the inventory control department.

When the inventory control department obtains the receiving report, the clerk uses the purchase update program to access the pending open purchase record and closes it out. In addition, the clerk updates the inventory file by posting the amounts received to the various inventory records affected.

When the accounts payable department clerk receives the invoice from the supplier, he matches it to the supporting purchase order and receiving report received from the purchasing and receiving departments, respectively. The clerk manually reconciles all three documents and prepares an AP record from the department terminal.

Finally, at the end of each day, the inventory control department and the accounts payable department create a hard-copy inventory summary and accounts payable journal voucher, respectively, reflecting the effects of all of the day's transactions. These documents are sent to the general ledger department, where they are reconciled and posted to their specific control accounts within the general ledger file.

Required:

a. Create a data flow diagram of the current system.
b. Create a system flowchart of the existing system.
c. Analyze the internal control weaknesses in the system. Model your response according to the six categories of physical control activities specified in the COSO internal control framework.
d. Prepare a system flowchart of a redesigned computer-based system that resolves the control weaknesses you identified.

7. Bait 'n Reel Superstore (Combination of Networked Computers and Manual System)

(Prepared by Matt Wisser, Lehigh University)
Bait 'n Reel was established in 1983 by Jamie Roberts, an avid fisherman and environmentalist. Growing up in Pennsylvania's Pocono Mountains region, Roberts was lucky enough to have a large lake right down the road, where he found himself fishing throughout the year. Unfortunately, he had to drive more than 15 miles to purchase his fishing supplies, such as lines, hooks, and bait. Throughout his early adulthood, Jamie frequently overheard other fishermen expressing their displeasure at not having a local fishing store to serve their needs. Roberts vowed to himself that he would open his own store if he could ever save up enough money.

By 1983, he had sufficient funds and the opportunity arose when a local grocery store went up for sale. He bought the building and converted it into the "Bait 'n Reel" fishing store. His early business involved cash-only transactions with local fishermen. By the mid-1990s, however, the building had expanded into a superstore that sold a wide range of sporting products and camping gear. People from all over the county shopped at Bait 'n Reel as Roberts increased his advertising efforts, emphasizing his ability to provide excellent service and a wide range of products. Roberts moved away from a cash-only business and began offering store credit cards to consumers. He also became a regional wholesaler to many smaller sporting goods stores.

With the help of a friend, Roberts installed a computer network. Although these computers helped automate the company's business processes and facilitated the sharing of data between departments, much interdepartmental communication continued to be via hard-copy documents.

Revenue increased sharply during the four years after the implementation of the computer system. In spite of this, Roberts had some questions about the quality of processes, as many of the subsidiary accounts did not match the general ledger control accounts. This didn't prove to be a material problem, however, until recently, when the computers began listing supplies on hand that were not actually on the shelves. This created problems as customers became frustrated by stock-outs. Roberts knew something was wrong, but he couldn't put his finger on it.

You have been hired by Roberts to evaluate Bait 'n Reel's processes and internal controls and make recommendations for improvement. Bait 'n Reel's expenditure cycle is described in the following paragraphs.

Expenditure Cycle

Purchases System

The process begins when the purchasing manager checks the inventory subsidiary ledger on his computer terminal each morning. When inventory is deemed to be too low, he reviews the valid vendor file, also from his terminal, to select vendors for items to be purchased. Once a vendor is found, he prepares an electronic version of the purchase order, in addition to two hard copies of the purchase order. One hard copy is sent to the vendor immediately, while the other is filed in the department. Immediately after this event, the electronic version of the purchase order is sent out to two terminals: one in the receiving department and one in the accounts payable department.

When the clerk in the receiving department receives the electronic purchase order, he reads over it once to make sure it seems correct. When the goods arrive, he makes a detailed inspection of them and reconciles the goods to the corresponding information contained in the electronic purchase order. If everything looks correct, the clerk manually prepares two hard copies of the receiving report. One of these copies accompanies the goods to the inventory control/storage department, where the clerk updates the inventory subsidiary account from his terminal; it is then filed after the goods are placed on the shelves. The other copy of the receiving report is sent to the accounts payable department.

Upon receipt of the receiving report, the accounts payable clerk matches it to the respective electronic purchase order on his terminal. He then updates the accounts payable subsidiary ledger from his terminal to reflect the transaction. The clerk temporarily files the receiving report until the invoice arrives from the vendor. Typically, vendors provide a photocopy of the original purchase order along with the invoice so that any discrepancies can immediately be identified. When the accounts payable clerk receives the invoice and purchase order copy, he pulls the receiving report from the temporary file and reconciles the three documents. At this time, the clerk updates the accounts payable control and the inventory control accounts in the general ledger on his terminal. The clerk the sends the invoice, receiving report, and the purchase order copy to the cash disbursements department.

Cash Disbursements System

Upon receipt of the documents from the accounts payable department, the cash disbursements clerk prepares a check for the invoiced amount. Once this is completed, he updates the check register, AP subsidiary account, and the general ledger from his

terminal. The three documents, along with the check, are then passed on to the assistant treasurer. As an additional control, the assistant treasure reviews the supporting documents and makes a photocopy of the check for record-keeping purposes. The treasurer and then signs the check, which is immediately sent to the vendor for payment. The invoice, purchase order copy, receiving report, and check copy are filed in the department.

Required:

a. Create a data flow diagram of the current system.
b. Create a system flowchart of the existing system.
c. Analyze the internal control weaknesses in the system. Model your response according to the six categories of physical control activities specified in the COSO internal control framework.
d. Prepare a system flowchart of a redesigned computer-based system that resolves the control weaknesses you identified.

8. Green Mountain Coffee Roasters, Inc. (Manual Procedures and Standalone PCs)

(Prepared by Ronica Sharma, Lehigh University)

Green Mountain Coffee Roasters, Inc., was founded in 1981 as a small café in Waitsfield, Vermont, roasting and serving premium coffee on the premises. Green Mountain blends and distributes coffee to a variety of customers, including cafés, delis, and restaurants, and currently has about 6,700 customer accounts reaching states across the nation. As the company has grown, several beverages have been added to its product line, including signature blends, light and heavy roasts, decaffeinated coffee and teas, and herbal teas. Green Mountain Coffee Roasters, Inc., has been publicly traded since 1993.

Green Mountain Coffee has a warehouse and manufacturing plant located in Wilton, Vermont, where it presently employees 250 full-time and part-time workers. The company receives its beans in bulk from a select group of distributors located across the world, with their largest supplier being Columbia Beans Co. Green Mountain Coffee also sells accessories that complement its products, including mugs, thermoses, and coffee containers that it purchases from its supplier, Coffee Lovers, Inc. In addition to Green Mountain purchases paper products such as coffee bags, coffee cups, and stirrers, which it distributes to customers.

Green Mountain's accounting system consists of manual procedures supported by standalone PCs located in various departments. Because these computers are not networked, they cannot share data digitally, and all interdepartmental communication is through hard-copy documents.

Green Mountain is a new audit client for your CPA firm. As manager on the assignment, you are examining its internal controls. The expenditure cycle is described in the following paragraphs.

Purchases System

Green Mountain Coffee purchases beans and blends from manufactures and then sells them to customer stores. Sara is in charge of inventory management in the warehouse. From her PC, she reviews the inventory ledger to identify inventory needs. When items fall to their preestablished reorder point, she prepares a purchase requisition. She keeps a copy in her department for use later, files one in the open purchase requisition file, and sends a copy to AP. At the end of the day, she uses the purchase requisitions to prepare a four-part purchase order. One copy is filed, two copies are sent to the supplier, and one copy is sent to Fayth in the AP department. When the goods arrive, Sara inspects and counts them and sends the packing slip to AP. Using a PC, Sara updates the inventory subsidiary ledger and, at the end of day, sends an account summary to Vic in the general ledger department.

After checking that the purchase requisition and purchase order exist to support the packing slip, Fayth files the documents in the AP pending file. The supplier's invoice is mailed directly to Fayth, who checks it against the documents in the pending file. Using a computer system, she updates the AP subsidiary ledger and records the transaction in the purchases journal. She then files the purchase requisition, purchase order, packing slip, and invoice in the open AP file. At the end of the day, she prepares a journal voucher, which is sent to Vic in the general ledger department. Using a separate computer system, Vic updates the control accounts affected by the transactions and files the summary and journal vouchers.

Cash Disbursements System Summary

Fayth reviews the open AP file for items due for payment, waiting until the last date to make a payment and still take advantage of the discount. From her PC, she then updates (closes) the appropriate AP subsidiary record, prints a two-part check, and records the payment in the check register file. At the close of day, Fayth mails the check to the supplier, files a copy, and prepares a journal voucher, which goes to Vic. Vic records the transaction in the affected general ledger accounts and files the journal voucher.

Required:

a. Create a data flow diagram of the current system.
b. Create a system flowchart of the existing system.
c. Analyze the internal control weaknesses in the system. Model your response according to the six categories of physical control activities specified in the COSO internal control framework.

d. Prepare a system flowchart of a redesigned computer-based system that resolves the control weaknesses you identified.

9. Holly Company—Payroll Systems (Small Company Uses Manual Procedures with PC Support)

Holly Company is a small, family-run manufacturer of wooden garden furniture, sheds, and storage containers. The company is located outside Pittsburgh, Pennsylvania, and currently employs 185 workers. Much of the manufacturing work involves casual labor in the lumber yard and sawmill. The work is hard, and employees often move on after a few months. Although the company does not issue audited financial statements, its owner has retained your firm to conduct a review of its internal controls. The focus of your review at this time is the payroll process.

Payroll Processing System

Holly employees use a time clock in an unsupervised area to record their time on the job. The time-keeping clerk tries to monitor the process, but is often distracted by other duties. Every Friday, the shop foremen collects the time cards for their subordinates, review and approve them, and deliver them to the payroll clerk.

The payroll clerk uses a standalone PC to record the employee earnings in the employee records and print a hard-copy payroll register. The payroll clerk sends one copy of the payroll register to the accounting department. The clerk then files the time cards and a copy of the payroll register in the payroll department.

The accounting department clerk receives the payroll register, reviews it for accuracy, and uses the department computer to record the transaction by posting to subsidiary and general ledger accounts, including wages expense, cash, and various withholding accounts. The clerk then prints the hard-copy checks, which are written on the general cash account. The clerk signs the paychecks and sends them to the foremen, who distribute them to the employees. Finally, the clerk files the payroll register in the department.

Required:

a. Create a data flow diagram of the payroll systems.
b. Create a system flowchart of the payroll systems.
c. Analyze the internal control weaknesses in the system. Model your response according to the six categories of physical control activities specified in the COSO internal control framework.
d. Make recommendations for improving the payroll procedures.

10. A&V Safety, Inc.—Payroll Processing System (Manual Process)

(Prepared by Aneesh Varma, Lehigh University)

A&V Safety, Inc., is a growing company specializing in the sales of safety equipment to commercial entities. It currently employs 200 full-time employees, all of whom work out of its headquarters in San Diego, California. During the summer, the company expands to include summer interns who are delegated smaller jobs and other errands. The A&V payroll process is presented in the following paragraphs.

A&V Safety, Inc., supervisors collect and review employee time cards, which they forward to the payroll department. During payroll processing, individual employee wage rates are manually pulled from the personnel file based on the employee ID . Interns working for A&V, however, do not receive employee identification cards and numbers because they are at the firm for only 10 weeks. In such cases, the immediate supervisor writes the wage rate on the time cards prior to submission to the payroll department.

The payroll clerk then manually prepares the payroll checks, updates the payroll register, and files the time cards in the department. She sends a copy of the payroll register to the AP clerk who updates the AP ledger for wages payable. The payroll clerk then sends a payroll summary to the general ledger. Finally, the payroll clerk sends the paychecks to the cash disbursement department, where they are signed and forwarded to supervisors, who distribute them to their respective employees.

The signed copies of the payroll checks are returned to the payroll department, where they are matched to the payroll register and filed locally. The cash disbursements clerk prepares a list of verified recipients. She sends one copy of the list to the AP department. The AP clerk uses the list to update the AP ledger to close out the wages payable account. The cash disbursements clerk sends a second copy of the list of recipients to the general ledger clerk, who reconciles it to the summary report and posts to general ledger.

Required:

a. Create a data flow diagram of the current system.
b. Create a system flowchart of the existing system.
c. Analyze the internal control weaknesses in the system. Model your response according to the six categories of physical control activities specified in the COSO control framework.
d. Prepare a flowchart of a redesigned computer-based system that resolves the control weaknesses you identified.

ACL Assignments

The files used for the following assignments are located in the **sampleproject. acl** that accompanies ACL. Some of the assignments employ the ACL's *Relation* and *Join* features. For detailed information on the use of these and other commands, consult ACL's online Help.

1. Open the **AP_Trans** (purchases) file and stratify it on the Quantity field. Print the last results window and comment on the action to be taken by the auditor.

2. Using the *Relation* feature, create a view from data in both the **AP_Trans** (purchases) and **Inventory** files that shows product details (**product description** and **quantity on-hand**). Print the view and comment on the results.

3. Open the **EMPMAST** (employee master file) and test for duplicate employee records. Prepare a last-results report that identifies anomalies or potential errors. Print the report and comment on the results.

4. Using the *Relation* feature, create a view of data from both the **Empmast** and **Payroll** files that test for paychecks to non-existent employees.

5. Using the *Join* feature, create a view of data from both the **Empmast** and **Payroll** files that tests for paychecks to nonexistent employees.

6. Bradmark Comprehensive Case.

Required:

Access the Bradmark ACL Case in the Student Resource section of textbook's Web site. Your instructor will tell you which questions to answer.

CHAPTER 11

Enterprise Resource Planning Systems

LEARNING OBJECTIVES

After studying this chapter, you should:

- Understand the general functionality and key elements of ERP systems.
- Understand the various aspects of ERP configuration including servers, databases, and the use of bolt-on software.
- Understand the purpose of data warehousing as a strategic tool and recognize the issues related to the design, maintenance, and operation of a data warehouse.
- Recognize the risks associated with ERP implementation.
- Be aware of the key considerations related to ERP implementation.
- Understand the internal control and auditing implications associated with ERPs.

Until recently, most large and midsized organizations designed and programmed custom information systems in-house. This resulted in an array of standalone systems that were designed to the unique needs of the users. Although these systems dealt efficiently with their designated tasks, they did not provide strategic decision support at the enterprise level because they lacked the integration needed for information transfer across organization boundaries. Today the trend in information systems is toward implementing highly integrated, enterprise-oriented systems. These are not custom packages designed for a specific organization. Instead, they are generalized systems that incorporate the best business practices in use. Organizations mix and match precoded software components to assemble an **enterprise resource planning (ERP)** system that best meets their business requirements. This means that an organization may need to change the way it conducts business to take full advantage of the ERP.

This chapter is composed of five major sections and an appendix. The first section outlines the key features of a generic ERP system by comparing the function and data-storage techniques of a traditional flat-file or database system to that of an ERP. The second section describes various ERP configurations related to servers, databases, and bolt-on software. The topic of the third section is data warehousing. A data warehouse is a relational or multidimensional database that supports online analytical processing (OLAP). The fourth section examines key risks associated with ERP implementation. The fifth section reviews the internal control and auditing issues related to ERPs and the discussion follows the COSO framework. The chapter appendix reviews the leading ERP software products. Some of the functionality and distinguishing features of these systems are highlighted.

WHAT IS AN ERP?

ERP systems are multiple module software packages that evolved primarily from traditional manufacturing resource planning (MRP II) systems. The Gartner Group coined the term ERP, which has become widely used in recent years. The objective of ERP is to integrate key processes of the organization such as order entry, manufacturing, procurement and accounts payable, payroll, and human resources. By doing so, a single computer system can serve the unique needs of each functional area. Designing one system that serves everyone is an undertaking of massive proportions. Under the traditional model, each functional area or department has its own computer system optimized to the way it does its daily business. ERP combines all of these into a single, integrated system that accesses a single database to facilitate the sharing of information and to improve communications across the organization.

To illustrate, consider the traditional model for a manufacturing firm illustrated in Figure 11.1. This company employs a **closed database architecture**, which is similar in concept to the basic flat-file model. Under this approach, a database management system is used to provide minimal technological advantage over flat-file systems. The database management system is little more than a private but powerful file system. As with the flat-file approach, the data remain the property of the application. Thus, distinct, separate, and independent databases exist. As is true with the flat-file architecture, there is a high degree of data redundancy in a closed database environment.

FIGURE 11.1   **Traditional Information System**

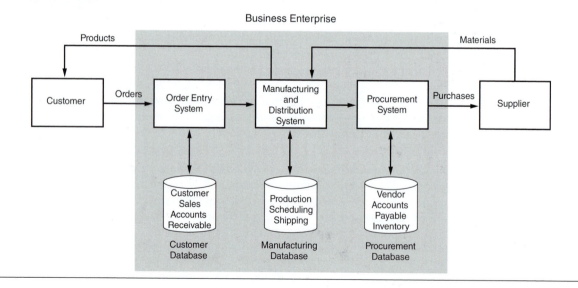

When a customer places an order, the order begins a paper-based journey around the company where it is keyed and rekeyed into the systems of several different departments. These redundant tasks cause delays and lost orders, as well as promote data entry errors. During transit through the various systems, the status of the order may be unknown at any point in time. For example, responding to a customer query, the marketing department may be unable to look into the production database to determine whether an order has been manufactured and shipped. Instead, the frustrated customer is told to call manufacturing. Similarly, the procurement of raw materials from suppliers is not linked to customer orders until they reach the manufacturing stage. This results in delays because manufacturing awaits the arrival of needed materials or in excessive investment in inventories to avoid stock-outs.

The lack of effective communication between systems in the traditional model is often the consequence of a fragmented systems design process. Each system tends to be designed as a solution to a specific operational problem rather than as a part of an overall strategy. Furthermore, because systems designed in-house emerge independently and over time, they are often constructed on different and incompatible technology platforms. Thus, special procedures and programs need to be created so that older mainframe systems using flat files can communicate with newer distributed systems that use relational databases. Special software patches are also needed to enable commercial systems from different vendors to communicate with each other as well as with custom systems that were developed in-house. Although communications between such a hodgepodge of systems is possible, it is highly fragmented and not conducive to efficient operations.

ERP systems support a smooth and seamless flow of information across the organization by providing a standardized environment for a firm's business processes and a common operational database that supports communications. An overview of ERP is presented in Figure 11.2. Data in the operational database are modeled, structured, and stored in accordance with the internal attributes of the data. They remain independent of any specific application. Extensive data sharing among users occurs through application-sensitive views that present the data in a way that meets all user needs.

ERP Core Applications

ERP functionality falls into two general groups of applications: core applications and business analysis applications. **Core applications** are those applications that operationally support the day-to-day activities of the business. If these applications fail, so does the business. Typical core applications include, but are not limited to, sales and distribution, business planning, production planning, shop floor control, and logistics. Core applications are also called **online transaction processing (OLTP)** applications. Figure 11.2 illustrates these functions applied to a manufacturing firm.

Sales and distribution functions handle order entry and delivery scheduling. This includes checking on product availability to ensure timely delivery and verifying customer credit limits. Unlike the previous example, customer orders are entered into the ERP only once. Because all users access a common database, the status of an order can be determined at any point. In fact, the customer will be able to check the order directly via an Internet connection. Such integration reduces manual activities, saves time, and decreases human error.

Business planning consists of forecasting demand, planning product production, and detailing routing information that describes the sequence and the stages of the actual production process. Capacity planning and production planning can be very complex; therefore, some ERPs provide simulation tools to help managers decide how to avoid shortages in materials, labor, or plant facilities. Once the master production schedule is

FIGURE 11.2	ERP System

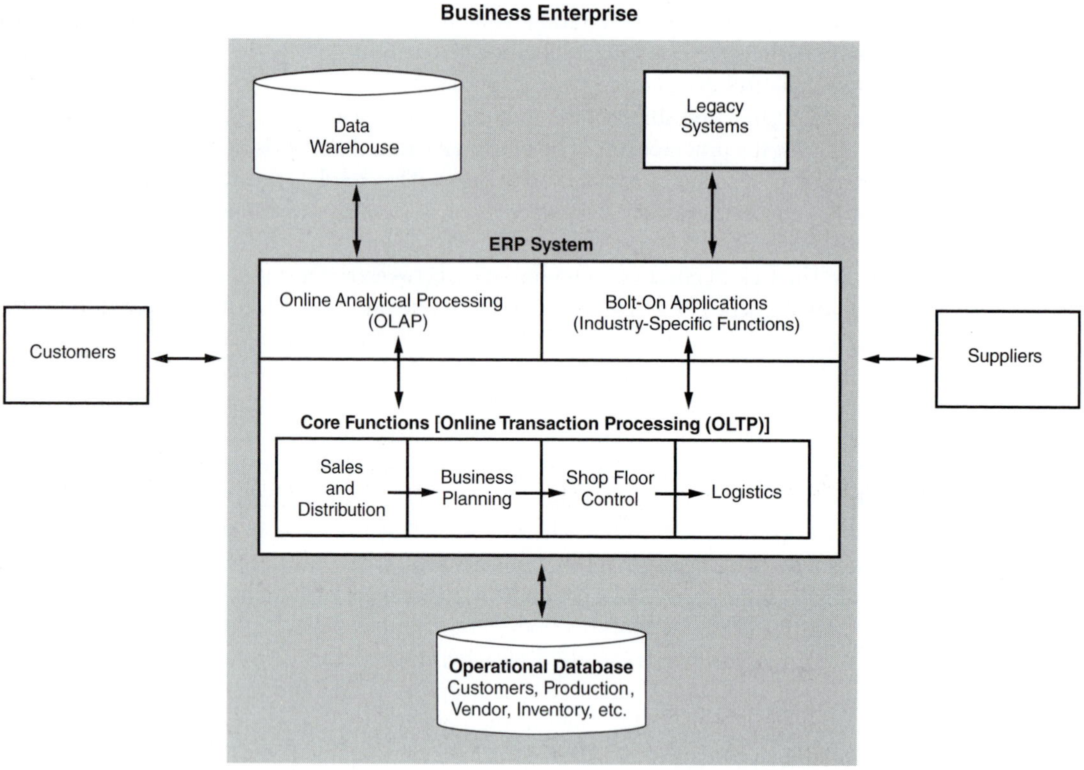

Business Enterprise

complete, the data are entered into the MRP (materials requirements planning) module, which provides three key pieces of information: an exception report, materials requirements listing, and inventory requisitions. The exception report identifies potential situations that will result in rescheduling production, such as late delivery of materials. The materials requirements listing shows the details of vendor shipments and expected receipts of products and components needed for the order. Inventory requisitions are used to trigger material purchase orders to vendors for items not in stock.

Shop floor control involves the detailed production scheduling, dispatching, and job costing activities associated with the actual production process. Finally, the logistics application is responsible for ensuring timely delivery to the customer. This consists of inventory and warehouse management, as well as shipping. Most ERPs also include their procurement activities within the logistics function.

Online Analytical Processing

An ERP is more than simply an elaborate transaction processing system. It is a decision support tool that supplies management with real-time information and permits timely decisions that are needed to improve performance and achieve competitive advantage. **Online analytical processing (OLAP)** includes decision support, modeling, information retrieval, ad hoc reporting/analysis, and what-if analysis. Some ERPs support these functions with their own industry-specific modules that can be added to the core system. Other ERP vendors have designed their systems to accept and communicate with specialized bolt-on packages that third-party vendors produce. Sometimes the user organization's decision support requirements are so unique that they need to integrate in-house legacy systems into the ERP.

However business analysis applications are obtained or derived, they are central to their successful function as a data warehouse. A **data warehouse** is a database constructed for quick searching, retrieval, ad hoc queries, and ease of use. The data are normally extracted periodically from an operational database or from a public information service. An ERP system could exist without having a data warehouse; similarly, organizations that have not implemented an ERP may deploy data warehouses. The trend, however, is that organizations that are serious about competitive advantage deploy both. The recommended data architecture for an ERP implementation includes separate operational and data warehouse databases. We will examine issues related to the creation and operation of a data warehouse later in the chapter.

ERP SYSTEM CONFIGURATIONS

Server Configurations

Most ERP systems are based on the **client-server model**, which will be discussed in detail in Chapter 5. Briefly, the client-server model is a form of network topology in which a user's computer or terminal (the client) accesses the ERP programs and data via a host computer called the server. The servers may be centralized, but the clients are usually located at multiple locations throughout the enterprise. Two basic architectures are the two-tier model and the three-tier model, as described in the following sections.

Two-Tier Model

In a typical **two-tier model**, the server handles both application and database duties. Client computers are responsible for presenting data to the user and passing user input back to the server. Some ERP vendors use this approach for local area network (LAN) applications for which the demand on the server is restricted to a relatively small population of users. This configuration is illustrated in Figure 11.3.

Three-Tier Model

The database and application functions are separated in the **three-tier model**. This architecture is typical of large ERP systems that use wide area networks (WANs) for connectivity among the users. Satisfying client requests requires two or more network connections. Initially, the client establishes communications with the application server. The application server then initiates a second connection to the database server. Figure 11.4 presents the three-tier model.

OLTP Versus OLAP Servers

When implementing an ERP system that will include a data warehouse, a clear distinction needs to be made between the competing types of data processing: OLTP and OLAP. OLTP events consist of large numbers of relatively simple transactions, such as updating accounting records that are stored in several related tables. For example, an

| FIGURE 11.3 | Two-Tier Client Server |

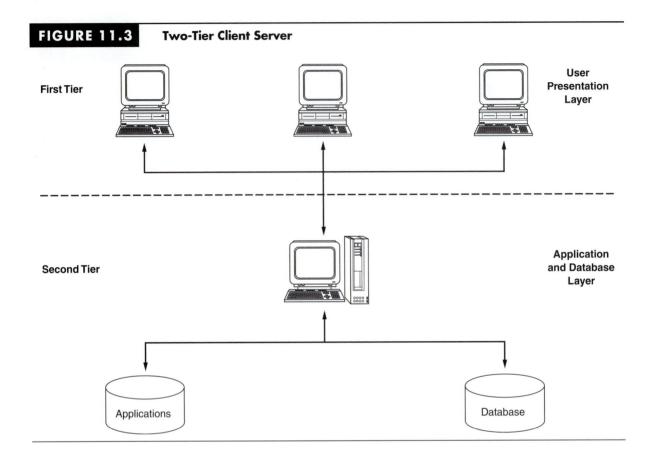

order entry system retrieves all of the data relating to a specific customer to process a sales transaction. Relevant data are selected from the Customer table, Invoice table, and a detailed Line Item table. Each table contains an embedded key (i.e., customer number), which is used to relate rows between different tables. The transaction processing activity involves updating the customer's current balance and inserting new records into the Invoice and Line Item tables. The relationships between records in such OLTP transactions are generally simple, and only a few records are actually retrieved or updated in a single transaction.

OLAP can be characterized as online transactions that:[1]

- Access very large amounts of data (e.g., several years of sales data).
- Analyze the relationships among many types of business elements such as sales, products, geographic regions, and marketing channels.
- Involve aggregated data such as sales volumes, budgeted dollars, and dollars spent.
- Compare aggregated data over hierarchical time periods (e.g., monthly, quarterly, yearly).
- Present data in different perspectives such as sales by region, by distribution channel, or by product.

---

1   The Queen's University of Belfast, Data Mining Techniques, http://www.pcc.qub.ac.uk.

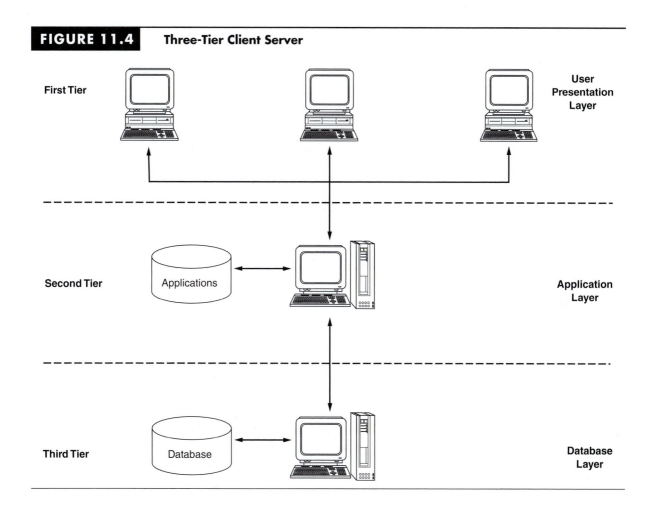

FIGURE 11.4   **Three-Tier Client Server**

- Involve complex calculations among data elements such as expected profit as a function of sales revenue for each type of sales channel in a particular region.
- Respond quickly to user requests so they can pursue an analytical thought process without being stymied by system delays.

An example of an OLAP transaction is the aggregation of sales data by region, product type, and sales channel. The OLAP query may need to access vast amounts of sales data over a multiyear period to find sales for each product type within each region. The user can further refine the query to identify sales volume by product for each sales channel within a given region. Finally, the user may decide to perform year-to-year or quarter-to-quarter comparisons for each sales channel. An OLAP application must be able to support this analysis online with rapid response.

The difference between OLAP and OLTP can be summarized as follows. OLTP applications support mission-critical tasks through simple queries of operational databases. OLAP applications support management-critical tasks through analytical investigation of complex data associations that are captured in data warehouses. OLAP and OLTP have specialized requirements that are in direct conflict. Figure 11.5 shows how the client-server architecture enables organizations to deploy separate and specialized

FIGURE 11.5	OLTP and OLAP Client Server

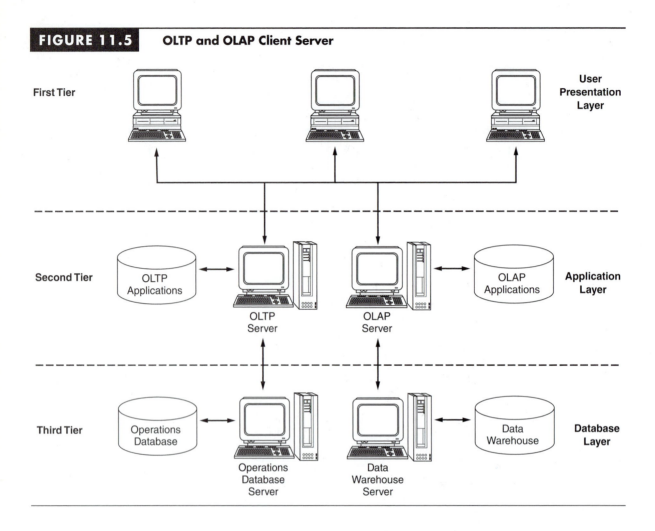

application and database servers to resolve these conflicting data management needs. OLAP servers support common analytical operations including consolidation, drill-down, and slicing and dicing.

- **Consolidation** is the aggregation or roll-up of data. For example, sales offices data can be rolled up to districts and districts rolled up to regions.
- **Drill-down** permits disaggregating data to reveal the underlying details that explain certain phenomena. For example, the user can drill down from total sales returns for a period to identify the actual products returned and the reasons for their return.
- **Slicing and dicing** enables the user to examine data from different viewpoints. One slice of data might show sales within each region. Another slice might present sales by product across regions. Slicing and dicing is often performed along a time axis to depict trends and patterns.

OLAP servers allow users to analyze complex data relationships. The physical database itself is organized in such a way that related data may be rapidly retrieved across multiple dimensions. Thus, OLAP database servers need to be efficient when storing and processing multidimensional data. Later in the chapter, data modeling and storage techniques that improve data warehouse efficiency will be examined. In contrast, relational databases for operations are modeled and optimized to handle OLTP applications. They concentrate on reliability and transaction processing speed, instead of decision support need.

Database Configuration

ERP systems are composed of thousands of database tables. Each table is associated with business processes that are coded into the ERP. The ERP implementation team, which includes key users and information technology (IT) professionals, selects specific database tables and processes by setting switches in the system. Determining how all the switches need to be set for a given configuration requires a deep understanding of the existing processes used in operating the business. Often, however, choosing table settings involves decisions to reengineer the company's processes so that they comply with the best business practices in use. In other words, the company typically changes its processes to accommodate the ERP rather than modifying the ERP to accommodate the company.

Bolt-On Software

Many organizations have found that ERP software alone cannot drive all the processes of the company. These firms use a variety of **bolt-on software** that third-party vendors provide. The decision to use bolt-on software requires careful consideration. Most of the leading ERP vendors have entered into partnership arrangements with third-party vendors that provide specialized functionality. The least risky approach is to choose a bolt-on that is endorsed by the ERP vendor. Some organizations, however, take a more independent approach. Domino's Pizza is a case in point.

Domino's Pizza

Domino's U.S. distribution delivered 338 million pizzas in 1998.[2] The company manufactures an average of 4.2 million pounds of dough per week in its eighteen U.S. distribution centers. A fleet of 160 trucks carries the dough along with other food and paper products to the 4,500 U.S. Domino's franchises. Domino's has no cutoff time for ordering supplies. Therefore, a franchise can call and adjust its order even after the truck has rolled away from the distribution center. To help anticipate demand, Domino's uses forecasting software from Prescient Systems Inc., which bolts on to their PeopleSoft ERP system. In addition, they use a system from Manugistics Inc. to schedule and route the delivery trucks. Each truck has an onboard computer system that feeds data into a time-and-attendance system from Kronos Inc., which connects to the PeopleSoft human resources module. Domino's also has an extensive data warehouse. To anticipate its market, Domino's performs data mining with software from Cognos Inc. and Hyperion Solutions Corp.

Domino's had been using these and other applications before it implemented an ERP. The company did not want to retire its existing applications, but discovered that the legacy system required data fields that the ERP did not provide. For instance, the routing system tells the truck drivers which stores to visit and in what order. The ERP

---

2   Slater, D. "The Ties That Bolt," Enterprise Resource Planning, *CIO Magazine* (April 15, 1999), 4–9.

system did not have a data field for specifying the delivery stop sequence. The warehousing system needs this information, however, to tell loaders what to put in the trucks and in what order. Having confidence in its in-house IT staff, Domino's management decided to take the relatively drastic step of modifying the ERP software to include these fields.

Supply Chain Management

Another development regarding the bolt-on software issue is the rapid convergence between ERP and bolt-on software functionality. **Supply chain management (SCM)** software is a case in point. The supply chain is the set of activities associated with moving goods from the raw materials stage to the consumer. This includes procurement, production scheduling, order processing, inventory management, transportation, warehousing, customer service, and forecasting the demand for goods. SCM systems are a class of application software that supports this task. Successful SCM coordinates and integrates these activities into a seamless process. In addition to the key functional areas within the organization, SCM links all of the partners in the chain, including vendors, carriers, third-party logistics companies, and information systems providers. Organizations can achieve competitive advantage by linking the activities in its supply chain more efficiently and effectively than its competitors.

Recognizing this need, ERP vendors have moved decisively to add SCM functionality to their ERP products. ERP systems and SCM systems are now on converging paths. SAP and Oracle have recently added an SCM module, while PeopleSoft has acquired smaller SCM vendors to integrate its SCM software into future releases. On the other hand, SCM software vendors are also expanding their functionality to appear more like ERP systems. As larger ERP vendors move into the midsize company market, the smaller SCM and ERP vendors will likely be pushed out of business.

DATA WAREHOUSING

Data warehousing is one of the fastest growing IT issues for businesses today. Not surprisingly, data warehousing functionality is being incorporated into all leading ERP systems. A data warehouse is a relational or multidimensional database that may consume hundreds of gigabytes or even terabytes of disk storage. When the data warehouse is organized for a single department or function, it is often called a **data mart**. Rather than containing hundreds of gigabytes of data for the entire enterprise, a data mart may have only tens of gigabytes of data. Other than size, we make no distinction between a data mart and a data warehouse. The issues discussed in this section apply to both.

The process of data warehousing involves extracting, converting, and standardizing an organization's operational data from ERP and legacy systems and loading it into a central archive—the data warehouse. Once loaded into the warehouse, data are accessible via various query and analysis tools that are used for data mining. Data mining is the process of selecting, exploring, and modeling large amounts of data to uncover relationships and global patterns that exist in large databases but are hidden among the vast number of facts. This involves sophisticated techniques that use database queries and artificial intelligence to model real-world phenomena from data collected from the warehouse.

Most organizations implement a data warehouse as part of a strategic IT initiative that involves an ERP system. Implementing a successful data warehouse involves installing a process for gathering data on an ongoing basis, organizing it into meaningful information, and delivering it for evaluation. The data warehousing process has the following essential stages:[3]

- Modeling data for the data warehouse
- Extracting data from operational databases
- Cleansing extracted data
- Transforming data into the warehouse model
- Loading the data into the data warehouse database

Modeling Data for the Data Warehouse

Chapter 8 stressed the importance of data normalization to eliminate three serious anomalies: the update, insertion, and deletion anomalies. Normalizing data in an operational database is necessary to efficiently and accurately reflect the dynamic interactions among entities. Data attributes are constantly updated, new attributes are added, and obsolete attributes are deleted. Even though a fully normalized database yields the flexible model needed for supporting multiple users in an operational environment, it would add unnecessary complexity and performance inefficiency to the operation of a data warehouse.

The Warehouse Consists of Denormalized Data

Because of the vast size of a data warehouse, such inefficiency can be devastating. A three-way join between tables in a large data warehouse may take an unacceptably long time to complete and may be unnecessary. In the data warehouse model, the relationship among attributes does not change. Because historical data are static in nature, nothing is gained by constructing normalized tables with dynamic links.

For example, in an operational database system, Product X may be an element of work-in-process (WIP) in Department A this month and part of Department B's WIP next month. In a properly normalized data model, it would be incorrect to include Department A's WIP data as part of a Sales Order table that records an order for Product X. Only the product item number would be included in the Sales Order table as a foreign key linking it to the Product table. Relational theory would call for a join (link) between the Sales Order table and Product table to determine the production status (i.e., which department the product is currently in) and other attributes of the product. From an operational perspective, complying with relational theory is important because the relation changes as the product moves through different departments over time. Relational theory does not apply to a data warehousing system because the Sales Order/Product relation is stable.

Wherever possible, therefore, normalized tables pertaining to selected events may be consolidated into denormalized tables. Figure 11.6 illustrates how sales order data are reduced to a single denormalized Sales Order table for storage in a data warehouse system.

Extracting Data from Operational Databases

Data extraction is the process of collecting data from operational databases, flat files, archives, and external data sources. Operational databases typically need to be out of service when data extraction occurs to avoid data inconstancies. Because of their large size and the need for a speedy transfer to minimize the downtime, little or no conversion of data occurs at this point. A technique called **changed data capture** can dramatically reduce the

---

3   P. Fiore, "Everyone Is Talking About Data Warehousing," *Evolving Enterprise* (Spring 1998), 2.

FIGURE 11.6 Denormalized Data

A. Normalized Representation for an Operational Database System

Customer Table

Customer Number	Name	Street	City	State
34675	John Smith	10 Elm	Bath	PA

Invoice Table

Invoice Number	Invoice Date	Shipped Date	Invoice Amount	Customer Number
8866376	06/12/09	06/23/09	600	34675

Line Item Table

Invoice Number	Item Number	Quantity	Price	Extended Price
8866376	j683	2	200	400
8866376	r223	5	40	200

B. Denormalized Representation for Data Warehouse System

Sales Order Table

Customer Number	Name	Street	City	State	Invoice Number	Invoice Date	Shipped Date	Invoice Amount	Item Number	Quantity	Price	Extended Price
34675	John Smith	10 Elm	Bath	PA	8866376	06/12/09	06/23/09	600	j683	2	200	400
34675	John Smith	10 Elm	Bath	PA	8866376	06/12/09	06/23/09	600	r223	5	40	200

extraction time by capturing only newly modified data. The extraction software compares the current operational database with an image of the data taken at the last transfer of data to the warehouse. Only the data that have changed in the interim are captured.

Extracting Snapshots *versus* Stabilized Data

Transaction data stored in the operational database go through several stages as economic events unfold. For example, a sales transaction first undergoes credit approval, then the product is shipped, then billing occurs, and finally payment is received. Each of these events changes the state of the transaction and associated accounts such as inventory, accounts receivable, and cash.

A key feature of a data warehouse is that the data contained in it are in a nonvolatile, stable state. Typically, transaction data are loaded into the warehouse only when the activity on them has been completed. Potentially important relationships between entities may, however, be absent from data that are captured in this stable state. For example, information about canceled sales orders will probably not be reflected among the sales orders that have been shipped and paid for before they are placed in the warehouse. One way to reflect these dynamics is to extract the operations data in slices of time. These slices provide snapshots of business activity. For example, decision makers may want to observe sales transactions approved, shipped, billed, and paid at various points in time along with snapshots of inventory levels at each state. Such data may be useful in depicting trends in the average time taken to approve credit or ship goods that might help explain lost sales.

Cleansing Extracted Data

Data cleansing involves filtering out or repairing invalid data prior to being stored in the warehouse. Operational data are dirty for many reasons. Clerical, data entry, and computer program errors can create illogical data such as negative inventory quantities, misspelled names, and blank fields. Data cleansing also involves transforming data into standard business terms with standard data values. Data are often combined from multiple systems that use slightly different spellings to represent common terms, such as cust, cust_id, or cust_no. Some operational systems may use entirely different terms to refer to the same entity. For example, a bank customer with a certificate of deposit and an outstanding loan may be called a lender by one system and a borrower by another. The source application may use cryptic or difficult-to-understand terms for a number of reasons. For example, some older legacy systems were designed at a time when programming rules placed severe restrictions on naming and formatting data attributes. Also, a commercial application may assign attribute names that are too generic for the needs of the data warehouse user. Businesses that purchase commercial data, such as competitive performance information or market surveys, need to extract data from whatever format the external source provides and reorganize them according to the conventions used in the data warehouse. During the cleansing process, therefore, the attributes taken from multiple systems need to be transformed into uniform, standard business terms. This tends to be an expensive and labor-intensive activity, but one that is critical in establishing data integrity in the warehouse. Figure 11.7 illustrates the role of data cleansing in building and maintaining a data warehouse.

Transforming Data into the Warehouse Model

A data warehouse is composed of both detail and summary data. To improve efficiency, data can be transformed into summary views before they are loaded into the warehouse.

FIGURE 11.7	Data Warehouse System

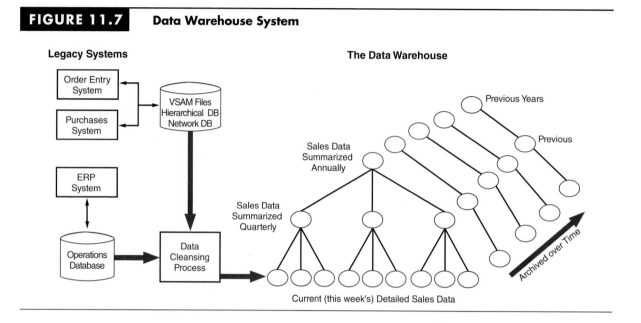

For example, many decision makers may need to see product sales figures summarized weekly, monthly, quarterly, or annually. It may not be practical to summarize information from detail data every time the user needs it. A data warehouse that contains the most frequently requested summary views of data can reduce the amount of processing time during analysis. Referring again to Figure 11.7, we see the creation of summary views over time. These are typically created around business entities such as customers, products, and suppliers. Unlike operational views, which are virtual in nature with underlying base tables, data warehouse views are physical tables. Most OLAP software will, however, permit the user to construct virtual views from detail data when one does not already exist.

A data warehouse will often provide multiple summary views based on the same detailed data such as customers or products. For example, several different summary views may be generated from sales order detail data. These may include summaries by product, customer, and region. From such views, an analyst can drill down into the underlying detail data. Many business problems require a review of detail data to fully evaluate a trend, pattern, or anomaly exhibited in the summarized reports. Also, a single anomaly in detail data may manifest itself differently in different summary views.

Loading the Data into the Data Warehouse Database

Most organizations have found that data warehousing success requires that the data warehouse be created and maintained separately from the operational (transaction processing) databases. This point is developed further in the next sections.

Internal Efficiency

One reason for a separate data warehouse is that the structural and operational requirements of transaction processing and data mining systems are fundamentally different, making it impractical to keep both operational (current) and archive data in the same database. Transaction processing systems need a data structure that supports performance, whereas data mining systems need data organized in a manner that permits broad examination and the detection of underlying trends.

Integration of Legacy Systems

The continued influence of legacy systems is another reason that the data warehouse needs to be independent of operations. A remarkably large number of business applications continue to run in the mainframe environment of the 1970s. By some estimates, more than 70 percent of business data for large corporations still resides in the mainframe environment. The data structures these systems employ are often incompatible with the architectures of modern data mining tools. Hence, transaction data that are stored in navigational databases and Virtual Storage Access Method (VSAM) systems often end up in large tape libraries that are isolated from the decision process. A separate data warehouse provides a venue for integrating the data from legacy and contemporary systems into a common structure that supports entity-wide analysis.

Consolidation of Global Data

Finally, the emergence of the global economy has brought about fundamental changes in business organizational structure and has profoundly changed the information requirements of business entities. Unique business complexities challenge decision makers in the global corporation. For example, they need to assess the profitability of products built and sold in multiple countries with volatile currencies. Such challenges add complexity to data mining. A separate centralized data warehouse is an effective means of collecting, standardizing, and assimilating data from diverse sources.

In conclusion, the creation of a data warehouse separate from operational systems is a fundamental data warehousing concept. Many organizations now consider data warehouse systems to be key components of their information systems strategy. As such, they allocate considerable resources to build data warehouses concurrently with the operational systems being implemented.

Decisions Supported by the Data Warehouse

By making the data warehouse as flexible and friendly as possible, it becomes accessible by many end users. Some decisions that a data warehouse supports are not fundamentally different from those that traditional databases support. Other information uses, such as multidimensional analysis and information visualization, are not possible with traditional systems. Some users of the data warehouse need routine reports based on traditional queries. When standard reports can be anticipated in advance, they can be provided automatically as a periodic product. Automatic generation of standard information reduces access activity against the data warehouse and will improve its efficiency in dealing with more esoteric needs.

Drill-down capability is a useful data analysis technique associated with data mining. Drill-down analysis begins with the summary views of data described previously. When anomalies or interesting trends are observed, the user drills down to lower-level views and ultimately into the underlying detail data. Obviously, such analysis cannot be anticipated like a standard report. Drill-down capability is an OLAP feature of data mining tools available to the user. Tools for data mining are evolving rapidly to satisfy the decision maker's need to understand the business unit's behavior in relation to key entities including customers, suppliers, employees, and products. Standard reports and queries

TABLE 11.1	**Applications of Data Mining**	
	Business Field	**Application**
	Banking/Investments	Detect patterns of fraudulent credit card use.
		Identify loyal customers and predict those likely to change their credit card affiliation.
		Examine historical market data to determine investors' stock trading rules.
		Predict credit card spending of key customer groups.
		Identify correlations between different financial indicators.
	Health Care and Medical Insurance	Predict office visits from historical analysis of historical patient behavior.
		Identify successful and economical medical therapies for different illnesses.
		Identify which medical procedures tend to be claimed together.
		Predict which customers will buy new policies.
		Identify behavior patterns associated with high-risk customers.
		Identify indicators of fraudulent behavior.
	Marketing	Identify buying patterns based on historical customer data.
		Identify relationships among customer demographic data.
		Predict response to various forms of marketing and promotion campaigns.

produced from summary views can answer many what questions, but drill-down capability answers the *why* and *how* questions. Table 11.1 summarizes some of the applications of data mining in decision support.

Supporting Supply Chain Decisions from the Data Warehouse

The primary reason for data warehousing is to optimize business performance. Many organizations believe that more strategic benefit can be gained by sharing data externally. By providing customers and suppliers with the information they need when they need it, the company can improve its relationships and provide better service. The potential gain to the giving organization is seen in a more responsive and efficient supply chain. Using Internet technologies and OLAP applications, an organization can share its data warehouse with its trading partners and, in effect, treat them like divisions of the firm. A few examples of this approach are outlined in the following extract.[4]

> Western Digital Corporation, a leading manufacturer of hard drives, plans to grant certain suppliers access to its data warehouse so suppliers can view performance data on their parts. Because Western Digital maintains a limited engineering staff, the company relies on its suppliers to act as strategic partners in product development. Providing suppliers with performance data allows them to make improvements and

---

4   B. Davis, "Data Warehouses Open Up," *Information Week Online News in Review* (June 28, 1999).

participate in the engineering process. The suppliers improve their parts, which in turn improves Western Digital's products.

The company's data warehouse holds more than 600 gigabytes of raw data collected from more than 100,000 drives that it manufactures each day. Approximately 800 attributes are collected on each drive, which can be analyzed using OLAP software. The systems feeding the warehouse include ERP applications, data from trouble-call centers, data from failure-analysis systems, and field test data from customer sites and service centers. The company routinely searches the data warehouse for failure information on every drive that it manufactures. All failures and their causes can be linked back to the supplier.

The General Motors (GM) supply-chain data warehouse is available via the Web to more than 5,000 suppliers worldwide. Suppliers can log on to a secure Web site and query information on the quantities of supplies shipped, delivery times, and prices. This information will help GM suppliers optimize their product planning, ability to source materials, and shipping-fulfillment processes.

MIM Health Plans Inc., an independent pharmacy benefits management company, lets its customers view warehouse data to promote better buying decisions. For instance, benefits managers can view reports and drill down into the warehouse to see claims costs, overall costs, the number of prescriptions ordered in a given time period, the number of brand versus generic drugs, and other decision metrics.

RISKS ASSOCIATED WITH ERP IMPLEMENTATION

The benefits from ERP can be significant, but they do not come risk-free to the organization. An ERP system is not a silver bullet that will, by its mere existence, solve an organization's problems. If that were the case, there would never be ERP failures, but there have been many. This section examines some of the risk issues that need to be considered.

Big Bang Versus Phased-in Implementation

Implementing an ERP system has more to do with changing the way in which an organization does business than it does with technology. As a result, most ERP implementation failures are the result of cultural problems within the firm that stand in opposition to the objective of process reengineering. Strategies for implementing ERP systems to achieve this objective follow two general approaches: the big bang and the phased-in approach.

The **big bang** method is the more ambitious and risky of the two. Organizations taking this approach attempt to switch operations from their old legacy systems to the new system in a single event that implements the ERP across the entire company. Although this method has certain advantages, it has been associated with numerous system failures. Because the new ERP system means new ways of conducting business, getting the entire organization on board and in sync can be a daunting task. On day 1 of the implementation, no one within the organization will have had any experience with the new system. In a sense, everyone in the company is a trainee learning a new job.

The new ERP system will initially meet with opposition because using it involves compromise. The legacy systems, which everyone in the organization was familiar with, had been honed over the years to meet exact needs. In most cases, ERP systems have neither the range of functionality nor the familiarity of the legacy systems that they replace. Also, because a single system is now serving the entire organization, individuals at data input points often find themselves entering considerably more data than they did previously with the more narrowly focused legacy system.

As a result, the speed of the new system often suffers and causes disruptions to daily operations. These problems are typically experienced whenever any new system is implemented. The magnitude of the problem is the issue under the big bang approach in which everyone in the company is affected. Once the initial adjustment period has passed and the new culture emerges, however, the ERP becomes an effective operational and strategic tool that provides competitive advantage to the firm.

Because of the disruptions associated with the big bang, the **phased-in** approach has emerged as a popular alternative. It is particularly suited to diversified organizations whose units do not share common processes and data. In these types of companies, independent ERP systems can be installed in each business unit over time to accommodate the adjustment periods needed for assimilation. Common processes and data, such as the general ledger function, can be integrated across the organization without disrupting operations throughout the firm.

Organizations that are not diversified can also employ the phased-in approach. The implementation usually begins with one or more key processes, such as order entry. The goal is to get ERP up and running concurrently with legacy systems. As more of the organization's functions are converted to ERP, legacy systems are systematically retired. In the interim, the ERP is interfaced to legacy systems. During this period, the objectives of system integration and process reengineering, which are fundamental to the ERP model, are not achievable. To take full advantage of the ERP, process reengineering will still need to occur. Otherwise, the organization will have simply replaced its old legacy system with a very expensive new one.

Opposition to Changes in the Business's Culture

To be successful, all functional areas of the organization need be involved in determining the culture of the firm and in defining the new system's requirements. The firm's willingness and ability to undertake a change of the magnitude of an ERP implementation is an important consideration. If the corporate culture is such that change is not tolerated or desired, then an ERP implementation will not be successful.

The technological culture must also be assessed. Organizations that lack technical support staff for the new system or have a user base that is unfamiliar with computer technology face a steeper learning curve and a potentially greater barrier to acceptance of the system by its employees.

Choosing the Wrong ERP

Because ERP systems are prefabricated systems, users need to determine whether a particular ERP fits their organization's culture and its business processes. A common reason for system failure is when the ERP does not support one or more important business processes. In one example, a textile manufacturer in India implemented an ERP only to discover afterward that it did not accommodate a basic need.

The textile company had a policy of maintaining two prices for each item of inventory that it sold. One price was used for the domestic market, and a second price, which was four times higher, was for export sales. The ERP that the user implemented was not designed to allow two different prices for the same inventory item. The changes needed to make the ERP work were both extensive and expensive. Serious system disruptions resulted from this oversight. Furthermore, modifying an ERP program and database can introduce potential processing errors and can make updating the system to later versions difficult.

Goodness of Fit

Management needs to make sure that the ERP they choose is right for the company. No single ERP system is capable of solving all the problems of all organizations. For example, SAP's R/3 was designed primarily for manufacturing firms with highly predictable processes that are relatively similar to those of other manufacturers. It may not be the best solution for a service-oriented organization that has a great need for customer-related activities conducted over the Internet.

Finding a good functionality fit requires a software selection process that resembles a funnel, which starts broad and systematically becomes more focused. It begins with a large number of software vendors that are potential candidates. Evaluation questions are asked of vendors in iterative rounds. Starting with a large population of vendors and a small number of high-level qualifier questions, the number of vendors is reduced to a manageable few. With proper questioning, more than half the vendors are removed from contention with as few as ten to twenty questions. In each succeeding round, the questions asked become more detailed and the population of vendors decreases.

When a business's processes are truly unique, the ERP system must be modified to accommodate industry-specific (bolt-on) software or to work with custom-built legacy systems. Some organizations, such as telecommunications service providers, have unique billing operations that off-the-shelf ERP systems cannot satisfy. Before embarking on the ERP journey, the organization's management needs to assess whether it can and should reengineer its business practices around a standardized model.

System Scalability Issues

If an organization's management expects business volumes to increase substantially during the life of the ERP system, then there is a scalability issue that needs to be addressed. **Scalability** is the system's ability to grow smoothly and economically as user requirements increase. The term *system* in this context refers to the technology platform, application software, network configuration, or database. Smooth and economical growth is the ability to increase system capacity at an acceptable incremental cost per unit of capacity without encountering limits that would demand a system upgrade or replacement. User requirements pertain to volume-related activities such as transaction processing volume, data entry volume, data output volume, data storage volume, or increases in the user population.

To illustrate scalability, four dimensions of scalability are important: size, speed, workload, and transaction cost. In assessing scalability needs for an organization, each of these dimensions in terms of the ideal of linear scaling must be considered.[5]

> *Size.* With no other changes to the system, if database size increases by a factor of x, then query response time will increase by no more than a factor of x in a scalable system. For example, if business growth causes the database to increase from 100 to 500 gigabytes, then transactions and queries that previously took 1 second will now take no more than 5 seconds.

---

5   R. Winter, "Scalable Systems: Lexicology of Scale," *Intelligent Enterprise Magazine* (March 2000), 68–74.

Speed. An increase in hardware capacity by a factor of x will decrease query response time by no less than a factor of x in a scalable system. For example, increasing the number of input terminals (nodes) from one to twenty will increase transaction processing time proportionately. Transactions that previously took 20 seconds will now take no more than 1 second in a system with linear scaling.

Workload. If workload in a scalable system is increased by a factor of x, then response time, or throughput, can be maintained by increasing hardware capacity by a factor of no more than x. For example, if transaction volume increased from 400 per hour to 4,000 per hour, the previous response time can be achieved by increasing the number of processors by a factor of ten in a system that is linearly scalable.

Transaction cost. In a scalable system, increases in workload do not increase transaction cost. Therefore, an organization should not need to increase system capacity faster than demand. For example, if the cost of processing a transaction in a system with one processor is 10 cents, then it should still cost no more than 10 cents when the number of processors is increased to handle larger volumes of transactions.

Vendors of ERP systems sometimes advertise scalability as if it were a single-dimension factor. In fact, it is a multifaceted issue. Some systems accommodate growth in user populations better than others. Some systems can be scaled to provide more efficient access to large databases when business growth demands it. All systems, however, have their scaling limits. Because infinite scalability is impossible, prospective users need to assess their needs and determine how much scalability they want to purchase up front and what form it should take. The key is to anticipate specific scalability issues before making an ERP investment and before the issues become reality.

Choosing the Wrong Consultant

Implementing an ERP system is an event that most organizations will undergo only once. Success of the projects rests on skills and experience that typically do not exist in-house. Because of this, virtually all ERP implementations involve an outside consulting firm, which coordinates the project, helps the organization to identify its needs, develops a requirements specification for the ERP, selects the ERP package, and manages the cutover. ERP consulting has grown into a $20 billion-per-year market. The fee for a typical implementation is normally between three and five times the cost of the ERP software license.

Consulting firms with large ERP practices at times have been desperately short of human resources. This was especially true in the mid- to late-1990s, when thousands of clients were rushing to implement ERP systems before the new millennium to avoid Y2K (year 2000) problems. As demand for ERP implementations grew beyond the supply of qualified consultants, more and more stories of botched projects materialized.

A frequent complaint is that consulting firms promise experienced professionals, but deliver incompetent trainees. They have been accused of employing a bait-and-switch maneuver to get contracts. At the initial engagement interview, the consulting firm introduces their top consultants, who are sophisticated, talented, and persuasive. The client agrees to the deal with the firm, but incorrectly assumes that these individuals, or others with similar qualifications, will actually implement the system.

The problem has been equated to the airline industry's common practice of overbooking flights. Some suggest that consulting firms, not wanting to turn away business, are guilty of overbooking their consulting staff. The consequences, however, are far graver than the inconvenience of missing a flight—a voucher for a free flight cannot compensate for the damages done. Therefore, before engaging an outside consultant, management should:

- Interview the staff proposed for the project and draft a detailed contract specifying which members of the consulting team will be assigned to which tasks.
- Establish in writing how staff changes will be handled.
- Conduct reference checks of the proposed staff members.
- Align the consultants' interests with those of the organization by negotiating a pay-for-performance scheme based on achieving certain milestones in the project. For example, the actual amount paid to the consultant may be between 85 and 115 percent of the contracted fee, based on whether a successful project implementation comes in under or over schedule.
- Set a firm termination date for the consultant to avoid consulting arrangements becoming interminable, resulting in dependency and an endless stream of fees.

High Cost and Cost Overruns

Total cost of ownership (TCO) for ERP systems varies greatly from company to company. For medium- to large-sized systems implementations, costs range from hundreds of thousands to hundreds of millions of dollars. TCO includes hardware, software, consulting services, internal personnel costs, installation, and upgrades and maintenance to the system for the first 2 years after implementation. The risk comes in the form of underestimated and unanticipated costs. Some of the more commonly experienced problems occur in the following areas.

Training. Training costs are invariably higher than estimated because management focuses primarily on the cost of teaching employees the new software. This is only part of the needed training. Employees also need to learn new procedures, which is often overlooked during the budgeting process.

System testing and integration. In theory, ERP is a holistic model in which one system drives the entire organization. The reality, however, is that many organizations use their ERP as a backbone system that is attached to legacy systems and other bolt-on systems, which support the unique needs of the firm. Integrating these disparate systems with the ERP may involve writing special conversion programs or even modifying the internal code of the ERP. Integration and testing are done on a case-by-case basis; thus, the cost is extremely difficult to estimate in advance.

Database conversion. A new ERP system usually means a new database. Data conversion is the process of transferring data from the legacy system's flat files to the ERP's relational database. When the legacy system's data are reliable, the conversion process may be accomplished through automated procedures. Even under ideal circumstances, a high degree of testing and manual reconciliation is necessary to ensure that the transfer was complete and accurate. More often, the data in the legacy system are not reliable (sometimes called dirty). Empty fields and corrupted data values cause conversion problems that demand human intervention and data rekeying. Also, and more importantly, the structure of the legacy data is likely to be incompatible with the reengineered processes of the new system. Depending on the extent of the process reengineering involved, the entire database may need to be converted through manual data entry procedures.

Develop Performance Measures

Because ERPs are extremely expensive to implement, many managers are often dismayed at the apparent lack of cost savings that they achieve in the short term. In fact, a great deal of criticism about the relative success of ERPs relates to whether they provide benefits that outweigh their cost.

To assess benefits, management first needs to know what they want and need from the ERP. They should then establish key performance measures such as reductions in inventory levels, inventory turnover, stock-outs, and average order fulfillment time that reflect their expectations. To monitor performance in such key areas, some organizations establish an independent value assessment group that reports to top management. Although financial break-even on an ERP will take years, by developing focused and measurable performance indicators, an operational perspective on its success can be developed.

Disruptions to Operations

ERP systems can wreak havoc in the companies that install them. In a Deloitte Consulting survey of sixty-four *Fortune* 500 companies, 25 percent of the firms surveyed admitted that they experienced a drop in performance in the period immediately following implementation. The reengineering of business processes that often accompanies ERP implementation is the most commonly attributed cause of performance problems. Operationally speaking, when business begins under the ERP system, everything looks and works differently from the way it did with the legacy system. An adjustment period is needed for everyone to reach a comfortable point on the learning curve. Depending on the culture of the organization and attitudes toward change within the firm, adjustment may take longer in some firms than in others. The list of major organizations that have experienced serious disruptions includes Dow Chemical, Boeing, Dell Computer, Apple Computer, Whirlpool Corporation, and Waste Management. The most notorious case in the press was Hershey Foods Corporation, which had trouble processing orders through its new ERP system and was unable to ship products.

As a result of these disruptions, Hershey's 1999 third-quarter sales dropped by 12.4 percent compared to the previous year's sales, and earnings were down by 18.6 percent. Hershey's problem has been attributed to two strategic errors related to system implementation. First, because of schedule overruns, it decided to switch to the new system during their busy season. The inevitable snags that arise from implementations of complex systems like SAP's R/3 are easier to deal with during slack business periods. Secondly, many experts believe that Hershey attempted to do too much in a single implementation. In addition to the R/3 system, it implemented a customer relations management system and logistics software from two different vendors, which had to interface with R/3. The ERP and these bolt-on components were all implemented using the big bang approach.

IMPLICATIONS FOR INTERNAL CONTROL AND AUDITING

As with any system, the internal control and audit of ERP systems are issues. Key concerns are examined next within the COSO framework.

Transaction Authorization

A key benefit of an ERP system is its tightly integrated architecture of modules. This structure, however, also poses potential problems for transaction authorization. For example, the bill of materials drives many manufacturing systems. If the procedures for the creation of the bill of materials are not configured correctly, every component that uses the bill of materials could be affected. Controls need to be built into the system to validate transactions before other modules accept and act upon them. Because of an ERP's real-time orientation, they are more dependent on programmed controls than on human intervention, as was the case with legacy systems. The challenge for auditors in verifying transaction authorization is to gain a detailed knowledge of the ERP system configuration as well as a thorough understanding of the business processes and the flow of information between system components.

Segregation of Duties

Operational decisions in ERP-based organizations are pushed down to a point as close as possible to the source of the event. Manual processes that normally require segregation of duties are, therefore, often eliminated in an ERP environment. For example, shop supervisors may order inventories from suppliers and receiving dock personnel may post inventory receipts to the inventory records in real time. Furthermore, ERP forces together many different business functions, such as order entry, billing, and accounts payable, under a single integrated system. Organizations using ERP systems must establish new security, audit, and control tools to ensure duties are properly segregated. An important aspect of such control is the assignment of *roles*, which is discussed in a later section.

Supervision

An often-cited pitfall of an ERP implementation is that management does not fully understand its impact on business. Too often, after the ERP is up and running, only the implementation team understands how it works. Because their traditional responsibilities will be changed, supervisors need to acquire an extensive technical and operational understanding of the new system. Typically, when an organization implements an ERP, many decision-making responsibilities are pushed down to the shop floor level. The employee-empowered philosophy of ERP should not eliminate supervision as an internal control. Instead, it should provide substantial efficiency benefits. Supervisors should have more time to manage the shop floor and, through improved monitoring capability, increase their span of control.

Accounting Records

ERP systems have the ability to streamline the entire financial reporting process. In fact, many organizations can and do close their books daily. OLTP data can be manipulated quickly to produce ledger entries, accounts receivable and payable summaries, and financial consolidation for both internal and external users. Traditional batch controls and audit trails are no longer needed in many cases. This risk is mitigated by improved data entry accuracy through the use of default values, cross-checking, and specified user views of data.

In spite of ERP technology, some risk to accounting record accuracy may still exist. Because of the close interfaces with customers and suppliers, some organizations run the risk that corrupted or inaccurate data may be passed from these external sources and corrupt the ERP accounting database. Additionally, many organizations need to import data from legacy systems into their ERP systems. These data may be laden with problems such as duplicate records, inaccurate values, or incomplete fields. Consequently, strict data cleansing is an important control. Special scrubber programs are used as interfaces between the ERP and the exporting systems to reduce these risks and ensure that the most accurate and current data are being received.

Independent Verification

Because ERP systems employ OLTP, traditional, independent verification controls such as reconciling batch control numbers serve little purpose. Similarly, process reengineering to improve efficiency also changes the nature of independent verification. For example, the traditional three-way match of the purchase order, receiving report, and invoice and the subsequent writing of a check may be completely automated in an ERP environment. The focus of independent verification thus needs to be redirected from the individual transaction level to one that views overall performance. ERP systems come with canned controls and can be configured to produce performance reports that should be used as assessment tools. Internal auditors also play an important role in this environment and need to acquire a thorough technical background and comprehensive understanding of the ERP system. Ongoing independent verification efforts can be conducted only by a team well versed in ERP technology.

Access Controls

Access security is one of the most critical control issues in an ERP environment. The goal of ERP access control is to maintain data confidentiality, integrity, and availability. Security weaknesses can result in transaction errors, irregularities, data corruption, and financial statement misrepresentations. Also, uncontrolled access exposes organizations to cybercriminals who steal and subsequently sell critical data to competitors. Security administrators therefore need to control access to the tasks and operations that process or otherwise manipulate sensitive corporate data.

Traditional Access Control Models

Traditionally, the owner of a system resources (data, functions and processes) grants access privileges individually to users based on the individual's trust level and job description. Access control is typically achieved via an **access control list** (or access token) within the user's application.[6] The access control list specifies the user ID, the resources available to the user, and the level of permission granted such as read-only, edit, or create. Although this model allows for the assignment of specific access privileges to individuals, it is quite inflexible. The sheer volume and variety of access privilege needs in modern ERP environments presents a significant administrative burden. Any access-granting model must efficiently keep up with new hires, changes to existing privileges

---

6   Access control list and access tokens were discussed in detail in Chapter 3 within the broader context of general controls.

FIGURE 11.8   Access Control List versus RBAC

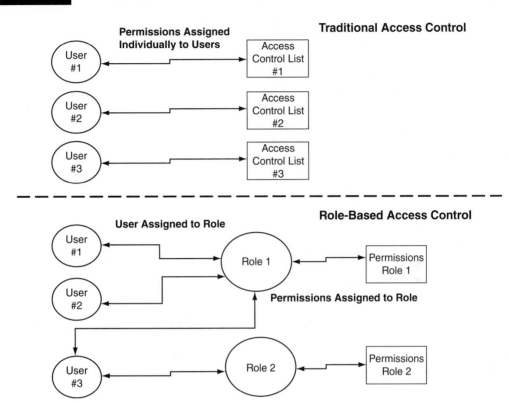

brought about by promotions and individuals transferring from one department to another, and personnel terminations. To meet these demands, modern ERP systems employ **role-based access control (RBAC)**, which is discussed next.

Role-Based Access Control (RBAC)

A **role** is a formal technique for grouping together users according to the system resources they need to perform their assigned tasks. For example, a system administrator could create a Sales Role for sales department personnel that permits access only to the ERP's Sales Module and certain documents such as customer orders, sales orders, and customer records. When an employee joins the sales department (whether a new hire or transfer from another department), he or she will be assigned to the Sales Role and, through it, can access to its pre specified resources. Figure 11.8 illustrates the difference between RBAC and the traditional access control list approach.

Notice from the figure how this technique assigns access permissions to the role an individual plays in the organization rather than directly to the individual. Therefore, more than one individual can be assigned to a role and a predefined set of access permissions. Also, an individual may be assigned more than one role, but can log into the system only under one role at a time. Thus, RBAC conveniently handles many-to-many relationships between users and permissions and facilitates dealing efficiently with vast numbers of employees.

FIGURE 11.9	**SAP Role Definition**

ERP Role Name: **AP Processing**   **Location: AP Department**

Role Goal: Data Entry of Customer Invoices and Check Requests

Knowledge, Skills: Knowledge of invoice processing from receipt to payment and relevant finance and procurement SAP modules, Vendor Master Data, P-card processes.   Understanding of IRS 1099 reporting & processing requirements.

Responsibilities/Tasks:

--Review and verify parked invoices and submit to Accounts Payable
--Park non-P.O. invoices (check request)
--Enter invoices for goods received into SAP; code invoices for payment (park)

SAP Security Considerations:

AP	Transaction Type		
FB03	Display Document	FB04	Display Changes
FBD3	Display Recurring Entry	FBL1	
FBL1N	Display Vendor Line Item	FBL3N	Account Line Item Display
FBV2	Change Parked Document	FBV3	Display Parked Documents
FCH1	Display Check Information	FCH2	Display Payment Document checks
FCHN	Check Register	FK10N	Vendor Balance Display
FV60	Park/Edit Invoice	PV65	Park/Edit Credit Memo
MIR4	Display Invoice Document	MIR5	Display List of Invoice

ERPs come with predefined roles with preassigned permissions. Administrators and line managers may also create new roles, modify existing roles, and delete roles that are no longer needed. Creating a role involves defining the following role attributes:

1. A stated set of business responsibilities to be performed within the role
2. The technical competencies needed to perform the role
3. The specific transactions (permissions) required to carry out the stated responsibilities

Figure 11.9 presents a SAP role definition for an accounts payable role in a hypothetical organization. The individual(s) assigned this role is governed in his or her access to specific SAP program modules (in this case AP) and to specific activities within the module by the transaction code list in the *SAP Security Considerations* section of the role definition.

Internal Control Issues Related to ERP Roles

Although RBAC is an excellent mechanism for efficiently managing access control, the process of creating, modifying, and deleting roles is an internal control issue of concern for management and auditors alike. The following points highlight the key concerns:

1. The creation of unnecessary roles
2. The rule of least access should apply to permission assignments
3. Monitor role creation and permission-granting activities

The Creation of Unnecessary Roles

The fundamental objective of RBAC is to provide access in accordance with an organization's needs, which derive from defined tasks rather than an individual's wants. Managers in ERP environments, however, have significant discretion in creating new roles for individuals. This may be done for employees who need access to resources for special and/or one-time projects. Such access-granting authority needs to be tempered with judgment to prevent the number of roles from multiplying to the point of becoming dysfunctional and thus creating a control risk. Indeed, an oft-cited problem in ERP environments is that roles tend to proliferate to a point at which their numbers actually exceed the number of employees in the organization. Policies need to be in place to prevent the creation of unnecessary new roles and to ensure that temporary role assignments are deleted when the reason for them terminates.

The Rule of Least Access

Access privileges (permissions) should be granted on a need-to-know basis only. Nevertheless, ERP users tend to accumulate unneeded permissions over time. This is often due to two problems:

1. Managers fail to exercise adequate care in assigning permissions as part of their role-granting authority. Because managers are not always experts in internal controls they may not recognize when excessive permissions are awarded to an individual.
2. Managers tend to be better at issuing privileges than removing them. As a result, an individual may retain unneeded access privileges from a previous job assignment that creates a segregation of duties violation when combined with a newly assigned role.

Policies should be in place to require managers to apply due diligence in assigning permissions to roles to avoid the granting of excessive access. They should assign privileges based on the task at hand and be aware of the individuals' existing permissions that may pose a control violation.

Monitor Role Creation and Permission-Granting Activities

Effective RBAC management demands procedures that that monitor role creation and permission granting to ensure compliance with internal control objectives. Verifying role compliance across all applications and users in an ERP environment, however, poses a highly complex and technical problem that does not lend itself to manual techniques. **Role-based governance** systems are available for this purpose. These systems allow managers to:

*   View the current and historical inventory of roles, permissions granted, and the individuals assigned to roles.
*   Identify unnecessary or inappropriate access entitlements and segregation-of-duties violations.
*   Verify that changes to roles and entitlements have been successfully implemented.

These systems can continually monitor for risk and issue alerts when violations are detected so that remedial action can be taken. In addition, role-based governance can maintain an audit trail to provide a record of violations and evidence of compliance.

Contingency Planning

The implementation of an ERP creates an environment with a single point of failure, which places the organization at risk from equipment failure, sabotage, or natural disaster. To control this risk an organization needs an effective contingency plan that can be invoked quickly in the event of a disaster. Two general approaches are outlined next.

Centralized organizations with highly integrated business units may need a single global ERP system that is accessed via the Internet or private lines from around the world to consolidate data from subsidiary systems. A server failure under this model could leave the entire organization unable to process transactions. To control against this, two linked servers may be connected in redundant backup mode. All production processing is done on one server. If it fails, processing is automatically transferred to the other server. Organizations that want more security and resilience may arrange servers in a cluster of three or more that dynamically share the workload. Processing can be redistributed if one or more of the servers in the cluster fail.

Companies whose organizational units are autonomous and do not share common customers, suppliers, or product lines often choose to install regional servers. This approach permits independent processing and spreads the risk associated with server failure. For example, BP Amoco implemented SAP's R/3 into seventeen separate business groups.

SUMMARY

This chapter opened by comparing the function and data storage techniques of a traditional flat-file or database system with that of an ERP. An important distinction was drawn between OLTP and OLAP applications. Similarly, the differences between the ERP's operational database and the data warehouse were discussed. Next, ERP configurations were examined related to servers, databases, and bolt-on software. We discussed SCM as an area of contention. ERP vendors are moving quickly to provide SCM functionality. Simultaneously, SCM vendors are encroaching on traditional ERP territory.

Data warehousing was the topic of the third section. A data warehouse is a relational or multidimensional database that supports OLAP. A number of data warehouse issues were discussed, including data modeling, data extraction from operational databases, data cleansing, data transformation, and data loading into the warehouse.

The fourth section examined common risks associated with ERP implementation. Among these are the risks associated with the big bang approach, internal opposition to changing the way a company does its business, choosing the wrong ERP model, choosing the wrong consultant, cost overrun issues, and disruptions to operations. Also presented were a number of issues to consider when implementing an ERP. These include selecting a system that is a good fit for the organization, understanding that the term *scalability* can mean different things to different people, potential problems associated with customizing the software, the need for assigning performance measures, and the need to control outside consultants. The chapter concluded with a review of the internal control and auditing issues related to ERPs.

Appendix

Leading ERP Products

The ERP market constitutes products from dozens of vendors of all sizes. This appendix reviews the key features and distinguishing characteristics of the industry leaders, including SAP, Oracle, Microsoft, and SoftBrands. The purpose is to provide overview and insight into the underlying philosophies of these vendors. Specific system characteristics and functionality, however, undergo changes on a regular basis. To obtain current and detailed information on these products, the reader should visit the vendors' Web pages.

SAP

Founded in 1972, SAP is the leader in providing collaborative business solutions. By April 2005, it had an estimated 12 million users worldwide with more than 88,700 installations and more than 1,500 partners. The customer list consists of firms of all sizes in twenty-six different industries, including aerospace, automobile, banking, chemicals, consumer goods, higher education, post office, and utilities.

For years, SAP R/3 software was the leading ERP software, providing comprehensive functions that integrate virtually all major business processes within the enterprise. Recently, SAP developed a family of mySAP products as replacements for R/3. SAP is offering upgrades from R/3 to mySAP for current R/3 customers. SAP R/3 customers who wish to continue with R/3 may do so, but SAP will stop supporting the system in 2012. New SAP customers, however, will be unable to purchase SAP R/3. In the future, mySAP will be the focus of all SAP sales activity.

Key Features and Functions

mySAP ERP comes with four individual solutions that support key business processes: mySAP ERP Financials, mySAP ERP Operations, mySAP ERP Human Capital Management, and mySAP ERP Corporate Service.

mySAP ERP Financials

Financial and Managerial Accounting. mySAP ERP Financials supports both financial accounting and managerial accounting. Financial accounting functions help users comply with international accounting standards, such as (GAAP) and International Financial Reporting Standards (IFRS). It also supports the legal and accounting requirements resulting from European market and currency unification.

Using the financial accounting functions, users can perform the activities of general ledger, accounts receivable and payable, fixed asset accounting, cash journal accounting, inventory accounting, tax accounting, accrual accounting, fast close, financial statements, and parallel valuation.

Using the managerial accounting functions of mySAP ERP Financials, users can perform the activities of profit center accounting, cost center and internal order accounting,

573

project accounting, investment management, product cost accounting, profitability accounting, and transfer pricing.

Corporate Governance.   The solution includes new tools that support corporate governance projects, including:

- Management of Internal Controls
  It certifies the accuracy of quarterly and annual financial statements and disclosures. Meanwhile, it designs, establishes, and maintains disclosure controls and procedures. Moreover, the solution evaluates and reports the effectiveness of those controls and procedures and indicates any significant changes, including discrepancies that have occurred since the most recent evaluation.
- Management of the Audit of Accounting Information System
  mySAP ERP Financials includes an auditor's toolbox to help users comply with corporate governance requirements, such as Sections 302 and 404 of the Sarbanes-Oxley Act. The solution enables audit trails to the document level, tests users' financial system security controls, and provides structure control reports for better auditing.
- Management of Whistleblower Complaints
  mySAP ERP Financials includes whistleblower functions that support Section 301 of the Sarbanes-Oxley Act, allowing stakeholders to send and analyze anonymous complaints.
- Management of Capital and Risk
  mySAP ERP Financials supports the requirements of Basel II by enabling users to evaluate the capital adequacy frameworks used to analyze risk levels and allowing users to create a reporting framework and analytical workbench that operate with central bank data.

Financial Supply Chain Management.   mySAP ERP Financials includes features and functions to support financial SCM activities, such as electronic invoicing and payments, dispute management, collections management, credit management, cash and liquidity management, and treasury and risk management.

mySAP ERP Operations

mySAP ERP Operations provides solutions for procurement and logistics execution, product development and manufacturing, and sales and service. The solution also provides powerful analytic tools for better decision making.

Procurement and Logistics Execution.   mySAP ERP Operations enables users to manage end-to-end logistics for complete business cycles, including purchase-to-pay and make-to-order cycles.

Product Development and Manufacturing.   mySAP ERP Operations enables core development and manufacturing activities. The solution provides features and functions in production planning, manufacturing execution, asset management, product development, and data management.

Sales and Services.   mySAP ERP Operations supports core sales and services processes, including sales order management, aftermarket sales and service, and global trade services across SAP and non-SAP systems. It also helps users manage incentive and commission programs.

mySAP ERP Human Capital Management

The solution provides integrated, enterprise-wide functionality in human resource management. It helps users to identify, recruit, and track most qualified employees. With SAP Learning Solution, it enables enterprises to manage and integrate business learning processes. It functions to integrate team and individual goals with corporate-level goals and strategies. Moreover, its performance management could link management objectives to performance review and appraisal and support a performance-oriented compensation process. In addition, mySAP Human Capital Management helps users to implement different reward strategies. Companies can perform comparative compensation package analysis based on internal and external salary data to ensure competitiveness in the marketplace.

Workforce Process Management. mySAP ERP Human Capital Management supports all basic processes related to personnel and employee information management. Through a centralized database, employees and management have instant access to up-to-date, consistent, complete information. The solution supports key processes for managing and disseminating organizational structure and policy information. It facilitates effective time management strategies and provides convenient tracking, monitoring, record keeping, and evaluation of time data. It also enables users to handle complex payroll processes.

The solution supports current legal regulations for more than fifty countries worldwide, besides ensuring compliance with regulatory requirements for reporting purposes. Accordingly, it supports all processes involved in international employee relocation, from the planning and preparation of global assignments to personnel administration and payroll for global employees. Advanced features address considerations such as national currency, multiple languages, collective agreements, and reporting.

Workforce Deployment. mySAP ERP Human Capital Management provides comprehensive support for project resource planning that ensures employees are assigned to appropriate jobs, projects, and teams. The solution uses a portfolio management paradigm to unify project management, time tracking, financial data, and employee skills information. It facilitates workforce deployment across other SAP solutions, which enables businesses to create project teams based on skills and availability, monitor project progress, track time, and analyze results. It supports call center scheduling, which is based on forecasted call volume and shift schedules. It schedules retail staff based on customer volume, shift schedules, and skills.

mySAP ERP Corporate Services

mySAP ERP Corporate Services supports and optimizes both centralized and decentralized administrative processes. It can be tailored to meet specific requirements for transparency and control, as well as reduced financial and environmental risk, in the real estate, project portfolio, travel and environment, and health and safety management. It also enables a unified approach to total quality management, delivering efficiencies that result from fewer product returns and improved asset utilization. It has strong quality control and maintaining function so that it could react quickly when unexpected issues arise throughout the product life cycle.

ORACLE | PEOPLESOFT

Founded in 1977 by Larry Ellison, Oracle was the first database management system to incorporate the SQL language. Oracle is also the first software company to develop and deploy 100 percent Internet-enabled enterprise software across its entire product line: database, business applications, and application development and decision support tools.

Oracle is the world's leading supplier of software for information management, and the world's second largest independent software company.

Oracle acquired PeopleSoft on January 18, 2005 (and PeopleSoft completed the acquisition of J. D. Edwards in July 2003). For the PeopleSoft Enterprise and J. D. Edwards EnterpriseOne product lines, the combined companies plan to develop and release a subsequent version of each over the next 2 calendar years. The combined company plans to continue to enhance and support the PeopleSoft product lines until at least 2013, and it extended support for J. D. Edwards EnterpriseOne versions XE and 8.0 until February 2007.

Oracle E-Business Suite

Oracle E-Business Suite is a complete and integrated set of enterprise applications. Oracle uses a single, unified data model that stores information for all applications in one place. Its Financial Services supports documentation and auditing for compliance with Sarbanes-Oxley and other regulations, and the Manufacturing/High technology provides option-dependent sourcing, automated spare parts return and repair processing, international drop shipment, and distribution planning.

PeopleSoft Enterprise Solutions

PeopleSoft Enterprise is built on its Pure Internet Architecture technology and designed for complex business requirements. It includes Campus Solutions, which the University of Michigan and other universities are using, Customer Relationship Management, Financial Management, Human Capital Management, Service Automation, Supplier Relationship Management, Supply Chain Management, Asset Management, and Enterprise Performance Management Product Modules.

J. D. Edwards EnterpriseOne

J. D. Edwards EnterpriseOne is a complete suite of modular, preintegrated, industry-specific business applications designed for rapid deployment and ease of administration on a pure Internet architecture. It is ideally suited for organizations that manufacture, construct, distribute, service, or manage products or physical assets. EnterpriseOne includes functionality of Asset Lifecycle Management, Customer Relation Management, Financial Management, Human Capital Management, Manufacturing and Supply Chain Management, Project Management, and Procurement Management.

MICROSOFT

Microsoft Dynamics is a family of integrated business applications for small and midsize organizations and divisions of large enterprises. It provides applications and services for retailers, manufacturers, wholesale distributors, and service companies. The Microsoft Dynamics series includes Dynamics GP, Dynamics AX, Dynamics SL, and others. These solutions are ready to work with widely used productivity applications, like Microsoft Office, and technologies such as Microsoft Windows Server System and Microsoft.NET.

Microsoft Dynamics GP

Microsoft purchased this accounting software package from Great Plains Software in 2001. Formerly known as Great Plains 8.0, Dynamics GP focuses on the business-process needs for lower midmarket businesses and is scalable to meet the requirements of complex business processes for upper midmarket and corporate firms. Dynamics GP offers integrated capabilities for financial management, distribution, manufacturing, project accounting, human resource management, field service management, and business analytics. Dynamics GP delivers deep access to decision-driving information and a rapid return on investment, as well as expert, dedicated customer service.

Microsoft Dynamics AX

Dynamics AX is a multilanguage, multicurrency ERP solution with core strengths in manufacturing and e-business together with strong functionality for the wholesale distribution and business services industries.

Dynamics AX offers a full range of functionality to control manufacturing and production. At any time, users can measure specific costs associated with employees, machinery, and products. Its capabilities regarding material planning help users project long-term needs, foresee fluctuations in demand, and adjust plans accordingly. Users can manage the shop floor more effectively by reducing manual entry, and enable employee information such as time registration and payroll to be accessed through a Web site.

By collecting and analyzing production-related information, such as work hours and production activities, users can improve cost control. For project management, Dynamics AX uses Gantt charts to provide a detailed illustration of scheduled elements. Users can define their own Gantt plans and envision the production flow from one machine to another. Because of the online configuration, products can be generated online and with greater precision. At the same time, users can open the system to customers and vendors so that they can configure their own products, submit orders, and view an expected delivery date via the Internet. The full graphical suite, including version control, helps users design and maintain bills of materials.

Microsoft Dynamics SL

Dynamics SL is a robust, flexible solution built to meet the needs of project-centric and distribution-driven companies. It also boosts employee efficiency by providing real-time data access through a Web-based interface.

SAGE SOFTWARE

Sage Software offers automated business management solutions including accounting, human resources, payroll, fixed asset management, customer relationship management, and e-commerce software. The most powerful member of the Sage software family is MAS 500.

MAS 500 is a complete enterprise management solution that was developed to help companies manage and streamline operations. This SQL server-based software system automates all areas of business management including Core and Advanced Financials, Customer Relationship Management (CRM), Project Accounting (including time and expense tracking), Wholesale Distribution, Discrete Manufacturing, Warehouse Management, Human Resources and Payroll, e-Business, and Business Intelligence.

MAS 500's recent version 7.0 includes new warehouse management and business intelligence modules that enhance workflow throughout an organization. MAS 500 Suite is the only application in the enterprise market developed from the start exclusively for Microsoft platforms and is designed to support the latest features of current Microsoft releases.

Distinguishing Features and Functions

Manufacturing

The program streamlines the entire manufacturing process and helps users respond quickly to customer demands. Advanced capabilities include project management, routings, bills of materials, work orders, MRP, scheduling, job costing, and labor reporting.

Distribution

Ideal for larger distributors with multiple warehouses, MAS 500 optimizes the supply chain, improving productivity and workflow. It also reduces inventory carrying and shipping costs and manages customer returns quickly and efficiently.

Project Accounting

MAS 500 gives project-driven businesses the control to reduce cost overruns, improve cash flow, closely track progress, and capture every billable hour.

SOFTBRANDS

SoftBrands is a leader in providing next-generation enterprise software for businesses in the hospitality and manufacturing sectors. It has more than 4,000 customers in more than sixty countries.

The Fourth Shift Edition for SAP Business One was provided by SoftBrands to meet the unique needs of dynamic small and midsize businesses. The Fourth Shift Edition enables emerging companies to streamline their operational and managerial processes with SAP-centric solution.

Distinguishing Features and Functions

Custom Products Manufacturing

Custom Products Manufacturing helps users plan and control make-to-order and engineer-to-order products. Users can price custom products by having retail prices established and, as the custom product is configured, roll up the retail prices for a final sales price. Users can alternatively price custom products based on accumulating the component costs and applying a markup. Users can easily estimate and track job costs, schedule production, control inventory and purchasing, manage job configurations, and improve customer order processing. Users can respond quickly to quotation requests and customer inquiries, which improves customer service. Users can promise valid delivery dates based on availability of material and meet users' promises using Fourth Shift to coordinate purchasing, manufacturing, and shipping activities. The Fourth Shift Edition could help users improve job cost estimating, quicken job configuration processes, manage job-related activities, and track job status and actual-versus-estimated job costs.

Trace and Serialization

The functions of Lot Trace and Serialization help users gain control over raw materials and finished goods to improve quality, prevent waste, and provide better customer service. Fourth Shift Edition Lot Trace/Serialization allows users to track lot-traced items throughout the manufacturing process, from receiving through shipping. Serial numbers can be assigned to items at the time of shipment. The Fourth Shift Edition could help users improve quality control, prevent waste, and improve customer satisfaction.

For further information, please visit the following companies' Web sites:

1. www.sap.com
2. www.oracle.com
3. www.microsoft.com
4. www.softbrands.com
5. www.sagesoftware.com

KEY TERMS

access control list

big bang

bolt-on software

changed data capture

client-server model

closed database architecture

consolidation

core application

data mart

data warehouse

drill-down

enterprise resource planning (ERP)

online analytical processing (OLAP)

online transaction
    processing (OLTP)

phased-in

role

role-based access control (RBAC)

role-based governance

scalability

slicing and dicing

supply chain management (SCM)

three-tier model

two-tier model

REVIEW QUESTIONS

1. Define ERP.
2. What is the closed database architecture?
3. Define core applications and give some examples.
4. Define OLAP and give some examples.
5. What is the client-server model?
6. Describe the two-tier client-server model.
7. Describe the three-tier client-server model.
8. What is bolt-on software?
9. What is SCM software?
10. What is changed data capture?
11. What is a data warehouse?
12. What is data mining?
13. What does data cleansing mean?
14. Why are denormalized tables used in data warehouses?
15. What is the drill-down approach?
16. What is the big bang approach?
17. What is scalability?
18. What is a role?
19. What is an access control list?
20. How is the access control list approach different from RBAC?
21. Search the Web: How is the Oracle Express database different from relational databases?
22. What is the OLAP operation called consolidation?
23. What is the OLAP operation of drill-down?
24. What is meant by the term *slicing and dicing*?

DISCUSSION QUESTIONS

1. How are OLTP and OLAP different? Provide some examples.
2. Distinguish between the two-tier and three-tier client-server models. Describe when each would be used.
3. Why do ERP systems need bolt-on software? Give an example of bolt-on software.
4. Your organization is considering acquiring bolt-on software for your ERP system. What approaches are open to you?
5. Explain why the data warehouse needs to be separate from the operational database.
6. Data in a data warehouse are in a stable state. Explain how this can hamper data mining analysis. What can an organization do to alleviate this problem?
7. This chapter stressed the importance of data normalization when constructing a relational database. Why, then, is it important to denormalize data in a data warehouse?
8. What problems does the data cleansing step attempt to resolve?
9. How are the summary views in a data warehouse different from views in an operational database?
10. Would drill-down be an effective audit tool for identifying an unusual business relationship between a purchasing agent and suppliers in a large organization with several hundred suppliers? Explain.
11. Disruptions to operations are a common side effect of implementing an ERP. Explain the primary reason for this.
12. ERP systems use the best-practices approach in designing their applications, yet goodness of fit is considered to be an important issue when selecting an ERP. Shouldn't the client just be able to use whatever applications the ERP system provides?
13. Explain the issues of size, speed, workload, and transaction as they relate to scalability.
14. Explain how SAP uses roles as a way to improve internal control.
15. How would you deal with the problem of file-server backup in a highly centralized organization?
16. How would you deal with the problem of file-server backup in a decentralized organization with autonomous divisions that do not share common operational data?
17. Distinguish between the OLAP operations of consolidation and drill-down.
18. When would slicing and dicing be an appropriate OLAP tool? Give an example.
19. Explain the risks associated with the creation of unnecessary roles and why it can happen.
20. What is the fundamental concept behind the rule of least access? Explain why this is a potential problem in an ERP environment.
21. What is the purpose of role-based governance software?

MULTIPLE-CHOICE QUESTIONS

1. Closed database architecture is
   a. a control technique intended to prevent unauthorized access from trading partners.
   b. a limitation inherent in traditional information systems that prevents data sharing.
   c. a data warehouse control that prevents unclean data from entering the warehouse.
   d. a technique used to restrict access to data marts.
   e. a database structure that many of the leading ERPs use to support OLTP applications.
2. Each of the following is a necessary element for the successful warehousing of data EXCEPT
   a. cleansing extracted data.
   b. transforming data.
   c. modeling data.
   d. loading data.
   e. all of the above are necessary.
3. Which of the following is typically NOT part of an ERP's OLAP applications?
   a. decision support systems
   b. information retrieval
   c. ad hoc reporting/analysis
   d. logistics
   e. what-if analysis
4. There are a number of risks that may be associated with ERP implementation. Which of the following was NOT stated as a risk in the chapter?
   a. A drop in firm performance after implementation because the firm looks and works

differently than it did while using a legacy system.

b. Implementing companies have found that staff members, employed by ERP consulting firms, do not have sufficient experience in implementing new systems.

c. Implementing firms fail to select systems that properly support their business activities.

d. The selected system does not adequately meet the adopting firm's economic growth.

e. ERPs are too large, complex, and generic for them to be well integrated into most company cultures.

5. Which statement is NOT true?

a. In a typical two-tier client-server architecture, the server handles both application and database duties.

b. Client computers are responsible for presenting data to the user and passing user input back to the server.

c. Two-tier architecture is for local area network applications where the demand on the server is restricted to a relatively small population of users.

d. The database and application functions are separated in the three-tier model.

e. In three-tier client-server architectures, one tier is for user presentation, one is for database and applications access, and the third is for Internet access.

6. Which statement is NOT true?

a. Drill-down capability is an OLAP feature of data mining tools available to the user.

b. The data warehouse should be separate from operational systems.

c. Denormalization of data involves dividing the data into very small tables that support detailed analysis.

d. Some decisions supported by a data warehouse are not fundamentally different from those that are supported by traditional databases.

e. Data cleansing involves transforming data into standard business terms with standard data values.

7. Which statement is LEAST accurate?

a. Implementing an ERP system has more to do with changing the way that an organization does business than it does with technology.

b. The phased-in approach to ERP implementation is particularly suited to diversified organizations whose units do not share common processes and data.

c. Because the primary reason for implementing an ERP is to standardize and integrate operations, diversified organizations whose units do not share common processes and data do not benefit and tend not to implement ERPs.

d. To take full advantage of the ERP process, reengineering will need to occur.

e. A common reason for ERP failure is that the ERP does not support one or more important business processes of the organization.

8. SAP, one of the leading ERP producers, makes several modules available to adopters. Which of the following is not a SAP module?

a. Business Process Support

b. Internet Development Support

c. Logistics

d. E-Commerce Support

e. Human Resources

9. Auditors of ERP systems

a. need not be concerned about segregation of duties because these systems possess strong computer controls.

b. focus on output controls such as independent verification to reconcile batch totals.

c. are concerned that managers fail to exercise adequate care in assigning permissions.

d. do not see the data warehouse as an audit or control issue at all because financial records are not stored there.

e. need not review access levels granted to users because these are determined when the system is configured and never change.

10. Which statement is most correct?

a. SAP is more suited to service industries than manufacturing clients.

b. J. D. Edwards's ERP is designed to accept the best-practices modules of other vendors.

c. Oracle evolved from a human resources system.

d. PeopleSoft is the world's leading supplier of software for information management.

e. SoftBrands provides enterprise software for the hospitality and manufacturing sectors.

PROBLEMS

1. Data Warehouse Access Control

You are the CEO of a large organization that implemented a data warehouse for internal analysis of corporate data. The operations manager has written you a memo advocating opening the data warehouse to your suppliers and customers. Explain any merit to this proposal. What are the control issues, if any?

2. Project Implementation

Your organization is planning to implement an ERP system. Some managers in the organization favor the big bang approach. Others are advocating a phased-in approach. The CEO has asked you, as project leader, to write a memo summarizing the advantages and disadvantages of each approach and to make a recommendation. This is a traditional organization with a strong internal hierarchy. The company was acquired in a merger 2 years ago, and the ERP project is an effort on the part of the parent company to standardize business processes and reporting across the organization. Prior to this, the organization had been using a general ledger package that it acquired in 1979. Most of the transaction processing is a combination of manual and batch processing. Most employees think that the legacy system works well. At this point, the implementation project is behind schedule.

3. OLTP Versus OLAP Servers

For each of the following processes, state whether OLTP or OLAP is appropriate and why.

a. An order entry system that retrieves customer information, invoice information, and inventory information for local sales.

b. An order entry system that retrieves customer information, invoice information, inventory information, and several years of sales information about both the customer and the inventory items.

c. An order entry system that retrieves customer information, invoice information, inventory information, and information to compare the current sale to sales across several geographic regions.

d. An order entry system that retrieves customer information, invoice information, inventory information, and accounts receivable information for sales within one marketing region.

e. An insurance company requires a system that will allow it to determine total claims by region, determine whether a relationship exists between claims and meteorological phenomenon, and why one region seems to be more profitable than another.

f. A manufacturing company has only one factory, but that factory employs several thousand people and has nearly $1 billion in revenue each year. The company has seen no reason to make comparisons about its operations from year to year or from process to process. Its information needs focus primarily on operations, but it has maintained backup of prior-year operations activities. Examination of prior-year financial reports have shown that the company, while profitable, is not growing and return on investment is decreasing. The owners are not satisfied with this situation.

4. Selecting a Consultant

You are the chief information officer for a midsized organization that has decided to implement an ERP system. The CEO has met with a consulting ERP firm based on a recommendation from a personal friend at his club. At the interview, the president of the consulting firm introduced the chief consultant, who was charming, personable, and seemed very knowledgeable. The CEO's first instinct was to sign a contract with the consultant, but he decided to hold off until he had received your input.

Required:

Write a memo to the CEO presenting the issues and the risks associated with consultants. Also, outline a set of procedures that could be used as a guide in selecting a consultant.

5. Auditing ERP Databases

You are an independent auditor attending an engagement interview with the client. The client's organization has recently implemented a data warehouse. Management is concerned that the audit tests that you perform will disrupt operations. Management suggests that instead of running tests against the live operational database, you draw the data for your analytical reviews and substantive tests of details from the data warehouse. Management points out that operational data are copied weekly into the warehouse and everything you need will be contained there. This will enable you to perform your tests without disrupting routine operations. You agree to give this some thought and get back to the client with your answer.

Required:

Draft a memo to the client outlining your response to their proposal. Mention any concerns you might have.

6. Big Bang versus Phased-In Approach

The Nevada Department of Motor Vehicles (DVM) is the agency responsible for licensing both drivers and vehicles in the state of Nevada. Until recently, legacy systems were used for both licensing needs. The legacy system for driver's licenses maintained the following information about each licensed driver: name, age, address, violation, license classification, organ donation, and restrictions. The vehicle licensing system maintained information about each vehicle, including cost, taxes, VIN, weight, insurance, and ownership. In the summer of 1999, over a 3-day weekend, information from the two legacy systems was transferred to a new ERP. The ERP and all new hardware were installed in every DMV across the state, and when employees returned from their long weekend, an entirely new system was in place.

The DMV employees were not well trained on the new system, and the system itself presented a few bugs. As a result of these obstacles, customers at the DMV faced excessively long lines and extended waiting times, and several of the employees simply quit their jobs because of frustrations with the system and difficulty dealing with irate customers. Knowing that the waiting times were so long, many drivers simply refused to renew licenses or obtain new licenses.

Assume that the ERP the DMV management selected was correctly configured and was capable of meeting all requirements of the DMV; consider data warehousing implications, business culture implications, and disruption to operations; and discuss the advantages and disadvantages associated with the decision to implement the new system using the big bang approach versus the phased-in approach.

7. ERP Failure

When an ERP implementation fails, who is to blame? Is it the software manufacture, the client firm, or the implementation strategy?

Required:
Research this issue and write a brief paper outlining the key issues.

8. ERP Market Growth

Because many large corporations implemented ERP systems prior to 2000, what direction will growth of the ERP market take?

Required:
Research this issue and write a brief paper outlining the key issues.

9. ERP Consultants

Do an Internet search of complaints about ERP consultants. Write a report about the most common complaints and cite examples.

10. ERP Bolt-On Software

Go to ten Web sites of companies that supply bolt-on software. Write a report containing URLs that briefly describe the software features and its compatibility with specific ERP systems.

CHAPTER 12

Business Ethics, Fraud, and Fraud Detection

LEARNING OBJECTIVES

After studying this chapter, you should:

- Understand the broad issues pertaining to business ethics.
- Understand what constitutes fraudulent behavior.
- Be able to explain fraud-motivating forces.
- Be familiar with typical fraud schemes perpetrated by managers and employees.
- Be familiar with the common anti-fraud techniques used in both manual systems and computer-based systems.
- Be familiar with the use of ACL in the detection of fraud.

Recent major financial frauds have heightened public awareness of frauds and to the terrible damage they can cause. The U.S. Congress passed the Sarbanes-Oxley Act of 2002 in an attempt to bring under legislation certain requirements to deter fraud and increase punishment for executives who commit financial frauds.

This chapter examines the two closely related subjects of ethics and fraud and their implications for auditing. We begin the chapter by surveying ethical issues that highlight the organization's conflicting responsibilities to its employees, shareholders, customers, and the general public. Organization managers have an ethical responsibility to seek a balance between the risks and benefits to these constituents that result from their decisions. Management and accountants must recognize the new implications of information technologies for such historic issues as working conditions, the right to privacy, and the potential for fraud. The section concludes with a review of the code of ethics requirements that SOX mandates.

The second section is devoted to the subject of fraud and its implications for accountants. Although the term *fraud* is very familiar in today's financial press, it is not always clear what constitutes fraud. In this section, we discuss the nature and meaning of fraud, differentiate between employee fraud and management fraud, explain fraud-motivating forces, outline the most common fraud schemes, and present audit procedures to detect fraud. It concludes with a review of ACL tests that can be performed to detect fraud.

ETHICAL ISSUES IN BUSINESS

Ethical standards are derived from societal mores and deep-rooted personal beliefs about issues of right and wrong that are *not* universally agreed upon. It is quite possible for two individuals, both of whom consider themselves to be acting ethically, to be on opposite sides of an issue. Often, we confuse ethical issues with legal issues. When the Honorable Gentleman from the state of ——, who is charged with ethical misconduct, stands before Congress and proclaims that he is "guilty of no wrongdoing," is he really saying that he did not break the law?

We have been inundated with scandals in the stock market, stories of computer crimes and viruses, and almost obscene charges of impropriety and illegalities by corporate executives. Using covert compensation schemes, Enron's CFO Andy Fastow managed to improve his personal wealth by approximately $40 million. Similarly, Dennis Kozlowski of Tyco, Richard Scrushy of HealthSouth, and Bernie Ebbers of WorldCom all became wealthy beyond imagination while driving their companies into the ground. Indeed, during the period from early 1999 to May 2002, the executives of twenty-five companies extracted $25 billion worth of special compensation, stock options, and private loans from their organizations while their companies' stock plummeted 75 percent or more.[1]

A thorough treatment of ethics issues is impossible within this chapter section. Instead, the objective is to heighten the reader's awareness of ethical concerns relating to business, information systems, and computer technology.

Business Ethics

Ethics pertains to the principles of conduct that individuals use in making choices and guiding their behavior in situations that involve the concepts of right and wrong. More specifically, **business ethics** involves finding the answers to two questions: (1) How do managers decide what is right in conducting their business? and (2) Once managers have recognized what is right, how do they achieve it?

Ethical issues in business can be divided into four areas: equity, rights, honesty, and the exercise of corporate power. Table 12.1 identifies some of the business practices and decisions in each of these areas that have ethical implications.

Making Ethical Decisions

Business organizations have conflicting responsibilities to their employees, shareholders, customers, and the public. Every major decision has consequences that potentially harm or benefit these constituents. For example, implementing a new computer information system within an organization may cause some employees to lose their jobs, while those who remain enjoy the benefit of improved working conditions. Seeking a balance between these consequences is the managers' **ethical responsibility**. The following ethical principles provide some guidance in the discharge of this responsibility.[2]

---

1   Robert Prentice, *Student Guide to the Sarbanes-Oxley Act*, Thomson Publishing, 2005, p. 23.

2   M. McFarland, "Ethics and the Safety of Computer System," *Computer*, February 1991.

TABLE 12.1	**Ethical Issues in Business**	
Equity	Executive Salaries	
	Comparable Worth	
	Product Pricing	
Rights	Corporate Due Process	
	Employee Health Screening	
	Employee Privacy	
	Sexual Harassment	
	Diversity	
	Equal Employment Opportunity	
	Whistleblowing	
Honesty	Employee and Management Conflicts of Interest	
	Security of Organization Data and Records	
	Misleading Advertising	
	Questionable Business Practices in Foreign Countries	
	Accurate Reporting of Shareholder Interests	
Exercise of Corporate Power	Political Action Committees	
	Workplace Safety	
	Product Safety	
	Environmental Issues	
	Divestment of Interests	
	Corporate Political Contributions	
	Downsizing and Plant Closures	

SOURCE: Adapted from the Conference Board, "Defining Corporate Ethics," in P. Madsen and J. Shafritz, *Essentials of Business Ethics* (New York: Meridian, 1990), 18.

- ***Proportionality.*** The benefit from a decision must outweigh the risks. Furthermore, there must be no alternative decision that provides the same or greater benefit with less risk.
- ***Justice.*** The benefits of the decision should be distributed fairly to those who share the risks. Those who do not benefit should not carry the burden of risk.
- ***Minimize risk.*** Even if judged acceptable by the principles, the decision should be implemented so as to minimize all of the risks and avoid any unnecessary risks.

Computer Ethics

The use of information technology in business has had a major impact on society and thus raises significant ethical issues regarding computer crime, working conditions, privacy, and more. **Computer ethics** is "the analysis of the nature and social impact of computer technology and the corresponding formulation and justification of policies for the ethical use of such technology.... [This includes] concerns about software as well as hardware and concerns about networks connecting computers as well as computers themselves."[3]

One researcher has defined three levels of computer ethics: pop, para, and theoretical.[4] Pop computer ethics is simply the exposure to stories and reports found in the

3   J. H. Moor, "What Is Computer Ethics?" *Metaphilosophy* 16 (1985): 266–275.
4   T. W. Bynum, "Human Values and the Computer Science Curriculum" (Working paper for the National Conference on Computing and Values, August 1991).

popular media regarding the good or bad ramifications of computer technology. Society at large needs to be aware of such things as computer viruses and computer systems designed to aid handicapped persons. Para computer ethics involves taking a real interest in computer ethics cases and acquiring some level of skill and knowledge in the field. All systems professionals need to reach this level of competency so they can do their jobs effectively. Students of accounting information systems should also achieve this level of ethical understanding. The third level, theoretical computer ethics, is of interest to multidisciplinary researchers who apply the theories of philosophy, sociology, and psychology to computer science with the goal of bringing some new understanding to the field.

A New Problem or Just a New Twist on an Old Problem?

Some argue that all pertinent ethical issues have already been examined in some other domain. For example, the issue of property rights has been explored and has resulted in copyright, trade secret, and patent laws. Although computer programs are a new type of asset, many feel that these programs should be considered no differently from other forms of property. A fundamental question arising from such debate is whether computers present new ethical problems or just create new twists on old problems. Where the latter is the case, we need only to understand the generic values that are at stake and the principles that should then apply.[5] However, a large contingent vociferously disagrees with the premise that computers are no different from other technology. For example, many reject the notion of intellectual property being the same as real property. There is, as yet, no consensus on this matter.

Several issues of concern for students of accounting information systems are discussed in the following section. This list is not exhaustive, and a full discussion of each of the issues is beyond the scope of this chapter. Instead, the issues are briefly defined, and several trigger questions are provided. Hopefully these questions will provoke thought and discussion in the classroom.

Privacy

People desire to be in full control of what and how much information about themselves is available to others, and to whom it is available. This is the issue of **privacy**. The creation and maintenance of huge, shared databases make it necessary to protect people from the potential misuse of data. This raises the issue of **ownership** in the personal information industry.[6] Should the privacy of individuals be protected through policies and systems? What information about oneself does the individual own? Should firms that are unrelated to individuals buy and sell information about these individuals without their permission?

Security (Accuracy and Confidentiality)

Computer security is an attempt to avoid such undesirable events as a loss of confidentiality or data integrity. Security systems attempt to prevent fraud and other misuse of computer systems; they act to protect and further the legitimate interests of the system's constituencies. The ethical issues involving security arise from the emergence of shared, computerized databases that have the potential to cause irreparable harm to individuals by disseminating inaccurate information to authorized users, such as through incorrect credit reporting.[7] There is a similar danger in disseminating accurate information to

---

5   G. Johnson, "A Framework for Thinking about Computer Ethics" in J. Robinette and R. Barquin (eds.), *Computers and Ethics: A Sourcebook for Discussions* (Brooklyn: Polytechnic Press, 1989), pp. 26–31.

6   J. H. Moor, "The Ethics of Privacy Protection," *Library Trends* 39 (1990): 69–82.

7   W. Ware, "Contemporary Privacy Issues" (Working paper for the National Conference on Computing and Human Values, August 1991).

persons unauthorized to receive it. However, increasing security can actually cause other problems. For example, security can be used both to protect personal property and to undermine freedom of access to data, which may have an injurious effect on some individuals. Which is the more important goal? Automated monitoring can be used to detect intruders or other misuse, yet it can also be used to spy on legitimate users, thus diminishing their privacy. Where is the line to be drawn? What is an appropriate use and level of security? Which is most important: security, accuracy, or confidentiality?

Ownership of Property

Laws designed to preserve real property rights have been extended to cover what is referred to as intellectual property, that is, software. The question here becomes what an individual (or organization) can own. Ideas? Media? Source code? Object code? A related question is whether owners and users should be constrained in their use or access. Copyright laws have been invoked in an attempt to protect those who develop software from having it copied. Unquestionably, the hundreds and thousands of program development hours should be protected from piracy. However, many believe the copyright laws can cause more harm than good. For example, should the look and feel of a software package be granted copyright protection? Some argue that this flies in the face of the original intent of the law. Whereas the purpose of copyrights is to promote the progress of science and the useful arts, allowing a user interface the protection of copyright may do just the opposite. The best interest of computer users is served when industry standards emerge; copyright laws work against this. Part of the problem lies in the uniqueness of software, its ease of dissemination, and the possibility of exact replication. Does software fit with the current categories and conventions regarding ownership?

Equity in Access

Some barriers to access are intrinsic to the technology of information systems, but some are avoidable through careful system design. Several factors, some of which are not unique to information systems, can limit access to computing technology. The economic status of the individual or the affluence of an organization will determine the ability to obtain information technology. Culture also limits access, for example, where documentation is prepared in only one language or is poorly translated. Safety features, or the lack thereof, have limited access to pregnant women, for example. How can hardware and software be designed with consideration for differences in physical and cognitive skills? What is the cost of providing equity in access? For what groups of society should equity in access become a priority?

Environmental Issues

Computers with high-speed printers allow for the production of printed documents faster than ever before. It is probably easier just to print a document than to consider whether it should be printed and how many copies really need to be made. It may be more efficient or more comforting to have a hard copy in addition to the electronic version. However, paper comes from trees, a precious natural resource, and ends up in landfills if not properly recycled. Should organizations limit nonessential hard copies? Can *nonessential* be defined? Who can and should define it? Should proper recycling be required? How can it be enforced?

Artificial Intelligence

A new set of social and ethical issues has arisen out of the popularity of expert systems. Because of the way these systems have been marketed, that is, as decision makers or replacements for experts, some people rely on them significantly. Therefore, both knowledge engineers (those who write the programs) and domain experts (those who provide the knowledge about the task being automated) must be concerned about their responsibility for faulty decisions, incomplete or inaccurate knowledge bases, and the role given to computers in the decision-making process.[8] Further, because expert systems attempt to clone a manager's decision-making style, an individual's prejudices may implicitly or explicitly be included in the knowledge base. Some of the questions that need to be explored are: Who is responsible for the completeness and appropriateness of the knowledge base? Who is responsible for a decision made by an expert system that causes harm when implemented? Who owns the expertise once it is coded into a knowledge base?

Unemployment and Displacement

Many jobs have been and are being changed as a result of the availability of computer technology. People unable or unprepared to change are displaced. Should employers be responsible for retraining workers who are displaced as a result of the computerization of their functions?

Misuse of Computers

Computers can be misused in many ways. Copying proprietary software, using a company's computer for personal benefit, and snooping through other people's files are just a few obvious examples.[9] Although copying proprietary software (except to make a personal backup copy) is clearly illegal, it is commonly done. Why do people feel that it is not necessary to obey this law? Are there any good arguments for trying to change this law? What harm is done to the software developer when people make unauthorized copies? A computer is not an item that deteriorates with use; so is there any harm to the employer if it is used for an employee's personal benefit? Does it matter if the computer is used during company time or outside of work hours? Is there a difference if some profit-making activity takes place rather than, for example, using the computer to write a personal letter? Does it make a difference if a profit-making activity takes place during or outside of working hours? Is it okay to look through paper files that clearly belong to someone else? Is there any difference between paper files and computer files?

Sarbanes-Oxley Act and Ethical Issues

Public outcry surrounding ethical misconduct and fraudulent acts by executives of Enron, Global Crossing, Tyco, Adelphia, WorldCom, and others spurred Congress into passing the American Competitiveness and Corporate Accountability Act of 2002. This wide-sweeping legislation, more commonly known as the Sarbanes-Oxley Act (SOX), is the most significant securities law since the SEC Acts of 1933 and 1934. SOX has many provisions designed to deal with specific problems relating to capital markets, corporate governance, and the auditing profession. Several of these have been discussed in previous chapters. At this point, we are concerned primarily with Section 406 of the act, which pertains to ethical issues.

---

8   K. C. Laudon, "Data Quality and Due Process in Large Interorganizational Record Systems," *Communications of the ACM* (1986): 4–11.

9   R. Dejoie, G. Fowler, and D. Paradice (eds.), *Ethical Issues in Information Systems* (Boston: Boyd & Fraser, 1991).

Section 406—Code of Ethics for Senior Financial Officers

Section 406 of SOX requires public companies to disclose to the SEC whether they have adopted a code of ethics that applies to the organization's CEO, CFO, controller, or persons performing similar functions. If the company has not adopted such a code, it must explain why. A public company may disclose its code of ethics in several ways: (1) included as an exhibit to its annual report, (2) as a posting to its Web site, or (3) by agreeing to provide copies of the code upon request.

Whereas Section 406 applies specifically to executive and financial officers of a company, a company's code of ethics should apply equally to all employees. Top management's attitude toward ethics sets the tone for business practice, but it is also the responsibility of lower-level managers and nonmanagers to uphold a firm's ethical standards. Ethical violations can occur throughout an organization, from the boardroom to the receiving dock. Methods must therefore be developed for including all management and employees in the firm's ethics schema. The SEC has ruled that compliance with Section 406 necessitates a written code of ethics that addresses the following ethical issues.

Conflicts of Interest. The company's code of ethics should outline procedures for dealing with actual or apparent conflicts of interest between personal and professional relationships. Note that the issue here is in dealing with conflicts of interest, not prohibiting them. Whereas avoidance is the best policy, sometimes conflicts are unavoidable. Thus, one's handling and full disclosure of the matter become the ethical concern. Managers and employees alike should be made aware of the firm's code of ethics, be given decision models, and participate in training programs that explore conflict of interest issues.

Full and Fair Disclosures. This provision states that the organization should provide full, fair, accurate, timely, and understandable disclosures in the documents, reports, and financial statements that it submits to the SEC and to the public. Overly complex and misleading accounting techniques were used to camouflage questionable activities that lie at the heart of many recent financial scandals. The objective of this rule is to ensure that future disclosures are candid, open, truthful, and void of such deceptions.

Legal Compliance. Codes of ethics should require employees to follow applicable governmental laws, rules, and regulations. As stated previously, we must not confuse ethical issues with legal issues. Nevertheless, doing the right thing requires sensitivity to laws, rules, regulations, and societal expectations. To accomplish this, organizations must provide employees with training and guidance.

Internal Reporting of Code Violations. The code of ethics must provide a mechanism to permit prompt internal reporting of ethics violations. This provision is similar in nature to Sections 301 and 806, which were designed to encourage and protect whistleblowers. Employee ethics hotlines are emerging as the mechanism for dealing with these related requirements. Because SOX requires this function to be confidential, many companies are outsourcing their employee hotline service to independent vendors.

Accountability. An effective ethics program must take appropriate action when code violations occur. This will include various disciplinary measures, including dismissal. Employees must see an employee hotline as credible, or they will not use it. Section 301 directs the organization's audit committee to establish procedures for receiving, retaining, and treating such complaints about accounting procedures and internal control violations. Audit committees will also play an important role in the oversight of ethics enforcement activities.

FRAUD AND ACCOUNTANTS

Perhaps no major aspect of the independent auditor's role has caused more controversy than their responsibility for detecting fraud during an audit. In recent years, the structure of the U.S. financial reporting system has become the object of scrutiny. The SEC, the courts, and the public, along with Congress, have focused on business failures and questionable practices by the management of corporations that engage in alleged fraud. The question often asked is, "Where were the auditors?"

The passage of SOX has had a tremendous impact on the external auditor's responsibilities for fraud detection during a financial audit. It requires the auditor to test controls specifically intended to prevent or detect fraud likely to result in a material misstatement of the financial statements. The current authoritative guidelines on fraud detection are presented in *Statement on Auditing Standards (SAS) No. 99*, "Consideration of Fraud in a Financial Statement Audit." The objective of SAS 99 is to seamlessly blend the auditor's consideration of fraud into all phases of the audit process. In addition, SAS 99 requires the auditor to perform new steps such as a brainstorming during audit planning to assess the potential risk of material misstatement of the financial statements from fraud schemes.

Definitions of Fraud

Although *fraud* is a familiar term in today's financial press, its meaning is not always clear. For example, in cases of bankruptcies and business failures, alleged fraud is often the result of poor management decisions or adverse business conditions. Under such circumstances, it becomes necessary to clearly define and understand the nature and meaning of fraud.

Fraud denotes a false representation of a material fact made by one party to another party with the intent to deceive and induce the other party to justifiably rely on the fact to his or her detriment. According to common law, a fraudulent act must meet the following five conditions:

1. **False representation**. There must be a false statement or a nondisclosure.
2. **Material fact**. A fact must be a substantial factor in inducing someone to act.
3. **Intent**. There must be the intent to deceive or the knowledge that one's statement is false.
4. **Justifiable reliance**. The misrepresentation must have been a substantial factor on which the injured party relied.
5. **Injury or loss**. The deception must have caused injury or loss to the victim of the fraud.

Fraud in the business environment has a more specialized meaning. It is an intentional deception, misappropriation of a company's assets, or manipulation of its financial data to the advantage of the perpetrator. In accounting literature, fraud is also commonly known as *white-collar crime, defalcation, embezzlement,* and *irregularities.* Auditors encounter fraud at two levels: *employee fraud* and *management fraud.* Because each form of fraud has different implications for auditors, we need to distinguish between the two.

Employee fraud, or fraud by nonmanagement employees, is generally designed to directly convert cash or other assets to the employee's personal benefit. Typically, the employee circumvents the company's internal control system for personal gain. If a company has an effective system of internal control, defalcations or embezzlements can usually be prevented or detected. Employee fraud usually involves three steps: (1) stealing something of value (an asset), (2) converting the asset to a usable form (cash), and (3) concealing the crime to avoid detection. The third step is often the most difficult. It may be relatively easy for a storeroom clerk to steal inventories from the employer's warehouse, but altering the inventory records to hide the theft is more of a challenge.

Management fraud is more insidious than employee fraud because it often escapes detection until the organization has suffered irreparable damage or loss. Usually management fraud does not involve the direct theft of assets. Top management may engage in fraudulent activities to drive up the market price of the company's stock. This may be done to meet investor expectations or to take advantage of stock options that have been loaded into the manager's compensation package. The Commission on Auditors' Responsibilities calls this performance fraud, which often involves deceptive practices to inflate earnings or to forestall the recognition of either insolvency or a decline in earnings. Lower-level management fraud typically involves materially misstating financial data and internal reports to gain additional compensation, to garner a promotion, or to escape the penalty for poor performance. Management fraud typically contains three special characteristics:[10]

1. The fraud is perpetrated at levels of management above the one to which internal control structures generally relate.
2. The fraud frequently involves using the financial statements to create an illusion that an entity is healthier and more prosperous than, in fact, it is.
3. If the fraud involves misappropriation of assets, it frequently is shrouded in a maze of complex business transactions, often involving related third parties.

The preceding characteristics of management fraud suggest that management can often perpetrate irregularities by overriding an otherwise effective internal control structure that would prevent similar irregularities by lower-level employees.

The Fraud Triangle

The **fraud triangle** consists of three factors that contribute to or are associated with management and employee fraud. These are:

(1) *situational pressure,* which includes personal or job-related stresses that could coerce an individual to act dishonestly;
(2) *opportunity,* which involves direct access to assets and/or access to information that controls assets, and;
(3) *ethics,* which pertains to one's character and degree of moral opposition to acts of dishonesty.

Figure 12.1 graphically depicts the interplay among these three forces. The figure suggests that an individual with a high level of personal ethics, who is confronted by low pressure and limited opportunity to commit fraud, is more likely to behave honestly than one with weaker personal ethics, who is under high pressure and exposed to greater fraud opportunities.

Research by forensic experts and academics has shown that the auditor's evaluation of fraud is enhanced when the fraud triangle factors are considered. Obviously, matters of ethics and personal stress do not lend themselves to easy observation and analysis. To

10   K. A. Forcht, "Assessing the Ethic Standards and Policies in Computer-Based Environments," in R. Dejoie, G. Fowler, and D. Paradice (eds.), *Ethical Issues in Information Systems* (Boston: Boyd & Fraser, 1991).

FIGURE 12.1   **Fraud Triangle**

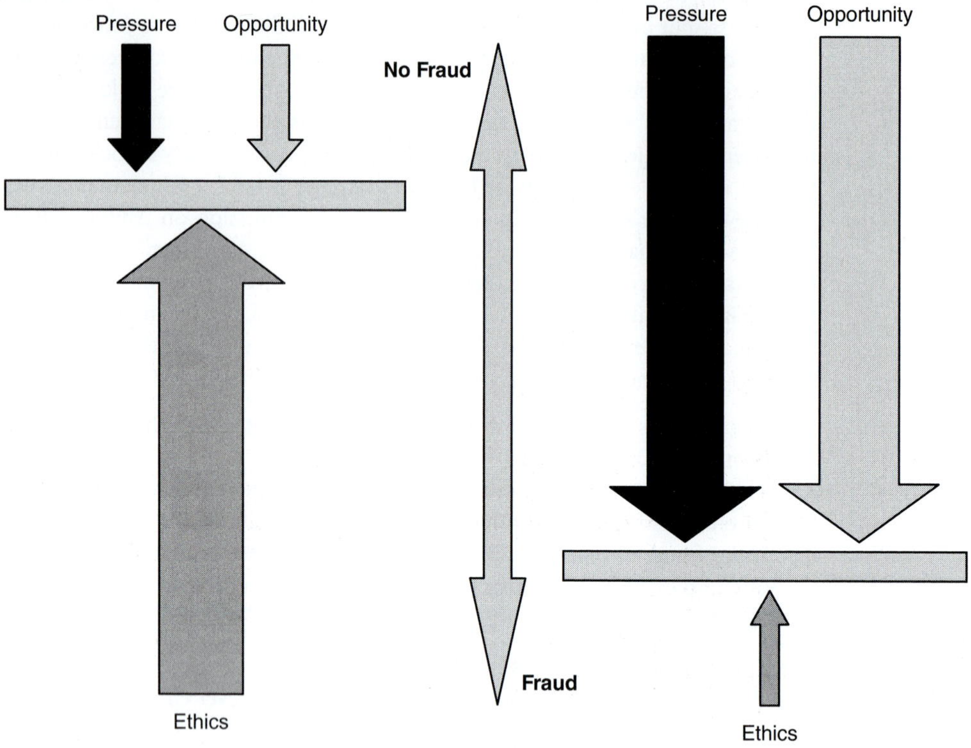

provide insight into these factors, auditors often use a *red-flag* checklist consisting of the following types of questions:[11]

- Do key executives have unusually high personal debt?
- Do key executives appear to be living beyond their means?
- Do key executives engage in habitual gambling?
- Do key executives appear to abuse alcohol or drugs?
- Do any of the key executives appear to lack personal codes of ethics?
- Are economic conditions unfavorable within the company's industry?
- Does the company use several different banks, none of which sees the company's entire financial picture?
- Do any key executives have close associations with suppliers?
- Is the company experiencing a rapid turnover of key employees, either through resignation or termination?
- Do one or two individuals dominate the company?

11   R. Grinaker, "Discussant's Response to a Look at the Record on Auditor Detection of Management Fraud," *Proceedings of the 1980 Touche Ross University of Kansas Symposium on Auditing Problems* (Kansas City: University of Kansas, 1980).

A review of some of these questions shows that contemporary auditors may need to use professional investigative agencies to run confidential background checks on key managers of existing and prospective client firms.

Financial Losses from Fraud

A research study published by the **Association of Certified Fraud Examiners (ACFE)** in 2008 estimates losses from fraud and abuse to be 7 percent of annual revenues. This translates to approximately $994 billion in fraud losses for 2008. The actual cost of fraud is, however, difficult to quantify for a number of reasons: (1) not all fraud is detected; (2) of that detected, not all is reported; (3) in many fraud cases, incomplete information is gathered; (4) information is not properly distributed to management or law enforcement authorities; and (5) too often, business organizations decide to take no civil or criminal action against the perpetrator(s) of fraud. In addition to the direct economic loss to the organization, indirect costs including reduced productivity, the cost of legal action, increased unemployment, and business disruption due to investigation of the fraud need to be considered.

Of the 959 occupational fraud cases examined in the ACFE study, the median loss from fraud was $175,000, while 25 percent of the organizations experienced losses of $1 million or more. The distribution of dollar losses is presented in Table 12.2.

TABLE 12.2	**Distribution of Losses**
Amount of Loss	**Percent of Frauds**
$1–$999	1.9
$1,000–$9,999	7.0
$10,000–$49,999	16.8
$50,000–$99,999	11.2
$100,000–$499,999	28.2
$500,000–$999,999	9.6
$1,000,000 and up	25.3

SOURCE: Adapted from the Association of Certified Fraud Examiners, *2008 Report to the Nation on Occupational Fraud & Abuse*, p. 9.

The Perpetrators of Frauds

The ACFE study examined a number of factors that profile the perpetrators of the frauds, including position within the organization, collusion with others, gender, age, and education. The median financial loss was calculated for each factor. The results of the study are summarized in Table 12.3 through 12.7.[12]

Fraud Losses by Position within the Organization

Table 12.3 shows that 40 percent of the reported fraud cases were committed by non-managerial employees, 37 percent by managers, and 23 percent by executives or owners.

---

12   *Ibid.*

TABLE 12.3

Losses from Fraud by Position

Position	Percent of Frauds	Loss
Owner/Executive	23	$834,000
Manager	37	150,000
Employee	40	70,000

Although the reported number of frauds perpetrated by employees is higher than that of managers and almost twice that of executives, the average losses per category are inversely related.

Fraud Losses and the Collusion Effect

Collusion among employees in the commission of a fraud is difficult to both prevent and detect. This is particularly true when the collusion is between managers and their subordinate employees. Management plays a key role in the internal control structure of an organization. They are relied upon to prevent and detect fraud among their subordinates. When they participate in fraud with the employees over whom they are supposed to provide oversight, the organization's control structure is weakened, or completely circumvented, and the company becomes more vulnerable to losses.

Table 12.4 compares the median losses from frauds committed by individuals acting alone (regardless of position) and frauds involving collusion. This includes both internal collusion and schemes in which an employee or manager colludes with an outsider such as a vendor or a customer. Although frauds involving collusion are less common (36 percent of cases), the median loss is $500,000 as compared to $115,500 for frauds perpetrated by individuals working alone.

Fraud Losses by Gender

Table 12.5 shows that the median fraud loss per case caused by males ($250,000) was more than twice that caused by females ($110,000).

TABLE 12.4

Losses from Fraud by Collusion

Perpetrators	Loss
Two or more (36%)	$500,000
One (64%)	115,500

TABLE 12.5

Losses from Fraud by Gender

Gender	Loss
Male (59%)	$250,000
Female (41%)	110,000

TABLE 12.6	Losses from Fraud by Age	
	Age Range	**Loss**
	< 26	$25,000
	26–30	50,000
	31–35	113,000
	36–40	145,000
	41–50	250,000
	51–60	500,000
	> 60	435,000

TABLE 12.7	Losses from Fraud by Educational Level	
	Education Level	**Loss**
	High school	$100,000
	College	210,000
	Post graduate	550,000

Fraud Losses by Age

Table 12.6 indicates that perpetrators younger than 26 years of age caused median losses of $25,000, while frauds perpetrated by individuals 60 years of age and older were approximately 20 times larger.

Fraud Losses by Education

Table 12.7 shows the median loss from frauds relative to the perpetrator's education level. Frauds committed by high school graduates averaged only $100,000, whereas those with bachelor's degrees averaged $210,000. Perpetrators with advanced degrees were responsible for frauds with a median loss of $550,000.

Conclusions to Be Drawn

While the ACFE fraud study results are interesting, they appear to provide little in the way of anti-fraud decision-making criteria. Upon closer examination, however, a common thread appears. Notwithstanding the importance of personal ethics and situational pressures in inducing one to commit fraud, opportunity is the factor that actually facilitates the act. Opportunity was defined previously as access to assets and/or the information that controls assets. No matter how intensely driven by situational pressure one may become, even the most unethical individual cannot perpetrate a fraud if no opportunity to do so exists. Indeed the opportunity factor explains much of the financial loss differential in each of the demographic categories presented in the ACFE study:

- *Position.* Individuals in the highest positions within an organization are beyond the internal control structure and have the greatest access to company funds and assets.

- *Gender.* Women are not fundamentally more honest than men, but men occupy high corporate positions in greater numbers than women. This affords men greater access to assets.
- *Age.* Older employees tend to occupy higher-ranking positions and therefore generally have greater access to company assets.
- *Education.* Generally, those with more education occupy higher positions in their organizations and therefore have greater access to company funds and other assets.
- *Collusion.* One reason for segregating occupational duties is to deny potential perpetrators the opportunity they need to commit fraud. When individuals in critical positions collude, they create opportunities to control or gain access to assets that otherwise would not exist.

Fraud Schemes

Fraud schemes can be classified in a number of different ways. For purposes of discussion, this section presents the ACFE classification format. Three broad categories of fraud schemes are defined: fraudulent statements, corruption, and asset misappropriation.[13]

Fraudulent Statements

Fraudulent statements are associated with management fraud. Whereas all fraud involves some form of financial misstatement, to meet the definition under this class of fraud scheme, the statement itself must bring direct or indirect financial benefit to the perpetrator. In other words, the statement is not simply a vehicle for obscuring or covering a fraudulent act. For example, misstating the cash account balance to cover the theft of cash is not financial statement fraud. On the other hand, understating liabilities to present a more favorable financial picture of the organization to drive up stock prices does fall under this classification.

Table 12.8 shows that whereas fraudulent statements account for only 8 percent of the fraud cases covered in the ACFE fraud study, the median loss due to this type of fraud scheme is significantly higher than losses from corruption and asset misappropriation.

Appalling as this type of fraud loss appears on paper, these numbers fail to reflect the human suffering that parallels them in the real world. How does one measure the impact on stockholders as they watch their life savings and retirement funds evaporate after news of the fraud breaks? The underlying problems that permit and aid these frauds are found

TABLE 12.8 ## Losses from Fraud by Scheme Type

Scheme Type	Percent of Frauds*	Loss
Fraudulent statements	10	$2,000,000
Corruption	27	375,000
Asset misappropriation	89	150,000

*The sum of the percentages exceeds 100 because some of the reported frauds in the ACFE study involved more than one type of fraud scheme.

13   *Report to the Nation: Occupational Fraud and Abuse,* Association of Fraud Examiners, 2004.

in the boardroom, not the mail room. In this section, we examine some prominent corporate governance failures and the legislation designed to remedy them.

The Underlying Problems.   The series of events symbolized by the Enron, WorldCom, and Adelphia debacles caused many to question whether our existing federal securities laws were adequate to ensure full and fair financial disclosures by public companies. The following underlying problems are at the root of this concern.

1. *Lack of auditor independence.* Auditing firms that are also engaged by their clients to perform nonaccounting activities such as actuarial services, internal audit outsourcing services, and consulting lack independence. The firms are essentially auditing their own work. The risk is that as auditors they will not bring to management's attention detected problems that may adversely affect their consulting fees. For example, Enron's auditors—Arthur Andersen—were also their internal auditors and their management consultants.

2. *Lack of director independence.* Many boards of directors are composed of individuals who are not independent. Examples of lack of independence are directors who have a personal relationship by serving on the boards of other directors' companies; have a business trading relationship as key customers or suppliers of the company; have a financial relationship as primary stockholders or have received personal loans from the company; or have an operational relationship as employees of the company.

    A notorious example of corporate inbreeding is Adelphia Communications, a telecommunications company. Founded in 1952, it went public in 1986 and grew rapidly through a series of acquisitions. It became the sixth largest cable provider in the United States before an accounting scandal came to light. The founding family (John Rigas, CEO and chairman of the board; Timothy Rigas, CFO, CAO, and chairman of the audit committee; Michael Rigas, VP for operation; and J.P. Rigas, VP for strategic planning) perpetrated the fraud. Between 1998 and May 2002, the Rigas family successfully disguised transactions, distorted the company's financial picture, and engaged in embezzlement that resulted in a loss of more than $60 billion to shareholders.

    Whereas it is neither practical nor wise to establish a board of directors that is totally void of self-interest, popular wisdom suggests that a healthier board of directors is one in which the majority of directors are independent outsiders with the integrity and the qualifications to understand the company and objectively plan its course.

3. *Questionable executive compensation schemes.* A Thomson Financial survey revealed the strong belief that executives have abused stock-based compensation.[14] The consensus is that fewer stock options should be offered than currently is the practice. Excessive use of short-term stock options to compensate directors and executives may result in short-term thinking and strategies aimed at driving up stock prices at the expense of the firm's long-term health. In extreme cases, financial statement misrepresentation has been the vehicle to achieve the stock price needed to exercise the option.

    As a case in point, Enron's management was a firm believer in the use of stock options. Nearly every employee had some type of arrangement where they could purchase shares at a discount or were granted options based on future share prices. At Enron's headquarters in Houston, televisions were installed in the elevators so employees could track Enron's (and their own portfolio's) success. Before the firm's

---

14   Howard Stock, "Institutions Prize Good Governance: Once Bitten, Twice Shy, Investors Seek Oversight and Transparency," *Investor Relations Business*; New York (November 4, 2002).

collapse, Enron executives added millions of dollars to their personal fortunes by exercising stock options.

4. *Inappropriate accounting practices.* The use of inappropriate accounting techniques is a characteristic common to many financial statement fraud schemes. Enron made elaborate use of special-purpose entities (SPEs) to hide liabilities through off-balance-sheet accounting. SPEs are legal, but their application in this case was clearly intended to deceive the market. Enron also employed income-inflating techniques. For example, when the company sold a contract to provide natural gas for a period of two years, they would recognize all the future revenue in the period when the contract was sold.

WorldCom was another culprit of the improper accounting practices. In April 2001, WorldCom management decided to transfer transmission line costs from current expense accounts to capital accounts. This allowed it to defer some operating expenses and report higher earnings. Also, through acquisitions, the company seized the opportunity to raise earnings. WorldCom reduced the book value of hard assets of MCI by $3.4 billion and increased goodwill by the same amount. Had the assets been left at book value, they would have been charged against earnings over four years. Goodwill, on the other hand, was amortized over a much longer period. In June 2002, the company declared a $3.8 billion overstatement of profits because of falsely recorded expenses over the previous five quarters. The size of this fraud increased to $9 billion over the following months as additional evidence of improper accounting came to light.

Sarbanes-Oxley Act and Fraud.   Congress enacted SOX into law in July 2002 to address plummeting institutional and individual investor confidence triggered in part by business failures and accounting restatements due to fraud.

The act establishes a framework to modernize and reform the oversight and regulation of public company auditing. Its principal reforms pertain to (1) the creation of an accounting oversight board, (2) auditor independence, (3) corporate governance and responsibility, (4) disclosure requirements, and (5) penalties for fraud and other violations. These provisions are discussed in the following section.

1. *Accounting oversight board.* SOX created the **Public Company Accounting Oversight Board (PCAOB)** to set auditing, quality control, and ethics standards; to inspect registered accounting firms; to conduct investigations; and to take disciplinary actions.

2. *Auditor independence.* The act addresses auditor independence by creating more separation between a firm's attestation and nonauditing activities. This is intended to specify categories of services that a public accounting firm cannot perform for its client. These include the following nine functions:

    (a) Bookkeeping or other services related to the accounting records or financial statements
    (b) Financial information systems design and implementation
    (c) Appraisal or valuation services, fairness opinions, or contribution-in-kind reports
    (d) Actuarial services
    (e) Internal audit outsourcing services
    (f) Management functions or human resources
    (g) Broker or dealer, investment adviser, or investment banking services
    (h) Legal services and expert services unrelated to the audit
    (i) Any other service that the PCAOB determines is impermissible

Whereas SOX prohibits auditors from providing the above services to their audit clients, they are not prohibited from performing such services for nonaudit clients or privately held companies.

3. *Corporate governance and responsibility.* The act requires all audit committee members to be independent and requires the audit committee to hire and oversee the external auditors. This provision is consistent with many investors who consider the board composition to be a critical investment factor. For example, a Thomson Financial survey revealed that most institutional investors want corporate boards to be composed of at least 75 percent independent directors.[15]

   Two other significant provisions of the act relating to corporate governance are: (1) public companies are prohibited from making loans to executive officers and directors and (2) the act requires attorneys to report evidence of a material violation of securities laws or breaches of fiduciary duty to the CEO, CFO, or the PCAOB.

4. *Issuer and management disclosure.* SOX imposes new corporate disclosure requirements, including:

   (a) Public companies must report all off-balance-sheet transactions.

   (b) Annual reports filed with the SEC must include a statement by management, asserting that it is responsible for creating and maintaining adequate internal controls and asserting to the effectiveness of those controls.

   (c) Officers must certify that the company's accounts "fairly present" the firm's financial condition and results of operations.

   (d) Knowingly filing a false certification is a criminal offense.

5. *Fraud and criminal penalties.* SOX imposes a range of new criminal penalties for fraud and other wrongful acts. In particular, the act creates new federal crimes relating to the destruction of documents or audit work papers, securities fraud, tampering with documents to be used in an official proceeding, and actions against whistleblowers.

Corruption

Corruption involves an executive, manager, or employee of the organization in collusion with an outsider. The ACFE study identifies four principal types of corruption: bribery, illegal gratuities, conflicts of interest, and economic extortion. Corruption accounts for about 10 percent of occupational fraud cases.

Bribery. **Bribery** involves giving, offering, soliciting, or receiving things of value to influence an official in the performance of his or her lawful duties. Officials may be employed by government (or regulatory) agencies or by private organizations. Bribery defrauds the entity (business organization or government agency) of the right to honest and loyal services from those employed by it. For example, the manager of a meat-packing company offers a U.S. health inspector a cash payment. In return, the inspector suppresses his report of health violations discovered during a routine inspection of the meat-packing facilities. In this situation, the victims are those who rely on the inspector's honest reporting. The loss is salary paid to the inspector for work not performed and any damages that result from failure to perform.

Illegal Gratuities. An **illegal gratuity** involves giving, receiving, offering, or soliciting something of value because of an official act that has been taken. This is similar to a bribe, but the transaction occurs after the fact. For example, the plant manager in a

---

15 *Ibid.*

large corporation uses his influence to ensure that a request for proposals is written in such a way that only one contractor will be able to submit a satisfactory bid. As a result, the favored contractor's proposal is accepted at a noncompetitive price. In return, the contractor secretly makes a financial payment to the plant manager. The victims in this case are those who expect a competitive procurement process. The loss is the excess costs the company incurs because of the noncompetitive pricing of the construction.

Conflicts of Interest.   Every employer should expect that his or her employees will conduct their duties in a way that serves the interests of the employer. A **conflict of interest** occurs when an employee acts on behalf of a third party during the discharge of his or her duties or has self-interest in the activity being performed. When the employee's conflict of interest is unknown to the employer and results in financial loss, then fraud has occurred. The preceding examples of bribery and illegal gratuities also constitute conflicts of interest. This type of fraud can exist, however, when bribery and illegal payments are not present, but the employee has an interest in the outcome of the economic event. For example, a purchasing agent for a building contractor is also part owner in a plumbing supply company. The agent has sole discretion in selecting vendors for the plumbing supplies needed for buildings under contract. The agent directs a disproportionate number of purchase orders to his company, which charges above-market prices for its products. The agent's financial interest in the supplier is unknown to his employer.

Economic Extortion.   **Economic extortion** is the use (or threat) of force (including economic sanctions) by an individual or organization to obtain something of value. The item of value could be a financial or economic asset, information, or cooperation to obtain a favorable decision on some matter under review. For example, a contract procurement agent for a state government threatens to blacklist a highway contractor if he does not make a financial payment to the agent. If the contractor fails to cooperate, the blacklisting will effectively eliminate him from consideration for future work. Faced with a threat of economic loss, the contractor makes the payment.

Asset Misappropriation

The most common fraud schemes involve some form of asset misappropriation in which assets are either directly or indirectly diverted to the perpetrator's benefit. Ninety percent of the frauds included in the ACFE study fall into this general category. Certain assets are, however, more susceptible than others to misappropriation. Transactions involving cash, checking accounts, inventory, supplies, equipment, and information are the most vulnerable to abuse. Table 12.9 shows the percent of occurrence and the medium value of fraud losses in eight sub-categories of asset misappropriation. The following sections provide definitions and examples of the fraud schemes listed in the table.

Skimming.   **Skimming** involves stealing cash from an organization before it is recorded on the organization's books and records. One example of skimming is an employee who accepts payment from a customer but does not record the sale. Another example is **mailroom fraud**, where an employee opening the mail steals a customer's check and destroys the associated remittance advice. By destroying the remittance advice, no evidence of the cash receipt exists. This type of fraud may continue for several weeks or months until detected. Ultimately, the fraud will be detected when the customer complains that his account has not been credited. By that time, however, the mailroom employee will have left the organization and moved on.

TABLE 12.9	**Losses from Asset Misappropriation Schemes**		
Scheme Type	**Percent of Frauds***		**Loss**
Skimming	17		$80,000
Cash Larceny	10		75,000
Billing	24		100,000
Check Tampering	15		138,000
Payroll	9		49,000
Expense Reimbursement	13		25,000
Theft of Cash	15		50,000
Non-Cash Misappropriations	16		100,000

*The percentages exceed 100 percent because some fraud cases in the ACFE study involved multiple schemes from more than one category.

Cash Larceny. **Cash larceny** involves schemes where cash receipts are stolen from an organization after they have been recorded in the organization's books and records. An example of this is **lapping**, where the cash receipts clerk first steals and cashes a check from Customer A. To conceal the accounting imbalance caused by the loss of the asset, Customer A's account is not credited. Later (the next billing period), the employee uses a check received from Customer B and applies it to Customer A's account. Funds received in the next period from Customer C are then applied to the account of Customer B, and so on.

Employees involved in this sort of fraud often rationalize that they are simply borrowing the cash and plan to repay it at some future date. This kind of accounting cover-up must continue indefinitely or until the employee returns the funds. Lapping is usually detected when the employee leaves the organization or becomes sick and must take time off from work. Unless the fraud is perpetuated, the last customer to have funds diverted from his or her account will be billed again, and the lapping technique will be detected. Employers can deter lapping by periodically rotating employees into different jobs and forcing them to take scheduled vacations.

Billing Schemes. **Billing schemes**, also known as **vendor fraud**, are perpetrated by employees who cause their employer to issue a payment to a false supplier or vendor by submitting invoices for fictitious goods or services, inflated invoices, or invoices for personal purchases. Three examples of billing scheme are presented below:

A **shell company** fraud first requires that the perpetrator establish a false supplier on the books of the victim company. The fraudster then manufactures false purchase orders, receiving reports, and invoices in the name of the vendor and submits them to the accounting system, which creates the allusion of a legitimate transaction. Based on these documents, the system will set up an account payable and ultimately issue a check to the false supplier (the fraudster). This sort of fraud may continue for years before it is detected.

A **pass-through** fraud is similar to the shell company fraud with the exception that a transaction actually takes place. Again, the perpetrator creates a false vendor and issues purchase orders to it for inventory or supplies. The false vendor then purchases the needed inventory from a legitimate vendor. The false vendor charges the victim company a much higher than market price for the items, but pays only the market price to the legitimate vendor. The difference is the profit that the perpetrator pockets.

A **pay-and-return** scheme is a third form of vendor fraud. This typically involves a clerk with check writing authority who pays a vendor twice for the same products (inventory or supplies) received. The vendor, recognizing that its customer made a double payment, issues a reimbursement to the victim company, which the clerk intercepts and cashes.

Check Tampering.   **Check tampering** involves forging or changing in some material way a check that the organization has written to a legitimate payee. One example of this is an employee who steals an outgoing check to a vendor, forges the payee's signature and cashes the check. A variation on this is an employee who steals blank checks from the victim company and makes them out to himself or an accomplice.

Payroll Fraud.   **Payroll fraud** is the distribution of fraudulent paychecks to existent and/or nonexistent employees. For example, a supervisor keeps an employee on the payroll who has left the organization. Each week, the supervisor continues to submit time cards to the payroll department as if the employee were still working for the victim organization. The fraud works best in organizations where the supervisor is responsible for distributing paychecks to employees. The supervisor may intercept the paycheck, forge the former employee's signature, and cash it. Another example of payroll fraud is to inflate the hours worked on an employee time card so that he or she will receive a larger than deserved paycheck. This type of fraud often involves collusion with the supervisor or timekeeper.

Expense Reimbursements.   **Expense reimbursement** frauds are schemes in which an employee makes a claim for reimbursement of fictitious or inflated business expenses. For example a company salesman files false expense reports, claiming meals, lodging, and travel that never occurred.

Thefts of Cash.   **Thefts of cash** are schemes that involve the direct theft of cash on hand in the organization. An example of this is an employee who makes false entries on a cash register, such as voiding a sale, to conceal the fraudulent removal of cash. Another example is a bank employee who steals cash from the vault.

Non-Cash Misappropriations.   **Non cash fraud** schemes involve the theft or misuse of the victim organization's non cash assets. One example of this is a warehouse clerk who steals inventory from a warehouse or storeroom. Another example is a customer services clerk who sells confidential customer information to a third party.

Computer Fraud

Because computers lie at the heart of most organizations' accounting information systems today, the topic of **computer fraud** is of special importance to auditors. Although the objectives of the fraud are the same—misappropriation of assets—the techniques used to commit computer fraud vary greatly.

We saw in a previous section of this chapter that fraud loss estimates for 2008 exceed $990 billion. How much of this can actually be traced to computer fraud is difficult to say. One reason for uncertainty is that computer fraud is not well defined. For example, we saw in the ethics section of this chapter that some people consider copying commercial computer software to be neither unethical nor illegal. On the other side of this issue, software vendors consider such acts to be criminal. Regardless of how narrowly or broadly computer fraud is defined, most agree that it is a rapidly growing phenomenon. For our purposes, computer fraud includes the following:

- The theft, misuse, or misappropriation of assets by altering computer-readable records and files.
- The theft, misuse, or misappropriation of assets by altering the logic of computer software.
- The theft or illegal use of computer-readable information.
- The theft, corruption, illegal copying, or intentional destruction of computer software.
- The theft, misuse, or misappropriation of computer hardware.

The general model for accounting information systems shown in Figure 12.2 portrays, conceptually, the key stages of an information system. Each stage in the model—data collection, data processing, database management, and information generation—is a potential area of risk for certain types of computer fraud.

Data Collection. **Data collection** is the first operational stage in the information system. The objective is to ensure that transaction data entering the system are valid, complete, and free from material errors. In many respects, this is the most important stage in the system. Should transaction errors pass through data collection undetected, the organization runs the risk that the system will process the erroneous data and that they will impact the financial statements.

FIGURE 12.2   **The General Model for Accounting Information Systems**

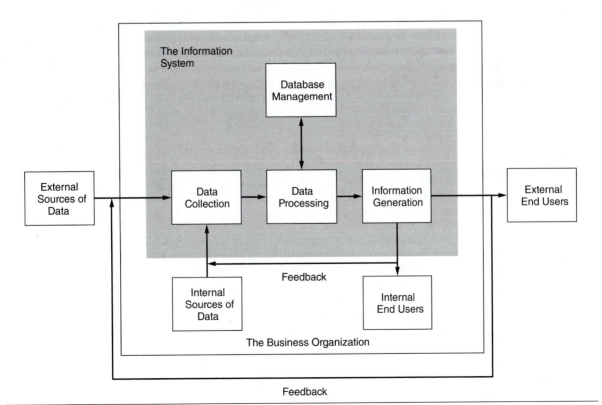

Two rules govern the design of data collection procedures: relevance and efficiency. The information system should capture only relevant data. A fundamental task of the system designer is to determine what is and what is not relevant. He or she does so by analyzing the user's needs. Only data that ultimately contribute to information are relevant. The data-collection stage should be designed to filter irrelevant facts from the system.

Efficient data-collection procedures are designed to collect data only once. These data can then be made available to multiple users. Capturing the same data more than once leads to data redundancy and inconstancy. Information systems have limited collection, processing, and data storage capacity. Data redundancy overloads facilities and reduces the overall efficiency of the system. Inconsistency among data elements can result in inappropriate actions and bad decisions.

The simplest way to perpetrate a computer fraud is at the data collection or data entry stage. Frauds of this type require little or no computer skills. The perpetrator need only understand the system and its control weaknesses. The fraudulent act involves entering falsified data into the system. This may involve deleting, altering, or creating a transaction. For example, to commit a payroll fraud, the perpetrator may insert a fraudulent payroll transaction along with other legitimate transactions. Unless the insertion is detected by internal controls, the system will generate an additional paycheck for the perpetrator. A variation on this type of fraud is to change the Hours Worked field in an otherwise legitimate payroll transaction to increase the amount of the paycheck.

Still another variant on this fraud is to disburse cash in payment of a false account payable. By entering fraudulent supporting documents (purchase order, receiving report, and supplier invoice) into the data-collection stage of the accounts payable system, a perpetrator can fool the system into creating an accounts payable record for a nonexistent purchase. Once the record is created, the system will presume it is legitimate and, on the due date, will disperse funds to the perpetrator in payment of a bogus liability.

Networked systems expose organizations to transaction frauds from remote locations. Masquerading, piggybacking, and hacking are examples of such fraud techniques. **Masquerading** involves a perpetrator gaining access to the system from a remote site by pretending to be an authorized user. This usually requires first gaining authorized access to a password. **Piggybacking** is a technique in which the perpetrator at a remote site taps into the telecommunications lines and latches onto an authorized user who is logging into the system. Once in the system, the perpetrator can masquerade as the authorized user. Hacking may involve piggybacking or masquerading techniques. **Hackers** are distinguished from other computer criminals because their motives are not usually to defraud for financial gain. They are motivated primarily by the challenge of breaking into the system rather than the theft of assets. Nevertheless, hackers have caused extensive damage and loss to organizations. Many believe that the line between hackers and the more classic computer criminals is thin.

Data Processing.   Once collected, data usually require processing to produce information. Tasks in the data processing stage range from simple to complex. Examples include mathematical algorithms (such as linear programming models) used for production scheduling applications, statistical techniques for sales forecasting, and posting and summarizing procedures used for accounting applications. Data processing frauds fall into two classes: program fraud and operations fraud.

Program fraud includes the following techniques: (1) creating illegal programs that can access data files to alter, delete, or insert values into accounting records; (2) destroying or corrupting a program's logic using a computer virus; or (3) altering program logic to cause the application to process data incorrectly. For example, the program a bank uses to calculate interest on its customers' accounts will produce rounding errors. This happens because the precision of the interest calculation is greater than the reporting precision. Therefore, interest figures that are calculated to a fraction of one cent must be rounded to whole numbers for reporting purposes. A complex routine in the interest-calculation program keeps track of the rounding errors so that the total interest charge to the bank equals the sum of the individual credits. This involves temporarily holding the fractional amounts left over from each calculation in an internal memory accumulator. When the amount in the accumulator totals one cent (plus or minus), the penny is added to the customer's account that is being processed. In other words, one cent is added to (or deducted from) customer accounts randomly. A type of program fraud called the salami fraud involves modifying the rounding logic of the program so it no longer adds the one cent randomly. Instead, the modified program always adds the plus cent to the perpetrator's account but still adds the minus cent randomly. This can divert a considerable amount of cash to the perpetrator, but the accounting records stay in balance to conceal the crime.

Operations fraud is the misuse or theft of the firm's computer resources. This often involves using the computer to conduct personal business. For example, a programmer may use the firm's computer time to write software that he sells commercially. A CPA in the controller's office may use the company's computer to prepare tax returns and financial statements for her private clients. Similarly, a corporate lawyer with a private practice on the side may use the firm's computer to search for court cases and decisions in commercial databases. The cost of accessing the database is charged to the organization and hidden among other legitimate charges.

Database Management. The organization's database is its physical repository for financial and nonfinancial data. **Database management fraud** includes altering, deleting, corrupting, destroying, or stealing an organization's data. Because access to database files is an essential element of this fraud, it is often associated with transaction or program fraud. A common fraud technique is to access the database from a remote site and browse the files for useful information that can be copied and sold to competitors. Disgruntled employees have been known to destroy company data files simply to harm the organization. One method is to insert a destructive routine called a logic bomb into a program. At a specified time, or when certain conditions are met, the logic bomb erases the data files that the program accesses. For example, a disgruntled programmer who is contemplating leaving an organization inserted a logic bomb into the payroll system. Weeks later, when the system detects that the programmer's name has been removed from the payroll file, the logic bomb is activated and erases the entire payroll file.

Information Generation. Information generation is the process of compiling, arranging, formatting, and presenting information to users. Information may be an operational document such as a sales order, a structured report, or a message on a computer screen. Regardless of physical form, useful information has the following characteristics: **relevance**, **timeliness**, **accuracy**, **completeness**, and **summarization**.

- *Relevance.* The contents of a report or document must serve a purpose. This could be to support a manager's decision or a clerk's task. We have established that only data relevant to a user's action have information content. Therefore, the information system should present only relevant data in its reports. Reports containing irrelevancies waste resources and may be counterproductive to the user. Irrelevancies detract attention from the true message of the report and may result in incorrect decisions or actions.
- *Timeliness.* The age of information is a critical factor in determining its usefulness. Information must be no older than the time period of the action it supports. For example, if a manager makes decisions daily to purchase inventory from a supplier

based upon an inventory status report, then the information in the report should be no more than a day old.

- *Accuracy.* Information must be free from material errors. However, materiality is a difficult concept to quantify. It has no absolute value; it is a problem-specific concept. This means that, in some cases, information must be perfectly accurate. In other instances, the level of accuracy may be lower. Material error exists when the amount of inaccuracy in information causes the user to make poor decisions or to fail to make necessary decisions. We sometimes must sacrifice absolute accuracy to obtain timely information. Often perfect information is not available within the decision time frame of the user. Therefore, in providing information, system designers seek a balance between information that is as accurate as possible, yet timely enough to be useful.
- *Completeness.* No piece of information essential to a decision or task should be missing. For example, a report should provide all necessary calculations and present its message clearly and unambiguously.
- *Summarization.* Information should be aggregated in accordance with a user's needs. Lower-level managers tend to need information that is highly detailed. As information flows upward through the organization to top management, it becomes more summarized. Later in this chapter, we shall look more closely at the effects that organizational structure and managerial level have on information reporting.

A common form of fraud at the information generation stage is to steal, misdirect, or misuse computer output. One simple but effective technique called **scavenging** involves searching through the trash cans of the computer center for discarded output. A perpetrator can often obtain useful information from the carbon sheets removed from multipart reports or from paper reports that were rejected during processing. Sometimes output reports are misaligned on the paper or slightly garbled during printing. When this happens, the output must be reprinted and the original output is often thrown in the trash.

Another form of fraud called **eavesdropping** involves listening to output transmissions over telecommunications lines. Technologies are readily available that enable perpetrators to intercept messages being sent over unprotected telephone lines and microwave channels. Most experts agree that it is practically impossible to prevent a determined perpetrator from accessing data communication channels. Data encryption can, however, render useless any data captured through eavesdropping.

AUDITOR'S RESPONSIBILITY FOR DETECTING FRAUD

The current authoritative guidelines on fraud detection are presented in SAS No. 99, *Consideration of Fraud in a Financial Statement Audit, which* pertains to the following areas of a financial audit:

1. Description and characteristics of fraud
2. Professional skepticism
3. Engagement personnel discussion
4. Obtaining audit evidence and information
5. Identifying risks
6. Assessing the identified risks
7. Responding to the assessment
8. Evaluating audit evidence and information
9. Communicating possible fraud
10. Documenting consideration of fraud

This list demonstrates how the external auditor must now think about fraud during every phase of the audit processes and seamlessly blend the auditor's consideration of fraud into the audit process. The auditor is also required to assess the risk factors related to both **fraudulent financial reporting** and the **misappropriation of assets**.

Fraudulent Financial Reporting

Risk factors that relate to fraudulent financial reporting are grouped according to the following classifications:

- *Management's characteristics and influence over the control environment.* These factors relate to the tone-at-the-top regarding internal control, management style, situational pressures, and the financial reporting process.
- *Industry conditions.* This includes the economic and regulatory environment in which the entity operates. For example, a company in a declining industry or with key customers experiencing business failures is at greater risk to fraud than one whose industry base is stable.
- *Operating characteristics and financial stability.* This pertains to the nature of the entity and the complexity of its transactions. For example, an organization involved with related-party transactions with organizations that are not audited may be at risk to fraud.

In the case of financial fraud (management fraud), external auditors should look for the following kinds of common schemes:

- Improper revenue recognition
- Improper treatment of sales
- Improper asset valuation
- Improper deferral of costs and expenses
- Improper recording of liabilities
- Inadequate disclosures

Misappropriation of Assets

Two risk factors are related to misappropriation of assets:

1. *Susceptibility of assets to misappropriation.* The susceptibility of an asset pertains to its nature and the degree to which it is subject to theft. Liquid assets, such as cash and bearer bonds, are more susceptible to misappropriation than nonliquid assets such as steel girders and physical plant equipment.
2. *Controls.* This class of risk factors involves the inadequacy or lack of controls designed to prevent or detect misappropriation of assets. For example, a database management system that does not adequately restrict access to accounting records increases the risk of asset misappropriation.

Examples of common schemes related to employee theft (asset misappropriation) include the following:

- Personal purchases
- Ghost employees
- Fictitious expenses
- Altered payee

- Pass-through vendors
- Theft of cash (or inventory)
- Lapping

Auditor's Response to Risk Assessment

The auditor's judgments about the risk of material misstatements due to fraud may affect the audit in the following ways:

- *Engagement staffing and extent of supervision.* The knowledge, skill, and ability of personnel assigned to the engagement should be commensurate with the assessment of the level of risk of the engagement.
- *Professional skepticism.* Exercising professional skepticism involves maintaining an attitude that includes a questioning mind and critical assessment of audit evidence.
- *Nature, timing, and extent of procedures performed.* Fraud risk factors that have control implications may limit the auditor's ability to assess control risk below the maximum and thus reduce substantive testing.

Response to Detected Misstatements Due to Fraud

To some degree, the risk of material misstatement due to fraud always exists. The auditor's response is thus influenced by the degree of assessed risk. In some cases, the auditor may determine that currently planned audit procedures are sufficient to respond to the risk factors. In other cases, the auditor may decide to extend the audit and modify planned procedures. In rare instances, the auditor may conclude that procedures cannot be sufficiently modified to address the risk, in which case the auditor should consider withdrawing from the engagement and communicating the reasons for withdrawal to the audit committee.

When the auditor has determined that fraud exists but has had no material effect on the financial statements, the auditor should

- Refer the matter to an appropriate level of management at least one level above those involved.
- Be satisfied that implications for other aspects of the audit have been adequately considered.

When the fraud has had a material effect on the financial statements or the auditor is unable to evaluate its degree of materiality, the auditor should

- Consider the implications for other aspects of the audit.
- Discuss the matter with senior management and with a board of director's audit committee.
- Attempt to determine whether the fraud is material.
- Suggest that the client consult with legal counsel, if appropriate.

Documentation Requirements

The auditor should document in the working papers the criteria used for assessing the fraud risk factors. Where risk factors are identified, the documentation should include (1) those risk factors identified and (2) the auditor's response to them.

FRAUD DETECTION TECHNIQUES

Because of the need to falsify accounting records, many fraud schemes leave a trail in the underlying accounting data that the forensic auditor can follow if he or she knows what to look for. For businesses with a large volume of transactions, however, finding the tell-tale trail using manual procedures may be impossible. Computer-based data extraction and analysis tools such as ACL are thus essential.

To find the trail in the masses of data, the auditor first develops a "fraud profile" that identifies the data characteristics that one would expect to find in a specific type of fraud scheme.[16] This identification requires an understanding of the enterprise's processes and internal controls (and their weaknesses). Once the fraud profile is developed, ACL can be used to manipulate the organization's data to search for transactions that fit the profile. In this section, we examine the operational and data characteristics of three common fraud schemes. The ACL features that are used here for fraud detection were discussed in Chapters 9 and 10 and explained in detail in the ACL workbook that accompanies the software license. The following discussion presumes that the reader is familiar with that material.

Payments to Fictitious Vendors

The purchasing function is particularly vulnerable to fraud and, for many organizations, represents a significant area of risk. A common fraud scheme involves making a payment to a fictitious company. A preliminary step in this scheme requires the perpetrator to create a phony vendor organization and establish it in the victim organization's records as a legitimate supplier. The embezzler then submits invoices from the fake vendor, which are processed by the accounts payable system of the victim company. Depending on the organizational structure and internal controls in place, this type of fraud may require collusion between two or more individuals. For example, the purchasing agent prepares a purchase order for items from the fake vendor, and the receiving clerk prepares a fictitious receiving report for the items. Accounts payable receives these documents, which appear to be legitimate, and matches them to the phony invoice when it arrives. An accounts payable is recorded and payment is subsequently made. In smaller organizations, a single individual with the authority to authorize payments can hatch a simpler version of the scheme. The fraud profile describing the false-vendor scheme and the audit procedures are described next.

Sequential Invoice Numbers

Since the victim organization is the only recipient of the invoices, the supporting invoices "issued" by the phony vendor may actually be in something close to an unbroken numerical sequence. The audit procedure is to use ACL to *sort* the records of the invoice file by invoice number and vendor number. This will highlight records that possess series characteristics, which can then be retrieved for further review.

Vendors with P.O. Boxes

Most legitimate suppliers have a complete business address. Since fake suppliers have no physical facilities, the perpetrator of the fraud will sometimes rent a P.O. box to receive payments by mail. Although it is also possible for a legitimate vendor to use a P.O. box,

16   D. Johnson, "Finding the Needle in the Haystack," *ACL Services Ltd. (internal publication)* (Vancouver BC, Canada, 1997).

these suppliers are candidates for further review. The audit procedure is this: Using ACL's expression builder, create a *filter* to select vendor records from the invoice file that use P.O. box addresses. From this list, verify the legitimacy of the vendor.

Vendors with Employee Addresses

Rather than rent a P.O. box, the perpetrator may use his or her home address on the invoice. Although it is also possible that an employee's home-based business is a legitimate supplier, this is not likely and should be investigated. The audit procedure is to use ACL to *join* the employee file and the invoice file using the address fields as the common key for both files. Only records that match should be passed to the resulting combined file. These records can then be reviewed further.

Multiple Companies with the Same Address

To divert attention away from excessive purchases made from the same vendor, a perpetrator may create several phony suppliers that share the same mailing address. As an audit safeguard, use ACL's *Duplicates* command to generate a listing of mailing addresses that are common to two or more vendors.

Invoice Amounts Slightly below the Review Threshold

Many organizations control disbursements by establishing a materiality threshold. A management review and signature is required for all checks that exceed the threshold. Those that fall below the limit are not reviewed. Knowing this, the perpetrator may falsify payments that fall just under the threshold to maximize his or her benefit from the fraud. The audit procedure for this situation is to use ACL's expression builder to *create* a value range around the control threshold. To highlight suspicious activity that warrants further investigation, sort payments records that fall within this range by vendor.

Payroll Fraud

The two common forms of payroll fraud are overpayment of employees and payments to nonexistent employees. The first scheme typically involves inflating the number of hours worked and/or issuing duplicate payroll checks. The second approach involves entering fictitious employees into the payroll system. A supervisor, who then receives the resulting payroll checks, usually perpetrates this type of fraud. A variation on this scheme is to keep a terminated employee on the payroll. Suggested audit procedures for detecting these frauds are described next.

Test for Excessive Hours Worked

Use ACL's *Expression Builder* to select payroll records that reflect excessive hours worked. The determination of what is excessive will depend on the nature of the organization and its policies. If moderate overtime is fairly common, then filtering records to identify instances where the hours worked field in in the payroll record is greater than 50 may uncover fraudulent situations. Using this filter to review employee records over time may disclose a pattern of abuse.

Test for Duplicate Payments

Use ACL's *Duplicates* function to search payroll records for employees with the following characteristics:

- Same employee number, same name, same address, etc. (duplicate payments)
- Same name with different mailing addresses

- Same name with different checking accounts
- Same name with different Social Security numbers
- Same mailing address with different employee names

Some duplicate records detected in the search will be due to natural phenomena (i.e., unrelated individuals who happen to have the same name). The results, however, provide the auditor with a basis for further review.

Test for Nonexistent Employees

Use ACL's *Join* feature to link the payroll and employee files using Employee Number as the common attribute. The resulting joined file should contain only those records from the payroll file that do not match valid employee records. These records need to be reviewed with management.

Lapping Accounts Receivable

Lapping was described earlier in the chapter as the theft of a customer's check received in payment on his account. The perpetrator then covers the theft in the following period by applying cash received from a second customer to the account of the first. The simplicity of this fraud technique is key to its success because it presents a very obscure fraud profile. The only evidence of fraud in the underlying data is in the timing difference between when payment is received and when it is recorded. Depending on how the organization structures its accounts receivable, this may be difficult to detect. The problem is illustrated by comparing two common methods of managing accounts receivable.

The Balance Forward Method

The **balance forward method** is used extensively for consumer accounts. Total sales to customers for the period are itemized and billed at the period end. Customers are required to pay only a minimum amount off the balance. The rest of the balance, plus interest, is carried forward to the next period.

Lapping is difficult to detect in this type of system. For example, assume the perpetrator embezzles a customer payment of $500. This amount would not be posted to the customer's account in the current period, and the balance carried forward to the next period would be overstated by $500. In the following period, cash taken from another customer would be used to cover this amount. Since balances carried forward are commonplace, an overstated amount does not draw attention internally. The customer, however, may complain that the payment was not recorded. If the embezzler himself deals with the complaint, he could explain that the payment was received too late to be reflected on the current statement but would show up in the next period.

The Open Invoice Method

The **open invoice method** is often used to manage trade accounts receivable (sales to other business organizations). Each invoice is recorded as a separate item in the invoice file. Checks received from customers are usually in payment of individual invoices. Since good credit relations between customer and supplier are critical, payments tend to be on time and in full. Partial payments resulting in balances carried forward are the exception rather than the norm.

To illustrate lapping in this situation, assume that Customer A remits a check for $1,523.61 in payment of an open invoice for the same amount. The perpetrator pockets the check but does not close the invoice. Therefore, the invoice balance is carried

TABLE 12.10	Sales Invoice File						
	Invoice Number	Customer Number	Invoice Amount	Sales Date	Due Date	Closed Date	Remittance Amount
	77885	23671	2,636.88	02/12/04	02/25/04	03/28/04	1,113.27

forward. In the next period, Customer B remits a check for $2,636.88 in full payment of an open invoice. The embezzler applies $1,523.61 of this payment to Customer A's open invoice, thus closing it. The remainder ($1,113.27) is applied to Customer B's invoice, which remains open. The balance of $1,523.61 is carried forward into the next period. To go undetected, the perpetrator must actively continue the lapping fraud from period to period. This carry-forward characteristic provides the forensic auditor with a basis for constructing a fraud profile. To illustrate, refer to invoice record structure in Table 12.10.

The Invoice Amount field in Table 12.10 is the accounts receivable amount due. The Due Date field is calculated at the time of the sale, and the Closed Date field is entered when the payment is received. The Remittance Amount field reflects the amount of payment received from the customer.

The audit procedure is as follows: Assuming the organization follows proper backup procedures, the invoice file will be copied frequently throughout the period under review, thus producing several archived versions of the file. Collectively, these files reflect the invoice amounts carried forward from month to month. If the auditor suspects lapping, he or she may employ the following ACL tests:

- Use ACL's *expression builder* to select items from each file version whose Remittance Amount field is greater than zero and less than the Invoice Amount field. These sets of records may contain legitimate items that are being disputed by the customers. For example, damaged goods, overcharges, and refused deliveries may result in customers making only partial payments. The auditor will need to sift through these legitimate issues to identify lapping.
- *Merge* the resulting carry-forward files into a single file reflecting activity for the entire period.
- Create a *calculated field* of the amount carried forward (Invoice Amount—Remittance Amount).
- Use the *duplicates* command to search the file for calculated carry-forward amounts that are the same. Following the example just illustrated, a carry-forward pattern of $1,523.61 will emerge.

SUMMARY

This chapter examined the two closely related subjects of ethics and fraud and their implications for auditing. It began by examining ethical issues that societies have pondered about for centuries. Good ethics is a necessary condition for the long-term profitability of a business. This requires that ethical issues be understood at all levels of the firm, from top management to line workers. In this section, we identified several ethical issues for auditors to consider in their fraud risk assessment.

The second section of the chapter examined a number of fraud issues. Although the term *fraud* is familiar in today's financial press, what constitutes fraud is not always clear. We examined the nature and meaning of fraud, differentiated between employee fraud and management fraud, and explained fraud-motivating forces. We then examined fraud schemes and the auditor's responsibility for fraud detection. Three general categories of fraud schemes were presented: financial misrepresentation (management fraud), corruption, and asset misappropriation (employee fraud). Management fraud typically involves the material misstatement of financial data to attain additional compensation or promotion or to escape the penalty for poor performance. Managers who perpetrate fraud often do so by overriding the internal control structure. Corruption involves using one's position to defraud another person or entity. Employee frauds are generally designed to direct cash or other assets directly to the employee's personal benefit. Typically, the employee circumvents the company's internal control structure for personal gain. However, if a company has an effective system of internal control, defalcations or embezzlements can usually be prevented or detected. The section presented an overview of SAS No. 99, which defines the external auditor's responsibilities for the detection of fraud during a financial audit. In addition, several risk-assessment factors related to management fraud and asset misappropriation were presented. The chapter concluded with a review of fraud detection techniques, including audit procedures employing ACL technology.

KEY TERMS

accuracy
Association of Certified Fraud Examiners (ACFE)
balance forward method
Billing schemes
bribery
business ethics
Cash larceny
Check tampering
completeness
computer ethics
computer fraud
computer security
conflict of interest
corruption
data collection
database management fraud
eavesdropping
economic extortion
employee fraud
ethical responsibility
ethics
Expense reimbursement
false representation
fraud
fraud triangle
fraudulent financial reporting

fraudulent statements
hackers
illegal gratuity
injury or loss
intent
justifiable reliance
lapping
mailroom fraud
management fraud
masquerading
material fact
misappropriation of assets
Non-cash fraud
open invoice method
operations fraud
ownership
pass-through
pay-and-return
payroll fraud
piggybacking
privacy
program fraud
Public Company Accounting Oversight
     Board (PCAOB)
relevance
SAS No. 99

scavenging
shell company
skimming
summarization

thefts of cash
timeliness
vendor fraud

REVIEW QUESTIONS

1. What is ethics?
2. What is business ethics?
3. What are the four areas of ethical business issues?
4. What are the main issues to be addressed in a business code of ethics required by the Securities and Exchange Commission?
5. What are three ethical principles that may provide some guidance for ethical responsibility?
6. What is computer ethics?
7. How do the three levels of computer ethics—pop, para, and theoretical—differ?
8. Are computer ethical issues new problems or just a new twist on old problems?
9. What are the computer ethical issues regarding privacy?
10. What are the computer ethical issues regarding security?
11. What are the computer ethical issues regarding ownership of property?
12. What are the computer ethical issues regarding equity in access?
13. What are the computer ethical issues regarding the environment?
14. What are the computer ethical issues regarding artificial intelligence?
15. What are the computer ethical issues regarding unemployment and displacement?
16. What are the computer ethical issues regarding misuse of computers?
17. What is the objective of *Statement on Auditing Standards No. 99*?
18. What are the five conditions that constitute fraud under common law?
19. Name the three fraud-motivating forces.
20. What is employee fraud?
21. What is management fraud?
22. What three forces constitute the triangle of fraud?
23. How can external auditors attempt to uncover motivations for committing fraud?
24. What is lapping?
25. What is collusion?
26. What is bribery?
27. What is economic extortion?
28. What is conflict of interest?
29. What is computer fraud, and what types of activities does it include?
30. At which stage of the general accounting model is it easiest to commit computer fraud?
31. Define check tampering.
32. What is billing (or vendor) fraud?
33. Define cash larceny.
34. What is skimming?

DISCUSSION QUESTIONS

1. Distinguish between ethical issues and legal issues.
2. Some argue against corporate involvement in socially responsible behavior because the costs incurred by such behavior place the organization at a disadvantage in a competitive market. Discuss the merits and flaws of this argument.
3. Although top management's attitude toward ethics sets the tone for business practice, sometimes it is the role of lower-level managers to uphold a firm's ethical standards. John, an operations-level manager, discovers that the company is illegally dumping toxic materials and is in violation of environmental regulations. John's immediate supervisor is involved in the dumping. What action should John take?
4. When a company has a strong internal control structure, stockholders can expect the elimination of fraud. Comment on the soundness of this statement.
5. Distinguish between employee fraud and management fraud.

6. The estimates of losses annually resulting from computer fraud vary widely. Why do you think obtaining a good estimate of this figure is difficult?

7. How has the Sarbanes-Oxley Act had a significant impact on corporate governance?

8. Discuss the concept of exposure, and explain why firms may tolerate some exposure.

9. If detective controls signal error flags, why shouldn't these types of controls automatically make a correction in the identified error? Why are corrective controls necessary?

10. Discuss the nonaccounting services that external auditors are no longer permitted to render to audit clients.

11. Discuss whether a firm with fewer employees than there are incompatible tasks should rely more heavily on general authority than specific authority.

12. An organization's internal audit department is usually considered an effective control mechanism for evaluating the organization's internal control structure. The Birch Company's internal auditing function reports directly to the controller. Comment on the effectiveness of this organizational structure.

13. Comment on the exposure (if any) caused by combining the tasks of paycheck preparation and distribution to employees.

14. Explain the five conditions necessary for an act to be considered fraudulent.

15. Distinguish between exposure and risk.

16. Explain the characteristics of management fraud.

17. The text identifies a number of personal traits of managers and other employees that might help uncover fraudulent activity. Discuss three.

18. Give two examples of employee fraud and explain how the thefts might occur.

19. Discuss the fraud schemes of bribery, illegal gratuities, and economic extortion.

20. Explain at least three forms of computer fraud.

21. Distinguish between skimming and cash larceny.

22. Distinguish between a shell company fraud and pass-through fraud.

23. Why are the computer ethics issues of privacy, security, and property ownership of interest to accountants?

24. A profile of fraud perpetrators prepared by the Association of Certified Fraud Examiners revealed that adult males with advanced degrees commit a disproportionate amount of fraud. Explain these findings.

25. Explain why collusion between employees and management in the commission of a fraud is difficult to both prevent and detect.

26. Because all fraud involves some form of financial misstatement, how is fraudulent statement fraud different?

27. Explain the problems associated with lack of auditor independence.

28. Explain the problems associated with lack of director independence.

29. Explain the problems associated with questionable executive compensation schemes.

30. Explain the problems associated with inappropriate accounting practices.

31. Explain the purpose of the Public Company Accounting Oversight Board.

32. Why is an independent audit committee important to a company?

33. What are the key points of the "Issuer and Management Disclosure" of the Sarbanes-Oxley Act?

34. In this age of high technology and computer-based information systems, why are accountants concerned about physical (human) controls?

MULTIPLE-CHOICE QUESTIONS

1. All of the following are issues of computer security except
   a. releasing incorrect data to authorized individuals.
   b. permitting computer operators unlimited access to the computer room.
   c. permitting access to data by unauthorized individuals.
   d. providing correct data to unauthorized individuals.

2. Which characteristic is not associated with software as intellectual property?
   a. uniqueness of the product
   b. possibility of exact replication
   c. automated monitoring to detect intruders
   d. ease of dissemination

3. For an action to be called fraudulent, all of the following conditions are required except
   a. poor judgment.
   b. false representation.

c. intent to deceive.

d. injury or loss.

4. One characteristic of employee fraud is that the fraud
    a. is perpetrated at a level to which internal controls do not apply.
    b. involves misstating financial statements.
    c. involves the direct conversion of cash or other assets to the employee's personal benefit.
    d. involves misappropriating assets in a series of complex transactions involving third parties.

5. Forces that may permit fraud to occur do not include
    a. a gambling addiction.
    b. lack of segregation of duties.
    c. centralized decision-making environment.
    d. questionable integrity of employees.

6. Who is responsible for establishing and maintaining the internal control system?
    a. the internal auditor
    b. the accountant
    c. management
    d. the external auditor

7. Which of the following indicates a strong internal control environment?
    a. The internal audit group reports to the audit committee of the board of directors.
    b. There is no segregation of duties between organization functions.
    c. There are questions about the integrity of management.
    d. Adverse business conditions exist in the industry.

8. Employee fraud involves three steps. Of the following, which is not involved?
    a. concealing the crime to avoid detection
    b. stealing something of value
    c. misstating financial statements
    d. converting the asset to a usable form

9. The importance to the accounting profession of the Sarbanes-Oxley Act of 2002 is that
    a. bribery will be eliminated.
    b. management will not be able to override the company's internal controls.
    c. firms are required to have an effective internal control system.
    d. firms will not be exposed to lawsuits.

10. The board of directors consists entirely of the CEO's close business associates and management of the organization. This
    a. indicates a weakness in the accounting system.
    b. is incompliant with the Sarbanes-Oxley Act.

c. is a red flag for auditors to review and report on executive compensation.

d. is a normal board structure and not an issue of audit concern.

11. Business ethics involves
    a. how managers decide on what is right in conducting business.
    b. how managers achieve what they decide is right for the business.
    c. both a and b.
    d. only a.

12. All of the following are conditions for fraud except
    a. false representation.
    b. injury or loss.
    c. intent.
    d. material reliance.

13. Management can expect various benefits to follow from implementing a system of strong internal control. Which of the following benefits is least likely to occur?
    a. reduced cost of an external audit
    b. preventing employee collusion to commit fraud
    c. availability of reliable data for decision-making purposes
    d. some assurance of compliance with the Foreign Corrupt Practices Act of 1977
    e. some assurance that important documents and records are protected

14. Which of the following situations is not a segregation of duties violation?
    a. The treasurer has the authority to sign checks but gives the signature block to the assistant treasurer to run the check-signing machine.
    b. The warehouse clerk, who has the custodial responsibility over inventory in the warehouse, selects the vendor and authorizes purchases when inventories are low.
    c. The sales manager has the responsibility to approve credit and the authority to write off accounts.
    d. The department time clerk is given the undistributed payroll checks to mail to absent employees.
    e. The accounting clerk who shares the record-keeping responsibility for the accounts receivable subsidiary ledger performs the monthly reconciliation of the subsidiary ledger and the control account.

15. What does the underlying assumption of reasonable assurance regarding implementation of internal control mean?
    a. Auditors are reasonably assured that fraud has not occurred in the period.
    b. Auditors are reasonably assured that employee carelessness can weaken an internal control structure.
    c. Implementation of the control procedure should not have a significant adverse effect on efficiency or profitability.
    d. Management assertions about control effectiveness should provide auditors with reasonable assurance.
    e. A control applies reasonably well to all forms of computer technology.

16. To conceal the theft of cash receipts from customers in payment of their accounts, which of the following journal entries should the bookkeeper make?

	DR	CR
a.	Miscellaneous Expense	Cash
b.	Petty Cash	Cash
c.	Cash	Accounts Receivable
d.	Sales Returns	Accounts Receivable
e.	None of the above	

17. Which of the following controls would best prevent the lapping of accounts receivable?
    a. Segregate duties so that the clerk responsible for recording in the accounts receivable subsidiary ledger has no access to the general ledger.
    b. Request that customers review their monthly statements and report any unrecorded cash payments.
    c. Require customers to send payments directly to the company's bank.
    d. Request that customers make the check payable to the company.

18. Providing timely information about transactions in sufficient detail to permit proper classification and financial reporting is an example of
    a. the control environment.
    b. risk assessment.
    c. information and communication.
    d. monitoring.

19. What fraud scheme is similar to the "borrowing from Peter to pay Paul" scheme?
    a. expense account fraud
    b. kiting
    c. lapping
    d. transaction fraud

20. Which of the following best describes lapping?
    a. applying cash receipts to a different customer's account in an attempt to conceal previous thefts of funds
    b. inflating bank balances by transferring money among different bank accounts
    c. expensing an asset that has been stolen
    d. creating a false transaction

21. Operations fraud includes
    a. altering program logic to cause the application to process data incorrectly.
    b. misusing the firm's computer resources.
    c. destroying or corrupting a program's logic using a computer virus.
    d. creating illegal programs that can access data files to alter, delete, or insert values.

PROBLEMS

1. **CMA 1289 3-Y6**
   Causes of Fraud
   The studies conducted by the National Commission on Fraudulent Financial Reporting (the Treadway Commission) revealed that fraudulent financial reporting usually occurs as the result of certain environmental, institutional, or individual influences and opportune situations. These influences and opportunities, present to some degree in all companies, add pressures and motivate individuals and companies to engage in fraudulent financial reporting. The effective prevention and detection of fraudulent financial reporting requires an understanding of these influences and opportunities while evaluating the risk of fraudulent financial reporting that these factors can create in a company. The risk factors to be assessed include not only internal ethical and control factors but also external environmental conditions.

   Required:
   a. Identify two situational pressures in a public company that would increase the likelihood of fraud.

b. Identify three corporate circumstances (opportune situations) where fraud is easier to commit and detection is less likely.

c. For the purpose of assessing the risk of fraudulent financial reporting, identify the external environmental factors that should be considered in the company's
   i. industry.
   ii. business environment.
   iii. legal and regulatory environment.

d. List several recommendations that top management should incorporate to reduce the possibility of fraudulent financial reporting.

2. Kickback Fraud

The kickback is a form of fraud often associated with purchasing. Most organizations expect their purchasing agents to select the vendor that provides the best products at the lowest price. To influence the purchasing agent in his or her decision, vendors may grant the agent financial favors (cash, presents, football tickets, and so on). This activity can result in orders being placed with vendors that supply inferior products or charge excessive prices.

Required:

Describe the controls that an organization can employ to deal with kickbacks. Classify each control as either preventive, detective, or corrective.

3. BOD Composition

A recent survey of institutional investors reveals that most of them want corporate boards to be composed of at least 75 percent independent directors.

Required:

Write an essay explaining why director independence has become such a high-profile issue and one of great importance.

4. Auditor Independence

The Sarbanes-Oxley Act addresses auditor independence by creating more separation between a firm's attestation and nonauditing activities.

Write an essay outlining the services that a public accounting firm cannot perform for its client. Conduct research to explain the rationale behind each of these prohibitions.

5. PCAOB Authority

The Sarbanes-Oxley Act created a Public Company Accounting Oversight Board (PCAOB). The PCAOB is empowered to set auditing, quality control, and ethics standards, to inspect registered accounting firms, to conduct investigations, and to take disciplinary actions.

Required:

Write an essay comparing the powers of the PCAOB with those of the AICPA. Describe how this initiative might affect the accounting profession.

6. Predictors of Fraud

A number of factors have been used to characterize the perpetrators of the frauds, including position within the organization, collusion with others, gender, age, and education.

Required:

Write an essay summarizing the usefulness of these factors as predictors of fraud within an organization.

7. CMA 1289 3-4
Evaluation of Internal Control

Oakdale, Inc. is a subsidiary of Solomon Publishing and specializes in the publication and distribution of reference books. Oakdale's sales for the past year exceeded $18 million, and the company employed an average of 65 employees. Solomon periodically sends a member of the internal audit department to audit the operations of each of its subsidiaries, and Katherine Ford, Oakdale's treasurer, is currently working with Ralph Johnson of Solomon's internal audit staff. Johnson has just completed a review of Oakdale's investment cycle and prepared the following report.

General

Throughout the year, Oakdale has made both short-term and long-term investments in securities; all securities are registered in the company's name. According to Oakdale's bylaws, long-term investment activity must be approved by its board of directors, while short-term investment activity may be approved by either the president or the treasurer.

Transactions

All purchases and sales of short-term securities were made by the treasurer. The long-term security purchases were approved by the board, while the long-term security sales were approved by the president. Because the treasurer is listed with the broker as the company's contact, all revenue from these investments (dividends and interest) is received by this individual, who then forwards the checks to accounting for processing.

Documentation

Purchase and sale authorizations, along with the broker's advices, are maintained in a file by the treasurer. The certificates for all long-term investments are kept in a safe deposit box at the local bank; only the president of Oakdale has access to this box. An inventory of this box was made, and all certificates were accounted for. Certificates for short-term investments are kept in a locked metal box in the accounting office. Other documents, such as long-term contracts and legal agreements, are also kept in this box. There are three keys to the box held by the president, the treasurer, and the accounting manager. The accounting manager's key is available to all accounting personnel should they require documents kept in this box. Documentation for two of the current short-term investments could not be located in this box; the accounting manager explained that some of the investments are for such short periods of time that formal documentation is not always provided by the broker.

Accounting Records

The accounting department records deposits of checks for interest and dividends earned on investments, but these checks could not be traced to the cash receipts journal, which is maintained by the individual who normally opens, stamps, and logs incoming checks. These amounts are journalized monthly in an account for investment revenue. The treasurer authorizes checks drawn for investment purchases. Both the treasurer and the president must sign checks in excess of $15,000. When securities are sold, the broker deposits the proceeds directly in Oakdale's bank account by an electronic funds transfer.

Each month, the accounting manager and the treasurer prepare the journal entries required to adjust the short-term investment account. There was insufficient backup documentation attached to the journal entries reviewed to trace all transactions; however, the balance in the account at the end of last month closely approximates the amount shown on the statement received from the broker. The amount in the long-term investment account is correct, and the transactions can be clearly traced through the documentation attached to the journal entries. There are no attempts made to adjust either account to the lower of aggregate cost or market.

Required:

To achieve Solomon Publishing's objective of sound internal control, the company believes the following four controls are basic for an effective system of accounting control:

- Authorization of transactions
- Complete and accurate record keeping
- Access control
- Internal verification
    a. For each of the four controls listed above, describe its purpose.
    b. Identify an area in Oakdale's investment procedures that violates each of the four controls.
    c. For each of the violations identified, describe how Oakdale can correct each weakness.

8. Fraud Scheme

A purchasing agent for a home improvement center is also part owner in a wholesale lumber company. The agent has sole discretion in selecting vendors for the lumber sold through the center. The agent directs a disproportionate number of purchase orders to his company, which charges above-market prices for its products. The agent's financial interest in the supplier is unknown to his employer.

Required:

What type of fraud is this, and what controls can be implemented to prevent or detect the fraud?

9. Fraud Scheme

A procurement agent for a large metropolitan building authority threatens to blacklist a building contractor if he does not make a financial payment to the agent. If the contractor does not cooperate, the contractor will be denied future work. Faced with a threat of economic loss, the contractor makes the payment.

Required:

What type of fraud is this, and what controls can be implemented to prevent or detect the fraud?

10. Mailroom Fraud and Internal Control

Sarat Sethi, a professional criminal, took a job as a mailroom clerk for a large department store called "Benson & Abernathy and Company." The mailroom was an extremely hectic work environment consisting of forty-five clerks and one supervisor. The clerks were responsible for handling promotional mailings, catalogs, and interoffice mail, as well as receiving and distributing a wide range of outside correspondence to various internal departments. One of Sethi's jobs was to open cash receipts envelopes from customers making payments on their credit-card balances. He separated the remittance advices (the bills) and the checks into two piles. He then sent remittance advices to the Accounts Receivable department, where the customer accounts were updated to reflect the payment. He sent the checks to the Cash Receipts department, where they were recorded in the cash journal and then deposited into the bank. Batch totals of cash received and accounts receivable updated were reconciled each night to ensure that everything was accounted for. Nevertheless, over a one-month period Sethi managed to steal $100,000 in customer payments and then left the state without warning.

The fraud occurred as follows: Because the name of the company was rather long, some people had adopted the habit of making out checks simply to "Benson." Sethi had a false ID prepared in the name of John Benson. Whenever he came across a check made out to "Benson," he would steal it along with the remittance advice. Sometimes people would even leave the payee section on the check blank. He stole these checks also. He would then modify the checks to make them payable to "J. Benson" and cash them. Since the accounts receivable department received no remittance advice, the end-of-day reconciliation with cash received disclosed no discrepancies.

Required:

    a. This seems like a foolproof scheme. Why did Sethi limit himself to only one month's activity before leaving town?

    b. What controls could Benson & Abernathy implement to prevent this from happening again?

11. Segregation of Duties

Explain why each of the following combinations of tasks should, or should not, be separated to achieve adequate internal control.

    a. Approval of bad debt write-offs and the reconciliation of the accounts receivable subsidiary ledger and the general ledger control account

    b. Distribution of payroll checks to employees and approval of employee time cards

    c. Posting of amounts from both the cash receipts and the cash disbursements journals to the general ledger

    d. Writing checks to vendors and posting to the cash account

    e. Recording cash receipts in the journal and preparing the bank reconciliation

12. Expense Account Fraud

While auditing the financial statements of Petty Corporation, the certified public accounting firm of Trueblue and Smith discovered that its client's legal expense account was abnormally high. Further investigation of the records indicated the following:

- Since the beginning of the year, several disbursements totaling $15,000 had been made to the law firm of Swindle, Fox, and Kreip.

- Swindle, Fox, and Kreip were not Petty Corporation's attorneys.

- A review of the canceled checks showed that they had been written and approved by Mary Boghas, the cash disbursements clerk.

- Boghas's other duties included performing the end-of-month bank reconciliation.

- Subsequent investigation revealed that Swindle, Fox, and Kreip are representing Mary Boghas in an unrelated embezzlement case in which she is the defendant. The checks had been written in payment of her personal legal fees.

Required:

    a. What control procedures could Petty Corporation have employed to prevent this unauthorized use of cash? Classify each control procedure in accordance with the COSO framework (authorization, segregation of functions, supervision, and so on).

    b. Comment on the ethical issues in this case.

13. Tollbooth Fraud

Collectors at Tollbooths A and B (see figure) have colluded to perpetrate a fraud. Each day, Tollbooth Collector B provides A with a number of toll tickets pre-stamped from Tollbooth B. The price of the toll from Point B to Point A is 35 cents. The fraud works as follows:

Drivers entering the turnpike at distant points south of B will pay tolls up to $5. When these drivers leave the turnpike at Point A, they pay the full amount of the toll printed on their tickets. However, the tollbooth collector replaces the tickets collected from the drivers with the 35-cent tickets provided by B, thus making it appear that the drivers entered the turnpike at Point B. The difference between the 35-cent tickets submitted as a record of the cash receipts and the actual amounts paid by the drivers is pocketed by Tollbooth Collector A and shared with B at the end of the day. Using this technique, Collectors A and B have stolen over $20,000 in unrecorded tolls this year.

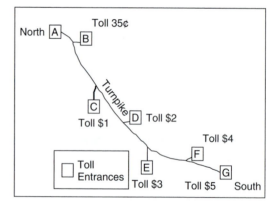

Required:

What control procedures could be implemented to prevent or detect this fraud? Classify the control procedures in accordance with the COSO framework.

14. Financial Aid Fraud

Harold Jones, the financial aid officer at a small university, manages all aspects of the financial aid program for needy students. Jones receives requests for aid from students, determines whether the students meet the aid criteria, authorizes aid payments, notifies the applicants that their request has been either approved or denied, writes the financial aid checks on the account he controls, and requires that the students come to his office to receive the checks in person. For years, Jones has used his position of authority to perpetrate the following fraud:

Jones encourages students who clearly will not qualify to apply for financial aid. Although the students do not expect aid, they apply on the off chance that it will be awarded. Jones modifies the financial information in the students' applications so that it falls within the established guidelines for aid. He then approves aid and writes aid checks payable to the students. The students, however, are informed that aid was denied. Since the students expect no aid, the checks in Jones's office are never collected. Jones forges the students' signatures and cashes the checks.

Required:

Identify the internal control procedures (classified per COSO) that could prevent or detect this fraud.

15. Evaluation of Controls

Gaurav Mirchandaniis is the warehouse manager for a large office supply wholesaler. Mr. Mirchandaniis receives two copies of the customer sales order from the sales department. He picks the goods from the shelves and sends them and one copy of the sales order to the shipping department. He then files the second copy in a temporary file. At the end of the day, Mr. Mirchandaniis retrieves the sales orders from the temporary file and updates the inventory subsidiary ledger from a terminal in his office. At that time he identifies items that have fallen to low levels, selects a supplier, and prepares three copies of a purchase order. One copy is sent to the supplier, one goes to the AP clerk, and one is filed in the warehouse. When the goods arrive from the supplier, Mr. Mirchandaniis reviews the attached packing slip, counts and inspects the goods, places them on the shelves, and updates the inventory ledger to reflect the receipt. He then prepares a receiving report and sends it to the AP department.

Required:

a. Prepare a systems flowchart of the procedures just described.
b. Identify any control problems in the system.
c. What kinds of frauds are possible in this system?

16. Evaluation of Controls

Matt Demko is the loading dock supervisor for a dry cement packaging company. His work crew is composed of unskilled workers who load large transport trucks with bags of cement, gravel, and sand. The work is hard and the employee turnover rate is high. Employees record their attendance on separate timecards. Demko authorizes payroll payments each week by signing the timecards and submitting them to the payroll department. The paychecks are then prepared by payroll and distributed to Demko, who distributes them to his work crew.

Required:

a. Prepare a systems flowchart of the procedures described above.
b. Identify any control problems in the system.
c. What kinds of frauds are possible in this system?

INTERNAL CONTROL CASES

1. Bern Fly Rod Company

Bern Fly Rod Company is a small manufacturer of high-quality graphite, fly-fishing rods. It sells its products to fly-fishing shops throughout the United States and Canada. Bern began as a small company with four salespeople, all family members of the owner. Due to the high popularity and recent growth in fly-fishing, Bern now employs a sales force of sixteen and for the first time employs nonfamily members. The salespeople travel around the country giving fly-casting demos of their new models. Once the sales orders are generated, inventory availability is determined and, if necessary, the salesperson sends the order directly to the manufacturing department for immediate production. Sales staff compensation is tied directly to their sales figures. Bern's financial statements for the December year-end reflect unprecedented sales, 35 percent higher than last year. Further, sales for December account for 40 percent of all sales. Last year, December sales accounted for only 20 percent of all sales.

Required:

Analyze the above situation and assess any potential internal control issues and exposures. Discuss some preventive measures this firm may wish to implement.

2. Breezy Company

(This case was prepared by Elizabeth Morris, Lehigh University.)

Breezy Company of Bethlehem, Pennsylvania, is a small wholesale distributor of heating and cooling fans. The company deals with retailing firms that buy small-to-medium quantities of fans. The president, Chuck Breezy, was very pleased with the marked increase in sales over the past couple of years. Recently, however, the company's accountant informed Chuck that although net income has increased, the percentage of uncollectibles has tripled. Due to the small size of the business, Chuck fears he may not be able to sustain these increased losses in the future. He has asked his accountant to analyze the situation.

Background

In 1998, the sales manager, John Breezy, moved to Alaska, and Chuck hired a young college graduate to take over the position. The company had always been a family business and, therefore, measurements of individual performance had never been a large consideration. The sales levels had been relatively constant because John had been content to sell to certain customers with whom he had been dealing for years. Chuck was leery about hiring outside of the family for this position. To try to keep sales levels up, he established a reward incentive based on net sales. The new sales manager, Bob Sellmore, was eager to set his career in motion and decided he would attempt to increase the sales levels. To do this, he recruited new customers while keeping the old clientele. After one year, Bob had proved himself to Chuck, who decided to introduce an advertising program to further increase sales. This brought in orders from a number of new customers, many of whom Breezy had never done business with before. The influx of orders excited Chuck so much that he instructed Jane Breezy, the finance manager, to raise the initial credit level for new customers. This induced some customers to purchase more.

Existing System

The accountant wrote up a comparative income statement to show changes in revenues and expenses over the last three years, shown in Exhibit A. Currently, Bob is receiving a commission of 2 percent of net sales. Breezy Company uses credit terms of net 30 days. At the end of previous years, bad debt expense amounted to approximately 2 percent of net sales.

As the finance manager, Jane performs credit checks. In previous years, Jane had been familiar with most clients and approved credit on the basis of past behavior. When dealing with new customers, Jane usually approved a low credit amount and increased it after the customer exhibited reliability. With the large increase in sales, Chuck felt that the current policy was restricting a further rise in sales levels. He decided to increase credit limits to eliminate this restriction. This policy, combined with the new advertising program, should attract many new customers.

EXHIBIT A BREEZY COMPANY COMPARATIVE INCOME STATEMENT FOR YEARS 2007, 2008, 2009

	2007	2008	2009
Revenues			
Net Sales	350,000	500,000	600,000
Other Revenue	60,000	60,000	62,000
Total Revenue	410,000	560,000	662,000
Expenses			
Cost of Goods Sold	140,00	200,000	240,000
Bad Debt Expense	7,000	20,000	36,000
Salaries Expense	200,000	210,000	225,000
Selling Expense	5,000	15,000	20,000
Advertising Expense	0	0	10,000
Other Expenses	20,000	30,000	35,000
Total Expenses	372,000	475,000	566,000
Net Income	30,000	85,000	96,000

Future

The new level of sales impresses Chuck and he wishes to expand, but he also wants to keep uncollectibles to a minimum. He believes the amount of uncollectibles should remain relatively constant as a percentage of sales. Chuck is thinking of expanding his production line but wants to see uncollectibles drop and sales stabilize before he proceeds with this plan.

Required:

Analyze the weaknesses in internal control and suggest improvements.

3. Whodunit?

(This case was prepared by Karen Collins, Lehigh University.)

The following facts relate to an actual embezzlement case.

Someone stole more than $40,000 from a small company in less than two months. Your job is to study the following facts, try to figure out who was responsible for the theft and how it was perpetrated, and (most important) suggest ways to prevent something like this from happening again.

Facts

Location of company: a small town on the eastern shore of Maryland. Type of company: crabmeat processor, selling crabmeat to restaurants located in Maryland. Characters in the story (names are made up):

- John Smith, president and stockholder (husband of Susan).
- Susan Smith, vice president and stockholder (wife of John).
- Tommy Smith, shipping manager (son of John and Susan).
- Debbie Jones, office worker. She began working part-time for the company 6 months before the theft. (At that time, she was a high school senior and was allowed to work afternoons through a school internship program.) Upon graduation from high school (several weeks before the theft was discovered), she began working full time. Although she is not a member of the family, the Smiths have been close friends with Debbie's parents for more than 10 years.

Accounting Records

All accounting records are maintained on a microcomputer. The software being used consists of the following modules:

1. A general ledger system, which keeps track of all balances i the general ledger accounts and produces a trial balance at the end of each month.

2. A purchases program, which keeps track of purchases and maintains detailed records of accounts payable.

3. An accounts receivable program, which keeps track of sales and collections on account and maintains individual detailed balances of accounts receivable.

4. A payroll program.

The modules are not integrated (that is, data are not transferred automatically between modules). At the end of the accounting period, summary information generated by the purchases, accounts receivable, and payroll programs must be entered into the general ledger program to update the accounts affected by these programs.

Sales

The crabmeat processing industry in this particular town was unusual in that selling prices for crabmeat were set at the beginning of the year and remained unchanged for the entire year. The company's customers, all restaurants located within 100 miles of the plant, ordered the same quantity of crabmeat each week. Because prices for the crabmeat remained the same all year and the quantity ordered was always the same, the weekly invoice to each customer was always for the same dollar amount.

Manual sales invoices were produced when orders were taken, although these manual invoices were not prenumbered. One copy of the manual invoice was attached to the order shipped to the customer. The other copy was used to enter the sales information into the computer.

When the customer received the order, the customer would send a check to the company for the amount of the invoice. Monthly bills were not sent to customers unless the customer was behind in payments (that is, did not make a payment for the invoiced amount each week).

Note: The industry was unique in another way: Many of the companies paid their workers with cash each week (rather than by check). It was, therefore, not unusual for companies to request large sums of cash from the local banks.

Performance of Key Functions by Individual(s)

John, president
Susan, vice president
Tommy, son and shipping manager
Debbie, office worker

	Individual(s) Performing Task	
	Most of the Time	**Sometimes**
1. Receive order from customers	John	All others
2. Oversee production of crabmeat	John or Tommy	—
3. Handle shipping	Tommy	John
4. Bill customers (entering sales into accounts receivable program)	Debbie	Susan
5. Open mail	John	All others
6. Prepare bank deposit tickets and make bank deposits	Susan or Debbie	All others
7. Record receipt of cash and checks (enter obtain collections of accounts receivable into accounts receivable program)	Debbie	Susan
8. Prepare checks (payroll checks and payments of accounts payable)	Susan or Debbie	—
9. Sign checks	John	—
10. Prepare bank reconciliations	John	—
11. Prepare daily sales reports showing sales by type of product	Susan	—
12. Summarize daily sales reports to obtain monthly sales report by type of product	Susan or Debbie	—
13. Run summaries of AR program, AP program, and payroll program at month end and input summaries into GL program	Susan or Debbie	—
14. Analyze trial balance at month end and analyze open balances in accounts receivable and accounts payable	Susan	—

When Trouble Was Spotted

Shortly after the May 30 trial balance was run, Susan began analyzing the balances in the various accounts. The balance in the cash account agreed with the cash balance she obtained from a reconciliation of the company's bank account.

However, the balance in the accounts receivable control account in the general ledger did not agree with the total of the accounts receivable subsidiary ledger (which shows a detail of the balances owed by each customer). The difference was not very large, but the balances should be in 100 percent agreement.

At this point, Susan asked me if I would help her locate the problem. In reviewing the computerized accounts receivable subsidiary ledger, I noticed the following:

a. The summary totals from this report were not the totals that were entered into the general ledger program at month end. Different amounts had been entered. No one could explain why this had happened.

b. Some sheets in the computer listing had been ripped apart at the bottom. (In other words, the listing of the individual accounts receivable balances was not a continuous list but had been split at several points.)

c. When an adding machine tape of the individual account balances was run, the individual balances did not add up to the total at the bottom of the report.

Susan concluded that the accounts receivable program was not running properly. My recommendation was that an effort be made to find out why the accounts receivable control account and the summary totals per the accounts receivable subsidiary ledger were not in agreement and why we were finding problems with the accounts receivable listing. Since the accounts receivable subsidiary and accounts receivable control account in the general ledger had been in agreement at the end of April, the effort should begin with the April ending balances for each customer by manually updating all of the accounts. The manually adjusted May 30 balances should then be compared with the computer-generated balances and any differences investigated.

After doing this, Susan and John found several differences. The largest difference was the following:

CUSTOMER ACCOUNT PER MANUAL RECONSTRUCTION

Dr.		Cr.	
Sale #1	5,000	Pmt. #1	5,000
Sale #2	5,000	Pmt. #2	5,000
Sale #3	5,000	Pmt. #3	5,000
Sale #4	5,000	—	—
Ending Balance	5,000		

CUSTOMER ACCOUNT PER MANUAL RECONSTRUCTION

Dr.		Cr.	
Sale #1	5,000	Pmt. #1	5,000
Sale #2	5,000	Pmt. #2	5,000
Sale #3	5,000	Pmt. #3	5,000
Ending Balance	0		

Although they found the manual sales invoice for Sale #2, Susan and John concluded (based on the computer records) that Sale #2 did not take place. I was not sure, so I recommended that they call this customer and ask him the following:

a. Did he receive this order?

b. Did he receive an invoice for it?

c. Did he pay for the order?

d. If so, did he have a copy of his canceled check?

Although John felt that this would be a waste of time, he called the customer. He received an affirmative answer to all of his questions. In addition, he found that the customer's check was stamped on the back not with the normally used "for deposit only" stamp of the company but with an address stamp giving only the company's name and city. When questioned, Debbie said that she sometimes used this stamp.

Right after this question, Debbie, who was sitting nearby at the computer, called Susan to the computer and showed her the customer's account. She said that the payment for $5,000 was in fact recorded in the customer's account. I came over to the computer and looked at the account. The payments were listed as follows:

Amount	Date of Payment
$5,000	May 3
$5,000	May 17
$5,000	May 23
$5,000	May 10

I questioned the order of the payments—why was a check supposedly received on May 10 entered in the computer after checks received on May 17 and 23? About 30 seconds later, the computer malfunctioned and the accounts receivable file was lost. Every effort to retrieve the file gave the message "file not found."

About five minutes later, Debbie presented Susan with a copy of a bank deposit ticket dated May 10 with several checks listed on it, including the check that the customer said had been sent to the company. The deposit ticket, however, was not stamped by the bank (which would have verified that the deposit had been received by the bank) and did not add up to the total at the bottom of the ticket (it was off by 20 cents).

At this point, being very suspicious, I gathered all documents I could and left the company to work on the problem at home, away from any potential suspects. I received a call from Susan about 4 hours later saying that she felt much better. She and Debbie had gone to Radio Shack (the maker of their computer program), and Radio Shack had confirmed Susan's conclusion that the computer program was malfunctioning. She and Debbie were planning to work all weekend reentering transactions into the computer. She said that everything looked fine and not to waste my time working on the problem.

I felt differently. How do you feel?

Required:

a. If you were asked to help this company, could you conclude from the evidence presented that an embezzlement took place? What would you do next?

b. Who do you think was the embezzler?

c. How was the embezzlement accomplished?

d. What improvements would you recommend in internal control to prevent this from happening again? In answering this question, try to identify at least one suggestion from each of the six classes of internal control activities discussed in this chapter (under the section "Control Activities"): transaction authorization, segregation of duties, supervision, accounting records, access control, and independent verification.

e. Would the fact that the records were maintained on a microcomputer aid in this embezzlement scheme?

ACL CASES

1. False Vendor Fraud

You are the auditor of a large company. You suspect that employees may have established themselves as false vendors. A copy of the Vendor and Empmast (employee master) files are located in the Sample Project that accompanies ACL. Perform the necessary audit tests to produce a list of employees that may be guilty of this fraud scheme.

The following Assignments are located in the **ACL Tutorial** folder in the Student Resources section of this textbook's website:

2. Fraud Tutorial 1

Required:

Complete this tutorial. The assignment involves performing five tests for detecting payroll fraud.

3. Fraud Tutorial 2

Required:

Complete this tutorial. The assignment involves performing six tests for detecting purchasing fraud, including employee theft and fictitious vendors.

4. Fraud Tutorial 3

Required:

Complete this tutorial. The assignment pertains to the identification of unusual trends in marketing salaries.

5. Bradmark Comprehensive Case

Required:

Access the Bradmark ACL Case in the Student Resource section of the textbook's web site. Your instructor will tell you which questions to answer.

Glossary

A

Access controls: Controls that ensure that only authorized personnel have access to the firm's assets. (1)

Access method: The technique used to locate records and to navigate through the database. (4)

Access tests: Tests that ensure that the application prevents authorized users from unauthorized access to data. (7)

Accounting records: The documents, journals, and ledgers used in transaction cycles. (1)

Accuracy: The need for information to be free from errors. (12)

Accuracy tests: Tests that ensure that the system processes only data values that conform to specified tolerances. (7)

Association of Certified Fraud Examiners (ACFE): A company that conducts studies to estimate losses from fraud and abuse. (12)

Attendance file: File created by the time-keeping department upon receipt of approved time cards. (10)

Attributes: Equivalents to adjectives in the English language that serve to describe the objects. (4)

Audit objectives: Audit goals derived from management assertions that lead to the development of audit procedures. (1)

Audit opinion: Opinion of auditor regarding the presentation of financial statements. (1)

Audit planning: Stage at which the auditor identifies the financially significant applications and attempts to understand the controls over the primary transactions that are processed by these applications. (1)

Audit procedure: Tasks performed by auditors to gather evidence that supports or refutes management assertions. (1)

Audit risk: Probability that the auditor will render unqualified opinions on financial statements that are, in fact, materially misstated. (1)

Audit trail: Accounting records that trace transactions from their source documents to the financial statements. (6)

Auditing: Form of independent attestation performed by an expert who expresses an opinion about the fairness of a company's financial statements. (1)

Authenticity tests: Tests verifying that an individual, a programmed procedure, or a message attempting to access a system is authentic. (7)

B

Backbone systems: Basic system structure on which to build. (5)

Balance forward method: A method in which total sales to customers for the period are itemized and billed at the period end. (12)

Base case system evaluation (BCSE): Variant of the test data technique, in which comprehensive test data are used. (7)

Batch control totals: Record that accompanies the sales order file through all of the data processing runs. (9)

Batch controls: Effective method of managing high volumes of transaction data through a system. (7)

Big bang approach: An attempt to switch operations from the old legacy systems to the new system in a single event that implements the ERP across the entire company. (11)

Bill of lading: Formal contract between the seller and the shipping company that transports the goods to the customer. (9)

Biometric devices: Devices that measure various personal characteristics, such as fingerprints, voice prints, retina prints, or signature characteristics. (4)

Bolt-on software: A company's use of a third-party vendor to perform a specialized function. (11)

Bribery: The influence of an official in the performance of his or her lawful duties. (12)

C

Call-back device: Hardware component that asks the caller to enter a password and then breaks the connection to perform a security check. (3)

Check digit: Method for detecting data coding errors. A control digit is added to the code when it is originally designed to allow the integrity of the code to be established during subsequent processing. (7)

Client-server model: A form of network topology in which a user's computer or terminal (the client) accesses the ERP programs and data via a host computer (the server). (11)

Closed database architecture: Database management system used to provide minimal technological advantage over flat-file systems. (11)

Compilers: Language translation modules of the operation system. (3)

Completeness tests: Tests identifying missing data within a single record and entire records missing from a batch. (7)

Completeness: The idea that no piece of information essential to a decision or task should be missing. (12)

Computer fraud: The use of a computer to commit fraud. (12)

Conceptual design: The production of several alternative designs for the new system. (5)

Conflict of interest: When an employee acts on behalf of a third party during the discharge of his or her duties or has self-interest in the activity being performed. (12)

Consolidation: The aggregation or roll-up of data. (11)

Control activities: Policies and procedures used to ensure that appropriate actions are taken to deal with the organization's risks. (1)

Control environment: The foundation of internal control. (1)

Control risk: Likelihood that the control structure is flawed because controls are either absent or inadequate to prevent or detect errors in the account. (1)

Core applications: Operations that support the day-to-day activities of the business. (11)

Corrective controls: Actions taken to reverse the effects of errors detected in the previous step. (1)

Corruption: The act of an official or fiduciary person who unlawfully and wrongfully uses his station or character to procure some benefit for himself or for another person, contrary to duty and the rights of others. (12)

Customer open order file: File containing a copy of the sales order. (9)

Customer order: Document that indicates the type and quantity of merchandise being requested. (9)

Cycle billing: Method of spreading the billing process out over the month. (9)

D

Data definition language (DDL): Programming language used to define the database to the database management system. (4)

Data dictionary: Description of every data element in the database. (4)

Data manipulation language (DML): Language used to insert special database commands into application programs written in conventional languages. (4)

Data mart: Data warehouse organized for a single department or function. (11)

Data structures: Techniques for physically arranging records in the database. (4)

Data warehouse: A relational or multidimensional database that supports online analytical processing (OLAP). (11)

Database administrator (DBA): The individual responsible for managing the database resource. (4)

Database authorization table: Table containing rules that limit the actions a user can take. (4)

Database lockout: Software control that prevents multiple simultaneous access to data. (4)

Database management fraud: The act(s) of altering, deleting, corrupting, destroying, or stealing an organization's data. (12)

Database management system (DBMS): Software system that controls access to the data resource. (4)

Deletion anomaly: The unintentional deletion of data from a table. (8)

Detailed design: Design of screen outputs, reports, and operational documents; entity relationship diagrams; normal form designs for database tables; updated data dictionary; designs for all screen inputs and source documents; context diagrams for overall system; low-level data flow diagrams; and structure diagrams for program modules. (5)

Detection risk: Risk that auditors are willing to take that errors not detected or prevented by the control structure will also not be detected by the auditor. (1)

Detective controls: Devices, techniques, and procedures designed to identify and expose undesirable events that elude preventive controls. (1)

Disaster recovery plan (DRP): Comprehensive statement of all actions to be taken before, during, and after a disaster, along with documented, tested procedures that will ensure the continuity of operations. (2)

Documentation: Written description of how the system works. (5)

Drill-down: The disaggregation of data to reveal underlying details that explain certain phenomena. (11)

E

Eavesdropping: Listening to output transmissions over telecommunication lines. (12)

Echo check: Technique that involves the receiver of the message returning the message to the sender. (3)

Economic extortion: The use (or threat) of force (including economic sanctions) by an individual or an organization to obtain something of value. (12)

Electronic data interchange (EDI): The intercompany exchange of computer-processable business information in standard format. (3)

Embedded audit module (EAM): Technique in which one or more specially programmed modules embedded in a host application select and record predetermined types of transactions for subsequent analysis. (8)

Employee file: A file used with the attendance file to create an online payroll register. (10)

Employee fraud: Performance fraud by nonmanagement employees generally designed to directly convert cash or other assets to the employee's personal benefit. (12)

Empty shell: Arrangement that involves two or more user organizations that buy or lease a building and remodel it into a computer site, but without the computer and peripheral equipment. (2)

Encryption: Technique that uses a computer program to transform a standard message being transmitted into a coded (ciphertext) form. (3)

End users: Users for whom the system is built. (5)

Enterprise resource planning (ERP): A generalized system that incorporates the best business practices in use. (11)

Entity: A resource, event, or agent. (4)

Error file: Transaction file that lists any detected errors. (7)

Ethics: The principles of conduct that individuals use in making choices and guiding their behavior in situations that involve the concepts of right and wrong. (12)

F

False representation: A fraudulent act involving a false statement or a nondisclosure. (12)

Firewall: Software and hardware that provide a focal point for security by channeling all network connections through a control gateway. (3)

Fraud: A false representation of a material fact made by one party to another party with the intent to deceive and induce the other party to justifiably rely on the fact that to his or her detriment. (12)

Fraud triangle: The combination of situational pressures, opportunities, and personal characteristics that can lead to the act of fraud. (12)

Fraudulent financial reporting: Fraud commonly committed by persons at the management level. (12)

G

Generalized audit software (GAS):   Software that allows auditors to access electronically coded data files and perform various operations on their contents. (7)

Grandparent-parent-child (GPC):   Backup technique used in sequential batch systems. (4)

H

Hacking: The act of breaking into a computer system. (12)

Hash total: Control technique that uses nonfinancial data to keep track of the records in a batch. (7)

Hashing structure: Structure employing an algorithm that converts the primary key of a record directly into a storage address. (8)

Hierarchical data model: A database model that represents data in a hierarchical structure and permits only a single parent record for each child. (4)

Hierarchical topology: Topology where a host computer is connected to several levels of subordinate smaller computers in a master-slave relationship. (3)

I

Illegal gratuity: The act of "rewarding" an official for taking a particular course of action. (12)

Indexed random file: Randomly organized file that is accessed via an index. (8)

Indexed sequential access method (ISAM):   Sequential structure used for large table files that can be accessed by an index. (8)

Indexed sequential file: Sequential file structure that is accessed via an index. (8)

Indexed structure: A class of file structure that use indexes for its primary access method. (8)

Inference controls: Controls that prevent users from inferring specific data values through normal query features. (4)

Inherent risk: Risk that is associated with the unique characteristics of the business or industry of the client. (1)

Injury or loss: The condition to a fraudulent act that the deception must have caused injury or loss to the victim of the fraud. (12)

Insertion anomaly: The unintentional insertion of data into a table. (8)

Integrated test facility (ITF):   Automated technique that enables the auditor to test an application's logic and controls during its normal operation. (7)

Intent: The condition to a fraudulent act that the intent to deceive or the knowledge that one's statement is false. (12)

Internal control system: Policies a firm employs to safeguard the firm's assets, ensure accurate and reliable accounting records and information, promote efficiency, and measure compliance with established policies. (1)

Internal view: The physical arrangement of records in the database. (4)

Interpreters: Language translation modules of the operating system that convert one line of logic at a time. (3)

Inverted list: A cross reference created from multiple indexes. (8)

J

Justice: The idea that the benefits of the decision should be distributed fairly to those who share the risks. (12)

Justifiable reliance: The condition to a fraudulent act that the misrepresentation must have been a substantial factor on which the injured party relied. (12)

L

Lapping: Use of customer checks, received in payment of their accounts, to conceal cash previously stolen by an employee. (12)

Logical key pointer: A pointer containing the primary key of the related record. (8)

M

Management assertions: Explicit or implicit statements made by management within the financial statements pertaining to the financial health of the organization. (1)

Management fraud: Performance fraud that often uses deceptive practices to inflate earnings or to forestall the recognition of either insolvency or a decline in earnings. (12)

Masquerading: A perpetrator gaining access to the system from a remote site by pretending to be an authorized user. (12)

Material fact: The condition to a fraudulent act that is a substantial factor in inducing someone to act. (12)

Misappropriation of assets: Fraud commonly committed by employees. (12)

Monitoring: The process by which the quality of internal control design and operation can be assessed. (1)

Mutual aid pact: Agreement between two or more organizations (with comparable computer facilities) to aid each other with their data processing needs in the event of a disaster. (2)

N

Navigational model: Model that possesses explicit links or paths among data elements. (4)

Network model: Variation of the hierarchical model. (4)

Network topology: Physical arrangement of the components. (3)

New systems development: Process that involves five steps: identifying the problem, understanding what needs to be done, considering alternative solutions, selecting the best solution, and implementing the solution. (5)

O

Object-oriented design: Building information systems from reusable standard components or modules. (5)

Objects: Equivalent to nouns in the English language. (5)

Online analytical processing (OLAP): A branch of ERP that includes decision support, modeling, information retrieval, ad hoc reporting/analysis, and what-if analysis. (11)

Online transaction processing (OLTP): Processes consisting of large numbers of relatively simple transactions. (11)

Open invoice method: A method in which each invoice is recorded as a separate item in the invoice file. (12)

Operations fraud: The misuse or theft of a firm's computer resources. (12)

Opportunity: A force within an individual's personality and external environment that can lead to the act of fraud. (12)

Ownership: The personal information a person owns. (12)

P

Packing slip: Document that travels with the goods to the customer to describe the contents of the order. (9)

Parallel simulation: Technique that requires the auditor to write a program that simulates key features of processes of the application under review. (7)

Parity check: Technique that incorporates an extra bit into the structure of a bit string when it is created or transmitted. (3)

Partitioned database approach: Database approach that splits the central database into segments or partitions that are distributed to their primary users. (4)

Password: Secret code entered by the user to gain access to the data files. (3)

Payroll fraud: The overpayment of employees and payments to nonexistent employees. (12)

Payroll imprest account: An account into which a single check for the entire amount of the payroll is deposited. (10)

Phased-in approach: The ERP systems are installed independently in each business unit over a period of time. (11)

Piggybacking: The action in which a perpetrator taps into the telecommunications line from a remote source and latches onto an authorized user who is logging onto the system. (12)

Pointer structure: A structure in which the address (pointer) of one record is stored in the field on a related record. (8)

Polling: Popular technique for establishing communication sessions in WANs. (3)

Preventive controls: Passive techniques designed to reduce the frequency of occurrence of undesirable events. (1)

Privacy: A matter of restricted access to persons or information about persons. (12)

Program fraud: A form of data processing fraud that involves creating illegal programs to alter accounting records, destroying a program's logic using a virus, or altering the program logic to cause the application to process the data incorrectly. (12)

Project planning: Allocation of resources to individual applications within the framework of the strategic plan. (5)

Project schedule: Document that formally presents management's commitment to the project. (5)

Public Company Accounting Oversight Board (PCAOB):   A company created by the Sarbanes-Oxley Act to set auditing, quality control, and ethics standards, to inspect registered accounting firms, to conduct investigations, and to take disciplinary actions. (12)

Public key encryption: Technique that uses two keys: one for encoding the message and the other for decoding it. (3)

R

Recovery operations center (ROC):   Arrangement involving two or more user organizations that buy or lease a building and remodel it into a completely equipped computer site. (2)

Redundancy tests: Tests that determine that an application processes each record only once. (7)

Reengineering: The identification and elimination of nonvalue-added tasks by replacing traditional procedures with those that are innovative and different. (9)

Relevance: The need for the contents of a report or document to serve a purpose. (12)

Replicated databases: Database approach in which the central database is replicated at each IPU site. (4)

Request-response technique: Technique in which a control message from the sender and a response from the sender are sent at periodic synchronized intervals. (3)

Reusable password: A network password that can be used more than one time. (3)

Ring topology: Topology that eliminates the central site. All nodes in this configuration are of equal status. (3)

Risk assessment: Risk factors included in the design of an audit report. (12)

Risk assessment: The identification, analysis, and management of risks relevant to financial reporting. (1)

Rounding error tests: Tests that verify the correctness of rounding procedures. (7)

Run-to-run controls: Controls that use batch figures to monitor the batch as it moves from one programmed procedure to another. (7)

S

Salami frauds: Fraud in which each victim is unaware of being defrauded. (7)

Sales order: Source document that captures such vital information as the name and address of the customer making the purchase; the customer's account number; the name, number, and description of product; quantities and unit price of items sold; and other financial information. (9)

SAS No. 99: Consideration of Fraud in a Financial Statement Audit: The current guidelines on fraud detection. (12)

Scalabilty: The system's ability to grow smoothly and economically as user requirements increase. (11)

Scavenging: Searching through the trash cans of the computer center for discarded output. (12)

Schema (conceptual view):   Description of the entire database. (4)

Segregation of duties: Separation of employee duties to minimize incompatible functions. (1)

Sequential structure: A data structure in which all records in the file lie in contiguous storage spaces in a specified sequence arranged by their primary key. (8)

Servers: Special-purpose computers that manage common resources, such as programs, data, and printers of the LAN. (3)

Shipping notice: Document that informs the billing department that the customer's order has been filled and shipped. (9)

Slicing and dicing: The process that enables the user to examine data from different viewpoints. (11)

Stakeholders: Entities either inside or outside an organization that have direct or indirect interest in the firm. (5)

Steering committee: An organizational committee consisting of senior-level management responsible for systems planning. (5)

Stock release (picking ticket): Document that identifies which items of inventory must be located and picked from the warehouse shelves. (9)

Structured design: Disciplined way of designing systems from the top down. (5)

Subschema (user view): User view of the database. (4)

Substantive tests: Tests that determine whether database contents fairly reflect the organization's transactions. (1)

Summarization: The idea that information should be aggregated in accordance with a user's needs. (12)

Supervision: A control activity involving the critical oversight of employees. (1)

Supplier's (vendor's) invoice: The bill sent from the seller to the buyer showing unit costs, taxes, freight, and other charges. (10)

Supply chain management (SCM): The convergence between ERP and bolt-on software to move goods from raw material stage to the consumer. (11)

System survey: Determination of what elements, if any, of the current system should be preserved as part of the new system. (5)

Systems analysis: Two-step process that involves a survey of the current system and then an analysis of the user's needs. (5)

Systems development life cycle (SDLC): Formal process consisting of two major phases: new systems development and maintenance. (5)

Systems planning: Linking of individual system projects or applications to the strategic objectives of the firm. (5)

T

Test data method: Technique used to establish application integrity by processing specially prepared sets of input data through production applications that are under review. (7)

Tests of controls: Tests that establish whether internal controls are functioning properly. (1)

Timeliness: The idea that information must be no older than the time period of the action it supports. (12)

Token passing: Transmission of a special signal (token) around the network from node to node in a specific sequence. (3)

Tracing: Test data technique that performs an electronic walkthrough of the application's internal logic. (7)

Transaction authorization: Procedure to ensure that employees process only valid transactions within the scope of their authority. (1)

Transcription errors: Type of error that can corrupt a data code and cause processing errors. (7)

Transposition errors: Error that occurs when digits are transposed. (7)

Trojan horse: Program that attaches to another legitimate program but does not replicate itself like a virus. (3)

Turnkey systems: Completely finished and tested systems that are ready for implementation. (5)

U

Update anomaly: The unintentional updating of data in a table, resulting from data redundancy. (8)

User views: The set of data that a particular user needs to achieve his or her assigned tasks. (4)

V

Valid vendor file: A file containing vendor mailing information. (10)

Validation controls: Controls intended to detect errors in transaction data before the data are processed. (7)

Vendor-supported systems: Custom systems that organizations purchase from commercial vendors. (5)

Virus: Program that attaches itself to a legitimate program to penetrate the operating system. (3)

W

Walkthrough: Analysis of system design to ensure the design is free from conceptual errors that could become programmed into the final system. (5)

Worm: Software program that "burrows" into the computer's memory and replicates itself into areas of idle memory. (3)

Index